GREAT AMERICAN
SPORTS AND
ADVENTURE
VACATIONS

D1050739

Fodor's Travel Publications, Inc.
New York • Toronto • London • Sydney • Auckland
http://www.fodors.com/

Fodor's Great American Sports and Adventure Vacations

Editor: Anastasia Redmond Mills
Editorial Contributors: Jonathan Abrahams, Steven R. Adang, Naomi Black, Erik Fair, Susan Farewell, Catherine Fredman, Rosemary Freskos, Beth Gibson, Bud Journey, Andrea Lehman, Michael B. McPhee, Peter Oliver, Peter Potterfield, Jeanne Ricci, Melissa Rivers, Linda K. Schmidt, Lee R. Schreiber, W. Lynn Seldon Jr., Jordan Simon, Lisa Skriloff, Bill Strickland, Dennis Stuhaug, Michael J. Sullivan, Scott S. Warren, Jonathan Weisel, Sandra Widener, Jane Zarem, Rena Zurofsky

Creative Director: Fabrizio LaRocca
Cover Photographs: background, John Telford; left spot, Magnus Rietz/Image Bank; middle spot, Glenn Moody/Vermont Bicycle Touring; right spot, Torsten Blackwood/HI-AYH
Design: Tigist Getachew

Special Sales

CONTENTS

ou're free-falling through 2,000 feet of perfectly clear Montana air. You're eye to eye with a school of Day-Glo fish alongside a reef on the Florida coast. You're scudding along in a sailboat, the New England salt air stinging your lips, or calling out "wagons ho-o-o!" from a canvas-topped covered wagon jolting down the Oregon Trail. You're shooting hoops with Magic Johnson, learning to lob on Nick Bollettieri's home turf, roaring down a Grand Prix racetrack in a BMW 325i at 135 mph.

No, you're not Walter Mitty. You've just joined the growing group of Americans who have learned that a vacation can be more than a trip to the beach—Americans who are taking advantage of the increasing number of trips and sports schools that make it possible for ordinary folks like you to spend a week or two or three learning—and performing—feats that you previously only fantasized about.

This guide will turn you on to hundreds of ways to do just that, enabling you to come away from your vacation with a lot more than a suntan. You will have cross-country skied to frozen waterfalls or watched, all alone, as Old Faithful blew off steam. You will have improved your golf swing or mastered the short game; sea-kayaked next to a breaching pod of whales or shot the continent's most awesome white water in a raft; or even mountain-biked through the Rockies, gaining an intimate understanding of their name.

Whether you're young or old, an athlete or a wannabe, alone or traveling with family or friends, you'll find a lifetime of great outdoor vacation ideas inside this book. These are mainly scheduled group trips and courses in the United States that last between 5 and 14 days. Keep in mind that in addition to the trips described here, there are many others scheduled: shorter trips, longer trips, trips to other parts of the country, and even trips to other countries. Also, most of the outfitters running these trips can set you up on a special tour, one that's customized for you and your family or a group of friends.

If you have special dietary or health needs don't forget to query the outfitter before you sign up. If you're traveling with your family, for instance, be sure to ask whether youngsters are allowed. Some trips and courses are just not suited to kids—they're too hard or too dangerous or require too much sitting still—and some trips are fine for 13-year-olds but would be horrible for toddlers.

If you're traveling solo, ask about the single occupancy policy. Most prices we quote are per person based on double occupancy. Almost all companies will charge you a single supplement if you request a single room; some companies charge you the extra fee even if you request a double but end up in a single.

Each chapter in this guide contains a comprehensive checklist of questions to help you choose the right trip. General questions to ask include:

How much of a deposit is required and when is the balance due? Most schools and outfitters require you to put down a deposit by a particular day in order to reserve your spot, then pay in full some time before the departure date.

What is the cancellation policy? You may get a full or partial refund if you cancel your reservation, and then again, you may not. Policies vary from full refunds offered up to 30 days before the trip to partial refunds offered up to 7 days before the trip to no refunds offered ever. Find out how far in advance you must cancel to get a full refund, and ask if any allowances will be made for cancellations due to medical emergencies. If the outfitter offers cancellation insurance,

always take it. You'll receive a full refund if for any reason you can't make the trip.

Are taxes and tips included in the cost? Generally, taxes and tips are not included, and these can add substantially to the cost of your trip. Be sure to ask who customarily gets tipped and about how much that tip should be.

Every care has been taken to ensure the accuracy of the information in this guide. All prices and dates quoted here are based on information supplied to us at press time, but this may change, and the prudent traveler will avoid inconvenience by calling ahead. Fodor's cannot accept responsibility for errors that may occur.

Fodor's wants to hear about your travel experiences, both pleasant and unpleasant. When a school or outfitter fails to live up to its billing, let us know and we will investigate the complaint and revise our entries where the facts warrant it. Send your letters to the editors of Fodor's Travel Publications, 201 E. 50th Street, New York, NY 10022.

Readers should also remember that adventure travel and outdoor vacations may entail certain risks. While outfitters, trip operators, and tour guides mentioned in this book have been carefully selected, the publisher makes no warranties regarding their competence, reliability, and safety practices and disavows all responsibility for injury, death, loss, or property damage that may arise from participation in their trips.

Baseball Fantasy Camps

By Michael B. McPhee

Updated by W. Lynn Seldon Jr.

hat baseball lover hasn't dreamed of a shot at the major leagues? It's the bottom of the ninth, and you're playing in front of a loyal home-team crowd. Runners on first, second, and third eye you tensely as you step up to the plate. The pitcher checks the signals, winds up, and hurls the ball . . . A moment later the stadium erupts in wild celebration as the ball you've clobbered drops cleanly over the right field fence.

For most of us, this scenario will always remain a fantasy, but those who want to get a little closer to the dream can join one of 20 baseball fantasy camps created by the major-league teams. You can go down to your favorite team's spring training facility for one week in the off-season and be coached in the game by some former greats. As best they can, the teams try to re-create the conditions major leaguers train under in the spring. There are also other types of similar camps and fan tours available at major-league parks and through other operators.

Want to learn a breaking pitch? Let Rollie Fingers show you how he does it. Or let Gary Carter demonstrate how to catch a breaking ball. Tommy Lasorda or Denny Doyle will show you signals, when to steal, when to swing or when to bunt.

Mornings are spent warming up, stretching, and exercising. Together, you're coached in all the fundamentals, then you're given a position and taught how to play it. Lunch usually follows. In the afternoon, the camp breaks into teams, and real games—complete with umpires, base coaches, and trash talking—are played. It all ends in the locker rooms, with showers, beers, and (for the men) banter with the pros about how the day went.

At the end of the week, more pros usually show up, and you play a team made up of former players. An awards banquet follows that night, with the Most Valuable Player award, the trainer's award (given to the player who spent the most time in the trainer's room), and dozens more.

All the teams emphasize that anyone can play, man or woman, experienced or not. The vast majority of participants are men, but women do come. The Red Sox camp, for example, usually gets 4 or 5 women each year. Some bring their husbands, but most are alone. And yes, the women do sometimes play better than the men. People come from all walks of life: carpenters, doctors, shopkeepers, and writers. The minimum age for most teams is 30, but a few allow anyone over 21 to play. The oldest participants are, typically, in their late seventies. And you don't have to be in great shape, just reason-

Outdoor writer Michael B. McPhee has contributed to the *New York Times,* the *Washington Post,* and the *Boston Globe.* Freelance writer and photographer Lynn Seldon has been a baseball fan since the Baltimore Orioles won the 1966 World Series. Lynn would wear Cal Ripken's number, eight, at a camp.

ably able to chase a grounder and run to first base. Some teams, such as the Mets, encourage people with disabilities to join. Every team emphasizes fun, and the high jinks and shenanigans that go on all week leave everyone laughing on the plane back home. Guests who aren't playing are usually welcome, and many teams have a special package for them.

Players need only bring a glove and spikes (rubber preferred), and the team will supply the rest, including your uniform with your name printed on it and the number of your choice. You also get lots of mementos—autographed baseballs, bats, trading cards of yourself at your position, warm-up jackets, and the like.

Prices are steep—typically between $3,000 and $4,000 for the week—but the accommodations are usually posh, the food is usually the same as what the major leaguers eat, and the price often includes rubdowns and a few drinks at night. As of mid-1995, most camp operators were still experiencing adverse effects of the baseball strike, but not severely enough to offer incentives to lure campers; most operators raised their prices, even though calls were estimated by one operator to be down by 30%.

CHOOSING THE RIGHT CAMP

The vast majority of people pick the camp of their favorite team or the one where a favorite player is supposed to show up, but whether you have a favorite team or not, here are some questions to ask:

How many years has the camp been run? The longer the camp's been running, the more likely it is to be run well. See if the camp has been run by the same operator for a number of seasons—a few camps have spotty on-again, off-again histories.

How large is the camp? The total size doesn't really matter so much as the size of the individual teams within the camp and the number of managers for each. Nine campers per team would be too few; 20, too many. Thirteen is about right, with 2 pro managers.

How many teams are there and how many playing fields? If the camp has more teams than fields, you may end up warming the bench more than you would like.

What pros have actually signed up for the camp? How many days will each of them be there, and how much time will I actually spend with them? In promoting themselves, camps can be loose with the names of pros. Find out who has actually signed on the dotted line, how many days the pros will be around, whether they will dine with you, stay at your hotel, or join you after practice in the locker rooms. The biggest names sometimes fly in for the Saturday game and then fly out again.

Who plays in the big Saturday game against the pros? In some camps, everyone plays; in others, it's just the two best teams.

What's the cost and what's included? Unless stated otherwise, all the prices given here are per person, double occupancy, and include accommodations, ground transportation between the hotel and the ballpark, breakfasts, lunches, and one dinner, usually a Saturday night awards banquet. Prices do not include airfare unless stated otherwise. If you want a private room, you must pay a few hundred dollars more.

What are the free-time activities? Some teams organize evening programs, with open bars, videos of the day's games, and conversation with the pros; some outfits take campers to local restaurants one night; and some camps simply leave you at the ballpark after practice with a see-you-tomorrow attitude. Don't worry too much about golf, tennis, swimming, and other activities—your days will be full and you'll be dead tired at night. But if you're into golf, it doesn't do any harm to ask if the pros will play with you.

What are accommodations like? Campers stay in generally upscale hotels or resorts. Ask for brochures that list facilities and describe rooms. Ask for the room you want—some face the beach, others the parking lot; some are upper-floor rooms with great views, others are lower down and noisier; some are single rooms, others are suites.

Is laundry service available? This could allow you to pack fewer clothes.

What's the food like? At most camps breakfast and lunch are served. You could be eating hamburgers and fries or lemon chicken and baked potatoes.

Are there any off-season events? Sometimes campers get together throughout the year to socialize or play ball. Sometimes they go to the sponsoring team's games during the regular season, and their presence in the stadium is announced before the game.

May I bring my spouse or a friend? Almost all week-long camps let you bring a nonplaying guest. Some offer your guest a complete package (usually Thursday through Sunday) that includes everything from rooms and meals to airfare; others have no special package but will help make arrangements. If you're bringing someone, make sure there's enough for him or her to do.

When does the camp take place, and how early do I need to sign up? Most of the camps are in late January or early February. As a rule, make reservations 2 months in advance; to play it safe, leave 4 months, particularly for the more popular camps—those run by the Cubs, Yankees, and Dodgers.

MAJOR PLAYERS

BASEBALL FANTASY CAMPS This organization operates camp for the Milwaukee Brewers and also runs the Field of Dreams camp. (Twin Lakes Park, 6700 Clark Rd., Sarasota, FL 34241, tel. 813/925–4855 or 800/336–2267, fax 813/922–3751).

BASEBALL HEAVEN The camps of the Atlanta Braves, the Cleveland Indians, the Cincinnati Reds, the New York Mets, and the Florida Marlins are run by this company (Box 1033, Southampton, PA 18966, tel. 215/938–5075, fax 215/938–5078).

DREAM WEEK Dream Week organizes the the Philadelphia Phillies camp and the Major League Baseball All-Star Dream Week camp, among other baseball events and trips. (Suite 203, Huntingdon Valley Federal Building, 2617 Huntingdon Pike, Huntingdon Valley, PA 19006, tel. 215/938–1200, fax 215/938–7746).

MAJOR SPORTS FANTASIES This outfit operates programs for the Boston Red Sox and the Minnesota Twins (Box 85, Waterbury, VT 05676, tel. 802/244–4100 or 800/226–7794, fax 802/244–5835).

RANDY HUNDLEY'S BASEBALL CAMPS The Chicago Cubs and the St. Louis Cardinals camps are run by this organization (675 North Court, Suite 160, Palatine, IL 60067, tel. 708/991–9595, fax 708/991–9471).

THE CAMPS

ATLANTA BRAVES The Braves' camp is held at the team's training facility in West Palm Beach, Florida, and games are played at the Municipal Stadium there. Former players who have participated in the camp include Darrel Chaney, Ralph Garr, Rod Gilbreath, Glen Hubbard, and Rick Mahler.

There are up to 90 campers, and the Braves welcome nonplaying guests. There are 2 postgame, locker-room bull sessions a week, which are the stuff of male fantasy: sitting around in towels, drinking beers and chatting with the pros.

Campers have a reunion at Fulton County Stadium, where their presence is announced prior to the game. *The Atlanta Braves Baseball Heaven, c/o Baseball Heaven, Inc., Box 1033, Southampton, PA 18966, tel. 215/938–5075 or 800/827–2837, fax 215/938–5078. Early Feb. in West Palm Beach, FL: 7 nights, $3,795. Price includes airfare from anywhere in the continental United States. Guest package: 3 nights, $695 (including airfare). Campers must be at least 30 years old.*

BOSTON RED SOX The Red Sox camp is held in Ft. Myers, Florida, in City of Palms Stadium. There are about 120 campers and about 25 former major leaguers. Bill Lee, Rico Petrocelli, Ted Williams, Johnny Pesky,

Bobby Doerr, Fergie Jenkins and Carlton Fisk have all played. Rick Garcia concurrently runs a minicamp for up to 20 umpire wannabes. There's also a coaching camp for up to 30 participants.

Everyone stays at the Sheraton Harbor Place (tel. 813/337–0300) in downtown Ft. Myers. The hotel has one tennis court and three pools. You're on your own for breakfast, but the price includes lunches, which are served in the park, and 5 dinners, including the awards banquet.

The pros eat dinner and socialize in the evening with you, which is a real plus; it's these sorts of informal gatherings that make baseball camps so memorable. In addition, Sox pros, led by Gary Bell, conduct a nightly kangaroo court, fining campers for dumb things they did during the day. The proceeds go to the Jimmy Fund, a children's charity. The camp ends with the camper teams playing against the pro mentors in general admission games at City of Palms Stadium. *The Boston Red Sox, c/o Major Sports Fantasies, Box 85, Waterbury, VT 05676, tel. 802/244–4100 or 800/226–7794, fax 802/ 244–5835. Early Feb. in Ft. Myers, FL: 7 nights, $3,500. Price includes lunches and 5 dinners but not breakfasts. Non-playing guest package: 7 nights, $750. Umpire program: 7 nights, $950. Coaching camp: 7 nights, $1,750. Campers must be at least 30 years old.*

CHICAGO CUBS What is it about those Cubs fans? This camp is so popular they have it 3 times a year, twice in January and once again in April. The campers all come down to train at Fitch Park in Mesa, Arizona, using the same facilities as the Cubs, then play their games in Ho Ho Kam Stadium nearby. Anywhere from 60 to 80 campers show up; capacity is 88. Roughly 12 major leaguers are on hand, including, in past years, Glenn Beckert, Ron Santo, Billy Williams, Jose Cardenal, and Joe Pepitone.

You stay at the Dobson Ranch Inn (tel. 602/831–7000), which is where the Milwaukee Brewers stay during their spring training. It's a plush resort on the edge of town,

with a top-ranked golf course, 20 tennis courts, and four pools. Nonplaying guests are welcome, but the Cubs don't have a guest package.

You eat breakfast at the hotel and lunch at the ball field. You're on your own for dinner. Videos of your games are shown every night. Many of the pros play golf, and campers are welcome to join them on the links or at the pool.

The Cubs also host a 3-day minicamp during the summer, held in Chicago at Wrigley Field and limited to 48 players. Campers have to find their own place to stay; fortunately, most of them live in Chicago. *The Chicago Cubs, c/o Randy Hundley's Baseball Camps, 130 S. Northwest Highway, Palatine, IL 60067, tel. 708/991–9595 or 800/766–4004, fax 708/991–9471. Jan. and late Apr. in Mesa, AZ: 7 nights, $2,995. Campers must be at least 30 years old. Chicago minicamp: 3 days, $1,895. Price includes lunches but not accommodations.*

CHICAGO WHITE SOX The Chicago White Sox are now running their own camp—8 days at the Ed Smith Sports Complex in Sarasota, Florida, the spring training home of the Sox. Four squads of players (44 campers) are each coached by two former White Sox major-league players, who might include Moose Skowron, Tom Packiorek, Rich Dotson, Ron Kittle, Dick Allen, Bill Melton, Billy Pierce, Gary Peters, Jim Landis, Greg Walker, and Ed Farmer. You stay in a private room at the Harley Sandcastle resort hotel on the Gulf of Mexico; optional half-day golf and fishing excursions are available. Breakfast and lunch is included, as well as opening and closing banquets. *The Chicago Fantasy Baseball Camps, Inc., c/o Aaron Michaelson, 3026 Carmel Dr., Flossmoor, IL 60722, tel. 708/799–2934, fax 708/799–2977. Late Jan. in Sarasota, FL: 7 nights for $2,325, airfare not included.*

CINCINNATI REDS The campers use the Reds' facilities in Plant City, Florida (east of Tampa), and games are played in the Plant City Stadium. Former Reds who have signed up in the past include Darrel Chaney, Don

Gullet, Jim Maloney, Joe Nuxhall, and Pat Zachry. Marge Schott and her dog have been known to drop by, as has Pete Rose.

The Reds take on a maximum of 96 campers. Breakfast is served at the hotel, and lunch is at the stadium. Dinners are not included, but the Reds host a cocktail party at the hotel every night with most of the pros in attendance. Guests not playing are welcome, and there's a good guest package.

Campers leave with an armful of Reds paraphernalia—the usual uniform, bats, balls, and videos. The team announces the campers to Reds fans prior to a regular-season game in Riverfront Stadium. *The Cincinnati Reds Baseball Heaven, c/o Baseball Heaven, Inc., Box 1033, Southampton, PA 18966, tel. 215/938–5075 or 800/755–7337. Late Jan. in Plant City, FL: 7 nights, $3,795 (including airfare). Guest package: 3 nights, $695 (including airfare). Campers must be at least 30 years old.*

CLEVELAND INDIANS The Indians hold their camp at their spring-training grounds at Chain-O'Lakes Stadium in Winter Haven, Florida. It's the complete facility used by the Indians, and all equipment is available to the campers. In the past, about 12 former major leaguers signed up, including Bob Feller, Mudcat Grant, Tito Francona, and Herb Score.

The camp has accommodated up to 120 campers. You stay at the Grenelefe Golf and Tennis Resort (tel. 813/422–7511) in Haines City, Florida, which is about 30 minutes from Orlando and 15 minutes from the ballpark. Should you bring a partner, or plan to stay on, the resort has three 18-hole golf courses, 20 tennis courts, and 4 pools. Campers stay in villa suites. Breakfast and lunch are served at the ballpark. You're on your own for dinner, except for the Saturday night banquet.

Campers are also treated to a reunion during the Indians' season at the Gateway facility in Cleveland. *The Cleveland Indians Baseball Heaven, c/o Baseball Heaven, Inc., Box 1033, Southampton, PA 18966, tel. 215/938–5075*

or 800/758–7423. Late Jan. in Winter Haven, FL: 7 nights, $3,795. Price includes airfare from anywhere in the continental United States. Guest package: 3 nights, $595 (including airfare). Campers must be at least 30 years old.

DETROIT TIGERS The Tigers have 2 week-long camps back-to-back at Tiger Town, their own training facility in Lakeland, Florida. Games are played in nearby Marchant Stadium. About 17 former players attend each camp; in the past the roster has included Mark Fidrych, Rocky Colavito, Al Kaline, and Mickey Lolich. Willie Horton, who is loved among the players for his barbecue, has also participated, playing and cooking.

Roughly 80 campers show up each week and are housed with the Tigers at the Holiday Inn-North in Lakeland (tel. 813/858–1411). The hotel has a pool but no tennis or golf. Campers are on their own for breakfast but are fed lunch at Tiger Town and five dinners at the hotel.

The Tigers are big on hosting evening social events, such as a championship night, where top teams are feted; and an autograph night, which features an open bar.

The Detroit camp is unique in that it has a large, very active alumni group. Former campers have games every other weekend during the season at a college in Detroit and sometimes take on the campers from the Cleveland Indians. The Tigers' campers have a luncheon every 6 weeks, publish a newsletter, and perform charity work. *Detroit Tigers Fantasy Camp, c/o Sports Fantasies, Inc., 28777 Northwestern Hwy., Suite 290, Southfield, MI 48034, tel. 810/353–5643 or 800/952–2671, fax 810/353–5641. Early Feb. in Lakeland, FL: 7 nights, $2,995. Price includes airfare from Detroit, lunches, and 5 dinners but not breakfasts. Guest package: 7 nights, $1,000 (including airfare from Detroit). Campers must be at least 21 years old. Register by Dec. 15.*

FLORIDA MARLINS The first ever camp for the Florida Marlins will be held in late January, 1996, in Melbourne, Florida, at Space

Coast Stadium. The current Marlins coaching staff, from both the major and minor leagues, and about a dozen players will be on hand. Campers will stay at the Hilton Rialto (407/768–0200) in Melbourne, a 242-room hotel near the airport with a restaurant, sports bar, pool, tennis court, and workout room. A total of 48 campers will participate in an opening night party, a closing banquet, and a "bull session" with the pros—an opportunity to ask questions about their careers. *The Florida Marlins Fantasy Camp, c/o Baseball Heaven, Box 1033, Southampton, PA 18966, tel. 215/938–5075, fax 215/938–5078. Late Jan. in Melbourne, FL: 7 nights, $3,595. Price does not include airfare. Guest package: $695 (3 nights). Campers must be at least 30 years old.*

LOS ANGELES DODGERS The Dodgers camp is unique in that the club owns its own 450-acre facility, including accommodations, dining room, conference center, 2 golf courses, and all the fitness equipment you would ever need. It's called Dodgertown and it's in Vero Beach, Florida.

There are 2 camps, one in November and one in February. About 15 former Dodgers, including some from the old Brooklyn Dodgers, show up. You meet and play ball with the likes of Ralph Branca, Carl Erskine, Steve Garvey, Clem Labine, and Duke Snider. Tommy Lasorda may show up for the big game on Saturday.

The camps sell out, with 96 campers in each. About 50% of the campers are repeat visitors—always a good sign. Because you stay at Dodgertown, you eat and sleep in the same facilities as the Dodgers. Spouses or friends aren't allowed to stay in players' rooms unless they're playing, too, but the Dodgers will help them find a room in town and will assist with transportation.

Nights are spent reviewing films and videos of the day's workout and of Dodgers World Series highlights.

Campers have a very strong alumni group, which travels and plays around the world. One year they traveled to Russia and played an exhibition game there. *Los Angeles Dodgers Adult Baseball Camp, Dodgertown, Box 2887, Vero Beach, FL 32961, tel. 407/569–4900 or 800/334–7529, fax 407/770–2424. Nov. and Feb. in Vero Beach, FL: 6 nights, $3,995. Price includes all meals. Campers must be at least 30 years old.*

MILWAUKEE BREWERS A relatively small number of campers—about 40—and up to 10 pros attend the Brewers' camp at Compadre Stadium in Chandler, Arizona, where the Brewers hold their own spring training. The camp might feature Rollie Fingers, Robin Yount, Gorman Thomas, Don Money, Jim Gantner, Mike Hegan, and Ken Sanders.

Accommodations are at the Dobson Ranch Inn (tel. 602/831–7000), a rather posh resort in a residential area outside Chandler, about 30 minutes from the stadium, and about 20 minutes east of Phoenix Airport. The two-story inn has a pool, and there's an 18-hole public golf course four blocks away. Breakfast is at the hotel and lunch is served at the stadium by the Brewers' kitchen staff. Dinner is on you until the Saturday night banquet. *The Milwaukee Brewers Fantasy Camp, c/o Baseball Fantasy Camps, Inc., Twin Lakes Park, 6700 Clark Rd., Sarasota, FL 34241, tel. 813/ 925–4855 or 800/336–2267, fax 813/922–3751. Mid Feb. in Chandler, AZ: 7 nights, $3,100. Price includes airfare from Milwaukee. Guest package: 3 nights, $750 (including airfare from Milwaukee). Players must be at least 30 years old.*

MINNESOTA TWINS The Twins' camp, under the same management as the Red Sox camp, is held in the Lee County Sports Complex in Ft. Myers, Florida. Although it's a minor-league facility, it has all the coaching and training equipment of a major-league camp, such as batting cages, pitching machines, and a clubhouse. The Twins also offer umpire and coaching schools.

Among the former Twins who have signed up in the past are Tony Oliva, "Mudcat" Grant, Frank Quilici, and Harmon Killebrew. The 60-odd campers stay at the Radisson Hotel in Ft. Myers (tel. 813/936–4300). The newly renovated Radisson is on Rte. 41

about 14 miles from the beaches. It has a two-story motel section, a five-story hotel, pool, tennis courts, and outdoor tiki bar. *The Minnesota Twins, c/o Major Sports Fantasies, Box 85, Waterbury, VT 05676, tel. 802/244–4100 or 800/226–7794 fax 802/244–5835. Late Jan. in Ft. Myers, FL: $3,500. Price includes all meals. Guest package: 7 nights, $750. Umpire camp in late Jan.: 7 nights, $950. Coaching camp in late Jan.: 7 nights, $1,750. Campers must be at least 30 years old.*

MONTREAL EXPOS At the Expos' (and the Atlanta Braves') spring training facility, Municipal Stadium in West Palm Beach, Florida, the likes of Gary Carter, Bill "Spaceman" Lee, Steve Rogers, Ken Singleton, Larry Parrish, Jeff Reardon, and Warren Cromartie teach the finer points of baseball to up to 78 fantasy camp participants. An outside company called PAS*SPORTS operates this program for the Expos. A coaching camp is run simultaneously; for half the price of the regular camp, you can serve as the assistant to a professional coach throughout the week.

After working on baseball techniques all day, campers socialize with the pros during four scheduled group dinners, participate in a trivia contest hosted by two Expos broadcasters, and join in the uproarious laughter at Warren Cromartie's outrageous kangaroo court.

Campers and the pros who don't live in the area stay at the comfortable MacArthurs Holiday Inn on I-95, the former spring training headquarters hotel for the Expos and just 10 minutes north of the ballpark.

Alumni reunite at two Expos games at Olympic Stadium. At one game, they have dinner and watch the game together; at the other, they come out onto the field in uniform in front of thousands of spectators and are introduced by name as their picture flashes on the scoreboard. *Montréal Expos Fantasy Camp, Box 8235, Warwick, RI 02888, tel. 401/785–2637 or 800/989–2267. Feb. in West Palm Beach, FL: 7 nights, $3,095. Price includes breakfasts, lunches,* *and 4 dinners. Guest package: 7 nights, $425 (including breakfasts, lunches, and 4 dinners). Coaching camp: 7 nights, $1,600 (including breakfasts, lunches, and 4 dinners). Campers must be at least 22 years old.*

NEW YORK METS The Mets play host to some enthusiastic campers in Port St. Lucie, Florida, and no wonder: As many as 30 former players return each year, and many of them stay in the same hotel as the campers. The roster has included Bud Harrelson, Ed Charles, Jerry Koosman, and Gary Carter. Games are played in the Thomas J. White Stadium, about 10 miles from the five-story Holiday Inn (tel. 407/337–2200), where both pros and campers stay. The hotel is on U.S. Hwy. 1 in Port St. Lucie, about 8 miles from the beach. The hotel has a pool and there are several 18-hole golf courses nearby. Guests are welcome, but there's no guest package.

About 100 campers show up each year, and space fills up early. The Mets camp is unique in that it encourages people with disabilities to attend. "Playing skills are not necessary—having a good time is," is their motto, and they make sure you get to play, regardless of your ability.

Breakfast is at the hotel, lunch is in the clubhouse, but you're on your own for dinners. There's also a reunion game in which campers play on the field before the big league game and then get announced to the crowd. *The New York Mets Fantasy Camp, c/o Baseball Heaven, Inc., Box 1033, Southampton, PA 18966, tel. 215/938-5075 or 800/898–6387. Early Feb. in Port St. Lucie, FL: 7 nights, $3,995. Price includes airfare from New York, breakfasts, and lunches. Campers must be at least 30 years old.*

NEW YORK YANKEES At the New York Yankees Spring Training Headquarters in Fort Lauderdale, a talented crew of baseball stars, which might include Ron Guidry, Jake Gibbs, Bucky Dent, Moose Skowron, Catfish Hunter, Mickey Rivers, John Blanchard, Bobby Mercer, Yogi Berra, Enos Slaughter, and former Yankee manager Hank Bauer teach 90 campers at each of three week-long programs in early spring and fall.

A private room is reserved for every camper at the Palm-Aire Spa Resort in Pompano Beach (tel. 305/972–3300 or 800/272–5624), 15 minutes from Fort Lauderdale International Airport. This is where the Yankees stay during spring training. The resort has 5 golf courses, 37 tennis courts, and a state-of-the-art health club.

The camp is big on loading campers up with lots of paraphernalia—more than just the standard uniform, balls, and cards. *Mickey Mantle's Week of Dreams, Box 7777, Grayson, KY 41143-7777, tel. 606/474–7771, fax 606/474–8008. Early May and late Oct.–early Nov. in Fort Lauderdale, FL: 7 nights, $4,200. Price includes airfare from New York (or a travel credit toward airfare from elsewhere), private room, breakfast at the hotel and lunch in the clubhouse. Guests stay free in campers' rooms. Campers must be at least 30 years old.*

PHILADELPHIA PHILLIES Campers can rub shoulders with their favorite Phillies players at the Carpenter Complex in Clearwater, FL, the team's winter home, during one of two special spring training weeks in which you live the life of a pro alongside the stars. At the end of the week, campers get to show their mettle in the Dream Game when they play against the pros in an all-star line-up at Jack Russell Stadium. Former Phillies who have participated include Larry Bowa, Dave Cash, Greg Luzinski, Kent Tekulve, Tony Taylor, Richie Allen, Rick Wise, John Callison, Grank Jackson, Gary Matthews, and Dallas Green. This is a popular camp, with 13 years behind it, so register early. Up to 104 campers attend each weeklong session. There are parties and dinners with the pros, and campers make a special appearance in uniform at Veterans Stadium during the regular season. *The Philadelphia Phillies, c/o Dream Week, Inc., Suite 203, Huntingdon Valley Federal Building, 2617 Huntingdon Pike, Huntingdon Valley, PA 19006, tel. 215/938–1200, fax 215/938–7746. Mid Jan. to early Feb. in Clearwater, FL: 7 nights, $3,995. Price includes airfare from Philadelphia, hotel, and all breakfasts and lunches. Campers must be at least 30 years old.*

PITTSBURGH PIRATES Campers come down to the Pirates' training facility in Bradenton, Florida, and games are played at McKechnie Field. About a dozen former players spend the week with you, and as many as 25 may show up for the game on Saturday. Possible players include Chuck Tanner, Al Martin, Jay Bell, and Bill Mazeroski.

A maximum of 72 campers stay at the Holiday Inn-Riverfront (tel. 813/747–3727) in downtown Bradenton, about 15 minutes from the field. The hotel has an outdoor pool but no golf or tennis; the beach is 9 miles away. Breakfast and lunch are served in the Pirate City cafeteria. Three dinners are taken at the hotel when the team hosts question-and-answer sessions and signs autographs. There's no package for nonplaying guests, but the Pirates will assist with arrangements.

The Pirates host a reunion during the regular season and introduce the campers in their uniforms during a game at Three Rivers Stadium. *Pittsburgh Pirates Camp Bradenton, c/o The Pittsburgh Pirates, 600 Stadium Circle, Pittsburgh, PA 15212, tel. 412/323–5025, fax 412/323–5024. Early Jan. in Bradenton, FL: 7 nights, $3,295. Price includes airfare from anywhere in the continental United States, breakfasts, lunches, and 3 dinners. Campers must be at least 30. Register by mid-Dec.*

ST. LOUIS CARDINALS The Cardinals have a 3-day summer camp held once a year in St. Louis, with games played in Busch Stadium. Up to 45 campers come to practice and play against 9 pros, including Bob Gibson and Curt Flood.

The biggest difference between this and other camps, other than its short duration, is that no accommodations are provided and most of the campers live in the St. Louis area. The pros usually stay at the Marriott Pavilion (tel. 314/421–1776) across the street from the stadium and may make dinner plans or have drinks with the campers, but nothing is planned by the camp. *The St. Louis Cardinals, c/o Randy Hundley's Baseball Camps, 130 S. Northwest Hwy, Palatine, IL 60067, tel. 708/991–9595, fax 708/991–9471. Sum-*

mer in St. Louis, MO: 3 nights, $1,795. Price includes lunch but no accommodations or ground transportation. Campers must be at least 21 years old.

SAN FRANCISCO GIANTS This popular camp, limited to 96 players, is held at Arizona's Scottsdale Stadium at Indian School Park, where the Giants go for spring training. Campers and pros stay together at the two-story Radisson Resort, Scottsdale (tel. 602/991–3800), which has tennis courts and a pool but no golf. Veteran pros include Dusty Baker, Bob Brenly, Orlando Cepeda, Jim Davenport, Mike Krukow, and Chris Speier. There's an almost 60% return rate, so be sure to register at least 6 months in advance. Early enrollees (all who register by September or the first 60 people) get to play at Candlestick Park following a Giants' game. A variety of packages are available for guests. *San Francisco Giants Fantasy Camp, Candlestick Park, San Francisco, CA 94124, tel. 415/330–2575 or 800/442–6874, fax 415/467–3803 or 415/330–2697. Early Feb. in Scottsdale, AZ: 7 nights, $3,995. Price includes airfare from San Francisco. Guest package: $600–$1,400. Campers must be at least 30 years old.*

TORONTO BLUE JAYS Begun in 1991, the Blue Jays camp is owned and operated by three current members of the Blue Jays organization: first-base coach Bob Bailor, minor-league manager Garth Iorg, and Ken Carson, director of Florida operations. About 15 former Blue Jays, including John Mayberry, Willie Upshaw, and Buck Martinez, assist in instructing a maximum of 70 campers at the Blue Jays' spring training facilities in Dunedin, Florida, 30 miles west of Tampa International Airport.

The program begins on Superbowl Sunday, so the highlight of the welcome party is the huddle around the TV to watch the game. For the rest of the week, though, the focus is baseball, baseball, baseball.

Accommodations may vary from year to year. Participants have stayed about 10 miles from the ballpark at the Adam's Mark Caribbean Gulf Resort (tel. 813/443–5714 or 800/444–2326) on the Gulf of Mexico. In their free time campers can go jet skiing and parasailing at the hotel, and tennis courts and golf courses are a few miles away. Many of the pros stay in the same hotel as the campers. Four nights during the week, special guests, who may include current Blue Jays, show up at the hotel for informal chats; in 1995, World Series MVP Pat Borders, former pitcher Dave Steib, and manager Cito Gaston fielded questions from campers.

Participants have been invited to a reunion during the old timers' game at the SkyDome, the Blue Jays' regular-season home. *Blue Jays Fantasy Camp, Box 957, Dunedin, FL 34697, tel. 813/736–0705 or 800/549–1992 or fax, 813/738–4531. Late Jan.–early Feb. in Dunedin, FL: 7 nights, $3,600. Price includes airfare, breakfasts, lunches, and two dinners. Guest package: 7 nights, $850 (including airfare but not meals). Campers must be at least 30 years old.*

MLB ALL STAR DREAM WEEK The Major League Baseball All Star Dream Week primarily caters to fans in cities without big-league teams. You get to practice and play every day with big-league coaches at the Carpenter Complex in Clearwater, Florida, one of the finest training facilities in baseball. You also get to play against the all-star pros at the end of the week in the Dream Game. Former All Stars who have participated include Bob Feller, Pat Kelly, Bob Gibson, Cookie Rojas, Paul Splittorff, John Mayberry, Lee May, Larry Bowa, George Foster, Don DiMaggio, Kent Tekulve, Steve Garvey, Bill Madlock, and Greg Luzinski. *The MLB All Star Dream Week, c/o Dream Week, Inc., Suite 203, Huntingdon Valley Federal Building, 2617 Huntingdon Pike, Huntingdon Valley, PA 19006, tel. 215/938–1200, fax 215/938–7746. Mid Jan. in Clearwater, FL: 7 nights, $3,995. Price includes hotel, all breakfasts and lunches, and parties and dinners with the pros; it does not include airfare. Campers must be at least 30 years old.*

BROOKS ROBINSON This camp, formerly the Baltimore Orioles' camp, is conducted by Baseball Fantasy Camps, Inc. This is one of the most popular, due to steady management and enthusiastic Baltimore Orioles fans. In the past enrollment has been capped at 130 campers, enough for 10 teams. A high percentage of the participants—more than 40%—are repeats. The big change now is that Hall of Famer Brooks Robinson will be at the camp all week. Other former Orioles scheduled to appear include Earl Weaver, Paul Blair, Mike Cuellar, Rich Dauer, Eddie Watt, and Hall of Famer Hoyt Wilhelm.

Everything takes place at Ed Smith Stadium in Sarasota, Florida. The park has 5 fields, a field house, and a variety of training equipment, including pitching machines and batting cages. The 10 teams play doubleheaders each day, leading up to the big game on Saturday against the former Orioles.

Accommodations are at the Harley Sand Castle Hotel (tel. 813/388–2181) on Lido Beach in Sarasota, Florida. It has two pools but no tennis courts; golf is 15 minutes away. Breakfast and lunch are taken at the ballpark, prepared and served by the Orioles' kitchen staff. Campers are on their own for dinner, except for the awards banquet.

A reunion night is held with each player from the fantasy camp, in uniform, announced in Camden Yards prior to an Orioles game. *The Brooks Robinson Fantasy Camp, c/o Baseball Fantasy Camps, Inc., Twin Lakes Park, 6700 Clark Rd., Sarasota, FL 34241, tel. 813/925–4855 or 800/336–2267, fax 813/922–3751. Early Feb.: 7 nights, $3,600. Price includes airfare from Baltimore. Guest package: 3 nights, $725 (including airfare from Baltimore). Campers must be at least 30 years old.*

FIELD OF DREAMS This camp is held each year over Labor Day Weekend in Dyersville, Iowa, using the actual field built for Field of Dreams, the popular 1989 baseball film. Campers play for 3 days in copies of 1919 White Sox uniforms, and they attend an awards banquet. Evening activities include a riverboat cruise on the Mississippi, a cookout, and a VIP reception. This camp has had an elite list of former major-league players, including Hall of Famers Brooks Robinson, Rollie Fingers, and Lou Brock.

The camp is limited to 45 campers, who are broken down into 4 squads. Two squads play an inning, then warm the benches while the other 2 play an inning, until the games are completed.

Everyone stays at the Best Western Dubuque Inn (tel. 319/556–7760), which is 26 miles from the stadium. The hotel has an indoor pool, and there are two golf courses within 3 miles. Breakfast is at the hotel and lunch is served at the field. Guests not playing are welcome, but there is no package for them. *Field of Dreams Baseball Camp, c/o Baseball Fantasy Camps, Inc., Twin Lakes Park, 6700 Clark Rd., Sarasota, FL 34241, tel. 813/925–4855 or 800/336–2267, fax 813/922–3751. Labor Day Weekend: 5 nights, $1,800 (airfare not included). Campers must be at least 30 years old.*

TEAMS WITHOUT CAMPS These are the teams that, as of mid-1995, had no camps of their own. You may want to call and ask about their future plans.

California Angels, Box 2000, Anaheim, CA 92803, tel. 714/937–7200.

Oakland Athletics, Oakland Coliseum, Oakland, CA 94621, tel. 510/638–4900.

Seattle Mariners, Box 4100, Seattle, WA 98104, tel. 206/628–3555.

Colorado Rockies, 1700 Hwy., Suite 2100, Denver, CO 80290, tel. 303/292–0200.

San Diego Padres, Box 2000, San Diego, CA 92112, tel. 619/283–7294.

Texas Rangers, Box 90111, Arlington, TX 76004-3111, tel. 817/273–5222.

Houston Astros, Box 288, Houston, TX 77001-0288, tel. 713/799–9708.

Chicago White Sox, 333 W. 35th St., Chicago, IL 60616, tel. 312/924–1000.

Kansas City Royals, Box 419969, Kansas City, MO 64141-6969, tel. 816/921–2200.

Basketball Fantasy Camps

By Michael J. Sullivan

Updated by Steven R. Adang

ou know your weekend game of hoops could be better. You know that somewhere deep inside you is a gravity-defying, in-your-face, slam-dunking machine. You know, as you watch your favorite NBA star pull off a lightning fast pick-and-roll and then duck and bob and weave and leap his way to the net, that you, too, could do that. Well, maybe, sort of. If somebody showed you how. With practice. Well, here's your chance.

At a basketball fantasy camp, usually held in the NBA's off-season, current and former professional players and coaches lead men and women through some fundamentals of the game in 4 or 5 days of serious workouts, coaching tips, practice drills, and competition—in short, total immersion in all things basketball. This is your chance to improve your game and get some insight into how the pros do it.

Basketball fantasy camps are a relatively new phenomenon, not nearly as widespread as their baseball counterparts. They should not be confused with the numerous basketball camps run for high-school players hoping for the attention of college team scouts. These camps are for adults. Unlike baseball fantasy camps, which are usually sponsored by individual teams, these camps are often independently run. NBA teams do, however, sometimes donate equipment and tickets to their games.

All camps follow the same basic format: You're teamed up with other players of similar ability, go through warm-up routines, run individual skill drills, and participate in everything from one-on-one to full-team competitions. Next you learn NBA plays and use them during a league-style series of games climaxing with a big match on the last day. Although none of the schools requires a particular skill level, you'll have a hard time keeping up if you don't play at least some hoops and aren't already in pretty good shape. All camps have you sign a liability waiver, and one asks for written verification from your doctor that says you're up to the intense workout.

In fact, the word *fantasy* ought to be taken with a few grains of salt. These camps aren't about basketball as a spectator sport—you are expected to work through the same drills and practice moves that the pros do. Your skills and stamina are tested to the limit and improved. Just don't expect to increase your hang-time by too much: Some moves are possible only if you're 7 feet tall.

CHOOSING THE RIGHT TRIP

Because there are so few basketball camps most people won't find one where their favorite team's players are sure to be. And since the instruction is top-notch across the board, you'll probably pick a camp because

Host of a weekly sports radio show on New York's Long Island, Michael J. Sullivan is a lifelong hoops fan and has written a book for children about Shaquille O'Neal. Steven Adang is still recovering from the retirement of Dr. J., the greatest of all time.

of the reputations of the camp leaders, the price, or the location. When choosing a camp, it's a good idea to ask the following:

Which NBA pros besides the camp leaders have signed on as staff? Every year different players help coach the camp teams. There is no guarantee that a particular player will return year after year, so if meeting your favorite basketball star is the only reason you plan to sign up, make sure he'll be there.

How large is the camp? As far as working on your game, the total number of campers won't matter so long as there is at least one coach for each group of players. One of the beauties of basketball is its flexibility: You have only 6 players? Fine, just play 3-on-3. If there are an even number of players up to 10, let the game begin. The size of the camp *will* make a difference, however, in the amount and quality of the time you spend on the court with whichever NBA stars you came to be near.

How much playing time can you expect to get? Get a sense of the ratio of time spent on drills and individual skill instruction, and how much is spent in scrimmages. If you have several hours of free time each day, find out what else there is to see and do in the area.

What's the cost and what's included? The Magic Johnson camp's per-day fee is more than twice that of the other two. This has a lot to do with location—Lake Tahoe and Aspen or Vail versus Maui—but is also a reflection of the luxuriousness of the camp. Unless otherwise noted, prices are per person, based on double occupancy (which means that you'll be rooming with another player unless you pay an additional fee) and include lodging, dinner, and either lunch or breakfast. T-shirts, shorts, basketballs, and sometimes even basketball shoes are all supplied.

What are accommodations like? Campers stay in generally upscale hotels. Ask for brochures that list facilities and find out which rooms campers are slated for.

What's the food like? Generally, you eat in the hotel restaurant.

How far in advance do I need to book? The camps we list require from 1 to 3 months advance booking.

THE CAMPS

THE ROCKIES

COLORADO **Fantasy Camp.** The Denver Nuggets started this fun-filled camp in Aspen in 1994; it wasn't held in 1995, but the camp is expected to be an annual event starting again in 1996.

The 4-day camp is held in late August or early September to escape the summer heat of the Rockies. You arrive on Thursday evening in time for a team dinner and a get-acquainted banquet with your 49 fellow campers (who have been between the ages of 22–53), who range from dedicated couch-potato Nugget fans to YMCA-court junkies.

Friday and Saturday are spent doing skill drills, skill competitions, one-on-ones, 3-point shooting, and playing 3-on-3 and 4-on-4 half-court games under the watchful eyes of respectively present and past Nugget coaches Bernie Bickerstaff and Dan Issel. Other previous instructors have been former Nugget great Walter Davis and current NBA players Bryant Stith, Rodney Rogers, and Scott Hastings.

All day Sunday is reserved for a round-robin tournament of full-court games followed by an awards dinner that concludes the camp.

Lodging is single accommodation in a plush Rocky Mountain resort, and many campers bring their families along for a vacation. As we went to press, hotel plans were not finalized but campers will most likely stay at one of Aspen Snowmass's 6 hotels (970/923–2010). All proceeds from the camp go to the team's community fund, which supports various youth organizations in the Denver area. Included in your weekend package is an authentic Nuggets jersey, sports bag, videotape of the weekend highlights, and a simulated NBA contract. *Denver Nuggets, 1635 Clay Street, McNichols Arena, Denver,*

CO 80204, tel. 303/893–6700, fax 303/893–3203. Late Aug.–early Sept. (1996): 4 days, $2,500. Price includes single accommodation and all meals.

THE SOUTHWEST

NEVADA **Cotton Fitzsimmons/Kurt Rambis/Connie Hawkins Fastbreak Fantasy Camp.** Since 1991, this fantasy camp held on the Nevada side of Lake Tahoe for a single 6-day session in early July has attracted a diverse group of 26 basketball fanatics, most of them devoted followers of the Phoenix Suns.

The big draw here is long-time Phoenix coach and local hero Cotton Fitzsimmons. Hall of Famer and Brooklyn schoolyard legend Connie Hawkins, and Kurt Rambis, one of basketball's great storytellers and a veteran of four NBA championships with the Lakers, fill out the roster. Past camps have drawn other present and former greats, including Charles Barkley and Lionel Hollins.

You're on the courts for 5 hours each day, in 2½-hour practice sessions, each packed with passing, dribbling, and shooting drills designed to increase your heart rate, strengthen your legs, and sharpen your eye. You also learn how to fight through picks and master the pick-and-roll. Practice and games take place at the Incline Village High School gymnasium, not far from the hotel.

You stay at the Hyatt Regency Tahoe in Incline Village. Breakfast and dinner, included in the package, are served at the hotel's restaurant; for lunch, you're on your own. Among the souvenirs you take home are your practice gear, a new pair of Nike basketball shoes, a team photo, and a video of the final game.

You must be 30 or older to attend, and you need a note from your doctor asserting that you're fit enough to play. *Cotton Fitzsimmons/ Kurt Rambis/ Connie Hawkins Fastbreak Fantasy Camp, Box 1369, Phoenix, AZ 85001, tel. 602/514–8246, fax 602/379–7922. July: 5 days, $3,200. Price includes airfare, ground transfers, and 2 meals per day.*

HAWAII

MAUI **Magic Johnson/Jerry West Executive Camp.** Don't get the idea that you come here just to watch a dazzling show of round-ball by two legendary former Lakers. This camp is about improving your overall conditioning and polishing up such basic skills as passing, shooting, and dribbling.

It is also pricey—but look at where it's held and who's leading it. Both Magic Johnson and Jerry West were on several championship Los Angeles Lakers teams—in different eras—and are among the best guards the game has ever seen. They now conduct a couple of 5-day basketball camps each July, on the west end of Maui, in the beach resort town of Lahaina.

You and your 29 fellow campers will be put through your paces by Johnson, West, and the other 5 past and present NBA pros on the staff. You also get personal attention from the stars, and Magic Johnson gets to know every camper.

Five hours a day are spent learning and going through the same drills and plays that Johnson and West used when they were with the Lakers. Each day is broken up into 2 on-court sessions—3 hours in the morning, then another 2 hours from 4 PM to 6 PM, allowing time in between to rest up, explore Maui, or practice what you learned before noon. Toward the end of the camp there are 3-on-3, free-throw, and 3-point-shot competitions.

You play on the courts at the Maui Civic Center gymnasium in Lahaina. On the fifth day your squad participates in a final game, with Lakers announcer Chick Hearn calling the play-by-play. There's a luau on the beach the night before the big game, and a closing and awards ceremony at a brunch banquet after it.

Lodging is in the Westin Maui hotel on Kaanapali Beach. Every camper gets his or her own room, and meals at the hotel restaurant are part of the package. The luau and banquet aside, there isn't much organized activity off the court, although socializing among campers and between campers and staff is commonplace. Those who can afford to come here tend to be successful business executives and Hollywood celebrity types. Bring your business cards—everyone else does. Film director Garry Marshall, like many campers, attends almost every year. Still, it's basketball not business that you've come for, and while schmoozing happens, it doesn't happen on the court and isn't the focus of the camp. Some campers even bring their families. The camp has sold out every year that it's been held (the past 8 years), so sign up well in advance.

You take home such mementos as a monogrammed Lakers uniform, practice gear, a new pair of basketball shoes, a sports duffle bag, photos of yourself with your fellow campers and with Magic Johnson and Jerry West, and the video—with Chick Hearn's play-by-play—of your final game. And camp ain't necessarily over when it's over; you are invited to a reunion game at the Lakers' home court in the Los Angeles Forum, where you play in front of the crowd gathered for that night's NBA matchup. *Magic Johnson Enterprises, Inc., 9100 Wilshire Blvd., West Tower Suite 1060, Beverly Hills,* *CA 90212, tel. 310/247–1994, fax 310/247–0733. July: 5 days, $6,100. Price includes a private room, 3 meals per day, and 2 adult tickets to each event; sign up at least 3 months in advance.*

SOURCES

There is no umbrella organization for basketball fantasy camps, so information about them can be hard to come by. To find out if any besides those listed above are being held this year, call your local or favorite NBA team and ask if any of its players or coaches are running a camp. Don't bother calling the NBA; its representatives will not have this information.

PUBLICATIONS The NBA's magazine, *Hoop* (355 Lexington Ave., New York, NY 10017, tel. 508/452–6310), sold at every franchise's arena, is one place to find out about upcoming basketball fantasy camps. You might also scrutinize the ads in the back pages of *Sports Illustrated* (Time-Life Building, Rockefeller Center, New York, NY 10020, tel. 212/522–1212).

Bicycling

By Bill Strickland

See the country by bike and you see it as no one else can. Cycling brings you closer to the landscape, the people, the wildlife—closer even to the spirit of the land. When cycling, you notice hills, dips, rough roads, and breezes; you pay attention to the weather. Bicyclists travel slowly enough to spot rare flowers, birds, and small animals, and quietly enough to happen upon deer and other large mammals. Locals will wave to cyclists, or stop to chat while you're refueling at the country store.

Still, you can travel long distances on a bike: You see more and cover more ground than you could on foot. A laid-back bike tour might cover 150 or 200 miles in less than a week. Big-ride sessions can go 600 miles. Yes, you can do it. Bike touring is easy on the body. Modern bikes are more comfortable than ever and have more gears for easier pedaling. On the right terrain, even an out-of-shape noncyclist can cover 30 miles or more before lunch. I once toured with a woman who hadn't been on a bike in five years; she rode 130 miles in a week. On another tour, I pedaled alongside a recreational rider who finished a 250-mile trek just one year after hip-replacement surgery.

The existence of commercial touring companies makes it possible for just about anyone to tour by bike. These organizations supply the expertise. There's no need for you to know how to plot a bike-friendly route, arrange food and lodging, customize your bike to carry equipment and luggage, or fix a flat tire. You don't even have to own a bike. You simply choose an area of the country you'd like to see, identify the companies that offer tours there, and ask a few questions to make sure you and the trip are a good match (*see* Choosing the Right Trip, *below*). And, of course, you have to pay: A bike trip with an outfitter can run from $130 to $250 per day, not including bike rental. If you want to cut costs, you can opt for a camping trip instead of an inn trip.

A typical touring company offers a selection of 2- to 10-day trips with preplanned routes, and usually provides at least 2 guides for every trip: One rides with the cyclists, and the other drives a support van along the route. This van transports your luggage to each destination and patrols the route, carrying water, snacks, repair equipment, and even tired cyclists. Most companies also rent bikes.

These organized trips have from 6 to 15 riders and range from day-long pedaling marathons to casual jaunts with many stops, in which the bike is mainly used to travel from one point of interest to another. Will you ride too fast or too slow to remain with the group? It doesn't matter. Most tours offer multiple options for each day's ride. You can go short or long, flat or hilly, hard or easy.

Bill Strickland, managing editor of *Bicycling* magazine, pedals his way to work every day and races mountain bikes frequently. In more than 10 years of riding he's toured every corner of the United States.

Whichever option you choose, you won't be alone. Just as there are no atheists in a foxhole, there are no enemies on a bike tour. Sharing physical challenges seems to bond people. I've yet to join a tour on which the participants didn't cheer each other on during the day and gather at night to share tales from the road. It seems that at least one close, lasting friendship is formed on every trip, and it's not uncommon for riders to meet a mate.

Of course, traveling as a group can be a drag. You're tied to a common schedule for everything from waking in the morning to eating dinner. Sometimes your meals must be selected from a limited menu. If the weather stinks, you can't hide in the lodge for another day. If you need a rest day, it's more often than not spent in the back of the support van—not exactly the best way to explore the country. See an inn you'd rather stay at, or enjoy a village so much you'd like to tarry there an extra day? Too bad.

Most tour veterans I've talked with, however, agree that the advantages of commercial trips outweigh these inconveniences. The few bad experiences I've heard about occurred when cyclists chose trips that didn't match their cycling ability. But if you'd still rather gather a group of friends and create your own itinerary, most bike-touring companies will be glad to guide you.

I said that anyone could complete a bike tour. I did not say that anyone could complete any bike tour. I had a great time one summer on a week-long trip that covered 850 miles. Maybe a 30-mile-per-day bike-and-shop through quaint New England towns is more your speed. Or maybe you're in excellent shape but don't want to grind out 100-plus miles per day—you'd prefer biking yourself senseless with 50 miles of Colorado mountain passes every morning.

It is important to match your physical ability and ambition to the trip. Don't sign up for the toddler trip along the Outer Banks and then complain that you aren't getting enough training miles at your target heart rate. Nor should you let your aspirations outweigh your common sense and land you in a West Coast hammerhead tour with ultra-fit riders when you just wanted to spin a few miles between sips of wine.

In the trip descriptions, we've tried to give you an accurate picture of how tough the riding will be. Don't judge toughness by mileage alone. I've been toasted senseless by 20 miles of hilly Pennsylvania roads, and walked away from 65 flat Florida miles whistling and wishing for more. Pay attention to other factors such as terrain description, number of off-bike activities (the more detours, the less strenuous the trip is likely to be), and even the time of year. Rolling Kentucky hills in September? Sign me up. Same territory in summer's dog days? Ugh.

The classic touring areas are New England (especially Vermont and the Massachusetts coast), Pennsylvania, North Carolina and Virginia, and California. They all deserve your consideration, but pay attention to the other listings, too. Tour companies have branched out in the past few years, and some of these gambles have led to the discovery of amazing new areas for bike touring. Any region seems fair game these days.

Also be honest about your level of comfort. Rugged camping trips sound admirable, but it's okay to spoil yourself on a pampered tour of plush resorts. Hey, it's a vacation.

Finally, there's food. Fuel. You burn a lot of calories on a week-long tour—up to 2,000 calories per day—so you must take in a lot simply to replace your energy stores. This means you get to eat and eat and eat and not feel one bit guilty. Gaining weight on a bike tour is almost impossible. Indulge: spicy Mexican meals, fresh seafood, hearty midwestern dinners, heapings of family-style Amish fare, campfire-grilled anything, homemade soups and breads. The secret's out. Sure you must eat to ride, but you can also ride to eat.

See you on the road. And, as the pros say, keep the rubber side down.

CHOOSING THE RIGHT TRIP

To be included in these listings, each touring company had to offer trips along preplanned, established routes; provide at least 2 mileage options each day; furnish some type of support (such as motorized route patrols, "sag" service for tired or injured riders, and luggage transport); provide or assist in arranging lodging; supply at least some meals; and require the use of helmets (you never appreciate a skid lid until you need it).

But before you buy, take some time to learn more about the company and the specific tour you're interested in. Don't be shy about asking questions. And if the organizers seem too busy to respond, that's a kind of response in itself.

How long has the company been in business? You take a trip with an outfitter in order to capitalize on its experience. Make sure it has enough, or at least the people running it do.

Who are the leaders, how old are they, and how are they trained? Sound a little nosy? Hey, you're putting your whole vacation in these people's hands. Make sure they're fit to hold it.

How tough is the trip? Find out as much as you can. Describe your riding experience and physical condition, then ask if the organizer thinks you can do the trip (or if you'll be bored). You'll get an honest answer: A miserable guest is not a repeat guest.

How much can the mileage be increased (or decreased)? Most companies will go beyond their stated limits.

What's the weather like when I want to tour? Some folks like it hot; others think cold is "fresh." In any case, you will have to bring the proper clothes.

What are the accommodations like? Be specific or be surprised. Some impressive bed-and-breakfast inns, for example, require you to share hallway bathrooms or telephone lines. If it's a camping trip, find out if you'll be in a campground with hot showers or in farmer Joe's field.

What are the meals like? Same idea. Also, most companies skip at least one lunch or dinner. We list these deletions but changes may occur.

Will laundry service be available? This could be the difference between one suitcase or two.

What's the cost and what's included? Costs vary from outfitter to outfitter, depending on the type of accommodations, the quality of the food, or simply the remoteness of the area where you'll be biking. Prices in these listings are per person and include double occupancy, lodging, meals, gratuities, entrance fees to parks and attractions, and, when applicable, camping fees.

Always ask whether there are extras: $75 for that hot-air balloon trip or $50 for the massage that was added shortly before the tour. Airfare, the cost of shuttle service between the airport and the trip starting and ending points, and the cost of renting bikes or other equipment are not included in prices we quote, unless we note otherwise.

What is the makeup of the touring group? You can find out the size of the group and the participants' ages, gender, marital status, and home states. This will keep you from being a third wheel in a couples-only tour.

Is this same tour available for singles (families, senior citizens, women, whatever)? You may prefer to pedal with your peers. Some companies offer reduced rates for kids and families.

How extensive is the support? Some companies make only one or two runs along a route; others patrol constantly. Find out how many guides work each trip. The more the better.

Can the leaders handle minor mechanical repairs (and is there a charge)? Something will break. Something always breaks. If it's just a wheel that needs minor truing, I'd expect a freebie. But be reasonable: If your bottom bracket and hubs must be overhauled, cough up a tip even if the guide doesn't charge you for 2 hours of labor.

What is the rental equipment like? Find out what brands of bikes are used, how many sizes they offer, and how old the fleet is. Between the sleek road bike and thrasher mountain bike lies an ideal touring compromise called a hybrid, or cross bike. These are equipped with flat bars (for an upright sitting position and more stability) and semi-wide tires (for a cushy but easy-spinning ride). Ask if the company has these. If you want special equipment—gel saddles or mixte frames—make sure you can get it. Ditto for camping equipment. Prices quoted in the listings for rentals get you a two-wheeler for the duration of the trip.

Do you offer free helmet use?

What extras are included? Many companies offer T-shirts, sweatshirts, water bottles, and other freebies.

Are any local events happening before or after the tour? I have biking buddies who only take tours when they can piggyback big events such as the Kentucky Derby or wine harvest festivals with their trips.

How far in advance must I book? The most popular trips may fill up a year in advance; others can be booked just a month before. Always call if you want to make a last-minute booking; cancellations are common.

Do you have references from past guests? To be honest, I never call the telephone numbers I get. But if a company ever refused to give me any names, it would make me wonder why.

MAJOR PLAYERS

When it comes to touring companies, bigger is usually better, although many small organizations run fine programs. The difference between small companies and the major players is scope. Where the small tour operator offers 6 yearly trips, the large organization runs 30. The small operator works within a state or a small multistate area. The major companies span whole geographic regions, coasts, maybe even the entire country. If one tour is booked, they can offer another (and another) with approximately the same flavor.

Following are descriptions of the major touring companies, the ones with the most consistent quality and widest variety of tours. If you can't find exactly what you're looking for in our listings, give these touring experts a call and ask about their other offerings.

BACKROADS This is the biggest touring company in the world. In business since 1979, it offers more than 90 different road and mountain biking trips, in the U.S. and abroad, each run several times per year. The company has a heavy West Coast and western U.S. bias, although it continues to expand.

Backroads is famous for its exquisite lunches, prepared by the guides in the company's fleet of custom-designed trailers. The full menu for trips reads like the bill of fare at a better big-city eatery: smoked salmon, homemade pasta with pesto, and fresh fruit cobbler. I've never eaten better than on a Backroads trip.

Accommodations include historic hotels, grand chateaux, comfortable lodges, and country inns with regional flavor and personality. Camping trips are also available.

Backroads rents its own line of touring bikes, made by Chimayo. The guides are generally young and knowledgeable about cycling and the area of the tour. I've never talked to anyone who's been disappointed with a Backroads trip, although some cyclists complain that the itineraries are too tame. (1516 5th St., Berkeley, CA 94710–1740, Suite B122, tel. 510/527–1555 or 800/462–2848, fax 510/527–1444).

VERMONT BICYCLE TOURING Going strong since 1972, Vermont Bicycle Touring (VBT) now runs 17 different tours in Vermont, 22 in other states, and 7 in other countries, serving 7,000 to 8,000 guests each year.

Accommodations on VBT's U.S. trips rival those of the other top-notch companies, and many of the same restaurants are used; 3–5 lunches are included with the price of each tour. The plentiful and tasty spreads are not quite as extravagant as those of Backroads, but neither are VBT's prices.

Typical VBT guests are casual cyclists, including lots of older riders, but the company also seems to attract riders who want to hammer, or ride a lot of miles fast. This last quality may be because—as several high-mileage friends have told me—the company is extremely willing to customize its routes. Overall, the mix of hammers and people just interested in noodling along is good. VBT has one more plus: Its fleet of rental bikes is always in top-notch condition (Box 711, Bristol, VT 05443, tel. 802/453–4811 or 800/ 245–3868, fax 802/453–4806).

BICYCLE ADVENTURES Although it specializes in West Coast touring, Bicycle Adventures also offers trips in British Columbia and Hawaii. I like this company because it was founded (in 1984) and is still staffed by Pacific Northwest natives who know the area well. It offers 18 different trips (Box 7875, Olympia, WA 98507, tel. 206/786– 0989 or 800/443–6060, fax 206/786–9661).

BIKE VERMONT This company runs 160 weekend and 5-day tours in Vermont, more than any other company. The organizers have run trips in New England since 1977 (Box 207, Woodstock, VT 05091, tel. 802/ 457–3553 or 800/257–2226, fax 802/457– 1236).

MICHIGAN BICYCLE TOURING This is the Michigan version of Bike Vermont. The company offers 18 different bike tours in Michigan and skiing tours in the off-season. It's been in business since 1978 (3512 Red School Rd., Kingsley, MI 49649, tel. 616/ 263–5885).

TIMBERLINE BICYCLE TOURS Aggressive riders like this company's big-mileage and high-altitude tours in the western U.S., northern Great Lakes, and Canada. These routes will wear out anyone (J, 7975 E. Harvard, Denver, CO 80231, tel. 303/759–3804).

FAVORITE TRIPS

THE NORTHEAST

MAINE Boothbay Harbor/Penobscot Bay. VBT offers 5-day tours in each of 2 coastal regions of Maine. They're similar trips. Seen from the air, Boothbay would look like the multi-toed foot of some strange animal. Those "feet" are tiny peninsulas, and each peninsula has its own character. You'll cycle between them, stopping at historic fishing villages, shopping towns, artist communities and lighthouses.

Penobscot Bay is Maine's largest harbor. You cycle around and near the harbor, stopping to go lobstering, sea kayaking, visiting a boatbuilding school, and shopping. There's also a chartered boat ride to Isleboro Island, home to celebrities such as Kirstie Alley and John Travolta.

The roads on both tours are flat, quiet, wind through forested regions, and hug the coast. A novice should have no problem pedaling the entire distance every day. Accommodations are at historic inns on the water. If you have to ask about the food, you're not using your imagination—fresh goodies from the sea every day. Daily distance is 20–35 miles. Each trip is run about 10 times per year. *Vermont Bicycle Touring, Box 711, Bristol, VT 05443, tel. 802/453–4811 or 800/245–3868, fax 802/453–4806. June– Oct.: 5 days, $1,095 (Boothbay), $995 (Penobscot). Price includes 3 lunches. Road- or hybrid-bike rental, $98.*

MASSACHUSETTS From the Vineyard to Nantucket. This 5-day ride is a classic cycling tour in VBT's home turf. The islands of Martha's Vineyard and Nantucket have been popular spots for pedaling vacations for years: The riding is easy—flat to rolling—and the traffic is never overbearing. These conditions combined with the Atlantic seaside scenery make it easy to understand why so many 2-wheeled tours take place here. This trip begins on the Vineyard, where you have 3 days to explore the harbor and back roads. It's a bit of a huff to get to the bluffs at the southwestern corner of the island, but the spectacular views are worth the effort. Much of the riding is on designated bike paths. You ferry to Nantucket for the final 2 days, cruising on more bike paths, some of which wind right through fishing villages.

On both islands you sleep in fine inns. Meals are predominantly fresh from the sea, but there's a variety of gourmet food. Though a bit touristy, this relaxing tour became a classic for a reason. See for yourself. The distance covered daily averages 22 miles. This trip is run about 12 times per year. *Vermont Bicycle Touring, Box 711, Bristol, VT 05443, tel. 802/453–4811 or 800/245–3868, fax 802/453–4806. May–Sept.: 5 days, $1,095. Price includes 3 lunches. Road- or hybrid-bike rental, $98.*

VERMONT **Connecticut River Valley.** This 5-day ramble follows the Connecticut River, the meandering border between Vermont and New Hampshire. It's one of my favorite Vermont tours, because the river is never far away, and you cross it several times.

You visit New Hampshire's Dartmouth College campus and explore a restored Shaker village. There's even hiking on some mountain trails. Yes, mountains. You have to endure some climbs, but the slopes are more steady than steep. This is an excellent introduction to Vermont cycling.

Nights are spent in historic New Hampshire and Vermont inns, as well as mountain lodges. Take your swimsuit. Daily distances range from 18 to 53 miles. This trip is run about 21 times per year. *Bike Vermont, Box 207, Woodstock, VT 05091, tel. 802/457–3553 or 800/257–2226, fax 802/457–1236. May–mid-June: 5 days, $585. Late June–mid-Sept.: 5 days, $655. Late Sept.–mid-Oct.: 5 days, $695. Late Oct.: 5 days, $655. Road-bike rental, $80.*

VERMONT **Classic Vermont Scenery.** It seems silly to praise a Vermont tour for its views—all trips in this state have knockout scenery—but this one receives exceptionally high marks. The 5-day tour begins and ends in Middlebury and wanders along the shore of Lake Champlain and into the Green Mountain National Forest. The terrain is rolling, through a landscape of farms, orchards, typical New England towns, and several lakes. All this is shadowed by the Adirondack peaks on the west and the Green Mountains on the east.

You sleep at an inn built by the family of Ethan Allen and at an old stagecoach stop. Delectable dinners might include smoked salmon over linguini with garden vegetables or breast of pheasant with a cherry brandy sauce. Daily distance options range from 13 to 45 miles. Beginners can tough it out; intermediate riders will just cruise and enjoy the views. This trip is run about 18 times per year. *Bike Vermont, Box 207, Woodstock, VT 05091, tel. 802/457–3553 or 800/257–2226, fax 802/457–1236. May 5–June 11: 5 days, $670. June 12–Sept. 17: 5 days, $720. Sept. 18–Oct. 15: 5 days, $765. Oct. 15–Oct. 27: 5 days, $720. Road-bike rental, $80.*

VERMONT **From the Capital to Stowe.** Backroads bills this 5-day trip as one of its most luxurious. Coming from a company where plush is the norm, that's saying something. The accommodations—country inns and manors—don't disappoint, and neither does the riding. It's vintage Vermont, with rolling roads through green hills. There are maple sugar houses where you can stop and sample before you buy, ski resorts with exceptional views and accommodations, and a trail-crossed countryside where you meet fellow autoless travelers—hikers and horseback riders.

The trip begins in Montpelier, the state capital, and hits Craftsbury Common, Stowe, and Waterbury. Daily distance options range from 17 to 51 miles. There's an optional rest day in Stowe and an optional tour of Ben & Jerry's ice-cream factory in Waterbury. (You're not doing all that riding for nothing.) About 8 trips are run per year. *Backroads, 1516 5th St., Suite B122, Berkeley, CA 94710–1740, tel. 510/527–1555 or 800/462–2848, fax 510/527–1444. Aug.–Oct.: 5 days, $1,398. Road-bike rental (flat or drop handlebar), $109.*

THE MID-ATLANTIC

MARYLAND **Chesapeake Bay.** In the past, almost all eastern "beach-and-bike" tours focused on the Carolina coasts. Here's a great alternative, especially for novices or families looking for flat riding.

This 5-day trip navigates the Chesapeake Bay, where you stop to explore ports and fishing villages. The trip includes a 1-day excursion on the *H.M. Krentz*, one of the sailing boats still used for actual (as opposed to tourist-oriented) oyster dredging. The *Krentz* is captained by a classic coastal character and human encyclopedia on the history and ecology of the bay. (Captain Ed Farley was one of author James Michener's chief sources for his book about the Chesapeake).

Accommodations are at historic inns and portside hotels that are often the architectural focal points of the tiny settlements centered around them. Meals? Of course you'll want fresh seafood—including some of those oysters off the *Krentz.* Daily distance is 15–35 flat miles per day. This trip is run about 7 times per year. *Vermont Bicycle Touring, Box 711, Bristol, VT 05443, tel. 802/453–4811 or 800/245–3868, fax 802/453–4806. April–Oct.: 5 days, $995. Road- or hybrid-bike rental, $98.*

PENNSYLVANIA **Delaware River Valley.** On this 5-day trip you cross into New Jersey but spend most of the week in the pastoral countryside of Bucks County, Pennsylvania. I do a lot of pedaling in this region, and I can attest to the lack of traffic and rolling hills that make for some of the finest road riding in the country. The scenery includes woodlands, old stone farmhouses and colonial buildings, mills, tiny towns along the Delaware, and even historic sites (you visit the spot where George Washington made his famous crossing). Don't worry, you're not overloaded with history. The historic sites are just another part of the landscape. The entire experience is soothing, and you feel farther from big-city civilization than you really are (New York is less than 2 hours away). The accommodations are bed-and-breakfasts and former private manors built during the 1800s.

I also like this tour company's rental bike: a Bridgestone XO-2, a hybrid with a "mous-tache" handlebar. Stylin'. Daily distance options range from 25 to 45 miles. Intermediate riders will have the most fun. There aren't any monster climbs, but the hills are steady. The trip is run twice each year. *Northstar Bicycle Tours, 113 Crawley Ave., Pennington, NJ 08534, tel. 609/737–8346, fax 609/737–3787. July–Aug.: 5 days, $780. Price does not include lunches. Hybrid bike rental, $90.*

PENNSYLVANIA **Lancaster County's Farms and Towns.** There are ritzier, plusher tours of this popular cycling area, but I like this one because it allows you to cover more ground. Pennsylvania Dutch country is a patchwork of Amish and Mennonite villages; fields, farmhouses, and barns; grassy valleys; and tourist towns rich in antiques shops, general stores, and gift shops.

You traverse the county in 5 days, traveling from inn to inn. Each day's ride is scenic and soothing, with minimum traffic: You're more likely to share the road with horse-drawn carriages than with autos. The route is hilly, though, and even an advanced rider could tire by the end of the week. Still, I wouldn't hesitate to recommend the tour to a beginner, because the roads are cyclist-friendly and the scenery is captivating.

The 19th-century inns where you stay are generally either in the middle of a lot of acreage or in tiny villages. Most meals are Amish family-style spreads of fresh vegetables, poultry or red meat, and warm breads. Daily distance options range from 25 to 40 miles. This trip is run 3 times per year. *Northstar Bicycle Tours, 113 Crawley Ave., Pennington, NJ 08534, tel. 609/737–8346, fax 609/737–3787. July–Aug.: 5 days, $775. Price does not include lunches. Hybrid bike rental, $90.*

VIRGINIA **Historic Sites Along the Colonial Parkway.** This is an underrated touring area that's especially suited for families. The terrain is mild, often flat, and the rich history of the region provides plenty of off-bike experiences. Whenever I've cycled in Virginia, I've been impressed by the lack of traffic and the general respect for cyclists exhibited by most auto drivers, especially on the parkways. This 5-day trip begins in Williamsburg and travels up and down the Colonial Parkway.

Much of the route passes through national parklands, and sometimes it winds through Revolutionary War battlefields. You see plenty of peanut and cornfields, as well as large stands of pine. Sound soothing? It is. One of the highlights of this tour is the final day's exploration of Jamestown.

Accommodations are in modern inns that provide more convenience than charm. Daily distance options range from 20 to 45 miles. If you're looking to jam out the miles—and you're not a history buff—you may get bored. About 10 trips are run each year. If you have extra time before or after the tour, check out the nearby Busch Gardens theme park. *Vermont Bicycle Touring, Box 711, Bristol, VT 05443, tel. 802/453–4811 or 800/245–3868, fax 802/453–4806. Apr.–Nov.: 5 days, $699. Price includes 3 lunches. Road- or hybrid-bike rental, $98.*

VIRGINIA **Challenging the Shenandoah.** This is a completely different Virginia: the Shenandoah Valley, 200 miles of rolling farmland and woodland, with the Shenandoah, Blue Ridge, and Allegheny mountain ranges serving as a backdrop. The terrain is challenging. It's constantly rolling, with a few significant climbs. Vacationers new to bike touring will fare okay on this 5-day trip if they're fit; experienced cyclists can take the longer routes and wear themselves out. Traffic is never a factor.

You sleep in historic inns, the best of which is probably the Jordan Hollow Farm Inn, a 200-year-old restored horse farm next to Shenandoah National Park. Horseback rides are available for an extra fee. Average daily distance is 33 miles. This trip is run about 6 times per year. *Vermont Bicycle Touring, Box 711, Bristol, VT 05443, tel. 802/453–4811 or 800/245–3868, fax 802/453–4806. May–Oct.: 5 days, $995. Price includes 3 lunches. Road- or hybrid-bike rental, $98.*

THE SOUTH

KENTUCKY **Bluegrass Country.** The bluegrass isn't just for hooves. My wheels have galloped through this region, and I can report that the sight of miles of white fences rolling over hills is as beautiful as any canyon vista. This 5-day trip begins in Bardstown and passes through Bernheim Forest, several Appalachian towns, and Pleasant Hill, a Shaker village. Most of the sparsely traveled roads are bordered by distinctive horse-farm fences, and you cycle to Keeneland Race Course, where you can watch the trainers at work. The riding is a bit tougher than you'd expect, but there are no major climbs.

The accommodations are in historic hotels and inns, many built to house early horse breeders and traders. The food? Just ask for spoonbread and cornsticks. Daily distance options range from 15 to 55 miles. About 4 trips are run each year. *Backroads, 1516 5th St., Suite B122, Berkeley, CA 94710–1740, tel. 510/527–1555 or 800/462–2848, fax 510/527–1444. May and Oct.: 5 days, $1,145. Road-bike rental, $109.*

LOUISIANA **New Orleans and the Plantations and Bayous Beyond.** I have to admit that my chief interest in this tour is the food: southern Louisiana Cajun-Creole cuisine. Nearly every meal served by the restaurants and hotels on the route includes cayenne, hot sauce, and crawfish.

Oh yeah, the riding. You spend at least 2 days in New Orleans, enough time to get a feel for the city. Your hotel here is sure to have patios decked with tropical plants, porches overhanging the streets, and fountains in the courtyards. You cycle through the Latin Quarter, which can be either an adventure or a misadventure, depending on the traffic.

Once you ease out of the Big Easy, the roads get more interesting. They travel around bayous, through gently rolling woods, and to small southern towns. There seem to be plantations around every corner, and many of them are open for tours.

Daily distance options are 30 to 50 miles. Beginners will have no problem. This 6-day trip is run about 3 times per year. *French Louisiana Bike Tours, 601 Pinhook Rd. E, LaFayette, LA 70501, tel. 800/346–7989. May, Sept., and Oct.: 6 days, $795. Price does not include lunches. Mountain-bike (with smooth tires) rental, $89.*

■MISSISSIPPI Antebellum Mansions to Civil War Battle Sites. This is one of my personal favorites, partly because most of the route is on the amazingly cyclist-friendly Natchez Trace Parkway—which has low speed limits, no commercial traffic, and no buildings to blot the southern landscape—and partly because the route passes through scenes of great historic interest.

You begin this 6-day tour in the small Mississippi River town of Natchez, which has more than a dozen antebellum mansions open for tours. From there you travel along the parkway to Port Gibson, Vicksburg, and other Civil War battle sites. Save your strength for the last day's 20-mile loop through Vicksburg's Military Park, where you tour the battlefield.

These Mississippi roads are flat or gently rolling—perfect for easy cruising or blow-your-lungs hammering. Where else could you time-trial from Civil War mansion to Civil War mansion? Those mansions, each of which is on the National Register of Historic Places, are where you sleep at night. The food includes catfish and southern barbecued chicken.

Daily distance options range from 20 to 45 miles. At the end of the trip, a hydrojet returns you to Natchez from upriver. About 7 trips are run each year. *Vermont Bicycle Touring, Box 711, Bristol, VT 05443, tel. 802/453–4806 or 800/245–3868, fax 802/453–4811. Mar., Apr., Oct., Nov.: 6 days, $1,195. Price includes 3 lunches. Road- or hybrid-bike rental, $106.*

■MISSISSIPPI Biking the Natchez Trace in Mississippi. This trip is aimed at beginner and intermediate riders, as well as cultural

enthusiasts. Rather than ride all 300 miles of the Trace, you pedal 4–5 hours a day, with lots of stops for mint juleps and history chats with museum curators. Emphasis is on plush accommodations, including colonial mansions and plantation houses, all filled with antiques and canopy beds. There's also a river boat ride down the Mississippi, a Dixie band concert, and a crawdaddy fest.

Another thoughtful touch: The trips are run to coincide with either the spring blossoms (the dogwoods and redbuds are nearly beyond belief), or the fall.

Daily distance ranges from 15 to 50 miles, with extra options for the energetic. About 6 trips are run per year. *Butterfield & Robinson, 70 Bond St., Toronto, Ontario, Canada M5B 1X3, tel. 416/864–1354 or 800/678–1147, fax 416/864–0541. June, Sept., and Oct: 7 days, $1,950. Price does not include 2 dinners and 1 lunch.*

THE MIDWEST

■MICHIGAN Mackinac Wayfarer. This region—with its rolling terrain, lakeside routes, and potential island adventures—could become one of bike touring's hot spots. For now, though, the roads are uncrowded and the countryside is still unspoiled, although tourist shops are popping up. Michigan is not known for its good weather, but the moderate temperatures of summer and fall make cycling here ideal. There's little humidity—or rain—to knock you off your bike in summer, and in fall (the best time to go) the colors burst from the trees and the days are cool.

This 5-day tour begins in Charlevoix, a village on the shores of Lake Michigan. You wind northward through hilly countryside that alternates between farmland, forest, and small tourist towns. A ferry takes you to Mackinac Island, which has interesting geological formations, Victorian architecture, and several fudge shops that are famous in the Midwest. Best of all, automobile traffic is banned. The biggest vehicles you encounter are horse-drawn carriages.

This is billed as MBT's most deluxe tour, and riders I've talked with have agreed. The lodging is in luxury-class hotels and inns. Lunch may be complemented by fresh local cherries, blueberries, or peaches.

Daily distance options range from 23 to 63 miles. Athletic beginners can handle the route, and there are enough side roads to keep even advanced pedalers busy. About 3 trips are run per year. *Michigan Bicycle Touring, 3512 Red School Rd., Kingsley, MI 49649, tel. 616/263–5885. June, late Aug., and late Sept.: 5 days, $750. Late Aug.: 5 days $835. Price does not include 2 lunches. Road-bike rental, $80; mountain-bike rental, $95.*

WISCONSIN **Door County.** This state's thumb-shaped peninsula, surrounded by Green Bay and Lake Michigan, has always been a haven for nautical folks, but we 2-wheeled types are beginning to feel at home here, too. Beginners are enticed by the flat to gently rolling terrain as well as the waterfront villages—on this peninsula you cannot escape waterfront villages—where the shops and sights provide plenty of diversion for those who tire of cycling. With its lighthouses and small towns, the area has been compared to Cape Cod—with slightly better biking.

This 6-day trip centers on Door County, far north on the peninsula. But don't worry—you move along back roads instead of the car-heavy thoroughfares. You'll explore southward, past limestone cliffs, shipyards, white-sand beaches, and working lighthouses, and you'll cross "Death's Door Passage" to Washington Island, the U.S.'s largest Icelandic settlement. There are plenty of potential stops for novices tired of long stretches of road.

Daily distance ranges from 24 to 40 miles. Accommodations are inns and historic hotels built in nautical styles, with widow's walks, fancy weathervanes, and large bay windows. Fish is the usual fare, but full midwestern meals—steak and potatoes—are also popular. This trip is run about 5 times per year. *Vermont Bicycle Touring, Box*

711, Bristol, VT 05443, tel. 802/453–4806 or 800/245–3868, fax 802/453–4811. July–early Sept.: 6 days, $995. Price includes 3 lunches. Road- or hybrid-bike rental, $98.

THE SOUTHWEST

ARIZONA **Going Downhill Through Canyonlands.** If this 5-day tour were run backward, it would be a killer of a climb. But as it stands, the route includes a couple of 10- to 15-mile descents amid a desert panorama that changes daily. It's good stuff for beginners—it's inspiring to ride these roads—with enough challenges to give more advanced spinners fits.

You begin in Oak Creek Canyon, go through Sedona, and stop overnight at Mormon Lake, the largest natural lake in the state. Leading to the lake, the trip is a collection of red-rock canyon eye poppers. After that, it becomes a kind of Tour de Lake. By the third day, you're at the lip of the purple-and-pink painted high desert. Later, on the way from Flagstaff to the Grand Canyon, you hit alpine country.

This is scenery usually reserved for mountain bikers or ultrafit road whippets. There's a detour through Walnut Canyon, which once sheltered the largest Native American cliff-dwelling habitat in the country. I also like the last day's scoot along the eastern section of the Grand Canyon. The road is closed to automobiles in the summer, so you're free to concentrate on the view.

The daily distance ranges from 40 to 80 miles, with about 50 being average. The toughest climb is a mile or so. There are a lot of rolling hills, but about an equal amount of flats or downhills. It's like this: I'd send my mother or my hammerhead buddies. Accommodations range from the rustic (old cabins at Mormon Lake) to the luxurious (bed-and-breakfast inns). At mealtimes, don't pass up the spicy Mexican dishes. This trip is run about 2 times each year. *Southwest Cycle Expeditions, Box 30731, Flagstaff, AZ 86003, tel. 602/526–4882. June and July: 5 days,*

$700. Price does not include lunches and 1 dinner. Road-bike rental, $100.

NEW MEXICO **Pedaling the Peaks.** This is a rider's tour—90-plus miles per day in macho territory. But here's the surprise: About half to two-thirds of the cyclists who take the 7-day trip are intermediates extending themselves—and succeeding.

The trip rolls through deceptively tough country. Don't get me wrong. This part of the state has some bonafide killer climbs to as high as 7,000 and 10,000 feet. But most of the terrain is simply rolly, rolly, rolly, and you don't realize how high you're climbing. The first day includes no major ascents or mountain passes, but you still climb about 4,000 vertical feet.

You start in the low flats of Albuquerque and climb to Santa Fe, then Las Vegas (New Mexico, that is), and on to the high mountain desert of Taos. You do the almost-mandatory routes, such as the Enchanted Circle road that rises above Taos, but for me this trip gets stars for its marriage of mileage and spectacular scenery. You can even stretch your workout by taking optional rides on the 2 rest days.

You have to arrange for accommodations yourself. About half the crowd camps, and the others stay in motels that set aside rooms for this trip. The average daily distance is about 75 miles. This trip is run only once each year. *Pedal the Peaks, 2878–H West Long Circle, Littleton, CO 80120, tel. 800/795–0898. June: 7 days, $325. Price does not include hotel, camp fees, or dinners. Rental bikes can be arranged through affiliated bike shops.*

NEW MEXICO **Hill-Hopping from Santa Fe to Taos.** Get out your climbing legs, folks. This is a Backroads trip with bite. You begin at 7,000 feet, on the Alameda mountain in Sante Fe, in the foothills of the Sangre de Cristo Mountains. The first of 5 days is spent tooling through the area in search of ancient adobes, museums, galleries (this entire region has become an arty mecca), and historic cathedrals and homes. Then the hill-hop-ping begins. I've talked to experienced cyclists who wore themselves out on the High Road climb, a curvy route with plenty of mountain scenery. Beginners will have to shuttle up in the support van or plan to arrive well after dinner.

Taos is your base for the rest of the trip. As you explore the surrounding areas, you'll avoid the biggest ascents (on the Enchanted Circle road, you cycle around New Mexico's highest mountain, 13,161-foot Wheeler Peak), but still face some lung-busters in the 9,107-foot Palo Flechado and 9,820-foot Bobcat passes. The payoff for all this effort, of course, is the background of New Mexico peaks and valley vistas—and the big-time descents. The restaurants are classic southwestern eateries, and, as usual, Backroads has found some dandies. The best day on this route is the long climb and descent to Red River, a mountain resort in Carson National Forest, north of Taos.

Daily distance options range from 20 to 55 miles. Most of us could hack 30 to 40 per day and still have enough energy left to explore at night, but this is a surprisingly tough trip for Backroads. On the last day, you ride only 21 miles; the rest of the day is spent on a Class III white-water raft trip down the Rio Grande, which lands you back in Santa Fe. About 11 trips are run annually. Do yourself a favor: Drink plenty of water. *Backroads, 1516 5th St., Suite B122, Berkeley, CA 94710–1740, tel. 510/527–1555 or 800/462–2848, fax 510/527–1444. May–Sept.: 5 days, $1,298. Road (with flat or drop handlebar) bike rental, $109.*

THE ROCKIES

COLORADO **Alpine Meadows in the San Juan Mountains.** The southwestern corner of Colorado is a mecca for mountain bikers, but the road riding is just as sweet. This 5-day trip is a good sampler of what draws so many cyclists to the area. The ride begins with a train ride: A workhorse locomotive chugs up 2,500 feet from Durango to Silverton on narrow-gauge tracks. The engine stops at 9,000 feet. The next 24 miles—over Red Mountain Pass—are up to you. This is the easiest day, but not the most scenic.

Honor goes to the second day's ride, which curves and climbs through alpine meadows covered with either wildflowers or yellowing aspen, depending on the season. The trip includes a rest day in Telluride. Even if you don't consider yourself a mountain biker, be sure to rent a mountain bike and spend a few hours exploring the trails around here. You may be converted. History buffs should enjoy the ride past the Anasazi ruins in Mesa Verde National Park.

Can you hack the climbing? Three mountain passes? I'd give an athletic beginner about a 50% chance of pedaling the whole trip. Daily distance options range from 24 to 100 miles. Accommodations are provided in hotels, inns, and lodges plush enough to have hot springs and hot tubs. This route is also done as a camping trip, and there are special dates for singles. About 7 trips are run each year. *Backroads, 1516 5th St., Suite B122, Berkeley, CA 94710–1740, tel. 510/527–1555 or 800/462–2848, fax 510/527–1444. Aug.– Sept.: 5 days, $1,195 inn, $749 camping. Road (with flat or drop handlebar) bike rental, $109.*

COLORADO **San Juans Alpiner.** Here's a tour of the San Juans for more athletic riders. This 7-day climbing odyssey is one of the reasons Timberline Bicycle Tours is gaining a reputation as a company catering to fit cyclists. The trip covers much of the same area as the Backroads tour listed above, but Timberline cyclists will pedal about twice as much—and twice as high. Every day includes at least one challenging climb, many of them to 10,000 feet and above. The 13-mile ascent to Red Mountain Pass is probably the toughest.

Accommodations are in restored Victorian hotels, national park inns, and mountain lodges. The tour ends with a long downhill back to its starting point in Durango.

Expect to grind out about 55 miles per day. I wouldn't attempt this unless I trained for

it. Natural climbers and the extremely fit should have fun. This trip is run twice a year. *Timberline Bicycle Tours, #J, 7975 E. Harvard, Denver, CO 80231, tel. 303/759–3804. Late June–early Sept.: 7 days, $1,150. Road-bike rental, $95.*

MONTANA **Glacier National Park.** This is a trip that will instill a feeling of real accomplishment in beginner bikers—how many people can say that they cycled to the spine of the Continental Divide?—but it requires more perseverance than pedaling power. At the same time, pedal slammers and hammerheads can choose to knock themselves out on these climbs.

The 6-day trip begins in West Glacier with a day of easy cruising. Then you go up and up and up. The main route is the Going-to-the-Sun Road, generally recognized as one of the most scenic cycling climbs in the country. How far up and how scenic? At times you're cycling above the cloud and fog line. On a clear day, you can stop for water atop 6,646-foot Logan Pass and look down on waterfalls, virgin evergreen forests, and alpine meadows. Don't forget those peaks in the distance, either.

Frequent riders in the area report spotting mountain lions, goats, bighorn sheep, and even the occasional grizzly. The brochures tout these sightings, but in truth you probably won't get that lucky.

The highlight of the lodge-and-inn accommodations is the final night's stay in the Glacier Park Lodge, which has a lobby supported by pillars of Douglas fir. You can cut costs almost in half by choosing the trip's camping option.

Daily distance options range from 28 to a downright scary up-and-down 91 miles crossing the Canadian border. About 21 trips are run each year. Special dates for singles are available. *Backroads, 1516 5th St., Suite B122, Berkeley, CA 94710–1740, tel. 510/527–1555 or 800/462–2848, fax 510/527–1444. June–Sept.: 6 days, $1,298 inn, $749 camping. Road (with flat or drop handlebar) bike rental, $109.*

THE WEST COAST

CALIFORNIA **Lassen Volcano Alpiner.** The climax of this 7-day trip is a hike to the summit of the southernmost volcano in the Cascades chain. You climb 4,000 feet in the first day's assault of Mt. Shasta, then spend the second day riding rollers southeast to the northern gate of Lassen Volcanic National Park. The third day begins the ascent of Lassen Volcano; you ride to 8,000 feet, then leave the bikes behind to hike a short trail to the crest. Timberline is a company that caters to fit cyclists: If you didn't infer that, you weren't paying attention.

The rest of the trip is spent exploring the national parks and rolling roads of this part of northern California. The traffic is surprisingly light; there are so many side roads that the tour avoids the main thoroughfares. And this area isn't overtoured; it still feels fresh.

Keep an eye peeled for Bigfoot: This is prime territory for sightings of the beast. Accommodations are provided at inns and lodges within the park. This trip, with an average daily distance of 60 miles, is run once a year. *Timberline Bicycle Tours, #J, 7975 E. Harvard, Denver, CO 80231, tel. 303/759–3804. Sept.: 7 days, $1,095. Road-bike rental, $95.*

CALIFORNIA **Cruising to Microbreweries.** Here's a (hic) fun alternative (burp) to the standard wine tours. Where else could you build up and try to cycle off a beer belly at the same time? This 6-day tour through the northern part of the state takes you to mid- and post-ride tastings at a number of microbreweries, including the Napa Valley Brewing Company, Anderson Valley Brewing, Downtown Joe's in Napa, Marin Brewing Company in Lakespur, and the Gordon Biersch Brewpub in San Francisco.

You cycle on rolling terrain over a varied route—along seaside cliffs, on quiet countrylike lanes, and, sometimes, in traffic. And because the tour begins and ends in San Francisco, you get a chance to pedal across the Golden Gate Bridge.

Accommodations are Backroads quality—luxurious and usually historic. Daily distances range from 11 to 75 miles. Beginners and heavy drinkers may need to rely on the support van. This trip is run about 7 times per year. *Backroads, 1516 5th St., Suite B122, Berkeley, CA 94710–1740, tel. 510/527–1555 or 800/462–2848, fax 510/527–1444. May–Nov.: 6 days, $1,275. Road (with flat or drop handlebar) bike rental, $109.*

OREGON **Ashland and Crater Lake.** On this 6-day tour beginners are introduced to the fine cycling of southern Oregon by being shuttled to the crest of the toughest climbs and left to enjoy the wooded landscape and rolling riding.

The trip begins in Ashland, just north of the California border, and heads farther into Oregon on a bike path that parallels Bear Creek. You skirt the foothills around Medford, then load the bikes into the van for a gas-powered trip to Crater Lake National Park (about 7,000 feet high). The quiet, little-traveled park roads make a relaxing loop. You cycle out of the park and follow the Rogue River before returning to Ashland.

The scenery includes small towns, historic mining-era villages, thick forests, covered bridges, and the Cascades looming in the distance. You skip the worst climbs, but the unrelenting rolling terrain can be tough. There's a layover day in Jacksonville, where you can explore the National Historic Landmark town or cycle through the Applegate Valley. Be sure to check out Ashland, where the tour begins and ends. It's a college town, site of a Shakespeare festival, and one of the best small cities on the West Coast.

On this trip, which is run about 3 times per year, peddlers bed down at historic inns and bed-and-breakfasts. Daily distances average 30 miles. *CycleWest, 75 Bush St., Ashland, OR 97520, tel. 503/482–1088 or 800/831–5016. July–Sept.: 6 days, $898. Free shuttle from Medford airport. Road bike (with drop or straight handlebar) rental, $97.*

OREGON **Crater Lake.** This 5½-day excursion through the mountain lakes region of southwestern Oregon covers some of the best cycling areas in the state. On wide-shouldered roads you roll past dozens of mountain lakes, evergreen forests, and bright orchards, then ascend to Crater Lake National Park for a ride around the rim.

As with the other Crater Lake trip we list, this one begins in Ashland, Oregon (just north of the California border), then travels north along quiet roads, creekside bike paths, and small-town lanes. This trip is set up to accommodate more energetic riders, however. The distances can be a little longer, going as much as 63 miles per day. (The average without options, however, is a reasonable 32-43.)

Days 5 and 6 are spent cycling around Crater Lake. The water is some of the bluest you'll ever see inland, and the 33-mile rim ride is spectacular. The final day is a fun, downhill spin followed by a shuttle to Ashland or Medford.

Accommodations are at resorts, historic hotels, and the newly renovated for '95 Crater Lake Lodge. You get lakeside rooms here. Enjoy. Lunches are quick picnics, but the dinners are scrumptious mixes of seafood and traditional fine-dining items such as steak or veggie dishes. The trip is run about 4 times per year. *Backcountry, Box 4029, Bozeman, MT 59772-4029, tel. 406/586-3556, fax 406/586-4288. Late Aug.-mid Sept.: 5 1/2 days, $1,095. Road- or mountain-bike rental, $129.*

OREGON **Oregon Coast.** This 7-day central Oregon trip covers territory new to bike touring. The national forests, rivers, and snow-clad peaks were once the sole domain of loggers—the lack of paved roads, and frequent closures to allow logging operation, discouraged tourism. Now the Forest Service has opened the woodlands to recreation.

You pedal along the Aufdeheide National Scenic Byway, wind through old-growth forests, follow the McKenzie and Willamette rivers, cross McKenzie Pass, and have many chances to stop and explore volcanic rock outcroppings. The riding is best suited to intermediate or advanced cyclists: There's a lot of up-and-down, and the mileage starts to pile up.

Accommodations include the Black Butte Ranch and Sun River Resort, both popular—and comfy—resorts. There's always a 2-day layover at one of the resorts, which gives you a chance for tennis, golf, rafting, or hiking. The fare includes seafood, veggie dishes, and most other requests. Expect to do 25–50 miles per day. This trip is run about 5 times per year. *Bicycle Adventures, Box 7875, Olympia, WA 98507, tel. 206/786-0989 or 800/443-6060, fax 206/786-9661. June–Oct.: 7 days, $1,278. Road- or mountain-bike rental, $118.*

WASHINGTON **Island Hopping in the San Juans.** Get lucky with the rain and you won't find a nicer place to ride than the islands in the Pacific Northwest's Puget Sound. Waterfront rambles, thick woodlands, beach cruises, craggy clifftop overlooks, and plenty of island hopping make this a 6-day variety tour.

The terrain can be mildly challenging but is nothing compared to that of the ever-present peaks in the background. While you roll over the islands just north of Seattle, the entire Olympic Mountain Range juts into sight. It's a rare treat for a bike rider to enjoy a view without having to conquer it.

There are hiking options and wildlife cruises; on one of the latter you might spot killer whales navigating the Sound. You spend your time on three islands: Lopez, Orcas, and San Juan. An advanced rider can burn big-time energy on Orcas; novices can keep themselves busy exploring the tourist shops after completing easier routes. Average daily distance is 33 miles.

You stay in historic inns; meals are usually fresh from the Pacific. This trip is run about 56 times per year. Special dates are available for singles. *Bicycle Adventures, Box 7875, Olympia, WA 98507, tel. 206/786-0989 or 800/443-6060, fax 206/786-9661. Apr.–Nov.: 6 days, $1,098. Road- or mountain-bike rental, $118.*

WASHINGTON **Whidbey Island and the Olympic Peninsula.** This 6-day Backroads jaunt is a slightly different take on Puget Sound. You can keep your mileage moderate because there are extremely low mileage options, so there's more time to check out the area's attractions—"quaint" villages, pier-side taverns, antiques stores, and historic forts.

Hammerhead cyclists won't be happy; the distances are too short, and the groups on this trip tend to be mellow recreational riders or tourists looking for two-wheeled adventure. But the scenery is no less impressive, and the air is no less fresh.

The tour begins and ends with a ferry trip between Seattle and Whidbey Island, and you pedal to other Puget Sound islands and harbors. You stay in inns that are typically Backroads: log buildings, rambling Victorian houses on bluffs, and renovated farmhouses, some with wood-burning fireplaces. A camping option is also available.

Daily distance options range from 7 to 53 miles. This trip is run about 10 times each year; go for the summer trips if you can. *Backroads, 1516 5th St., Suite B122, Berkeley, CA 94710–1740, tel. 510/527–1555 or 800/462–2848, fax 510/527–1444. June–Sept.: 6 days, $1,298 inn, $749 camping. Road (with flat or drop handlebar) bike rental, $109.*

ALASKA

SOUTHEAST **Crossing the Frontier.** Whoa, is this still America? Cycling friends who've crossed this state tell me there is simply no territory for two-wheeled road travel that's more wide-open or wild. This 7-day trip gives you the opportunity to explore the wilderness while enjoying some of Backroads's trademark cushiness. The tour begins and ends in Anchorage. You roll out on the Glenn Highway, following the Matanuska River into the wilderness, and you raft back down the river the next day.

The route traverses spruce forest, alpine meadows, several small mountain passes with gradual upgrades, and even a few glaciers. You pedal by 14,000-foot Mount Wrangell, the state's largest active volcano. There's also a ferry ride into Prince William Sound, where you might spot moose, bald eagles, seals, porpoises, and killer whales.

As you'd expect in such a big state, the rides encompass big miles. Two rest days are thrown in, but the week's total could still top 350 miles, including one killer century (100-mile ride) on day 5. Don't panic if you're closer to the energetic beginner side of the cycling spectrum: The rest days and low-mileage options can get you through.

The food is regional—salmon and halibut barbecues, homemade pies—and the accommodations range from rustic pioneer-style roadhouses to luxurious mountain lodges. Lots of extras are available: horseback rides, flyovers in a Piper Cub, and scenic chair lifts over glaciers. About 8 trips are run each year. *Backroads, 1516 5th St., Suite B122, Berkeley, CA 94710–1740, tel. 510/527–1555 or 800/462–2848, fax 510/527–1444. June–Aug.: 7 days, $1,698. Price includes white-water rafting but not other off-bike activities. Road (with flat or drop handlebar) bike rental, $129.*

HAWAII

THE BIG ISLAND **Lava Flows and Snorkeling.** This is one trip where the bike is in danger of becoming just an accessory, but you can scoot around the Big Island of Hawaii on 2 wheels better than on 4, so we'll keep the bicycles, thank you. Tropical rain forests, sugar cane fields, rolling pastures, white and black sand beaches, surf, lava flows, mountain vistas. What more could you ask?

The southern half of the island is your base for 6 days. You pedal from Hilo to Kona, spending 2 days at the base of the Kilauea Volcano, where you can see the live lava flow (check it out at night if you can). There's also an optional one day of hiking to the crater. At Kona, you spend a day snorkeling.

The riding here is tougher than you might think because of the hilly terrain. There are some climbs, and you should average about 48 miles per day. Accommodations are in inns, where the restaurants serve regional fare—pig roasts and I-can't-believe-it fruit salads. This tour is run about 8 times per year. *Bicycle Adventures, Box 7875, Olympia, WA 98507, tel. 206/786–0989 or 800/443–6060, fax 206/786–9661. May–Oct.: 6 days, $1,150. Road- or mountain-bike rental, $126.*

SOURCES

ORGANIZATIONS **Adventure Cycling Association** (Box 8308, Missoula, MT 59807, tel. 406/721–1776) runs long tours, sells cycling maps, and provides information about touring. It publishes *The Cyclists' Yellow Pages* and *BikeReport*. **American Youth Hostels** (Box 37613, Washington, DC, 20013–7613, tel. 202/783–4943) runs long tours and provides inexpensive accommodations. **League of American Bicyclists** (Suite 120, 190 W. Ostend St., Baltimore, MD 21230–3755, tel. 410/539–3399), an organization of cycling enthusiasts, runs events, provides touring information, and publishes *Bicycle USA*. **Rails to Trails Conservancy** (Suite 300, 1400 16th St. NW, Washington, DC, 20036, tel. 202/797–5400) promotes conversion of abandoned railroad land to cycling paths and provides touring information.

PERIODICALS League of American Bicyclists publishes *Bicycle USA* 8 times per year, which it distributes to members. Every issue contains at least one touring feature and lots of rides and events. *Bicycling*, a how-to magazine, features numerous touring articles throughout the year and a special touring issue. It's published 11 times annually (Rodale Press, 33 E. Minor St., Emmaus, PA 18098, 610/967–8093 for information, 515/242–0286 to subscribe). *The Cyclists' Yellow Pages*, an annual publication distributed to Adventure Cycling members, lists sources of touring information and maps. *California Cyclist*, published 11 times per year, lists rides and events f or the northern part of the state (Suite 304, 490 2nd St., San Francisco, CA 94107, tel. 415/546–7291). *Sports Etc/Northwest Cyclist* catalogs rides and events in the Pacific Northwest. It's published 10 times per year (Box 9272, Seattle, WA 98109, tel. 206/286–8566).

BOOKS Pick up a copy of *500 Great Rail Trails* (Living Planet Press) to discover the U.S. rail-trail system, a series of abandoned rail lines that have been converted to bike trails. Researched and written by long-time cycling writer Dennis Coello, the *Bicycle Touring Series: Arizona, Colorado, Utah* (Northland Publishing) maps out the best routes in each state, pointing out attractions along the way. Some of the best touring books available are those in the *Bicycling the Back Roads Series: Northwest Oregon, Northwest Washington, Pacific Coast, Southwest Washington* (The Mountaineers Books). Each book is compiled by local experts, with detailed route directions, sightseeing tips, and lodging and food recommendations. Two other series, *The Best Bike Rides: Pacific Northwest, New England* and *Short Bike Rides: Cape Cod, Central Massachusetts, Connecticut, Eastern Pennsylvania, Long Island, New Jersey, New York City, Rhode Island, Washington, D.C., Western Washington* (both published by Globe Pequot), are of 200- to 300-page comprehensive handbooks to touring the covered area.

ALSO SEE There's no need to keep your two wheels on the road: This country has trails where you can lose your inhibitions. The Mountain Biking chapter will put you there.

Canoeing and Kayaking in Flat Water

By Dennis Stuhaug

Updated by W. Lynn Seldon Jr.

anoeing or kayaking in flat water invites contemplation; without the need to constantly study the river to anticipate sudden changes in white-water areas, you have the time to notice and appreciate your surroundings. The pleasures of flat-water paddling are serene ones: stroking crisply across a remote lake, drifting across a placid, forest-rimmed pond, or floating down a quiet river in dappled sunshine. Best of all, these pleasures are accessible to even novice paddlers, who lack the carefully acquired and honed skills of the white-water paddler. Paddling trips are a good introduction to life in the woods for outdoors novices because as both canoes and kayaks can carry considerable gear, the level of comfort can range from pleasant to downright luxurious, compared to, say, backpacking trips.

If you've never done any canoeing or kayaking, you might start with short guided trips on nearby waters. If you catch paddling fever, then sign up for a weeklong guided group canoeing trip (widely available in the west), or go to one of the hundreds of outfitters that thrive in the country's major flatwater canoeing and kayaking areas—the Adirondacks or the Boundary Waters Canoe Area of northern Minnesota—and have an outfitter put together a longer camping-and-canoeing trip for you. Typically, outfitters in such areas can plan a route to suit your tastes and abilities; equip you with map, canoes or kayaks, paddles, personal flotation devices, and all camping gear (including tents, sleeping bags and pads, stoves and cookware, and more); and supply you with an assortment of fresh and freeze-dried food as well as the necessary permits.

Outfitters can also supply you with a guide, who can help with camp chores or provide wildlife or historical information. On slow, easy-paddling rivers where you can't possibly get lost, a guide might seem a needless expense (at about $90 to $130 a day), but if you lack basic camping and outdoor experience, there are definite advantages to going with an expert—and these apply whether you go with a scheduled group outing or opt for a custom trip.

Paddling with a guide is an ideal introduction to the world of canoes and kayaks. Under the tutelage of veteran outdoors people, you can learn by example. By copying their economical paddle strokes, you learn to move your canoe more easily through the water. After breaking camp and stowing gear once or twice, you find your own packing becoming quicker and neater. With their expert instruction, you learn how to make your craft go where you want it to, and very quickly, you are able to read routes down river channels.

Longer paddling trips have a predictable rhythm. The first day is hectic as you discover how to pack the canoe most efficiently,

Dennis Stuhaug, the managing editor of *Canoe and Kayak Magazine,* is a former white-water and flat-water instructor. An avid boater and a freelance writer and photographer, Lynn Seldon recently drove from Virginia to Maine to buy a canoe.

master new strokes or re-learn old ones, and get accustomed to your paddling partner and to the group. A smooth rhythm emerges within a day or so, and with it, a sense of confidence on the water. You learn how a 6-hour paddling day feels and how to slice into the wind or deal with crosscurrents, and you ultimately come to feel at ease on the water. When you're not paddling—on layover days, at lunchtime, or after you've beached the canoes and readied your campsite at day's end—you can spend your time fishing, hiking, swimming, or lazing around camp.

For both scheduled group trips and custom expeditions, most outfitters start out with a rendezvous at an inn or local paddling center, where they introduce you to your craft, fit you for paddles and life jackets, and discuss what to expect on the journey. On independent and custom outfitted trips, you also discuss your route, your gear, and your food packs. Then it's off to the embarkation site or, in paddling terms, the put-in (the end of the trip is, appropriately enough, called the take-out). Some outfitters shuttle you to the put-in; others ask that you provide your own transportation.

Don't expect smooth going all the way, even in flat water. Mother Nature exacts her own tolls in the form of rapids, beaver dams, shallows, and occasional dry spots that must be hiked over to get to the next patch of water; the boat must be carried around the obstacle, in a maneuver known as the portage, from the French word porter, "to carry," used by the French-Canadian voyageurs who first explored the continent's inland waterways. Helping hands are not only appreciated but usually expected—and there are plenty of paddles and packs that need to be transported, in addition to the boats; the sooner they are moved, the sooner you're back on the water.

More and more flat-water outfitters use kayaks as well as canoes (seldom both on the same trip). Often equipped with seats with adjustable backrests, kayaks are more comfortable than canoes. However, they're harder to portage, since they weren't designed to be carried. While a canoe can be hoisted onto the shoulders of a single schlepper with relative ease, kayaks take two people to carry. Consequently, kayaks are more frequently found on long river trips rather than on lake-to-lake itineraries.

The cost of these excursions usually runs about $100 per person per day for scheduled group trips, and about $175 a day for a custom expedition—varying considerably depending on the number of guides and the quality of the provisions, as well as whether you camp or stay at one or more inns, whether paid permits are required in the wilderness area where you paddle, and whether the outfitter's price includes shuttle service to and from put-in and take-out.

CHOOSING THE RIGHT TRIP

Before you open your wallet, open your mouth and start asking questions. A reputable outfitter or school will be glad to answer any you put forth.

How long has the company been in business? As a general matter, stick with an outfitter who has been in business for several years. That's not a rap on new businesses, but an acknowledgment that the company with a few years in its wake has already met the questions and challenges that you're liable to throw at them. As you grow in experience and knowledge, you can look to alternative sources. Ask about the outfitter's current operating license, and the professional organizations the company belongs to. At the least, it should be an active member of such professional groups as America Outdoors or the North American Canoe Liveries and Outfitters Association (NACLO), umbrella organizations that set minimum standards to which members must agree.

How experienced are the guides? The better the guide, the better the trip. Your guide should be certified by either the American Canoe Association (ACA) or the British Canoe Union (BCU) and able to administer emergency medical aid, including CPR. The certification process ensures that the instructor can teach the right strokes the right way and has the necessary wilderness skills such as route-finding and navigating on a river. A guide's ability to identify plants, animals, and geological phenomena is also a decided bonus.

What about safety and insurance? Mostly you paddle at your own risk. On-water liability insurance is not mandatory for NACLO members, for instance. If an outfitter is operating on state or federal property, though, they are required to be insured as part of the permit process. NACLO distributes a seven-minute safety video which most members show prior to the trip. It's always a good idea to check your own insurance coverage, medical or homeowners/renters, for personal articles before any trip.

How strenuous is the trip? Some trips can be a leisurely float while you're waited upon hand and foot. On other trips, you may be expected to help with portages, pitch in while making camp, and grab a paddle to power the boat. Mileage doesn't count as much as hours on the water and paddling conditions, so be sure to ask about wind, waves, and weather. Don't set yourself up for an experience beyond your physical abilities to enjoy. Be honest with yourself—how strenuous a trip do you want?

How many people are in the group? The more there are, the less sense of wilderness you may have. Ten is common. Still, a group of about 20 can be companionable and offer diverse socializing off-river.

What is the ratio of paddlers to guides? Usually there are 4 or 5 paddlers per guide, but on trips with a support crew to do camp chores and cooking, the ratio may be lower.

What's the cost and what's included? Make sure the costs are precisely spelled out, and that you understand exactly what is and what is not included. Unless otherwise noted, the prices for all trips described below include your guide and basic instruction, canoes or kayaks, life preservers, all meals, and accommodations while you're canoeing—either tents on camping trips or your room on inn-based trips. Unless we specify to the contrary, sleeping bags and pads are included in the cost of custom trips but not in that of scheduled group trips; if they're not, and you need them, find out whether the outfitter will rent them and for what fee.

There is considerable variation as to whether transportation to and from the put-in and take-out and more than basic instruction are included; be sure to find out your outfitter's policy.

What are the meals like? There's enough room in a canoe to pack a cooler, so you can usually expect a good supply of fresh fruits and vegetables and frozen meat or chicken. Breakfasts usually encompass the range of typical camping specialties: hot cereal, granola, pancakes. Lunches "on the paddle" (in which your paddle doubles as a serving platter) are often a smorgasbord including cheese, peanut butter, and fruit. Dinners can be ambitious or fairly basic. If you care, ask to see sample menus.

What are accommodations like? Some canoe trips have you going from lodge to lodge, but they are unusual and none are described here. If you hear of one that interests you, be sure to query the operator as to the style and comfort level of the properties on the itinerary. Most canoe trips involve camping; if you don't supply your own equipment, make sure that the gear you get from the outfitter is up to the conditions. Are the sleeping bags warm enough? Are they made of down, which loses its insulating properties when wet, or of a synthetic that can keep you warm even if it's had a dousing? Are the tents modern and easy to set up? And is their mosquito netting free of holes?

What do you do when you're not paddling? Few river trips involve more than 6 hours per day or so on the water. Ask what happens the rest of the time, and find out whether hikes, nature walks, wildlife watching, or photography are planned and what the countryside is like off the river.

Is the trip suitable for singles? Most canoes are powered by 2 paddlers and a single person may not always be matched with an appropriate partner. If you're traveling solo, find out what the policy is before you sign up. Similarly, most camping trips put 2 people in a tent. If you're without a partner, ask whether you have a choice of having a tent of your own or whether you'll be paired up with another tripper.

How far in advance is booking required? Although it's possible to sign up for a trip at the last minute, most outfitters prefer your booking as much as 90 days in advance or even more. This is primarily so that they can be sure of having enough participants before making the complicated arrangements involved in planning a trip.

If the outfitter you want to go with can't take you, contact local chambers of commerce or the state tourist offices for recommendations of others in the area. Their addresses and telephone numbers follow the information for outfitters serving that trip. These agencies are also good sources for canoeing areas in which scheduled group trips are uncommon or nonexistent and where most paddlers use outfitters to set them up on independent or custom trips.

MAJOR PLAYERS

Canoe outfitters are an independent lot, and they concentrate on serving the rivers near their home base. Operators who offer trips throughout a broad area are unusual.

DVOŘÁK'S KAYAK AND RAFTING EXPEDITIONS
Bill and Jaci Dvořák's family-owned outfit, founded in 1969, is one of the finest in the country; while they offer a considerable number of white-water rafting trips, they also have numerous flat-water canoeing and kayaking trips. Canoe trip offerings range from a half-day on the Arkansas River to 12 days on the Colorado. On canoe trips, meals tend to be southern-style cooking, and most involve camping rather than overnights in inns. The number of participants ranges from

10 to 25, with 3 guides for every 10 guests. Guides have up to 10 years of experience as well as first-aid and CPR certification; they're known for their energy, enthusiasm, and respect for the environment. Rates are around $150 per day (17921 U.S. 285, Nathrop, CO 81236, tel. 719/539–6851 or 800/824–3795, fax 719/539–3378).

LAUGHING HEART ADVENTURES California's federally designated Wild and Scenic Rivers—the Eel, Smith, Trinity, and Klamath—are the prime paddling grounds of this well-established company, founded in 1987. Over 50% of their clients are returning customers or referrals. Most guides have 10 years of experience and all are ACA-certified and have advanced first-aid training; there are usually 2 on every trip, which have with up to 10 participants. Meals are typically hot, wholesome, and filling, providing the calories you need after strenuous days on the river. You're not expected to help with camp chores unless you wish. Rates average $100 per day, not including tents, sleeping bags, and pads, which are available for rent (Box 669, Willow Creek, CA 95573, tel. 916/629–3516 or 800/541–1256 outside of California, fax 916/629–2206).

FAVORITE TRIPS

THE NORTHEAST

MAINE **Expedition on the Great Allagash.** The Allagash is Maine's own river, with the state owning the shoreline for the 96 miles of the Allagash Wilderness Waterway. Probably one of the most popular paddling areas in the East, the Waterway extends back 500 feet from the riverbank on each side, creating the illusion of near-wilderness despite its being remarkably accessible—and despite a century of active logging. You see an occasional road end and an occasional camp, but for the main part you canoe through dense stands of balsam fir and spruce, camping in sheltered nooks among the dark trees. Mergansers sail in flotillas along the shore. It's possible to see moose, and an occasional whitetail deer is visible, along with geese, ducks, ospreys, great blue herons, bald eagles, the splash of a beaver, the shadow of a mink, and the blue dive-bomb of a kingfisher. While the best fishing is early in the year, you can still land your dinner as the summer heats the river. Classic northwoods paddling, the river alternates between swift, stony stretches and long, sluggish pools. The riffles and little drops demand your attention as you pick and choose a path down areas of thin water; if you miscalculate, you'll hear a decisive thump as you glance off a submerged boulder. But for the most part, the waters are not beyond the abilities of the beginner.

On this fully outfitted 9-day trip you have plenty of time to explore the mud bars, poke into eddies and creek mouths, watch for wildlife, and learn the tips and tricks that let a canoe drop gracefully down a riffle. Maine Sport Outfitters, founded in 1976, usually provides a pair of river professionals for each party of 10. The guides are naturalists with a broad range of plant, bird, and animal knowledge, and they give you plenty of paddling points and tips. (They're also registered Maine guides, with wilderness first-aid training.) Once ashore, they transform into camp crafters—setting tents, laying a fire, and starting dinner with a speed guaranteed to amaze. Their culinary wizardry produces breakfasts of bacon and eggs with fried potatoes or pancakes with Maine maple syrup, soup-and-sandwich lunches, and dinners of steak with onions and mushrooms, barbecued chicken, or sautéed scallops, shrimp, and lobster.

The outfitter's season begins in July, a bit after the first paddlers of the season go down the river, and extends until September, when the weather is excellent and the river uncrowded, and there's still plenty of water to move a canoe downstream. *Maine Sport Outfitters, Box 956, Rte. 1, Rockport, ME 04856, tel. 207/236–8797 or 800/722–0826, fax 207/236–7123. Maine Publicity Bureau, Box 2300, Hallowell, ME 04347, tel. 207/582–9300 or 800/533–9595. July–Sept.: 9 days, $849. Sign up 1 month in advance.*

■MAINE■ **Northwoods Paddling on the Machias.** When ticking off the list of Maine's scenic waterways, the Machias has to be near the top of the list—along with the Allagash, Penobscot, and St. John. What does it have to offer? Start with swamps, marshes, and lakes, some sporty rapids that throw a bucket of spray in the bow person's face, ledges, portages—the full mix of classic northwoods paddling that defines canoeing's heritage. Free-flowing (no obstructions or dams) from Fifth Machias Lake to the sea, about 75 miles, it is flanked by near-wilderness. While logging roads do extend along the river, only a handful of cabins mark human presence. Frosting on the canoeing cake is that the Machias is much less heavily traveled than the Allagash and much more accessible than the St. John.

Trips down the river from Maine Sport Outfitters are scheduled for June, when conditions are optimum. As on the outfitter's Allagash trips, there is at least 1 guide for each 6 guests, and a typical party is a pair of professionals guiding a party of 10. Only one Machias trip is planned each year, depending on water conditions. Meals are similar to those served on the outfitter's Allagash trip. *Maine Sports Outfitters, Box 956, Rte. 1, Rockport, ME 04856, tel. 207/236–8797 or 800/722–0826, fax 207/236–7123. Maine Publicity Bureau, Box 2300, Hallowell, ME 04347, tel. 207/582–9300 or 800/533–9595. June: 5 days, $495. Sign up 1 month in advance.*

■NEW YORK■ **Quietwater in Adirondack Park.** Less than a century ago the Adirondacks were the nation's chosen destination resort, a network of hundreds of miles of rivers, streams, ponds, and lakes that attracted canoeists from all over the country. J. Henry Rushton, the father of American canoe design, grew up on an Adirondack river and placed his stamp on modern American canoe building from his boat shop just north of the present park. Nineteenth-century author Nessmuk, less well known as George Washington Sears, wrote his incredibly popular woodcraft stories based on cruises in the Adirondacks. And the founders of the American Canoe Association camped at Lake George to create the organization in 1880.

McDonnell's Adirondack Challenge puts together paddling vacations throughout the area; one of its most popular trips takes you through the stream-connected Saranac Lakes chain. With its many bays, points, islands, marshes, and ponds, it would take a summer to adequately explore the waters of this area.

Rather than offering a roster of group trips, McDonnell's sets up a special departure for every party, with one guide for about 6 guests. Since each trip is customized, prices vary; average is $75 per person per day including guide, boats, camping equipment, and meals, but the figure could go up or down depending on where you paddle, how many in your party, and what you do en route. If you want to bring your own boat and camping equipment or just want a map and directions, McDonnell's will work with you. Working with its sister company, All Seasons Outfitters, McDonnell's provides experienced guides and top-of-the-line equipment for a variety of wilderness adventures. *McDonnell's Adirondack Challenge, All Seasons Outfitters, 168 Lake Flower Ave., Saranac Lake, NY 12983, tel. 518/891–6159. Saranac Lake Area Chamber of Commerce, 30 Main St., Saranac Lake NY, 12983, tel. 518/891–1990 or 800/347–1992. May–Oct.: 2 days–2 weeks, about $100 per person per day. Sign up 1 month in advance.*

THE SOUTH

FLORIDA **Wilderness Waterway in Florida's Backcountry.** Although the Everglades is one of the most visited and most studied areas in the National Park system, the 99-mile inside water route through the backcountry from Everglades City on the Gulf of Mexico to Flamingo on the Florida Bay has a much lower profile. Known as the Wilderness Waterway, this subtropical trail passes through America's most extensive mangrove forest, and an array of exotic varieties of tropical vegetation. Nearly every kind of marine life found in the Caribbean is displayed here. You may even have the chance to see elusive wildlife such as a bobcat, bear, panther, alligator, or manatee as you paddle through the green jungle and past ancient Calusa Indian shell mounds.

Because of tides and winds, the park service recommends you plan on covering no more than 10 miles a day and that only experienced canoeists undertake the trip. Permits are required and special regulations are enforced to preserve the park area. Nautical charts are necessary to find your way. Campers have three choices of sites: coastal beaches, interior bay and river ground sites, and chickees, which are wooden platforms located along interior rivers and bays that lack dry land. Water has to be carried as there is no fresh water available along the whole trail. The best time to visit is in the winter when it seldom rains, temperatures are above 60 degrees, and the insects are less bothersome (but good mosquito netting is still a must). An important note: the Everglades backcountry is shared by canoeists and powerboaters alike, although motorboats have to detour some areas. *Florida Bay Outfitters, Box 2513, Key Largo, FL 33037, tel. 305/451–3018. Dec.–April: $699 for 7 days. The Everglades National Park, Box 279, Homestead, FL 33030, tel. 305/242–7700. Florida National Parks and Monuments Association, Box 279, Homestead, FL 33030, tel. 305/247–1216.*

FLORIDA AND GEORGIA **The Free-Flowing Suwannee River.** The Suwannee River, originating in the Okefenokee Swamp, Georgia, flows south for over 200 miles through northwestern Florida to the Gulf of Mexico, fed by 22 major springs. (Some of those springs, including those at Manatee Springs State Park, offer diving and other recreational opportunities). The upper trail begins in White Springs, and the lower trail begins at Suwannee River State Park. The U.S. Department of the Interior considers the Suwannee to be one of the foremost free-flowing streams of its type in the Southeast.

A run of the entire river could take from two to three weeks, so most paddlers prefer to travel shorter portions; there are many access points. The area with the most abundant wildlife and least traffic is the 46-mile stretch between Fargo, Georgia, and White Springs, Florida, although several rocky shoals in this section might give beginners trouble. The river widens downstream of Suwannee State Park where river traffic increases, so most paddlers take out there. The best seasons to go are spring and fall. River water is not potable, so plan on bringing your own.

Suwannee Canoe Outpost, an outfitter, is in the Spirit of Suwannee Park on a 500-acre full-service campground. They tailor rates according to trip length, group size, and camping services. *Suwannee Canoe Outpost at the Spirit of Suwannee Park, Rt. 1, Box 98A, Live Oak, FL 32060, tel. 904/364–4991 or 800/428–4147. Year round: camping and canoe rentals (no meals), $35 per day. Sign up at least 2 weeks in advance.*

GEORGIA **The Okefenokee: Black-Mirror Waters and Trembling Earth.** This 600-square-mile wilderness in the southern part of the state—far from being the smelly, foul basin that the word swamp might suggest—provides a paddling experience that's simply not to be missed. The preserve's eastern reaches, where Wilderness Southeast begins its 5-day paddling trips, is made up of expanses of water-based prairie patched here and there by solid and not-so-solid islands known as hammocks. Composed of densely matted floating vegetation bound together by a network of roots, some of these hammocks shiver when trod upon (which is why the Indians who named the swamp called it "the land of the trembling earth"). In the west are dense forests of cypress, whose roots have stained the swamp's pure water the color of dark tea; in shady areas, it is quite black and perfectly reflects the lush green overhanging vegetation and the lacy trails of Spanish moss to magical effect. The Okefenokee's shallows and backwaters shelter thousands of alligators; the preserve is also the territory of deer and otter, dozens of

kinds of snakes, and hundreds of species of birds.

While rental canoes are readily available at key visitor areas on the fringes of the swamp, Wilderness Southeast trips are particularly rewarding since they are led by naturalist-guides who give you background about the swamp's fascinating ecosystem.

Moreover, in addition to the some 40 miles of stillwater paddling in the swamp, there's another 10 down the Suwannee River, which begins in the Okefenokee. Camping is within the Okefenokee National Wildlife Refuge, one of the public lands within the swamp; you set up tents on wooden platforms. With savory dishes like vegetarian chili and stir-fried shrimp and rice on the menu, the meals are surprisingly tasty. Usually a pair of guides accompany 14 guests. Wilderness Southeast, founded in 1973, is a nonprofit educational corporation.

If you go in spring, you will find flowers in bloom, nesting birds, the gators at their most active, and a lot of other people. In fall, you can sign up for special photo-workshop trips with lodging in cabins rather than in tents. *Wilderness Southeast, 711 Sandtown Rd., Savannah, GA 31410, tel. 912/897–5108, fax 912/897–5116. Okefenokee National Wildlife Refuge, Rte. 2, Box 338, Folkston, GA 31357, tel. 912/496–3331. Apr. and Nov.: 5 days, $440. Sign up 3–4 months in advance.*

MISSISSIPPI **Southern Hospitality on the Wolf River.** Snow-white sand beaches and sparkling clear water reflecting magnolia, cypress, and oak: It sounds like a promotional piece for paradise. In fact, though, the images describe the Wolf River in the southern part of the state, one of the cleanest and least developed rivers in the South, yet one that even beginning paddlers can handle. The water is basically placid, with only a few scattered, easy-to-negotiate riffles marring the surface. A 5-day cruise takes you through lush forests, with a beach around every bend; you share the scenery with the deer, raccoons, owls, great blue herons and even flocks of wild turkeys. Under the surface, you can find bass, catfish, sunfish, and the occasional prowling gar; bring your fishing tackle.

On this slow and beautiful river, you won't find long, scheduled group trips, and few paddlers feel the need of a guide, but if you do, Wolf River Canoes can supply one, along with your canoe, paddles, personal flotation devices, and shuttle to put-in (camping equipment can be rented). *Wolf River Canoes (Joseph Feil), 21652 Tucker Rd., Long Beach, MS 39560, tel. 601/452–7666. For additional resources, contact America Outdoors, Box 1348, Knoxville, TN 37901, tel. 615/524–4814, fax 615/524–3784. Year round: 5 days, $595. Price does not include food, tents, stove, cookware, or sleeping bags and pads; sign up 1 month in advance.*

THE MIDWEST

MINNESOTA **Boundary Waters Canoe Area Wilderness.** The lure to paddlers of this 150-mile arc of woodlands across northeast Minnesota is powerful: 1,175 lakes dotting 1.1 million acres of forests inhabited by more than 225 species of birds and 55 species of mammals (moose, deer, bear, coyote, fox, otter, mink, bobcat, lynx, marten, and wolf); and 2,200 campsites, give or take a few, scattered along at least 1,500 miles of canoe routes. There are no roads and no cabins. No airplanes can land, and motorboats are permitted only in a very small area. Abutting the BWCA across the border to the north is Quetico Provincial Park, whose pristine acreage doubles the amount of wilderness beckoning the paddler. A system of permits, in effect on both sides of the border, limits the number of visitors and keeps them widely dispersed so that you can easily go for days without seeing other paddlers.

Lakes are connected by a system of streams, rivers, and portages; ponds and bogs sparkle among the conifers. It's classic northwoods flat-water canoeing, as good as it gets. There are some challenging, if not downright dangerous, rivers, and most of the rivers have at least riffles. However, well-established trails give you the choice of portaging around difficult spots. You can spend a lifetime in the area and not exhaust its possibilities nor tire of its beauty.

Typically, in this area, you sign up with an outfitter, who provides boats, food, all camping equipment, and the necessary permits and campsite reservations. Tom & Woods' Moose Lake Wilderness Canoe Trips is typical (a frill here is that lodging before and after your trip is included). As is usual among local outfitters, this one also helps you plan a route that suits your paddling ability and camping experience and takes in the waterfalls, wildlife, islands, and other natural features that you travel to the area to experience. The outfitter sets you up with Mad River Kevlar canoes and Eureka tents, plus everything else you need; all you have to bring is your clothing and fishing gear.

Summer is the best time to visit, though if the itinerary you plan takes in a river or stream, you may prefer to travel in late spring or early summer, when water levels are higher, or after the start of the fall rains. *Tom & Woods' Moose Lake Wilderness Canoe Trips, Box 358, Ely, MN 55731, tel. 218/365–5837 or 800/322–5837, fax 218/365–6369. Minnesota Office of Tourism, 375 Jackson St., 256 Skyway Level, St. Paul, MN 55101, tel. 612/296–5029 or 800/657–3700. May–Sept.: $143–$182 per day. Sign up 3–7 months in advance.*

MINNESOTA **Another Approach to the Boundary Waters Canoe Area.** One of the favorite trips among canoeists who sign up for Top of the Trail's outfitting services is a relatively easy, laid-back course through the BWCA's northwest corner. But you won't rub elbows with your neighbors given the vast amounts of space as you loop around Saganaga Lake, skirt the international boundary between the United States and Canada from Saganaga through Knife Lake and on to Birch, then make a left turn through a chain of small lakes and ponds to Thomas Lake. At that point, you swing northeast, crossing Kekebabic and Ogishkemuncie lakes and the Seagull River as you return to Saganaga. The paddling delivers a little bit of everything the BWCA promises—big lakes, ponds, little rivers, great scenery, no matter which way you're looking, and 39 brief portages. (And if this route doesn't sound appealing, Top of the Trail can design any number of others.)

Top of the Trail, a member of the Minnesota Canoe Association and the United States Canoe Association, was established in 1987. Fresh foods mix with freeze-dried foods on your menu, which includes omelettes, French toast, pancakes, granola, and cereal for breakfast; summer sausage sandwiches, bagels, and spaghetti for lunch; and steak, lasagna, and turkey tetrazzini for dinner. While most paddlers opt for an independent trip, guides are also available; they all have extensive paddling experience and first-aid training, and they leave it up to you as to whether you help with camp chores or just go fishing. The total outfitting fee varies depending on the size of your group, when you go, and what kind of canoes you use—several are available, and the lighter, easier-to-portage models nudge your tab to the higher end of the scale. *Top of the Trail Canoe Outfitters, Saganaga Lake, Box 1001, Gunflint Trail, Grand Marais, MN 55604, tel. 218/388–2255 or 800/869–0883. Minnesota Office of Tourism, 375 Jackson St., 256 Skyway Level, St. Paul, MN 55101, tel. 612/296–5029 or 800/657–3700. May–Sept.: $138–$160 per day. Sign up 2 months in advance.*

THE SOUTHWEST

ARIZONA **Canyons and Hot Springs along the Colorado.** As fall slowly drains into the dark hours of the year, it's time to head for the desert. One of the most spectacular, thoroughly enjoyable, and little-known paddle trips in North America is along the Black Canyon of the Colorado River below Hoover Dam. Picture steep canyon walls vaulting up from the big, smooth river; bighorn sheep looking down on the canoes; yourself stretched back in a bubbling hot spring soaking your paddle-weary muscles. And the best part of the trip is yet to come.

Summertime, traditionally, is vacation time. Most people hoard their free time jealously, and burn it off in a single grand splurge. Summer, though, is not the best time to poke around the Lake Mead National Recreation Area south of Las Vegas and downstream of Hoover Dam. It's hot! Really hot. But if you wait until November is about ready to fall off the calendar, temperatures subside into the comfortable. You can venture out into the noonday sun without sloshing sunblock over each square inch of bare skin. Fish no longer flee to the deepest depths, and are more than interested in trying out the selection of lures or baits you offer.

Best of all, there's another natural vacation break at the tail end of the month—Thanksgiving. Squeeze another day onto the 4 days of Thanksgiving weekend, and you have just enough time for one of Laughing Heart Adventure's fabulous Thanksgiving expeditions, with a multicourse holiday meal—from turkey with all the fixings to sweet-potato pie for dessert.

Below Hoover Dam, the Colorado is big but placid and crystal-clear, rolling on its way toward the Gulf of California. This is flatwater canoeing country, with plenty of emphasis on the flat. You definitely earn the miles between each campsite.

Expect a maximum party size of 10 guests, supported by at least a pair of ACA-certified guides. Meals are filling: huevos rancheros, Dutch-oven lasagna, and an assortment of homebaked cakes. After dinner, you can relax, since guests are not required to help with camp chores. If you can't make the Thanksgiving journey, try for the similar trip that Laughing Heart mounts over the Easter weekend, with a similar banquet spread on the riverbank. The price of the trip includes round-trip transportation from Las Vegas. *Laughing Heart Adventures, Trinity Outdoor Center, Box 669, Willow Creek, CA 95573, tel. 916/629–3516 or 800/541–1256 (outside California), fax 916/629–2206. Thanksgiving and Easter: 5 days, $425. Sign up 2–3 months in advance.*

UTAH **Paddling the Green through Red-Rock Country.** With the orange-red sandstone just outside Canyonlands National Park soaring upward from the river's edge, the Green River in Utah can be a photographer's paradise. It's hard to beat this 5-day, 70-mile paddle between Green River, Utah, and Mineral Bottom, at the confluence of the Green and the Colorado rivers—a trip offered by Southwind Kayak Center, founded in 1987. The river's course runs through sheer canyons and past inviting side canyons, and abandoned mines and cabins.

Southwind makes the trip both with canoes and kayaks. With its gentle current, this is cruising country for kayaks—great for beginners—and easy strokes power you across or up the river and build speed downstream atop the current. While leisurely for kayaks, the stream is strenuous for canoeists, requiring far harder paddling and a fair amount of experience, although it is certainly within the reach of even moderately competent paddlers. There are approximately 20 paddlers and 5 guides per outing. Guides have from 2 to 5 years of professional training in instruction and leadership, and all are certified in first aid and CPR; most also have advanced wilderness medical training.

Paddle rafts accompany the trip, and the support crew of 3 whips up western-style meals such as salmon grilled with herbs, barbecued steak or chicken breast, with fresh salads and vegetables, hot soup, and warm bread. After dinner, the crew sets up comfortable camps on remote beaches while you explore the nearest canyons in the company of your two naturalist-guides.

The Green is navigable year-round, but spring and fall are the best seasons, as the water is warm enough for swimming and high enough to move swiftly but not too high to submerge good campsites on the riverbanks and islands. Winter temperatures can dip to the 20°F to 60°F range, and summer days top out at 110°-plus (albeit with far cooler nights). Price includes transportation to and from Los Angeles. *Southwind Kayak Center, 17855 Sky Park Circle, #A, Irvine CA 92714, tel. 714/261–0200 or 800/768–8494, fax 714/261–8728. July: 5 days, $995. Sign up 3 months in advance.*

THE ROCKIES

COLORADO **Classical Music on the Dolores.** On this 8-day trip down the great Dolores, which surges through the deserts of the Southwest, through alpine forests and past ancient Anasazi sandstone caverns, outfitter Bill Dvořák invites musicians from the Los Angeles Philharmonic, who ride in rafts and provide nightly concerts while you're on the river. Canoers and kayakers are welcome as well as rafters, and the outfitter provides your boat. You can portage around the few Class III rapids along the route or you can ride through on a raft while a guide takes your boat through.

The Classical Music Trip is immensely popular, and early reservations are strongly suggested. For specifics on the food and outfitting style, see River Rafting. *Dvořák's Kayak and Rafting Expeditions, 17921 U.S. 285, Nathrop, CO 81236, tel. 719/539–6851 or 800/824–3795, fax 719/539–3378. June: 8 days, $1,650. Price does not include tent or sleeping bag; sign up 9–12 months in advance.*

THE WEST COAST

CALIFORNIA **An Easy Trip down the Gentle Eel.** Back in 1850, explorer Josiah Gregg had a broken skillet and a hankering for fresh food. Bivouacked by a northern California river, a member of his party successfully swapped the broken pan to a party of local Native Americans for a mess of fresh eels. Even though the natives already had a name for the river, Weeyot, Gregg immediately renamed it Eel to commemorate the meal.

Today, this gentle stream is California's longest wilderness river. The main Eel rises at the foot of Bald Mountain in the Mendocino National Forest and heads south for 20 miles before turning northwesterly through the

Coast Range to the Pacific, wiggling through a land of towering old growth redwood forests, with only a few roads in sight. In the presence of these ancient trees, many paddlers whisper in awe. Deer may gingerly step out onto the wide gravel beaches in search of a drink, or a raccoon may be glimpsed in the water at the mouth of a tributary, watching the canoes pass as he hunts for a meal.

Laughing Heart Adventures' 7-day canoe expeditions on this stream, the longest of several available, usually have no more than 10 guests, supported by at least a pair of guides, sometimes 3. They tend to know much more than just the techniques of shepherding their flock down the river. If you find a track at the river's edge, they can describe the animal and as likely as not show you where to watch for a glimpse of it. They can identify a bird from its song, point out a nearly hidden nest in a tree, and spin a tale about the rich coastal environment. When you encounter the modest white-water stretches, they provide enough thorough but low-key coaching to help get novices through without a hitch. Off the river, their accomplishments really shine: The guides pride themselves on the ability to whip up a fabulous meal while guests relax on the riverbank. Signature dishes include huevos Mexicanos at breakfast and lasagna made in the Dutch oven at dinner.

The Eel, whose average annual 90 inches of precipitation fall mostly from November through March, shrinks to a thread meandering down the wide gravel banks and bars by April. Riding the boundary between the cool, moist Pacific air and the heat of inland California, the Eel gets strong upriver winds most afternoons; Laughing Heart trips avoid the winds by starting early in the morning and making camp early on the river's beautiful sandy beaches. *Laughing Heart Adventures, Trinity Outdoor Center, Box 669, Willow Creek, CA 95573, tel. 916/629–3516 or 800/541–1256, fax 916/629–2206. Mar.–July: 7 days, $700. Sign up 2–3 months in advance.*

CALIFORNIA **Splashing through the Trinity Alps.** The name Alps conjures up images of rugged mountains, lush meadows, and sparkling streams—and for the paddler venturing into the Trinity Alps of northern California the imagery is fully justified. The Trinity River splashes down through steep-walled canyons, turning and twisting among stands of towering evergreens as it works its way from the spine of California to where it meets the Klamath River and dashes to the sea. This is superb canoeing water, alternating between long, placid pools mirroring the dark needles of the conifers and the rugged rocks and bouncing waves and gleaming white water in the easy drops.

On this canoeing trip from Laughing Heart Adventures, it takes 6 easy days to paddle the 75 miles from Hawkins Bar near Willow Creek to the mouth of the Klamath River, where it pours into the Pacific Ocean near Klamath Glen in Redwood National Park. The upper stretches of the trip are paralleled by road, which is generally unobtrusive. Below the confluence of the Trinity and Klamath rivers, downstream from the Hoopa Reservation, the dense forests of the Coast Range close in, and the river works its way through near-wilderness. Along the riverbanks you might glimpse deer, raccoon, even a shy black bear. Birds of prey glide overhead, especially during the salmon runs.

With a maximum party size of 14 and at least 2 guides, there's plenty of time to absorb the guides' knowledge. Want to improve your paddling? Or learn the difference between Douglas fir, hemlock, and pine? Curious about the tiny, clawed footprint in the sand? Want to lean back and enjoy the changing skies at the end of the day, with the smells of food in the air? That's what this trip is all about.

River levels on the Klamath are not as critical as on some rivers; an upstream dam keeps the flow even. However, the upper stretches cross California's interior, and air and water temperatures can be quite warm from mid- to late summer. *Laughing Heart Adventures, Trinity Outdoor Center, Box 669, Willow Creek, CA 95573, tel. 916/629–*

3516 or 800/ 541–1256, fax 916/629–2206. May–Sept.: 6 days, $660. Sign up 2–3 months in advance.

SOURCES

ORGANIZATIONS Membership organizations set standards for river guides and outfitters and are good sources for referrals and for checking references. Among them are **America Outdoors** (Box 1348, Knoxville, TN 37901, tel. 615/524–4814), the national association for river guides, and the **National Association of Canoe Liveries and Outfitters** (NALCO—U.S. 27 and Hornbeck Roads, Box 248, Butler, KY 41006, tel. 606/472–2205). Another good source for information about guides and outfitters and listings of local clubs, the backbone of paddling sports today, is the **American Canoe Association** (7432 Alban Station Blvd., Ste. B226, Springfield, VA 22159, tel. 703/451–0140), which publishes the "American Canoeist" newsletter. Clubs focus on everything from white water to placid river drifts to fierce surf competition to Olympic sprints to long-distance sea kayaking. There are hundreds of them in the United States.

PERIODICALS *Canoe and Kayak Magazine* 3146, Kirkland, WA 98083, tel. 800/692–2663), another source for an up-to-date list of local paddling clubs, covers flat water and white water, canoes and kayaks, trips and techniques. The quarterly *Paddler* (Box 775450, Steamboat Springs, CO 80477, tel. 303/879–1450) covers a broad spectrum of canoe and kayak trips and runs product reviews and tips on paddling skills.

BOOKS *Canoeing,* prepared by the American National Red Cross, is the basic book on canoe technique. If you don't have access to a canoe club or other paddling instruction, it is your best source of safety information. *Basic Canoeing* is an abridged version of the full book. *Canoeing Made Easy,* by I. Herbert Gordon, is a manual for beginners with plenty of tips for the most experienced of

boaters. *Canoeing & Rafting: The Complete Where-to-Go Guide to America's Best Tame and Wild Waters,* by Sara Pyle, is a state-by-state list of canoe and kayak waters with notes on difficulty and optimum paddling times; it's valuable despite its somewhat dated livery and outfitter information.

In the summer of 1930, a pair of Minnesota teenagers paddled a canoe from Minneapolis to Hudson Bay, 2,250 miles away. *Canoeing With The Cree,* by Eric Sevareid, describes their 4-month journey on the wilderness waterways made famous by fur traders. A great yarn, Sevareid's narrative portrays the North Woods before civilization encroached. *The Complete Wilderness Paddler,* by James West Davidson and John Rugge, is a ripping tale of a great adventure, paddling down the Moisie River in Labrador. Each step of the trip is carefully dissected, giving the reader insights into the skills needed for paddling a canoe virtually anywhere. A must-read for anyone interested in canoe tripping. *A Guide to Big Water Canoeing,* by David Alan Herzog, is an introduction to the techniques of paddling North America's large lakes, bays, and salt water. An invaluable resource. *Pole, Paddle & Portage: A Complete Guide to Canoeing,* by Bill Riviere, distills the experience and Northeast viewpoint of this respected outdoors writer and former Maine canoe guide into a readable introduction to canoeing. *Rivers Running Free: Canoeing Stories by Adventurous Women,* edited by Judith Niemi and Barbara Wieser, is an anthology. Necessary reading if you're planning on an Everglades trip is *A Guide to the Wilderness Waterway,* by William G. Truesdell.

ALSO SEE If you like flat-water canoeing and kayaking, you may want to tackle white water, either in a canoe or kayak (*see* Canoeing and Kayaking in White Water) or on a raft (*see* River Rafting). Or you may want to try canoeing in flat water under the aegis of a wilderness program such as Outward Bound (*see* Major Players in Wilderness and Survival Schools).

Canoeing and Kayaking in White Water

By Dennis Stuhaug

Updated by W. Lynn Seldon Jr.

ith a quick draw, the paddler in the bow swings the canoe away from the rock and down the smooth tongue of water flowing out of the glistening white water of the rapid. The evergreens arch over the narrow tunnel of the river, and there is a half-shadowed movement in the bankside brush that may have been a nervous deer. A kayak slips through the water after the canoe, its paddler laughing as the boat bursts through the waves in a cloud of spray into a smooth, placid pool.

This is classic white-water river paddling. Virtually anyone can master the basics in a few lessons under the guidance of a seasoned instructor. The strokes and combinations of strokes that allow a boat to move forward, backward, or sideways, or turn, are simple to grasp. The art of finding a route through a boulder garden is readily acquired. Your kayak is upended? Many people can learn to roll a kayak right side up in a single lesson. Your canoe is swamped? Maneuver yourself around to the upstream side of the canoe and hang on as the canoe runs the rapids.

Instruction is available both on learn-as-you-go group trips down rivers across the country and in organized white-water paddling schools. Typically, the former involves a classic wilderness camping-trip format, with guides to teach paddling skills and handle camp chores; the cost includes food, equipment, instruction, and lodging (usually a tent) at about $125 to $150 per person per day.

During organized classes, you spend from 3 days to a week in a single location, usually at the school's base camp or headquarters, and learn strokes, reading the river, and ways to get out of the water if you get in (one of them, the Eskimo roll, involves using your paddle to flip your kayak right side up); the cost runs about $75 a day per person, including equipment and lunch but not breakfast, dinner, and lodging. If you wear contact lenses, you may want to bring a pair of swim goggles.

On a typical first day, you meet early in the morning over breakfast and get a brief description of what you'll do during the week, followed by a detailed description of what you'll learn that day. Then it's down to the water for step-by-step demonstrations of the techniques on the docket, and lots of practice. Many schools videotape you in action, and play the videotapes at the end of the day, after you've showered, cleaned up, and had dinner.

You can do this type of white-water boating in either canoes or kayaks. A small number of programs are exclusively for those who

---

Dennis Stuhaug, the managing editor of *Canoe Magazine,* is a former white-water and flat-water instructor and a longtime sport and recreational paddler. Freelance writer and photographer Lynn Seldon learned white-water paddling with the Nantahala Outdoor Center in North Carolina and Class VI River Runners in West Virginia.

use kayaks or traditional canoes, while others use one or the other depending on the preferences of those who have signed up. Instructional programs use canoes and kayaks with equal frequency nationwide. What's the difference, practically speaking, between canoes and kayaks? Canoes are usually open on top; you kneel or sit relatively high in the craft and power the boat with a single-bladed paddle. Kayaks are enclosed, and the paddler sits low and propels the craft with a double-bladed paddle. Unlike long, stable sea kayaks (a.k.a. touring kayaks), which average about 17 feet in length, white-water kayaks are short, typically under 13 feet, with a low center of gravity so that they respond instantly to the paddler's command—a responsiveness that in the hands of a novice equals extreme tippiness. Whether you learn one or the other is a matter of personal taste; some people don't like the idea of sitting in kayaks because they're enclosed, and opt for the open-decked canoe.

The opportunity to travel in the company of a professional guide who not only knows how to get you down the river but can also point out the natural features of the landscape is reason enough to sign up for a group white-water trip rather than strike out on your own. Being able to lean back after a day on the river in anticipation of a superb meal, without having to do the cooking, is another. And facing the challenge of a complex rapid—and accomplishing the last mile into camp—are the pleasures that quickly make new paddlers into devotees.

CHOOSING THE RIGHT TRIP

Before you leap to sign up, start asking questions—and the more, the better. A reputable outfitter or school will be glad to tell you anything you want to know.

How strenuous is the trip? On point-to-point trips, you may be waited upon hand and foot—or you may be expected to help with portages and pitch in making camp. In terms of sheer toughness, mileage doesn't count as much as the number of hours on the

water and paddling conditions, so be sure to ask about wind, waves, and weather. Unless otherwise noted, all the trips described below are available for people of all paddling levels.

Also, familiarize yourself with white-water classifications, the shorthand code that paddlers use to describe the relative difficulty of rivers. The classification goes in increasing order of difficulty from Class I to Class VI. Class I connotes moving water with riffles and small waves, runnable by practiced beginners. Obstructions, if any, may be easily avoided. Class II signals easy rapids with waves up to 3 feet. Channels are wide and clear, and the routes may be easily identified from a boat without scouting. Some maneuvering is required. Class II waters are runnable by intermediate paddlers. Class III waters contain narrow passages and high, irregular waves capable of swamping an open canoe. Complex maneuvering and scouting from shore may be required. You need experience. Class IV rapids are long and difficult, with constricted passages, often requiring precise maneuvering in turbulent waters. These waters are generally impassable for open canoes. A high degree of paddling skill is essential. Class V rapids are long and violent, nearly always requiring scouting from shore. Rescue conditions are difficult, and any mishap causes a significant hazard to life. Only a team of experts should undertake these waters. Class VI waters approach the limit of navigability; they are nearly impossible, very dangerous, and suitable only for teams of experts and only after close study and with all precautions taken.

Remember when choosing a trip that river conditions are not static. A change in water level and river flow can transform a stream. In some cases, a very challenging rapid may disappear when higher water floods a channel. In others, a simple section of river at low water may turn into a cauldron as the volume of water increases.

How long has the company been in business? As a general matter, stick with an outfitter or school that has been in business for several years when you're a beginner. The company with a few years' experience under its belt has already dealt with the challenges that you're liable to throw them. Ask about the outfitter's current operating license, and find out which professional organizations the company belongs to. At the least, it should be an active member of such professional groups as America Outdoors, the National Association of Canoe Liveries and Outfitters (NACLO), or the American Canoe Association (*see below*). These organizations set minimum standards for the profession.

How experienced are the guides and instructors? The better the guide, the better the trip. Instructors and guides should be certified by either the American Canoe Association (ACA) or British Canoe Union (BCU). The certification process ensures that the instructor can teach the right strokes the right way and that the guide knows the necessary wilderness skills. Also ask whether guides are experienced naturalists, and find out how well they know the region. One guide in each group should be able to administer emergency medical aid, including CPR. A knowledge of plants, animals, and geological phenomena is a decided plus.

What about safety or insurance? Mostly you paddle at your own risk. On-water liability insurance is not mandatory for NACLO members, for instance. If an outfitter is operating on state or federal property, though, they are required to be insured as part of the permit process. NACLO distributes a seven-minute safety video, which most members show prior to the trip. But it's always a good idea to check your own insurance coverage—medical or homeowners/renters for personal articles—before any trip.

How many people are in your group? The more there are, the less sense of wilderness you may have. Ten is common on group trips, though a group of about 20 can be companionable and offer diverse socializing off-river.

What is the ratio of paddlers to guides or instructors? Usually, on trips, there are 4 or 5 paddlers per guide, but on trips with a support crew to do camp chores and cooking, the ratio may be higher. In instructional setups, the greater the number of guides, the more personal attention you will have.

How much time do you spend on the water? This is especially relevant when you're signing up for a clinic or school. The usual range is 5 to 6 hours; you may get tired after that if you don't start out in great shape.

What do you do when you're not paddling? Few river trips involve more than 6 hours or so on moving water. Ask what happens the rest of the time, and find out whether there are plans for hikes, nature walks, wildlife watching, or photography.

What's the cost and what's included? Make sure it's precisely spelled out, and that you understand exactly what is and what is not included. Typically, and for the operations described below unless otherwise noted, paddling schools include instruction, equipment, and lunch only, with accommodations, breakfasts, and dinner extra. On point-to-point trips, the price you pay includes instruction and guiding, all meals while you're on the river, boats, life preservers, wet suits if you need them, and camping equipment, including tents but not sleeping bags and pads. Anything you need that is not supplied is usually available for rent if you don't have your own equipment. Find out if you will need a wet suit and ask whether it's included.

What are the meals like? On point-to-point trips, ask for sample menus. In general, because there's enough room in a canoe to pack a cooler, you can usually expect a good supply of fresh fruits and vegetables as well as frozen meat, fish, or chicken. Breakfasts are generally the standard camping fare: hot cereal, granola, pancakes, and the like. Lunches are often a smorgasbord of cheese, peanut butter, fruit, and perhaps something canned. Dinners may stick with simple but satisfying lasagna and pasta—but can aspire to culinary heights; in some regions, there's an informal competition among river guides as to who can produce the more elaborate fare.

What are the accommodations like? If accommodations are not included, ask about what's available nearby; then call the properties themselves and find out about the establishment's rooms and facilities. If the outfitter is providing camping gear, make sure it's of a quality you'll be happy with; you don't want a sleeping bag that isn't warm enough or a tent that you have to wrestle with to set up. Also ask about the campsites and shower and latrine arrangements.

Is this program suitable for singles? Most canoes are powered by 2 paddlers and a single person's luck of the draw may not always match them up with an appropriate partner. Find out what the outfitter's policy is before you sign up. Similarly, most camping trips routinely put 2 people in a tent. If you're without a partner, ask whether you have a choice of having a tent of your own or whether you'll be automatically paired up with another tripper.

Do you have references from past guests? If you have qualitative questions about a program you're considering, there's no better way to get them answered than to chat with someone who's paddled the waters and spent time with the staff.

How far in advance do I need to book? Count on a week to several months ahead, depending on the season, the type of program, and its location.

MAJOR PLAYERS

ARTA RIVER TRIPS ARTA, or American River Touring Association, a nonprofit corporation, has been running rivers since 1963, providing safe, exciting river adventures that cultivate an appreciation of the natural environment. ARTA runs trips on a variety of western rivers through five states, including the Yampa, Green, Colorado, Salmon, Rogue, and Upper Klamath. Wilderness camping is cushioned a bit by riverside cuisine prepared by guides. In addition to their cooking skills, ARTA's guides display diverse talents in fly fishing, playing banjo, or discussing the history and geology of a river canyon. The company offers unusual trips from year to year, too, covering topics such as archaeology and Native America history. ARTA has several special interest programs for families and people with disabilities. Trip lengths range from 3 to 13 days, with an equally wide range of trip costs. (24000 Casa Loma Rd., Groveland, CA 95321, tel. 209/962–7873 or 800/323–ARTA, fax 209/962-2819).

DVORAK'S KAYAK AND RAFTING EXPEDITIONS Bill and Jaci Dvořák, well-known for their flat-water canoeing trips and rafting trips, are also well known for their 1- to 12-day white-water instructional clinics, staged on Class II and Class III waters such as the Arkansas, Colorado, Dolores, Green, Gunnison, Rio Chama, Rio Grande, and North Platte. (Their rafting trips are usually accompanied by several inflatable kayaks.) Clinics are held either at the Dvořák base on the Arkansas River or on another one of the western rivers they run; white-water kayaking and canoeing trips are offered on a variety of western rivers. Instructional programs, available for beginners, intermediates, and experts, have a 4:1 student-to-instructor ratio. A support raft goes along on kayak trips, which means that meals incorporate lots of fresh fruits, vegetables, and meats, as well as whole grains. The operation was founded in 1969 and has been going strong ever since, growing by leaps and bounds every year (17921 U.S. 285, Nathrop, CO 81236, tel. 719/539–6851 or 800/824–3795, fax 719/ 539–3378).

NANTAHALA OUTDOOR CENTER Founded in 1972 and now employee-owned, this member of America Outdoors and the North American Liveries and Outfitters Association is one of the country's top paddling schools and river runners. Both on trips and in schools, groups are limited to 10 with 2 instructors who are ACA-certified with advanced wilderness first-aid and CPR training and 5 years of experience or more. Boats are modern, since the fleet is replaced every year. NOC instruction programs, which run from March through October and cost from $134 to $147 per day, take place on the Chattooga, French Broad, Little Tennessee, Nantahala, Nolichucky, Ocoee, Oconaluftee, and Tuckaseigee; depending on the course's level and length, you may experience up to 4 of these streams. Specialized instruction programs are available for people with mobility impairments, quick learners, timid learners, women, children, and people on tight budgets, among others. Meals, included in prices for both trips and schools, are hearty; during instruction programs, they're served family-style and dinners may star a salad flecked with edible flowers from the NOC garden. Accommodations are available in NOC's modern-rustic bunkhouse, which has a limited number of shared rooms with shared baths; there are campgrounds and motels nearby (13077 Hwy. 19W, Bryson City, NC 28713, tel. 704/ 488–6737, fax 704/488–2498).

OUTDOOR CENTRE OF NEW ENGLAND In 1991, nine years after this central Massachusetts school was established on the Connecticut River, *Paddler* magazine recognized founder Tom Foster as "the godfather of contemporary paddling instruction in the United States." The school is very technically oriented, emphasizing Olympic-style techniques that reflect the latest knowledge about the use of the human body to propel a craft through the water. Typically, students spend as much as 6 hours on just a mile of river, working on eddy turns, peelouts, and other maneuvers, and zooming in and out of waves and across troughs. However, the OCNE staff can also teach you wilderness canoe tripping, freestyle canoeing, downriver kayak or canoe racing, and open-water kayaking. Group workshops and private instruction are available at all ability levels. Staffers are all ACA-certified, and are not only excellent technical paddlers but also experienced teachers; the student-to-instructor ratio is a low 3:1. OCNE has its own guest house with two guest rooms for couples, and a dorm-style, air-conditioned lodge with bunk beds that accommodates up to 18 people in two large rooms (bring your own linen). The all-you-can-eat breakfasts and lunch buffets charge you up for the days to come. Prices vary; there's a waiting list for

all courses (10 Pleasant St., Millers Falls, MA 01349, tel. 413/659–3926, fax 413/659–3464).

SUNDANCE KAYAK SCHOOL AND EXPEDITIONS Instruction and paddling facilities are second to none at this school, founded in 1973 and based on the banks of the Rogue River, in southern Oregon's Siskiyou Mountains. Imagine 5 days of personalized kayak teaching, capped with 4 days of paddling on one of the most spectacular of the United States's Wild and Scenic Rivers. That's the basic beginner's kayak school at Sundance, and it's just one of the school's programs. Other offerings range from 4 or 5 days of intermediate and advanced instruction on Oregon's North Umpqua or Illinois River to multi-day trips on the Middle Fork of Idaho's Salmon River or a run down the Colorado through the Grand Canyon. All instructors have worked at Sundance at least 5 years (8 to 12 years is more usual), a year of that as an apprentice to learn the school's teaching techniques. The Sundance Riverhouse, on the last piece of privately owned property upstream of the Wild and Scenic section of the Rogue River, has a huge skylighted dining room, an oversized living room, and accommodations in both traditional rooms and more unusual digs—jumbo dome tents set up on carpeted decks and fitted out with beds, chests of drawers, and electricity. The outdoor hot tub is one focal point of student socializing (14894 Galice Rd., Merlin, OR 97532, tel. 503/479–8508, fax 503/476–6565).

ZOAR OUTDOOR PADDLING SCHOOL Bruce Lessels, a nationally acclaimed paddler and writer who wrote the Appalachian Mountain Club's definitive *Whitewater Handbook,* is the director of this operation on the shores of the Deerfield River in the northern part of Massachusetts' Berkshires; the school offers 1- to 5-day white-water classes and river trips for all levels of paddlers. All instructors are ACA-certified with 5 to 7 years of paddling experience; they're chosen as much for their ability to communicate their love of the sport as for their ability to handle canoes and kayaks. While there's some classroom work, with video presentations to help instructors make their points, 85% of the time is spent on the water. Equipment is state-of-the-art, with new boats purchased every other year. The variety of programs enables the school to put together courses of students with similar goals and experience and to fine-tune the material covered to suit each group. A river rescue course is among several special-interest programs (Mohawk Trail, Box 245, Charlemont, MA 01339, tel. 800/532–7483 or 413/339–4010, fax 413/337–8436).

MAJOR SCHOOLS AND TRIPS

THE NORTHEAST

MAINE **Kayak School on the Androscoggin River.** Rising in Maine's Rangeley Lakes and looping into New Hampshire before curling back into southern Maine and the sea, this is one of the few rivers in New England with constant white water. From its outpost at Errol, the Northern Waters white-water school offers beginner and intermediate kayakers both an introduction to the pleasures of white water and a sound basis in kayaking fundamentals.

The program begins with a brief talk that familiarizes new paddlers with the jargon of the river as well as with an overview of what they will be learning. Starting on a placid section of the river, paddlers learn how to exit an overturned kayak (if you're not pushing your limits, you're not learning, and if you are pushing, you'll take an occasional swim). You also learn to rescue yourself and aid in the rescue of others.

Then it's off down a section of river matched to your level of paddling skills. Under the tutelage of skilled instructors, you'll soon learn to maneuver at will across the current, zip in and out of eddies, and read the currents. Each day you expand on what you learned the preceding one. A strong group, with a good grasp of skills, voyages into spicier water; a group moving more sticks to easier stretches. By the program's conclusion on the fifth day, paddlers know how to

roll their boats and comfortably run Class III water. Kayak classes are typically limited to 6 boats. Other programs are available for those who want to work with traditional open canoes; 4 boats are the usual maximum here.

A restaurant and motel are nearby; many paddlers stay at the campsites at the paddling school, which have showers, shops, and a rec hall where you can watch videos on river safety and paddling techniques. *Northern Waters, Saco Bound, Box 119-C, Center Conway, NH 03813, tel. 603/447–2177, fax, 603/447–6278. May–early Sept.: 5 days, $390. Price does not include food; sign up 2 months in advance.*

MAINE **Playboating on the Kennebec and Penob.** These two streams, about 5 hours from Boston and home to some of New England's favorite white water, are the destination of this Outdoor Centre of New England trip, one of the few that ventures away from its central Massachusetts base. The Kennebec is known for the spectacular, steep-walled Kennebec Gorge, with its Class III and IV rapids; the West Branch of the Penob, for the awesome 2-mile-long Ripogenus Gorge, where the river descends a stomach-dropping 70 feet per mile over Class V rapids with names like the Exterminator, and the white-water maze called the Cribworks. It takes a good paddler to handle these waters, and this trip is open to experienced paddlers only. Off the river, you can spot wildlife—moose, osprey, bald eagle, and the like. And you can swim in these rivers, despite the latitude, since they drain from shallow lakes and run warmer than those in some other parts of the country. Leaders are OCNE owner Tom Foster, along with Kel Kelly, a national medalist in women's solo freestyle. The student-to-instructor ratio is 3:1; groups usually have about 6 students. OCNE arranges for group campsites. *Outdoor Centre of New England, 10 Pleasant St., Millers Falls, MA 01349, tel. 413/659–3926, fax 413/659–3464. July: 4 days, $295. Price does not include meals; sign up 1 month in advance.*

MAINE **Canoeing on the St. John.** The great explorer Samuel de Champlain sailed into the mouth of the St. John on June 24, 1604, the feast day of St. John the Baptist, and from the calendar gave the river its name. If he had been there just a month earlier, he might have noted it as one of the great paddling rivers of the Northeast, for in May, the 128 miles of river from Fourth St. John Pond to what is now the bridge at Dickey offers white-water canoeing that is unparalleled east of the Mississippi. Then, during high water, many of its rapids and riffles are easier to run, with rocks and ledges deeper under the surface. It's certainly easier to pick your way down a stony stretch without a firm thump to remind you that you miscalculated the depth of a boulder. The river banks display mile after mile of vast timberlands managed for timber and pulp, and you often sight deer, moose, loons, and eagles.

The 8-day canoeing trips run by Maine Sport Outfitters, founded in 1976, are fully outfitted, so all you need to bring are your clothes and personal items. Guides double as instructors on the river and cooks ashore, and in their company you rough it in comfort and have great down-home cooking, often with fish just pulled out of the river. The standard ratio is 6 guests per guide; as often as not this means a pair of guides with a party of 10. *Maine Sport Outfitters, Box 956, Rte. 1, Rockport, ME 04856, tel. 207/ 236–87907, fax 207/236–7123. May: 8 days, $795. Sign up at least 1 month in advance.*

MASSACHUSETTS **Learning to Kayak on the Deerfield.** Offering some of southern New England's easiest yet most rewarding paddling, the northern Massachusetts sections of this stream are a good bet for beginners. Zoar Outdoor Paddling School kayak classes put in on one of the Class I sections, near the towns of Charlemont and Florida, and gradually move into Class II water as paddlers become more confident. Both a beginner and an intermediate program are offered, each available in 2- and 3-day sessions. For more aggressive paddlers, or quick learners who

start with some skills, the second or third day out may be in Class III waters. All classes start at 8 in the morning and last an entire day—take-out is at 5!

Classes are also available for those who want to paddle traditional open canoes. Camping facilities and a number of motels and bed and breakfasts are nearby. *Zoar Outdoor Paddling School, Mohawk Trail, Box 245, Charlemont, MA 01339, tel. 413/339–4010, or 800/532–7483, fax 413/337–8436. Apr.– early Sept.: 2–3 days, $160–$235. Sign up 1 month in advance.*

MASSACHUSETTS **Paddling Workshop in the Berkshire Foothills.** Even drought years don't cancel workshops run by the Outdoor Centre of New England, since the primary teaching rivers—the Ashuelot, West, Millers, and Deerfield, ranging from Class I to Class IV—are downstream from dams that release water regularly and keep the paddling lively. The 4- and 5-day workshops for beginners and intermediates are a terrific introduction to the world of paddlesports. A good variety of craft is available, with something for every body type, and the enthusiasm of the staff, who live and breathe paddling, is infectious. The first day begins early with gear checkout, and, after an orientation, a trip to a calm-water practice site, where the group is divided by ability levels. Subsequent instruction, which runs from early morning until 5 every day with a break for lunch, addresses appropriate paddling points—effective upper and lower body movement, boat leans, self-rescue, and more. The point is to help you become an efficient paddler. A variety of shorter workshops is also available, including beginner–intermediate workshops for those over 50, for women, and for those who want to earn an ACA instructor certification. The student-to-instructor ratio is usually 3:1. *Outdoor Centre of New England, 10 Pleasant St., Millers Falls, MA 01349, tel. 413/659–3926, fax 413/659–3464. July–Aug.: 4 days, $189; 5 days, $329. Price includes instruction, boat, meals, and accommodations; sign up 1 month in advance.*

THE MID-ATLANTIC

PENNSYLVANIA **Playing Around on the Youghiogheny.** Just because you can spell it or pronounce it (a hint: yock-a-GAIN-nee) doesn't mean you can paddle it. While the Middle Yough is on the mellow side, the Lower is definitely spicy: The 7-mile stretch from the village of Ohiopyle, Pennsylvania, down to Stewarton has hosted 2 Open Canoe National Championships as well as a host of other competitive events, and the swirling, bouncing watercourse lives up to its reputation as one of the Northeast's premiere white-water playgrounds. But the Youghiogheny is within your grasp with a little careful coaching, a bit of tutelage on rolling, technique, and the opportunity to follow an expert from Riversport School of Paddling in Confluence, Pennsylvania.

First item on the agenda is a trip to a nearby lake, where paddlers learn, relearn, or hone Eskimo-rolling skills. After lunch, it's off to the Yough to put your skills to work on moving water—the destination varies with the strength and goals of the class. The Yough is dam-controlled, with regular releases, so there's plenty of white water throughout the year. Summer and fall are the most popular times.

Interested in paddling solo-decked canoes or open canoes? Or slalom racing or squirt-boating, the river equivalent to freestyle mogul skiing? Have a yen to learn more about river and boating safety? Want to instruct? Special-interest clinics are a regular feature at Riversport. *Maximum class size is 6 per instructor, and as often as not the number is more like 4 or 5. Riversport School of Paddling, Box 95, 213 Yough St., Confluence, PA 15424, tel. 814/395–5744. Mar.–Oct.: 1 day, $100; 3 days, $270; 4 days, $360; 5 days, $425. Price includes 3 meals a day and camping; sign up 1 month in advance.*

WEST VIRGINIA **Kayak School on the New.** The river's name is a misnomer—on a geological scale it's possibly the oldest river in North America and, at 65 million years, one of the oldest in the world. Today 53 miles of this ancient river are preserved as the New River Gorge National River under the jurisdiction of the National Park Service. The river flows through a rugged canyon that's 1300 feet at its deepest, over rocks as old as 330 million years. White-water thrills are plenty on the New, with rapids ranging from Class I to Class IV. The scenery is majestic: fast-growing, deciduous forests hide the evidence of the coal boom of times past. At one time, the riverside was dotted with coal towns, abandoned as the mines played out.

The New River begins high in the Blue Ridge Mountains of North Carolina, flows north into Virginia, turns northwest into southern West Virginia, and then heads west to meet the Gauley River. At Gauley Bridge, the New and Gauley Rivers join together forming the Kanawha River. White-water rafting, with dozens of outfitters available, is immensely popular on the New, Gauley, and several other wild and wonderful West Virginia rivers.

For folks who'd like to learn to ride the rivers with confidence and skill, Class VI River Runners offers kayak clinics. These programs are designed for beginners and intermediates, and offer personalized instruction with no more than two students to one instructor. Clinics range in length from one to six days, but multi-day clinics are recommended to build solid skills. The first day begins with classroom instruction and an equipment orientation. The remainder of the day is spent on a calm stretch of water practicing the basics of maneuvering, wet exiting, and Eskimo rolls. On the second day, you learn how to read water and execute eddy turns, peel outs, and ferrying. Additional days provide time to practice these skills in increasingly challenging white water.

Kayaking is only one adventure available to those visiting the New River Gorge. Class VI customizes trips and also offers a high-adventure trip that mixes kayaking, rafting, rock climbing, mountain biking, hiking, and horseback riding. Those who sign up for any of Class VI's courses can camp or stay in hotels, inns, or state park cabins. *Class VI River Runners, Ames Heights Rd., Box 78, Lansing, WV 25862-0078, tel. 304/574-0704 or 800/252-7784, fax 304/574-4906. May–Sept.: 1–6 days, $150–$810; 3 or more people, $350–$400 per group per day.*

THE SOUTH

NORTH CAROLINA **Learning to Kayak in the Wake of Olympic Paddlers.** Like most kayaking programs, the Nantahala Outdoor Center's 7-day intensive river kayaking course starts on placid water—in this case, the warm waters of Lake Fontana. The half- to full-day session, depending on group skills and needs, covers basic strokes and acquaints paddlers with how strokes work and link together to control and move a kayak. Everyone is going to turn over, both to learn how to slip out under a capsized craft and to roll up and continue paddling without the inconvenience of a swim.

Then it's off to the river! During most sessions, the first river to toss a few drops into your face is the Little Tennessee, one of the jewels of the Great Smoky Mountains. Relax for a minute on this Class I stream and look up at the mountains. In spring the banks explode with the colors of blossoming rhododendrons and laurel. The possibility of wildlife lurks around every bend, even though the rivers selected for beginner programs don't descend through wilderness. (Virtually every beginner river over the week has a road winding alongside. In the rare event of a mishap, it's easy to get off the river.)

Don't think this class is just a tranquil drift. Under the watchful eyes of the instructors, group skills are constantly assessed and new adventures planned. Paddlers learn route-finding both by listening to instructors and by following them from eddy to eddy, from wave to tongue of water. Then you move from the gentle Little Tennessee to the bouncy Nantahala, with its outstanding play spots and popular slalom race sites. Crown-

ing the program, for the vast majority of the intensive classes, are runs on the Ocoee River, site of white-water slalom races for the 1996 Summer Games in Atlanta. While that particular course is not readily accessible (or, for that matter, really within the skills of most fresh-out-of-the-box paddlers), it still offers a chance to claim, truthfully, that you paddled the river the gold medal contenders slalomed. Lodging is in the modern-rustic NOC lodge. *Nantahala Outdoor Center, 13077 Hwy. 19W, Bryson City, NC 28713, tel. 704/488–6737, fax 704/488–2498. Mar.–Oct.: 7-day intensive course, $995. Price includes NOC lodging and all meals; sign up 1–2 months in advance.*

THE SOUTHWEST

TEXAS **Kayaking Classes on the Rio Grande.** If you're an intermediate or advanced kayaker, the Rio Grande's 90-mile-long Lower Canyons and Regan Canyon section is the place to come in spring to hone your skills for the white-water season ahead. But beginners can learn to tame the waters as well. Bill and Jaci Dvořák run laid-back 7-day instructional seminars here from mid-March through late April, when the desert is blanketed in spring blooms, daytime temperatures range between 70°F and 90°F, and river water is a comfortable 60°F to 70°F.

Starting at La Linda, Mexico, the river's course winds through the lonely, silent chasms, rocky flats, and desert mountains along the Texas–Mexico border. There are some quiet stretches, but you'll bounce through some good rapids as well. After a few hours on the river each day, you'll have plenty of time to hike up the side canyons to explore local landmarks ranging from old homesteads to the mysterious Candelilla ruins. The trip is among the company's most popular for beginners and intermediates, suitable for anyone who has never been in a canoe or kayak before. Starting with the basics of kayak design and how to choose a paddle and a personal flotation device and helmet, you cover types of paddling, carrying methods, self-rescue methods, and white-water safety techniques such as how to swim in white water with and without your boat. *Dvořák Kayak and Rafting Expeditions, 17921-B U.S. Hwy. 285, Nathrop, CO 81236, tel. 719/539–6851 or 800/824–3795, fax 719/ 539–3378. Mid-Mar.–late Apr.: 7 days, $925. Sign up 1–2 months in advance.*

THE ROCKIES

IDAHO **Running Salmon River White Water.** Born high in the snowy Sawtooth Mountains of Idaho, the Salmon River today is one of the most sought-after white-water runs in the entire United States. One of the very first rivers to be protected under the federal government's Wild and Scenic Rivers Act, its 200 miles of fabulous white water, ranging from a laid-back Class II to a spray-in-your-face Class V, is one of the longest stretches of unspoiled river remaining on the continent. American explorers Lewis and Clark saw the rapids in the 19th century (and, having seen the waters' fearsome power, continued their epic journey on foot); but people have lived in the area for at least 8,000 years, and when you venture into the wilderness back from the river, you may discover petroglyphs and ancient tools as well as signs of more recent habitation. You'll also discover prime fishing: This is the spawning ground for chinook salmon and Dolly Varden, rainbow, and cutthroat trout—these last known as redsides among locals.

Flowing as clear as the snows from which it springs, the Middle Fork of the Salmon cascades from the confluence of Marsh and Bear creeks and runs for about 125 miles through the rocky canyons and dense woodlands of the River of No Return Wilderness area of the Salmon National Forest to join the Main Salmon. The smooth flow of the river is broken by Class IV–V Velvet Falls, Redsides, and Rubber.

The thrills don't let up once you paddle out into the Main Salmon. From there down to Vinegar Creek—90 miles—there are 65 named rapids up to Class V. And yet, with raft support and 6 guides accompanying each party of no more than 24 people, it is a safe and practical trip for paddlers familiar with big white water. You run through the second-deepest gorge in North America on your passage through the mountains (the deepest is Hells Canyon on the Snake River, with the torrents from the Salmon flowing into the Snake and helping it in its massive excavation). The scenery is truly spectacular.

With this outfitter, you get a choice of 6 days on the Middle Fork, 6 days on the Main, or 12 days on both. You paddle a vigorous 10 to 15 miles a day, soak away tired muscles in one of the many natural hot springs that line the river, cast a lure out in the peace of the evening as the guides clean up from a dinner of prime rib cooked in a Dutch oven, fresh vegetables, and just-made desserts—there is an informal but very real competition among the guides on this river as to who can put together the best menu and meal.

Guests fly via bush plane from Boise to put-in and back to Boise from take-out when the adventure is over. Guides carefully screen guests who want to kayak; if you lack white-water paddling skills, you can go along for the ride in the support rafts.

When's the best time to paddle the river? Depending on the weather, the river opens in early May. Melt off from mid-May and into June sends flows soaring, and the river becomes a fierce torrent. Weather in July and August is normally the best, and the river is clear and spunky. Declining flows can reduce the rapids in September. *Mackay Bar–Wilderness River Trips, 3190 Airport Way, Boise, ID 83705, tel. 800/635–5336 or 208/344–1881, fax 208/344–1882. May–Oct.: 6 days on the Middle Fork, $1,165; 6 days on the Main Salmon, $995; 12 days on both, $1,850. Price includes sleeping bags; sign up 4–6 months in advance.*

THE WEST COAST

CALIFORNIA **Kayaking in Gold Mining Country.** The Salmon River is virtually unknown except to die-hard kayakers. During the California gold rush, it was a key river, but now only the rare miner or occasional boater is seen on it. One of California's Wild and Scenic Rivers, it offers class II through IV runs in the late spring and early summer. The Salmon has three forks—the South, Main and North—and is a narrow, steep-sided, snow melt river set in breathtaking scenery. The Middle Fork offers 100 miles of clear water, hotsprings, and excellent rapids. The current is swift, constant and often interrupted by long technical rapids which are challenging early in the season.

Serving the Salmon and Klamath rivers is the Otter Bar Kayak School, an outfit routinely lauded in paddling and outdoor publications for its excellent programs and its remote, pristine location in the Klamath National Forest. They offer a tempting combination: the comfort of an intimate resort with ambitious cuisine and outstanding white-water instruction. Week-long programs of groups averaging a dozen paddlers are offered at beginning through advanced levels and use a fleet of kayaks that is new every year. The school was founded in 1981. *The Otter Bar Kayak School, Box 210C, Forks of Salmon, CA 96031, tel. 916/462–4772, fax 916/462–4788. $1290 for 7 days and nights, all inclusive. Sign up 1 month in advance.*

OREGON **A Learning Trip down the Rogue.** Some rivers achieve a mythic existence, a perceived reality above and beyond the water, the channels, and the drops. Even their names become legends, and their rapids become catchphrases in the lexicon of river paddlers. Right at the top of this list is Oregon's Rogue River; a stretch if it is so popular that access to it is by permit only, and long lines form each year as individuals, clubs, and commercial operations vie for the few open slots. The 40 sparkling miles of the Rogue that cause all this commotion have been designated Wild and Scenic, and burst from Oregon's warm interior and flow out to the cool, breezy Pacific shoreline.

One of the best ways to experience the Rogue is on Sundance Kayak School and Expedition's 9-day combination instruction program–river trip, available for both beginners and more advanced paddlers. The standard beginner's program kicks off with 5 days of top-level kayaking instruction near Sundance's own riverfront lodge near the town of Galice. Neophytes learn basic kayak strokes and braces, the fundamentals of the Eskimo roll, and how to exit from an overturned boat and choose a route through currents and rapids. Such basic techniques as entering and leaving eddies and ferrying across a current become second nature in the warm, quickwater sections of the upper Rogue. By the fifth day, virtually everyone is proficient in their kayaks, and certainly capable of taking on the Class III white water waiting in the designated Wild and Scenic sections of the Rogue, 4 miles downstream of the Sundance Riverhouse.

Graduation is definitely the icing on this vacation cake. Up to a dozen students, accompanied by 4 instructors and a pair of raft guides, set off down the Rogue. Days are spent playing in the river, riding waves like a surfboarder in the ocean while instructors glide among the covey of neophytes, offering bits of advice and words of encouragement. Nights are spent camped on the riverbanks under a canopy of unbelievably bright stars. Meals are on the gourmet end of the scale, with a tilt toward the healthful.

If your time is short, you can skip the Rogue run and sign up simply for the 5 days of instruction. *Sundance Kayak School and Expeditions, 14894 Galice Rd., Merlin, OR 97532, tel. 503/479–8508, fax 503/476–6565. Mid-May–mid-Sept.: 9 days (including 5 days of lodge-based kayaking instruction and a 4-day raft-supported trip), $1,305; 5 days of instruction only, $725. Price of all programs includes lodging during instructional section of program and all meals; sign up 1 month in advance.*

SOURCES

ORGANIZATIONS Setting standards for the outfitters and guides are several organizations: **America Outdoors** (Box 1348, Knoxville, TN 37901, tel. 615/524–4814), the association for national river guides; the **American Canoe Association** (7432 Alban Station Blvd., #B226, Springfield, VA 22150 tel. 703/451–0140), which publishes the "American Canoeist" newsletter; and the **National Association of Canoe Liveries and Outfitters** (NACLO, U.S. 27 and Hornbeck Rds., PO Box 248, Butler, KY 41006, tel. 606/472–2205). For lists of paddling clubs, the backbone of paddling sports today, contact *Canoe & Kayak Magazine* (tel. 800/692–2663) or the American Canoe Association.

PERIODICALS *Canoe & Kayak Magazine* (Box 3146, Kirkland, WA 98083, tel. 800/692–2663), the leading paddle sports magazine in North America, focuses on both flatwater and white-water canoeing and kayaking, on both rivers and lakes. It covers both international and North American canoeing and kayaking destinations and offers a look into the nooks and crannies of local paddle-sports trips. Regular columns offer tips and techniques for all levels of paddling. Each bimonthly issue includes sections listing paddling schools and major outfitters. The quarterly *Paddler* (Box 775450, Steamboat Springs, CO 80477, tel.

303/879–1450) covers a broad spectrum of both major and easily accessible canoe and kayak trips, and includes product reviews and pieces on paddling skills and techniques.

BOOKS *Canoeing & Rafting: The Complete Where-to-go Guide to America's Best Tame and Wild Waters,* by Sara Pyle, is a valuable state-by-state compendium of canoe and kayak routes, with notes on degree of difficulty and the best time to paddle; the information on equipment rentals is a little dated. The ultimate reference guide for river running nationwide, *The Complete Whitewater Sourcebook,* by the Boat People (tel. 408/258–7971), lists phone numbers, water levels, regional guidebooks, access points, and permit requirements; the book is a must if you're planning a trip of your own and need a reliable source for names of outfitters. *Whitewater Canoeing,* by William Sandreuter, reflects on the author's 35 years of white-water canoeing.

ALSO SEE If you love peaceful paddling, look over Canoeing and Kayaking in Flat Water. If it's the spray in your face that draws you, check out River Rafting.

Caving

By Naomi Black

Updated by Jeanne Ricci

aving, or spelunking, as it is also called, is not for everyone. It's a dark, dirty, often cold and wet excursion into a fragile, hostile environment. Spelunkers would not even call it a sport. They consider it a science, with rules originated and safeguarded by a small community of serious cavers who will ostracize anyone who caves recklessly. And for good reason: Caving is dangerous. People die or injure themselves in caves every year. No one should go caving alone.

Why do they do it? Because when you're caving, spelunkers say, you enter into a world apart, a dimly lit world of primitive beauty—not at all like the fully illuminated "show caves" most tourists see. In wild caves, you have to look hard for spectacular speleothems (mineral formations), and their subtle colors seem dull compared to their show-cave counterparts. But beyond the geology—and the biology and the history—of the caves lies the excitement of the experience: the adventure of coming to terms with the dark, the cold, the pervasive damp, and your latent claustrophobia.

Caves are not the place for thrill-seekers. Getting around on muddy, uneven ground is slow and slippery; duck walks and belly crawls are common. It's vital to be in good shape; walking a half mile in a squat can be murder on the thigh muscles. If you suffer from a fear of heights or dark water, think

again about spelunking. Some of the most interesting caves require technical climbing skills involving equipment or wading through midriff-high cold water.

Anyone who wants to try the sport should get in touch with the National Speleological Society (NSS), which has about 10,000 members (*see* Sources, *below*). This is the organization to join for information on recreational caving, and joining it is, without question, the best way to get started. You can also take a short course in speleology at Western Kentucky University (*see* Favorite Courses, *below*). The NSS, which owns the rights of entrance to many caves, sponsors regional "grottoes," or local chapters. An individual can become a member of a grotto without joining the NSS, but membership facilitates entree to other grottoes throughout the country.

Grotto members are loath to reveal the whereabouts of caves to outsiders, so associating with a grotto is virtually the only way to learn about interesting local caves and to join group excursions led by members to distant caves. Most caving trips involve a single day or a weekend, but many grottoes plan at least one week-long excursion a year, with car-pool transportation. There are also professional guides, but the practice of leading people on caving expeditions for pay is a controversial issue. The NSS and most spelunkers in the grottoes look down on

New York City–based Naomi Black writes frequently about the outdoors. A member of the National Speleological Society, she has caved in the Northeast and in California. Jeanne Ricci is an adventurous travel writer currently living in California.

these guides, so commercial trips have not been covered in this chapter.

Through the NSS and its grottoes, novices can learn the basics of cave safety and etiquette from experienced members and are able to join not only grotto trips but also other programs led by members. The personality of the grottoes differs from one to the next, and their activities vary from region to region. Typically, however, a grotto publishes a newsletter, offers practice sessions for such skills as knot tying and vertical ascents and descents, gives classes for first-aid certification and rescue training, and organizes cleanups of local caves in addition to scheduling trips for members of all abilities. Grotto activities are normally free or provided at cost to members (whose annual dues are usually under $25).

Underground formations have survived for hundreds if not millions of years, but a single fingerprint can stop the growth of a stalactite or turn it black. Cavers are, therefore, understandably concerned about educating anyone who wants to explore underground. A good leader will insure that you learn conservation, as well as proper technique and the history and geology of the caves.

The time it takes to traverse a cave always varies, depending on the pace of the slowest person and on the activities planned inside (exploring side tunnels, practicing skills, etc.). Even a fairly short beginners' cave takes half a day to get through. That allows for exploration time down small tunnels or up craggy passageways. Leaders also make time for rest and for "black-out" periods when cavers stay still, stop talking, and turn out their lights.

There are wet caves where stalactites and stalagmites grow, like stone icicles and obelisks—made of minerals deposited by the slow drip of water. There are dry caves and mazelike horizontal caves where no climbing is necessary, and three levels might cross over one another in a 3-D network of tunnels; and there are up-and-down caves where vertical drops might be as high as 300 feet. You can expect to see speleothems of all sorts—mineral formations, mostly crystalline, in various shapes: There are gypsum crystals, blood-red gypsum flowers, and selenite needles, as well as stalactites and stalagmites and hefty columns where the two meet. You might encounter manganese oxide lining some caves, a sticky black goo that's impossible to wash out of clothes. (Don't worry: You wear coveralls.) Honeycomb formations of calcite cover ceilings; huge calcite crystals coat walls, like alligator skin 11 inches thick.

In addition to the richly decorated limestone caves like Carlsbad and Mammoth that are found in many states, there are sandstone cliff dwellings and rare gypsum caves in arid areas of the Southwest, littoral (or sea) caves on the coasts, lava tubes in Hawaii and California, and caves made from fallen boulders and debris. Once you have some experience, you'll be able to enjoy the variety of caves this country has to offer. Grottoes often welcome visiting groups or individual NSS members from other states.

CHOOSING THE RIGHT TRIP

At the beginning, don't be particular about where you go underground. Wherever your grotto is headed, just go. Any cave should make you happy. But choosing to cave with a group or guide who is safety-oriented and aware of cave etiquette can make the difference between a successful trip that's fun and a potentially dangerous or uncomfortable trip. For that reason, you should ask the following questions before going.

Has the leader arranged to give the group's exact whereabouts and anticipated time of departure from the cave to a responsible person aboveground? If so, in the event of a serious delay, someone will come after you.

Is there an orientation covering etiquette and conservation for this particular trip? The trip will be most rewarding if you are briefed beforehand on the geology of the cave, its biology (will you see bats, small animals, fish?) and what is necessary to protect its ecology.

Does the leader have permission from the landowner to enter the cave? The NSS frowns on groups entering private caves without permission. Sometimes a landowner will give blanket permission to one grotto but one only; sometimes the owner might close a cave if someone has been injured or if cavers have been careless with human waste or trash (a pee bottle and plastic bags are indispensable accessories on lengthy or overnight cave trips).

Is the leader bringing a carbide, electric, or miner's lamp as a primary light source? Each person brings three light sources on a caving trip: one (or two) attached to the helmet, one in hand, and sometimes a spare. Flashlights are not good enough for a leader, who needs a brighter, more reliable source of light to lead the way and examine speleothems close-up.

Does someone in the group have first-aid training? Rescue training? Will you bring a first-aid kit? Can you rig up a heat tent for emergencies? If the leader of the group has not had first-aid training, make sure another group member has. An emergency first-aid kit is de rigueur, as is a tented enclosure to be used, in case of injury, to prevent hypothermia.

What conditions can I expect? Temperatures in caves hardly fluctuate at all. In the Northeast they typically range from about 50°F to 56°F; in central California, 55°F to 58°F; and in Oregon, as low as 42°F. Caves can be running with water and covered with mud, and there are some crystalline caverns that are nothing but ice, and therefore much colder. The temperature is 55°F in Mammoth Cave, 56°F in Carlsbad.

FAVORITE COURSES

THE SOUTH

KENTUCKY **Speleology.** This 7-day course at Western Kentucky University, taught by spelunker and author (*The Longest Cave*) Roger Brucker, investigates the basics of cave science, delving into geology, biology, chemistry, hydrology, and ecology. The building blocks taught here help cavers discover new passageways wherever they are and teach beginners to appreciate just how fragile an environment a cave is. At least 60% of course time is spent in the Mammoth Cave system, much of it in undeveloped areas. The caving is rigorous, so students must be fit.

As in the Exploration of Mammoth Cave course, *below,* students are responsible for their own meals and lodging (although the school will help coordinate camping and bunkhouse reservations) and for transport to Nashville, Tennessee. This course can also be taken for credit, at additional cost. *Speleology, c/o Dr. Nick Crawford or Dr. Chris Groves, Center for Cave and Karst Studies, Department of Geography and Geology, Western Kentucky University, Bowling Green, KY 42101, tel. 502/745–4555. June: 7 days, $290. Price includes rental of lights but not room and board. Sign up 2–3 months in advance.*

KENTUCKY **Exploration of Mammoth Cave.** Students in this week-long course, given by Western Kentucky University, study the longest cave system in the world, and the history of its exploration, mining, and commercialization. The passageways at Mammoth cover nearly 330 mapped miles beneath the 52,700 acres of Mammoth Cave National Park. Although it's not as decorative as Carlsbad and other show caves, Mammoth does reveal beautiful rust-colored speleothems, among them classic stalactites and stalagmites, translucent ribbons running along the ceiling, flowstone, draperies, and formations nicknamed Frozen Niagara, Moonlight Dome, and Crystal Lake.

Some trips to Mammoth follow tourist trails within the cave (now closed to the general public) and historic connecting routes, while other adventures require strenuous hiking and crawling for up to eight hours. The class decides which route to take. All students must be in excellent physical condition.

Most activities not in the cave—lectures, meals, and food preparation—take place at

Maple Springs Research Center in the Park. Participants make their breakfasts and bag lunches in the big kitchen-and-meeting-room building and then convene at 8 in the morning to go to the cave. There's an hour or two before each evening's lecture when students can prepare their dinner, take a walk, or just relax.

Lodging is not included but can be arranged, in simple dormitory-style single-sex rooms in the bunkhouse with shared baths and hot showers, or at campsites within 100 yards of the buildings. Camping is free, and the bunkhouse costs $2 a night. Students are responsible for getting to the research center (closest airport is in Nashville, Tennessee) and for their own food. The course can be taken for credit for an additional fee. *Exploration of Mammoth Cave, c/o Dr. Nick Crawford or Dr. Chris Groves, Center for Cave and Karst Studies, Department of Geography and Geology, Western Kentucky University, Bowling Green, KY 42101, tel. 502/745–4555. June: 7 days, $290. Price includes light rental but not room and board. Sign up 2–3 months in advance.*

SOURCES

ORGANIZATIONS The **American Cave Conservation Association, Inc.** (Box 409, Horse Cave, KY 42749, tel. 502/786–1466) is a national, nonprofit organization founded in 1977 for the purpose of protecting caves, karstlands, and groundwater. It is responsible for the planning and development of the American Cave and Karst Center & Museum in Horse Cave, Kentucky. Membership costs $25 ($15 for students) and includes a year's subscription to *American Caves* magazine.

The **National Speleological Society** (2813 Cave Ave., Huntsville, AL 35810, tel. 205/852–1300), affiliated with the American Association for the Advancement of Science, was founded in 1941. Membership (ages 17 and over) costs $25 and includes a year's subscription to two publications. The **National Caves Association** (4138 Dark Hollow Rd., McMinnville, TN 37110, tel. 615/668–3925) produces a brochure that identifies 91 tourist caves in 25 states, Puerto Rico, and Curaçao. Some have adventure tours to caves that require scrambling. The nonprofit educational **National Outdoor Leadership School** (288 Main St., Lander, WY 82520, tel. 307/332–6973; *see* Climbing and Mountaineering) teaches such caving skills as route-finding, passage-memorizing, rope work, technical climbing, first aid, and rescue.

PERIODICALS *American Caves* (Box 409, Horse Cave, KY 42749, tel. 502/786–1466), published three or four times a year by the American Cave Conservation Association, covers subjects of interest, archaeological and otherwise, to both academic and recreational spelunkers. *NSS Bulletin*, published semiannually by the NSS (*see* Organizations, *above*) is a scholarly journal with technical articles on speleology. *NSS News*, published monthly, prints articles on recreational caving and provides a forum for such controversial issues as caving for pay.

BOOKS The following are available through Speleobooks (Box 10, Schoharie, NY 12157, tel. 518/295–7981): *Caving Basics*, by Tom Rea for the NSS; *Adventure of Caving: A Practical Guide for Advanced and Beginning Cavers*, by David McClurg; *American Caves and Caving: Techniques, Pleasures, and Safeguards of Modern Cave Exploration*, by William R. Halliday, MD; *The Longest Cave*, by Roger W. Brucker and Richard A. Watson; *Speleology: The Study of Caves*, by George W. Moore and G. Nicholas Sullivan; *Karst Hydrology: Concepts from the Mammoth Cave Area*, by William B. White and Elizabeth L. White.

ALSO SEE The chapter in this book on Climbing and Mountaineering contains information on programs that can teach you skills you need in some caves, while the Wilderness and Survival Schools chapter covers a couple of programs that include cave exploration among their activities.

Climbing and Mountaineering

By Peter Potterfield

ou don't have to be among the fortunate few to experience the many pleasures of climbing: the satisfying bite of the ice axe as you crampon across a steep glacier beneath towering peaks; the solidity of a smooth rock face as you reach for a hold on its warm granite, adrenaline pumping, confidence high; or the tranquillity you feel when you're deep in the wilderness en route to a remote alpine peak or standing atop a high, quiet summit on a clear summer day.

By taking a course or two on basic rock climbing or mountaineering at any of a dozen quality climbing schools all over the country, almost anyone who is moderately fit can experience the excitement of this sport. In just a couple of days, they can have a beginner climbing pretty well or put a climber of medium abilities on harder routes. These schools offer a range of experiences, from a few days of rock climbing instruction at California's Yosemite or on New York's Shawangunk Cliffs to week-long alpine programs that include ascents of major peaks such as Mount Rainier or month-long attempts on Alaska's Mount McKinley.

Each climbing course concentrates on a different facet of the sport; some address several. *Rock climbing* can be done in almost all parts of the country, not necessarily in the mountains; many towns and cities have cliffs, quarries, crags, or even indoor climbing walls where beginners can learn and experts can practice. It's an activity that you can pursue after work or on weekends, since you have to travel only as far as the nearest steep rocky surface to be able to do it. When you take a rock climbing course, you learn to recognize hand- and footholds in rocks that may appear quite smooth, and to use these holds to ascend rock faces of anywhere from 20 to 3,000 feet. Many of the skills you acquire in a basic rock climbing course are used in other forms of climbing, including ice climbing and mountaineering. *Ice climbing* involves climbing frozen waterfalls, traveling on glaciers, or ascending steep slopes covered with snow or ice, using special equipment (and additional skills). Snow and ice techniques are a must in Alaska and the higher elevations of the Rockies, the Cascades, and the Sierra. Few beginners start out learning to handle ice; it's a skill that climbers acquire as they gain experience. *Mountaineering* involves traveling on foot to a summit in mountainous terrain, heading into the alpine zone, the area near and above timberline. This may require skills in both rock and ice climbing, so thorough mountaineering courses will cover the basics along with other skills you need to spend extended time in the wilderness. The wilderness experience is one of the rewards of mountaineering—but to get it, you must live near the mountains or travel to them and commit to a block of time.

Seattle-based Peter Potterfield, author of *Selected Climbs in the Cascades* and *Chimney Rock*, has climbed from Alaska and the Sierra to Nepal. Formerly the editor of *Pacific Northwest Magazine*, he has contributed to *Condé Nast Traveler, Summit, Outside*, and other magazines.

To choose among America's hundreds of climbing programs, it is best to decide what you want to learn and where you want to learn it. Do you want to stay close to home or travel to an area you've always wanted to visit? No two climbing areas are quite alike. The landscape is different, and—more to the point for rock climbers—the terrain is different. In some areas you may have to contend with difficult weather conditions, while others are regularly warm and sunny. The quality of the rock also varies from one area to another, requiring you to master different skills. Where you find cliffs of fractured or broken rock, you acquire a whole repertoire of ways to grasp the protrusions. Where the local rock is smoother, you may learn crack techniques, different approaches to sticking your hands and feet into cracks in the rock; or you may concentrate on friction climbing, which involves using your weight and balance to ascend a smooth rock face without holds. Basic skills such as rappelling and belaying are standard elements of the curriculum in most locations.

Most U.S. climbing schools operate pretty much in their home region, although some offer courses around the country and a few travel worldwide. Many operate year-round, changing their location with the season and their curriculum with the location. You usually overnight in local motels and campgrounds and eat meals in local restaurants, except when courses are held partially or entirely in the backcountry; then you camp out or spend the night in a high-country guide hut. Tuition ranges from $50 to $150 per day, with the average course costing about $110 per day.

CHOOSING THE RIGHT TRIP

While there are a lot of questionable operations in the mountain-guiding game, most climbing schools are run by competent climbers and guides. However, you can't be too careful, since you could be injured or even killed while learning to climb. The schools and courses we list are all quality operations, but they are not the only good ones. Asking a few key questions will help you find the school that's right for you.

Is the school accredited by the American Mountain Guides Association? It's not necessarily a bad sign if it isn't, since accreditation is a relatively new function for this organization, which is dedicated to developing and maintaining high standards of mountain guiding and climbing instruction (*see* Sources, *below*). However, AMGA accreditation does assure you that the school's safety practices are appropriate for its activities. If the school you're interested in is not accredited, ask about the safety record.

How long has the school been in business? Longevity provides some assurance that it's not a fly-by-night operation.

What are the instructors' qualifications? If you're serious about acquiring climbing skills, go for a program whose instructors are experienced teachers as well as experienced climbers. If you're told where the instructors have climbed, don't be impressed before you ask: "But can they teach?" If all you want is a taste of the sport, you may prefer to hang out with a hotshot climber who can regale you with sagas of climbs in the Himalayas and other exotic locales.

What's the cost and what's included? Unless otherwise noted, your fee for courses listed below includes instruction, transportation between course venues, and any necessary technical climbing equipment (such as ropes, helmets, and harnesses), but not meals, accommodations in motels or campgrounds, sleeping bags and pads, tents, camp stoves, and personal gear such as backpacks.

Be sure to ask whether the outfitter provides special rock shoes, crampons, ice axes, and double plastic boots (climbers' standard footwear, resembling ski boots, in snow and ice environments); there is considerable variance from one operation to the next. (When the necessary equipment is not included, outfitters may provide it on a rental basis.) Also find out whether your bunk and food while lodging in guide huts or backcountry lodges is included.

What are food and accommodations like? When you attend most courses, you lodge and dine in establishments available in the mountain town nearest the course venue. Often, motels are simple and restaurant offerings basic—but exceptions exist. On backcountry trips, ask about the menu.

What experience is required for the course? For beginner courses—and all those described below, unless otherwise noted—no previous climbing experience is required, but you should be at least moderately fit: It will quickly become obvious if you're out of shape. As one wise man observed, climbing would be great, a truly wonderful thing, if it weren't for all that damn climbing.

What is the school's stated purpose or philosophy? Some schools emphasize minimum impact wilderness travel, others teach you to climb using lightweight gear, still others concentrate on pragmatic outdoor skills.

Can you supply references from past students? Call a few. Ask how they liked their instructors, and make sure that the program seemed competently run.

How far in advance do I need to book? Every school has different sign-up dates, ranging from 2 weeks to 6 months before the course begins.

MAJOR PLAYERS

ALPINE SKILLS INTERNATIONAL For most climbing schools, speed isn't a high priority and the weight of the equipment used isn't a major concern. This AMGA-accredited operation, established in 1979 with a distinctly European flair, is different, teaching a unique style of climbing that empasizes going fast and light. If you're a purist in other endeavors and fit enough to handle the extra challenges that this climbing style demands, go for it. The school offers a full range of mountain experiences year-round, including rock climbing, ice climbing, and mountaineering courses (Box 8, Norden, CA 95724, tel. 916/426–9108, fax 916/426–3063).

AMERICAN ALPINE INSTITUTE *Outside* magazine called this AMGA-accredited organization, founded in 1975, the best all-around climbing school and guide service in the country. Certainly, the AAI is one of the biggest, offering a variety of rock climbing, alpine mountaineering, and guided ascents in North America, Asia, Europe, and South America; courses in the United States are in Alaska and on its home turf in the North Cascades (1515 12th St., Bellingham, WA 98225, tel. 360/671–1505).

EASTERN MOUNTAIN SPORTS CLIMBING SCHOOL This is the oldest professional climbing school in the eastern United States, founded in 1968 under the aegis of the Eastern Mountain Sports retail operation. The school's varied courses take place in several eastern locations year-round (at press time, western locations were being considered); guided climbs and programs for women and teens are also available. It's accredited by the AMGA (Box 514, North Conway, NH 03860, tel. 603/356–5433, fax 603/356–9469).

EXUM MOUNTAIN GUIDES It was 1931 when Glen Exum made the first ascent of the ridge in Wyoming's Grand Tetons that now bears his name. In the same year, he founded this guide service, now one of the oldest in the United States. Exum guides are the only ones authorized to lead climbs of all routes and all peaks within Grand Teton National Park. They also offer instruction in rock climbing and mountaineering, snow and ice climbing, and winter mountaineering as well as a range of guided climbs (Box 56, Moose, WY 83012, tel. 307/733–2297).

NATIONAL OUTDOOR LEADERSHIP SCHOOL This private nonprofit operation founded in 1965 is not a climbing school as such. Its courses impart a wide range of outdoor skills and safety practices, with a strong emphasis on minimum-impact wilderness travel; in a NOLS course, you learn climbing as you learn a lot of other things, including general outdoor skills, teamwork, and safety practices. NOLS is one of the most respected organizations in its field, enrolling some 2,000 students every year in its huge array of courses staged from the Rockies to the Sierra Nevada, the Cascades, and Alaska. Though most courses last from 2 weeks to 3 months and many are for teens, there is a good selection of shorter courses geared specifically toward adults, and all NOLS climbing and mountaineering courses are accredited by the AMGA (288 Main St., Lander, WY 82520-0579, tel. 307/332-6973, fax 307/332-3631).

PACIFIC CREST OUTWARD BOUND Teaching climbing is just one of the ways that this AMGA-accredited school, based in Portland, Oregon, and founded in 1966, furthers its larger goal: to help students grow spiritually by meeting the challenge of acquiring apparently difficult new skills. Courses are staged up and down the West Coast, from Washington State's North Cascades and California's Sierra Nevada southward to Joshua Tree National Monument (0110 Southwest Bancroft St., Portland, OR 97201-4050, tel. 800/547-3312, fax 503/274-7723).

RAINIER MOUNTAINEERING, INC. RMI founder Lou Whittaker is a charming raconteur and celebrated climber who holds court on the mountain at some of his courses. His guides have been taking aspiring climbers up Mt. Rainier since 1968. Guided ascents and seminars on the mountain's Disappointment Cleaver route are some of its best-known programs; winter seminars, advanced climbing instruction, and climbing expeditions in other parts of the United States and abroad are among its other activities (535 Dock St., Suite 209, Tacoma, WA 98402, tel. 206/627-6242, fax 206/627-1280; in summer, Paradise, WA 98398, tel. 360/569-2227).

YOSEMITE MOUNTAINEERING SCHOOL The sole climbing school and guide service in Yosemite National Park, founded in 1969, this AMGA-accredited operation has taught rock climbing and mountaineering to thousands of visitors. The varied terrain here allows for a wide range of climbing activities, for climbers of all levels of ability and experience. The school, primarily known for its day-long programs, is based in Yosemite Valley in spring and fall, and at Tuolumne Meadows in summer (Yosemite National Park, CA 95389, tel. 209/372-8344, fax 209/372-1330).

FAVORITE COURSES

THE NORTHEAST

NEW YORK Basics on the Shawangunks. The 'Gunks, a 90-minute drive north of Manhattan, is one of the outstanding climbing venues in the United States thanks to its fractured rock. One of the draws of Eastern Mountain Sports Climbing School's 4-day Basic Rock Program here—actually 4 single-day courses offered consecutively as a package—is the wide variety of rock of different textures and the kinds of holds you are exposed to. It's a thorough introduction to rock climbing that will give you some proficiency fairly quickly. Instructors, 1 for every 3 students, teach the basics of everything from equipment to knots, and the fundamentals of belaying, climbing, and rappelling. You begin climbing on relatively easy rock faces, then move on to multipitch routes that call for more difficult moves, using more sophisticated techniques. Lodging and meals are up to you; there are campgrounds, bed-and-breakfasts, hotels, and restaurants in the vicinity. *Eastern Mountain Sports Climbing School, Box 514, North Conway, NH 03860, tel. 603/356-5433, fax 603/356-9469. May–Sept.: 4 days, $375-$550. Sign up at least 1 week in advance.*

NEW YORK Beginning Ice Climbing in the Adirondacks. Adirondack Rock and River Guide Service's 4-day novice ice-climbing course is one of the best introductions to the sport of climbing hard-water ice, such as waterfalls. Held in the mountains of upstate New York, this program introduces the aspiring ice-climber to the use of ice tools, ice screws and other protection, crampons and ropes. Belaying, climbing, descending and protecting the route are all covered in this comprehensive 4-day introduction to the exciting sport. The course finale is ascending a 700-foot frozen waterfall in the company of one of the instructors. Winter-camping or other cold-weather experience is helpful. The client to guide ratio is 2:1. You'll need double plastic boots (which can be rented). Climbers have the option of overnighting in local campgrounds or lodging in the school's own comfortably rustic lodges, one of which has an indoor climbing wall. Adirondack Rock and River has been teaching since 1988 and is accredited by the AMGA. *Adirondack Rock and River Guide Service, Box 219, Keene, NY 12942, tel. 518/576-2041. Dec.–Mar.: 4 days, $320. Sign up 1 month in advance.*

THE ROCKIES

COLORADO **Rock Camp in Rocky Mountain National Park.** Colorado Mountain School's wide-ranging 7-day course, held in and around Rocky Mountain National Park, takes you quickly from the basics to multi-pitch rock climbs. Even on the first day, after going over knots, protection, belaying, and rappelling, you get in some climbing. But the climbing is continuous during the next 2 days, as you develop your skills and learn new ones. On the fourth day, you begin preparing for 2 more days of climbing on big, multipitch walls and an ascent of one of the rock spires in the park's high country. The student-to-instructor ratio ranges from 6:1 at the beginning to 3:1 later on.

Dormitory lodging and some meals are available in CMS's Climbers' Lodge for an additional cost; campgrounds, motels, hotels, and restaurants are in the town of Estes Park, which is where you'll probably buy the fixings for the brown-bag lunch you're asked to bring every day.

Colorado Mountain School, founded in 1982, offers a full program of instruction, from beginner to advanced, in all types of climbing. The school is accredited by the AMGA, and is the concessioned guide service for Rocky Mountain National Park. *Colorado Mountain School, Box 2062, Estes Park, CO 80517, tel. 303/586-5758. May–Oct.: 7 days, $960–$1264. Sign up 1–2 months in advance.*

COLORADO **Rock Week in Steamboat Springs.** The off-season charm of the laid-back ski resort of Steamboat Springs is a definite plus for Rocky Mountain Ventures' Rock Week, 6 days of intensive instruction and guided climbing that will make you competent at high-angle rock work; the course covers everything from knots and simple rope systems to complex anchors, hanging belays, lead-climbing skills, and self-rescue. An indoor climbing wall and video are used to practice and analyze your progress; the student-to-instructor ratio is 3:1 or 4:1.

Unusual among climbing schools, this one provides everything you need, including not only the instruction, technical equipment, and the guided climbing that are part of the course but also a climbing manual, meals, condominium-quality lodging (other accommodations, including campgrounds, are available for those who want to provide their own food and lodging), even use of a health club. Accredited by the AMGA, Rocky Mountain Ventures offers a full curriculum of rock and ice climbing courses, as well as guided trips into the nearby Mount Zirkel Wilderness of Routt National Forest. *Rocky Mountain Ventures, Box 775046, Steamboat Springs, CO 80477, tel. 303/879-4857. Jun.–Sept.: 6 days, $885 with meals and accommodations, $440 without; sign up 1–2 months in advance.*

WYOMING **Basic and Intermediate Climbing with Ascent of the Grand Teton.** In less than a week, Exum Mountain Guides can put you atop the 13,770-foot Grand Teton, the centerpiece of the national park of the same name and one of those alluring peaks that all climbers want to scale; access to the approaches to the summit is relatively short, and the mountain's granite and gneiss is sturdy. Exum starts you with a basic climbing course, which is held in the park on moderately angled rock faces and covers the fundamentals of rock climbing and mountaineering. Short ascents of varying difficulty on the low-angled slabs expose you to the realities of the sport and let you try out different skills and moves. Then you go on to Exum's intermediate course, to learn techniques for climbing steeper faces and handling multipitch climbs as well as methods of anchoring and placing protection; there's also more rappelling. The precise route taken to the summit of Grand Teton varies depending on conditions, weather, and participating students' expertise; usually it includes a boat ride across Jenny Lake and a night at the Exum Grand Teton Hut at the mountain's 11,600-foot Lower Saddle.

Most students take a week to complete the pair of courses and climb the Grand, although the combination can be done in 4 or 5 days with good weather. Lodging and meals are available in Grand Teton National Park and in nearby Jackson. *Exum Mountain Guides, Box 56, Moose, WY 83012, tel. 307/ 733–2297. June–Aug.: 4–5 days, $565– $670. Sign up 2–3 months in advance.*

WYOMING AND SOUTH DAKOTA **Beginning Climbing in the Black Hills and Devils Tower.** No one who saw the movie *Close Encounters of the Third Kind* will forget Devils Tower, that distinctively shaped plug of rock jutting out of the western plains. It's where you spend the last 2 days of a 5-day introduction to climbing program from Sylvan Rocks Climbing School & Guide Service, founded in 1989. The first 3 days are spent a few hours' drive away, in the forested Needles area of South Dakota's Black Hills, notable for its roughly textured rock and for its low elevations and resulting low incidence of severe storms. Because it's remote, the area is not overrun by climbers as are the Shawangunks and Yosemite. Here you get a solid introduction to basic climbing moves, rappelling, and anchor systems, and then acquire more sophisticated skills, such as handling self-equalizing anchors and ropes, self-rescue, and multipiece hardware placements. This prepares you for the ascent of Devils Tower, where you learn sophisticated

crack techniques on the Tower's superb rock and solidify your mastery of the fundamentals. Though most students are beginners, many acquire a very high level of climbing skills. Student-to-guide ratios range from 3:1 to 1:1, and Sylvan Rocks, founded in 1989, is accredited by AMGA. Lodging and meals are available near both sites. *Sylvan Rocks Climbing School & Guide Service, Box 600, Hill City, SD 57745, tel. 605/574–2425. May– Oct.: 3- to 5-day packages, $450–$1,000. Sign up 2 months in advance.*

THE WEST COAST

CALIFORNIA **Rock Faces of Yosemite.** After 5 days of Yosemite Mountaineering School, you won't be ready to climb El Capitan, but as you make your way through the basics of rock climbing and on to a guided ascent, you will definitely get a feel for the crisp granite that has made this park one of the world's most famous climbing destinations. The 5-day Alpencraft course is actually 5 day-long courses offered as a package.

Your first day, an overall introduction to rock climbing, ends with a short climb on one of Yosemite's distinctive rock faces. Over the next 2 days you progress through basic climbing techniques and equipment to more advanced skills; you learn to use belay anchors, nuts and runners, and more difficult holds and techniques, then set up rappel anchors and rig secure rope positions. The fourth day covers basic snow and ice techniques, including glissading and the use of ice axes and snow belays, and on the final day, you make a guided ascent of one of the peaks in the vicinity, depending on the expertise of participating students.

You must provide your own meals and lodging. Yosemite is immensely popular—nearly overcrowded in summer—and even a campsite must be reserved many months in advance. Meals are easy to come by at the many food concessions in the valley. The student-to-instructor ratio ranges from 6:1 to 3:1. *Yosemite Mountaineering School, Yosemite National Park, CA 95389, tel. 209/*

372-8344. May–late Oct.: 5 days, $320. Sign up 5 months in advance.

CALIFORNIA **Fast and Light above Donner Pass.** Alpine Skills International's 5-day Rock Skills Seminar teaches you a specific approach to rock climbing: fast and light, with a minimum of equipment. Suitable for experienced as well as novice climbers, the intensive course is carefully planned and covers both face and crack climbing techniques, as well as the placement and removal of protection anchors in multipitch climbing. You also get instruction in direct aid—how to put climbers' hardware directly into the rock to use as hand- and footholds (something that fewer and fewer climbers do nowadays)—and you learn the protocol required when you function as the lead climber in a group (something taught only in advanced courses at most schools). At regular intervals, your instructor videotapes you and then analyzes the tape to help you refine your climbing technique. The mountain above Lake Tahoe where much of the climbing is done, Donner Summit, offers more than 300 possible ascents ranging from easy to the most challenging anywhere, as well as weather that stays pleasantly cool even in summer. The area is well-known among climbers, but perhaps more widely famed as the site of the starvation, death, and cannibalism of the ill-fated Donner Party of pioneers, who attempted to cross the pass in the winter of 1846–1847. Present-day visitors are likely to have a happier experience.

Climbing always requires a certain level of fitness; the Alpine Skills approach demands even better physical condition, and the staff will question you carefully about your fitness level before they sign you up. The course is held at Alpine Skills' Donner Spitz Hutte, a favored destination of day-trippers, who often drop in for espresso and wine while they're out on the trail. Breakfast and dinner are served at the chalet, and although most accommodations are in dorms, it's possible to snag a private room, a real luxury when you're in climbing school. The student-to-instructor ratio is 8:1 maximum. *Alpine Skills International, Box 8, Norden, CA 95724, tel. 916/426–9108, fax 916/426–3063. June–Oct.: 5 days, $498. Price includes dormitory accommodations but no climbing gear besides harnesses; sign up at least 3 weeks in advance.*

CALIFORNIA **Mountaineering in the Sierra Nevada.** Pacific Crest Outward Bound's 14-day Alpine Mountaineering Course takes place at and above timberline, from 9,000 to 10,000 feet, at various locations in the High Sierra's Sequoia and Kings Canyon National Park. Focusing on mountaineering, backcountry travel, and rock climbing, it challenges you in a variety of activities and terrain to master a variety of skills—among them low-impact travel. The ultimate goal is personal growth. A typical day involves many hours on the trail and lots of teamwork, and is physically and mentally rigorous. This Outward Bound is open only to adults 21 and up. The student-to-instructor ratio is 4:1 or 5:1. Meals are nutritious and wholesome, and unlike many operations that rely on freeze-dried and other prepackaged foods, Outward Bound uses staples such as beans, rice, pastas, and seasonings. *Pacific Crest Outward Bound School, 0110 SW Bancroft St., Portland, OR 97201-4050, tel. 800/547-3312, fax 503/274–7723. June–July: 14 days, $1,695. Price includes meals, sleeping bag and pad, backpack, rain gear, and other necessary equipment; sign up 6 months in advance.*

CALIFORNIA **Winter Rock Seminar in the Desert.** Joshua Tree National Monument is southern California's equivalent of the 'Gunks: It's close to where large numbers of climbers live; the granite is outstanding; and the weather is good in winter, when cold makes climbing uncomfortable farther north. Wilderness Connection's introductory rock climbing course, which is held here in winter, crams so much information, instruction, and experience into 5 days that even absolute beginners can advance rapidly. You start by covering the basics, including terminology, safety systems, and knots; progress to climbing and rappelling on low-angle faces; and gradually move on to more sophisticated climbing moves, belaying, and hardware placements.

Motels and campgrounds are convenient to Joshua Tree National Park and to Tahquitz and Suicide Rocks, areas in the San Bernardino National Forest not far from the town of Idyllwild, where the course is held in summer. Suicide Rocks, which has some 200 routes, is in the sun most of the day, and Tahquitz, which has relatively long routes and plenty of crack climbing, remains cool and shady. The Wilderness Connection, established in 1989, is AMGA-accredited, and the student-to-instructor ratio is 3:1 or 4:1. *Wilderness Connection, Box 29, Joshua Tree, CA 92252-0029, tel. 800/890-4745, fax 619/366-9315. Year-round: 5 days, $420. Sign up 2 weeks in advance.*

OREGON **Mountaineering on Mount Hood.** The realm of snow and ice atop this celebrated peak is the setting for this 5-day program, one of several offered by this company. In this course, you immediately travel by Sno-Cat from the grand, WPA-vintage Timberline Lodge at 5,000 feet to the 8,500-foot level; from here, you pack your gear to 9,300 feet, where you set up a base camp at Illumination Saddle. In the morning you begin with basic snow-climbing instruction, including the use of ice axe, crampons and rope handling. In the next days, you progress to more advanced instruction, including intermediate snow and ice climbing and crevasse rescue techniques. On your last day you ascend Mount Hood in the company of a guide, via the challenging Leuthold's Couloir if conditions are good. *Timberline Mountain Guides, Box 23214, Portland, OR 97281-3214, tel. 503/636-7704, fax 503/636-0344. Apr.–July: 5 days, $625. Price includes camping gear and food, as well as Sno-Cat transport; sign up 6–8 weeks in advance.*

OREGON **Rock Camp in the Desert.** This six-day rock camp is one of the most extensive rock-climbing seminars anywhere. It's held at Oregon's Smith Rock State Park, considered one of the best climbing areas in the United States. For quality of rock and length of climbing season—its location in sunny eastern Oregon creates perfect conditions spring through fall—the area is frequently compared to California's Yosemite Valley.

The course takes you through basic, intermediate, and advanced rock climbing skills, including knots, ropes, hardware placements, and climbing moves. An unusual feature of this seminar is that its curriculum also includes direct-aid climbing—ascending smooth rock faces by using hardware—and big-wall climbing techniques. The course ends with a guided ascent of Monkey Face, the most famous climb in the park.

Food and accommodations are not provided, but are available in both nearby Redmond and Bend. Tents are available for those students who wish to camp in the park. Timberline offers a full range of other climbing courses and guided climbs throughout the Cascades and elsewhere. Timberline's instructional program is accredited by the AMGA. *Timberline Mountain Guides, Box 23214, Portland, OR 97281-3214, tel. 503/636-7704, fax 503/636-0344. Mar.–Oct.: 6 days, $450–$570. Price does not include transportation to Smith Rock State Park or rock-shoe rental; sign up 4–6 weeks in advance.*

WASHINGTON **17 Days of Mountaineering on Mount Rainier.** This 17-day program, designed for adults, is one of the shorter offerings from the National Outdoor Leadership School (NOLS). Like all those from this organization, it isn't specifically a climbing course—the emphasis is on minimum-impact wilderness travel, camping skills, teamwork, and safety. But you do learn a lot about climbing, because climbing and mountaineering skills are a requisite on Rainier.

Initially the pace is slow as you move through the forests and rivers surrounding the mountain and master the NOLS leave-no-trace camping methods. In a few days, however, you move to the incredible world above timberline, high on the heavily glaciated slopes. There, for the next 2 weeks, you learn map-reading and route-finding as well as safety and emergency procedures, and your days are packed with instruction in glacier travel, rope systems, crevasse rescue, and ice-axe and crampon use. You set up a new camp every 2 or 3 days, but there is plenty of climbing and plenty of time for reflection.

Meals are heavy on grains, pasta, and beans, and draw on the NOLS trail cookbook; macaroni and cheese, and beans and rice embellished with spices are typical fare. Students do the cooking, with some guidance. *NOLS, 288 Main St., Lander, WY 82520-0579, tel. 307/332-6973, fax 307/ 332-3631. Aug.: 17 days, $2,050. Price includes meals, group camping equipment, and tents; sign up 3-5 months in advance.*

WASHINGTON **Snow and Ice Climbing Seminar and Mount Rainier Ascent.** This 14,410-foot dormant volcano is the second highest mountain in the Lower 48 (after California's Mount Whitney). Its terrain is diverse, and its slopes are heavily glaciated, so it is unsurpassed as a site for teaching glacier travel, snow climbing, and even vertical ice climbing, the subject matter of this 5-day program. Because the course also includes an ascent to Rainier's summit, it's a strong option if you're training for a climb in Alaska or the Himalayas, or if you know rock climbing and want to get a feel for a big, glacier-covered volcano. Even an ambitious beginner in at least moderately good shape can complete the course.

The seminar generally begins with a trek from the Paradise Visitor Center at 5,000 feet to Camp Muir, a small plateau at 10,000 feet on Rainier's South Side. There's a ranger station here, a guide hut with a bunkhouse, and an open area where climbers not on this RMI trip pitch their tents. At Camp Muir, you spend 3 days working on basics—snow and ice climbing techniques, including self-arrest and team-arrest, belays, roped travel, snow anchors, knots, route-finding, crevasse rescue, and technical ice climbing. The terrain here is truly awesome, and the glaciers are huge. Usually by the fourth day everyone has acclimated to the thin air of this elevation, and, weather permitting, the summit attempt begins.

A big plus of the course is the Camp Muir bunkhouse: Basic as it is (4 walls and a roof),

it beats squatting at the door to a tent trying to get your camp stove lighted in the wind— especially in bad weather, which can blow in at any time on this mountain. You don't even have to do the cooking; the RMI staff does it for you: oatmeal for breakfast, sandwiches for lunch, stew for dinner, and other plain but nutritious fare. *Rainier Mountaineering, Inc., 535 Dock St., Suite 209, Tacoma, WA 98402, tel. 206/627-6242, fax 206/627-1280; in summer, Paradise, WA 98398, tel. 360/569-2227. May–Aug.: 5 days, $667.12. Price includes bunkhouse meals and lodging; sign up at least 12-16 weeks in advance.*

WASHINGTON **12 Days of Alpine Mountaineering in the North Cascades.** The North Cascades, home turf for the American Alpine Institute (AAI), offers an array of alpine terrain unmatched in the Lower 48: peaks over 10,000 feet, deep canyons, more than 300 glaciers, varied fauna and flora, and hundreds of mountain lakes and streams. AAI's 12-day mountaineering program is held in the heart of the area, largely above timberline, in the rugged alpine areas of North Cascades National Park and the Glacier Peak Wilderness Area in Snoqualmie National Forest. Up here, among the glaciers, the craggy rock spires, and the hidden meadows, you learn the fundamentals of rock, snow, and ice climbing and how to travel in the alpine environment without harming it. You also learn to identify avalanche hazards and other risks, and acquire self-rescue and minimum-impact camping skills. Although climbing experience isn't required, it's helpful to have done some backpacking. You camp out in tents, usually on snow or glaciers, and prepare meals in camp. Food, which you supply (with some AAI coaching), should be nutritious enough to fuel your exertions without weighing down your pack—something worth considering since the base camp moves several times. Group sizes range from 3 to 5 students with 1 instructor, to 6 to 10 students with 2 instructors. The natural follow-up to the course is a 4- to 10-day AAI expedition in the Cascades or Canada. *AAI,*

1515 12th St., Bellingham, WA 98225, tel. 360/671–1505, fax 206/734–8890. May– early Oct.: 12 days, $1,390. Sign up 3 months in advance.

ALASKA

CENTRAL **23-Day Mountaineering Seminar and Mount McKinley Ascent.** Every year, hundreds of climbers ascend this mountain, also known as Denali ("the high one"). Yet it's a serious undertaking. Making it as safe and as enjoyable as possible is this program from Alaska Denali Guiding, which has earned a reputation as one of the best guide services on Denali. Along with alpine-mountaineering instruction, the program includes an ascent of the mountain by the West Buttress route. Though the least difficult approach to McKinley, it still involves very high altitude, arctic conditions, crevasses, steep ice slopes, and unpredictable weather.

The climb begins at 7,200 feet, on the Kahiltna Glacier, accessible via a breathtaking bush plane flight from Alaska Denali Guiding's base in the hamlet of Talkeetna. From here, you learn knots, rope care and management, placement of snow and ice anchors, belay techniques, glacier travel, use of ice axe and crampons, and sophisticated snow and ice techniques. A major camp is established at 14,000 feet, and a high camp, from which the summit attempt is made, at 17,000 feet; intermediate camps are put in as required. With 23 days, there is plenty of time for teaching, and with more than 13,000 feet of elevation to gain, plenty of opportunity for practice. You are not just a student but also a key member of an expedition and an integral part of the team.

Some previous climbing experience is required, and a very high fitness level is essential to reach the summit, since the work of climbing the mountain is substantial.

Alaska Denali Guiding, founded in 1982, offers many other adventure trips in the state, including mountaineering trips and guided climbs throughout the Alaska Range, guided treks across the tundra, ski-mountaineering trips on the Ruth Glacier, as well as custom guided climbs and expeditions. *Alaska Denali Guiding, Box 566, Talkeetna, AK 99676, tel. 907/733–2649, fax 907/733– 1362. May–July: 23 days, $2,600. Price includes meals, tents, and stoves; sign up at least 6 months in advance.*

SOURCES

ORGANIZATIONS The **American Mountain Guides Association** (Box 2128, Estes Park, CO 80157, tel. 303/586–0571) can provide a list of members and accredited schools and guides and can help you find the guide service to meet your needs. In addition, you can contact local climbing shops in areas where you want to climb.

PERIODICALS The bimonthly *Climbing* (Box 339, Carbondale, CO 81623, tel. 303/ 963– 9449) covers this sport exclusively. The monthly magazines *Outside* (1165 N. Clark, Chicago, IL 60610, tel. 303/447–9330), *Summit* (1221 May Street, Hood River, OR 97031, tel. 503/387–2200), and *Backpacking* (33 E. Minor St., Emmaus, PA 18098, tel. 215/967–5171) regularly run articles on mountaineering.

BOOKS *Climbing in North America,* by Chris Jones, is the best overview of climbing in and around the continent. *Fifty Classic Climbs,* by Steve Roper and Allen Steck, gives you a glimpse of the varied climbing available in the United States and Canada. *Mountaineering, Freedom of the Hills,* edited by Don Graydon, is the standard reference on climbing techniques, equipment, ethics, and more.

ALSO SEE Like the feel of testing your limits and coming to grips with your fears? *See* Wilderness and Survival Schools.

Covered Wagon Trains

By Melissa Rivers

agons, ho-o-o-o!" The call goes out and your wagon lurches forward, canvas cover flapping against the frame. Burly wagon masters bark instructions to the sturdy horses as you're jostled this way and that on the dusty, bumpy trail. Atop a ridge, you forget the dust and saddle sores and take in the beauty of the scenery that beckoned you here. The horizon widens, waving grass ebbs and flows on the warm, sage-scented breeze, and distant pink-and-buff-colored spires reach for the deep blue sky. Here, all appears as it was in the 1800s.

Join a modern wagon train to go back in time, to step out of the hectic 20th century and experience, if only for a few days, what the tens of thousands of brave emigrants of the westward movement endured. Most trips are run from June through early September on trails throughout the Southwest and the Rockies. The terrain varies widely—from the dry desert of Arizona and the red-rock arroyos of Colorado to the lushly forested mountains or grassy plains of Wyoming—and should be a major consideration when choosing your trip. Some wagon trains follow historical byways, such as the Pony Express route or the rough Overland, Mormon, and Oregon trails, while others utilize gentler logging roads through protected parklands.

For some outfitters, the authenticity of their wagon train is the most important element: Their wagons are authentic replicas, with wooden- or steel-rimmed wheels and canvas tops that roll up for visibility and down for shade. Other outfitters put comfort first, providing modernized wagons with shock absorbers, rubber wheels, and foam-padded seats to relieve some of the uncomfortable bounce of the trail. They also provide camp amenities such as tents, folding stools, portable potties, and solar showers (as opposed to pit toilets and warm water in a basin for sponge bathing on most "authentic" trips). You're usually responsible for bringing a sleeping bag, water canteen, flashlight, and binoculars.

Trail guides and cooks—most of them professional cowboys with ranching or rodeo backgrounds—can wrangle horses, rattle off cowboy poetry, lecture on the flora and fauna seen along the trail, and rustle up surprisingly delicious campfire meals (heavy on the steaks, stews, biscuits, and cobblers). They are usually between 20 and 60 years old, very amiable, and decked out in jeans, boots, hats, and bandannas.

A typical day on the trail is long. You rise to the sound of the morning bell (usually around 7:30) and gather for breakfast from the chuck wagon before packing and hitching up the teams for the day's journey. Board one of the canvas-topped wagons or ride the gentle saddle horses for a trek of 6 hours or more, which might cross rivers, prairies, or rocky passes in sight of ghost towns and

---

Although she didn't make the trip by covered wagon, Melissa Rivers, a freelance writer, did migrate west and now lives comfortably near the end of the famous Oregon Trail.

herds of wild horses and antelope. Stop to take photographs or gather round for historical talks at sites along the route. At "nooning," you get a break for cool water and sack lunches while the teams rest up for the remaining journey.

When you "circle up" the wagons in the late afternoon, the horses are unhitched and tents are set up by the trail hands while you rest, hike, swim, hunt for arrowheads, or lend a hand with chores (not a requirement) until the dinner bell, when everyone gathers around a crackling campfire to eat and be regaled with stories and songs of the Old West. After your hard day, you'll probably want to take an early leave and head to a tent, tepee, or wagon, or simply stretch out under the stars and drift off to sleep, serenaded by coyotes baying at the moon.

Covered wagon trains appeal to a cross section of nostalgic dudes, but there are often young families—college-educated baby boomers and their kids—along for the ride. A trip can cost from $600 to $900, but many outfitters have reduced rates for children. Most people come with little or no riding or camping experience and are here to live out their Western fantasy, or just get closer to nature. The rewards of healthy outdoor fun and the chance to relive pioneer history must be carefully weighed against frustrations such as bug bites, lack of indoor plumbing, and disagreeable weather and dust.

CHOOSING THE RIGHT TRIP

In choosing a trip, consider whether authenticity or comfort is more important to you, as well as what type of topography and scenery you would most enjoy. Here are some questions you should ask:

How long has the company been in business? Chances are that you're not going to find a fly-by-night covered wagon train operation; however, because you're going to be on the dusty road for up to a week, the more knowledge and experience the guides have the better.

Are the wagons authentic reproductions? Are wheels wooden-rimmed, steel-rimmed, or rubber? Are seats padded for comfort? Try to gauge what your tolerance for discomfort is when choosing a trip. Of course, this is a gritty activity to begin with—all part of the experience—but pads on the seats can make your ride that much smoother.

Is there the option of riding in wagons and on horseback? Is riding experience necessary? Usually, you have a choice of riding in a wagon or on a horse; it's often more interesting to break the trip up by trying both. If you *have* to spend part of the time on a horse, however, it would be wise to learn how good a rider you have to be.

What will the accommodations be like? Digs vary from padded bunks in the wagons to tepees and tents (some with foam-padded bottoms).

What kinds of showers and toilets are provided? Just how outdoorsy are you? For some, the thought of communing that closely with nature for a week is too much. For others, a portable toilet would be too representative of the present to enjoy the trip into the past.

What kind of meals are provided? Can the outfitter meet special dietary requirements? A lot of the menus on these trips have meat as the main course. There are usually side dishes and salads as well, but if you have dietary restrictions, it's a good idea to find out what the options are.

What is the maximum group size? The groups range in size from 20 to 45. As people sign up for the trip, wagons, which carry around 8 people apiece, can be added on. The more people on a trip, the more interesting it can be—but more than 45 people might prove too large as the train gets longer.

What chores, if any, are guests required to do? The trail hands generally help set up camp and saddle the horses, but what is expected of you can vary—cooking, caring for horses, pitching tents, and so on. Find out what is required and decide how willing you are to pitch in.

What are the free-time options? The areas around the trails that you ride on offer a wide variety of activities, from swimming to fishing to hiking. Make sure that there are opportunities to take advantage of them.

What's the cost and what's included? All outfitters listed below supply accommodations and meals for would-be pioneers. Some supply sleeping bags and pads, but some don't, so be sure to ask. You will have to bring your own boots, binoculars, and canteen. Although occasionally a trip will run in a circle, most covered wagon trains move from a starting point to a different finish point. Outfitters will either transport you back to the starting point or arrange to have your car driven to the finish point; this is included in the trip price. Inquire also about seasonal and youth discounts.

Do you have references from past guests?

How far in advance do I need to book? Make a reservation as early as possible; by spring, outfitters are often booked for the year.

FAVORITE TRIPS

THE MIDWEST

NEBRASKA **Oregon Trail Wagon Train.** History buff Gordan Howard's 6-day covered wagon trek couldn't be more authentic. Your group of up to 40 can ride on long, uncushioned benches in traditional wooden wagons that Howard's family constructed. Or, if you get tired of bouncing uncomfortably with 3 to 15 other passengers (wagons vary in size but none has shock absorbers), you can switch to the scout horses or walk alongside as the pioneers usually did. As you travel, Howard—a 60-year-old farmer-turned-trail-guide—shares his extensive knowledge of early American history and the Oregon Trail.

The wagon train starts out at a base camp 2 miles outside Bayard and follows the section of the Oregon Trail that cuts through the panhandle of Nebraska, between Chimney Rock—a towering rock spire that was a "sign post" to pioneers heading west—and Scotts

Bluff National Monument. The prairie schooners roll through a wide, rolling valley covered in sage, blue stem, and buffalo grass and hemmed in by bluffs to the south and the Platte River to the north. Along the trail, you can walk in worn wagon ruts and search for artifacts such as Indian beads, arrowheads, shards of pioneer crockery, and broken utensils left by those who passed this way in the 1850s. You can learn to load and fire a black powder rifle, square dance on the prairie, and take part in an "Indian encounter." At the end of the day, you sit around the campfire and chow down on typical trail meals—buffalo hump or ham and beans. Jump in the water tank to cool off. You can lend a hand with the camp chores (though this is not mandatory) or crawl toward sleep in your short-walled tent, similar to those used by the pioneers. The primary concession to comfort is the custom potty wagon with chemical toilet. Otherwise, this trip is so authentic that a northeastern college will give you graduate credits in history for participating. *Oregon Trail Wagon Train, Rte. 2, Box 502, Bayard, NE 69334, tel. 308/586–1850, fax 308/586–1848. May–Sept.: 6 days, $600. Sign up 30 days in advance.*

THE SOUTHWEST

ARIZONA **Wagons Ho Wagon Train.** The spirited 78-year-old Ruth C. Hefner founded Wagons Ho Wagon Train almost 30 years ago in Kansas, and her company is one of the most experienced outfitters in the business. It's also the only outfitter that operates year-round, running during the winter in the Phoenix-Scottsdale area and in the Grand Canyon area throughout the summer months. The winter trip, with temperatures ranging from 45°F to 75°F, runs in the Sonoran Desert, in the foothills of the McDowell Mountains, with no towns in sight. You're surrounded by saguaro cactus and mesquite, cottonwood, and cedar trees, and you might see gophers, coyote, and jackrabbits along the route. The summer trip takes you up into forested country on an abandoned Indian trail across private ranch land. The heat is tempered by the higher elevations along the route, so it's quite pleasant for you and all the deer, cattle, rabbits, and quail.

Over the decades, Ruth has found a happy medium between authenticity and comfort on her 4-day journeys. A train of 4 to 12 covered wagons, complete with steps and cushioned seats, travels along the summer and winter trails. Knowledgeable guides accompany you and your group of up to 46, explaining the flora and fauna and discussing the historical stagecoach stops. A trail hand shares his Native American lore, a Pony Express rider delivers mail, a stagecoach intercepts your group, and there's always the chance of an "Indian encounter." Your evenings are filled with square- and round-dancing, storytelling, roping demonstrations, and songs of the Old West, sung to the accompaniment of a guitar or accordion. Afterward, you bed down either in a tent or in one of the wagons' padded bunks. Portable restrooms and solar showers are part of the train, and most of the food (pioneer recipes and more modern fare) is prepared in kitchens and trucked to the site. Ruth has thought of everything, down to sunbonnets and prairie dresses for women who want to get into the frontier spirit. *Wagons Ho Wagon Train, Box 60098, Phoenix, AZ 85082, tel. 602/230–1801 or 602/ 977–7724, fax 602/974–3282. June–mid-Sept. and Oct.–mid-May: 4 days, $975. Sign up 2–4 weeks in advance.*

THE ROCKIES

WYOMING **Along the Oregon Trail.** In 1988, when horsewoman Nona Reid couldn't find an outfitter that provided short covered wagon train tours, she started Trails West, which now specializes in 3-day slices of pioneer life on the Oregon Trail. Four custom-built, steel-wheeled, oak-plank wagons carry 20 people down a 70-mile stretch of trail. (The wagons are extra wide for wheelchair access—Trails West is probably the only operator with wagons built specifically to accommodate travelers with disabilities.)

Here the Oregon, Overland, and Mormon trails come together through the South Pass to cross the Continental Divide. During the 8 to 10 hours spent on the trail each day, you try everything from panning for gold and pink garnets in the Sweetwater River to examining rocky eagle nesting sites to drinking pure water from underground springs. You stop at the boomtown of Lewiston, St. Mary's stage stop, and a Mormon graveyard, where the victims of a 1856 blizzard are buried. Evening camp is set up by the trail crew at Diamond Springs, an old Shoshone campground; here you are treated to hearty campfire meals of 16-oz. steaks and fresh berry cobblers before retiring to photogenic Crow-style tepees with triangular doorways and tall ridgepoles. *Trails West, Inc., 65 Main St., S. Pass City, WY 82520, tel. and fax 307/332–7801 or tel. 800/327–4052. June–Aug.: 3 days, $400. Sign up 6 weeks in advance.*

WYOMING **Along the Sweetwater River.** Family-owned and operated, Great Divide Tours has been running horseback vacations in Wyoming since 1985. In celebration of the Oregon Trail Sesquicentennial, the firm now offers a 30-person, 6-day trek that covers 150 miles of the famous trail. Under incredibly blue skies, authentic, steel-wheeled wagons pulled by mighty draft horses and accompanied by mounted outriders follow the grassy high plains of central Wyoming along the Sweetwater River to South Pass, gateway to the "land of opportunity." You'll be led by knowledgeable guides in period costume during the 5 or 6 hours spent on the trail each day, passing through stands of aspen, pine, and cedar, and expanses of sagebrush, wildflowers, and blooming cacti. Antelope and herds of wild mustangs roam through the area. In the evening, living history programs, cowboy poetry, dances, and raucous musical reviews recreate life among the emigrants of the 1800s. Foam-padded, two-person tents, solar showers, and portable "privies" provide the modern-day touches. Great Divide also offers the Outlaw Trail Horseback trip in the Big Horn Mountains, a week-long expedition to the Hole-in-the-

Wall made famous by Butch Cassidy and the Wild Bunch. *Great Divide Tours, 336 Focht Rd., Lander, WY 82520, tel. 307/332–3123 or 800/458–1915, fax 307/332–4510. Mid-July and mid-Aug.: 6 days, $1,095–$1,295. Sign up 30 days in advance.*

WYOMING **Teton Country Covered Wagon Adventure.** The lush Bridger-Teton National Forest and Mt. Leidy Highlands in the northwest corner of Wyoming are the setting for Wagons West's 6-day journeys. The 15-person train is run by a trio of seasoned partners with the wagon covers rolled back so you can better view the spruce, pine, and aspen trees; the high country wildflowers; and the deer, elk, moose, and eagles. You spend half of each 6-hour day on the trail in comfortable, converted hay wagons (with rubber tires and heavy-duty shocks) and the other half on horseback (though full-day horseback options are available at additional cost), following the trail as it opens up to panoramic views of the Grand Tetons, the Gros Ventre River, and the Wind River mountain range. After circling up the wagons in the early afternoon, you have time to hike, sunbathe, take pictures, or ride to a nearby stream for a cool dip. The guides share their knowledge of Western history and philosophy, while the cook prepares typical cowboy meals that passengers fondly describe as "hearty, ample, and brown." A cowboy crooner entertains later in the evening, before you drift off to sleep in a tepee, tent, or padded bunk. *American Wilderness Experience, Box 1486, Boulder, CO 80306–1486, tel. 303/444–2622 or 800/444–0099, fax 303/444–3999. June–Aug.: 6 days, $700–$750. Sign up at least 2 weeks in advance.*

WYOMING **Teton Prairie Schooner Holiday.** Nick Wilson was a boy when he first passed through the untamed West into Jackson Hole, Wyoming, in the mid-1800s. As he got older, he rode for the Pony Express and the Overland Stage company, and he was among the first to drive covered wagons over Teton Pass into Jackson Hole. Today, his great-grandson Bill Thomas continues the tradi-

tion, leading modern adventurers through the wildlands of northwest Wyoming. Thomas's prairie schooners, modeled after the old Conestoga wagon (with the addition of rubber tires and padded seats), carry you along backcountry roads through the pine forests of Targhee National Forest between Grand Teton and Yellowstone national parks. The Pony Express delivers the mail and you visit with Indians and a mountain man. Each evening, you roll out your sleeping bags and pitch your foam-padded tents in a new camp, near scenic high-mountain lakes where you can fill your free time canoeing, swimming, hiking, and photographing the bountiful wildlife. Later on, you sit around the campfire enjoying Dutch-oven meals and cowboy yarns. *Bar-T-Five Inc., Box 3415, Jackson, WY 83001, tel. 307/733–5386 or 800/772–5386, fax 307/739–9183. Late June–Aug.: 4 days, $595. Price does not include transportation from Jackson. Sign up 3–8 months in advance.*

SOURCES

ORGANIZATIONS You can learn about wagon trains from the **National Trail Ride and Wagon Train Association** (c/o Art Howell, Box 8625, Gadsden, AL 35902).

BOOKS To get a feel for the historical significance of covered wagon train travel, you might enjoy reading about life on the trails. *The Oregon Trail,* by Francis Parkman, a fascinating account of the route's emigrants in 1846. The *Journal of Travels,* by Joel Palmer, is an interesting picture book with quotes from pioneers' diaries illuminating life on the trail. *On the Oregon Trail,* by Jonathan Nicholas and Ron Cronin, is a coffee table book, filled with distinctive pictures of life on the trail and quotes from pioneers.

ALSO SEE If this type of rough-and-tumble, true-to-life Western experience is for you, check the Working Farms, Ranches, and Cattle Drives chapter for other vacation options in the same spirit.

Cross-Country Skiing

By Rosemary Freskos and Jonathan Weisel

Updated by W. Lynn Seldon Jr.

Picture a skier in skintight leggings with neon-pink stripes racing past you on short high-tech skating skis. Up ahead, an instructor wearing black stretch pants, a nylon windbreaker, and dark goggles digs her metal-edged skis into the snow, accomplishing a nearly perfect telemark turn. Behind her, another skier, dressed in wool knickers and a fisherman's sweater, glides along on machine-set tracks, basking in the sunshine and breathing deep the dry, cold air.

Scenes like this one, which you'll see at cross-country ski areas across the United States, say volumes about how the sport has grown in the past 50 years. With so many ways to enjoy it, cross-country skiing has become appealing to a large assortment of people. It's one of the top sports for low-impact cardiovascular exercise, and a good way to enjoy the wintery outdoors.

You learn about nature while cross-country skiing. You see animals; you come to know what the flow of clouds may mean for weather the next day; and eventually you can guess the temperature based on the sound of your skis gently rubbing on the snow (rule of thumb: The higher-pitched the squeak, the colder it is). Furthermore, when you cross-country ski, you don't make much noise, you don't burn fossil fuels, and you don't really need much money.

A cross-country trip is usually cheaper than a downhill-ski vacation. You can pay as little as $7 for a daily trail pass instead of the $25 to $48 for a lift ticket, and rentals run about $12 as opposed to $20 for alpine skis. Moreover, there are many out-of-the-way lodges and inns with cross-country networks, and these are relatively inexpensive, whereas in downhill-ski areas the price of accommodations tends to be inflated.

To keep costs really low, rent a pair of skis from a local shop and try them out in your backyard or at a nearby golf course. Or take a few lessons with a professional instructor who can help you outsmart your feet—show you how to move with fluid grace across the flats, ascend the hills, descend the hills, and turn. It's best to learn at a cross-country ski resort, where the trails are machine-groomed with tracks. That means the snow is compacted into a consistent surface and two parallel grooves, or tracks, are cut into it so that your skis can't go anywhere but forward. Tracked trails allow anyone to experience the thrill of speed with confident control at any pace, and the trail systems are so well marked and signed, it takes both talent and effort to get lost.

But there's a lot more to cross-country skiing than machine-groomed tracks. You can scuttle through the backcountry on virgin snow on wider, more stable skis; speed

Rosemary Freskos has been writing about snow sports for some two decades. Jonathan Wiesel has visited more than 300 North American cross-country ski areas. Lynn Seldon heads to West Virginia to cross-country ski after every heavy snowfall.

down hard-packed skating lanes using short skis to step-and-glide forward much as you would on ice skates; or don heavier, metal-edged skis to descend lift-served slopes, lunging forward on one knee in a telemark position.

In this chapter we cover several types of cross-country ski vacations to ensure we address the variety of ski experiences available for novices and experts alike. We tell you about entire areas devoted to the sport, such as Jackson, New Hampshire, and Royal Gorge, California, where there are several connected trail systems; we cover individual hotels and ranches with their very own trail networks; and we add a few organized guided trips by outfitters who will take you from lodge to lodge or hut to hut.

Keep in mind that you can have many different experiences at various cross-country ski areas, which are wildly diverse in size and emphasis. If you choose a large area, you have a large choice of accommodations and your trail pass gives you access to a big network with a wide variety of trails. Individual hotels, lodges, and ranches, on the other hand, may have small trail networks but more personality. Some accept only a dozen overnight guests; others have three score lodgers and hundreds of day skiers. Many include trail fees in multiday packages, but the day visitor pays $10 to $15 for a few hours of skiing. Guided trips with outfitters make it easy: You pay one price and they take care of just about everything. Guide companies generally emphasize service rather than challenging terrain, and they usually offer a combination of track and touring, or even stick just to groomed trails.

Because there's still some confusion about the nomenclature of cross-country skiing, the Cross Country Ski Areas Association, a national organization representing cross-country ski operators and suppliers, has come up with some standard definitions. Nordic skiing is an all-inclusive term comprising every kind of skiing other than alpine skiing: track, skating, backcountry,

and telemarking—all using skis that are of lighter weight than alpine and boots and bindings that leave your heel free. The organization uses the term cross-country more exclusively, to refer to skiing on machine-groomed surfaces—both tracks and compacted lanes—although most people use cross-country interchangeably with Nordic. Ski touring is off-track skiing, from fooling around on skis at a local golf course to trekking in the Tetons. Ski touring can be variously described as bushwhacking, mountaineering, or backcountry skiing, but it always refers to skiing on ungroomed trails.

Note: In most cases, cross-country skiers measure distance in kilometers (km) rather than miles. To convert kilometers into miles, divide by 1.6.

CHOOSING THE RIGHT EXPERIENCE

Cross-country ski areas have a justified reputation for hospitality, comfort, and culinary excellence; guided tours can be either plush or primitive. If you're researching the ideal site or tour, it's helpful to ask the following questions.

How long has the resort or hotel been operating as a cross-country destination? How long has the guide service been in business? Experience gives any business the knowledge it needs to work out problems with its operation and to meet the needs of all its customers.

Are the trails groomed or ungroomed? If you are going on a guided tour, the answer to this question will tell you a lot about the trip. You won't find groomed trails leading to a backcountry hut.

How many km of machine-groomed track are there? Are the tracks single or double and is there a skating lane? Obviously, more track means more skiing terrain to keep you busy. Some individual hotels might have only up to 20 km of groomed track, which is probably enough for a beginner, but more advanced skiers will be happier at a place with 50 km or more. Single-track trails accommodate only one skier going in one direction, which makes them ideal for those looking for solitude. Double tracks are set so that skiers can travel in both directions. Skiers who want to skate will need a skating lane, a wide flat trail of packed snow.

Are all the trails groomed or are there backcountry trails as well? Backcountry skiers visiting a resort or hotel should make sure that there are plenty of marked, ungroomed trails where they can get into the wilderness they love.

Is the system connected to other systems, and if it is, does your trail pass cover the connected systems? Some inns and hotels have trail networks that connect with other networks where you are allowed to ski using the same trail pass. This means you get more skiing area for your dollar.

What's the cost and what's included? Is professional instruction included? Guide service? In this chapter, costs quoted for packages and guided tours are generally per person and include double occupancy accommodations, meals (but not alcoholic beverages), and trail fees, unless stated otherwise. Guided trips with outfitters also include the services of a guide, who often gives the group instruction.

Many cross-country ski areas and even individual inns and ranches supply a limited number of group lessons as well as some short guided tours and clinics gratis; others don't. Paying extra for lessons and tours can add substantially to the cost of your trip. In all cases, you have to pay extra for private lessons and longer guided tours. Rental equipment is not included in the prices we quote unless stated otherwise.

Keep in mind that the multiple-day packages that we list are not your only option. At some resorts you can simply buy a daily trail pass (we list the price of this when it's available); at others, the trails are open only to overnight visitors, but you can pay for accommodations and a trail pass, without

the meals, lessons, and guide that are included in the package.

What are the accommodations like? Hotel rooms vary tremendously, and guided tours may lead you to primitive huts or comfortable country inns. Backcountry treks may also mention staying in a yurt—a round, semi-permanent structure stronger than a tent and similar to a hut.

What are the meals like? You could be dining in four-star restaurants, or eating beans around a wood stove.

Are the resort or hotel's instructors certified by the Professional Ski Instructors of America? What experience do the outfitter's guides have? Certification by PSIA assures that instructors have the necessary skiing and communication skills required to teach effectively. If a guide is going to lead you into the backcountry, make sure that guide has been there before. Also see that at least one guide has first-aid and CPR training.

What kind of equipment is available? Does the rental shop have waxable skis? What type of binding systems are on the rental skis? Lots of skiers bring their own skis, but if you're renting, you want to be sure the resort has the kind of skis you need. If you want to practice skating and it stocks only touring skis, you'll be out of luck. Many ski shops offer only waxless skis, so more advanced skiers, who prefer to choose a wax to match the skiing conditions, may be left unsatisfied. Also, if you bring your own boots but don't want to carry your own skis, you should be sure that your boots will fit on the rental ski bindings. New skiers might want to ask about the latest innovation, the micro ski, which is only three-quarters the length of older models and makes turning and learning a breeze on packed snow.

What is base elevation? What is the highest point on your trip likely to be? People who don't do well at high elevations should not pick ski areas in the mountains, and if you have limited time, you may want to avoid areas with high altitudes, where it's important to acclimate. When traveling from sea level to an elevation of 6,000 feet or higher, you should avoid strenuous exertion the first day or two. Remember that alcoholic beverages affect you twice as fast at higher elevations, and headaches are often a symptom of oxygen depletion.

What other recreation is available on site? Is there downhill skiing nearby? It's always fun to have other options.

What kids' programs and facilities are available? Almost half the adults out on the trails have children under 18. When you bring a child skiing you have to be sure that the kid won't be bored. Ask about day care and baby-sitting, a snow-play area, children's rental equipment, narrowly set tracks for smaller skis and legs, and the availability of insulated sleds that you can use to pull your tiny tot along the trails as you ski.

Are there former guests that I can call as a reference? There's nothing as good as word of mouth to ensure the quality of experience.

How far in advance do I need to book?

MAJOR PLAYERS

BACKROADS Backroads has been running cross-country skiing programs since 1991. They offer heli-skiing in the Canadian Rockies, Nordic skiing in the Colorado Rockies, terrific tours for novice skiers in the California Sierra and Washington's Methow Valley, and postcard-perfect tours in northeastern Vermont. Activities such as snowshoeing to sleigh rides round out your vacation (Backroads, 1516 5th St., Berkeley, CA 94710-1740, tel. 510/527–1555 or 800/462–2848, fax 510/527–1444).

OFF THE BEATEN PATH In addition to customizing trips in the Rocky Mountain West, Off the Beaten Path has scheduled cross country ski trips in the Tetons, Yellowstone National Park, Glacier National Park, and the Canadian Rockies (Off the Beaten Path, 109 East Main St., Bozeman, MT 59715, tel. 406/586–1311, fax 406/587–4147).

FAVORITE TRIPS

THE NORTHEAST

NEW HAMPSHIRE **Resort Skiing on 15,000 Acres.** The appeal of the Balsams ski resort is more a matter of quality than size. There are few ski establishments that offer the attention to service, architectural character, and culinary accomplishments that you find at The Balsams, a classic Grand Hotel founded in 1866. Set on a 15,000-acre private holding in far northern New Hampshire, it has top ratings and has been named a Historic Hotel of America by the National Trust for Historic Preservation. And to make it easier for you to have a good time here, the management includes just about all activities in the price of the Balsams America Plan.

This is beautiful, rugged country, closer to Montreal than Boston, and because The Balsams sits 600 feet higher than the surrounding area, it gets 250 inches of snow annually, 100 inches more than lower-lying lands. The 76-km groomed cross-country trail system, with both tracks and a skating lane, is complemented by 30 km of backcountry trails. The system provides more than 1,000 feet of vertical change, with trails passing through heavy stands of birch and maple. Trails can generally be skied in either direction, effectively doubling the system's length. Although the facilities are open to day visitors, you won't find crowds of skiers.

The Balsams also has a small alpine ski area (with a 1,000-foot vertical drop) with good telemark instruction and a snowboard half-pipe. There's ice skating, snowshoeing trails (equipment and instruction available), and horse-drawn hayrides, too. And yes, it's all included in the cost.

The hotel's ski learning center has a staff of instructors and guides, many certified by the Professional Ski Instructors of America. Guides lead several free tours, including a Thursday luncheon tour and a naturalist tour where participants study the tracks of rare pine marten, moose, and fox. The area boasts a peregrine falcon population, and if you come during the spring nesting season you might get a glimpse of one. Both alpine and cross-country skiers can take advantage of several warming shelters with heaters. Toilets are located at various points along the trails.

The property has just about everything you need, including a movie theater, ballroom, nightclub, piano bar, and a free nursery for infants to 5-year-olds. The atmosphere in the dining room is somewhat formal—men wear sports jackets—but co-owner and chef Phil Learned makes a poached salmon fillet that's worth dressing up for. Sunday-to-Friday ski packages include accommodations, breakfasts, dinners, use of both cross-country and alpine facilities and many guided tours. The on-site ski shop also provides rentals, sales and general ski merchandise; lessons are extra. *The Balsams/Wilderness, Dixville Notch, NH 03576, tel. 800/255–0600, fax 603/255–4221. Mid-Dec.–late Mar.: midweek 5-night package, $400–$650. Trail fee: $7 (included in package).*

NEW HAMPSHIRE **A Trail System in Classic New England.** Because the elevation ranges from 750 to 4,000 feet, there's an unusually high number of trails rated "most difficult" in this cross-country ski area, but the grooming is first-rate, with a mix of tracks and skating lanes. Back in the 70s, when the town came on hard times, Jackson made a calculated decision to establish a grand cross-country trail system twining through and around itself. It competes with Stowe, Vermont, in the Northeast for Nordic supremacy (although Stowe is better known for alpine skiing).

Jackson has 28 groomed trails totalling 91 km, ranging from a dozen shorties of less than 1 km to one that's 17.8 km. It also has an additional 90 km of backcountry routes. Conditions are variable, typical of the Northeast.

The area is controlled by the Jackson Ski Touring Foundation, headed by long-time director Thom Perkins. The Foundation maintains the trails and organizes lots of events, demonstrations, races, day tours, and clinics. It sponsors a Women's Weekend

as well as a 5-km hot chocolate loop. It will also tailor treks anywhere from 3 km to 15 km, an hour to a full day. Groups of up to 10 people are escorted by one guide. There's a guided orientation tour every Monday at 10:30. The area's Jack Frost Nordic Shop offers group and private lessons and also rents skis.

The town of Jackson is classic New England, complete with covered bridge. It's in the Mt. Washington Valley below the Presidential Range, about 2½ hours north of Boston. No matter what type of lodging you choose in Jackson—inn, hotel, B&B, condo, or motel— you will be able to step out your door onto the trails, which span 3 river valleys and 60 square miles in the White Mountain highlands. Two alpine ski areas, Wildcat and Black Mountain, are connected to the system, so you can telemark down their runs at no extra cost. If you want to ride the lift, however, you will need to buy a downhill pass, but you'll get that at a discount when you show your cross-country pass.

When you're not skiing, you can linger in the town's taverns, fine restaurants, and galleries or head south to North Conway for a shopping spree in the factory outlet stores. Visitors can also take sleigh rides or try ice skating for free on several small rinks in town or for $5 on Emerald Lake. *Jackson Ski Touring Foundation, Rte. 16, Box 216, Jackson, NH 03846, tel. 603/383–9355 or 800/XC–SNOWS. Jackson Lodging Bureau, tel. 800/ 866–3334. Mid-Dec.–late Mar. Trail fees: $7–$9.*

VERMONT **A Taste of Tyrol.** The first cross-country ski resort in North America, Trapp Family Lodge (owned by the von Trapp family of *Sound of Music* fame) was founded in 1968 at Stowe, Vermont, a well-known alpine ski area and one of the biggest Nordic areas in the Northeast. There are 3 other cross-country ski centers totalling 135 km of groomed trails around Stowe, but Trapp Family Lodge is the kingpin. It has 55 km of groomed trails, single-tracked with a skating lane, and access to 50 km of ungroomed routes. The elevation change between Skaters Waltz, on the low southern end of the network, and the Slayton Cabin, near the northern end, is more than 1,000 feet. Trails meander through meadows and forests of sugar maple, pine, and birch, with occasional grand views of the Green Mountain peaks.

Trapp's trail network connects with both Topnotch (20 km, groomed) and Mt. Mansfield (35 km, groomed), and Edson Hill Manor (25 km, groomed) is easily accessible by car. All areas honor each other's trail passes when you ski from one to the next, giving you the greatest concentration of groomed tracks in New England. You can start at the easier trails of, say, Topnotch, and graduate to the more advanced skiing at Trapp's in the same day. Both the groomed and wilderness trails are well mapped.

The fine staff of 6 full-time instructors has been rigorously trained by long-time Nordic director Charlie Yerrick. Naturalist and teacher Dick Smyth leads 1½- to 2-hour nature tours over easy terrain weekdays, studying everything from animal tracks to forest types ($5; sign up at lodge or ski shop). Guided backcountry day treks for groups of up to 6 can run as much as 20 km (prices vary), not necessarily tough skiing but a certain stamina is required. There are no overnight tours.

The original Trapp Family Lodge, built in 1941, burned down in 1980; it was replaced by a less idiosyncratic Tyrolean-style structure that sits grandly on Luce Hill, with an annex and guest houses nearby. The 93 lodge rooms all have a balcony and a view, but they're smaller and slightly more expensive than the 100 guest house apartments, which have kitchenettes and fireplaces and are also offered as time-share units. The lodge, however, is more convenient to restaurants.

Hot drinks and snacks are available at the cross-country center; you can get a soup-and-sandwich lunch along the trail at the Slayton Cabin; and the Austrian Tea Room and Bar serves light entrées and sandwiches. The lodge restaurant specializes in Austrian cuisine. Dinner is accompanied by harp,

piano, or guitar music. Since both trails and restaurant are open to the public, and Trapp Family Lodge is one of Stowe's best-known sightseeing destinations, staying here is not an intimate experience.

When you're not skiing tracks, you can try the downhill slopes, snowshoe, or go for a horse-drawn sleigh ride. The lodge has a fitness center with indoor pool, massage, sauna, and exercise room, and the charming though touristy town will satisfy the serious shopper. *Trapp Family Lodge, Stowe, VT 05672, tel. 802/253–8511 or 800/826–7000 (reservations). Mid-Dec.–early Apr.: 5-day package for 2, $840. Trail fee: $10 (included in package).*

VERMONT **From Craftbury Common to Stowe.** This 5-night trip includes stays in 2 fine Vermont inns near extensive trail networks. Guides lead you on daily tours from the inns, but if you would rather ski your own route you are free to do so. Instruction is offered for less-experienced skiers, and intermediates and experts can polish up on their skating and striding techniques.

The trip begins at the colonial village of Craftsbury Common, where you spend 3 nights at the elegant Inn on the Common, known for its 5-course dining feasts. Guides lead you on trails from the Craftsbury Nordic Ski Center through woods and open fields and around icy lakes. The 100-km system is groomed with side-by-side trails for skating and for diagonal striding. You're shuttled to Stowe, and if conditions are right you ski on the Recreation Path, an 8½-km ungroomed route that runs from the village, along a river, and is part of a 150-km trail system. By day's end you arrive at the Edson Hill Manor, a Georgian colonial-style inn. From here you do day-trips on the 50-km Mount Mansfield network, and if you want to hit the alpine slopes, Backroads will shuttle you back to Stowe.

Situated on 220 acres of rolling countryside, Edson Hill Manor has 25 rooms, 16 in the carriage house and 9 in the main manor house. Backroads groups usually stay in the carriage house rooms, which have pine paneling and raised brick fireplaces. Its restaurant serves innovative American cuisine, including a delicious grilled rabbit with cornbread stuffing and pecan chili sauce.

This tour includes 3 daily meals, lodging, guides, lessons, gratuities, a horse-drawn sleigh ride, and shuttle to Stowe and back to Craftsbury Common. There's a $50 charge for rental skis, and a $50 charge for round-trip van transfer from Burlington (either the airport or downtown). A maximum of 20 skiers are escorted by 2 guides. *Backroads, 1516 5th St., Suite B112, Berkeley, CA 94710-1740, tel. 510/527–1555 or 800/462–2848, fax 510/527–1444. Feb.: 6 days, $1,298.*

VERMONT **Five Days in Colonial Inns.** Inn-to-inn trips used to be a famous pastime of Vermont winters—leisurely guided jaunts with baggage transported for you, fine food and drink awaiting in century-old hostelries, rooms furnished with antiques, and goose-down comforters spread on old brass beds. Although many of the operators of these tours have long since gone under, the Viking Ski Touring Center has survived. It is one of New England's oldest cross-country ski centers, founded in 1970, and its touring company, Viking Inn-to-Inn Tours, still runs 5-day inn-to-inn trips that combine skiing with hospitality and fine food in the atmosphere of 18th- and 19th-century buildings. These trips are tailored to weather conditions and the experience level of the guests.

Novice skiers can handle most of these trails, although intermediates are likely to ski—and see—rather more. A mix of groomed and ungroomed paths run through farmland and birch, pine, and maple forest. Terrain is more gentle than at many Vermont resorts, and views are of rolling hills and up to the Green Mountain peaks. A maximum of 8 people accompanied by 1 or 2 guides—depending on the cohesiveness of the party—ski between 4 country inns.

The group starts at Viking's Londonderry guest house, a 4-bedroom B&B converted from an 1860s farmhouse. The first hour is spent with a brief review of technique, with the staff evaluating skiers to make sure side trips match skiers' abilities. It's as little as 5 km, but no more than 10 km, from one inn to the next, but trips on ungroomed routes to downhill play areas and viewpoints can double the distance skied daily.

Other accommodations include the 200-year-old Colonial House, near Weston, which is known for its made-to-order omelets; Rowell's Inn, a former stagecoach stop near Simonsville; the Village Inn, near the tiny town of Landgrove, which offers a sleigh ride and a hot tub; and on the final night, Londonderry's Highland House, the newest of these 4 (built in 1842) and the most posh, with a lovely post-and-beam dining room and many antiques. Breakfasts at the inns include fresh baked goods. Lunches, eaten on the trail, include sandwiches, fruit, hot drinks, brownies, and cookies. For dinner there's a variety of meat and fish entrées. All meals, baggage transportation, and a sleigh ride are included in the cost of this tour.

The Viking Ski Touring Center is in south central Vermont, near Bromley, Stratton, and Okemo ski areas. Its own 40 km of trail, which you'll use if you extend your stay, are double tracked but lack a skating lane; grooming is good. Three km of trail are lighted on Saturday nights. *Viking Inn-to-Inn Tours, 287 Rt. 100, Weston, VT 05161, tel. 802/824–6286, fax 802/824–3934. Jan.–early Mar.: 5 days, $535. Trail fee: $11 (included in package).*

THE MIDWEST

MINNESOTA **Backcountry Trekking in Boundary Wilderness.** The Gunflint Trail, tucked up in the northeast corner of Minnesota, is about as far north as you can go before entering Canada. It's a wild land of lakes and forest broken by rolling hills. The region is best known for the Boundary Waters Canoe Area Wilderness, long winters, moose, and timber wolves. When snow falls, it stays—and stays dry.

The region also has 4 cross-country trail networks with more than 200 km of ski trails:

the 100-km Upper Gunflint Trail connected by the 29-km straight-run Banadad Trail to the 55-km Central Gunflint Trail. And then there's the Pincushion Trail, whose unconnected 25 km are about 25 miles south of the Central Gunflint. The entire system is spread out along the 63-mile highway known as (what else?) the Gunflint Trail. These ski trails lace around or over a half dozen lakes, over hills (300-foot elevation change throughout the system), past impressive cliffs, and by spruce bogs. Most are double tracked, but some combine single track and a skating lane. The Gunflint area has 6 lodges, one B&B, the Ollie Cabin, and the Banadad yurts.

Boundary Country Trekking can help you customize a self-guided, cross-country, lodge-to-lodge, yurt-to-yurt, or lodge-to-yurt trip. You can also choose to stay at just one lodge, from which you can take day-trips. The company makes your reservations, maps out a route for you, and arranges to have your car and luggage driven to each destination. You can take meals at the lodges or yurts or bring your own food. There is no instruction and no guide on these tours, but if you choose at least one night at the Bearskin Lodge, you can take advantage of its free group lessons.

One popular option is a night in a woodstove-heated yurt shared by 4 to 6 persons. A yurt host brings overnight gear and prepares a hearty Mongolian hot pot dinner, with platters of veggies and meat cooked in steaming broth and served fondue-style.

The distance between lodges is generally 8 km to 12 km, but you can take longer routes or even travel part of the way by car. *Boundary Country Trekking, 590 Gunflint Trail, Grand Marais, MN 55604, tel. 218/388–9972 or 800/322–8327, fax 218/388–4487. Thanksgiving–early Apr.: about $115 per day. The larger the group, the lower the rate.*

MINNESOTA **Little Norway on the Prairie.** With its collection of items as varied as historical depot signs and neon clocks, and accommodations ranging from a remodeled chicken coop to a small lodge, Maplelag is nothing if not eclectic. This is a ski resort with a style of its own, and owners Jim and Mary Richards take pride in the high percentage of repeat visitors they get each year.

In rural northwestern Minnesota, 20 miles from Detroit Lakes and about an hour's drive from Fargo, North Dakota, Maplelag is at the edge of a dense forest. Just a few miles west, the prairie begins, so Maplelag is probably the last (or first) cross-country ski area east of the Rockies. The resort has 53 km of groomed trails winding through forest and an excellent telemark practice area about a half mile from the main lodge. Most loops are gentle and groomed only for diagonal stride, with double tracks; Wavy Gravy has a good deal more up-and-down. There are 6 km of skating trail maintained for race training and as a technical challenge, and a new 1½-km lighted loop.

Instruction by 4 staff members, 2 of whom are Norwegian, tends toward the informal. Classes are usually small, sometimes only 2 or 3 in a group, and cost $7 per person, per hour; private lessons cost $10 per hour. You can request to join a guided introductory tour of the trails, which is offered free. Free mid-week tours to nearby Tamarack Wildlife Refuge and Itasca State Park are also available.

You can spend winter days and nights skiing, snowshoeing, ice fishing, and ice skating, and the 500 pounds of sunflower seeds distributed at feeding stations along the trails annually make for excellent birdwatching. You might also see deer and, occasionally, moose and bobcats, and you will probably come across wolf tracks.

To soothe sore muscles, you can relax in one of the 2 saunas, the Turkish steam bath, or the 30-person outdoor hot tub, then make the plunge into the 8-foot swimming hole cut into the icy lake. As a reward for this feat, you are allowed to buy a T-shirt proclaiming your achievement. On Saturday nights you can dance to a DJ, and if you really want to get away, the Shooting Star Casino on White Earth Reservation is just a half-hour's drive.

The word Maplelag reflects the owners' interest in Norway and the fact that this used to be a working maple syrup farm. The Richards collect and display Norwegian folk art, stained glass windows, homemade Scandinavian skis, metal lunch boxes, neon clocks, and railroad signs. There is a range of accommodations for the 180 guests; you might stay in a small lodge with modern furnishings and a private bath, or you could choose a remodelled Finnish sauna or a former chicken coop, which don't have private baths. All guests must either bring linens or a sleeping bag or rent linens for $30 per week.

Meals are served family-style in the main lodge dining area, which is reserved for overnight guests. Dinners often follow an ethnic theme—Italian, Greek, Chinese, or German—and there is always a vegetarian option. The rich desserts include double fudge brownies and hot fudge sundaes. For breakfast you might feast on Swedish pancakes with lingonberries; for Sunday brunch you are treated to a Scandinavian smorgasbord. *Maplelag, Rte. 1, Box 52, Callaway, MN 56521-9741, tel. 218/375–4466 or 800/654–7711 (reservations). Mid-Dec.–mid-Mar.: 5 nights, $260 (extra nights, $46). Price does not include $30 per week for linens.*

THE SOUTHWEST

ARIZONA **Grand Canyon's North Rim.** At this northern Arizona lodge you can have the overwhelming silence, space, and awesome beauty of the Grand Canyon almost to yourself. Although more than 400,000 visitors come to the area in summer, in winter the backcountry Kaibab Lodge has no more than 50 guests. Located just 5 miles north of Grand Canyon National Park's North Rim entrance station, it is accessible only by enclosed tracked SnowVan, a 1½-hour, 26-mile trek south from the Jacob Lake junction, where U.S. 89A and Rte. 67 intersect.

The lodge is home to the North Rim Nordic Center, founded in winter 1988–89, and sits on the 1,500-square-mile Kaibab Plateau, towering a vertical mile over the desert and up to 9,200 feet above sea level. The snow is reliable, and the sunshine abundant.

You ski on the center's 60 km of mostly intermediate trail, groomed with both double tracks and a skating lane, or on the 23 km of forested backcountry trails, which are marked but ungroomed. In addition, you can try telemarking on the groomed telemarking hill and take free group lessons in classic, skate, or telemark skiing from the small ski school staff of 3 certified instructors.

If you're feeling more adventurous, you can join one of the free guided tours, which range from 10 km up, or choose to pay $25 to $60 extra for special tours to canyon overlooks that include meals and, in some cases, SnowVan transportation, snowshoes, and overnight stays in huts. No more than 8 skiers are accompanied by one guide.

If you stay at Kaibab for 5 days, consider taking the overnight expedition to Grand Canyon's Point Imperial. You ski along 23 km of groomed trail to a sleeping hut at the edge of Saddle Mountain Wilderness, just outside the park. The views from Saddle Mountain are incredible: You can see Shiva Temple, Echo Cliffs, and Marble Canyon. To reach Point Imperial, you have to ski 3½ km more—on marked but ungroomed trails through old-growth forest. This trip can be taken by 5 to 8 skiers. Each pays $25, which includes the guide, one dinner, one breakfast, 2 box lunches, and transportation of some equipment.

Back at the Kaibab Lodge, you can choose to sleep in cabin rooms with one or two double beds, private bath, and hot showers, or heated yurts with eight bunk beds (bring your own sleeping bag, pillow, and towel) and outhouses. Both are comfortable but far from luxurious. The main lodge has a dining room, where you eat all your meals, and a great room with a fireplace, where skiers socialize. There's also a television room, beer and wine bar, gift shop, hot tub, and ski rental and repair shop.

Keep in mind that the lodge is at high altitude. Children over 5 who can ski will probably have fun, but there's no day care here and no special facilities for kids. *North Rim Nordic Center at Kaibab Lodge, Box 2997, Flagstaff, AZ 86003, tel. 502/ 526–0924 or 800/525–0924 (outside Arizona), fax 502/527–9398. Dec. 22 and 29: 5 days, cabin for $600 per person, group yurt for $520. Jan.–Mar.: 5 days, cabin for $560, yurt for $480.*

THE ROCKIES

COLORADO **A Ranch with a Trail System.** Characterized by good taste and natural beauty, Vista Verde has been transformed from mighty fine to superb. Founded as a working cattle ranch in 1920, the 540-acre spread was purchased in 1991 by John and Suzanne Munn, who dramatically improved the facilities. They added to and redecorated the cabins, built a new lodge, and created a lake, but they've wisely kept vital staff, including chef Jacques Wilson, famous for his desserts (try the chocolate raspberry torte).

Vista Verde has 30 km of 2-way trail, groomed by Sno-Cat with a skating lane and double tracks so that you can ski side-by-side with a friend. Although the network is on the small side, it is an unusually gentle and scenic system, which the Munns are expanding. Trails wind across meadows and through conifer and aspen groves, and offer views of the Continental Divide. The system connects with 50 km of marked trails and virtually unlimited backcountry opportunities in the surrounding Routt National Forest. You can count on more than 300 inches of snow annually.

The ranch is situated at 7,800 feet, 25 miles from Steamboat Springs, and a free shuttle makes runs to the airport and into town. The 8 log cabins and 3 lodge rooms can accommodate 36 guests, but there are seldom more than 20 except at Christmas. The cabins are nestled among aspen on a hillside, only a moment's walk from the ski trails. Deer, elk, fox, and other wildlife are often visible in the meadow below.

There are two telemark areas and a sledding course, or you can try snowshoeing or horseback riding if the weather is good. So you won't forget that this is one of Colorado's finest working ranches, you are encouraged to take the sleigh, drawn by 2 black draft horses named Doc and Dillon, out to help feed the herd of horses.

There are several 5-night packages for novice or expert that include lessons by certified instructors, fun events such as a treasure hunt and an obstacle course competition, moonlight or lamplight skiing, all equipment, lodging, three daily meals, snacks, and transportation to and from Steamboat. *Vista Verde Ranch, Box 465, Steamboat Springs, CO 80477, tel. 970/879– 3858 or 800/526–7433, fax 970/879–1413. Mid-Dec.–mid-Mar.: 1 night, $155 ($195 for the holiday season). Jan. and Mar.: 5-night package, $645.*

COLORADO **10th Mountain Division Huts.** Colorado contains the greatest number of ski-in huts and yurts in North America, but its crown jewel is the 10th Mountain Division trail and hut system—14 huts set in the White River National Forest between Vail, Aspen, and Leadville and connected by 400 miles of trail.

Although it's possible to arrange your own trip to the area by calling the 10th Mountain Division Hut Association (tel. 303/925– 5775), you will need at least one experienced backcountry navigator with map and compass skills (and a bit of self-confidence and common sense about backcountry winter travel). Another option is to go with Vail-based Paragon Guides, a company that has been leading groups through the area since 1978.

Paragon's overnight tours run from 3 to 8 days and are rated Level I, Level II, and Level III. When arranging your trip, be very honest about your experience and skiing ability. A maximum of 8 skiers are escorted by 2 guides. Transportation to and from the trailheads, meals, hut fees, backcountry and telemark instruction, sleeping bag, and community equipment are provided. Sleeping bags and food are transported to the huts by Paragon to lighten your load to a 20- to 30-pounds. A pretrip orientation and acclimation day is spent at the Arrowhead Ski Area, near Vail, where participants are given a lift ticket, Nordic skills lessons, use of backcountry ski equipment, and a briefing on the trip, all part of the trip cost.

This is a high and light-filled land of dramatic contrasts, where most of the huts lie above 11,000 feet and the term dry powder is an understatement. Aspen groves spill down hillsides, conifer stands and meadow are intermingled, and there are bowls, glades, and endless vistas. Add crisp air that should be bottled for sale on city store shelves, and you have a skier's dream of heaven.

You ski on average from 6 miles to 8 miles each day, with elevation gains and losses of 700 to 3,000 feet, depending on the route chosen. At least one layover day is incorporated into most trips so you can relax, tour, telemark, or summit a nearby peak.

The huts are 2-story log buildings sometimes described as backcountry chateaus. Mattresses line the upstairs bunks, which can sleep up to 16 people. The heating and cooking are done with wood stoves, and water comes from melting snow. Large south-facing solar panels provide the energy to light the main areas of the hut, but flashlights are needed to navigate your way to the outhouse at night.

The trail is named after the 10th Mountain Division Army Ski Troop that trained at nearby Camp Hale during World War II. Make your reservation early to ensure the trip of your choice. *Paragon Guides, Box 130, Vail, CO 81658, tel. 907/926–5299, fax 907/926–5298. Late Nov.–mid-Apr.: 3–8 days, $510–$1,400.*

COLORADO **A Resort for Kids.** Here's a cross-country resort that not only accepts children but also caters to them. The kids get their own programs, such as wildlife tracking and ski games, and they even have a winter playground called Knickerknickerland over which they rule (adults are denied entry unless accompanied by a child). Unique among cross-country areas, C Lazy U Ranch hires a certified teacher to tutor children in English, history, math, science, and French, so you don't have to feel guilty if your kids are missing a few days of school.

Since the ranch is at 8,300 feet, you have to take some time to acclimate, but once you do, you can take advantage of nearly 40 km of groomed trail with a single track and a skating lane, as well as an area especially groomed for beginner telemarking. C Lazy U's trails run from 1 km to 8 km, and grooming is good. There are also backcountry routes and hills for advanced telemarking.

Ranch guides lead a series of free tours, including a 5-km round-trip to the top of Baldy Mountain, with 60-mile vistas. One 15-km round-trip backcountry tour for intermediate and advanced skiers winds through a forest of subalpine fir, spruce, and lodgepole pines along the Continental Divide. You may see elk, moose, red fox, coyote, ermine, snowshoe hare, eagles, and hawks. The number of skiers and guides varies with each tour, but there are seldom more than 4 guests per guide. The ranch's rental equipment is generally new, and there are more touring skis than track or telemark, but it's all lent out gratis.

C Lazy U Ranch is a 2-hour drive from Denver's Stapleton Airport via I–70 and Route 40, which continues to Steamboat Springs. You pass over Berthoud Pass, from which you can see paths carved through the mountains by avalanches, through the Fraser Valley, and on to Granby, 6 miles from the ranch.

As many as 100 guests are accommodated in a medley of cabins, none of which has TV or phone. Food is served in the dining room, where 10 guests sit at each table. Two entrées are offered for dinner: a customary hearty western platter, perhaps rack of lamb with fresh rosemary apricot glaze, and a lighter dish, such as turkey with cranberry sage sauce.

Ranch facilities are entirely reserved for overnight guests, so faces become familiar in short order. There's plenty of recreation on the more than 2,000 private acres and 3,000 acres of surrounding national forest: sleigh rides, a ½-mile sled run, daily shuttles to alpine skiing at Winter Park and Silver Creek, snowshoeing, dogsledding, sauna and hot tub, moonlight tours, trap and skeet shooting, skating parties, racquetball, and even bingo and billiards for the more sedentary. *C Lazy U Ranch, Box 379, Granby, CO 80446, tel. 303/887–3344, fax 303/887–3917. Mid-Dec.–late Mar.: 1 night, $95–$160. Ask about minimum-stay requirements.*

IDAHO **Backcountry Trekking on Alpine Lakes.** On this 3-day trip beginning in the Sawtooth Valley you stay in both a yurt and a walled tent and tour above the tree line. You pass through a coniferous forest of pines and furs and through stands of aspen. The terrain is alpine rugged, with peaks above 10,000 feet, but you ski in a valley and along a ridge on a relatively easy trail.

The tour begins in world-famous Sun Valley, Idaho, and you are driven by van 1 hour and 15 minutes north to the hut trailhead in the Sawtooth Valley. It's just 3½ miles, about a 3-hour ski, to Fishhook Hut, a Mongolian-style yurt in Fishhook Valley with views of the Sawtooth Mountains. You enjoy an early afternoon lunch at the hut, then guides take you out on backcountry tours chosen to match your group's skiing abilities.

The next day you climb to Bench Hut, a walled tent at an elevation of 7,500 feet. You cover 5 miles of relatively easy terrain on gentle switchbacks that lead to a low-angle ridgeline from which you can look east across the Sawtooth Valley to the White Cloud Mountains. Red Fish Lake, created by glaciers, is directly below you. You arrive at Bench Hut in time for lunch. The afternoon is spent touring near the hut, or climbing the slopes for lessons in telemark ski techniques.

The trip's highlight is the third day's 4-mile loop around the 5 alpine lakes above Bench Hut. You use climbing skins to scamper up the low ridge behind the hut, and tour across

or around the small alpine lakes. At the highest point, you can look up at the imposing vertical towers of Mt. Heyburn. You eat a late lunch back at Bench Hut and then ski 6 downhill miles out.

The huts are easy to get to and backcountry sleighs with provisions are pulled by the guides so skiers can spend most of their time on the trail carrying a backpack containing only personal items and a sleeping bag.

The company takes pride in its reputation for good food, which is prepared by a trained chef. Meals may include homemade pizzas, feta cheese salad, or a savory basil lemon chicken dish with rice pilaf. The huts are in the Sawtooth National Recreation Area, where permanent structures are prohibited. The Spartan accommodations have lodgepole pine bunk beds with foam mattresses; covered pit toilets with warm seats are nearby. Fishhook Hut has the added luxury of a hot tub, and Bench Hut has a sauna.

A maximum of 12 skiers are led by 2 guides. The standard tour includes guiding, instruction, meals, transportation to and from the trailhead, ski equipment, and avalanche transceiver. The company supplies a variety of the latest equipment on the tour, so people can try out different skis. *Sun Valley Trekking, Box 2200, Sun Valley, ID 83353, tel. 208/788–9585, fax 208/788–9585. Mid-Nov.–mid-Apr.: standard tour, $125 per person per day. Price includes ski rentals.*

IDAHO AND WYOMING **Dog Sleds and Sleigh Rides in the Tame Tetons.** This exclusive 8-night trip run by Off the Beaten Path takes you on several adventures in the Targhee and Bridger-Teton national forests of Idaho and Wyoming. There is enough variety to satisfy most winter recreation appetites.

The trip begins in the resort town of Jackson, but 3 days are spent on the sunny side of the mountains at Teton Ridge Ranch, a small and brilliant skiing gem near tiny Tetonia, Idaho. Composed of 4,000 acres of varied terrain, the ranch has more than 20 km of trail groomed with both double tracks and a skating lane. Trails are designed to be pleasurable rather than challenging, with 2 distinct kinds of terrain. One loop series leads east through conifer country, climbing into Wyoming before returning to the lodge. Routes heading south and west wind gently downhill, following a series of miniature valleys, crossing small intervening aspen-clad ridges. You may spot moose, deer, and coyote tracks but seldom the animals themselves.

Off the Beaten Path books the entire ranch for its tours. The 10,000-square-foot log lodge accommodates only 10 guests in 5 bedrooms, with a whirlpool, steam shower, and wood stove; meals are superb.

From Teton Ridge Ranch, skiers are conveyed to the splendid but little-known Absaroka Mountains on the northeast edge of Jackson Hole, along the Continental Divide. Dog sled teams carry you in to historic Brooks Lake Lodge, base for three days of backcountry adventure, with tours reaching close to 10,000 feet and great downhill play areas.

You return to Jackson for 2 days, where activities include a tour into Grand Teton National Park (moose sightings in the park are a sure thing), a sleigh ride through the world's largest elk herd, and a visit to the magnificent new National Wildlife Art Museum. Accommodations are in the Alpine House, a B&B owned and operated by former U.S. cross-country team members Hans and Nancy Johnstone. All meals, lodging, guide service, and ground transportation to and from Jackson Hole Airport are included. *Off The Beaten Path, 109 E. Main St., Bozeman, MT 59715, tel. 406/586–1311 or 800/445–2995, fax 406/587–4147. March: 7 nights, $2,275.*

■MONTANA■ **Big Sky, Big Ranch.** Lone Mountain Ranch is a giant of the winter guest-ranch genre, with 75 km of trail groomed with double tracks and a skating lane. Located 15 minutes from burgeoning Big Sky alpine ski area and 40 miles southwest of Bozeman, it's less isolated than other ranches. And since Lone Mountain's trails and dining area are open to the public,

you're likely to meet more skiers here than at other ranches, where facilities are restricted to overnight guests.

Skiing begins at 6,700 feet, so you must think about acclimating. Virtually every groomed route gives views of 11,166-foot Lone Mountain Peak, which dominates the region. Most trails involve a fair amount of climbing and turns and are suited to eager intermediates or to less experienced skiers with time on their hands.

Open since 1977, Lone Mountain offers a great diversity of tours. A number of all-day snowcoach trips take guests into Yellowstone National Park, where you ski over mostly gentle terrain. Fawn Pass, on the fringe of Yellowstone, is a delight in spring, when you have a chance of seeing grizzlies. One overnight trip goes by Sno-Cat to a backcountry yurt in the Spanish Peaks and includes guided skiing and meals. On all Lone Mountain tours, group size is usually limited to 7 skiers with one guide, and tour length ranges from about 5 km to 19 km.

Up to 50 guests stay in the ranch's 23 different cabins clustered around a mountain stream right beside the ski trails. These log structures house from 2 to 9 people; they have private baths, western-style furnishings, and electric heat. Some have fireplaces. Dining in the main lodge is headed up by European-trained chef Gerard van Mourik, whose rack of lamb has become a local legend. There is, however, always a lighter option, such as grilled breast of chicken.

Lone Mountain packages include airport shuttle, an on-snow buffet that's a gastronomic and visual treat, and a sleigh ride to the North Fork Cabin. Here, you and 40 to 50 other guests are seated at tables of 8 to 10 and served an elegant, family-style prime rib dinner, cooked on an old-fashioned wood stove, with cheesecake for dessert. You are entertained by such lively acts as the singer and guitarist Walking Jim Stoltz.

Consider making January reservations, when coldest temperatures are offset by driest snow. Keep in mind that the ranch's ski retail shop is top of the line, and its rentals are state of the art. *Lone Mountain Ranch, Box 69, Big Sky, MT 59716, tel. 406/995–4644, fax 406/995–4670. Early Dec.–early Apr.: 7-day package, $1,900 per couple.*

MONTANA Amtrak and Ski Tracks. Halfway between the towns of East and West Glacier lies tiny Essex, Montana, home of Izaak Walton Inn, the only American cross-country area with doorstep delivery by Amtrak. This is wild country: The inn is a stone's throw from Glacier National Park, trails border the Great Bear Wilderness, and the vast Bob Marshall Wilderness is almost next door. It's a region known for wildlife, including cougar, elk, eagle, moose, and wolf; bears have been known to prowl the trails early on April mornings.

Backcountry enthusiasts have spectacular touring opportunities in Glacier National Park and the adjoining Flathead National Forest. Small groups of 8 to 10 skiers with 2 guides are led on 10- to 20-km tours that include transportation to and from the trailhead and lunch. The Avalanche Creek tour through Moose Country, on the southern tip of Glacier, is ideal for beginners, and intermediates will enjoy practicing turns on the numerous hills of the Autumn Creek tour, which has awe-inspiring views of the crest of the Continental Divide. The Snyder Lake tour will challenge more advanced skiers.

For those who prefer to stay close to the inn, there are more than 30 km of trails groomed with double tracks and a skating lane on mostly gentle terrain. These run along the Middle Fork of the Flathead River and photogenic Essex Creek at a comfortable altitude below 4,500 feet. There's 1 km of lighted trail for night skiing, as well as a telemark hill that can be skied at night even though it's not lit. Snow around Essex is extremely dependable, with about 450 inches each year.

The half-timbered, 3-story hotel, built in 1939 to accommodate crews for the Great Northern Railroad, has 31 rooms, and additional lodging is in beautifully renovated 4-person cabooses with minikitchens, set on a hilltop overlooking the inn. A 5-night package includes luggage transfer from the train, 2 daily meals, trail privileges, sauna, a lesson, and a tour of Glacier National Park.

The railroad theme is maintained throughout the inn. Lodging is decorated with photos of trains and lanterns, and the Flagstop Bar and the Dining Car have railroad memorabilia on the walls. Be sure to try the succulent huckleberry cheesecake pie. For a change of pace, you can drive an hour from the inn to Big Mountain, an excellent downhill skiing complex. *Izaak Walton Inn, Box 653, Essex, MT 59916, tel. 406/888–5700, fax 406/888–5200. Mid-Nov.–mid-Apr.: 5 nights, $548; 7 nights, $727.*

MONTANA Comfortably Seeing Yellowstone on Skis. Off the Beaten Path has hired two guides—a naturalist and a Nordic ski specialist—to lead this 8-day trip through Yellowstone National Park, which in winter is the closest you can get to an African game park without crossing the ocean. Bison roam sheltered valleys; elk graze around the steaming geysers and mud pots, where the snow has melted; otter frolic in the icy streams; and bighorn sheep make appearances on the rocky ledges.

The guides recount Yellowstone's history, teaching you about forest regeneration after the great fires of 1988 and discussing park controversies such as destructive grazing caused by elk and bison overpopulation, and the recent reintroduction of the timber wolf.

The trip starts in Bozeman, and you are transported by van to the park. You spend 3 nights at the Mammoth Hot Springs Hotel, which is surrounded by open country and relatively easy skiing terrain. The first full day ends with a soak in the Boiling River Hot Springs. You are transported by snowcoach 75 miles south along the spectacular Grand Canyon of the Yellowstone to the Old Faithful Lodge, where you stay for another 3 nights in comfortable cabins. Here you ski the Upper Geyser Basin, stopping at Morning Glory Pool and Lone Star Geyser. The snowcoach then takes you another 30 miles to the town of West Yellowstone, where you spend an afternoon skiing the famous Rendezvous Trail tracks. Saturday's lodging is at the handsome and historic Gallatin Gateway Inn near Bozeman.

Plan to ski from 13 to 19 km per day over gentle terrain. Some trails are groomed sporadically. A maximum of 8 skiers are escorted by 2 guides. You should have some experience on cross-country skis or be an intermediate alpine skier. All meals, lodging, guide service, instruction, and ground transportation are included. *Off the Beaten Path, 109 E. Main St., Bozeman, MT 59715, tel. 406/ 586–1311 or 800/445–2995, fax 406/587–4147. Late Jan. through Feb.: 8 days, $1,950.*

WYOMING The Sunny Side of the Tetons. You can ski on the sunny, quiet side of the Tetons if you book a trip with Rendezvous Ski Tours, founded in 1987 by Glenn Vitucci and Carole Lowe. The company offers customized tours for both beginner and expert skiers using its own spacious guest house and 3 yurts in Targhee National Forest, along the Idaho-Wyoming border and near the Jedediah Smith Wilderness and Grand Teton National Park.

The terrain is typical of the west slope of the Tetons: wide open, low-angle bowls and broad ridges that you can cruise for miles, as well as high-angle powder bowls and relatively easy summit peaks that offer spectacular views. Snowfall is steady and reliable with more than 500 inches of champagne powder between November and April. The skiing is less steep and there are shorter runs than in Jackson, but the region has few of the sub-zero temperature inversions that plague the Jackson side of the Tetons.

Most groups are composed of fewer than 8 skiers with one guide. Daily distances and level of difficulty varies with each group; however, it's a 3- to 4-mile ski from the base guest house to each of the yurts, which sleep

8 on bunk beds with sleeping bags. The yurts lie a couple of thousand feet lower than Colorado's 10th Mountain Trail cabins, so there's less time needed for altitude acclimation.

Rendezvous's guest house, with its wonderful canyon views, is near Driggs, Idaho. It can sleep up to 12 skiers and has a hot tub. Package tours include van shuttle from either Jackson, Wyoming, or Idaho Falls airports, as well as accommodations, most meals, instruction, and use of light backpack (10–25 lbs.), climbing skins, and avalanche transceivers, if necessary. The town of Jackson Hole, with its huge alpine ski area, and Grand Teton National Park, are 45 minutes by car over the pass. *Rendezvous Ski Tours, 219 Highland, Victor, ID 83455, tel. 208/ 787–2906. Late Nov.–early Apr.: 4–7 days, $395–$695.*

THE WEST COAST

CALIFORNIA 9,000 Acres at Royal Gorge. Skiers often argue over which alpine ski resort is the largest, but in the world of cross-country skiing there's no doubt who is Big Daddy. By any criterion, Northern California's Royal Gorge leads the pack by a long kilometer—largest, most famous, and most popular.

Just off I–80 on the way to Lake Tahoe, Royal Gorge spreads over 9,000 acres; it has 8 track systems with 83 trails and 321 superbly groomed kilometers, the equivalent of skiing from San Francisco to the crest of the Sierras. Annual snowfall here averages 400 inches, but when the snows don't fall, the resort covers up to 15 km with artificial white powder. Trails have double tracks and a skating lane, and changes in temperature and snow type have relatively little effect on skiing quality because the resort's grooming is the best in the business.

Royal Gorge is one of those rare areas that was selected for its aesthetic appeal rather than merely added onto a preexistent facility. Trails slip around ridges, undulate through meadows and along frozen lakes.

They are well marked for ability levels and distances and have enough variety to please beginners and challenge experts. From Summit Station views west are dominated by spectacular Devil's Peak (7,704 feet), while craggy Castle Peak looms to the north, reaching almost 10,000 feet. From Point Mariah you can see the precipitous 4,400-foot drop into the Royal Gorge itself, on the North Fork of the American River. Three unique short surface lifts allow you to practice downhill techniques and save you from having to climb from low-lying trails to higher routes (there's 1,600 feet of vertical change).

Instructors certified by the Professional Ski Instructors of America offer a program of group lessons with 6 to 8 skiers and private instruction, including telemark and skating clinics. Guided tours may be arranged at the ski school (fees vary). Ski hosts are stationed at Summit and patrol the trails, giving advice and directions. You can break up your skiing day with stops at the area's 10 warming huts, 4 cafés, and 2 hotels.

If you're not on skis, you have to take a Sno-Cat-drawn sleigh about 6 km to reach the 35-room post-and-beam Wilderness Lodge. Rooms here have wood paneling and quilts on the beds; the restaurant serves French country cuisine. Rainbow Lodge, a 1920s B&B on the Yuba River, is at the far end of the resort's 22-km Interconnect Trail. You can drive your car to this property, which has 32 rooms with old-fashioned furnishings, wood-paneled walls, and chintz comforters. There are no TVs or phones, and some rooms share a bath. The excellent restaurant serves Continental and Italian cuisine.

Be aware that the resort's size does have its downside: On weekends and holidays there can be too many skiers around the trailheads, although after the first few kilometers, the crowds thin out. There are 3 alpine ski areas within a 3-mile radius of the resort, and gaming at Incline Village on Tahoe is only 40 minutes away. *Royal Gorge Cross Country Ski Resort, Box 1100, Soda Springs, CA 95728, tel. 916/426–3871 or 800/634–* *3086 (outside N. California), fax 916/426–9221. Mid-Nov.–mid-May: 5-day ski week (using Wilderness Lodge), $460 (not available on major holidays). Trail Fees: $13.50 half day and $17.50 full day, weekends and holidays; $12.50 half day and $15.50 full day, weekdays (included in package).*

CALIFORNIA **Sierra Tahoe Tour.** On this 5-day Backroads tour you sample 4 different cross-country areas in Northern California—Royal Gorge, Tahoe Donner Cross-Country Ski Resort, Lakeview, and Squaw Creek. Groups of 12 to 20 skiers are escorted by 2 leaders certified in Nordic ski instruction. Three hotels are used as bases from which the guides lead day trips.

At Royal Gorge you have more choices than at any other resort in North America. You can ski the easy and intermediate terrain around the open meadows of the Van Norden track system or though the woods of the Summit Station track system. You ski the broad, flat meadows of Euer Valley at the Tahoe Donner Cross-Country Ski Resort, and if you feel ambitious you can try the more challenging slopes. Then you go gliding at Lakeview Cross-Country Ski Area along Lake Tahoe's lovely north shore. Time is set aside on the last day of the trip for skiing the gentle trails of Squaw Creek's Cross-Country Center.

Royal Gorge's Rainbow Lodge, the 1873 vintage Truckee Hotel, and the modern Resort at Squaw Creek are your accommodations for this trip. Equipment rental costs $50. *Backroads, 1516 5th St., Suite B122, Berkeley, CA 94710, tel. 510/527–1555 or 800/462–2848, fax 510/527–1444. Jan.–Feb.: 5 days, $1,398.*

WASHINGTON **Lodge-to-Lodge in a Nordic Mecca.** The Cascade Mountains of Oregon and Washington aren't precisely a Nordic byword, so why add Methow Valley to your list of places to know? Well, how about 175 km of groomed trail with more in the works, hut-to-hut and lodge-to-lodge skiing, lots of cold powder, helicopter skiing, telemarking, and a million acres for touring? Add truly spectacular views (the Cascades may reach up to only 7,000 feet locally, but the valley floor is only 2,000 feet), negligible altitude acclimation, plus 200 days of sunshine a year and voilá! A Nordic mecca.

This Backroads lodge-to-lodge tour begins just 10 miles outside the town of Winthrop, at the 78-room Sun Mountain Lodge, a resort with 360° views of the valley and the Sawtooth Wilderness. The lodge has outdoor hot tubs to soothe sore muscles, and Backroads guests are treated to a relaxing evening sleigh ride. The gourmet dinner served in the lodge might include hickory applewood smoked duckling or rainbow trout roasted on bamboo leaves with an almond crust.

Sun Mountain Lodge is accessible to the 175-km trail system maintained by the Methow Valley Sport Trails Association and is the centerpiece of the valley. Backroads guides lead you through the mostly flat and rolling farm and woodlands. All skiing abilities, from novice to expert, can be accommodated. You can ski from 3 km to 20 km each day, stopping on the trail to eat the lunch Backroads packs for you. Although you have to pay more for the privilege, try to arrange to take a lesson with Don Portman, one of the lodge's outstanding instructors.

From Sun Mountain you follow the New Methow Trail down the valley into Winthrop, spending the night at the Rio Vista Hotel, which overlooks the Methow River. It's an easy ski through these lower lands before you head to the Mazama Country Inn, a wilderness lodge that's the stopping point for the plows that clear the highway to it.

On the final day of the tour you can choose to ski through rolling woodlands to a warming hut or take a skating lesson. Two certified Nordic instructors lead the group of up to 20 skiers and give daily lessons to those who want them. Rentals cost $50. *Backroads, 1516 5th St., Suite B122, Berkeley, CA 94710-1740, tel. 510/527–1555 or 800/462–2848, fax 510/527–1444. Jan.–Feb.: 5 days, $1,298.*

SOURCES

ORGANIZATIONS The **Cross Country Ski Areas Association** (259 Bolton Rd., Winchester, NH 03470, tel. 603/239–4341) promotes the sport and aims to protect the interests of operators and skiers. It serves as a clearinghouse of information on where to go and how to get started skiing cross-country.

PERIODICALS *The Best of Cross Country Skiing*, a directory published by the Cross Country Ski Areas Association, provides a verbal and pictorial introduction to the sport. Its concise listings cover size of trail system, additional recreation, availability of accommodations, kids' attractions, and more. Published five times per winter, *Cross Country Skier* (1823 Fremont Ave. S, Minneapolis, MN 55403, tel. 612/377–5105 or 800/827–0607) is a wide-ranging magazine, covering U.S. (and a few Canadian) ski destinations, technique, equipment, waxing, and touring tips. *Ski Trax* (2 Pardee Ave., Suite 204, Toronto, Ontario M6K 3H5, Canada, tel. 416/530–1350), is a Canadian publication covering both U.S. and Canadian cross-country skiing that provides much of the same information as *Cross Country Skier* but has a greater emphasis on racing. It's published 4 times per winter.

BOOKS In *Cross Country Ski Inns, Northeastern U.S. & Quebec* (Robert Reid Associates), Marge Lamy describes 37 hostelries and their trail systems. Her pleasant prose is complemented by excellent color photographs. *Gene Kilgore's Ranch Vacations* (John Muir Press) includes a substantial section on ranches with winter operations.

ALSO SEE Once you've learned to ski cross-country, it may be time to work on your downhill technique. The Ski Schools chapter of this book will help put you on the slopes. Or perhaps you'd rather skip the hills and speed things up on the flats: check out Snowmobiling. Or try tripping cross-country behind a pack of yipping huskies—look into Dogsledding.

Dogsledding

By Susan Farewell

Updated by Jeanne Ricci

Hike!" commands a musher as he releases a brake. They don't call it mushing for nothing. The word is from the French *moucher,* meaning "to go fast." And the dogs do. On command, a team of surprisingly small, amazingly strong huskies charge off, howling and yowling excitedly. Of all the wild sporting adventures out there, dogsledding may be the wildest—not only because it's exotic, but because you're literally out in the wilds with pack animals, just like a polar explorer.

Dogsledding, like most adventure sports, is not for everyone. For one thing, you have to like the cold. "How cold?" you ask. Let's just say sled dogs start to get uncomfortable when the temperature rises above zero. You also have to like roughing it. Even the nicest accommodations aren't far removed from camping out (here, luxury means a wood stove in your tent), and with camping out comes cooking out—any rib-sticking cuisine that can be cooked in a pot.

Most importantly, you have to like dogs—a lot. Out in the wilderness, with nothing but snow as far as the eye can see, it's you, a handful of other campers and guides, and a pack of 35- to 55-pound dogs. Contrary to the romantic image you may have of sled dogs, they're not all cuddly, clean Siberian huskies. They're often mutts (a little malamute, a little timber wolf, some Samoyed, German shepherd, you name it), not particularly clean, and, in some cases, downright smelly. Some outfitters maximize your contact with the dogs, having you help with everything from harnessing to feeding to untangling snarled sled lines, while others take care of everything for you. In any case, there's something very special about the experience of working with animals. One week with the same dozen or so dogs and you can't help but get attached.

Your trip will probably begin when you meet the other participants at a central location, often an airport. From there, you move on to the wilderness area you're going to traverse. The first day is usually reserved for general instruction on mushing—learning how to harness and unharness the dogs and getting a feel for the movement of the sled. Expertise is gained on the trail. Most outfitters take you out for a short run the first day to leave you eager to get started in earnest. Cross-country skiing and snowshoeing are combined with mushing on some trips, and some introduction to these sports is included in your orientation.

You'll be mushing through some of the country's most scenic landscapes—from the woods of Maine to the wilds of Minnesota—areas inhabited by birds and beasts most people see only on TV. And traveling by sled, there's nothing between you and

---

Freelance writer Susan Farewell first learned about dogsledding in Greenland, when she hitched a ride on one to the local airport. Jeanne Ricci is an adventurous travel writer currently living in California.

nature's handiwork. Most trips are structured with 2 to 3 hours of mushing in the morning and 3 to 4 hours after lunch.

Meals are always big and fortifying, with lots of carbohydrates to give you energy on the trail: You'll find everything from beef bourguignon to spaghetti. The level of service—from the amount of work done by the guides to the sophistication of the meals—varies with each outfitter.

The distance covered each day is usually between 15 and 35 miles, depending on the stamina of the group and the trail and weather conditions (heavy snow can slow things down). This may sound arduous, but the dogs do most of the work, and the clean crisp air rushing past you makes 7 or 8 miles an hour feel like flying.

Driving a team of dogs is an experience all ages can enjoy, although some outfitters do set a minimum age. All sorts of individuals are attracted to the sport, including singles, married couples, and families with older children. If you want to sample the experience without committing a whole vacation to it, look into the handful of winter resort areas where you can go out for a shorter outing. The following trips are at least 5 days, although some of the outfitters offer shorter and longer trips as well.

CHOOSING THE RIGHT TRIP

To choose the right trip, be sure to ask the following questions.

Will I be driving my own team of dogs? If you're not interested in skiing or snowshoeing, make sure you pick an outfitter who gives each member of the party a sled. You may need to consider your level of physical fitness if you're going to be cross-country skiing.

What kind of accommodations are provided? Accommodations on dogsledding trips generally aren't luxurious, but they can vary from tarps spread out in the open to heated cabins. Don't count on privacy.

What is the food like? Expect hearty meals from every outfitter, but ask for more specifics. Some outfitters offer a catered vacation, with each meal prepared by a staff member; others expect participants to plan, prepare, and clean up communally.

How many miles are covered each day? Get a good idea of how strenuous each outfitter's pace is.

What will my responsibilities be on the trip? If you're expecting a relaxing vacation, make sure you don't pick an outfitter who'll have you doing everything from hitching up the dogs to pitching the tents.

What's the cost and what's included? The prices of trips we list include accommodations, meals, and all major equipment—sleds, tents, and cookware. For these trips, sleeping bags and pads are also provided, but on some trips you will need to bring your own. Some outfitters also provide insulated jackets and other cold-weather wear that you might not own.

How long has the company been in business? Generally, a company with several years experience has learned how to deal with all kinds of problems.

Do you have references from past mushers? If you have questions about what the experience is like, there's no substitute for a chat with someone who has been on the trip and dealt with the outfitter.

How far in advance do I need to book? It's often necessary to reserve a spot on a dogsledding trip at least 3 months in advance—but there could be room for you on a trip that leaves tomorrow.

FAVORITE TRIPS

THE NORTHEAST

MAINE **Touring the Northern Woods.** The northern woods of Maine, home to the Mahoosuc Guide Service, is an area of unmatched wild beauty, featuring the state's highest peak (Mt. Katahdin), biggest state park (Baxter), and largest lake (Moosehead). Year-round residents include black bears, moose, bobcats, and flocks of birds. If you've ever wanted to climb into one of those snowy paperweights, this is for you.

Your 5-day trip through Rapid River country begins at Mahoosuc's headquarters in tiny Newry, just north of Bethel. The night before you set out, maps and routes are discussed; gear, including boots, parkas, and backpacks, is issued; and a video is shown providing instruction on everything from how to harness and handle the dogs to how to set up a winter camp. You spend the first night in a bed-and-breakfast and then rise early for the 45-minute drive to Richardson Lake, where your journey begins.

Mahoosuc's groups are intimate (8 to 10 people), and each party is accompanied by 2 or 3 guides. There are enough sleds on each trip to accommodate everyone, with 2 mushers per sled. You take turns driving, and sometimes you have to run alongside your sled. There's time for cross-country skiing and snowshoeing at the end of the day and on the one rest day.

Most gear is piled on a sled, but you have to carry a light pack containing your sleeping bag, pad, and clothes. You sled along Richardson Lake and Rapid River onto the frozen Umbagog Lake, taking in a landscape filled with spruce and fir trees, streams and lakes, and a menagerie of wildlife.

Campers take part in preparing meals; you might be asked to chop a hole in the ice for water or gather wood for a fire. Mahoosuc specializes in vegetarian dishes; one favorite, called Rubaboo, is a traditional Maine logger's stew, dense with split peas and barley. Home-baked desserts, such as chocolate-chip and oatmeal cookies, elicit "oohs" and "aahs" from campers at the end of each meal. At night, you retire to your sleeping bag in a canvas tent heated by a wood stove. The dogs sleep outside, under the stars, periodically howling in unison, snouts pointed to the sky.

Mahoosuc Guide Service is owned and operated by Polly Mahoney and Kevin Slater, committed outdoorspeople, former Outward Bound leaders, and state-registered Maine Guides. They offer sledding trips in Maine, New Hampshire, and Canada that range from day trips to 2-week expeditions. Most equipment (including the ashwood dog sleds) is handmade, using techniques developed by Native Americans; some of the trips are conducted by Native American guides. Many of the dogs were raised in Alaska, and several are veterans of the 1,049-mile, Anchorage-to-Nome Iditarod sled race.

All equipment is provided, including camping gear, parkas, snowshoes, extra-warm boots, and skis with special bindings to accommodate those boots; serious Nordic skiers may want to bring their own equipment. *Mahoosuc Guide Service, Bear River Rd., Newry, ME 04261, tel. 207/824–2073. Dec.–May: 5 days, $700. Book at least 3 months in advance.*

THE MIDWEST

MINNESOTA **Following the Voyageur's Highway.** One week with Boundary Country Trekking in Minnesota's Boundary Waters Canoe Area and you'll be thinking about buying yourself a team of huskies and a sled. Arleigh Jorgenson, one of North America's leading mushers and racers, heads up this dogsledding program, and you'll be driving your own team. His unflagging enthusiasm and knowledge of dogsledding make this trip especially worthwhile.

This 5-day trip begins in Ely, Minnesota, with an evening orientation session, when you watch a video filmed from a sled so that you get an excellent feel for movement on the trail. The first day is spent getting familiar with the dogs and sleds. After you learn the basics of harnessing the team, using the brakes, turning the sleds, and understanding the dogs, it's time for a short ride. For your first run you use a small team (3 or 4 dogs) that you are able to physically reign in if you have problems commanding them. By the end of the trip you'll be able to handle a full team of 7 or 8.

The first 2 nights are spent in modern cabins with indoor plumbing. Then you begin exploring the historic Voyageur's Highway on the border of the United States and Canada. The Highway, a series of lakes connected by portages, was used for centuries by Native Americans who traveled between lakes to trade and hunt. In winter the frozen lakes are prime dogsled terrain.

Each day, you and as many as 7 other mushers and a guide spend an average of 6 hours on the trail, covering between 20 and 40 miles a day. Much of the time, you ride on the runners of the sleds, which requires good balance and a workout for muscles you may not generally use. In some areas, you have to run alongside and guide the sleds: While it's usually pretty smooth going over the frozen lakes, some of the portages can get a little rough. You stop often to give the dogs time to catch their breath or for some advice from your guide on upcoming terrain.

At the end of the day you settle in camps set up in advance by the Boundary Country staff. Sleeping quarters are basic tents and cabins that accommodate 2 to 4, and yurts— canvas structures that look like huge marshmallows with a plexiglass skylight on top. All accommodations are furnished with mattresses, tables, chairs, and wood stoves; yurts also have gas lights. Meals on the trail are high in carbohydrates and protein; the staff outdoes themselves to concoct palatable entrées such as grilled rainbow trout, beef bourguignon, and shish kebabs.

Other Boundary Country destinations include the Gunflint Trail on the north shore of Lake Superior and the wilds of the Canadian Arctic. Trips range from 2 days to 2 weeks in length. Boundary Country provides everything but personal clothing. *Boundary Country Trekking, 590 Gunflint Trail, Grand Marais, MN 55604, tel. 218/388–4487 or 800/322–8327. Mid-Nov.–late-Apr.: 5 days/6 nights, $1,385. Sign up 2 months in advance.*

MINNESOTA **Outward Bound in the Boundary Waters Canoe Area.** The intensely scenic Boundary Waters Canoe Area, 2 million acres of forests scattered with more than 100 lakes, is the setting for a dogsledding and cross-country skiing expedition sponsored by Outward Bound, known for its wilderness education program. The course, which takes place in December or January, is not only a physically challenging adventure but also an inspiring emotional experience: Meeting the challenges of the wilderness and working together with others results in personal growth.

The group assembles in Duluth, Minnesota, then moves on to the base camp in Ely for an orientation. A "sleeping warm" seminar on the first afternoon teaches you to use insulated sleeping bags and pads to conserve body heat and survive Minnesota's bitterly cold nights, a lesson you quickly put to good use. The 3 instruction sessions on the second day have you out cross-country skiing, running sled dogs, and performing ice rescues: The trip traverses frozen lakes and rivers, and it's important to be prepared for emergencies. How much time you spend in Ely depends on the group: With Outward Bound, you never move faster than the slowest person. Once everyone is ready, you head for the woods and spend the next 6 days alternately mushing and cross-country skiing across frozen lakes and portages, 3 to 15 miles a day.

On the trail, you begin every day with breakfast at 6 and stop for snacks every couple of hours—but never for long, since your body temperature drops when you stop moving. When skiing, you travel ahead of the sleds, learning to navigate the trails, reading the safety of the ice, and breaking trail for the dogs. At 3 or 4, you stop and set up camp for the night. You cook meals communally over an open fire: The fare is usually simple but filling dishes such as spaghetti, macaroni and cheese, chili, or vegetarian casseroles. You sleep under a tarp on one of the frozen lakes.

Outward Bound provides everything but personal clothing, though a parka and wind jacket can be supplied on request. Participants are encouraged to go on the trip individually, rather than with a friend or relative, as group dynamics are a big part of the experience. You must also be open to new experiences and in good physical condition; a medical exam within the year is required. Minimum age is 16, and most participants are in their 20s and 30s. *Voyageur Outward Bound School, 10900 Cedar Lake Rd., Minnetonka, MN 55305, tel. 612/542–9448 or 800/ 328–2943. Dec.–Jan.: 8 days, $970. Sign up 2 months in advance.*

ALASKA

NORTHWEST **Exploring the Gates of the Arctic National Park.** Sourdough Outfitters will take you mushing through this park, which, with 8,300,000 acres above the Arctic Circle, is one of the last great wilderness areas in the world. Within its boundaries, the 600-mile-long Brooks Range weaves between glassy rivers and scattered lakes. The area teems with wildlife, including the caribou, black bears, Dall sheep, moose, wolves, wolverines, lynx, grizzlies, eagles, falcons, and many migratory birds.

This company offers several 6- and 8-day sledding trips here between January and mid-April. This is one of the most beautiful times of year in Alaska; the days are 14 or 15 hours long and the Northern Lights dance at night. Daytime temperatures generally are in the teens or twenties, although it can drop well below zero at night.

Your trip begins with a day of orientation in Bettles, where you learn the history of dogsledding and get familiar with equipment: how to set the brake, tie the reins, load the sled, and keep the runners clean of ice. Then it's time to get to know your dogs. Going beyond harnessing them and giving commands, you learn to perceive the pecking order of each team—which dog is the leader and which are the followers. On a short ride around Bettles, your team follows the guide's lead team, allowing you to get a feel for driving. (By the end of the trip you'll take a turn as the leader.) Upon your return, you get a lesson in unharnessing and feeding the teams.

In the morning you're off and running, driving your team over 15 to 30 miles (in 4 to 8 hours) of trail a day, stopping periodically for photo opportunities or to give the dogs a rest. At day's end, you help set up the tent camp, gather firewood, melt snow for water, and unharness, feed, and care for the dogs. Nights are spent in large, army-style canvas tents that sleep 3 or 4 and are heated with wood-burning stoves. Meals are lasagna, meat loaf, stews, chili, and spaghetti with Italian sausage.

Sourdough provides all camping gear plus special boots, heavy-hooded parkas, insulated wind-proof mittens, and snowshoes. *Sourdough Outfitters, American Wilderness Experience, Inc., Box 1486, Boulder, CO 80306, tel. 303/444–2622 or 800/444–0099, fax 303/ 444–3999. Jan..–Apr.: 8 days, $1,980; 6 days, $1,660. Sign up 3 months in advance.*

SOURCES

ORGANIZATIONS The **International Sled Dog Racing Association** (Box 446, Nordman, ID 83848, tel. 208/443–3153) provides information on races and other dogsled activities and publishes a magazine called *Info* ten times a year. Membership is $20 a year.

PERIODICALS *Mushing* is a bimonthly magazine that covers all aspects of dogsledding, including how-to information and articles on health and ethics (Stellar Communications, Box 149, Ester, AK 99725, tel. 907/ 479–0454).

BOOKS *Cold Nights, Fast Trails*, by Dave Olesen; *Dog Driver: A Guide for the Serious Musher*, by Mike and Julie Collins; *The Joy of Running Sled Dogs: A Step-by-Step Guide to Training and Enjoying Sled Dogs*, by Noel Flanders; and *Travelers of the Cold: Sled Dogs of the Far North*, by Dominique Cellura provide detailed information on the how-tos and experience of dogsledding.

ALSO SEE If you think you need some survival coaching before you tackle winter camping, turn to the Wilderness and Survival Schools chapter.

Fishing Camps and Fly-Fishing Schools

By Bud Journey

Updated by W. Lynn Seldon Jr.

he reason for all the fly-fishing schools scattered around the country is simple: It is not easy to cast a bulky line, a flimsy leader, and a feather-light fly between trees, against the wind, away from the back of your neck, and into position just in front of a fish's nose. The fly must land without frightening the fish and must look natural, or the fish will see it for what it is: a deceitful attempt by an antagonist to entice it into ingesting a bundle of feathers, fraught with peril, containing no food value at all.

Therein lies the allure of fly-fishing: It's a challenge that's rewarding when you succeed and that teaches you humility when you fail. Spin-casting, trolling, and bait-fishing have a similar attraction, and the type of angling you choose has nothing to do with a right method or a wrong method. It has more to do with personal preference and what's available.

If you'd like to spend a week's vacation learning to fish, a fishing school can teach you the rudiments, supply the equipment, and see that you get a chance to practice your newly developed skills on nearby streams or ponds—for a price. A 2-day course can run from $95 to $500. If you're a seasoned angler, you can sign up for an advanced class, or choose one of the camps, charter boats, or guide services.

Fishing schools and fishing camps are not always discrete entities; in fact, their elements often overlap. The operators of most fishing schools also usually offer guide service for a day's fishing or can recommend local guides, who will show you where, when, and how to fish specific bodies of water. On the other hand, although most fishing camps don't offer formal instruction, their guides are usually willing and quite able to provide what brief, on-the-spot tips the novice or intermediate fisherman will need during the trip. Though you can fish by yourself, the guides know all about the local waters and the best ways to extract their inhabitants; sometimes they even provide equipment. They charge hefty sums per day ($75–$350) for their expertise, but many anglers feel they are worth it.

Camps often house and feed you, but usually do not supply equipment; most anglers prefer to use their own. It is common for fishing schools to furnish all or most of the necessary gear while you're in class, and they frequently provide lunch, but for other meals and lodging you're usually on your own—though the operators will help you make arrangements. Guide services and charter boats, which usually charge by the day, can put together a 5-day or week-long package for a vacation, but you often have to forage for nearby food and lodging.

Bud Journey, who lives in Montana, has won outdoors-writing and photography contests and claims to have caught a 10-lb. 9-oz. walleye. Freelance travel writer and photographer Lynn Seldon has fished rivers throughout the United States.

Almost all fishing camps are independently run, as are most fishing schools, although some are set up in conjunction with a manufacturer or a merchant such as Orvis or L.L. Bean. Bigger is not necessarily better, nor is the instruction superior or more personalized. It makes more sense to book a school in an area you want to visit than to go out of your way to attend a school with a big-name sponsor.

If you're working on a limited budget, it might be best to forget the school altogether and look for a fishing camp that can provide a few minutes of instruction before you go out onto the water. Some camps cost less than $100 per day. Be forewarned, however, that if you're fly-fishing, those few minutes of instruction are not likely to make you more than barely competent. If it's what you can afford, though, go for it; a crash course in the fishing camp may be enough.

No matter what method of fishing you prefer, and whether you're at a school or camp, you soon become familiar with the concept of catch-and-release. Because the populations of some species have been diminished by over-fishing, short growing seasons, low reproduction, loss of habitat, and other factors, most schools and camps encourage the practice of carefully releasing uninjured or slightly injured fish. At some, this practice is mandatory.

Although fly-fishing skills are generally considered the hardest to master, you must know a few basics for any kind of fishing. Consider the following: You must (1) get a lure in front of a fish and (2) entice that fish to take the lure into its mouth. The fish will do so because: (1) it wants to eat the lure or (2) it wants to attack the lure. Sometimes both.

A fly fisherman almost always tries to simulate food for the fish. A bait fisherman actually offers the fish real food. Anglers who cast artificial lures (cast-and-retrieve) or who troll, slowly dragging a lure behind a boat, are trying to imitate food or provoke an attack. It's the same with jiggers, who sit over their quarry in a boat or on a bank and bounce their lures up and down, and also with little children who fish with safety pins on the end of a string. Their varying degrees of success depend on their skill and on the willingness of the fish to take the lure. As all anglers learn, the disposition of the fish can be affected by weather, barometric pressure, water temperature, pH factor, fishing pressure (the number of people fishing a particular area), the food supply, and just plain cussedness.

For some, the allure of fishing is in the challenge. Making a perfect cast into a tiny pocket of open water, amid weeds, willows, and overhanging limbs; fooling a wily game fish into striking; then deftly guiding it to the net through an underwater labyrinth of weeds, roots, and rocks is the ultimate satisfaction. For me, however, fishing is renewal. It recharges me after the pressures of the modern world have sucked the vigor from me. Sometimes I catch fish; sometimes I don't. But it's not the catching that counts, it's the process: a renaissance that only a fisherman knows. You'll have to try it to understand. And with apologies to the anonymous person who first said it, I would like to remind you that if you're too busy to go fishing, you're too busy.

CHOOSING THE RIGHT OUTFIT

No matter how well you check a school or a camp out, it may not meet your expectations. You can minimize that possibility, however, by asking the right questions.

On which species do you focus? Different fish inhabit different parts of the country, and anglers have their preferred species. If you want trout, you might go to the Rockies; for bass, try the South. Northern pike lurk in Minnesota lakes and in much of the West and Midwest; salmon stay on the coasts.

What method do you teach? Ask schools whether they teach just fly-fishing or can also instruct you in other methods, such as jigging, spin-casting, and trolling. Remember that learning a method of fishing is just the beginning. A school can give you a glimmering of these skills, but you must go fishing again and again to refine them. A school can teach you to read water—to recognize the kinds of places fish like to stay and feed—but only by hunting a species time after time do you discover its ways and habits.

Do you provide actual on-site fishing opportunities for real fish in natural conditions? That's a question that's essential to ask any fishing school you're considering. Casting and fishing on a stocked or sterile pond is a far cry from fishing in the wild for wild fish on a swiftly moving stream, surrounded by vegetation and other obstructions.

What's the cost and what's included? Unless otherwise noted, the cost of camps includes food and lodging but not guiding; schools' prices include instruction only; and guide services provide guiding only. All prices are per person unless otherwise noted.

Tackle is provided at schools unless otherwise noted, but not usually for the time you spend fishing on your own after completing the school. Camps and guides seldom provide tackle, but may be able to lend or rent it to you. Boats may or may not cost extra.

When accommodations are not provided, most outfits can steer you to a variety of lodging in a range of prices. The cost of your fishing license is almost always extra.

How do I get there? Some fishing camps are very remote, and getting there can be pricey and time-consuming. Some operators have shuttles; in remote areas you'll often be transported by river boat, airplane, float plane, horseback, and the like. Sometimes the cost is extra, sometimes it is included in the rate.

What are accommodations like? The best surprise is no surprise, so be sure you know what you're paying for. If you're staying at a fishing camp, ask what the guest quarters and public spaces are like; they could be stylishly rustic and sturdy or they could be cheap motel rooms with paper-thin walls. If you're camping, find out about the campsites and the shower and latrine arrange-

ments. Before you sign up to use the outfitter's tents or sleeping bags, make sure they are suited to the location.

What's the food like? Although ambitious cuisine is unusual, plain American fare, which you are most apt to find, can seem extraordinarily tasty when your appetite is sharpened by a day in the fresh air. Still, some outfitters and camps do better in the kitchen than others. If what you eat matters to you, make sure you know what to expect.

Is a guide available? What is the fee? How many guests per guide? Guides' fees can often be split by as many as 3 people, although with fly-fishing, 2 anglers per guide is the most you want.

What equipment is required? What else will I need? Make sure your equipment matches the requirements of the camp or school you are considering. For fly-fishing in streams you probably need waders, which are not always provided, although in hot weather in some waters, you can wade in sneakers and shorts or jeans.

In a fly-fishing camp, are fly-tying facilities available? You might want to try to "match the hatch" of insects that are emerging while you are there.

What is the weather like? Is it buggy? The weather can range from snowstorms in the Rockies in June, though they're rare, to hot and humid in Florida, which is usual. Mosquitoes are always around in woods and swamps, but some seasons are worse than others.

What is there for nonfishing companions to do? Many schools and camps are near cities large enough to have the usual complement of amusements; at schools in the wilderness, you'll have to be content with such rural pursuits as hiking, bird-watching, identifying wildflowers, and other nature studies. There's often riding, swimming, and exploring ghost towns or historic sites.

How long have you been in business? Can you provide references? Longevity should not necessarily be the deciding factor. Everybody has to start sometime, so if other things are favorable, don't let the operator's lack of experience discourage you. It's best to get a word-of-mouth recommendation from an independent source, but if none is available, calling people on a list provided by the operator is better than nothing. Chances are that if the anglers you call are satisfied, you will be too.

How far in advance must I book? You can ordinarily sign up anywhere from a month in advance to a year ahead. The more famous and the more remote locations tend to fill up faster. If you have your heart set on a specific location or program, however, give a call and you may snag a cancellation.

MAJOR PLAYER

ORVIS This long-established Vermont fishing-tackle manufacturer sponsors mid-priced fly-fishing schools in Vermont, Wyoming, New York, Virginia, Massachusetts, Pennsylvania, and California. Most of the courses are shorter than 5 days, but virtually all Orvis schools can help you round out a week's vacation by arranging guided or unguided fishing trips for the remainder of your time. The schools provide Orvis equipment and all follow the same formula for successfully teaching all levels of angler—as individuals or in groups—how to hook, land, and release a fish. The courses are often booked by companies as corporate entertainment for clients or executives, and classes are noncompetitive; each student progresses at his or her own pace. Orvis publishes a newsletter and a pamphlet describing the various schools (Historic Rte. 7A, Manchester, VT 05254, tel. 800/235–9763, fax 802/362–3525).

FAVORITE TRIPS

THE NORTHEAST

MAINE **Colonial Sportsman's Lodge.** Variety, economy, and home cooking set this fishing lodge apart. Owner-operator Pat Takach believes her camp in rural northeastern Maine is unique: Here, guests can fish for land-locked salmon from the front yard on the bank of Grand Lake Stream. Pat also cooks and serves the meals, in which she takes great pride. Guests can take a full American plan and eat at the lodge or choose basic housekeeping cabins. There are cooking facilities in 5 of the 6 cabins.

Besides land-locked salmon, you can fish for lake trout, smallmouth bass, brook trout, white perch, and several varieties of panfish, including crappie. But you must bring your own equipment; rentals are not available. You can fish from the bank or rent a boat for $35 per day. The fishing guides charge $125 per day for 2 people and use locally manufactured 20-foot-long Grand Lake canoes to get to the best fishing waters. Fly-fishing is a major activity at this site, but you can cast lures, troll, and bait-fish, if you prefer. Catch-and-release fishing is encouraged but not required. Free-time activities include swimming and tennis. *Colonial Sportsman's Lodge, Grand Lake Stream, ME 04637, tel. 207/796–2655. May–Sept.: 5 days, $125 housekeeping units; $425 with meals. Sign up 2 months in advance.*

NEW YORK **Tightlines Charters.** Nobody knows trolling with downriggers better than John Oravec. He fishes for species that spend their time suspended between the surface and the bottom. A 10- to 12-pound lead ball tied to his line keeps the bait at the proper depth, and the line releases when the fish takes the lure. Oravec is a full-time charter captain who fishes for king salmon, steelhead trout, brown trout, lake trout, coho salmon, and Atlantic salmon in the western basin of Lake Ontario. Oravec also writes articles and conducts seminars for fishing enthusiasts, so instruction is one of his fortes. He provides hands-on learning for his fishing clients, both beginners and experienced anglers, but does not house or feed them.

The intriguing aspect of Oravec's operations is that he also goes for muskies and walleyes in the St. Lawrence and Niagara rivers with downriggers, which is a departure from the traditional methods. People usually cast-and-retrieve for muskies, and go jigging, bait-fishing, and trolling without downriggers for walleyes. There's also fly-fishing in local streams and the Niagara River for brown trout, king salmon, and steelhead, and Oravec will set up a variety package or "safari" for you, using all these different methods for different species in different waters. He uses a state-of-the-art, 33-foot charter boat for his downrigger fishing, as well as smaller boats for shallower waters, and provides all the necessary equipment for up to 6 guests. Children fish free.

Oravec's base of operations is Point Breeze, in the Lake Plain region of upstate New York, which is an apple-growing area between the Finger Lakes and Niagara Falls. Local lodging runs from pricey waterfront motels to budget bed-and-breakfasts, and meals range from fast food to fine dining on the water. Free-time activities include swimming, jet-skiing, golf, camping, and shopping. *Tight-lines Charters, 913 Sunset Beach Rd., Waterport, NY 14571, tel. 800/443–2510, fax 716/682–3037. Mid-Apr.–mid-Sept.: 5 days, $625 per person with small boat (2 person min.), $500 with large boat (4 person min.). Price includes equipment but not food and lodging; sign up 3–6 months in advance.*

NEW YORK **Beaverkill Valley Inn.** This family-oriented inn sits in an undeveloped area of Catskill State Park, within a stone's throw of the Beaverkill and near other classic trout streams, surrounded by eastern hardwoods and flowering shrubs. Whitetail deer, foxes, bears, coyotes, and other animals also live in the area.

The Victorian lodge, built in 1895 and now renovated, has 20 rooms, 12 with private bath. It has an indoor swimming pool, a self-serve ice-cream parlor, children's playroom, and 2 private tennis courts, along with a casting pond stocked with trout. Breakfast and lunch are buffets, and dinner has a set menu. You might have corn chowder, loin lambchops, fresh vegetables, bread baked on the premises, and black-and-white chocolate mousse. Guests hike and mountain-bike

on 25 kilometers of maintained trails, and photography is also popular.

You fish free in the casting pond, on a private 1-mile stretch of the Beaverkill or in numerous other public waters in the vicinity. The inn contracts with several local fishing guides, whose fees vary from $75 to $200 per day. The famous Wulff School of Fly-fishing, which offers top-quality 2-day schools, is less than a mile away. *Beaverkill Valley Inn, Lew Beach, NY 12753, tel. 914/ 439–4851, fax 914/439–3884. Apr.–Sept.: 5 days, $825 ($700 shared bath). Sign up a month in advance.*

VERMONT **Orvis Fly-Fishing School.** The Orvis Company's main school is in Manchester, the site of its fly rod factory and executive offices. This is a scenic, rural region of southern Vermont, between the Green and the Taconic mountains. Continuity and longevity are two of the school's hallmarks: It has been around for nearly 30 years, and Rick Rishell has been at the helm since 1978. Much of its business comes from word-of-mouth recommendations.

You can take either of the two sessions that are given each week: Friday, Saturday, and half of Sunday; or Tuesday, Wednesday, and half of Thursday. A parent-child program runs for two weekends in April. The focus is on casting, fly selection and entomology, knots, equipment, and reading water. And casting for trout in Orvis's stocked ponds gives you a chance to put your skills to work on real fish. The school handles classes of up to 36 students and keeps the student to instructor ratios at reasonable levels for the various aspects of the course—3:1 or 4:1 on the casting ponds; 18:1 for fly-selection lectures; and about 8:1 for knot-tying seminars. If you're interested, also ask about their women-only sessions.

After completing the course, students fill out their vacations by fishing sections of the Battenkill through Orvis-owned access points. The school can also lend you equipment and provide guides, if you want. The area is oriented toward tourism, and besides fishing, you can play golf or tennis, go shopping, visit museums and antiques shops, and go to summer theater.

Orvis can arrange lodging at the plush Equinox Hotel or at other local hotels and B&Bs. *Orvis Fly-Fishing School, Box 798, Manchester, VT 05254, tel. 800/235–9763, fax 802/362–3525. Early Apr.–late Aug.: 5 days, $395. Sign up 2 months in advance.*

VERMONT **Streamline Fly-Fishing School and Guide Service.** Peter Cammann is so into fly-fishing that he runs a fly-fishing school, guides, sells equipment, and broadcasts and writes about fly-fishing as well. In keeping with the technical aspects of the sport, he limits his classes to a maximum of 2 people per instructor. His young but experienced crew (some have appeared on ESPN fly-fishing shows) believes in hands-on instruction in a real setting, so you learn on an actual stream, where such variables as wind, changing currents, and streamside vegetation complicate the mechanics of convincingly getting a fly in front of a fish. Fees for classes include lunch and a handbook, *Fly Fishing for Trout,* and all equipment except waders during the course.

A good 5-day vacation is to take 2 days of fly-fishing instruction with Cammann or one of his instructors, then go on day-trips, armed with a copy of his *Fishing Vermont's Streams and Lakes,* to try out your new fishing skills on one of the many nearby bodies of trout water. Cammann can put you in touch with a local canoe-rental service and he can supply you with an experienced guide. The staff can also help you arrange accommodations: The varied local lodging ranges from B&Bs to motels and condos, and the dining runs toward fine restaurants, with a few pizza places thrown in.

The school is in the rural, forested Mad River Valley of northern Vermont, where a convenient mixture of 6 first-class trout streams, numerous tennis courts, a famous golf course, horseback riding, hiking, canoeing, and other sports can make a lively vacation. *Streamline Fly-Fishing School, Box 1218, Waitsfield, VT 05673, tel. 802/496–5463, fax 802/496–5463. Early Apr.–late*

Oct.: 5 days, $425. Price includes lunch; sign up 1–2 weeks in advance.

THE MID-ATLANTIC

PENNSYLVANIA **Fishing Creek Outfitters.** In the foothills of the Endless Mountains of northeastern Pennsylvania, Allen and Iris Johnson offer one-day fly-fishing schools at two levels, and a guide service for trout fishing along Fishing Creek. The basic school for beginners is made up of 6 students and 2 instructors; the next level is a custom-tailored course with 1 or 2 advanced students per instructor.

The basic class focuses on fly-casting technique, with additional instruction on the bugs fish eat and the whys and hows of equipment. The first 2 casting sessions take place on a spacious grassy area where instruction can go on with a minimum of extraneous complications, but the third round is under real fishing conditions: on the creek. The casting sessions are punctuated with classroom instruction, and equipment is provided. The advanced class concentrates on any of the myriad aspects of fly-fishing that the student chooses: casting technique, reading the water, fly selection, appropriate equipment, or any other.

Combining a class with 4 days of guided fishing ($150 per day, $225 for 2) on private stretches of several area streams makes a nice vacation. The Johnsons can recommend local motels and B&Bs. *Fishing Creek Outfitters, RD 1 Box 310–1, Benton, PA 17814, tel. 717/925–2225, fax 717/925–5644. May–June and Oct: 5 days, $750. Price includes lunch; sign up 3–4 months in advance.*

VIRGINIA **Orvis Roanoke.** Robert Bryant runs his operation on 800 acres of mountainous private land with 2 casting ponds fed by springs. Guests spend 2 days in fly-fishing school and 3 days (or as many as they wish) on guided trips on the Smith and Jackson rivers, fishing for rainbow trout, brown trout, and smallmouth bass. Both the Jackson and the Smith are tailwater streams: They're below dams, which makes for the good, cold water the fish need. The Jackson runs through mountainous terrain, and the Smith flows in the Piedmont area. Your guide will arrange transportation.

The school covers casting mechanics, proper equipment, knots, entomology, reading water, and the other basics of fly-fishing. The instructors, led by Lou Barlow, all have 5 years or more experience, and the student-to-teacher ratio is 4:1. The school can take a maximum of 13 students, preferably older than 12, though younger children who can handle a full day of fishing are accepted. Equipment is provided.

The guide service (catch-and-release fishing only) provides float-fishing for bass and wading for bass and trout, with no more than 2 anglers per guide and equipment provided, though you're welcome to bring your own ($150 per day, $225 for 2).

Bryant can help you find lodging and meals; there is a wide variety of each in the Roanoke area. *Orvis Roanoke, 19 Campbell Ave., Roanoke, VA 24011, tel. 703/345–3635. Late Mar.–early Sept.: 5 days, $750. Price includes lunch and guide service; sign up 1 month in advance.*

VIRGINIA **Murray's Fly Shop.** Harry Murray, author of numerous magazine articles and the books *Fly Fishing for Smallmouth Bass* and *Trout Fishing in the Shenandoah National Park,* runs his fly shop and on-the-stream schools from his base on the scenic Shenandoah River in Edinburg, Virginia. He offers 2-day schools, up to 5 days of personal instruction, and guided trips. Murray runs approximately 20 schools a year and restricts class size to 10 so he can personally instruct his students. The smallmouth bass schools are held on either the North or South Fork of the Shenandoah River; he covers casting, selecting tackle, leader demands and techniques for fishing nymphs, streamers, and surface bugs. The Mountain Trout Schools are held on the Rapidan River and cover casting, entomology, reading the water, proper fly selection, and how to fish drys, nymphs, and streamers for trout in freestone streams.

Because Murray runs a fly shop, students can try free a broad assortment. Those who aren't part of the schools may rent any amount of equipment for $30 per day.

For local lodging, you have several B&Bs and motels to choose from. Personal instruction and/or guide fees are $150 per day for the first person, $50 per person for up to 3 extra people. *Murray's Fly Shop, Box 156, Edinburg, VA 22824, tel. 540/984–4212, fax 800/984–4895. Mar–Oct. 2-day school: $275; does not include food or lodging.*

WEST VIRGINIA **Cheat Mountain Outfitting and Guide Service.** This new outfitter is in the heart of the 900,000-acre Monongahela National Forest, atop Cheat Mountain and along the Shavers Fork River, a well-known trout stream. Championship fisherman Treve Painter heads the outfitting service and offers instruction on casting techniques, equipment use, knots, and other basics of fishing. His outfit can take you on 1-, 3-, and 5-day guided trips, fly fishing or spinning on some of West Virginia's famous blue ribbon trout streams for rainbow, brown, and brook trout; or they can steer you to the nearby Greenbrier and Tygart Valley Rivers, which are top-rated producers of trophy smallmouth bass.

Lodging is available at the historic Cheat Mountain Club, just a quarter mile away, or at one of the many B&Bs or motels in the area. *Cheat Mountain Outfitting & Guide Service, Inc., Box 217 (at Cheat Bridge), Durbin, WV 26264, tel. 304/456–4023, fax 304/456–4073. Apr.–Oct. 5 days: $600. Price includes shuttle to fishing sites and lunches; accommodations are additional.*

THE SOUTH

FLORIDA **Gypsy Guide Service/Suncast Fly-Fishing College.** Captain Pete Greenan uses fly-fishing equipment and other light tackle to fish for tarpon, snook, redfish, sea trout, and a few other species in the Charlotte Harbor area of southwest Florida. He concentrates on the mild backwaters for most of the action but will venture farther out for the hard-fighting tarpon. His busiest time is in winter, but the fishing is better in the spring and fall—even in the summer, if you can put up with the heat and humidity.

Captain Greenan finds that even experienced anglers are often unprepared for the special requirements of saltwater fly-fishing. He is willing to help with on-the-spot instruction, but too much of it cuts into the fishing time; consequently, he now runs a 3-day school in October and April to properly prepare his saltwater clients, and combines it with 2 days of guided fishing. Greenan normally takes out only 2 fly-fishermen or 3 spincasters at a time, but he can accommodate larger groups with the assistance of another guide. The fee per day is $350 for up to 3 people, and all equipment is provided. Children are welcome if they are truly interested in fishing.

The setting is typical of southwest Florida, with white sand beaches and mangrove islands where eagles, ospreys, and other wildlife are often in evidence. Free-time activities include swimming, bicycling, and sightseeing in and around Sarasota. There's a wide assortment of lodging and dining options, and Greenan can put you in contact with an affordable motel or make reservations for you. *Gypsy Guide Service/Suncast Fly-Fishing College, 2416 Parson Lane, Sarasota, FL 34239, tel. 813/ 923–6095. Oct. and Apr.: 5 days, $1,195. Price includes lunch; sign up 1–2 months in advance.*

TENNESSEE **McClintock's Guide Service.** Fred McClintock has set up his low-key, one-man operation to accommodate 1 or 2 serious adult anglers who are up for long, hard days of fishing primarily for trophy fish. He uses a 20-foot bass boat to go after smallmouth bass, walleyes, and rainbow trout in Dale Hollow Lake and striped bass in the Cumberland River—both in north central Tennessee, in a rural mountainous region of mostly hardwood forest, with some cedar and poplars.

A typical day would run 8 to 12 hours on the water, casting lures and trolling, so free time is limited. Most guests simply relax when they're not fishing, but country music fans might make a beeline for Nashville, 100 miles southwest.

Most guests bring their own fishing equipment, but loaners are available if necessary. There's a wide variety of lodging, from modest motels to expensive houseboats, and you eat at small, family restaurants or fast-food places. When you're fishing on the lake, you can buy lunch at an island restaurant, but a bag lunch is needed for the river. *McClintock's Guide Service, 6422 Livington Hwy., Celina, TN 38551, tel. 615/243–2142. Year-round: 5 days, $1,000 (1 or 2 people). Sign up 3 months in advance.*

THE MIDWEST

SOUTH DAKOTA **Custom Caster.** Larry and Jan Weeks arrange guided fishing trips in the Black Hills region of western South Dakota for people who want to catch rainbow trout, brown trout, brook trout, northern pike, smallmouth and largemouth bass, crappies, bluegills, and perch.

The method of fishing is your choice: fly-fishing, casting, and bait-fishing are all available. If you need help with your technique, Larry and Jan can provide impromptu instruction for $20 per hour. That won't get you on the professional fishing tour, but it will acquaint you with the basics of fishing in western South Dakota. The Weekses have enough guides at their disposal to accommodate 12 anglers in the summer and 6 in the winter. The angler-to-guide ratio is 2:1, and the guides use canoes, float tubes (an inner tube with a suspended seat), and wading to exploit the wide variety of fishing waters in the region. If you don't have your own fishing equipment, rentals are available. Kids 10 and over are welcome, provided they are avid anglers and don't need supervision; those under 13 fish free.

The Black Hills are actually fair-sized mountains, covered with pine and aspen forests and drained by many streams, including spring creeks. Free-time activities include hiking, mountain biking, swimming, and golf. If you want bright lights, you can go gambling in Deadwood, 3 miles away.

Lodging choices range from campgrounds and RV parks to expensive and inexpensive motels, and you can go in for fine dining or settle for fast food. *Custom Caster, 316 W. Main, Lead, SD 57754, tel. 605/584–2217. Year-round: 5 days, $500. Sign up 90 days in advance.*

THE SOUTHWEST

NEVADA **Reno Fly Shop Fly-Fishing School.** The Reno-Tahoe area has long been known for its year-round resort atmosphere, casinos, entertainment, and snow and water sports. But there is more, especially for the avid fly angler. From the crystal clear waters of high Sierra lakes and streams to the desolate beauty of Pyramid Lake, this area offers some of the most challenging and diverse fly fishing opportunities in the West.

The Reno Fly Shop is a small, informal operation offering courses in fly fishing, fly tying and rod building. You can choose from a variety of full-length, regularly scheduled classes, customized individual or group lessons, or professional guide services. Classes consist of basic instruction in fly-fishing, after which you go on guided fishing trips for such trout species as rainbow, brown, cutthroat, and brook. After classroom work, Dave Stanley and Dave Bryeans conduct the casting segments of these courses in schoolyards and parks, which have none of the brush, rocks, and other hazards of streams.

The school is basically a custom weekend class for up to 20 students, with instructors focusing on individual needs—each teacher handles no more than 6 students. Reno Fly Shop can provide you with plenty of equipment if you need it. All aspects of fly-fishing, from knot-tying to equipment and fly selection, are covered, but at least half of each day is spent on casting. After completing the course, you can take Reno Fly Shop's guided fishing trips for as many days as you wish, to a variety of waters, including the Truckee River and Lake Tahoe ($185 per day for 1 or 2 people). *Reno Fly Shop Fly-Fishing School, 294 E. Moana La., No. 14, Reno, NV 89502,* *tel. 702/825–3474, fax 702/825–5610. Mar.– July: 5 days, $650. Price includes lunch on guided trips; sign up 1 month in advance.*

TEXAS **Lake Fork Marina Fishing Camp.** Keith and Darla Blair run a camp for serious anglers at their marina on the shore of Lake Fork Reservoir in northeast Texas. Many consider this the prime bass lake in the state: It has produced 37 of the top 50 bass ever taken in Texas, averaging more than 14 pounds each. The marina is in a rural setting of gently rolling mountains with forests of mixed hardwoods and pines.

The Blairs provide lodging in motel-style rooms with small fridges and set you up with experienced full-time guides. The family-style meals in the restaurant are not included in the cost, but the price is moderate: breakfast, lunch, and a dinner with fried catfish, quail, hamburgers, or chicken-fried steak run no more than $20 per day.

The guides take you out in comfortable, well-equipped 19- and 20-foot bass boats, 1 or 2 guests per guide. Most of them can provide equipment, but they prefer that you bring your own. The favorite kinds of fishing are cast-and-retrieve, jigging, and bait-fishing for bass and crappie. You can buy bait and any supplies you might need at the marina. The best, and busiest, months are February, March, and April (during the spawn), September (during the bass-fishing tournament), and October.

There's not much to do except relax and swap fishing stories during the few waking hours that you're not on the water. Because the reservoir is full of stumps, it's good for fishing, but awful for swimming. *Lake Fork Marina, Unit One, Box 2, Alba, TX 75410, tel. 903/765–2764, fax 903/765–3369. Year-round: 5 days, $1,375 (1 or 2 people). Price includes lodging but no meals; sign up 8 months in advance.*

THE ROCKIES

BRITISH COLUMBIA **Horsepacking Near Banff with Elk Valley Bighorn Outfitters.**

This camp, run by Bob Fontana, is beside the Elk River in the southeast corner of British Columbia, near the Alberta line. It's about 40 miles by gravel road north of Elkford, but within a day's drive for many residents of Idaho, Washington, and Montana. Because the high-mountain cutthroat trout populations are fragile, all fishing is catch-and-release, and only artificial lures are used, since they are easier to release and thus less damaging. You do your fishing from the banks of streams and lakes.

Fontana's camp, easily the wildest in this chapter, is surely in the most awe-inspiring territory. His guiding area, hundreds of square miles in size, lies just south of Banff National Park. Here, high rocky peaks dominate the landscape, and coniferous forests and meadows cover the lower mountains and valleys. High-mountain lakes dot the region, drained by pure, clear streams.

Fontana and a wrangler use horses to transport guests and supplies to the backcountry, which is accessible only this way or on foot. The outfitter has several camps set up with small cabins, bunks, and cook shacks, and he supplies all your needs except sleeping bags and fishing equipment. He usually accommodates between 4 and 10 people, including children (ask about family rates), and 1 or 2 guides do the work. Food is cooked over a campfire or a portable wood cookstove, but it is plentiful and of high quality: You might dine on turkey, vegetables, salad, and strawberries.

You're likely to see elk, mountain goats, bighorn sheep, moose, coyotes, wolves, deer, black bears, grizzly bears, wolverines, mountain lions, water fowl, or grouse—not all species on every trip, but you will always see lots of wildlife.

Fontana can also set up a 7-day combination trip that includes both backcountry fishing and lower-elevation float fishing in the Elk River and the North Fork of the Flathead River. *Elk Valley Bighorn Outfitters, Box 275, Cranbrook, BC V1C 4H8, Canada, tel. 604/ 426–5789. Late June–late Aug.: 5 days,* *$660; 6 days, $775; 7 days, $875. Sign up 6– 12 months in advance.*

BRITISH COLUMBIA **Fernie Wilderness Adventures.** Kim Sedrovic's camp in southeastern British Columbia lies within a day's drive of most of Montana and Idaho. You fly into Kalispell, Montana, or Cranbrook, British Columbia, and Kim picks you up from either airport. The lodge, a large, old log building in a wooded setting, accommodates 12 people. All meals are provided, including excellent shore lunches while you're on float trips. Children are welcome.

Sedrovic uses platform rubber rafts and MacKenzie River boats (a standard hard-sided design that accommodates a guide in the middle and an angler on each end) to float the North Fork of the Flathead River and the Elk River for Westslope cutthroat trout and bull trout, a close relative of the Dolly Varden trout. (This is one of the few places you can still catch trophy bull trout.) He prescribes a cast-and-retrieve technique for both species, and when the conditions are right he switches to fly-fishing. The guest-to-guide ratio is 2:1.

The guided float trips go through extremely wild and scenic country, including the Flathead Valley, which skirts the west side of Waterton National Park. Competition from other anglers is light or nonexistent, and photo opportunities abound. It's not unusual to see deer, moose, elk, black bears, grizzly bears, wolves, and coyotes while floating the rivers.

It's best to provide your own fishing equipment, but Kim has some loaners and can help you with lure selection. He can also, at no extra cost, provide fundamental instruction on how to fish these rivers. In addition, he runs a 7-day trip that includes 3 days of float-fishing and 3 days of backcountry horseback riding, camping, and fishing. *Fernie Wilderness Adventures, 9 Ridgemont Ave., Fernie, BC V0B 1M2, Canada, tel. 604/423–6704. Mid-June–late Sept.: 5 days, $659; 6 days, $800; 7 days, $900. Sign up 4 months in advance.*

IDAHO **Adventure in Hell's Canyon.** Here is an opportunity to combine fishing with adventure in Hell's Canyon, the deepest gorge in North America. Steve Wieber takes you in jet boats through some spectacular white water on your way to great fishing for rainbows, steelhead, smallmouth bass, catfish, and that dinosaur of the water, the sturgeon.

Wieber runs his service in the Hell's Canyon National Recreation Area, which encompasses 67½ miles of the gorge separating northeastern Oregon from western Idaho. Mule deer and bighorn sheep are seen almost daily, as are waterfowl and birds of prey.

Guests use their own equipment for fly-fishing and cast-and-retrieve to catch trout and bass, and use cut-bait and worms for catfish and sturgeon—the lodge supplies equipment for the latter. Children of all ages are welcome, and those under 50 pounds pay half price. Catch-and-release is required for sturgeon and recommended for bass and steelhead.

The outfitter can accommodate up to 22 people at the lodge, and takes them out in its 4 boats in groups of 4 to 6 to fish for the day. If you're after sturgeon, which live at the upper end of the gorge, 2½ hours away, you charter a boat ($1,000 for up to 4 people) for an overnight at a tented camp, which is set up for you by the boat driver, who also cooks. Most guests do this as part of a 5-day package.

The log-cabin lodge, on the Snake River 40 miles south of Lewiston, has a deck, 2 baths, and 7 carpeted rooms—singles, doubles, and bunks. The home-cooked food is excellent and plentiful: salads, barbecued chicken, rib steak, game hens, and halibut. In your free time you can go hiking or swimming, play volleyball or pitch horseshoes, or visit historic pioneer and Native American sites.

The lodge also offers drop-off service: For $450 it will transport as many as 12 anglers with their own food, camping gear, and tackle to the upper gorge or another fishing site, and pick them up whenever they spec-

ify. *Cougar Country Lodge, 805 Snake River Ave., Lewiston, ID 83501, tel. 208/746-3546 or 800/727-6190. Mar.–Dec.: 5 days, $775 at lodge, $750 at lodge and camp (plus boat charter). Sign up 1 month in advance.*

MONTANA **Montana River Outfitters.** Owner Craig Madsen likes to give his clients a variety of fly-fishing options on 3 of the greatest trout-fishing streams in the world. You can fish for rainbows, browns, and cutthroats on day-trips in drift boats on the upper Missouri or choose 5- to 7-day float trips in inflatable rafts on the Smith River for rainbows and browns or on the South Fork of the Flathead River for native cutthroats.

Fishing equipment is available for rent on all trips, each guide takes care of only 1 or 2 guests, and children are welcome. On the Missouri River day-trips, the fishing is good despite the fact that the river winds through farming and ranching country near Wolf Creek, and you're never far from civilization. The Smith River trip is more remote, but you are driven to the put-in and from the take-out. The trip to the South Fork, in the heart of the huge Bob Marshall Wilderness Area, is about as remote as it gets in the lower 48 states; you ride in 20 miles on horseback. The scenery on these trips runs from spectacular to breathtaking.

On the Missouri trips, groups as large as 20 can stay in the outfitter's cabins and motel units at Wolf Creek and eat at a local restaurant (at extra cost). On the trips into backcountry, where the groups are 4 to 8 people, everything is included except your sleeping bag and fishing equipment. The guides set up tents and cook the meals on a campstove. The food is fresh—you might have salad, potatoes, steak, and strawberry shortcake. *Montana River Outfitters, 1401 5th Ave. S, Great Falls, MT 59405, tel. 406/761-1677 or 406/235-4350, fax 406/452-3833. Mar.–Oct.: 5 days on the Missouri River, $1,425 ($1,575 for 2 people); 5 days on the Smith River or South Fork, $1,775; 6 days, $2,075; 7 days, $2,375. Prices include lodging but no meals; sign up 2–4 months in advance.*

MONTANA **Catch Montana.** John Adza's camp is strictly for those who want the best fly-fishing and the best accommodations available. You don't have to be an advanced fly-caster to fish with Catch Montana, but it caters only to people who take fly-fishing seriously and who respect Montana's fragile trout fisheries by practicing catch-and-release.

Adza and the other guides help you work out the glitches in your technique—assistance you probably need before you can properly fish the sometimes fickle waters of western Montana. They use platform rubber rafts to fish for rainbows, browns, cutthroats, and brook trout in the fabled waters of the Bitterroot River, Clark Fork River, and Rock Creek. A stone fly hatch on the Bitterroot in late March or early April provides a unique early spring dry-fly fishing opportunity for those who can't wait until summer. The valley is flanked on both sides by mountains, and the Selway-Bitterroot Wilderness in the Clearwater and Nez Perce National Forest lies only a few miles west. Whitetail deer, water fowl, beavers, grouse, ospreys, and other wildlife are in evidence.

It's best to bring your own fishing equipment, but loaners are available. Guides work with a maximum of 2 guests per boat. Young people age 16 and up are welcome, if they've come to fly-fish. *Catch Montana, Box 428, Hamilton, MT 59840, tel. 800/882-7844. Late Mar.–mid-Oct.: 5 days, $1,550 ($1,250 for guided fishing only for 1 or 2 people). Sign up 6 months in advance.*

THE WEST COAST

CALIFORNIA **Clearwater House.** Dick Galland runs this fly-fishing school and camp out of a refurbished turn-of-the-century farmhouse next to Hat Creek, a prime trout stream in a sparsely populated part of northern California.

The school generally runs from Wednesday to Sunday, but shorter sessions are available. All classes take place on Hat Creek in natural fishing conditions, and video cameras are used to help fine-tune your skills. The beginners' class covers equipment, knot-tying, casting fundamentals, reading trout habitat, fly selection, and tips on how to play a trout. Intermediates learn how to catch large trout using sinking line and underwater flies called nymphs, and also how to make long casts and natural-looking floats with dry flies. The advanced class covers the technical fine points, teaching the most versatile and refined casting skills.

Clearwater House is in Cassel, in a scenic mountainous area between Burney and Fall River Mills, fewer than 40 miles from Lassen Volcanic National Park. It's a great place to spend a fishing vacation. You can go sightseeing and hiking in your free time, and Clearwater also offers guide service ($250 per day) and accommodations to other anglers. *Clearwater House, Box 90, Cassell, CA 96016, tel. 916/335-5500 (off-season 415/381-1173). Late Apr.–mid-Nov.: 5 days, $795 beginners and intermediates, $895 advanced. Prices include room and board; sign up 3 months in advance.*

CALIFORNIA **Lewiston Inn.** In the high mountains of northwest California, 30 miles west of Redding and a short skip east of Weaverville, lies the historic mining town of Lewiston. The inn is at the headwaters of the Trinity River (in the fly-fishing only, catch-and-release section), where it is surrounded by great fishing country in the heart of Bigfoot territory. Don't worry: There has never been a verified case of Bigfoot eating a fisherman.

The inn's 7 rooms are in 2 restored mining buildings of the handful left in town; the main one was built in 1875. Connor Nixon, the owner, caters to anglers, especially fly-fishermen, and 50% of his guests are typically return customers. The rooms are furnished with antiques, all have baths, and some have private entrances and decks. Fifteen guests can be accommodated; children of all ages are welcome. Fishing packages of different lengths can be arranged, with guides or without, but all include food and lodging. A full breakfast is usually served on the back deck, overlooking the Trinity River; lunch is packed for your day of fishing; and dinner is taken at the Lewiston Hotel, a former stagecoach stop in town.

Lodge guests are free to do unguided shore fishing and wading fishing, and many of them bring their own float tubes. If you choose to fish with a guide ($200 per day for 1, $250 for 2), the maximum number of anglers is 3. All the guides give casting instruction for an additional charge, and though some have loaner fishing tackle, it's best to bring your own. Guided trips include fishing from a drift-boat on the Trinity River and from a power boat on Lewiston Lake; the craft used range from aluminum boats and platform rafts to float tubes and a 13-foot Boston Whaler.

The setting is coniferous forests, drained by many streams and rivers, and the inn is only 10 minutes away from the Trinity Alps. Free-time activities include hiking, bicycling, bird-watching (bald eagles, ospreys, and waterfowl), and sitting around in the hot tub. *Lewiston Inn, Box 688, Lewiston, CA 96052, tel. 800/286–4441 or 916/778–3385, fax 916/778–0309. Year-round: 5 days, $495 ($560 for 2). Sign up 1 month in advance.*

CALIFORNIA **Oasis Springs Lodge.** If solitude is what you crave, you will like Warren and Linda Quan's fly-fishing resort. It's on a grassy 3,000-acre ranch in northern California, next to the South Fork of Battle Creek, about 30 miles east of Red Bluff—you can see both Lassen Peak and Mount Shasta from some spots. The resort's 6 miles of private water assures that even the most reclusive will find uncrowded fishing here.

The very modern lodge was completed in 1992; the air-conditioned rooms have television, ceiling fans, and some fireplaces. You can stay for as little as 2 days or as long as you like; there's room for 20 people. The meals are served family-style; there's a Continental breakfast, a hearty lunch, and such dinner fare as steak, chicken, salmon, halibut, turkey, and barbecues.

You can fish on your own, or go with a guide ($200 per day for up to 4 people), and begin-

ners can also take 3 hours of private instruction ($65 for up to 3 people). Only catch-and-release fly-fishing is done here; you fish from the bank or wade, and 90% of what you catch is rainbow trout, the rest browns. The ranch has some equipment to lend, but it's best to bring your own gear.

Though there are no amusements or services nearby, there's plenty to do; the resort has a hot tub, a swimming pool, and a tennis court, and you can hike, or go horseback riding at a neighboring ranch ($15 per hour). The region has mountain lions and eagles. *Oasis Springs Lodge, Box 454, Payne's Creek, CA 96075, tel. 510/521-1801 or 800/ 642–4150, fax 510/521–3039. Late Apr.– mid-Nov.: 5 days, $495–$795 per person double occupancy. Sign up 1–2 months in advance.*

CALIFORNIA **Trinity Canyon Lodge.** This is a good place for those who want to focus strictly on fishing in a backwoods environment. It is in a remote part of northwest California, west of Weaverville and next to the Trinity Alps Wilderness Area. The Trinity River has been designated a Wild and Scenic River, and Highway 299, which parallels it, is an official National Scenic Byway. The Trinity River Canyon is just wide enough for the river and the road, with very few open spots; the Trinity Canyon Lodge occupies one, with river frontage and a magnificent grove of oak trees. The river is considered one of the west's premier salmon, trout, and steelhead streams.

The lodge, run by Joe and Diane Mercier, has a rustic appearance and has been here for decades. It can accommodate about 25 people in 7 housekeeping cabins and 3 motel units. The cabins are completely outfitted— you need only groceries—and must be rented for 2 nights or longer. Nearby restaurants and cafés provide meals for those in the motel units.

The Merciers offer half-day ($160 for 2 people) and full-day workshops ($250 for 2, including lunch) on fly-fishing for trout, steelhead, and salmon. More than half the workshops are attended by families (i.e., parent and child, husband and wife). Bring your own equipment; there's a limited supply of loaners.

Guided fishing is also available, but the local guides are not part of the lodge operation. They use drift boats or rafts, and their fees average around $225 per day for 1 or 2 people, including lunch. The majority do strictly fly-fishing, but some of them use other methods also. You can fish in the high alpine lakes of the wilderness area as well as in the river.

In your free time you can tour a nearby ghost town dating from the California gold rush, visit ancient Native American villages, go hiking, white-water rafting, or tubing on the river (the lodge provides portage), dunking in private swimming holes, berry picking, or wildlife watching. Or you can drive to Weaverville to see the bright lights of a small town. *Trinity Canyon Lodge, Box 51, Helena, CA 96048, tel. 916/623–6318, fax 916/623–3306. Year-round: 5 days, $590 cabin (1 or 2); $275 motel unit (1 or 2). Price does not include meals; sign up 2 weeks in advance.*

CALIFORNIA **Fly-Fishing Outfitters Clinics.** These Bay Area clinics are run from the Fly-Fishing Outfitters shops in Lafayette and San Francisco. Some instruction actually takes place in the city, in locations that run from alleyways to first-rate casting ponds, depending on what's available at the time of the class. For sessions that include actual fishing, however, students provide their own transport (1 to 3 hours inland) to such appropriate waters as Putah Creek, the Yuba River system, and the Stanislaus River.

Fly-fishing guru Bryan Noguchi offers programs that range from a very basic 2½-hour class that hits on knots, casting, reading water, fly selection, and other fundamentals, to a comprehensive 2-day school that takes place in the Sierra, 100 miles away. These longer schools are intensive, with no more than 4 pupils per instructor. You cover everything from dry-fly fishing and nymph fishing to streamer techniques and other advanced methods. Customized trips of 5 or more days can be arranged.

These clinics have been offered since 1985, a large percentage of repeat students sign up, and classes fill earlier each year. Lunch and rods and reels are provided. You can stay in nearby motels, but the instructors usually camp, and students are invited to join them (and bring their own food), a good idea if you want to fraternize with the experts.

Free-time activities include all the urban amenities that the Bay Area can offer and the usual outdoor pursuits of the Sierra. *Fly Fishing Outfitters, 3533 Mt. Diablo Blvd., Lafayette, CA 94549, tel. 510/284–3474, fax 510/284–3314; 463 Bush St., San Francisco, CA 94108, tel. 415/781–3474. June–Sept.: Clinics start at $230 and go up, depending on length. Sign up 1 month in advance.*

CALIFORNIA **Bishop Creek Lodge.** At an elevation of 9,000 feet in the scenic Bishop Creek Canyon of the southeastern Sierra is a rustic lodge run by Gary and Suzie Olson. It's about 25 minutes by car northwest of Bishop and about 5 minutes from a trailhead into the High Sierra wilderness. The lodge offers no fishing classes and has no guides; its primary function is to house wilderness hikers and anglers in pursuit of the native golden trout. This rare and beautiful species is found in both the lakes and streams of the High Sierra, the country in which all golden trout originated.

Twelve cabins, all with bath and kitchen, can accommodate up to 45 in all; kids are welcome. A minimum stay of 2 days is required; a free day is allowed for each 7 consecutive paid days, and Continental breakfast is included in the price. A restaurant, bar, store, and laundry take care of virtually all your needs. The lodge sells fishing equipment; no rentals are available.

Free-time activities are essentially limited to outdoor pursuits like hiking and horseback riding, unless you want to make the 25-minute drive into Bishop. *Bishop Creek Lodge, Rte. 1, S. Lake Rd., Bishop, CA 93514, tel. 619/873–4484, fax 619/872–1213. Mid-Apr.–late Oct.: 5 days, $275 (cabin for 2)–$675 (cabin for 8). Prices do not include lunch or dinner; sign up 6 months in advance.*

CALIFORNIA **California School of Fly-Fishing.** When Ralph and Lisa Cutter are not teaching a fly-fishing school in Truckee, they are taking groups of up to 10 on 5-day horseback-fishing trips. Their destination is the Ansel Adams Wilderness, next to Yosemite National Park in the backcountry of the eastern High Sierra, where there are many streams and natural lakes, some as high as 12,000 feet.

Two wilderness camps have been set up for the season by a pack outfitter; the first is about 4 hours' ride from the starting point, and the second about 4 hours' ride from that. From the camps, you walk or ride horses to fishing places within a 1- or 2-hour radius, returning at night to a dinner fixed by backcountry chefs. The tented camps are remote but comfortable, with pit toilets and solar showers; the food is plentiful and good—salads, vegetables, chicken, and steaks. Everything is provided except sleeping bags and fishing equipment.

The main activity is catch-and-release fly-fishing for rainbow, brown, and brook trout, as well as the beautiful golden trout. These are not really instructional trips, but Ralph and Lisa are happy to provide brief on-the-spot tips to help you fish these high mountain waters. Many guests just go along for the ride, concentrating on photography, wildflower identification, bird-watching, and other naturalist activities. *California School of Fly-Fishing, Box 8212, Truckee, CA 96162, tel. 916/587–7005, fax 916/587–6686. May–June: 5 days, $895. Sign up 8 months in advance.*

CALIFORNIA **Sierra Bright Dot.** Fred Rowe runs Sierra Bright Dot out of Mammoth Lakes in east-central California. His services vary from half-day fishing trips around Mammoth Lakes to a 5-day guided horseback-fishing trip into the High Sierra. A major focus on these backcountry trips is catching golden trout, native only to this specific area in the ultra-high country, though rainbows, brook, and brown trout are also plentiful. Fred, a good teacher, will instruct you on appropriate techniques for the waters you will be fishing; you wade and fish from the bank of the streams and lakes. Children who are eager to fish and learn are welcome.

Sierra Bright Dot contracts with a packer, who owns the horses and hires the wranglers who do the work, bringing in supplies every couple of days. The base camp is set up on the Clark Lakes, where you spend 2 nights; you then move on to the second camp, at Alger Lakes. These are wilderness camps, with tents and chairs and portable toilets with tarps for privacy. If you want a shower, bring a solar one with you.

Food and all supplies except sleeping bags and fishing gear are provided, though some equipment rentals are available. The food is good; you might have steak, lasagna, or chicken, and fajitas one night for a change of pace. Though golden trout is always catch-and-release, you might have rainbows and brookies for dinner. Vegetables, salads, and fruit round out the meals; beer, wine, and sodas are included. Dinner is early, so you can fish in the evenings; then you come back for coffee, hot chocolate, and dessert around the campfire.

Mammoth Lakes is a ski area in the winter, and before you leave on the wilderness trips and after you return, you can find a variety of accommodations, from camping to motels to condo rentals, at off-season prices. The same is true for restaurants.

You can also go sailing, snow-skiing, and waterskiing there. One ski-lift will take you and your mountain bike up to the top for a sweat-free ride back down. *Sierra Bright Dot, Box 9013, Mammoth Lakes, CA 93546, tel. 619/934–5514. May–Oct.: 5 days, $750. Sign up 6 months in advance.*

CALIFORNIA **Bass Fishing Instructional Service.** Gary Harrison runs his business (more a guide service than a school) on the legendary Lake Castaic, perhaps the only body of water on earth where you have a chance of catching a world-record fish every time you dip your line. From January through July of 1993, for example, Harrison's clients landed 82 largemouth bass over 10 pounds. To put that in perspective, the state record for largemouths in Montana is barely 8 pounds. (Harrison's biggest fish is 18 lbs. 2 oz., and the lake record is 22 lbs. 1 oz. The existing world record is 22 lbs. 4 oz.)

Harrison provides all the equipment and bait; anglers need only bring themselves and a lunch. The 2 primary methods of fishing are cast-and-retrieve and trolling, both with live bait. There is not a lot to learn. The main requirement for success is patience and a knowledge of how to land heavy fish. Harrison's style is one of informality with a personal touch, and having fun supercedes all else. His bass boat is a fully equipped 18-foot Ranger that comfortably accommodates his limit of 2 adults, or 2 adults and 1 child (children under 16 free). He prohibits drinking alcohol in his boat and strongly urges catch-and-release.

Lodging can be found at a nearby campground or neighboring motels and hotels; ethnic eateries and family restaurants provide the local dining. *Bass Fishing Instructional Service, 16643 Gazeley St., Canyon Country, CA 91351, tel. 805/251–2277. Year-round: 5 days, $800–$900 ($1,100–$1,300 for 2 people). Sign up 1–2 months in advance.*

ALASKA

SOUTHWEST **Wood River Lodge.** This premium fishing camp, about 35 miles north of Dillingham, is accessible only by air or a long boat trip. The Agulawok River, which runs right by the lodge, reputedly contains more rainbow trout per mile than any other Alaska River, along with other species. Owners John and Linda Ortman, however, don't depend just on the Agulawok; they also fly you to other waters in a float plane, to fish for northern pike, Dolly Varden, arctic char, rainbow trout, lake trout, and all of Alaska's species of salmon.

Fly-fishermen and cast-and-retrieve anglers are both welcome here, but catch-and-release fishing is necessary for all species

except spawning salmon (who will soon die anyway). The cost of the camp includes everything you'll need, and although it's usual to bring your own equipment, tackle is included at no charge. Fishing excursions for the next day are individually planned between the guests and the head guide each evening. There are never more than 2 or 3 guests per guide, and you fish from boats or wade, depending on where you go and which species you're after.

This is a true wilderness camp, surrounded by forests and mountains, with a plethora of wildlife, including grizzly bears, caribou, moose, waterfowl, and eagles. The camp can accommodate up to 14 guests. You stay in spacious private cabins, and go to the main lodge for social activities and meals. The 5- and 7-course dinners might feature prime rib, steak, ham, or any of several varieties of salmon. Children are welcome. About three-quarters of the guests are return visitors.

The long days on the water and communal feasts don't leave much free time, but people play cards, watch wildlife, take photographs, and exchange fish stories with other guests. *Wood River Lodge, Box 1369, Dillingham, AK 99576, tel. 907/842–5200 or 800/842–5205 (in winter, 406/862–2305), fax 907/842–5200 (summer only). Mid-June–Sept.: 7 days, $4,500. Sign up 6–12 months ahead.*

SOURCES

ORGANIZATIONS **American Bass Association, Inc.** (886 Trotters Trail, Wetumpka, AL 36092, tel. 334/567–6035) is an advocacy group that works on improving bass fisheries and sponsors fishing tournaments. It publishes *American Bass News*. The **Federation of Fly Fishers** (Box 1595, Bozeman, MT 59771, tel. 406/585–7592) focuses on conservation, education, and restoration and publishes *The Quill*. The **National Fresh Water Fishing Hall of Fame** (Box 33 Hall of Fame Dr., Hayward WI 54843, tel. 715/634–4440), an advocacy group, keeps track of record fish and publishes *Official*

World Fresh Water Angling Records. **North American Fishing Club** (12301 Whitewater Dr., Minnetonka, MN 55343, tel. 612/936–9333) publishes *North American Fisherman.* The **International Game Fish Association** (1301 E. Atlantic Blvd., Pompano Beach, FL 33060, tel. 305/941–3474), an advocacy group, also maintains a book of fish records and publishes *World Record Game Fishes.* **Trout Unlimited** (1500 Wilson Blvd., #310, Arlington, VA 22209, tel. 703/522-0200) is "dedicated to conserving, protecting, and restoring wild trout and salmon and their habitat throughout North America."

PERIODICALS How-to magazines include *Bass Fishing* (88 Moors Rd., Gilbertsville, KY 42044, tel. 502/362–4304) and *Bassin' and Crappie* (Natcom, 15115 S. 76th E. Ave., Bixby, OK 74008, tel. 918/366–4441). *California Angler* covers where-to and how-to (all species, all techniques) for California and Baja (1921 E. Carnegie, Suite 3N, Santa Ana, CA 92705, tel. 714/261–9779). *Fishing Holes* (17021 N.E. Woodinville-Duval Rd., Woodinville, WA 98072, tel. 206/489–2919) is about where-to, how-to, and personal experience (all species, all techniques) in the northwestern United States. *Fishing & Hunting News* (511 Eastlake Ave. E, Seattle, WA 98109, tel. 800/488–2827), about where to fish in the West (all species), is published weekly. *Fishing World* (700 W. 47th St., #310, Kansas City, MO 64112, tel. 816/531–5730) is a magazine on destinations in the United States, Canada, Mexico, the Bahamas, and the Caribbean. *Fly Fisherman* (4 High Ridge Park, Stamford, CT 06905, tel. 800/435–9610) is a how-to, where-to (all species), and personal experience magazine. *Fly Rod & Reel* (Box 10141, Des Moines, IA 50340, tel. 800/888–6890) covers how-to and where-to for all species. *In-Fisherman* (2 In-Fisherman Dr., Brainerd, MN 56401, tel. 218/829–1648) is all about freshwater fishing for all species,

all techniques. *Salt Water Sportsman* (280 Summer St., Boston, MA 02210, tel. 617/439–9977) is about sport-fishing (all species), including fishing boats and tackle.

BOOKS National or even regional guides to fishing resources are scarce. (Most such guides are done by states, and good sources for them are the state agencies that administer fishing, for example: the California Department of Fish & Game, Vermont Fish & Wildlife Division, Washington Department of Wildlife, and the Virginia Department of Game & Inland Fisheries.) However, how-to and where-to guides are not nonexistent. *Angler's Guide to Montana* (Falcon Press Publishing), by Michael Sample, is a brief text locating species and type of water. *Chris Batin's 20 Great Alaska Fishing Adventures* (Alaska Angler Publications), by Christopher Batin, is on glossy paper, with lots of color photographs of the author and friends fishing. *Fly Tying Made Clear and Simple* (Frank Amato Publications), by Skip Morris, is a large-format book with step by step photographs in color. *Joan Wulff's Fly Fishing* (Stackpole Books), by Joan Wulff, is a good book on the fundamentals, with photographs, by the co-owner of the famous Wulff School of Fly-Fishing. *Knee Deep in Montana's Trout Streams* (Pruett Publishing), by John Holt, is a where-to and how-to book with humor. *Scientific Anglers Guidebook to Fly Fishing Mastery* (Scientific Anglers), by Howard West and Mike Dry, is a large-format paperback, with line drawings and photographs in color and black-and-white of people demonstrating techniques.

ALSO SEE If you'd rather make fishing a smaller part of your vacation, you can bring your rod along on a thrilling rafting trip or on a relaxing flatwater canoeing journey. Turn to the River Rafting and Canoeing and Kayaking in Flat Water chapters to find out more.

Golf Schools

By Jonathan Abrahams

ow's your golf game? You hate that question, don't you? It's humbling; *nobody's* golf game is as good as they'd like it to be. You're forced to look squarely in the eye at some of your greatest personal weaknesses: slicing, hooking, shanking. The yips. So your game needs a little work, huh? You're not alone. Whether you're threatening par or threatening to quit, your game would love some special attention. How about a week at a golf school? Imagine—an entire week devoted solely to you and your game. The game's best teachers, a plush setting, golf during every daylight hour—sounds good, doesn't it? Maybe you could even get rid of that nasty slice. So what are you in for?

There are a few things you can expect no matter what golf school you choose to attend. Whether the school is part of a large franchise, like John Jacobs', or independently operated, like The Academy of Golf Dynamics, the instruction will almost always be excellent. That's because it's rare to find faculty at a school that isn't made up entirely of Class A PGA Professionals. Almost all schools are at or near an upscale resort with a quality golf course. Return students and word-of-mouth are essential to a school's business, so they can't afford less than excellent accommodations. The food will be good, and there will be a pool and tennis courts and maybe even a health club. All this, of course, costs money: Golf school is pricey—four days can cost anywhere from $700 to $3,000; chances are your fellow students will be established businesspeople. More than a few business cards will change hands over lunch during your stay. Above all, you'll spend a lot of time with a golf club in your hand, perhaps more time than you ever have.

Most schools spend 4 to 6 hours a day covering all aspects of the game, from driving to putting. After breakfast, students convene on the driving range to warm up. If the group is more than 10, students most likely are divided into two or more groups, usually based on handicap. Typically, a group of 18 may be divided into three groups. All three groups participate in a warm-up, led by the instructors. After the preliminaries, Group 1 works on full-swing fundamentals, Group 2 on chipping and pitching, and Group 3 has their swings videotaped and analyzed. By mid-morning, the groups rotate stations; after lunch, they rotate again. In the late afternoon (usually after 3 PM), students usually are given the option to play. The process starts over on day two, except now the stations are trouble play, sand shots, and your mind-set. By the end of the week, students have been immersed in every possible aspect of the game. It's a lot of golf. Expect to get blisters and for those blisters to turn into calluses.

The bottom line is, most schools are credible: good golf, good vacation. But not all schools are the same. There are plenty of distinguish-

---

Jonathan Abrahams, a freelance golf writer, is a former instruction editor at *Golf Magazine*. His 3 handicap continues to survive despite his New York City residence.

ing factors; it just depends on what you're looking for. If you're willing to spend a little more money for higher-end accommodations, try Nicklaus/Flick, which holds schools at the country's most exclusive resorts. If you're concerned with activities geared toward the non-golfer, choose a location where golf is not the focal point. Your family, for instance, will have more options in Vail, Colorado, than in Myrtle Beach, South Carolina. Most schools have a minimum student:teacher ratio of 4:1; more personal attention is available at La Costa (in Carlsbad, CA), where Carl Welty and his assistant, Jennifer McFalls, have been known to give lessons with a student:teacher ratio as low as 1:2. For the carefree, Golf Digest includes everything in its package price—transportation to and from the airport, all meals, all golf—so you don't have to worry about money while you're there. Specialization is also becoming popular. Dave Pelz's school is for the short game only. Sports Enhancement Associates' program emphasizes blending the mental and physical aspects of the game.

Now, what *not* to expect: Don't think, no matter which school you attend, that you'll have magically cut 5 strokes off your handicap by the end of the week. Many students look back at their golf experience months later and realize, with disappointment, that their scores are no better than before they attended. There are no quick fixes to your golfing ills. You will pick up a number of fundamentals at golf school that provide clues to some of the game's mysteries, but they will do you no good unless they're applied through consistent practice. Truly dedicated students will consult a local PGA professional before choosing a school, so the experience fits in smoothly with regular lesson plans. Make your choice carefully. Remember, it's your vacation—your golf game might make you crazy, but the goal is, still, to have fun.

CHOOSING THE RIGHT SCHOOL

Is this school suited to my playing style? Is there a specific swing method taught? If your pro teaches a big-muscle method in the style of Jim McLean, it might be a mistake to go to a school with a small-muscle philosophy like Nicklaus/Flick's. If you've taken any lessons, it's important that you find a school that complements the method that you've been using.

What is the maximum class size? Most people prefer a smaller class because you get more personal attention. A lot of schools will limit the size to 18, but there are a few that don't.

What is the student:teacher ratio? This actually is more important than the class size. You don't want to have a ratio higher than 8:1. The lower the ratio, the more attention you're going to get.

What percentage of instruction time is spent on the golf course? You'll spend most of the day working on the range or practice green until around 3 or 4 in the afternoon, when you can go play for a couple of hours, depending on the sun. As a general rule, the more on-course work, the better.

How extensive is the practice facility? Questions to bear in mind: How big is the driving range? Is there a putting green? How big is it? Is there a short-game area? Is there a bunker? All of these facilities will allow you to concentrate on different parts of your game.

Are there indoor facilities in case of rain?

What is the cost and what is included? Prices listed here include lodging, meals, and instruction unless otherwise noted. Also, find out if carts and greens fees are included in the package price. Most schools don't provide transportation between the airport and the hotel. This could mean renting a car or taking the hotel's airport shuttle.

What are the accommodations like? All schools put their guests up in hotels, although the degree of luxury of the rooms and the facilities can vary quite a bit.

What is the food like?

Will laundry service be available? This could save you a suitcase.

Are there non-golf activities available during off-hours? Does the school plan nightly social activities?

Is there a spousal or non-golfing guest rate? What activities are available for non-golfing guests?

How far in advance do I need to book?

How long has the school been in business? If the school is new, be particularly careful to find out about the people in charge and their plans for the program. Make sure that their teaching experience is credible, and that the instruction seems well-conceived and well-organized.

Do you have references from past guests?

MAJOR PLAYERS

GOLF DIGEST INSTRUCTIONAL SCHOOLS

"Hey," some insightful editor at *Golf Digest* must have said long ago, "wouldn't it be terrific if we got all the great teachers that contribute to our magazine together so they could actually teach people face-to-face?" Well, *somebody* liked that idea, and in 1971 the Golf Digest Instructional Schools were formed. Indeed, they served as a showcase for some of the game's great teachers. Guys like Bob Toski, Jim Flick, and Davis Love Jr. worked together for years, feeding off each other's knowledge, learning to specialize their instruction according to the student's needs, and in the process made a big name both for themselves and *Golf Digest*.

Today, experts such as Scott Davenport, Jack Lumpkin, and John Elliot are among the large and highly qualified staff of professionals that teach at the Golf Digest Schools; they can be found at top destinations like Sea Island, Georgia; Scottsdale, Arizona; and Vail, Colorado. The basic philosophy is to identify the student's needs and qualities, and shape a program around them. No "swing method" is forced on anyone.

Digest's flexible philosophy is reflected in the variety of schools it offers. In addition to the standard 3-day schools for all golfers, it offers specialized programs for commuters, low-handicappers, parents and children, women, and those interested in short-game work only. There's also a "VIP School," for those who want to live a little better, get a little more attention, and don't mind paying a little more.

Speaking of attention, Golf Digest distinguishes itself from most other schools in the country with its hospitality. While others might send you directions from the airport in the mail and ask you to take care of at least one meal a day by yourself, Digest takes complete care of you. For the 3-day program, they pick you up at the airport, pay for all of your meals, and make sure you get back to your flight on time when the school is over (5520 Park Ave., Box 395, Trumbull, CT 06611–0395, tel. 203/373–7130 or 800/243–6121, fax 203/373–7088).

JOHN JACOBS' PRACTICAL GOLF SCHOOLS

John Jacobs' is huge. A former Tour Player, Ryder Cupper, and Walker Cup captain, Jacobs hooked up with fellow professional Shelby Futch in 1970 to run a golf school. Today, there are 800 John Jacobs' schools, each running 2–5 days, at 30 different locations worldwide.

What makes this man and his schools so popular? The answer lies in his teaching philosophy. It's highly personalized. Instead of forcing a student to adapt to a particular "swing method," Jacobs' instruction is designed to adapt itself to the student and his or her natural game. The goal is not learning how to swing like Fred Couples, but how you can improve your own swing. It's less intimidating for the student, and gives him or her the feeling that improvement is most certainly within reach.

One thing to expect at a John Jacobs' school is large classes. But Jacobs has a large number of PGA Class A Professionals on staff at each site, so the student:teacher ratio never gets out of hand. Just don't expect to get to know all your fellow students. At Marriott's Seaview Resort in New Jersey, for example, a class will get as many as 50 students. But with 10 instructors, everyone gets their fair share of attention. Five hours per day are spent on instruction, including video analysis; all aspects of the game are covered. On-course work comes afterwards. And as a parting gift, students get a copy of the *John Jacobs' Instruction Manual* to take home.

Specialization is also a big thing at John Jacobs'. Just a golf school? No. How about a golf school for women in business, or a school devoted only to the short game? What do you need? Jacobs will take care of it (7825 E. Redfield Rd., Scottsdale, AZ 85260–6977, tel. 602/991–8587 or 800/472–5007, fax 602/991–8243).

NICKLAUS/FLICK GOLF SCHOOLS Does Jack actually teach here? No, but the guy who *teaches* Jack teaches here. And that's only a sliver of his résumé. Jim Flick may be a slight man—he'll be sure to tell you after he belts a 270-yard drive—but his accomplishments as a teacher of golf are on a scale larger than that of just about anybody in the business. The college roommate of Arnold Palmer at Wake Forest, he moved on to help guide the then-fledgling Golf Digest Schools to prominence in 1972. In 1990, when he began to work with Nicklaus on his game, the Golden Bear found Flick's ideas so much like his own that they formed the Nicklaus/Flick Golf Schools. To this day, Flick has personally taught more than 900 classes—more than anyone else alive.

Flick's teaching philosophy has endured—and will continue to do so—for a few reasons. It focuses on the golf club and its motion, rather than various positions the body should or shouldn't be in. Flick's method does not espouse absolutes dictating the correct golf swing, but rather allows the student to concentrate on quality of contact and ball flight. It's a "user-friendly" system that pays as much attention to the student's mind and emotional state as his shoulder turn. "Students must be prepared emotionally before I can prepare them physically," says Dean Reinmuth, coach to Phil Mickelson and a member of Flick's top-notch staff. These people really know how to teach.

The instruction program is broken up into 4 sessions: Master Golf I, II, III, and IV. The sessions get shorter and more advanced as they progress, with the focus becoming on-course play. The student's entire golfing life is examined: short game, long game, state-of-mind, equipment evaluation, and fitness. Each student receives a videotape and the *Master Golf Workbook,* a manual written by Nicklaus, Flick, and Ken Bowden. There are never more than 18 students and the student:teacher ratio is never more than 6:1.

Nicklaus/Flick schools are also distinguished by their locations; they're absolutely top-shelf. Pebble Beach, Ibis Golf and Country Club (West Palm Beach, FL); Boyne Highlands Resort (Harbor Springs, MI), The Scottsdale Princess—all are at the top of their class in terms of golf, accommodations, and dining. You will live well at Nicklaus/Flick (11780 U.S. Hwy. One, N. Palm Beach, FL 33408–9809, tel. 407/626–3900 or 800/642–5528, fax 904/322–2567).

FAVORITE SCHOOLS

THE MID-ATLANTIC

NEW JERSEY John Jacobs' Practical Golf Schools. The Seaview Resort is officially a Marriott, but don't expect the standard 10-story hotel with lots of lights and a red roof. Years ago, Seaview was a very exclusive private club with guest quarters for members who came in from Philadelphia and New York for the weekend. It did lose a little of its old private club charm, however, when Marriott acquired the property and expanded the existing accommodations to 300 rooms.

Students prowl a large buffet breakfast before they hit the plush 22-acre practice facility at 9 AM. Each practice session is personalized, focusing on the individual's needs, with lots of video analysis. There can be as many as 50 students, but the student:teacher ratio is never greater than 5:1. Lunch—also included in the package price—breaks up the daily 5-hour instruction, then it's back to work until 3 PM, when students are allowed to go play.

Seaview has a couple of fine golf courses: The Bay, a Donald Ross classic from 1915, and The Pines, a newer, tougher track built in 1942.

Wagers on the course should be kept to a minimum, because only 10 minutes away lies Atlantic City and all its trappings. For less costly fun, the hotel itself has swimming pools, tennis courts, game and exercise rooms, and a health club. Several malls dot the area, but antiques aficionados will want to head to the small town of Smithville, just a few minutes away. Wrap the day up with dinner at Marriott's main dining room, which has a Friday seafood buffet that's the best in the area. *John Jacobs' Practical Golf Schools, 7825 E. Redfield Rd., Scottsdale, AZ 85260–6977, tel. 602/991–8587 or 800/ 472–5007, fax 602/991–8243. May–Sept.: 4 days, $1195–1675; 2 days, $760–$965. Price does not include dinner. Non-golfing companion rate (includes 2 meals): 2 days, $235; 4 days, $690.*

THE SOUTH

FLORIDA **Ben Sutton Golf Academy.** Twenty-five years ago, a retired Hoover engineer decided to get a bunch of buddies together and go on a golf vacation. The group didn't just want an ordinary golfing trip; they wanted their games to improve at the same time. So they took along a few pros, and the first golf school was born. The engineer's name was Ben Sutton, and he is the pioneer of the modern golf school.

Today, the Ben Sutton Golf Academy continues to operate in the same progressive spirit. Unlike most schools, which spend the majority of instruction time teaching the student how to swing the club, Ben Sutton's program is specifically designed around playing the game. Other schools have "player's" programs, usually for those with handicaps of 15 or less, that include extra playing time. But Ben Sutton goes beyond that. In its 5-day program (there's also a 3-day and 8-day) the majority of time, regardless of the student's ability, is spent on the 9-hole teaching

course. Working on long irons on the range is one thing; hitting long iron shots to an elevated green with a lake on the left is something completely different. By working on shots under playing conditions, students eliminate the need to bridge the gap between practice tee and course.

That's not to say there's no time spent on the range. Ben Sutton's range is a 360° grass practice tee that's totally exclusive to the school. There's the requisite putting green and short-game area, as well, but most of the work is done on the practice course.

After 6 hours of instruction, students are free to play Sun City Center's 27-hole private golf course, a challenging layout that is relatively hilly for Florida. Carts and greens fees are taken care of by the school. Students stay at the Sun City Center Hotel, a typical resort with swimming pools, tennis courts, and a solid (if unspectacular) restaurant. Breakfast and dinner, eaten at the hotel, are included in the package; lunch is at the country club and is extra. Students may bring guests, who are welcome to everything the students are—golf, meals, all but instruction.

One drawback: Ben Sutton's schools are so popular that they occasionally get crowded. There can be as many as 150 students at one school, and although they have 32 Class A PGA Professionals on staff, the student:teacher ratio can get as high as 7:1. *Ben Sutton Golf School, Box 9199, Canton, OH 44711, tel. 216/453–4350 or 800/225–6923, fax 216/453–8450. Year-round: 3 days, $625–$685; 5 days, $1035– $1115; 8 days, $1475–$1635. Non-golfing companion rate (includes meals and golf): 3 days, $285; 5 days, $525; 8 days, $750.*

FLORIDA **Dave Pelz Short Game School.** "How can I cut strokes off my scores?" Despite all the swing theories and golf gurus running around, there's only one real answer to this question, no matter who you are: Work on your short game. Improve your chipping, pitching, sand play, and putting (especially putting), and your scores will go down. Why? The golf swing itself is not the easiest motion for the average Joe. The short game swings, on the other hand, are simple. Anybody can make a putting stroke. Hit it all over the park with a grotesque swing but putt well, and you'll be a good player. Hit everything down the middle but putt lousy, and you're just another also-ran. P.S.: The secret to good putting is hitting your chips, pitches, and sand shots close to the hole.

It doesn't take a rocket scientist to figure that out, but one did anyway; as a result, the Dave Pelz Short Game School was born. Pelz spent 14 years as a research scientist for NASA; 16 years ago he decided to devote his life completely to golf—specifically, the short game. As you might imagine, Pelz's teaching philosophy is pretty cutting edge. Unlike other golf schools that merely include the short game, Pelz's school covers the short game *only* and uses a method that's uniquely his own. He espouses one swing motion for all wedge shots, systematically broken down into different lengths, according to the length of shot. He recommends carrying at least three wedges of different lofts in your bag: Some of his disciples on Tour (and he's got a few) carry as many as four. He's got two authentic robots, Perfy (a putting specialist) and Wedgy (a wedge wizard), to demonstrate his theories.

Pelz's schools are 3 days long, with about 8 hours of instruction daily, divided between indoor learning sessions and outdoor execution sessions. Players of all abilities are represented at the school—there's sometimes even a Tour pro or two—because Pelz's fundamentals are applicable to any player. He's a big believer that improvement is closely linked with knowledge of proper execution, so there's a good deal of time spent in the classroom. Maximum enrollment is 16, and the student:teacher ratio is never greater than 4:1.

Pelz offers three types of sessions: The Signature, headed by Pelz himself, includes three nights of lodging at the Boca Raton Resort and Club. Pelz doesn't show for the lower-priced Regular Session, but his partner, former PGA Tour player Tom Jenkins, does, and he teaches all the same stuff. The

Alumni session focuses more on on-course situations. It's expensive, but the Boca resort is very impressive. Two great golf courses, tennis courts, a beach club with private beach, a marina, three fitness centers—this place is stocked. *Dave Pelz Short Game School, The Boca Raton Resort & Club, Box 5025, Boca Raton, FL 33431-0825, tel. 407/395-3000, ext. 3753 or 800/833-7370, fax 512/261-5391. Year-round: 3 days, $2010-$2700; Price does not include meals. Non-golfing companions stay at no extra charge to single occupancy rate.*

FLORIDA **Doral Golf Learning Center with Jim McLean.** If you're looking for someone on the cutting edge of golf instruction, you've found him in Jim McLean. A former college teammate of Bruce Lietzke and John Mahaffey, and a teaching editor at *Golf Magazine*, McLean is one of the most successful teachers in the industry. His focus is on controlling the swing with the big muscles of the hips, back, and shoulders. He regularly instructs a number of PGA Tour players, most notably Tom Kite, who worked with him over several months prior to his 1992 U.S. Open victory.

Doral offers several programs for various levels of players, but the best of the best is McLean's 5-day Players' School. Here, instructors work with golfers with a handicap of 15 or better on actually playing the game. Classes are limited to 12 students, and the student: teacher ratio is 3:1. Five rounds on a number of Doral's 99 holes is included. McLean helps each student establish a personal goal for the week, then charts his or her progress as the session continues. He and his very capable teaching staff rely heavily on video analysis and a wide range of teaching aids. At the end of the week, students receive a videotape that includes footage of their swings, plus some personalized instruction from McLean. There's a whole lot of technology going on at Doral, which is indicative of McLean's attitude toward teaching. He's always trying to learn something new.

One of the week's highlights is the opportunity to play the Blue Monster, the best and toughest of the courses on the complex, and the site of the annual Doral Ryder Open. The entire spread at Doral is fairly plush. Rooms are spacious, but lodging is not included in the package price; reserve early. Breakfast and lunch, served at the Champions Club each day, is a bit more adventurous than your standard club food. Dinner is up to the students, although one night during the week, McLean and a few staff members have been known to take the group out for stone crabs. That meal is on McLean, and you should take your freebies when you can. Doral is expensive, and although there are other hotels in the vicinity, life is much easier if you're staying on-site.

Non-golfers, paying standard resort prices, can play tennis, indulge in the luxury of the Doral-Saturnia spa, or hit Miami proper. The ocean is right nearby, and South Beach, the trendiest strip on the east coast, is a few minutes' drive. *Doral Golf Learning Center with Jim McLean, 4400 N.W. 87th Ave., Miami, FL 33178, tel. 305/ 591–6409 or 800/723–6725, fax 305/599–2890. Year-round: 5 days, $2500. Price does not include lodging or dinners.*

NORTH CAROLINA **Pinehurst Golf Advantage Schools.** Pine trees, water sports, tennis, constant activity—takes you back, doesn't it? Camp Menohapatanga? At The Pinehurst Golf Advantage Schools, there's a definite summer-camp feel. Set in the self-proclaimed "golf capital of the world" at Pinehurst, North Carolina, the Advantage Schools put their students up in a grand old hotel built in 1901 and provide them with 3 meals a day. The breakfasts are buffets and the dinners are 5-course gourmet meals (probably better than what you got at Menohapatanga).

Pinehurst is a sprawling complex. In addition to the 7 golf courses and 24 tennis courts, there's a marina, high-end croquet courts, and a gun club (for those of you who really get frustrated with your game). The World Golf Hall of Fame is at Pinehurst, as well.

Headed by PGA professional John Reeves, the instruction program covers all areas of the student's game, and adds a bonus: club-fitting. Including this was a smart move. Few people, pros included, give club-fitting the attention it deserves. Fact is, without properly fitted clubs—and it's a very precise process—you're not going to play your best golf. There's also video analysis, unlimited range balls, and a daily clinic, in addition to 3 hours of daily work on your game. Maximum class size is 20 and the student:teacher ratio is never higher than 5:1.

Three hours is less time on the practice tee and putting green than most other schools provide, but there's a good reason for it. Students head to the golf course at 2:30 PM to apply what they've learned during the morning hours. Carts and greens fees are included in the package, which brings us to perhaps the best part of the Advantage Schools. Among the facility's 7 courses is Pinehurst No. 2, widely regarded as one of the finest courses in the world. Designed by Donald Ross near the turn of the century, this course is a timeless classic that can be enjoyed by all levels of golfer. It hosted the Tour Championship from 1991-92 and in 1995 was the site of the U.S. Open. It'll cost a bit extra to play, but the experience is well worth it. *The Pinehurst Golf Advantage Schools, Box 4000, Pinehurst, NC 28374, tel. 919/295–8128, fax 919/295–8110. Mar.–May, Sep.–Oct.: 4 days, $1,360–$1,675; 6 days, $1,840–$2,300. June–Aug.: 4 days, $1,130–$1,315. Price does not include premiums for playing on courses No. 2 and No. 7. Non-golfing companion rate: 4 days, $575; 6 days, $895.*

SOUTH CAROLINA **The Phil Ritson Golf School.** "Less is more" might be the best description of this school's philosophy. Unlike other schools that boast of their ability to administer a golf overdose during the course of a week, Ritson believes that no golfer should have to endure more than 3½ hours of instruction a day. The 5-day school, set on Pawley's Island, a half hour from Myrtle Beach, is typically made up of 3 half-day sessions at the practice facility, covering everything from driving to putting, and two 9-hole playing lessons. Classes are small—4 students, 1 teacher—so students aren't trying to connect to a number of different teachers.

Phil Ritson has been around for a very long time. Not only has he taught a lot of PGA Tour pros, he's taught a few of the guys who teach the Tour pros. He produced a very successful videotape called "Golf Your Way," a good indication of his teaching philosophy: Take whatever skills and swing the student has, and build upon them. With a sprawling practice facility, including a covered hitting area and an indoor teaching center, Pawley's Plantation provides an ideal arena to showcase his talents.

The only thing is, it's not his talents. It's his partner, Mel Sole, who does the teaching. They met in their native South Africa almost 30 years ago, and have been working together since 1969. Sole is a highly qualified professional, so expect the instruction to be top-notch.

Students have the option to play golf on the Jack Nicklaus signature course during the free half of the day. However, if you choose to come to Ritson's school during "high season" (March to May), you'll have to pay your own greens fee. During other times of the year, the school covers the tab. According to Sole, students are so worn out after half a day of instruction that they tend to cancel any tee times they've made in favor of lounging by the pool, anyway. Maybe you buy that, maybe you don't. In any case, you buy the tee times if you want to play extra golf.

The highlight of this school is the accommodations. Students are put up in luxury villas that have views of the ninth fairway. Two and three bedrooms, two full baths with Jacuzzis, a full working kitchen. For non-golfers, there are water sports, Civil War memorabilia, and country music—the best of the coastal South. *The Phil Ritson Golf School, Pawley's Plantation Golf & Country Club, Hwy. 17, Box 2580, Pawley's Island, SC 29585, tel. 803/237–4993 or 800/624–4653, fax 803/237–8397. Nov.–Feb.: 5 days, $970; Mar.–Jun., $1,245. Price does not include breakfast, dinner, or golf during* peak months. Non-golfing companion rate fluctuates according to group size.

THE MIDWEST

MICHIGAN **Rick Smith Golf Academy.** "Myrtle Beach of the North" is what people are calling Northern Michigan, the country's newest hotbed of golf activity. Courses are popping up everywhere–good courses designed by people like Fazio, Dye, Trent Jones, and Nicklaus. There's a lot of desirable real estate and the cool climes are ideal for growing bent grass, which makes for wonderfully fast, well-manicured greens. One of the centerpieces in this new golf mecca is the Treetops Sylvan Resort in Gaylord, home of the Rick Smith Golf Academy. There are 3—count 'em—18-hole courses: The Treetops original, designed by Robert Trent Jones; another 18, designed by Tom Fazio, who never, *ever* makes a weak design; and another course, designed by Rick Smith himself (insiders say it's the best of the three). Add a 9-hole par-3 course, designed by Smith, and you're in Golf Land. The best part: Students have free access to it all.

This guy Smith may have an average name, but he's one of the hottest young teachers in golf today. Besides being a top-notch architect, he's making quite a dent on the PGA Tour, teaching players like Billy Andrade and the 1993 U.S. Open winner, Lee Janzen. Rumor has it he's also been working with that other guy, Nicklaus.

Great courses, great teacher—sounds too good to be true. So, here's the catch. While it's Rick Smith's Academy, he doesn't teach the 3-day program. That is the job of Henry Young, a PGA pro of 20-plus years, who doesn't teach on tour and doesn't design big-name golf courses. But he has been working with Smith since Smith was a teenager, so it's safe to say that Young was instrumental in shaping Smith's teaching philosophy.

Class starts at 4 PM on Friday. Four students, no more, and Henry gets things started by doing some full-swing work and video analysis. Henry Young, like Smith, is the kind of teacher who isn't married to a particular method, but who shapes his lesson around the student's individual needs and qualities. Saturday and Sunday mornings are split between short game and putting from 8:30 to 10:30 and full swing from 10:30 to 12:30. An hour for lunch, then the students are set free to experience any one of the resort's golf courses. This is a very straightforward, fundamental approach: Practice in the morning, play in the afternoon. There's not a lot of attention paid to on-course work or mental training. But in the span of 2½ days, Rick Smith (and Henry Young) offer about the right amount of instruction. And with only 4 students, there's more individual attention here than just about anywhere else.

Unlike some other schools, breakfast and dinner are included in the package, while lunch is extra. Treetops, aside from their better-than-average rooms, offers swimming, tennis, and daycare. Children sightsee and shop on nearby scenic Mackinac Island or Traverse City while their parents play golf in peace. *Rick Smith Golf Academy, 3962 Wilkinson Rd., Gaylord MI 49735, tel. 517/732–6711 or 800/444–6711, fax 517/732–6595. May–Sept.: 3 days, $831. Price does not include lunches.*

THE SOUTHWEST

ARIZONA **Tour Golf Schools.** Formerly known as Sports Enhancement Associates, Tour Golf Schools is the baby of Chuck Hogan, an unusual golf professional who has dedicated himself to teaching golf based not just on perfecting the swing, but on increasing the level of "human performance"—which is to say, using your body and your mind together for an optimal performance. The idea is to help the student practice more effectively, overcome jitters, and manage inconsistency, as well as master technique. Rather than learning to work hard, Hogan believes the student should learn to play hard. It's a marriage of the mental and physical aspects of the game, and since 1984, it has produced a golf school program unlike any other.

Hogan isn't teaching in 1995-1996, but has left the reigns to three of his professionals—Billy McDonald, Dale McDermid, and Stan Sayers. Classes have a limit of 18 students, the student:teacher ratio is never more than 6:1, and all levels of ability are represented.

Hogan's a studious guy, and his school reflects it. Forty percent of the student's time is spent in the classroom, discussing concepts, determining the student's needs, and developing a strategy to address them. That takes most of the morning. After lunch, the group heads out to the practice tee, where the teachers implement the strategies they formulated in the classroom. Over the 5 days, students will play 27 holes of supervised golf, in addition to any golf they choose to play in the late afternoon. Greens fees and carts are included.

The setting for the 4½-day school is Sedona, Arizona, a tourist-oriented arts-and-crafts center surrounded by some of the most picture-perfect, red rock landscapes in the Southwest. The Sedona Golf Resort has an 18-hole championship course designed by Gary Panks and David Graham. Accommodations are not included in the package price. Students have the option of booking rooms at the upscale Los Ebrigedos Hotel ($165 per night, discounted), or the more modest Bell Rock Inn ($80 per night, discounted). Either way, students take care of their own breakfasts and 3 dinners. Lunch is provided by the school, and there are 2 gourmet dinners preceded by cocktail receptions at Los Ebrigedos. Non-golfers can experience Sedona as well: Do a little shopping, go horseback riding, hike the scenic trails. *Tour Golf Schools, Box 2788, Sedona, AZ 86336, tel. 602/284–9000 or 800/345–4245, fax 602/284–1948. Spring and Fall: 4½ days, $1,695. Price does not include lodging or some meals.*

TEXAS **The Academy of Golf Dynamics.** Austin, Texas, is home to a few of golf's greatest names. Ben Crenshaw and Tom Kite get their mail here. Nicklaus has a house at Lakeway, but he's got a house just about everywhere. In any case, with this illustrious roster of residents, it seems only right that there be a first-rate golf facility.

The Academy of Golf Dynamics, at the Hills of Lakeway development, is just that. With a 500-yard range, sprawling putting green, practice bunkers, and 3 practice holes in addition to one of Jack Nicklaus's most charming courses, the Academy has a facility for learning that outdistances most of the competition.

The Academy's director, PGA pro Bill Moretti, teaches with a progressive philosophy. Like many others, he's not married to any swing "method," but he also believes in letting a student's personality help shape the individual lesson plan. Everybody is videotaped, but some students will connect with technology more than others. As a result, some will spend a good deal of time with teaching and training aids, while others will learn more through plain old personal advice, and the good old beating of balls.

The big advantage here are the 3 practice holes, which allow the teachers to work on-course with the students daily. Fundamentals are covered, of course, but there is a much greater emphasis on actually playing the game than at most schools. Moretti is a big believer in creating the perfect learning environment. As a result, he guarantees a teacher:student ratio of no more than 3:1—lower than most. After experimenting with different session lengths, Moretti decided to make all his schools 3 days. Students spend the mornings working on fundamentals and the afternoons working on on-course situations. At 3 PM, you are free to go play (price included); if you choose not to, teachers are available for further instruction. It's an extremely complete program. The Academy also offers a parent and child session, as well as corporate and private packages.

The base price for the Academy does not include lodging. There are different choices for accommodations, from The Lakeway Inn, an unassuming hotel set above Lake Travis, to course-side villas. The school will fill you in on the details. Breakfast and lunch are included—standard country-club

fare at the Hills Club—but not dinner. Most of the non-golf action takes place on Lake Travis. If you're not into water sports, you're going to be hard-pressed to find something to keep you busy. Austin is a city first, a tourist attraction (a distant) second. *The Academy of Golf Dynamics, 45 Club Estates Pkwy., Austin, TX 78738, tel. 512/261–3300 or 800/879–2008, fax 512/261–8168. March–Oct.: 3 days, $860–$1,045 midweek, $975–$1,215 weekend. Price does not include lodging or dinner.*

THE ROCKIES

COLORADO **Golf Digest Instruction School at Vail.** You're guaranteed to add at least 10 yards to your drive at Golf Digest's Vail school. The catch is, you won't take that distance home with you. The Vail Valley lies high in the Rocky Mountains, more than 8,000 feet above sea level. The air is thinner, so resistance is lower and the ball flies farther. But the thin air won't cure your slice. That's the job of the pros from Golf Digest. Maximum class size is 21, and the student:teacher ratio is never greater than 7:1.

But the setting of the Vail school is so breathtaking that you probably won't care what happens to your game. First of all, you're surrounded by mountains. Then there are the Aspen trees and wildflowers that blanket the mountainsides. Throw in the winding creeks and rivers and you might just want to put your clubs down, grab a comfortable chair, and soak it all in.

You might—if you weren't practicing and playing golf at Sonnenalp Golf Club, once known as Singletree. Sonnenalp was designed by Jay Morrish in the early 1980s, when Morrish was Jack Nicklaus's top design man. (Morrish has since joined forces with Tom Weiskopf). Morrish didn't get a lot of credit for his work on the course, and Sonnenalp doesn't get much attention compared to Country Club of the Rockies, Nicklaus's creation across the street. Don't be fooled: It's one of the best courses in Colorado. It carves its way in and out of the foothills of the town of Edwards, and features dramatic changes in elevation, great views of the Vail Valley, and superbly manicured greens. With 4 sets of tees, it's a fair but challenging test for all levels of golfer.

The course is about 15 minutes down the road from the Vail Village and the Sonnenalp Inn, where students stay. There's a Bavarian motif at Sonnenalp, and it is reflected in each of their 3 restaurants. Golf Digest's all-inclusive policy means that meals are included. There's a spa and luxury boutique here for the non-golfer, but there's so much more to do outside the hotel. Go hiking, fishing, white-water rafting, horseback riding, take a chair lift up one of the mountains. There are endless ways to have a fabulous vacation in Vail. Just take it slow at first—the thin air takes a few days to get used to. *Golf Digest Instruction Schools, 5520 Park Ave., Box 395, Trumbull, CT 06611–0395, tel. 203/ 373–7130 or 800/243–6121, fax 203/373– 7088. June–Aug: 3 days, $2,575–$2,685. Non-golfing companion rate (includes all meals): $725.*

THE WEST COAST

CALIFORNIA **La Costa Golf School.** Over the years, golf schools have tended to develop into something more commercial and less personalized. Not at La Costa. Here, you choose who you want to take the school with (no more than 4 students), when to take it, and for how long. It's extremely private. You can come for a single day, or as many as 8. PGA professionals Carl Welty and Jennifer McFalls are the only instructors. The worst student:teacher ratio is 2:1. But it could be as good as 1:2, because even if you're alone, Welty and Eifrid will give you their undivided attention.

Welty may be the video maven of golf instruction: You're on camera from the moment you get there. The first thing every student does is play 9 holes under video surveillance. The tape is then analyzed to determine the student's strengths and weak-

nesses and to design a lesson plan around them. After that, it's 6–8 hours of instruction daily, broken down into equal thirds of on-course work (videotaped), practice drills and lessons (videotaped), and time in the classroom (video analysis). It almost never rains at La Costa, but Welty favors indoor instruction at times. When students can't see where the ball goes, they concentrate more on form and technique and less on result.

Unlike most schools, La Costa does not let you pay in package form. You've got to do the breakdown yourself, which means paying Welty and Eifrid between $35 and $85 per hour for their services, depending upon the number of golfers in your group (fewer golfers, more money). Rooms at La Costa are $200 a night. Do some quick arithmetic and the cost of a 3-day school for 2 comes out to about $2,700. Meals are not included. (Did we say this one was a bit less commercial?)

Yes, it's pricey. But it's perhaps the most personalized school around, offering the most individual attention, and furthermore, La Costa is not just another resort. The golf course is great: 18 of its 36 holes host the PGA Tour's Tournament of Champions each year. There are men's and women's spas, a fitness center, as well as the usual tennis court and swimming pool facilities. You're free to choose your meals during your stay, and 5 on-site restaurants offer plenty of dining options. (You'd better have a fat wallet.) And if you're a traditionalist, La Costa is the place for you, as well: They run their school the way they used to in the good old days. *The LaCosta Golf School, Costa del Mar Rd., Carlsbad, CA 92009, tel. 619/438–9111, ext. 4258, or 800/ 653–7888, fax 619/438–3758. Year-round custom-length sessions: $140 per hour for 4 students, $120 for 3 students, $100 for 2, $85 for 1. Price does not include meals or lodging. Rooms at the resort start at $200 double occupancy.*

CALIFORNIA **Nicklaus/Flick at Pebble Beach.** It's important to remember that Pebble Beach is not only a golf course, but a town as well, because this Nicklaus/Flick school is not at Pebble Beach the golf course. It's at the Inn at Spanish Bay, in Pebble Beach the town, only a few minutes from Pebble Beach Golf Course. All of which is set on the fabulous Monterey Peninsula.

Two different 3-day sessions are held from May to September. Master Golf I features a full day of instruction at Spyglass Hill plus 9 holes of golf daily at 1 of the 3 area courses (Spyglass, Pebble Beach, or Spanish Bay). Master Golf III limits practice sessions to a single half-day. Three 18-hole rounds are included. Students stay at the Inn at Spanish Bay, and again, it's not Pebble Beach—but it's just as good, if not better. The rooms are huge, with fireplaces and beautiful views of the ocean and the Links at Spanish Bay. There are also tennis courts and a health spa. Here, the living is very, very plush.

Breakfast is at the Inn each morning at 7 AM. The students are brought to Spyglass Hill Golf Club, considered the toughest of the Peninsula courses, where they take advantage of the club's extensive practice facility. There are never more than 18 students per school, and they are broken up into 3 groups according to handicap. Maximum student:teacher ratio is 6:1—higher than some schools, but Jim Flick's in-your-face teaching style narrows the gap considerably. A lunch of the usual sandwiches and salads is at Spyglass, while dinner is left up to the student. Good thing, because the Peninsula is filled with restaurants as spectacular as the ocean views. *Nicklaus/ Flick Golf School, 11780 U.S. Highway One, North Palm Beach, FL 33408-9809, tel. 407/626-3900 or 800/642-5528, fax 407/626-4104. May–Sept.: 3 days, $3,350– $4,250 (Master Golf I) or $3,250–$4,150 (Master Golf III). Price does not include dinners or extra rounds of golf. Non-golfing companion rate (includes meals): $725 for Master Golf I, $750 for Master Golf III.*

SOURCES

ORGANIZATIONS The **National Golf Foundation** (tel. 407/744-6006) isn't golf's governing body, but it is golf's largest research resource, and it has its collective finger on the pulse of just about everything that's happening in the game. It also happens to publish a list of the country's golf schools.

Before you commit to any golf school, be sure that those teaching the golf swing are members of the **Professional Golf Association of America** (tel. 407/624-8400). Class A certification by the PGA of America indicates that teachers know what they're doing. This is important not only in choosing a golf school, but when taking individual lessons, as well. Your local PGA chapter has a list of certified pros in your area.

PERIODICALS The leading golf magazines rarely run school listings anymore, but they do showcase the instruction of many of the teachers at the major schools. To catch a glimpse of some of the material you may learn at school, take a look at *Golf Magazine* (2 Park Ave., New York, NY 10016, tel. 800/876-7726); *Golf Digest* (Box 395, Trumbull, CT 06611-0395, tel. 800/727-4653); and *Golf Tips Magazine* (12121 Wilshire Blvd., Suite 1220, Los Angeles, CA 90025-1175, tel. 310/820-1500).

BOOKS For a complete listing of just about all the golf schools in this country and others, try *The Guide to Golf Schools & Camps*, published by ShawGuides Inc., or *Golf Schools—The Complete Guide*, by First Person Press. Both list all the basic information for the golf-school shopper. For a more personalized look, author Robin McMillan reviews several major schools in his book, *The Golfer's Home Companion*, published by Simon & Schuster. Fodor's publishes *Golf Digest's Best Places to Play*, the results of the magazine's reader survey, which chronicles more than 4,000 courses in the United States, Canada, and the Caribbean.

Hang Gliding

By Erik Fair

ang gliding is the flyingist flying there is. Hang glider pilots eschew the confines of cockpit or cabin and hang out in the breeze. They feel airspeed with their skin and hear its whisper in their ears. The silent, swooping sensations hang glider pilots feel recall the flight of mythological Icarus, whose wax wings carried him toward the sun.

Hang gliders, which weigh 50 to 75 pounds, are the only fabric-and-frame aircraft light enough to be foot-launched by a human being. The size of the hang glider (often called a wing) varies according to the pilot's weight. Solo pilots fly wings with 130 to 175 square feet of sail area; tandem pilots require 180 to 220 square feet of sail to support the weight of two people.

One common misconception is that a hang glider is powered by fickle wind. The wings are actually powered by gravity, which causes them to fly downward through whatever air mass they are in. A hang glider can climb away from the ground only if the air mass is rising faster than the glider is flying downward through it. Hang gliders can stay aloft in the wide band of air that is deflected upward when wind strikes the face of a cliff. They also climb away from the ground in masses of hot air (thermals) that rise faster than 200 feet per minute.

Wind direction, velocity, and degree of turbulence affect safety during launch and landing. Most pilots don't fly in winds greater than 25 mph, and experience teaches them how to predict and avoid turbulence. A beginner's inexperience at judging wind conditions is one of two main reasons why professional instruction is a must. The other is that trial-and-error learning is especially stupid in any form of aviation.

There are a variety of safe, enjoyable ways for you to try hang gliding for the first time. One option is bunny-slope training, which typically costs from $50 to $125 for a half- or full-day lesson. You spend the first few hours running around on flat ground, learning how to control the glider as it floats overhead. After you develop a feel for the friendly way the glider tugs up at your pants, you try a take-off on a gentle slope. Gravity and lift work their magic and suddenly you're moon-walking, then *really flying*, just a few feet off the ground. Several heartbeats later, you gape at your feet, knowing—though not quite believing—they actually left the ground. You need at least average strength, aerobic capacity, and flexibility to enjoy slope training. Avoid it if you have leg or back problems that keep you from running.

If the bunny slope sounds a little tame, you may opt for a tandem flight. For $100 to

Adventurer and writer Erik Fair is the author of *California Thrill Sports* and winner of the 1991 Max Karant Award for Excellence in Aviation Journalism. He's taught hundreds of folks how to fly a hang glider and wrote a book for them called *Right Stuff for New Hang Glider Pilots*.

$150 you will spend half an hour in ground school practicing launch procedures, then, safely under the wing of your instructor, trot off a mountain top or cliff for a high-altitude dance with blue space. A tandem flight gives you ground clearances of several hundred to several thousand feet, plus 10 to 60 minutes of air time on your first excursion. Experienced tandem pilots turn the glider over to you following launch. With your pilot in the "driver's ed." instructional position, you are suddenly in command. If you live in the flatlands, modern towing techniques will allow you and your instructor to safely launch, via tow-rope and winch, from the back of a boat or truck. Tandem is great for those who weigh less than 200 lbs. Some pilots will fly 200- to 225-pound passengers in strong wind conditions.

Vicarious thrill-seekers can have fun just watching others carve circles in the sky. Observation is free. Call the nearest hang gliding school, ask where and when the flying is, get directions to the LZ (landing zone), and show up an hour early. If it's a cliff site, just start asking questions and watch. If it's a mountain site, offer to serve as a driver and notice how popular you become. Hang glider pilots gladly befriend anyone willing to ride with them to the launch site and drive their car back to the LZ. You'll get a great taste of hang gliding and make a new friend, too.

No matter how you start out, you'll learn that relaxation is the heart and soul of hang gliding. That's because a hang glider literally follows your spine. With your body hanging in a hammocklike harness attached to the glider's center of gravity, you pull your weight forward to fly faster and push it backward to slow down. Nudge yourself to the right or left and the glider will follow your lead. When you relax your grip and just hang there, the glider flies straight and level, just above the minimum speed required to sustain flight.

If you want to become capable of soloing, you'll need to train a few days a week for several weeks. You might learn the *skills*

necessary to fly by yourself during a two-week vacation, but you won't develop the judgment needed to fly safely without professional supervision.

To earn a United States Hang Gliding Association (USHGA) Hang I (beginner) rating, you must demonstrate the ability to perform 3 consecutive smooth launches, followed by 3 soft landings on your feet into the wind. You will also have to demonstrate the ability to fly straight with good airspeed control. Some folks can do this in a single half-day lesson, but most require 2 to 4 lessons. A Hang I rating simply means you can launch and land on a bunny slope under professional supervision. To earn a Hang II (novice) rating—which allows you to fly under your own supervision in mild conditions—you also have to perform precise, linked 90- and 180-degree turns and land within 100 feet of a target. Naturals have been known to accomplish these feats in 3 lessons, but most people require between 4 and 12.

Fortunately, it is very easy to incorporate 2 or 3 days of hang gliding into a week-long vacation. California, particularly Southern California and the Bay Area, offers the best year-round conditions and training areas. But there are a number of good seasonal places in New England, the Southeast, the Southwest, and the Rocky Mountains. And developments in towing technology (launch via truck, boat, or ultralight air-tug) have opened up the vast flatlands of the Midwest to hang gliding.

Because many hang-gliding sites are threatened by development or liability considerations, secure locations are the sport's most treasured commodity. A secure site is one where the landowner formally acknowledges and permits hang gliding. These sites usually have bathrooms, launch ramps, picnic areas, and other conveniences.

Most schools will have you sign a liability release form, which says that you are willing to assume the risks associated with leaving the ground under your own power. A good school will make sure you clearly understand this document before you sign it.

CHOOSING THE RIGHT SCHOOL

You should choose a hang gliding school primarily on its adherence to the regulations that govern the sport. The certification of a school's hang gliders by the Hang Glider Manufacturers Association (HGMA) insures that they are strong, sophisticated aircraft, thoroughly tested for structural strength and aerodynamic stability. Certification of a school's instructors by the United States Hang Gliding Association (USHGA) guarantees that they are experienced hang glider pilots who have taught at least 10 days on a training hill under the supervision of a certified instructor, attended a 4-day training-and-certification seminar, and passed a written test. Ask these questions before you pay money or sign a liability release form:

Are your instructors certified by the USHGA? The only acceptable answer is yes. All schools listed below employ only certified instructors.

Will I be flying a glider that is certified by the HGMA? Don't take no for an answer, unless the glider has been specially modified for use on a bunny slope. HGMA-certified gliders are about five times stronger than they need to be to withstand normal flight loads in normal weather conditions. Since instructors of first- and second-day students teach only in very mild conditions, they will sometimes install lighter frame parts in a training glider. Even then, the glider is twice as strong as it needs to be and will save you 5 to 10 pounds of extra baggage on the hill.

Is this a secure site? Avoid schools who use "bandit" sites, where there's a good chance that a badge-toting "smokey" will run you off mid-lesson.

What kind of instruction do you offer? Whether you are interested in tandem flights or slope training (or some combination of the two), make sure the school you choose offers what you want. All schools listed below offer tandem flights as well as bunny-slope training.

How long has your company been in business, and how long have you been teaching? Experience means a lot. It's the only way you learn to read the wind.

What is the best time of year to hang glide here? With the exception of California—where blue skies, sunshine, predictable windflows, and varied terrain make for some of the world's best year-round hang gliding—most areas have definite gliding seasons.

What other attractions are in the area? This is especially important if you're traveling with non-pilots.

How far in advance do I need to book? Although some schools accept walk-in students when not fully booked, it's best to make reservations at least two weeks in advance. In these listings, chamber of commerce telephone numbers are given for assistance in finding accommodations near the schools.

Do you have references from former students?

FAVORITE SCHOOLS

THE NORTHEAST

NEW HAMPSHIRE **Morningside Flight Park.** Morningside is the finest hang gliding training area in the Northeast. Its centerpiece is a 250-foot gently sloping hill, wide enough to accommodate 20 gliders side by side. The hill is manicured and drained, like a golf course, and a big bull's-eye is painted in the landing area for students practicing spot landings. One amenity beloved by novices and veterans alike is the fleet of all-terrain vehicles (ATVs) that owner Jeff Nicolay has rigged to shuttle pilots and gliders from bottom to top between flights.

First-day bunny-slope students can expect quite a few 10- to 20-second flights from 15 to 40 feet up the slope—as many flights as will fit in the 4-hour lesson. Morningside also offers on-site tandem flights in which instructor and passenger are towed to altitude by an ultra-light aircraft pilot named Hungry Joe. That's good news for those who just want to say "I did it!" An excellent observation opportunity is found 10 miles away at Mt. Ascutney, one of the most popular mountain-soaring sites in the East.

Morningside Flight Park has been going strong since 1975, when owner Phil Haynes's love of hang gliding led him to lease his dairy farm to veteran pilot Jeff Nicolay. The school is in Western New Hampshire, about 2 hours from Boston. The lilac blossoms of spring and the vibrant colors of a New England fall make May, September, and October the best times of year to visit. The school closes when the ground freezes (usually after Thanksgiving), and reopens after the spring thaw in early April.

Morningside has a spring-fed pond for swimming, and a petting zoo with ducks, geese, horses, and Tennessee Fainting Goats. (Though these goats pass out when they're startled, they have grown accustomed to hang gliders—so you can, too!) There are also tent camping facilities and bathrooms with hot showers. The retail store stocks local maple syrup as well as hang gliding T-shirts and gear. *Morningside Flight Park, 357 Morningside Lane, North Charleston, NH 03603, tel. 603/542-4416. Claremont Chamber of Commerce, tel. 603/ 543-1296. Apr.–Nov. (lessons by appointment only): 4-hour bunny-slope lesson, $95; tandem flight (aero-tow to 2,500 ft.), $95.*

THE SOUTH

GEORGIA **Lookout Mountain Flight Park.** This is the school to choose if you want to become a solo pilot. Owner Matt Taber discourages the "looky loo" crowd from taking single-day, bunny-slope lessons at the 65-foot training hill in Lookout Valley. Taber favors a method that is not aimed at providing flights after one lesson. If you decide to take slope lessons at this school, you'll probably be talked into a 2- or 3-day lesson package, and there will be earnest talk of turning you into a hang glider pilot. If that's not on your agenda, by all means take a tandem flight with these guys; Taber and his instructors give 200 to 300 a year.

Lookout Mountain is one of the highest points on a 21-mile "soarable" ridge above Lookout Valley. This northwestern corner of Georgia is covered by hardwood trees that make the fall foliage season a beautiful time to hang glide here. Come for the crisp mountain air and the "wonder winds"—gentle upward drafts caused by warm air rising from the valley—that increase during the fall and spring seasons. The top of Lookout Mountain is directly accessible by Georgia Highway 189, and it's a convenient place to watch hang glider pilots as they perform exciting high-wind launches or get wafted up 1,000 feet by the evening wonder winds.

Another great observation opportunity is The Great Race, held here each spring. It's a pedal-to-the-metal contest that runs from the end of the ridge and back—a total of more than 40 miles. The best pilots from all over the country tune-up their high-performance gliders and show up for the party.

A pro-shop next to the launch ramp sells film, T-shirts, postcards, and snacks, and is a good place to watch some of the best hang glider pilots in the country begin their flights. For the rest of the family, the Chattanooga, Tennessee (about 20 minutes away) vicinity has an excellent fresh-water aquarium and Ruby Falls, an underground cavern with a waterfall. White-water rafting is an hour away on the Ocoee River, site of the 1996 Olympic Kayak Run. *Lookout Mountain Flight Park, Rte. 2, Box 215H, Rising Fawn, GA 30738, tel. 706/398-3541. Closest accommodations at the Lookout Inn, tel. 706/820-2000, or call the Chattanooga Chamber of Commerce, tel. 615/756-2121. Closed Wed. Year-round (lessons by appointment only): 2-day bunny-slope weekend package, $199; tandem flight (aero-tow to 2,000 ft.), $99.*

NORTH CAROLINA **Kitty Hawk Kites.** This is, without question, the world's foremost hang gliding school, giving 10,000 to 15,000 bunny-slope lessons a year. Kitty Hawk employs up to 30 certified instructors during the peak months of June, July, August, and September, so it can maintain a 5:1 student:instructor ratio. Even during slower months, there are 15 instructors here to handle the load. Lighter crowds, combined with the cooler northeasterly winds that are more comfortable for pilots, make the spring and fall prime times to visit Kitty Hawk. You can buy a lesson here any day of the year (except Christmas Day), weather permitting.

The school is in Jockey's Ridge State Park, part of North Carolina's Outer Banks, and lessons center around the East Coast's highest (110 feet) natural sand dune. You spend half an hour in ground school, then move on to a 3-hour lesson; here you're guaranteed to take 5 flights off the dune.

Although the emphasis at Kitty Hawk is on bunny-slope lessons, the instructors also offer tandem flights using modern aero- and boat-towing techniques. Aero-towing takes place at an airstrip in Kurrituck, about 40 minutes from the shop. An ultra-light aircraft will tow you and an instructor to 1,000 or 2,000 feet then cut you loose to glide down. Boat-tows are on Albamarle Sound near the town of Duck (that's right, Duck!), about 20 minutes from the shop.

Mother's Day Weekend has been special at Kitty Hawk since 1972, the first year of the annual Hang Gliding Spectacular. This gathering of eagles includes sand-skimming races and duration contests. At the end of the weekend, Francis Rogallo—the man who designed the first flexible wing (which was later used to create the hang glider) for NASA in the 1940s—joins Kitty Hawk owner John Harris in giving out awards to the winners.

Kitty Hawk's retail store is an attraction in itself. In addition to hang gliding and flying souvenirs and apparel, the store provides an area with toys for the kids to play with, a playground with tube slides and ball pits, an indoor rock wall for climbing, and rollerblade lessons and rentals. There are opportunities for kayaking, sailing, and windsurfing lessons on Albamarle Sound for those who prefer to keep it on the ground. *Kitty Hawk Kites, Box 1839, Nags Head, NC 27959, tel. 919/441–4124 or 800/334–4777. Outer Banks Chamber of Commerce, tel. 919/441–8144. Closed Christmas Day. Year-round (lessons by appointment only): 3-hour bunny-slope lesson (5 flights), $69; tandem aero-tow flight (1,000 or 2,000 ft.), $85–110, Tandem boat-tow flight (1,000 or 2,000 ft.), $99–125. Beginner Pilot lesson package (eight sand-dune lessons), $469. Novice Pilot lesson package (18 dune lessons, 18 tandem tows, and 2 solo tows for $999.*

THE MIDWEST

WISCONSIN **Raven Sky Sports.** Who says the Midwest is too flat to have a first-class hang gliding school? Not Raven Sky Sport owner Brad Kushner, a man who has parlayed unique local terrain and modern towing technology into a little bit of hang gliding heaven in Whitewater, Wisconsin. The center of the school is a private airport where Kushner houses his two Dragonflys, a motorized, ultra-light aircraft that's a cross between a hang glider and an airplane. It's specially designed for towing hang gliders to altitude, just as airplanes tow sailplanes. Kushner and crew will use one of two runways to tandem air-tow you to 2,500 feet for a smooth flight down.

Kushner has been flying for 20 years and teaching for 17. His methods include special instruction for people with disabilities, using equipment that permits rolling takeoffs and landings. This method also allows Kushner to train large folks (up to 300 pounds), a unique service in a sport where 200 pounds is the usual cutoff.

Whitewater is surrounded by dozens of grassy little 30- to 80-foot bunny slopes that face all different wind directions. Kushner selects a training hill based on weather conditions, and then meets students there in his Isuzu Trooper II, which tows a custom-designed Hang Trailer containing training equipment as well as a supply of hang gliding books, T-shirts, and souvenirs.

Although decidedly rural, Whitewater stands at the center of a densely populated triangle, an hour from Milwaukee and Madison, Wisconsin, and 2 hours from Chicago. You can go swimming, fishing, and boating at Lake Koshkonong or at Lake Geneva, a playground for Chicago's well-to-do that is famous for its bed-and-breakfasts. Nearby Whitewater Lakes Recreation Area offers camping and watersports. *Raven Sky Sports, Box 101, Whitewater, WI 53190, tel. 414/ 473–8800. Whitewater Chamber of Commerce, tel. 414/473–4005. Whitewater Lakes Recreation Area, tel. 414/473–6427. Mar.– Nov. (lessons by appointment only): 1-day bunny-slope lesson, $95; 5-day package, $350; tandem flight (aero-tow to 2,500 ft.), $105; 5-day novice training package (with 10 tandem flights), $1,150.*

THE SOUTHWEST

UTAH **Wasatch Wings.** You can learn to hang glide twice as fast at Wasatch Wings. It's one of the few places in the country where you can earn a Hang I (beginner) rating in a single week, or a Hang II (novice) rating in 2 weeks. The wind conditions at Point of the Mountain, Utah—which sits astride the narrowest portion of Salt Lake Valley—make this possible. The morning wind funnels straight up its 300-foot south-facing slope, and the afternoon wind funnels straight up its 1,000-foot north-facing slope, enabling owner Zac Majors to give more experienced students 2 lessons a day. At most schools you can only take 2 to 4 lessons a week. Majors reports that student pilots from all over the country come to Point of the Mountain to refine their skills. Many are accompanied by certified instructors from out of state who want to take advantage of the intense training the conditions allow.

The area is especially breathtaking in the fall, when the red-and-orange scrub oak and yellow sage of the Salt Lake Valley stand out against the green pines of the Wasatch Mountains. You can enjoy the views on tandem flights that Majors gives from 4,600-foot Frances Peak and 3,000-foot Camel Pass. Mountain biking, hiking, and swimming are available throughout the area, most notably at Deer Creek Lake. Salt Lake City is 30 miles away. *Wasatch Wings, 10889 South Shady Dell Drive, Sandy, UT 84094, tel. 801/277– 1042. Mountain Shadows Campground, tel. 801/ 571–4024. Salt Lake City Chamber of Commerce, tel. 801/364–3631. Apr.–Nov. (lessons by appointment only): 3- to 4-hour bunny-slope lesson (8–10 flights), $75; tandem flight (from 3,000–4,600 ft.), $125.*

THE ROCKIES

COLORADO **Golden Wings.** This is the only full-service hang gliding center in the Rockies. Because of a relatively short gliding season (early April through early October), and summer winds that can change from weak to wicked in a matter of minutes, this isn't the ideal location for a hang gliding school. Golden Wings makes it work, using a mobile training unit that gives instructors total control over training conditions for first- and second-day students.

Co-owners Ludwig Goppenhammer and Terry Hackbart have built a remarkable hang gliding flight simulator on the back of a flatbed truck. You hook into a glider tethered to the truckbed by lines that allow you to fly a few feet in the air before running out of slack. One instructor stands in front of you and issues commands that help you float up, up, and away to where you can practice basic controls to your heart's content. The other instructor drives the truck down the road fast enough for the wind to lift you and the glider into the air. If you have any problems, the instructor uses the tethers to pull you back into correct form.

After a few sessions on the truck simulator, you proceed to North Boulder, a 350-foot training hill about 20 miles from the shop. Or, you can take a foot-launched tandem flight from a 2,000-foot mountain. Head instructor Mark Windsheimer, who has been flying and teaching since 1972, is supremely qualified to supervise your flying experience.

The best times to hang glide in this area are early spring and early fall, when the temperatures are milder and the winds are smoother. Beer fans will be happy to note that Golden Wings is within minutes of the Coors Brewery. The town of Golden has a definite Old West flavor, complete with an old-fashioned Main Street. It's just a few minutes from downtown Denver and within striking distance of some of the best hiking, mountain biking, and white-water rafting in the United States. *Golden Wings, 15401 West 9th Ave., Suite A, Golden, CO 80401, tel. 303/278–7181 or 800/677–4449. Golden Chamber of Commerce, tel. 303/279–3113. Early Apr.–early Oct.: full-day flatbed simulator lesson, $75; slope lesson (350-ft. hill), $95; mountain tandem flight (2,000 ft.), $100.*

THE WEST COAST

CALIFORNIA **The Hang Gliding Center.** John Ryan and his wife Amy live with their two children in an environmentally correct home called an "Earth Ship" that has been fashioned out of old tires. An adjacent trailer houses John and Amy's hang gliding shop that has been serving the greater San Diego area for nearly twenty years. John provides individualized instruction year-round by appointment only. Unusually, he normally instructs 2–4 students per day on the bunny hills near Little Black and Otay mountains east of San Diego. He'll take 1–3 students per day out to Horse Canyon, Laguna Mountain, and Big Black for mountain-launched tandem flights or first solos. Most of the sites used by John are in or around the Anza Borrego desert (particularly beautiful in March when the wildflowers bloom) or Cleveland National Forest (always good for stunning panoramic vistas of desert mountains and valleys).

Sea World, the world famous San Diego Zoo, and Balboa Park are all within an hour's drive. Torrey Pines Park, on the coast near La Jolla, is a great place to watch local experienced pilots soar high above coastal cliffs, often mixing it up with radio control model sail planes and, on especially windy days, even real sail planes. *The Hang Gliding Center, Box 1049, Lakeside, CA. 92040, tel., 619/561–1009. Accommodation referrals available upon request or call San Diego Chamber of Commerce, tel., 619/456–4092. Year-round service by appointment only. Beginner Package: 3 days of bunny-slope lessons, $270. Novice Package; 6 days of bunny-slope lessons and a graduation solo flight, $515. Foot-launch tandem flights (from 1,000 ft to 3,400 ft), $175.*

CALIFORNIA **Mission Soaring.** Since learning to fly in 1972 owner Pat Denevan has dedicated himself to the development of safe, user-friendly, state-of-the art hang gliding equipment and instructional technique. Pat's school, in Milpitas near San Jose, has extra-light, extra-slow, and extra-easy crafts, and training harnesses specially designed with student comfort in mind.

Mission Soaring's Hollister training site has bunny slopes that allow straight-into-the-wind launches in different directions. Consistently gentle wind conditions, a huge landing area, and enough roadway to allow tandem and solo tow-launch via truck and winch make the Hollister site an ideal place to learn how to fly. Mission Soaring shows a 15-minute video entitled "First Flight," which introduces you to the techniques and exercises you'll be exposed to in your first few lessons at Hollister. You can watch this video at the shop or buy it for $20. If you buy the video, your $20 will be credited to your first lesson when you take it.

Mission Soaring's retail shop is a hang glider pilot's paradise. A custom hang gliding simulator for trying on harnesses, a huge topographical map showing all of Northern's California's flying sites, an impressive hang gliding picture gallery, and a big screen television set for viewing the latest videos will make you feel like kicking back here for hours at a time. Mission's service department is arguably the finest in the country.

Monterey, Santa Cruz, and San Jose are all within an hour's drive. A little less than two hours will get you to San Francisco. *Mission Soaring, 1116 Wrigley Way, Milpitas, CA 95035, tel., 408/262–1055, fax, 408/262–1388. Milpitas Chamber of Commerce, 408/262–2613. Lessons by appointment year round. Retail shop open Wednesday through Saturday. One 5-hour day on the bunny slope; $120. Novice Package (5 5-hour days on the bunny slope); $500. Inquire about tandem flights.*

CALIFORNIA **Windsports Hang Gliding School.** You may have already seen Windsports owner Joe Greblo fly a hang glider: He is one-half of Stunt Wings, the TV-and-film industry's most frequently employed hang gliding stunt team. He is also a USHGA regional director and one of the developers of the USHGA's Tandem Rating Program.

Greblo has been running Windsports, one of the oldest continuously operated hang gliding schools in the United States (and perhaps the world), since it opened in 1974. The school has three components: a 1,500-square-foot Pro Shop in Van Nuys, a bunny slope in the San Fernando Valley, and a more advanced launch site 3,500 feet above Joe's vacation home at the base of Los Angeles's Kagel Mountain.

You start with an hour of ground school at the shop, then spend an afternoon working with instructors on the 150-foot slope called Simi Valley. The slope is so gentle that your instructor can run right alongside you while you skim for hundreds of feet, just 3 to 5 feet above the ground. Joe supervises the more advanced lessons at Kagel Mountain, where the landing site is maintained by the City of Van Nuys. Greblo helped develop the Flight Park here, which includes a parking area, picnic tables, horseshoe- and barbecue-pits, and portable toilets. Tandem flights are offered at Windsports only to those who spend an afternoon on the bunny slope.

If you come fly with Windsports, Joe will have you picked up at the airport, provide you with a written syllabus of your course, and even rent you a room in his own house. Universal Studios is just 10 minutes away and Magic Mountain Amusement Park is 20 minutes from Greblo's home. *Windsports, International, 16145 Victory Blvd., Van Nuys, CA 91406, tel. 310/474–3502 or 818/988–0111. Van Nuys Chamber of Commerce, tel. 818/989–0300. Closed Mon. Year-round (lessons by appointment only): bunny-slope lesson, $99; tandem flight, $125; complete Hang Gliding Introduction (ground school, day on bunny slope, tandem flight), $199; 7-day package with lodging at Joe Greblo's house, 4 slope lessons, and one tandem flight, $625 per person.*

SOURCES

ORGANIZATIONS **United States Hang Gliding Association** (Box 8300, Colorado Springs, CO 80933, tel. 719/632–8300) provides general information on ratings, services, certification, and membership. Its official monthly publication, *Hang Gliding Magazine,* features an annual New Pilot Edition for beginners.

PERIODICALS *Hang Gliding Magazine* (6950 Aragon Cr., Suite 6, Buena Park, CA 90620, tel. 714/994–3050) has articles and photographs of interest to hang glider pilots of all skill levels.

BOOKS *Right Stuff for New Hang Glider Pilots* (Publitec Editions), by Erik Fair, is primarily aimed at people already enrolled in hang gliding lessons, but it also gives outsiders an inside look at some of the zanier aspects of hang gliding's offbeat culture. Peter Cheney's *Hang Gliding for Beginning Pilots* is thorough and well-illustrated, the best written resource available to the novice hang glider pilot. Both can be ordered through the United States Hang Gliding Association (*see* Organizations, *above*).

ALSO SEE People who like to fly may like to jump and fly. The Skydiving chapter tells you how to get started.

Hiking and Backpacking

By Peter Oliver

If horse racing is the sport of kings, hiking is the sport of the populace. So elementary and plodding is hiking that even considering it a sport might be doing an injustice to the whole premise of sport as athletic exercise and expression. No special skills are required, nor is extraordinary physical condition. No snazzy sporting gear or apparel is needed, either.

Hiking isn't defined by rules or much restricted by any specific parameters, other than the fact that you need reasonably solid ground to walk on. Perhaps it is because hiking involves the most rudimentary of human motor skills that it can be recast under so many different headings: trekking, walking, backpacking, tramping, scrambling, rambling, and so on. Such semantic excess. Let's just call a hike a hike.

Although hiking is something you can easily do under your own guidance, and most hikers do just that, organized trips also make sense: While selecting a route, planning an itinerary, getting the right gear and maps, planning meals, and making other necessary preparations have some hikers toiling with expeditionary zeal, signing up with a trip organizer returns trip preparations to the basics. All you need to do is decide where to go and how strenuous you want the trip to be, then choose a trip to match.

Your choices are virtually limitless. On the one hand, there is backpacking—the pervading image of hiking as a sport, trekking into the wilderness bearing your housing and food on your back. This is hiking at its most demanding, where you earn your reward, say, the chance to experience the blissful solitude of sunset in some remote wilderness. Then again, the weather can be miserable or the bugs unrelenting; your equipment could fail or your feet might blister; and the food is seldom anything to write home about: It has to be light in weight and therefore involves quantities of dried ingredients like rice, as well as nuts, dried fruits, and freeze-dried coffee and prepared foods. Backpacking is a quest for exhilaration that isn't for everyone.

But for anyone unwilling to accept the possibility that things can and do go wrong, there are alternatives—for instance, naturalist-led day hikes covering relatively flat terrain, with nights in comfortable beds in country inns and meals in cozy or elegant dining rooms where the fare tends toward the elegant—for instance, apple-pecan pancakes at breakfast, spinach quiche or hearty sandwiches on homemade bread at lunch, beef bourguignon, salmon doused with beurre blanc or sorrel sauce, or grilled boneless chicken breasts with a Dijon mustard sauce. Such trips are often organized with elderly hikers in mind (though not exclusively) and often come with a naturalist bent—bird-watching, flora identification, and so on. The only gear you need is a camera and sun block, and often opportunity is

---

Outdoors writer Peter Oliver has hiked all over the United States. His favorite destinations are New Hampshire's White Mountains and grizzly country in Montana.

provided, for those who want it, to cut a day's hike short and return to the inn porch to fall asleep reading a book.

Another option is llama trekking, wherein beasts of burden carry most camping equipment and food, allowing hikers to cover more terrain than if carrying their own gear, and making for campsite meals that by backpacker standards would be considered decadent—with fresh meats, poultry, fruits, and vegetables, at least at the beginning of the trip, and even wine to wash it down. Pack animals other than llamas, which are particularly well suited to travel in mountainous terrain, are sometimes used.

Some organizers combine hiking with biking, river rafting, horseback riding, antiquing, or fishing. About the only ancillary activities that can be ruled out are those rooted in a mechanized, televised, electronically digitized rat race from which any hike is at its essence an escape.

Such a wide range of options not surprisingly engenders a wide range of prices. There's a direct correlation between comfort and cost on the trail; a straightforward, simple, carry-all-your-own-gear 6-day trip with the Sierra Club, say, runs as little as $330, while an inn-to-inn jaunt, complete with van transport to the trailhead and sumptuous meals, is easily thrice the price.

No matter what the trip you'll need appropriate footwear: Sometimes walking or running shoes will do, but more probably a sturdy pair of hiking boots will be required, especially in the mountains and particularly if off-trail scrambling is involved.

CHOOSING THE RIGHT TRIP

Your primary concern ought to be safety, especially for longer, more rigorous trips. Guides should have the proper technical and first-aid gear and be well-trained in such emergency procedures as CPR as well as safety procedures, for instance, what to do if you're caught above the tree line in a lightning storm. This may be difficult to determine, because no governing body certifies trail guides or rates guided hiking tour operators, and the value of the regional groups' efforts to do so is debatable. In some areas, specifically national parks, the number of outfitters may be restricted, and in such cases there is at least some assurance that an outfitter is a responsible one. The larger trip organizers (*see* Major Players, *below*) do make some attempt to separate the wheat from the chaff.

So ask questions—lots of them—to be sure the outfitter is reputable and the particular trip is right for your abilities, interests, schedule, and budget. Start with these:

How long has the company been in business? Chances are that a company that has been around for a few years has ironed out all the kinks and has already answered the questions and met the challenges that you throw at them.

What are your guide's qualifications? The better the guide, the better the trip, simple as that. Find out how long the guides have been hiking in the area and how long they have been guiding groups, and ask about any other abilities or fields of expertise. Knowledge of local plants, animals, and geological phenomena is a decided plus. Make sure at least one guide with your group is certified in first aid and can administer CPR.

What size is the group, and who are its constituents? Trips often set out with as many as 16 hikers. If a group gets much larger, you lose the sense of remoteness and isolation that is one of the sport's great rewards. Group members' age, physical fitness, and hiking experience determine what a group can and can't do. Some trips are organized with families, women, men, or teens in mind—and if you don't fit in, you might not have a good time.

With smaller groups, there's the flexibility to change the itinerary if you want to. In some cases, outfitters encourage suggestions and participation by group members in the trip planning. And if you really want to keep your group small and to create your own itinerary, many organizers will arrange custom trips—for a premium price, of course.

How long is each day's hike, and how strenuous? A 10-mile hike through flat or rolling countryside may be easier than 3 miles in the mountains. Most trip organizers rate their trips, but unlike river rafting or rock climbing, hiking has no standard rating scale to determine a hike's relative difficulty. A trip that one organization considers moderate may be strenuous according to another. Be sure to question the outfitter carefully.

What are accommodations like? If you're staying at inns or resorts, find out what the rooms are like and ask about facilities. If you're camping, ask what kind of shower and latrine arrangements are usual. Before you sign up to use the outfitter's tents or sleeping bags, check that they are suited to the location.

What's the food like? Don't expect anything spectacular, except on llama-trekking journeys or inn-to-inn trips. But some outfitters make more of an effort to bring choice foods along the trail, and some are more virtuosic in their preparation of dried foods than others.

What's the cost and what's included? Typically (and for the trips described below unless otherwise noted), your trip fee includes guide service, all meals, any transfers after the group has assembled, and accommodations during inn- or lodge-based trips, but not tents, sleeping bags and pads, backpacks, and other camping gear for backpacking trips; sometimes the outfitter can rent you what you need. Most trip organizers provide lists of necessary gear. Meals and motel lodging before the trip heads off down the trail and after the walk's conclusion may be included—or they may not.

Ditto for transportation from the nearest airport, which is important only if you're not driving to the assembly point; if transfers are not included (as is usually the case), you may need to rent a car. Airfare into the area is always extra.

Do you have references from past guests? To answer qualitative questions about the outfitter's operation, there's no substitute for polling past guests. Ask for references even if you have no questions: A company's willingness to give them to you is an indication that the feedback you get will be positive.

How far in advance do I need to book? Usually you'll need to make your plans at least 3 months in advance, primarily so that outfitters can be sure there are enough participants before making the complex preparations involved in setting up a trip. (Trips may be canceled if not enough people sign up.) On the other hand, you may get lucky and find an open slot just a few days before trip time. The advance-booking times included in this chapter are those recommended by individual outfitters.

MAJOR PLAYERS

AMERICAN WILDERNESS EXPERIENCE This company, founded in 1971, is a trip wholesaler representing numerous smaller outfitters. As a result its trip offerings are all over the block. Hiking is just one of several activities in the AWE fold, and the relative difficulty, luxury, and cost of any trip varies from one outfitter to the next. There are llama trekking trips, backpacks, hikes with pack stock, lodge-based trips, and more. AWE is a good starting point for anyone interested in what's possible under the broad banner of "adventure travel" (Box 1486, Boulder, CO 80306, tel. 303/444–2622 or 800/444–0099, fax 303/444–3999).

HIKING HOLIDAYS This outfitter focuses its attention primarily on the eastern United States, although trips to Europe and New Zealand are also offered. For the most part, the hiking is at a relaxed pace over easy to moderate terrain, with options usually provided for those who prefer to bypass more arduous parts of a hike, such as a climb to a mountain summit. Hiking Holidays is thus a good choice for senior hikers or anyone more interested in a little exercise and a lot of fresh air rather than the physical exertion of backpacking. Lodging is in country inns of a fairly high order, and meals in some cases can be quite spectacular. Given the relative level of luxury, trip costs tend toward the higher end (Box 750, Bristol, VT 05443, tel. 802/ 453–4814 or 800/245-3868, fax 802/453–4806).

HOSTELLING INTERNATIONAL/AMERICAN YOUTH HOSTELS This organization is probably better known for its cycling program. However, the venerable AYH, founded in 1934 and now renamed, also conducts several hiking tours in the western United States, as well as in Canada and Europe. Hiking trips usually rely on vans to shuttle hikers from hostels to trailheads. Accommodations and meals in hostels, whose amenities and character vary, help to keep trip costs reasonable. Most HI/AYH hiking trips are moderately difficult and run from 9 days to 2 weeks. Many trips are for adults and seniors (733 15th St. NW, Suite 840, Washington, DC 20005, tel. 202/ 783–6161, fax 202/783–6171).

MOUNTAIN TRAVEL-SOBEK Primarily an international adventure-travel operator, this organization focuses its attention on exotic locales such as African rivers and Patagonia. However, it does offer some North American trips, mainly in Alaska and the Southwest. The emphasis in most is on a combination of adventure and cultural experience, although the balance of that equation differs, and trips range from fairly relaxed affairs to serious expeditions. Prices are in the mid- to high range; accommodations vary. A number of trips of 2 weeks and longer are available (6420 Fairmount Ave., El Cerrito, CA 94530, tel. 510/527–8100 or 800/227–2384, fax 510/525–7710).

REI ADVENTURES Affiliated with the outdoor gear and clothing chain, REI Adventures spans the adventure-travel spectrum: hiking, biking, kayaking, mountaineering, and the like, with trip difficulty ranging from moderate to expeditionary. REI's scope is international, but the company does have some trips in the Pacific Northwest and Alaska (Box 1938, Sumner, WA 98390, tel. 212/891–2631 or 800/622–2236, fax 206/891–2523).

SIERRA CLUB OUTINGS DEPARTMENT The Sierra Club also has perhaps the most extensive adventure-trip list of any organization anywhere, including around 100 hiking and backpacking trips. Precise offerings vary from year to year; destinations change, leaders may change, trips with the same leader to the same destination use different routes, or trips with a special focus are replaced by trips with a different focus to the same area or by trips with the same focus into a different area. As might be expected from a leader of the environmental movement, the preponderance of trips involve roughing it. However, not all is strenuous backpacking; some trips involve tent camping at a base just a short walk from the nearest trailhead, and several trips are designed specifically with families, small children, and senior hikers in mind. Groups usually hit the trail with about 15 hikers. Tent camping and campsite dining help to keep most trip costs low to moderate, and meals and guiding are always included but not backpacks, tents, sleeping bags and pads, and other camping equipment. In addition to regular backpacking and hiking trips, the Club also oversees a service program, in which hikers can do their thing with a purpose, from archaeology to trail maintenance. Enrollment for most trips begins in January; sign up as soon as possible after that (730 Polk St., San Francisco, CA 94109, tel. 415/ 923–5630, fax 415/776–4868).

TIMBERLINE BICYCLE TOURS This bike-tour specialist, founded in 1982, also offers hiking tours and several hiking-biking combos, primarily in the West. Lodging is in inns and mountain lodges, tending toward upscale, with meals of comparable quality (7975 E. Harvard, #J, Denver, CO 80231, tel. 303/ 759–3804).

WALKING THE WORLD Walking the World specializes in hiking trips for people over 50. While the organization's trips range in difficulty, the it doesn't soft-peddle hiking under the assumption that older people are less fit. Accommodations vary from trip to trip—inns and B&Bs in some cases, camping in others (Box 1186, Fort Collins, CO 80522, tel. 303/225–0500).

FAVORITE TRIPS

THE NORTHEAST

MAINE **Acadia National Park with Toddlers.** For the most part, hiking is an activity for which small children—or parents with small children—need not apply. That's what makes this 7-day Toddler Tromp from Sierra Club Outings noteworthy: It is designed specifically with kids in mind. Rather than long, demanding hikes from one destination to another, it consists of shell-collecting, blueberry picking, and campfire sing-alongs near the base camp. The most strenuous activity is the easy hike to the summit of 1,530-foot Mt. Cadillac.

Acadia National Park epitomizes all that is Maine: mountains and islands; a rocky, jagged coastline; small, yacht-filled harbors; and lobster boats. August is the height of the tourist season, and the park can be crowded, so this trip is hardly a wilderness escape. But August is also a month when the weather is most agreeable, another factor to consider for young and inexperienced campers. *Sierra Club Outings, 730 Polk St., San Francisco, CA 94109, tel. 415/923–5630, fax 415/776–4868. Mid-Aug.: 7 days, $570 adults, $380 children. Sign up 6–7 months in advance.*

MAINE **The Coast for Active Seniors.** Walking the World organizes trips exclusively for people 50 and older. That is to say, *active* people 50 and older: While this 8-day trip is certainly less strenuous than many in this chapter, it is hardly a piece of cake.

The moderate hiking does not follow a continuous trail; Maine's ruggedly indented coast would hardly permit it. Instead, you take short boat and van rides to trailheads for the coastal and island hikes, which average from 6 to 9 miles. The most extended are in Acadia National Park, where mountainous islands meet the sea. For the most part, this is not a complete wilderness escape: One of the attractions of the area is its Down East culture of clapboard homes, lobster boats, and leatherneck sea-

men; in September and October, there's also the changing foliage. Accommodations are in comfortable bed-and-breakfasts. Group size is 12 to 18. *Walking the World, Box 1186, Fort Collins, CO 80522, tel. 303/225–0500 or 800/340-9255, fax 303/225–0538. Sept., Oct.: 8 days, $1,395. Price does not include 4 dinners; sign up 6–8 months in advance.*

MASSACHUSETTS **The Berkshires.** As mountains go, the Berkshires aren't much more than rolling hills, but they are *impressive* rolling hills. Their flanks are densely and frangrantly forested and are laced with fast-running streams, hiking trails, and back roads. What gives the Berkshires their special character is a sense of history—a pre-Revolutionary spirit that remains remarkably intact in the architecture of the region and even, at times, in the spirit of the people.

The hiking, at around 6 miles a day, is fairly easy, although more challenging options are available. Much of the trip time is devoted to exploring the old, clapboard towns, such as West Stockbridge, that give the region its sense of historic rootedness. Nights are spent in country inns that tend toward the posh side, with meals to match. The best times to go are May, for wildflowers, and October, for the fall foliage. *Hiking Holidays, Box 750, Bristol, VT 05443, tel. 802/453–4816 or 800/245–3868, fax 802/453–4806. May-Oct.: 5 days, $895. Sign up 2 months in advance.*

NEW HAMPSHIRE **Day-tripping in the White Mountains.** Hiking in the White Mountains doesn't have to be rugged. Below tree line, the White Mountains can be positively tame, with their mixed forests, waterfalls, deep gorges, and occasional stunning views. Representative of the more leisurely opportunities in the area is this 5-day trip offered by Stonehurst Manor, a very stylish, turn-of-the-century 25-room inn outside North Conway. From here you make 4- to 14-mile group day hikes both below and above timberline in the Mt. Washington area, with daily itineraries varying according to the weather and the group's fitness level and interests. Your non-hiking traveling companions can relax back at the manor—read, swim, and the like—or explore North Conway's shops. A feeling of intimacy is maintained by restricting the group size to 8. The trip cost varies depending on whether you go for a standard room or opt for a deluxe version with a fireplace. *Stonehurst Manor, Box 1937, Rte. 16, North Conway, NH 03860, tel. 603/356–3271 or 800/525–9100, fax 603/356–3217. Apr.–Nov.: 5 days, $432– $582. Sign up 2–3 months in advance.*

NEW HAMPSHIRE **Hut-to-Hut in the White Mountains' Presidential Range.** The Presidential Range of the White Mountains, capped by 6,288-foot Mt. Washington, is the most uncompromising stand of peaks in the Northeast. The highest wind speed ever (231 mph) was recorded at the Mt. Washington summit's weather station, and it's brutally cold in winter and only occasionally warm in summer. But its austere beauty is unlike anything else in the Northeast: a weather-scoured succession of peaks, mostly above tree line and presenting panoramas of more than 100 miles in any direction.

This 4-day trip from the Appalachian Mountain Club is shorter than others in this book but deserves inclusion because it is a classic. Not an *easy* classic though—the hiking is strenuous, and while the mileage (5 to 8 miles a day) might not seem especially challenging, vertical gains of several thousand feet a day, involving some steep climbing, can be. The AMC's hut system along the Presidential Range is also a classic, unparalleled in the East and reminiscent of the old, stone huts and auberges found in the Alps. Meals are served family-style and lodging dormitory style, for which you need your own sheets or sleeping bag. This might be roughing it a bit, but wait until you step out the door in the morning to watch the sun rise from a horizon 100 miles away. If you want to extend your trip, check at the AMC's visitor center at Pinkham Notch for other hiking programs. *Appalachian Mountain Club, Box 298, Gorham, NH 03581, tel. 603/ 466–2727, fax 603/466–2720. June–July: 4*

days, $315 ($283.50 for AMC members). Sign up two months in advance.

NEW YORK **High Peaks Traverse in the Adirondacks.** It was in these mountains of upstate New York that the early apostles of America's environmental conscience, including Ralph Waldo Emerson, searched for intimacy with the wilderness. Theodore Roosevelt and other later adventurers also made frequent visits. The High Peaks, crowned by 5,543-foot Mt. Marcy, are the reason for many hikers' efforts here.

This 5-day program from the Adirondack Mountain Club focuses on trails in the checkerboard of public and private land known as Adirondack Park, the largest park in the country outside Alaska. The main base camp is the Adirondak Loj, a bunkroom-style log retreat, named by an early proponent of phonetic spelling, near Lake Placid. From here, groups go out on day hikes according to participants' fitness and inclination. With groups numbering from 4 to 8, this is a good choice for families with children or other hikers who might not be up to the challenge of strenuous summit hikes but still appreciate being surrounded by the great outdoors. Meals and bunkroom accommodations are nothing fancy, but neither is the tab. The Loj sleeps up to 46. *Adirondack Mountain Club, Box 867, Lake Placid, NY 12946, tel. 518/523–3441, fax 518/523–3518. July–Aug.: 3 days, $175– $220 adults, $115 children under 12; 5 days, $270–$320 adults, $210 children. Sign up 3–4 months in advance.*

VERMONT **The Long Trail.** This 200-mile footpath completely traverses Vermont from north to south and crosses all of the state's high peaks. But it is often not especially good for backpackers (although many backpackers do take it on) because campsites are in short supply and water is hard to find along the ridgetop in summer. However, because it leads with regularity from mountain summits to settled valleys and back, it is ideally suited for inn-to-inn hikers who enjoy demanding hikes by day and comfortable country inns by night.

Like almost all trips along the Long Trail, this one bites off only a small segment—in this case in central Vermont—and includes 6-to 10-mile day hikes through both rugged and not-so-rugged terrain. Accommodations and meals are in country inns tending more toward the casual end of the elegance scale. There are never more than 10 hikers. Fall trips, the most popular, are also the most expensive. Late May and early June, when spring is still in blooming evidence at higher elevations, is a good alternative, but be ready for the black flies. *Country Inns along the Trail, RR#3, Box 3115, Brandon, VT 05733, tel. 802/247–3300, fax 802/247–6851. May–Oct.: 5 days, $699–$799. Sign up 3–4 months in advance.*

VERMONT **The Lake Country.** You hear a lot of old-time Vermonters claim that the state has become overly gentrified—that it is now less rural than suburban. That certainly isn't true of Vermont's far north, a world of exceedingly small towns and hundreds of small lakes and ponds, where dirt roads are more common than paved ones. Words like "resort" and "condominium" are used relatively infrequently.

This Hiking Holidays trip through the area begins, ironically, in Stowe, a town driven by tourism in general and skiing in particular, and at the Green Mountain Inn, a model of gentrified, country-inn luxury. But from there the trip leads along back roads into Vermont's backwoods. The going is fairly easy, with mileages of from 4 to 6 a day, although there are a couple of climbs to summits overlooking fjordlike Lake Willoughby. All nights are in country inns with excellent food, including vegetarian lasagna and a Mexican buffet. Late September and early October are probably the best times to go—for the foliage—and as a result these trips are likely to fill up early. *Hiking Holidays, Box 750, Bristol, VT 05443, tel. 802/453–4816, fax 802/453–4806. June–early Oct.: 6 days, $898. Sign up 2 months in advance, 4 months for fall trips.*

THE MID-ATLANTIC

VIRGINIA **Shenandoah Mountains.** While Shenandoah is one of the United States' most visited national parks, the overwhelming majority of the visiting horde remains car-bound, and this most crowded of parks isn't particularly crowded with hikers, especially given the fact that there are more than 100 trail miles.

This 6-day trip from Hiking Holidays is offered in May, when the spring bloom of dogwoods and azaleas is the main feature, and in October, when the highlight is the fall foliage. The Shenandoah Mountains run as a long ridge rising above the Virginia flatlands to the east, and summit views tend to be of the sweeping, panoramic variety. The hiking is not especially strenuous, usually 4 to 7 miles per day: The few optional ascents to summits above 4,000 feet can be bypassed. Nights are in country inns with private baths, putting this trip fairly high on the luxury level, showing off the civilized, old-world gentility of rural Virginia. Group size ranges from 10 to 18. *Hiking Holidays, Box 750, Bristol, VT 05443, tel. 802/453–4816 or 800/245–3868, fax 802/453–4806. May, Oct.: 6 days, $995. Sign up 3 months in advance.*

WEST VIRGINIA **Volunteering in Monongahela National Forest.** There is something mysterious and brooding about West Virginia, something bred deeply in a conspiracy of geology and human history. You don't need to know much about the geology of the Appalachians to get a sense that here, in West Virginia, the mountains have eroded and compressed upon themselves through aeons of time. The contrast of the deep forests of the Dolly Sods Wilderness and the bald-rock openness of the Flat Rock Plains provide a dramatic lesson in the different ways in which the ancient forces of geology worked.

This trip is included in the Sierra Club's "service" program, meaning that you'll have to do some trail repair—moving rocks, building bridges, clearing brush, etc.—to earn your way. That might not be everybody's idea of fun, but it is not brutally hard work. And with it comes not only a sense of accomplishment but also the bonding rewards of working together as a group. There is one free day to do your own exploring. The Sierra Club's service trips in particular change frequently, depending on where trail repair is most urgently needed. One bonus of joining a service trip is the low cost, in acknolwedgement of the volunteer effort participants put in. *Sierra Club Outings, 730 Polk St., San Francisco, CA 94109, tel. 415/923–5630, fax 415/776–4868. Mid-Aug.: 7 days, $160. Sign up 6–7 months in advance.*

THE SOUTH

FLORIDA **Camping and Canoeing on the Florida Trail.** A hiking trip in February? A hiking trip in Florida? Incongruities, perhaps, but a rare opportunity to experience a wild Florida that contrasts strikingly with the Florida of golfing communities and Cadillacs. This 6-day Sierra Club trip is in this wilderness, specifically in the Ocala National Forest, the southernmost national forest in the United States, on the 1,100-mile Florida Trail, which crosses forest land en route from the Panhandle in the north to Big Cypress National Preserve in the south. The trail is one of the country's least publicized long trails, partly because some sections are not yet fully developed.

Daily hiking distances are under 10 miles, the terrain is flat, and food is stored along the route, to somewhat lighten your backpack (but only somewhat; this trip does call for carrying a pack of some size and camping out at night). Insects, intolerable in summer, are minimal at in February. After 4 days of backpacking, you pick up canoes for 2 days of canoeing at crystal-clear Juniper Springs. This much is guaranteed: you *will* see herons and alligators. Group size is 12. *Sierra Club Outings, 730 Polk St., San Francisco, CA 94109, tel. 415/923–5630, fax 415/776–4868. Mid-Feb.: 6 days, $435. Sign up 6–7 months in advance.*

NORTH CAROLINA **Blue Ridge Mountains.** At 6,684 feet, Mt. Mitchell is the highest mountain in the United States east of the Mississippi. Yet its distinction comes with almost total anonymity. No doubt, the reasons for this are the fame of New Hampshire's Mt. Washington and its notorious weather, and the immense popularity of Great Smoky Mountains National Park just to the west of Mt. Mitchell and ticky-tacky Gatlinburg, Tennessee, nearby. In this context, people tend to overlook the rugged and commanding upthrust of the Blue Ridge Mountains, of which Mt. Mitchell is king.

On this 6-day trip from Hiking Holidays, day tramps of 4 to 7 miles through deep, wild Linville Gorge and up Grandfather Mountain combine to provide a moderate amount of physical exertion. But since nights are spent at local inns, there is no need to transport heavy packs. A predominant feature of mountains at this latitude is the rhododendron cover, and the spring bloom makes April the preferable time to hike here; in fall, foliage is obviously the main attraction, although color shows may be more spectacular farther north. Group size is limited to 14 hikers. *Hiking Holidays, Box 750, Bristol, VT 05443, tel. 802/453–4816 or 800/245-3868, fax 802/453–4806. Apr., Oct.: 6 days, $895. Sign up 2 months in advance.*

THE MIDWEST

MICHIGAN **Lake Superior Shoreline.** Michigan's upper peninsula is a kind of land between, framed by a trio of Great Lakes (Superior, Huron, and Michigan) and suspended between the rest of the United States and Canada. The Lake Superior shoreline is the peninsula at its most scenic, with long, relatively deserted beaches and the cliff formations of Pictured Rocks National Lakeshore.

The going here is fairly easy—5 to 6 miles a day over flat terrain, making this more a trip for foliage fanciers and photographers than hard-core hikers. There's even a visit to an abandoned lighthouse, to spice up the hike with a bit of spookiness. Backpacking and camping are involved, but an aerobophilic level of physical fitness is not required. Group size is around 15. *Sierra Club Outings, 730 Polk St., San Francisco, CA 94109, tel. 415/923–5630, fax 415/776–4868. Mid-Sept.: 6 days, $360. Sign up 6–7 months in advance.*

THE SOUTHWEST

ARIZONA **Grand Canyon's South Rim.** About 90% of the nearly 4 million people who visit the Grand Canyon each year approach the national park from the south. The vast majority drive up, look out over the inspiring vista, take a few photos, and depart. Relatively few actually venture down into the canyon, to the banks of the Colorado River more than 4,000 feet below—despite the fact that doing this is the best way to understand the Canyon's geological history, complexity, and dimension.

This 5-day trip is one of those rare outings where going downhill may be more demanding than going up. The South Kaibab Trail from the rim to the river is extremely steep, covering 4,400 vertical feet in 6 miles, and its route is an acrophobe's nightmare. There's hiking in Havasu Canyon, whose waterfalls make it the Grand Canyon's most spectacular tributary canyon. On this trip, you overnight at Phantom Ranch, the only lodging within the canyon, and at Supai Lodge on the Havasupai Indian Reservation. Be prepared for encounters with mule-pack groups descending and climbing the canyon-wall trails. *Timberline Bicycle Tours, 7975 E. Harvard, #J, Denver, CO 80231, tel. 303/ 759–3804, fax 303/368–1651. April/May, Sept./Oct.: 5 days, $995. Sign up 3–4 months in advance.*

ARIZONA **Land of the Navajo.** Not all camping trips involve arduous treks with heavy packs, or even long, daily hauls from one camp to the next. On this 7-day Earth Treks trip in the northeast part of the state, there is walking and camping, but it's not particularly demanding, with only a mile or two a day, since the primary focus here is cultural.

It is a chance to experience first-hand the current and historical cultures of tribes of the Southwest, not only the Navajo but also the Anasazi, Hopi, and Zuni. Among the highlights of the trip is a hike in Canyon de Chelly, a 700-foot-deep sandstone gorge that contains Anasazi ruins, which has developed a cult following in recent years. The gorges, deserts, and mesas are a stunning backdrop. Group size is no more than 8; and camping equipment is available to rent. *Earth Treks, RFD 2, Box 785, Thorndike, ME 04986, tel. 207/589–4311. Early July, early Aug.: 8 days, $750. Sign up two months in advance.*

ARIZONA AND UTAH **Paria Canyon Wilderness.** Not all southwestern canyons are alike. While the most famous of all canyons, the Grand Canyon, cuts a deep, wide swath out of the Arizona landscape, in other places rivers have carved out deep canyons seemingly no wider than alleyways. Appropriately, these narrow canyons are called "slot" canyons, and the Paria River, beginning in southern Utah and reaching into Arizona, races through one of the most spectacular slot canyons in the country. Side trips include treks into smaller, even narrower slot canyons and a hike to Wrather Arch, another example of the way erosion has turned the arid Southwest into a world of natural sculpture.

The hiking on this trip is fairly easy—5 to 6 miles a day—but in addition to having to shoulder your own backpack, you'll need to be prepared for several stream crossings. The trip does, however, include two free days for exploring and photography. Petroglyphs and the end of the spring bloom—in addition to the canyon's own, inherent beauty—are reasons to bring a good camera and plenty of film. *Sierra Club Outings, 730 Polk St., San Francisco, CA 94109, tel. 415/923–5630, fax 415/776–4868. Mid-May: 7 days, $525. Sign up 6–7 months in advance.*

NEW MEXICO **Carson National Forest's Pecos Wilderness.** The Pecos Wilderness of the Carson National Forest sprawls for

225,000 acres across the Sangre de Cristo range, the southern terminus of the Rocky Mountains. With mountain bases at around 9,000 feet, this high area remains relatively cool in summer despite its southern latitude. The high-alpine lakes seem more characteristic of mountains farther north.

This 5-day trip makes the going easier (you leave the packing to llamas); trails are easy to moderate, with daily elevation gains averaging about 1,000 feet and daily distances from 4 to 6 miles. Designed with families in mind, it offers the experience of tent camping and wilderness hiking without the rigors of backpacking. A bonus for adults as well as kids: To identify wildlife and wildflowers, a naturalist accompanies each group, which numbers from 6 to 8. Try to add a couple of extra days to your trip to visit Santa Fe and get a taste of southwestern culture. *Farmer Llama Treks, Box 1254, Pampa, TX 79065, tel. 800/451–0583. June–Sept.: 5 days, $650. Sign up 1 month in advance.*

UTAH Bryce and Zion National Parks and the Grand Canyon's North Rim. These parks, about 80 miles apart in the southern part of the state, are great examples of the different ways in which erosion and geology can shape the landscape. Bryce is known for its hoodoos, rock spires sculpted by erosion with a delicate artistry. Zion is rockier, with cliffs rising as much as 3,000 feet above the various forks of the Virgin River.

This 6-day trip is lodge-based and van-supported—that is, nights are spent in relatively small but comfortable lodges near the parks and the 6 to 12 hikers in each group are shuttled by van to and from trail heads. On any given day, you may have several different hiking options, from short and easy to long and more difficult. Rather than pushing from one point to the next, the objective here is to explore, to appreciate the mazelike and intricate beauty of canyons and side canyons, and to understand the forces of nature that created them. This trip also includes a visit to the North Rim of the Grand Canyon. The weather, insufferably hot in summer, offers warm days and crisply

cool nights in spring. *American Wilderness Experience, Box 1486, Boulder, CO 80306, tel. 303/444–2622 or 800/444–0099, fax 303/ 444–3999. Apr., May, June: 6 days, $1,000; single supplement, $245. Sign up 3 months in advance.*

UTAH Rainbow Bridge. Called a rainbow of stone by the Navajo, Rainbow Bridge is the world's largest natural stone arch and a highlight of this 8-day Earth Treks trip in southernmost Utah, where canyons, deserts, rivers, and mountains converge. The itinerary also skirts the southern periphery of Lake Powell, the most dominant physical feature in the area, formed by the damming of the Colorado River. Exploring side canyons through the ancient bedrock and cresting the plateau for mountain and canyon views are the elements that give this trip its character. And unlike the canyons in the national parks to the north, these canyons see relatively few visitors. Backpacking and camping are involved, but the going is fairly easy, with daily averages of 3 to 6 miles and only moderate changes in elevation—less than 1,500 feet. May is ideal, with warm days, cool evenings, and some wildflowers and cacti still in bloom. Cooler weather returns again in October, although the fall trips obviously lack the bloom of spring. Maximum group size is 9. *Earth Treks, RFD 2, Box 785, Thorndike, ME 04986, tel. 207/589–4311. May, Oct.: 8 days, $740. Sign up 2 months in advance.*

THE ROCKIES

COLORADO Hiking and Biking San Isabel National Forest's Holy Cross Wilderness. All right—so this isn't purely a hiking trip, but it does provide an idea of what's possible when hiking is combined with other activities—in this case mountain biking. This 6-day trip from Roads Less Traveled starts in one of Colorado's most famous and overdeveloped mountain resorts, Vail. From here, the trip proceeds deep into the mountains, where huts provide lodging for 2 days of hiking. The area's predominant feature is Mt. Elbert, at 14,433 feet the highest mountain in the Colorado Rockies. In fact, with several peaks topping 14,000 feet, this entire range of mountains represents the Rockies at their loftiest. The hiking portion of the trip, which traverses a stretch of the 470-mile Colorado Trail, is followed by 2 days of mountain biking southward from Leadville along the Continental Divide, with lodging and dining in country inns along the way.

In many ways, this is a good trip for someone wanting to test the adventure-travel waters without making a full commitment. For one thing, it is relatively short. It also includes a sampling not only of different modes of travel but of different lodging styles, from fancy digs at Vail, to small inns, to backcountry mountain huts. Some travelers might prefer the slower, quieter pace of hiking; others might be more appreciative of the greater amount of terrain that can be covered by bike. An average active adult can handle the challenges. *Roads Less Traveled, Box 8187, Longmont, CO 80501, tel. 303/ 678-8750, fax 303/678-5568. July–Sept.: 6 days, $935. Sign up 3 months in advance.*

COLORADO San Juan Mountains for Seniors. The San Juans are a striking swath at the edge of the mesas and deserts to the south and west. Many people consider them the jewels of the Colorado Rockies because of their impressive upthrust and deep, aspen-gladed valleys. That's a matter of opinion; what is indisputable is that they are high, with several peaks above 14,000 feet. Even valleys tend to be around 9,000 feet.

But they are not the exclusive domain of young, well-conditioned backpackers. Still, this 8-day trip for 12 to 15 active people over 50, offered by Walking the World, an organization catering exclusively to active people over 50, is far from easy, though the use of llamas to schlepp the load moderates the steepness and elevation that make the San Juans such a visual spectacle. Daily mileages range from 6 to 8, with elevation gains moderate, up to 1,000 feet. Among the highlights are excellent fishing and abundant wildflowers at higher elevations. *Walking the World, Box 1186, Fort Collins, CO 80522, tel.*

303/225-0500 or 800/340-9255, fax 303/ 225-0538. July.: 7 days, $1,295. Sign up 3–5 months in advance.

COLORADO Vail and Aspen Wilderness. Putting "wilderness" in the same phrase with "Vail" and "Aspen" might strike some outdoor enthusiasts as treason, or at least a contradiction in terms. These famed resort towns, after all, are perhaps *the* major hubs of Rocky Mountain resort development. However, surrounding and between them in several national forests is a quartet of large, officially designated wilderness areas—the Gore Range Wilderness, Hunter Frying Pan Wilderness, and, for the most part, Holy Cross Wilderness—and it can be relatively quick and easy to get away from the resort scene into high-alpine country. Mostly you're above 9,000 feet, but the tree line in this part of the Rockies is at 11,000 feet. Evergreen forests account for much of the terrain you might expect to be above the tree line, although open meadows and tundra occupy a large percentage as well.

Paragon Guides offers 3- to 7-day llama-trekking trips in the area, with nights spent at backcountry tent sites. Because llamas bear most of the load, this is a good choice for parents interested in introducing children to the joys and challenges of backcountry travel. Before signing up with your kids, however, contact the outfitter to make sure they will be up to the task—usually 3 to 8 miles of hiking and 700 to 3,000 feet of altitude changes, depending on the route. *Paragon Guides, Box 130, Vail, CO 81658, tel. 970/926-5299, fax 970/926-5298. July– Sept.: 3–7 days, $590–$1,580. Sign up 2 months in advance.*

COLORADO AND WYOMING Mountain Parks of the West. Using a van to travel among three national parks—Rocky Mountain, Grand Teton, and Yellowstone—this 15-day trip is great for first-time visitors to the Rockies. As a national park sampler, it can also provide lessons in the subtle and obvious differences among mountain ecosystems—from a geological and ecological standpoint, all mountains are not created equal.

A ranger-led program introduces each park. Thereafter the program consists of 5- to 10-mile day hikes over hilly terrain—though the walking is always tailored to participants, who may even be involved in itinerary planning. Nights are spent in dormitories in simple but comfortable hostels. Meals are comparably simple, and vans are used to shuttle hikers to and from trail heads as well as between parks. One departure is for those 50 and older and the minimum age for others is 15. Groups usually include about 9 participants, and the trip begins and ends in Estes Park, Colorado. *Hostelling International/American Youth Hostels, 733 15th St. NW, Suite 840, Washington, DC 20005, tel. 202/783–6161 or 800/444–6111, fax 202/783–6171. July– Sept.: 15 days, $1,150. Price does not include sleeping bag or sheet sleep sack, necessary in hostels; sign up at least 1 month in advance.*

IDAHO AND MONTANA **River of No Return Wilderness.** The largest expanse of designated wilderness area in the continental United States, this vast forestland sprawling through 7 national forests takes in classic Rocky Mountain country: high mountains, deep valleys, lakes, meadows, and streams. Although summits typically average about 2,000 feet lower than Colorado summits, the mountains are big, wild, and as spectacular as anyplace in the Rockies.

One of the interesting aspects of this 8-day adventure is its nod to ecological education, in the form of a day-long seminar on the ecology of the northern Rockies. The 7 days that follow hold particular appeal for those who appreciate solitude and remoteness, not easily come by elsewhere in the Rockies in the middle of the summer. Those are privileges that must be earned, however, by carrying a sizable backpack distances of 8 to 10 miles, with up to 1,500 feet of elevation changes in any given day. However, there are 2 layover days. Camping is at beautiful high-mountain lakes and occasionally you are lucky enough to glimpse elk, bighorn, mountain goat, and other native species; moose are frequently sighted. Group size is never more than 8. *Wild Horizons Expedi-*

tions, 5663 West Fork Rd., Darby, MT 59829, Dept. F, tel. 406/ 821–3747. Mid-July: $850. Tents, backpacks, and sleeping bags and pads provided; sign up 1 month in advance.

IDAHO AND OREGON **The Snake River.** If asked what the deepest gorge in North America is, you'd probably answer the Grand Canyon, and you'd be wrong. The deepest gorge is carved by the Snake River as it runs through Hell's Canyon, more than 8,000 feet from river to rim at one point. That might sound more like rafting country than hiking country, and indeed it is—or has been until River Odysseys West came up with the idea of raft-supported hiking.

The idea here is to hike 5 to 8 miles a day, guided by naturalists, while rafts transport camping supplies downriver. The naturalist-led hiking is of moderate difficulty; there is no scrambling up 8,000-foot canyon walls, but the going in places can be narrow and steep. Fortunately, because the rafts take care of the heavy gear, you need only be encumbered by a daypack. The camping is comparable to raft-trip camping, which is to say, pretty luxurious as camping goes. Most camps are set up on beaches along the river, and because of the weight the rafts can carry, meals include things usually considered camping extravagances—fresh meats and produce, beer and soft drinks. One other bonus that could probably go without saying—the fishing is excellent. *River Odysseys West, offered through American Wilderness Experience, Box 1486, Boulder, CO 80306, tel. 303/444–2622 or 800/444–0099, fax 303/444–3999. May, Sept.: 5 days, $825. Sign up 3 months in advance.*

MONTANA **Glacier National Park.** The preserve's celebrated backcountry chalets, now indefinitely closed, provided not only fairly comfortable overnight lodging, but also safe haven from grizzly bears, who could rightfully be considered the park's dominant species. Anyone traveling in the Glacier backcountry always had to be particularly wary of bear encounters; now, without the chalets, overnight travelers must redouble their caution.

This is perhaps the best reason to sign on with an experienced guide service such as Glacier Wilderness Guides, which offers 6-day backpacking trips in summer. Itineraries vary according to current trail conditions and the desires and physical fitness of a particular group, but daily distances typically range between 6 and 8 miles, with moderate elevation gains, and daily itineraries provide a sampling of the glacially sculpted rock walls and parapets that are Glacier's glory—as they are the glory of Waterton National Park, Glacier's adjoining sister park across the Canadian border. Other highlights are tramps through high alpine basins, past waterfalls and ice caves, and berry picking. And yes, glaciers—not enormous, but still rare within the continental United States.

If you're disinclined to lug a 35-pound pack, you have the option of hiring a "Sherpa" to do the job (at an additional cost of $100 per day). Trips that include horse packing or rafting in addition to backpacking are also available. *Glacier Wilderness Guides, Box 535F, West Glacier, MT 59936, tel. 406/888–5466 or 800/521–7238, fax 406/862–5333 (summer) or 406/862–4802 (winter). May–Sept.: 6 days, $510. Sign up 4–5 months in advance.*

WYOMING **The Shoshone National Forest's Absaroka Wilderness.** The Absarokas aren't exactly a forgotten land, but with Yellowstone National Park to the north and west, these mountains in the Shoshone National Forest are often bypassed by visitors seeking the twin spectacles of geology and nature. In a way, the national park acts as a kind of decoy for the Absarokas, diverting visitor interest. Yet they are one of the highest and wildest ranges in the northern Rockies, including 12,000-foot peaks and some of the biggest expanses of alpine tundra south of Canada. And they contain literally hundreds of lakes and thousands of waterfalls.

This 6-day trip is a good way to experience the wild nature of the region during the height of the tourist season, when the park itself tends to be heavily populated. It's not for people who aren't in good shape:

Although there are 2 layover days, you normally cover 6 to 7 miles a day with a backpack, with up to 2,000 feet in elevation changes, and about half of the hiking is through high open country off-trail. Nor is this trip for those who have problems at higher altitudes, or for those who worry about bears, since the wildlife roster of the region includes grizzlies (though the chances of a bear encounter are remote, especially when traveling with an experienced guide). You do, however, usually see elk, moose, and bighorn sheep. Groups usually set out with 6 to 8 hikers. *Wild Horizons Expeditions, 5663 West Fork Rd., Dept. F, Darby, MT 59829, tel. 406/821–3747. Aug.: 6 days, $650. Price includes sleeping bags and pads, backpacks, and tents; sign up 1–2 months in advance.*

WYOMING **The Tetons' Western Slope.** The Tetons are not the tallest mountains in the West; it is just their extraordinary, rocky forcefulness that makes them seem so. It is probably a fair guess to assume they are the most photographed mountains in America, as an embodiment of the lore of Western wilderness. They have served as the backdrop for hundreds of commercials; if you want to make a statement about how rough-and-tough your product is, having the Tetons in the background amplifying your cause with a chorus of Rocky Mountain ruggedness is a can't-miss gimmick.

Most Teton visitors approach the mountains from the east, through Jackson, Wyoming, and Grand Teton National Park. In mid-summer, that can mean crowds—minimal, perhaps, once you're a half-mile or so from any trailhead, but enough to intrude upon your sense of backcountry solitude. Approach from the west, however, and the mountains are still there in all of their glory but without nearly as many people. The western slope, which receives more snow and rainfall, is a world of rushing streams and wildflowers in mid-summer, capped by that famous Teton rock.

On this 7-day Sierra Club trip, pack animals lug the equipment from one site to the next, and the itinerary includes 3 layover days to allow plenty of time for fishing, photography, or more hikes. Unfortunately, like all Sierra Club Outings trips, this one may well be unavailable when you get ready to sign up. *Sierra Club Outings, 730 Polk St., San Francisco, CA 94109, tel. 415/923–5630, fax 415/776–4868. July: 7 days, $1,025. Sign up 6–7 months in advance.*

WYOMING **The Wind River Range.** While the Tetons are Wyoming's most famous mountains, outdoor enthusiasts in the Jackson area prefer the Wind Rivers, to the east, when they want a more private backcountry experience. Unlike trails in Grand Teton National Park, those in the Wind Rivers get relatively little traffic, at least in their interior reaches. Part of the reason is that the going can be fairly rugged for those determined to reach the range's highest summits, including 13,804-foot Gannett Peak, the highest mountain in Wyoming. Daily distance averages 8 to 9 miles.

This strenuous 7-day trip is a full-bore mountain country backpack. The route includes steep climbs and rugged off-trail exploring. Such effort, however, yields the best of the Wild River backcountry: high alpine lakes and basins, craggy mountainous features, and glaciers that are a rarity in most other ranges of the lower 48. There is also wilderness solitude, a sense of physical accomplishment, and some terrific fishing for those so inclined. The group size is limited to 8. *Wild Horizons Expeditions, 5663 West Fork Rd., Dept. F., Darby, MT 59829, tel. 406/821–3747. Aug.: 7 days, $750. Price includes sleeping bags and pads, backpacks, and tents; sign up 1 month in advance.*

WYOMING **Yellowstone National Park.** Yellowstone is the oldest and perhaps most famous park of the national-park system, yet what do most people really know about it? That Old Faithful spouts punctually every hour and that bison roam freely. That's not much, and that's because most visitors stick to the roads and familiar tourist attractions. Despite the fact that 3 million people visit Yellowstone each year, most of the park's 2

million plus acres see little or no human traffic. Yellowstone presents a far greater opportunity to explore and experience true wilderness than you'd ever expect in a place so popular.

September is an ideal time to visit. Most tourists are gone, the mosquitoes are in retreat, elk are engaged in their fall rut, and trees and meadow grasses are beginning to take on the hues of autumn. This 7-day trip explores the lakes, geysers, meadows, and forests of the Yellowstone high country. You might not be far from the park's most famous attractions as the crow flies, but the Yellowstone backcountry feels far removed from their bustle. There is little strenuous climbing involved here, but this is an extended backpacking trip, and you'll be required to transport a sizable pack. Among the highlights of the trip is visiting forest sections ravaged by the fires of 1988. These forests are now in their early stages of rebirth—a fascinating lesson in ecological life cycles. Groups number no more than 8. *Wild Horizons Expeditions, 5663 W. Fork Rd., Dept. F, Darby, MT 59829, tel. 406/821–3747. Sept.: 7 days, $750. Price includes the use of sleeping bags and pads, backpacks, and tents; sign up 1 month in advance.*

THE WEST COAST

CALIFORNIA **Ansel Adams Wilderness and Yosemite National Park.** August in Yosemite may well conjure up images of an RV parking lot and people taking photos at designated photo stops. True enough, but there are still hundreds of square miles of spectacular countryside in Yosemite and the neighboring Ansel Adams Wilderness to explore. You may have to bypass the famed highlights of Yosemite—El Capitan and the rest—but what you get in exchange is the solitude of the wilderness, along with rock formations, high mountains, and deep forests that certainly do not lack for natural beauty.

This trip reaches to the park's southern Extreme, the remote Harriet Lake Basin. A

40-mile jaunt over passes above 10,000 feet might sound like a strenuous way of getting away from the Yosemite crowds. In fact, this is a relatively easy trip, with pack animals doing much of the hard work of lugging heavy camping supplies. In addition, four days of this 9-day trip are layover days—to relax, fish, take photos, or head off on your own day hikes. *Sierra Club Outings, 730 Polk St., San Francisco, CA 94109, tel. 415/923–5630, fax 415/776–4868. Aug.: 9 days, $1,100. Sign up 6–7 months in advance.*

CALIFORNIA **National Parks of the Sierra Nevada.** Yes, there are other national parks in California besides Yosemite. South of Yosemite are the adjoining Sequoia and King's Canyon national parks, famed for tall mountains and tall trees. The highest peaks of the Sierras, reaching above 14,000 feet, are the backdrop, while giant redwoods and virgin forest comprise the more immediate surroundings.

This is country popular among serious backpackers and climbers, but this trip takes a less strenuous approach to hiking. All hikes start and end at the Montecito-Sequoia Lodge, providing rustic but comfortable accommodations and meals featuring the best of California cuisine. The hiking is easy to moderate—perhaps 6 miles a day on average, with minimal climbing—with ample opportunities for other recreational activities. Without question, the trees are the highlight, especially in Redwood Canyon, which contains the largest grove of giant Sequoias in the world. *American Wilderness Experience, Box 1486, Boulder, CO 80306, tel. 303/444–2622 or 800/444–0099, fax 303/444–3999. May, Sept., Oct.: 7 days, $749. Sign up 3 months in advance.*

CALIFORNIA **The Northern Coast.** Despite areas of heavy development, the coastline of this part of the state remains Mother Nature's world. The forests of Point Reyes National Seashore reach to the dunes and the sea, a place that speaks a mood of splendid desolation when the chilling fog rolls in. Muir Woods, closer to San Francisco, while not as desolately beautiful nor as unpopulated, also has plenty going for it.

Backroads' 16- to 20-person trip spends 6 days exploring the dunes, the forests, the deep canyons, the wind-raked promontories. Nights are in local inns—fairly elegant ones, with dinners (this being on the periphery of California wine country) accompanied by quality cabernet or chardonnay. In summer, variations in temperature can also be wild. Temperatures exceeding 90°F inland can make the fog-cooled 50s by the sea seem refreshing or frigid, depending on your state of mind and dress. Go ahead—this is not a rugged trip for backcountry purists but for those who want only to appreciate surprisingly wild country so near to civilization. *Backroads, 1516 5th St., Berkeley, CA 94710, tel. 510/527–1444 or 800/462–2848, fax 510/527–1444. May–Oct.: 6 days, $1,345; $749 if camping. Sign up 2 months in advance.*

CALIFORNIA **Lake Tahoe.** Lake Tahoe might well be famous for its casinos, but almost all of that tinsel is concentrated around the lake's southern shore. Once you have escaped the confines of South Lake Tahoe, the natural spectacle of this region reveals itself in classic Sierra Nevada style: Snow-capped peaks and evergreen forests that spill down to the bluest lake waters imaginable.

This 6-day trip concentrates on the northern reaches of the lake—not exactly wilderness but an area rich in both natural beauty and early California history. Highlights include hiking along the shores of aptly named Emerald Bay and visiting Donner Pass, site of the famous pioneer tragedy. Groups moves at a fairly relaxed pace: Hikes cover about 6 to 10 miles a day, with options to shorten or lengthen the mileage. Regardless of how far you go each day, you get to recover in the evening in luxurious digs, such as the posh and modern Squaw Valley Inn. This is a good trip for those who appreciate the sybaritic pleasures of a comfortable bed and an elegant meal after a full day of fresh air and physical activity. *New England*

Hiking Holidays, P.O. Box 1648, North Conway, NH 03860, tel. 603/356–9696 or 800/869–0949. June–July: 6 days, $889. Sign up 2–3 months in advance.

WASHINGTON **Backpacking in Mt. Rainier National Park.** Among the volcanic domes that stretch from California to Washington, Mt. Rainier is the highest and most heavily glaciated. According to climatatologists, the summit is so cold and snowy that it has yet to emerge from the most recent ice age. Yet at its lower elevations, the site of this 35-mile backpacking, Mt. Rainier is a world of dense forests, wildflower-filled meadows, cascading waterfalls, and abundant wildlife.

This trip makes a loop through a northern section of the park, for a while following a part of the famed Wonderland Trail, which makes a complete, 93-mile rounding of the mountain. If you've never had a close encounter with an active glacier, this trip offers the opportunity, as well as an opportunity to test your balance negotiating, with backpack, a suspension bridge. Fear not—the guides are excellent sources of instruction on backcountry travel, as well as information about minimum-impact camping, wilderness safety, and navigation. *REI Adventures, Box 1938, Sumner, WA 98390, tel. 206/891–2631 or 800/622–2236, fax 206/891–2523. July–Sept.: 7 days, $795. Price includes tents and other group camping gear, but not sleeping bags and backpacks; sign up 2–3 months in advance.*

WASHINGTON **A Lodge-based Trip in the Olympic Peninsula.** While Olympic National Park's mountainous interior, capped by 7,995-foot Mt. Olympus, is pretty much the domain of backpackers, a lot of spectacular terrain can be reached on relative easy day hikes from the nearby towns of Lake Crescent, Forks, and Quinault. And there is certainly something to be said for having the roof of a comfortable lodge over your head when damp weather rolls in, as can happen on this 6-day trip from Backroads.

Not *all* of the peninsula is particularly rainy, though. One of the highlight hikes of this trip is along the relatively rain-free Hurri-

cane Ridge near the northern coast. This is mountainous hiking made relatively easy. A road leads to the ridge, and from there the hiking is mainly flat and even downhill. On clear days, Hurricane Ridge affords a terrific view of the peninsula's glaciated interior. The rain forests near Lake Quinault show the other side of the peninsula's character: huge trees, a dense canopy of green upon green upon green.

The hiking is at a fairly relaxed pace, ranging from 3 to 12 miles a day. Nights are in lodges that tend to be in the mode of rustic elegance. Meals can be quite fancy—even by the standards of this region, which is renowned for its seafood. Group size is up to 20. *Backroads, 1516 5th St., Berkeley, CA 94710, tel. 510/ 527–1555 or 800/462–2848, fax 510/527–1444. July–Aug.: 6 days, $1,295. Sign up 3–4 months in advance.*

ALASKA

CENTRAL **Wildlife Safari.** The prospect of taking on the Alaskan wilderness can seem daunting to those without experience in wilderness travel. The sheer size of the terrain and the possible hazards (getting lost, encountering inhospitable wildlife) seem to insist upon special backcountry awareness and skills. This 11-day Mountain Travel-Sobek trip to Denali National Park and the Kenai Peninsula, on the coast south of Anchorage, is proof that that needn't be so.

Denali National Park, of course, is home of Mt. McKinley, at 20,320 feet the highest mountain in North America. But such big, glaciated mountains are only part of what southern Alaska is all about. This trip also explores vast tundra meadows and glacially cut fjords that lead to the Gulf of Alaska, and as a safari of sorts, focuses equally on seeking out wildlife and photographing them—caribou, grizzly bears, Dall sheep, sea mammals, and eagles. Overnights are in cabins, and walks are on the easy to moderate side, with an average of 5 miles of hiking each day with minimal elevation changes. A short raft trip on the Kenai River and a sailing excursion to Kenai Fjords National Park are also part of the itinerary. Groups are limited to 16. *Mountain Travel-Sobek, 6420 Fairmount Ave., El Cerrito, CA 94530, tel. 510/527–8100 or 800/227–2384, fax 510/525–7710. July–Aug.: 11 days, $2,990. Sign up 3–6 months in advance.*

ARCTIC **Gates of the Arctic National Park.** The Sierra Club once referred to Gates of the Arctic as "the ultimate national park." You might rightfully wonder: What are the qualifications for ultimateness? Austere mountain wilderness; abundant wildlife, including caribou, wolves, and grizzly bears; fast-running rivers; open, tundra terrain presenting few obstacles for free-spirited hikers; and mountains that, because of their unusual mix of rock varieties, continue to astonish geologists. This is, indeed, the park with everything—except, perhaps, many trails or people.

This is not country for wilderness novices to venture in unguided. Even experienced hikers who join guided trips must be ready to face the inevitable challenges presented by such a remote and unforgiving place. This 8-day backpacking trip led by Sourdough Outfitters through the granite spires of the Arrigetch Peaks (listed on the National Register of Natural Landmarks) is rated moderate because the hiking itself is not extraordinarily tough. But this *is* backpacking, and it *is* a rugged, remote wilderness. Don't expect fancy meals—the treat here is to feast your eyes on the ultimate world around you. *Sourdough Outfitters, offered through American Wilderness Experience, Box 1486, Boulder, CO 80306, tel. 303/444–2622 or 800/444–0099, fax 303/444–3999. June-Aug.: 8 days, $1,250. Sign up 3 months in advance.*

HAWAII

KAUAI, MAUI, AND THE BIG ISLAND **Island-hopping in Paradise.** Hawaii's landscape amazes both for its sheer beauty and for its variety. Far from the broad sand beaches and bikinis, in the islands' mountainous interior,

dense jungle, active volcanoes, peaks rising above 10,000 feet, and waterfalls dropping more than 400 feet astonish and enchant those adventurous enough to penetrate it.

This 10-day, island-hopping trip starts on Kauai, along the Na Pali Coast and Waimea Canyon. This is one of the world's rainiest places—a fact that might do little for anyone seeking a deep, dark Hawaiian tan but one that adds considerably to the dense jungle and floral spectacle of this dramatically mountainous shoreline. From here, the trip leads to the island of Maui and on to Hawaii, to explore volcanic landscapes and to learn about traditional Hawaiian life. Hikes are generally short and relatively easy; in addition to hiking, days are filled with sea kayaking, swimming, and other activities. Accommodations vary, from oceanfront campsites to rustic cabins to modern hotels. Wherever you bed down for the night, expect to eat well—Hawaii's climate is ideal for growing fresh fruits and vegetables—and you finish off the trip with a celebratory luau. Group size ranges from 4 to 12. *American Wilderness Experience, Box 1486, Boulder, CO 80306, tel. 303/444–2622 or 800/444–0099, fax 303/444–3999. Apr.-Dec.: 10 days, $1,550. Sign up 3 months in advance.*

SOURCES

ORGANIZATIONS **American Hiking Society** (Box 20160, Washington, DC 20041, tel. 703/255–9304, fax 703/255–9308) is an advocacy group promoting proper trail management throughout the United States and is also a general clearinghouse on hiking information. **Appalachian Mountain Club** (5 Joy St., Boston, MA 02108, tel. 617/523–0636, fax 617/523–0722) is the leading hiking organization in the Northeast. The club maintains backcountry huts and lodges in New Hampshire's White Mountains as well as the Catskills of New York and the Berkshires of Massachusetts. The club is also active in maintaining trails in these areas and offers an extensive program of outings, seminars, and workshops. **National**

Audubon Society (700 Broadway, New York, NY 10003, tel. 212/ 979–3066, fax 212/353–0377) is primarily a naturalist organization, which is to say, it focuses mostly on birdlife and wildlife rather than outdoor recreation or broader environmental issues. Short outings, typically for bird-watching, are organized through local society chapters; longer trips and international outings are arranged through the national organization. The Society is an active book publisher; its magazine, *Audubon,* issued as part of club membership, does an excellent job of covering wildlife-related issues. **Sierra Club** (730 Polk St., San Francisco, CA 94109, tel. 415/923–5630, fax 415/776–4868) is one of the preeminent advocacy groups in the United States promoting responsible environmental and wilderness management. It also offers perhaps the most extensive trip schedule of any organization in the country, although technically the club doesn't organize trips itself; trips are organized by individuals and outfitters under the club's auspices. The club magazine, *Sierra,* issued as a part of club membership, is first-rate in covering environmental issues.

PERIODICALS The publication of the American Hiking Society, *American Hiker* (Box 20160, Washington, DC 20041, tel. 703/385–3252) reports on hiking-related issues and hiking destinations. The monthly magazine *Backpacker* (Rodale Press, 33 Minor St., Emmaus, PA 18098, tel. 215/967–5171) is the leading magazine in the United States devoted specifically to hiking and backpacking. It is an excellent source of information on trips and equipment, including boots, clothing, and camping gear. Also included is a classified-ad section with organized-trip listings. The foremost magazine in the country on outdoor and adventure recreation, hiking, and backpacking is *Outside* (1165 N. Clark St., Chicago, IL 60610, tel. 303/447–9330). There are personal narratives, cap-

sule reports on recommended trips, product reviews, and articles on environmental issues. The classified-ad section includes extensive listings of trip organizers. It's published monthly.

BOOKS The *Backpacker's Sourcebook 2,* by Noelle Liebrenz, is helpful. *The Complete Walker III,* by Colin Fletcher, gives the last word on the pleasures and techniques of the sport. *Hiking and Backpacking: A Complete Guide,* by Karen Berger, delivers just what the title promises—a guide to everything from finding a good backpack to finding a good place to use it.

The Appalachian Mountain Club (*see* Organizations, *above*), publishes, among other books, trail guides for many parts of the Northeast. Backcountry Publications (The Countryman Press, Box 175, Woodstock, VT 05091, tel. 802/457–1049, fax 802/457–3250) publishes guides to hiking, cycling, and skiing in the eastern United States. Among its best offerings for hikers is the series "50 Hikes in," with the areas covered ranging from Maine to West Virginia. Guidebooks from the Mountaineers (306 2nd Ave. W, Seattle, WA 98119, tel. 206/284–6310, fax 206/284–4977) cover the Northwest, including the Northern Rockies, California, and British Columbia. Books and trail guides from the Sierra Club (*see* Organizations, *above*) focus primarily though not exclusively on areas in the West. Wilderness Press (2440 Bancroft Way, Berkeley, CA 94709, tel. 510/843–8080, fax 510/548–1355), which publishes guides covering California and other parts of the West, stands out for its coverage of the Pacific Crest Trail.

ALSO SEE If you like to feel the trail under your feet and enjoy mountain vistas from on high, see Climbing and Mountaineering. Wilderness and Survival Schools covers still other ways to push yourself to the limit on the trail.

Horse Packing and Trail Riding

By Scott S. Warren and Andrea Lehman

Before the car, there was the horse, and despite nearly a century of competition from its mechanized cousin, the horse hasn't needed to make any improvements to maintain its status as the best mode of transportation for getting away from it all. Breathe in fresh mountain air or the gentle scents of the desert augmented by the smells of leather and horse, not the exhaust of the car in front of you. There are no traffic jams, no full campgrounds, and no scenic vistas framed by tour buses and RVs. You can ride for days and see nary another soul, and because your horse watches the trail, you can concentrate on the scenery. The farther into the wilderness you go, the more untouched and spectacular the landscape usually is. And you can cover a lot more ground, with less effort, than you can backpacking.

Taking a horseback vacation is also one of the best ways to experience another time. It's hard to get a feel for the Old West, for example, from the climate-controlled comfort of a late-model auto, but on a horse you can imagine the pioneers, outlaws, and Native Americans who shaped the land. Many trips focus not only on the scenery and activities of the wilderness but also on the culture and history of the area in which they operate.

Because horses demand a fair amount of care both before and after their day's work, there's more downtime for riders than on rafting, mountain biking, backpacking, and other wilderness trips—time you can spend exploring the area on foot, angling, taking photographs, or just recovering from bowed legs and saddle soreness. Yes, there may be a little discomfort if you haven't ridden much before spending your first long day in the saddle, but you soon get used to it.

One of the biggest pluses of traveling with horses is that you don't have to leave creature comforts back in civilization. On *horse pack trips,* where you travel from campsite to campsite or inn to inn, animals or vehicles carry equipment and supplies, so you can enjoy luxuries others might leave behind when venturing into the woods. On *trail riding trips,* which involve making day rides out of a base camp, the comfort quotient is even greater. In either case, guides usually handle the particulars of setting up camp and meal preparation.

Most horse pack outfitters operate in the West, whose vast wilderness lands make for superb riding. But you can also take overnight horse trips in parts of New England and the mid-Atlantic, experiencing the different scenery and trip styles that come with those regions. So saddle up and hit the trail. You're sure to have an adventure to remember.

Writer-photographer Scott Warren makes his home in Durango, Colorado, not far from where he took his first horse pack trip. Now living in New Jersey, writer, editor, and horse-lover Andrea Lehman swears there's still pine tar stuck in her clothes from many pack trips and trail rides in Montana.

CHOOSING THE RIGHT TRIP

All outfitters who operate on federal lands (and that includes most of the outfitters of the trips listed below) are required to have a permit. If you strike out on your own, make sure that the outfitter you ride with does. Here's a sample list of questions to help you decide which trip is right for you:

How large is the group and how many guides are there? To lessen groups' impact on the environment, most are limited to 12 riders. Some go down to just 3 or 4. Most outfits post at least 2 wranglers per dozen guests; some bring along another person to act as cook and assistant wrangler.

What about the horses and saddles? Unless you're a very experienced rider and are looking for a steed with a little extra spunk, stock should be well tempered, comfortable with greenhorns, and steady with adverse trail and weather conditions. You'll be trusting your horse to pick his or her way through potentially rough terrain, so you want an animal you can trust. If you have a preference for riding English or western, make sure the outfitter can accommodate you. Not surprisingly, western tack predominates in the West, and, you guessed it, English is more common in the East.

How much time is spent in the saddle each day and how difficult is the riding? Six hours is a long day in the saddle; usually, it's much less—about 4 hours. Most trips move at a walk, and there may be varying opportunities to trot, lope (western-speak for canter), and even gallop. There's usually little in the way of formal instruction, but eager riders can learn a lot by asking questions.

How many layover days are there? A layover involves spending an additional night in the same campsite. Because there's considerable work involved in moving from one place to another—that is, for the outfitter—a trip with more layover days feels more leisurely. In addition, a layover allows you to spend time getting to know a small area relatively well. If your prime interest is in covering the most ground, and in getting as far into the wilderness as possible, look for a trip without layovers.

What is there to do when you're not riding? Though some trips comprise almost an entire day of riding, most build in time to explore an area at your leisure—hiking, climbing, fishing, or just relaxing. Nearer to civilization, especially in inn-based treks, activities include shopping, playing tennis, swimming, or taking high tea. At night there may be sing-alongs or slide shows. Find out whether trip leaders plan activities for down time or leave you on your own.

Is riding experience or any other strength or skills required, and why? Different pack trips have different levels of difficulty. Unless otherwise noted, the following trips are suitable for riders with no more than basic experience on a horse. This does not mean that you will miss the spectacular scenery. Rather, it indicates that you will cover fewer miles in a day and follow better-established trails. Trips for more experienced riders entail more riding time, rougher terrain, more spirited mounts, and a faster pace, perhaps galloping cross-country. If you're not sure of your riding level, discuss your experience and your fears with the outfitter. Regardless of your riding ability, however, you should be in reasonably good physical condition. In addition to the saddle-soreness issue, there's the altitude factor: Many trips in the West visit elevations above 10,000 feet, which can be fatiguing.

What are the wranglers' qualifications? Guides should be experienced backcountry travelers; at least one member of the group should have first-aid training, if not wilderness first-aid training. Knowledge of area flora and fauna, as well as its history, geology, and ecology, is a big plus.

How many years has the outfitter been in the business? Experience counts. Also find out how long the outfitter has been packing in the area you will be exploring. Guides should know the weather conditions, where to find the best fishing and swimming holes and the choice spots for wildlife viewing and photography as well as shelter when storms blow up (as they do with predictable suddenness in the mountains). Many outfitters are third-generation ranchers and know all the local lore.

What are the meals like? On trips into the wilderness, the food is generally straightforward cowboy fare, cooked over a campfire or cook stove: steak, chili, biscuits, fresh-caught fish, and beans. Usually vegetables and other perishables are more in evidence earlier in the trip. Outfits that truck food into camp are often better supplied with fresh vegetables, but a cook who's a whiz with a Dutch oven can make you forget you ever missed something. While a cook goes along on some trips, guides often pull double duty in the kitchen on others. A little help from group members is always appreciated. On inn-based trips, you're normally treated to gourmet cuisine. Lunches on almost all rides are picnic affairs, but even they vary. If you care, ask what's planned. And of course, if you have any dietary restrictions, make arrangements beforehand; many trip operators are happy to accommodate vegetarians and others with special needs.

What are accommodations like? Don't allow yourself to be surprised. If you're staying at inns or motels, find out what the rooms are like and ask about the availability of any facilities you may want to use. If the trip involves camping, ask about the campsites and about shower and latrine arrangements. If you plan to use the outfitter's tents or sleeping bags, make sure they are suited to the location. Tents are generally either lightweight backpacking tents or roomier wall tents.

What's the cost and what's included? Prices run about $120 to $200 per person per day; inn-based trips hover near the high end of that range. The price for most trips, and for all those below unless noted otherwise, includes all meals while you're on the trail, guide service, your horse, and your tent but not a sleeping bag and pad. Also indicated in the profiles is whether first and last

nights' motel stays are included; they often are. Some trips have different single and double accommodation rates (doubles are assumed in listings); charge higher prices for certain trips, such as those during fall foliage season; or offer discounts for certain ages, families or other groups, or guests who help out on the trip or bring their own food or equipment. Make sure you know exactly what equipment is required, and whether any is available to borrow or rent. If you have to buy a hard hat, boots, sleeping bag, or rain gear that you're unlikely to use again, it can jack up the cost of your vacation considerably.

Trips generally start at a ranch or inn or, in California, a pack station, from which you are then trucked to the trailhead; be sure to find out whether the outfitter will pick you up at the nearest airport and transport you to the starting point or whether you'll have to arrange and pay for your own transportation. Note that it is standard policy to tip the head wrangler to divide among the staff, usually 3%–5% of the cost of your trip if it has been a good one, up to 10% if it has been outstanding—but it's a very personal matter. Sometimes tax and gratuities are already included in the price. The bottom line is: Calculate what the bottom line is before signing up, and you'll avoid any unhappy surprises.

How far in advance is it necessary to book? Most outfitters prefer to book their trips at least 3 months in advance. However, some trips are so popular that it's wise to reserve 6 months ahead. Of course, last-minute cancellations always crop up—large organizations like American Wilderness Experience can almost always slot you in somewhere—but the itinerary may not be your first choice.

MAJOR PLAYERS

By their very nature, pack outfitters are an independent lot. They typically offer rides in one particular region or area established by the U.S. Forest Service, Bureau of Land Management, or other government agency that issues outfitting permits. However, there are three larger organizations—booking agents, basically—worth investigating. (Many of the Favorite Trips listed below can be booked through these companies.) Each offers a catalog of trips that have been carefully checked out, and each is happy to provide consulting, to help you find a trip that's suited to your abilities, interests, and budget. Also, many of the outfitters listed in Favorite Trips lead a wide range of rides in the area they serve. So if you have your heart set on exploring a particular destination, but the trip you wanted is full, or too long or short, or at the wrong time of year, just check around a little more.

AMERICAN WILDERNESS EXPERIENCE As its name suggests, AWE focuses on backcountry adventure in North America. Founded in 1971, the company offers a wide range of trips, from backpacking to white-water rafting. Among its equine adventures, there's a good mix of moving pack trips and basecamp trail-riding vacations, and prior experience is not usually a requirement. In addition, there are a handful of combo adventures, such as horseback riding and rafting. Since the emphasis is on wilderness, AWE trips are more likely to involve camping than those of Equitour or FITS. A separate catalog covers dude ranch vacations (Box 1486, Boulder, CO 80306, tel. 303/444–2622 or 800/444–0099, fax 303/444–3999).

EQUITOUR This enterprise, like FITS, offers horse holidays only, but the folks at Equitour also raise and train horses, lead rides themselves, maintain a herd of 165 horses, and give riding instruction at their Wyoming ranch. Although most of its trips are overseas, Equitour has about 10 U.S. trips, generally contracted through local outfitters. Rides are aimed at an upscale crowd, so pleasant country inns and ranch houses are used for overnights in addition to wilderness campsites. Equitour trips generally assume at least a basic knowledge of riding. Rides are coded by suggested riding ability (Box 807, Dubois, WY 82513, tel. 307/455–3363 or 800/545–0019 outside WY, fax 307/455–2354).

FITS EQUESTRIAN Its name stands for "Fun in the Saddle"—the ultimate goal. FITS getaways are similar to Equitour's (indeed some can be booked by either organization): They're for riders with some riding experience, they're not short on comfort, and they're mainly in Europe. Minimum competence level on the dozen or so U.S. trips runs from basic to intermediate. FITS is also a full-service travel agency, so you can make all your travel arrangements through them (685 Lateen Rd., Solvang, CA 93463, tel. 805/688–9494 or 800/666–3487, fax 805/688–2943).

FAVORITE TRIPS

THE NORTHEAST

NEW HAMPSHIRE **Monadnock Highlands Inn-to-Inn Trek.** Imagine riding 5–6 or more hours a day, covering 18–24 miles through landscape seemingly untouched since the Colonial period, and perhaps cantering along 200-year-old byways. Each night you arrive at a different B&B, where your horse is stabled and you can enjoy epicurean dinners, full country breakfasts, and even an evening in a renowned blues and jazz club. (Lunches are normally picnics en route.) These are the hardships you face on this 6-day trip that tour operator Aline Coutu describes as "a touch of Europe in the heart of New England."

The beginning and ending point is Honey Lane Farm in Dublin, between Manchester and Keene. From there, you ride over gentle hills and old dirt roads, through forests and meadows—even some nature preserves—on your way to three historic inns, with amenities ranging from whirlpool baths to bedroom fireplaces. Massage is available for an additional charge. Not advised for beginner riders, the trip takes a maximum of 6 guests with 2 guides. You are expected to groom and tack up your own horse. *FITS Equestrian, 685 Lateen Rd., Solvang, CA 93463, tel. 805/688–9494 or 800/666–3487, fax 805/688–2943. Late May–Oct.: 6 days, $995 (May–mid-Sept.), $1,195 (fall foliage rides:*

mid.–Sept.–Oct.). Sign up 6 months in advance.

NEW YORK **Cold River Trail Ride.** Sprawling over 6 million acres, the Adirondack Mountains, in upstate New York, represent one of the largest tracts of wilderness in the East. They include forested valleys, secluded lakes, quiet streams, and 5,244-foot Mt. Marcy, the highest point in New York State. This 4-day ride explores just a fraction of this vast wilderness—the Cold River area. Fittingly, it's conducted by the Cold River Ranch, which has been offering trips since 1971. The updated turn-of-the-century lodge, 20 miles west of Lake Placid, can accommodate 9 guests.

Each night of the trip is spent in semi-permanent camps that include roomy cook tents and rustic lean-tos, part of the Adirondack Mountain Club hut system. Each day's ride brings excellent vistas of the surrounding mountains and forest, plus the chance to spot such wildlife as beaver, white-tailed deer, and black bear. Horses are gentle, well-broken, and sure-footed. Food runs toward the hearty and simple: eggs and pancakes for breakfast, sandwiches made with tuna or canned chicken with mayo for lunch, steak or fried chicken cooked over the fire for dinner. Groups set out with 6 or 7 participants and 2 or 3 wranglers with several years of guiding experience and CPR and basic first-aid training. *Cold River Ranch, Coreys, Tupper Lake, NY 12986, tel. 518/359–7559. June–late Oct.: 4 days, $640. Sign up 1 month in advance.*

VERMONT **Green Mountain Inn-to-Inn Ride.** Mix equal parts New England countryside and well-appointed, historic inns, and you get this 6-day trip, offered by Kedron Valley Stables, that's about as far as you can get from roughing it. By day, you ride from inn to inn and valley to ridge top, through tranquil farmlands and stands of birch, past stone fences and serene lakes, and along wooded hillside trails and dirt country lanes. By night, you relax in lodgings that date to as early as the 18th century but that still manage to provide such modern comforts as spas, gourmet dinners, tennis, and boating. Fall foliage trips are a leaf peeper's dream.

Arrive Sunday for dinner at the 1828 Kedron Valley Inn. The next morning you're matched to a horse and set off on your first of 4 days of riding, consisting of about 5½–6½ hours in the saddle and covering 20–25 miles. After riding through the lakes region, you arrive at the Echo Lake Inn, which has played host to President Coolidge and Thomas Edison, among other dignitaries. Next it's on to the Inn at Weathersfield, whose innkeepers are musicians and gourmet cooks; then to the Juniper Hill Inn, on the National Register of Historic Places; before returning on Thursday to South Woodstock and Kedron Valley.

Trail riding with Paul Kendall, an eighth-generation Vermonter, is fast paced and entertaining. He delights in recounting stories of the area, while Barbara Kendall makes picnic lunches that enormously exceed brown-bag expectations. On chilly days, you might even be fortified with hot tomato soup until you can ride to that night's inn and collapse beneath an heirloom quilt. Prices include gratuities and taxes. *Kedron Valley Stables, Box 368, South Woodstock, VT 05071, tel. 802/457–1480 or 800/225–6301, fax 802/457–3029. Mid-May–Oct.: 6 days, $1,300 double, $1,350 single (May–mid-Sept. and late Oct.); $1,500 double, $1,700 single (fall foliage rides: mid-Sept.–mid-Oct.). Sign up 2 months in advance.*

VERMONT **Sugarbush Tölt Trek.** This 5- or 6-day trip in the Mad River Valley of the Green Mountains also winds its way from charming upscale inn to charming upscale inn. Rides past flowering meadows, postcard-perfect villages, and, in the fall, fabulous foliage displays are rounded out with free time spent shopping, in hot tubs, with an on-call massage therapist, and savoring lavish meals. What sets this ride apart is the mounts—small but sturdy, purebred Icelandic horses, known for their stamina, their gentle disposition, and their *tölt*. A tölt is a gait, a sort of running walk that is particularly smooth and, therefore, great for long days in the saddle (some special tölting saddles are even available).

The ride begins on a Monday at the Vermont Icelandic Horse Farm, from which groups of 2–10 riders plus guides set out to the Mad River and over wooded trails and dirt roads. Lunches range from a picnic beside a stream to a refueling at a local country store. Most of the riding time is spent tölting, though there is some walking and cantering. To keep from getting saddle sore, you can hike leading your horse and take a dip in a swimming hole. Since there are alternate routes to each night's inn, pace and distance can be determined by the riders, though 15 or so miles a day is typical. On Friday, the 5-day riders depart, while 6-day participants stay on for more views of the surrounding ski areas and farmlands and lunch at the Sugarbush Airport, where you can watch gliders soar.

This is a trip for true horse-lovers—and experienced riders at that. *Vermont Icelandic Horse Farm, Box 577, Waitsfield, VT 05673, tel. 802/496–7141, fax 802/496–5390. Late May–late Oct.: 5 days, $925; 6 days, $1,095 (May–mid-Sept. and late Oct.); 5 days, $1,025; 6 days, $1,215 (fall foliage rides: mid-Sept.–mid-Oct.). Sign up 6 months in advance.*

THE MID-ATLANTIC

PENNSYLVANIA **Camping in Grand Canyon Country.** Carved by Pine Creek, Pennsylvania's 800-foot-deep Grand Canyon winds among the more pristine tracts of forest land in the mid-Atlantic region. The Mountain Trail Horse Center, founded in the 1970s and under its current ownership since 1982, does custom trail-riding trips out of backcountry camps. It's a true wilderness adventure, and you ride over all sorts of terrain—on trails or logging roads or bushwhacking through different parts of surrounding state forest lands, all in the company of a guide.

Overnight rides range from 2 to 5 days, and there is some flexibility in the amount of time spent in the saddle. There's also variety to the pace, from walking and trotting to cantering and galloping. Keep an eye peeled for wildlife: deer, black bears, eagles, or even coyotes, which you'll doubtless hear before seeing. Camp is usually moved at least once on longer trips, and there are no more than a dozen riders at the base camp at any given time. Guides have training in mountaineering as well as first aid. Horses are varied enough to accommodate participants' different tastes and riding experience.

You can opt for economy, basic, or deluxe packages. If you sign up for the economy package, you provide the camping gear and food. Basic packages include both, but the fare is simple—like hot dogs and beans. If you go with the deluxe package, wranglers set up camp before you arrive, and hors d'oeuvres and cold beer or wine are served before dinners that include steaks and fish, grilled over an open fire, as well as homemade pies and desserts. Don't fail to reserve well ahead for trips in fall, which is particularly colorful in the area, and for departures in June, when blossoming mountain laurel transforms the hills into a sea of pink. Prices vary by the number of people in your group and by days of the week (weekdays are cheaper than weekends). The price below is based on a group of 5 or 6 and includes tax. *Mountain Trail Horse Center, R.D. 2, Box 53, Wellsboro, PA 16901, tel. 717/376–5561, fax 717/376–2453. Apr.–Nov.: 5 days, $371 economy, $525 basic, $582 deluxe. Price does not include food or gear on economy trips; sign up 6 months in advance.*

WEST VIRGINIA **Fall Foliage in the Greenbrier Valley.** This 7-day riding adventure combines the charms of an elegant British-style B&B with the beauty of the relatively undiscovered West Virginia countryside. Home base is Swift Level, whose double-porticoed main house was built by Col. Samuel McClung II in 1827 and is listed on the National Register of Historic Places. Accommodations are here, in an adjacent cottage called the Bunk House, which was originally the ice house, and in the two-bedroom Log Cabin, in a field surrounded by brood mares and foals. (The owners raise thoroughbreds, quarter horses, and Connemara ponies.) A phone and fax are available, but there's no TV—just great views.

You arrive on Sunday, get acquainted with your horse (previous riding experience is helpful), and set out on Monday, across Muddy Creek Mountain into Blue Sulphur Springs, past 19th-century mill sites, cemeteries, pioneer homesites, and pastures of sheep and cattle—and perhaps to a cabin for some genuine mountain music at the end of the day. The valley was well traveled by many Native American nations and settled (not without bloodshed) in the 1700s by Irish, Scottish, and German newcomers. On the ride through the Greenbrier Valley, which George Washington surveyed, you pass many Civil War trenches and old telegraph lines, left standing as testimony to the separation of the Virginias. Ride leaders are well versed in the lore of the land.

After the first 3 nights at Swift Level, you spend 2 nights at the Current, a wonderful, informal B&B on the Greenbrier River. It's deep in Pocohontas County, where timber barons and railroads turned pristine wilderness into a worker's nightmare. Still, plenty of West Virginia beauty remains, especially at fall foliage time. The trip finishes, having covered 100 miles, back at Swift Level for the last night.

The ride is limited to 6 people, and days average 6 hours with a stop for a picnic lunch. Tack is English for the most part. Transportation to and from the Greenbrier Valley–Lewisburg Airport or the train in White Sulphur Springs is included, and a therapeutic massage can be arranged with advance notice. Other trips at different times of the year will very likely be offered. *Equitour, Box 807, Dubois, WV 82513, tel. 307/455–3363 or 800/545–0019 outside WV, fax 307/455–2354. Oct.: 7 days, $1,125. Sign up 3 months in advance.*

THE MIDWEST

SOUTH DAKOTA **Badlands National Park.** This vast, stunning wilderness in western South Dakota, filming location for parts of *Dances with Wolves,* is a haunting place, with its high grassy prairies, strangely eroded cliffs, and plentiful wildlife (especially pronghorn antelope). On this 4-day trip run by Dakota Badland Outfitters, and bookable through American Wilderness Experience, guides can tell the area's tall tales—of General Custer, pioneer wagon trains, and Sioux warriors for whom the land was sacred. Partly to make the trips seem more authentic, a horse-drawn chuck wagon accompanies riders on the fall departures, which comprise day rides out of a base camp along the Cheyenne River. Spring departures involve horse packing to remote regions of the park. Each day you journey 8–12 miles; at day's end, a comfortable camp awaits, complete with a campfire and cowboy coffee. Taking the ride in the spring reveals some spectacular wildflowers; autumn brings on delightfully warm afternoons and cool, starry nights. Group size is usually between 6 and 8. *American Wilderness Experience, Box 1486, Boulder, CO 80306, tel. 303/444–2622 or 800/444–0099, fax 303/444–3999. Mid-May–early June and Sept.–early Oct.: 4 days, $605. Sign up 4–6 months in advance.*

THE SOUTHWEST

ARIZONA **Cacti and Pine in the Superstition Wilderness Outside Phoenix.** This area of the Tonto National Forest, just east of Phoenix, is one of the country's best backcountry destinations in winter or early spring. This 6-day trip begins at the Peralta trailhead, at the edge of the wilderness, and heads through stands of giant saguaro cactus en route to the first night's camp at JF Ranch, a privately owned cattle spread. The next day you trail over Tortilla Pass and into beautiful Angel Basin, a stream-crossed meadow at the intersection of two canyons, and explore a nearby prehistoric cliff dwelling. The next night's camp is at Reavis Ranch, the turn-of-the-century homestead, now abandoned, of an eccentric hermit.

The Southwestern terrain ranges from cactus-studded deserts and rugged canyons to fragrant pine forests and breezy mountain ridges, which you cover at about 8–12 miles per day; there are 2 layover days. Camps are comfortable but in primitive settings, and meals are of the cowboy-campfire, steak-or-stew ilk with extras like salads and fruit. Group size is 8–10. *American Wilderness Experience, Box 1486, Boulder, CO 80306, tel. 303/444–2622 or 800/444–0099, fax 303/444–3999. Feb.–Apr.: 6 days, $855. Sign up 3–6 months in advance.*

ARIZONA A Week in the White Mountains. In midsummer, when the rest of Arizona is sweltering, this high country in the eastern part of the state is a comfortable 55°–85°. Arizona's second-highest range, the White Mountains comprise a wonderful mix of forests, meadows, streams, lakes, and rivers.

This 7-day excursion, recommended for intermediate and advanced riders, starts with a drive in vans from Gallup, New Mexico. You saddle up at Hannegan Meadow, near Alpine, and ride to the first night's camp at Lake Sierra Blanca. The next day you ride along the Black River, a beautiful little stream. Following its west fork, you climb to jewellike Big Lake, surrounded by broad, grassy meadows and known for its fishing. Of the trails you ride on succeeding days, most travel through gigantic pine forests; you also follow the Mogollan Rim, a geological fault that extends from central Arizona to northwestern New Mexico, with fine views over the Apache reservation. You're almost always at an elevation of 6,000–8,000 feet, and you are apt to spot deer and, if you're lucky, elk. On a typical day, you spend 5 or 6 hours astride the outfitter's quarter horses, covering around 20 miles; there are 2 layover days. Group size ranges from 15 to 30, with 4 staffers. The food is hearty, long on meat and potatoes—burgers, pork chops, chicken, and the like, all cooked over an open fire. *Equitour, Box 807, Dubois, WY 82513, tel.* *307/455–3363 or 800/545–0019 outside WY, fax 307/455–2354. July–Aug.: 7 days, $1,000. Sign up 3 months in advance.*

ARIZONA AND UTAH Monument Valley with a Navajo Guide. The towering mesas, buttes, and thin, knobby spires of this area, part of the Navajo Nation, have served as the backdrop for many John Ford westerns, and to the Navajo it is a land of legend and lore, as you'll learn from your Navajo guide over this 8-day trip.

After being picked up at the airport and overnighting in Gallup, New Mexico, you stop at the historic Hubbell's Trading Post en route to the your trailhead, in Monument Valley. From there, you travel around the North Window, where a pair of buttes frame a spectacular view of the distant desert, and to the foot of Thunderbird Mesa, where there's a well-equipped base camp with cots, bedrolls, sheets, pillows, tables, campfire chairs, and hot showers. Each day you ride out at about 9 and return at 5, averaging 5–6 hours in the saddle and taking in such landmarks as the Totem Pole, Rooster Rock, Hunt's Mesa, and Ford's Point, as well as unnamed natural arches, prehistoric cliff dwellings, and petroglyphs. On the penultimate day, a ride to the top of Mitchell Mesa reveals a magnificent panorama of the whole valley as well as portions of four states.

Meals are wholesome and hearty and include dinners of barbecued brisket or turkey with all the fixings, and evenings are capped off by cowboy entertainment. Because Monument Valley is part of the Navajo Nation, alcoholic beverages are not permitted. Group size ranges from 12 to 30 but is usually at the upper end. A couple of 5-day trips do not include the first and last nights' lodging nor airport transport but are otherwise similar. *American Wilderness Experience, Box 1486, Boulder, CO 80306, tel. 303/444–2622 or 800/444–0099, fax 303/444–3999. Mid-May–early June and Mid-Sept.–Mid-Oct.: 5 days, $1,005; 8 days, $1,405. Sign up 3–6 months in advance.*

NEW MEXICO Through the Mountainous Gila National Forest. This half-million acres in southwest New Mexico's Gila National Forest, a spectacular land of deep canyons and forested mountain ridges, was the first area in the United States to be designated a wilderness area. Today it serves as a magnificent setting for this 8-day horse pack trip.

The trip begins in Glenwood, New Mexico, where you overnight in a motel. The next day, you saddle up and head off into the high country east of town. Over the next 6 days you ride from semi-arid hills covered in piñon pine into forests of ponderosa pine and aspen surrounding the 10,600-foot high Mogollon Baldy Lookout, an abandoned fire lookout tower atop the region's highest peak. Typically, you spend 5–6 hours in the saddle and cover 8–10 miles per day. The fishing is superb in many of the streams, and you may spot deer, elk, antelope, mountain lion, and black bear, as well as the occasional eagle soaring on the air currents high above the mountains. Two layover days, one each at your first and second camps, give you time to explore at your own speed. Meals involve lots of Dutch oven cooking. Usually there are 8–12 people in each group. Your final night is spent back at Glenwood, and both the first and last nights' accommodations are included in the price. Transportation to and from El Paso is available for an additional $100. *American Wilderness Experience, Box 1486, Boulder, CO 80306, tel. 303/444–2622 or 800/444–0099, fax 303/444–3999. Mid-July–early Aug.: 8 days, $1,005; $955 youths 8–16 and senior citizens 65 or over. Sign up 3–6 months in advance.*

NEW MEXICO **Woman's Rite of Passage.** This 5-day pack trip, designed specifically for women over 37, is offered by the Taos Indian Horse Ranch, an educational facility in northern New Mexico's Sangre de Cristo range. The ranch has been around since 1969, and its aim is to turn riders "from tourists to active participants in history." Included in the trip is instruction in caring for horses, camp living, tracking, wilderness survival, and other aspects of Plains Indian culture that relate specifically to women. Dream interpretation is also part of the curriculum, and self-examination is emphasized.

Group size is limited to 7, and the warm camaraderie that develops during the course of the trip stands out. Riding consists of about 10 hours a day astride well-trained horses; 10–30 miles is typically covered. Steaks and chops are on the menu, along with vegetarian fare and wild mushrooms and asparagus that you harvest yourself. Overnights are in lean-tos. A recent doctor's statement of good health is required of each participant, as well as a short essay explaining your reasons for wanting to sign up. *Taos Indian Ranch, Box 3019, Taos, NM 87571-3019, tel. 505/758–3212 or 800/659–3210, fax 505/758–3212. Sept.: 5 days, $3,000. Sign up 6–8 months in advance.*

UTAH **Mountain Lakes and Vistas in the High Uinta Range.** Stretching across northeastern Utah, the Uintas Mountains, the only major range of the Rockies that runs from east to west, include Utah's highest summits, among them 13,526-foot Kings Peak. Piute Creek Outfitters operates custom trips in the western portion of the range, primarily in the 80,000-acre lake region—which means good fishing for small rainbow trout and opportunities for stunning photographs. Itineraries vary, but many trails pass through lush spruce and fir forests and across verdant meadows with terrific mountain vistas and, especially in July, an explosion of wildflowers. Deer, elk, and other species of wildlife abound.

Meals make virtuosic use of the Dutch oven: One night, there may be meat loaf, and another you chow down "runaway horse," an everything-but-the-kitchen-sink concoction based on ground beef and macaroni; there's always a steak dinner with corn-on-the-cob and homemade sourdough bread. Your mounts are all quarter horses, raised by the Arnolds, who run Piute Creek Outfitters and have been leading trips in the area since 1974. Foals go out on trips with their mothers even when they're very young, so horses are accustomed to following the leader. Trips are all custom; the Arnolds take out as few as 4 or as many as 8. If you can't assemble a party of at least 4 or want to go out with another group, they try to match you up with someone else who wants to travel at roughly the same time and for the same number of days. Usually there are 3 or 4 wranglers on each trip. Fees, which include sleeping bag and pad, vary depending on how long you stay out; if you make a commitment to help the Arnolds with the grooming and other heavy chores, you get a 20% discount. *Piute Creek Outfitters, 3000 North 900 East, Kamas, UT 84036-9509, tel. 801/783–2982 or 800/225–0218. July–Aug.: 3 days, $506; 5 days $801; 7 days, $1,046. Sign up 6 months in advance.*

UTAH **Exploring the Canyonlands.** Led by Perri Philip, this adventurous journey explores the beautiful canyonlands east of Moab, near Arches National Park. The region is filled with pink slickrock, sheer cliffs, sandy washes, mesas, and mountains as well as Anasazi petroglyphs and ruins.

The first and last nights of the trip are spent at a motel in Moab, and feature get-acquainted and farewell dinners for the group (lodging, meals, and transfers from Moab airport included). Apart from those nights—and one spent camping on a high mesa—you stay in log cabins at the Fisher Valley ranch of the pioneer Taylor family, chowing down on good, western fare. Each day, riding 5–7 hours at a slow to moderate clip, you explore all the area has to offer: spectacular desert canyons, aspen-forested slopes, and old cattle and uranium trails. In the fall, along with enjoying the colors, you can join in moving the Taylor cattle down a steep and rocky trail. The spring ride may substitute additional riding in the lower desert for the camp-out on the high mesa, and weather might dictate other changes in itinerary.

Groups of 4–6 riders, with a basic knowledge of riding, are accompanied by a pair of staff members. Both Western and English saddles are available. *FITS Equestrian, 685 Lateen Rd., Solvang, CA 93463, tel. 805/ 688–9494 or 800/666–3487, fax 805/688– 2943. Mid-May and late Sept. (other dates can be arranged): 7 days, $1,250. Sign up 6 months in advance.*

THE ROCKIES

COLORADO **Stunning Lake Scenery Near Aspen.** In the Maroon Bells–Snowmass Wilderness in the White River National Forest, near jet-setting Aspen, 13,000- and 14,000-foot snow-capped peaks frame aspen-covered valleys. This is the setting for an 8-day trip from A.J. Brink Outfitters, a firm that has built a solid reputation in the area since its founding in 1975.

The riding begins by following East Maroon Creek to a camp just below 12,450-foot Triangle Pass, where you spend 2 nights; on your second day out, you ride over to Copper Lake and then over another high pass before returning to camp. The next day sees you stopping in the old mining town of Gothic en route to a camp in Rustlers Gulch, where you spend 2 more nights; the second layover day gives you time to visit the old mines in the area. Then it's on to the Crystal River Valley, beautiful Snowmass Lake, and picture-perfect Crater Lake. Given the quality of the outfitting and the stunning scenery, this is one classy trip. You cover 8–12 miles a day on average and typically spend 4–6 hours astride quarter horses. Group size ranges from 10 to 15. Meals are fresh and homemade—with bacon and eggs, eggs Benedict, or French toast and sausage for breakfast, make-your-own sandwiches at lunch, and, for dinner, ham and sweet potatoes, Chinese stir-fries, pork chops with stuffing, and even roast beef along with the usual fried chicken and steaks. *A.J. Brink Outfitters, Glendevey Route Colorado, Jelm, WY 82063, tel. 303/ 435–5707. July–Aug.: 8 days, $860. Sign up 6 months in advance.*

COLORADO **Roosevelt National Forest's Rawah Wilderness.** In its day, the historic Glendevey Lodge, in the beautiful Laramie River Valley across from the northwest corner of Rocky Mountain National Park, served as a stagecoach stop, a hunting lodge, and an inn used by lumberjacks who were in the area to cut ties for the nation's railroads. Today it's the simple but cozy point of departure for this 7-day trip.

After spending 2 days at the lodge, you trade its comfort for a rather posh base camp at Housmer Creek, where tents come equipped with cots and stoves for heating. For the next 3 days, you make day rides out of camp to explore forested canyons, linger alongside lakes and streams teeming with trout, and poke around the foothills of some breathtaking peaks. Usually you spend 5–6 hours in the saddle, covering distances of 10–12 miles. Meals are hearty and western style, with dishes such as fried chicken and Dutch apple pie served in the lodge, and stews and steaks and potatoes whipped up by the wranglers on the trail. Group size is generally 6–8. Round-trip airport transfers from Laramie, Wyoming, cost $20 per carload. *American Wilderness Experience, Box 1486, Boulder, CO 80306, tel. 303/444–2622 or 800/444–0099, fax 303/444–3999. July–Aug.: 7 days, $1,195 single, $1,085 double. Sign up 3–6 months in advance.*

COLORADO **Bushwhacking in the Sangre de Cristo Wilderness for the Advanced Rider.** This 5-day foray through a saw-toothed range of formidable 13,000- to 14,000-foot peaks is for the serious rider. Referred to as the "ultimate pack trip," it travels well into rugged wilderness, keeping away from main trails and other humans. Bushwhacking your way back and forth across the spine of the Sangres—through hidden valleys and over isolated passes, cresting the mountains several times—you're rewarded by incredible views of alpine lakes, pine forests, and native wildlife. Expect long days (6–7 hours) in the saddle, covering 10–15 miles; there is 1 layover day. You're expected to care for your own horse. Meals are gourmet camp fare. Most groups number under 8. *American Wilderness Experience, Box 1486, Boulder, CO 80306, tel. 303/444–2622 or 800/444–0099, fax 303/444–3999. July–early Sept.: 5 days, $605. Sign up 4–6 months in advance.*

COLORADO **Forested Canyons of the San Juan Mountains—Along the Continental Divide.** Take a deep breath before leaving for this trip from San Juan Outfitting, a firm founded in 1975: You won't enjoy this much oxygen again for the next 8 days. The San Juans are the most rugged range of the Rockies. Since you're constantly above timberline among 13,000-foot peaks, the views are as good as they get. The start of the trip, at the top of 10,850-foot Wolf Creek Pass, and its end point in Silverton, the famous mining town, are both on the 2,700-mile Continental Divide Trail; the route between them takes in alpine lakes; glacial cirques; stretches of tundra that drop off into deep, forested canyons; the half-million acre Weminuche Wilderness in the San Juan National Forest; and 2 landmarks used by the Spaniards when they mined for gold in the area: the Rio Grande Pyramid, a triangular rock formation, and the Window, a notch in the rocks that looks just like what you'd expect. No wonder there's a 2-year waiting list for the trip.

Daily riding distances are 11–23 miles, requiring an average of 4–8 hours in the saddle, but there are 2 layover days. Mounts represent all breeds, including Arabians, Morgans, and quarter horses. Meals feature stuffed Cornish game hen, Navajo tacos, breaded pork chops, shrimp stir-fries, New York strip steaks, and the occasional homemade apple pie. No more than 6 riders saddle up for each departure, accompanied by 3 or 4 wranglers. *San Juan Outfitting, 186 County Road 228, Durango, CO 81301, tel. 303/259–6259. Aug.: 8 days, $1,800. Sign up 2 years in advance.*

COLORADO **Native American History in the Ute Mountain Ute Tribal Park.** Located just south of Mesa Verde National Park in southwestern Colorado, the 150,000-acre Ute Mountain Ute Tribal Park is rich in archaeological treasures and Native American history, as quickly becomes evident on this trip from Rapp Guides and Packers. You begin at Weber Canyon Ranch, then follow Weber Canyon for 13 miles along the Mancos River to a base camp at the mouth of Morefield

Canyon. Over the next several days, you go out on day trips led by a Ute guide—to unexcavated Anasazi cliff dwellings and ruins built some 700 years ago. Rock art abounds, as do a variety of artifacts, including pottery shards and skeletal remains, tools and arrowheads, and bits of yucca fibers the Indians used for sandals. The Utes, who now own this land, are not related to the ancient ruin dwellers, but have their own culture and traditions, which your guide may share with you, with a little coaxing.

On most days you spend 4–8 hours in the saddle, covering 3–13 miles. Horse- and mule-drawn wagons bring gear and groceries to camp, nestled in a grove of 300-year-old box elder trees, where wall tents provide the accommodations. For dinner there are T-bone steaks with corn on the cob and green chilies on the side, grilled swordfish, and Navajo tacos and beans; desserts are fresh out of the Dutch oven. Deluxe trips sport a gourmet chef and all the trimmings. The typical group numbers 8–12. *Rapp Guides and Packers, 47 Electra Lake, Durango, CO 81301, tel. 970/247–8923, fax 970/247–1255. Apr.–May and Sept.–Oct.: 4 days, regular $1,295, deluxe $1,595; plus $200 park fee. Sign up 6 months in advance.*

COLORADO **Riding and Trout Fishing in Weminuche Wilderness.** At a half-million acres, the Weminuche Wilderness, named for one of the seven bands of the Ute Indians, encompasses a good portion of the San Juan Mountains, whose 10,000-foot average elevation makes them the highest mountain range in all of North America. Be glad you're not hiking, as this 6-day ride from Rapp Guides and Packers climbs quickly to the Continental Divide and trails along the crest to a base camp at the head of Starvation Gulch. The beautiful, high, elk-filled meadow was named for the unfortunate experience of a group of winter explorers who wandered through here in the 1800s. You spend 3 nights and the intervening days exploring the alpine terrain of the surrounding Rio Grande and San Juan national forests, and you may want to wet a line and go for rainbows, brookies, or cutthroat trout

at a number of superb fishing spots. On the fourth day, camp is moved into the area alongside steep-banked Elk Creek, where you spend the trip's last 2 nights. If you opt to pay extra, you can return to Durango or Silverton and civilization aboard the coal-fired Durango & Silverton Narrow Gauge Railroad, known for its spectacular route carved into the mountainsides.

Most days have you in the saddle for about 4 hours, covering 10 miles. Meals rely heavily on fresh ingredients—steaks, fish, vegetables, and the like. Group size usually ranges from 4 to 7, and a staff of 2 or 3 wranglers goes along. *Rapp Guides and Packers, 47 Electra Lake Rd., Durango, CO 81301, tel. 970/247–8923, fax 970/247–1255. Aug.: 5 days, $1,095; 6 days, $1,295. Sign up 6 months in advance.*

COLORADO AND WYOMING **The Great Colorado-to-Wyoming Trail Ride.** Northern Colorado's Zirkel Range, in the heart of the Rockies, provides some truly pleasurable riding, thanks to beautiful scenery and well-maintained trails. This 6-day ride through the area is staged by Steamboat Lake Outfitters, a company founded in 1983. It starts at Steamboat Lake, 25 miles north of the ski resort town of Steamboat Springs, and follows the north fork of the Elk River before entering the Mount Zirkel Wilderness in the Routt National Forest.

With your Appaloosa or quarter horse doing the huffing and puffing, you cross the Continental Divide and then drop down to the Encampment River. From a 2-night camp on the Wyoming state line, you take a day ride to West Fork Lake. Then it's off through the Medicine Bow National Forest's Encampment Wilderness, an unspoiled area guaranteed to expand your wildlife-spotting experience.

Usually you spend 4–6 hours in the saddle; mileage varies depending on the group and the weather. The last night is at the secluded Water Valley Ranch, where comfortable suites and western meals of steak and prime rib top off your wilderness excursion. Meals on the trail are similar western fare, starring steaks and chicken, with entertainment in the form of cowboy songs and a lesson in lassoing after dessert. Group size is usually 10–20, with 5–10 staffers as necessary. *Steamboat Lake Outfitters, Box 749, Clark, CO 80428, tel. 303/879–4404, fax 303/879–5147. July–Aug.: 6 days, $1,250. Sign up 3 months in advance.*

IDAHO **Edna Lake and the Sawtooth National Forest's Sawtooth Wilderness.** Idaho's Sawtooth Mountains, in the central Rockies, rake the horizon like the blade of the crosscut saw for which they were named. The folks at the Mystic Saddle Ranch, which has been doing pack trips since 1969, can provide you with gentle, easygoing horses—and a comfortable introduction to the area from a base camp at jewellike Edna Lake, at the headwaters of the South Fork of the Payette River, in the heart of the Sawtooth Wilderness. From the camp, you can climb nearby peaks, cast flies into the area's blue-ribbon lakes, photograph wildflowers, or simply stretch out on a boulder and catch a few rays. Most trips are guided, though there is one drop-off trip that has travelers exploring on their own. Day trips are in the vicinity of 10 miles, usually with about 4 hours in the saddle.

Breakfasts star homemade cinnamon rolls along with the usual eggs and hotcakes; at dinner, you might be served salmon, smoked pork chops, pork tenderloin, chicken Kiev or teriyaki. Group size is usually 8–12, with a staff of 2–3. Longer and shorter custom trips are also available. *Mystic Saddle Ranch, Stanley, ID 83278, tel. 208/774–3591, fax 208/774–3455. July–Sept.: 5 days, $795. Sign up 6–9 months in advance.*

IDAHO **Wildlife Spotting and Trout Fishing in the Rugged Bitterroot Mountains.** Outfitter Jim Renshaw, one of Idaho's most experienced guides, leads the way to the rugged, vast, and unspoiled Bitterroot Mountains, another range of the Rockies. Four generations of his family have lead pack trips; Renshaw has owned his own outfit since 1953, making him Idaho's longest-operating licensed outfitter. On this 7-day trip in the

Clearwater and Nez Perce national forests, you ride good, gentle mountain horses to alpine lakes and streams where the fishing for native cutthroat and rainbow trout is excellent and so is the scenery. Wildlife is plentiful, and there's a good chance of spotting elk, deer, moose, and beaver. Typically, you ride for 4 hours a day over 12–16 miles and move camp only a couple of times to allow for plenty of leisure to explore each area. Trips can be tailored to suit the group. Meals feature home-style cooking: steaks, chicken, pork chops, and, of course, trout. *Renshaw Outfitting, Inc., Box 1165, Dept. A, Kamiah, ID 83536, tel. 208/926–4520 or 800/452–2567, fax 208/935–0788. July–Aug.: 7 days, $900. Sign up 2 months in advance.*

MONTANA **Bob Marshall Wilderness for Beginners and Kids.** Extending south from Glacier National Park in northern Montana, "the Bob," in the Flathead and Lewis & Clark national forests, is a gem in the nation's wilderness system. It not only encompasses some amazing mountain terrain headlined by the Chinese Wall (a natural granite escarpment almost 13 miles long), but also is rich in wildflowers and wildlife, including grizzly bear. Several outfitters serve the Bob with countless itineraries. This 5-day ride run by Lass and Ron Mills up the Dearborn River is both a good introduction to the area and to trail riding. The Mills have been doing pack trips in the vicinity since 1968.

The trip begins with a 10-mile ride through Devil's Glen along the Dearborn River, where you set up base camp for the entire trip. Here, you can go fishing, take riding lessons, or saddle up for guided group trips to higher country for spectacular vistas of the Dearborn drainage and beyond—usually with about 4–5 hours in the saddle and mileages of 6–8. In addition, special short outings are offered for youngsters. Groups usually number 6–8, and chow is campfire cooking. *American Wilderness Experience, Box 1486, Boulder, CO 80306, tel. 303/444–2622 or 800/444–0099, fax 303/444–3999. Late June: 5 days, $930. Sign up 6–8 months in advance.*

MONTANA **Custom Trips in Yellowstone National Park.** Yellowstone is everything you've heard—an expansive wonderland of forests, meadows, mountains, geysers, and wildlife. Though most visitors do little more than get out of their vehicle occasionally to snap a few pictures, a more breathtaking Yellowstone is just a few hours away by horseback. Enter Mike Thompson of R.K. Miller's Wilderness Pack Trips, who customizes 3- to 14-day pack trips to the interests of his groups (4–12 riders) and can arrange for either full-service trips or drop camps.

As a guide, Mike is known for his quiet manner and keen eyesight, pointing out elk, bear, birds of prey, and the occasional wolf. He is at home in the mountains and enjoys sharing that world with groups. His wife, Erin, provides three hearty meals a day, including marinated tenderloin steak, fresh vegetable salads, noodle and rice dishes, and home-baked desserts. There's also been a fair number of cutthroat trout cooked over an open fire, since Mike tailors trips for those who fly-fish as well. The other key member of the entourage is your mount, one of 18 surefooted and well-mannered horses picked to match your level of experience. The price of a 7-day trip, below, includes 2 nights' lodging. *R.K. Miller's Wilderness Pack Trips, c/o Mike Thompson, Box 5299, Bozeman, MT 59717, tel. 406/586-6702. July–Sept.: 7 days, $1,650.*

WYOMING **The Outlaw Trail Comes to Life.** A ride with some real flavor, this 8-day trip offers the opportunity to relive a bit of the Old West. This part of northern Wyoming was the lair of many outlaws, including Civil War deserters and Butch Cassidy and the Sundance Kid's Wild Bunch, as well as bands of Sioux, Arapaho, and Cheyenne. During the ride, you meet local ranchers, whose tales of past generations bring the area's rich history to life.

The adventure begins in Riverton, Wyoming. Your first dinner is at the home of Skip, your guide, and your first night is spent at a motel (included in price). The next day you're transported by vehicle to Buffalo Creek Canyon, which serves as base camp for 2 nights. (Hearty meat-and-potatoes fare includes burgers, chicken, and pork chops.) From here, you ride into the foothills of the Bighorn Mountains and around Buffalo Creek Canyon. Though the terrain can be rough, there are spots each day for experienced riders to cut loose and gallop. Continuing on to subsequent camps, you ride on and around the 50-mile-long rock formation known as the Red Wall (the wall of Hole-in-the-Wall Gang fame) and the venerable Shepardson Ranch. In September, you may be able to help drive cows down from the high country. At the end of the trail, you're driven back to your motel, and a farewell dinner with western dancing proves a fitting finale.

A maximum of 16 intermediate or better riders, accompanied by 4 staffers, ride mixed-breed horses of various temperaments. Typical days cover about 20 miles in 4–6 hours. *Equitour, Box 807, Dubois, WY 82513, tel. 307/455-3363 or 800/545-0019 outside WY, fax 307/455-2354. Late May–June and Aug.–Sept.: 8 days, $1,145, plus $125 single supplement. Sign up 3–4 months in advance.*

WYOMING **Frontier-Era Spirit Along the Pony Express/Oregon Trail.** The 1,900-mile Pony Express route originally stretched from St. Joseph, Missouri, to Sacramento, California, and riders used to cover it in 8 days. This trip, too, takes 8 days (6 of riding), but you and your horse cover a fraction of the distance at a much slower pace—around 15–20 miles a day with 4–6 hours in the saddle. And you won't encounter such distractions as Indian and outlaw ambushes!

The trip begins and ends in Riverton, with 2 nights in a motel included. Riding out of Sweetwater Station, a onetime Pony Express stop, you travel along the Pony Express and Oregon Trail corridors, through desert, sagebrush plain, and woods, set against a backdrop of the snowcapped Wind River Range. Wild horses and antelope are common sights. Along the way, you can indulge in non-horse-related activities, from swimming and fishing in the Sweetwater Canyon to touring historic South Pass City, one of the few towns that grew up along the Oregon Trail; it's preserved as something of a living museum, so that you can see how settlers lived, worked, and prepared their meals.

Each night is spent in a different camp, which is trucked in and set up, so riders (strong intermediates advised) can have nice long trots and canters unfettered by pack animals. Usually the ride is split into two groups, with more experienced riders traveling faster along a longer route to the next camp. Dinner is good and plentiful, but nothing fancy, and is often followed by a sing-along around the campfire. Mid-trip, you're driven into the old gold-mining town of Atlantic City for a night out, and your last evening is devoted to a farewell dinner and two-step dancing at a local night club.

Groups have no more than 16 riders, with 6–8 staffers riding shotgun. Mounts are local ranch-bred quarter horses. *Equitour, Box 807, Dubois, WY 82513, tel. 307/455–3363 or 800/545–0019 outside WY, fax 307/455–2354. July–Aug.: 8 days, $1,095, plus $125 single supplement. Sign up 2 months in advance.*

WYOMING **Women of the Wild, Wild West.** Because they realized that most of the riders on their trips—not to mention most of their best riders—were women, Great Divide Tours offers a trail ride for women, by women, and about women. It is truly a women-only trip, from the participants to the guides, wranglers, and camp crew (no promise is made as to horses' gender). And this is not just a pretty ride through the countryside; it's a riding seminar about the women who played a part in the Old West.

Each of the 5 nights on the trail, there is a campfire presentation on a different personality—Native Americans, missionaries, ranch owners, ladies of the evening. On the first night, for example, you make camp on Battle Mountain, where a member of the Arapaho tribe tells, from a women's point of view, about the exchange between cavalry

and Indians 120 years ago. You also hear the romantic story of a young teacher from the East who came to Wyoming to a one-room schoolhouse and was courted by a friend of Butch Cassidy.

A maximum of 12 riders, accompanied by 3 or 4 staff, spend 4–6 hours atop their horses as they explore this piece of history. The first night's lodging is in nice, new bunkhouses at the Horseman's Holiday Ranch (transfers from Riverton airport included); after that, you move on to a different camp each night. *FITS Equestrian, 685 Lateen Rd., Solvang, CA 93463, tel. 805/688–9494 or 800/666–3487, fax 805/688–2943. Early July and early Aug.: 6 days, $1,095. Sign up 6 months in advance.*

WYOMING **Rolling Valleys and Hidden Streams in the Wind River Mountains.** Because most tourists head for the better-known Tetons nearby, the Wind Rivers—some of the grandest mountains in the West—are also some of region's least explored. You have ample opportunity to try your luck with rod and reel in some of the high-country lakes and to explore hidden streams. You can also rub elbows with a number of granite summits along the Continental Divide on this 7-day trip from the Skinner Brothers—Wyoming-raised Monte, Bob, and Courtney, old hands here (having been outfitting trips since 1956), with a real love of sharing the area with others. You ride through rolling valleys, alpine meadows, and fields of wildflowers; there are a thousand lakes in the area and stunning high mountain peaks.

Usually you cover around 10 miles a day, and spend between 4 and 5 hours in the saddle; there are 3 layover days. The menu is basic western fare—hotcakes, eggs, and sausage for breakfast, sandwiches at lunch, and for dinner, steaks, roasts, fish, and chicken, followed up with pie or some canned fruit. Both groups and individuals can be accommodated. *Skinner Brothers, Box 859, Pinedale, WY 82941, tel. 307/367–2270 or 800/237–9138, fax 307/367–4757. Aug.: 7 days, $900. Sign up 1 month in advance.*

WYOMING **Camp Excursions in the Gros Ventre Mountains.** Most visitors who land in Jackson, Wyoming, head straight to either Grand Teton or Yellowstone National Park. But a third area nearby is often overlooked: the Gros Ventre Mountains, which rise east of town in the Bridger-Teton National Forest, practically in Yellowstone's backyard.

On the first day of this 5-day trip, you ride to a "luxurious" pre-set forest camp, complete with walled tents, a shower, and a heated mess tent with log-hewn furniture. By mid-week, you ride over the ridge to a second camp. From each base, daily excursions permit gazing at the surrounding mountains, exploring the Flat and Granite creek drainages (the fishing is terrific), and visiting Turquoise Lake and Sleeping Indian Mountain. Wildlife abounds, and you might spot elk and moose. Most day rides are 8–10 miles, with about 6–7 hours in the saddle, though tailoring is available. Meals are cooked on camp stoves or over the open fire—steaks perfumed with mesquite, stews, and Dutch oven biscuits and cobblers. The typical group saddling up includes 8 riders. *American Wilderness Experience, Box 1486, Boulder, CO 80306, tel. 303/444-2622 or 800/444-0099, fax 303/444-3999. July–early Sept.: 5 days, $830; $805 for groups of 4 or more. Sign up 3–6 months in advance.*

THE WEST COAST

CALIFORNIA **Mendocino Coast Inn-to-Inn Ride.** This 7-day trip along the northern California coast—a long string of hidden coves, steep headlands, and crashing surf—offers breathtaking scenery each day and comfortable bed-and-breakfasts with hot tubs each night. The ride leaves the Ricochet Ridge Ranch, near Fort Bragg; skirts bluffs high above the Pacific; ventures into dark and misty redwood forests; and allows time for galloping through the surf. Though absolute beginners can be accommodated, this trip is designed for more experienced riders. You spend an average of 5 hours in the saddle each day, covering around 20 miles.

Lunches, served on the trail, are build-your-own sandwiches, with your choice of 3 cheeses, 3 mustards, and 3 breads. Breakfasts include fresh berries, homemade baked goods, and eggs. With the exception of a salmon barbecue, which is served outdoors, you eat dinner in restaurants; appetizers, entrées, and wine are included in the trip price, along with 3 evenings' entertainment by a classical guitarist, a classical pianist, and a local Mendocino music group. Most groups have between 14 and 16 riders and 3 staffers. The ranch, in business since 1972, has been offering these inn-to-inn rides since 1985. *Ricochet Ridge Ranch, 24201 North Highway 1, Fort Bragg, CA 95437, tel. 707/964-7669, fax 707/964-9669. June–Oct.: 7 days, $1,580. Sign up 3–6 months in advance.*

CALIFORNIA **Day Trips in the High Sierras.** Having been in business since 1915, the folks at Mammoth Lakes Pack Outfit are almost intimately familiar with the rugged stretch of the Sierra Nevada range in which they operate. Fully catered 4- and 5-day vacations start with a climb up 10,750-foot high Duck Pass, whereupon you enter the Inyo National Forest's John Muir Wilderness, full of high lakes and streams, and travel 9–15 miles into the backcountry. Here you establish base camp, setting up tents and a kitchen.

Each day you go out for a day ride covering up to 8 miles, taking in exposed granite peaks, pine forests, and grassy meadows; typically you spend up to 4 hours in the saddle. Horses, matched to riders' abilities, are trail-wise and dependable. There's plenty of time for hiking, photography, fishing, and nature study, especially during lunch stops.

Breakfast might be banana pancakes and fresh trout or scrambled eggs, and you're served sandwiches for lunch, trailside, and steak, barbecued chicken, potatoes, and fresh vegetables for dinner, perhaps topped off with strawberry shortcake. Most departures set out with 6–12 riders and 2–3 staff members. *Mammoth Lakes Pack Outfit, Box 61, Mammoth Lakes, CA 93546, tel. 619/*

934–2434, fax 619/934–3975. July–early Sept.: 4 days, $600; 5 days, $750. Price does not include tents; sign up 3–4 months in advance.

CALIFORNIA **Eating Well in Kings Canyon National Park.** Like Yosemite, Kings Canyon encompasses an astounding range of high Sierra terrain, including jagged summits, deep canyons, glacial cirques, tumbling waterfalls, and thick forests. Yet it's far less known than its national park cousin. Following the Pacific Crest Trail, this 7-day trip between Pine Creek and the Bishop Pass trailhead takes in such scenic places as Evolution Valley, Le Conte Canyon, and the South Fork of the Kings River, and crosses a number of high passes, including 12,000-foot Muir Pass. You spend 4–6 hours a day on your gentle, well-mannered mountain horse and cover 8–10 miles; there are 3 layover days.

The western-style fare here stands out: 3 hearty meals with plenty of fresh fruits and vegetables. For breakfast, sourdough hotcakes, eggs served rancheros style with chili, French toast topped with blueberries or raspberries, or biscuits and gravy might put in an appearance; for dinner, you might have enchiladas, lasagna, and sourdough or garlic bread, followed by chocolate mousse or just-baked carrot cake or apple pie. Most groups have 4–11 riders with a minimum of 3 guides. A longer trip to Kings Canyon is often run in September. *Pine Creek Pack Station, Box 968, Bishop, CA 93515, tel. 619/387–2797. Aug.: 7 days, $735. Sign up 2–3 months in advance.*

WASHINGTON **A Base Camp in the Pasayten Wilderness.** North Cascade Safaris' owner Claude Miller grew up in these mountains and knows their summits, valleys, and hidden lakes inside and out. Beginning at the Billy Goat Corral, this 5-day ride heads directly to Hidden Lakes, where you set up in a base camp. Here, you can try your luck among numerous fishing holes, go for guided day hikes, or saddle up your gentle, good-natured horse for a morning on the trail with the guide, to look for elk and

mountain goat or visit flower-filled meadows such as those in the Tatoosh Buttes area. There are 2 or 3 layover days. Rides cover anywhere from 10 to 12 miles a day, with around 5 hours in the saddle. Meals are western-style with Continental touches: The scrambled eggs are made with peppers, for instance, and there's beef stroganoff and chicken cacciatore for dinner. Most groups number between 4 and 9, with 2 staffers. Miller has been in business since 1970. *North Cascade Safaris, c/o Claude Miller Pack Trips, Box 250, Winthrop, WA 98862, tel. 509/996–2350. June–Sept.: 5 days, $750. Sign up 2 months in advance.*

WASHINGTON **Prisitne Alpine Terrain Along the Pacific Crest Trail.** The northern Washington section of this famed backcountry route, 35 miles extending from Manning Park at the Canadian border in the north to Harts Pass in the south, cuts through some of the more pristine alpine terrain of the North Cascades. This 10-day trip run by Claude Miller follows 14 miles of the trail, beginning at 6,197-foot Harts Pass. From there, the route crosses Frosty Pass, a meadow at 7,200 feet, and eventually returning to Harts Pass by way of the middle fork of the Pasayten River. Most days you ride 10–12 miles, with about 5 hours in the saddle; there are 3 layover days—one near Frosty Pass and the others along the Pasayten, both sites good for fishing and just relaxing. Meals are western-style with Continental touches. Groups usually consist of 4–9 riders with 2 wranglers. *North Cascade Safaris, c/o Claude Miller Pack Trips, Box 250, Winthrop, WA 98862, tel. 509/996–2350. July–Sept.: 10 days, $1,500. Sign up 2 months in advance.*

ALASKA

CENTRAL **In the Shadow of Denali.** An orientation dinner kicks off this 6-day adventure (a 4-day option has a different itinerary) around the park that is home to 20,320-foot Mt. McKinley. In fact, riding starts 22 miles south of park headquarters, and, weather permitting, you get breathtaking views of the country's tallest peak on the first and last days of the trip. In between, you and no more than 5 others cover 10–16 miles per day in 6–8 hours as you follow seldom-used trails into Dall sheep country, across 2 major passes, up to a glacier, and through lush river valleys, wildflower meadows, and delicate tundra. A mineral lick provides a good opportunity for close-range wildlife observation. Lunch stops and 1 layover day are great times to fish the crystal-clear streams and lakes for grayling and Dolly Varden trout.

Professional outfitter Kirk Martakis, owner of the Wolf Point Ranch, recommends that you add 2 days on either end of your trip to fly to and from Anchorage and take the 8-hour Anchorage–Denali train ride. Many people decide to add additional days to explore the park in other ways. The outfitter picks you up at the Denali station and takes you to your accommodations; lodgings in nearby Cantwell and Anchorage can be arranged, but the cost is not included. *American Wilderness Experience, Box 1486, Boulder, CO 80306, tel. 303/444–2622 or 800/444–0099, fax 303/444–3999. June–early Aug.: 6 days, $1,355; 4 days, $915. Sign up 4–6 months in advance.*

SOURCES

ORGANIZATIONS There is no national association of horse-packing outfitters, but regional organizations provide information on outfitters in their respective states. Try **Colorado Outfitters Association** (Box 440021, Aurora, CO 80044-0021, tel. 303/841–7760), **Idaho Outfitters and Guides Association** (Box 95, Boise, ID 83701, tel. 208/342–1919 or 800/847–4843, fax 208/338–7830), **Montana Outfitters and Guides Association** (Box 1248, Helena, MT 59604, tel. 406/449–3578, fax 406/443–2439), **Washington Outfitters & Guides Association** (22845 N.E. 8, Suite 331, Redmond, WA 98053, tel. 206/392–6107, fax 206/392–0111), and **Wyoming Outfitters Association** (Box 2284, Cody, WY 82414, tel. 307/527–7453, fax 307/587–8633). Or contact the national park, forest, or wilderness area you're interested in for suggestions.

ALSO SEE If you want to ride but prefer hard work—and possibly a cost savings—to simple pleasure, see Working Farms, Ranches, and Cattle Drives. If you like the idea of being around horses and exploring the Old West but you or your family don't want to ride your own steeds, see the Covered Wagon Trains chapter.

Mountain Biking

By Bill Strickland

ountain bikes are time machines. Ride one and you become a kid again. Splash through mud, ride through grass, jump a rock, color outside of the lines. It's improvisation and freedom, jazz instead of classical.

And boy can it take you places. I've watched black bears scamper up the sides of hills. I've lain on mountaintops while lightning storms raged seemingly only inches from my head. I've gotten lucky and looked out from the top of Washington's Capitol Peak on a clear day that revealed all the state's volcanic ranges in one sweeping view.

But guess what? I'm not even that good a mountain biker. I've only been riding off-road for about a year. That's the other incredible thing about mountain biking. Although its image is that of the gnarly, muddy dude thrashing a way-wicked trail and slinging lingo unintelligible to humans not on an adrenaline spike, its reality is me and you. Regular people who discover how easy it is to move among forests, over deserts, up hills, into canyons, through creeks.

Sure, you need real skill to hack the most technical stuff. Make a mistake in certain sections of the rides we list and you could die. Easily. But there are plenty of simple and safe rides for absolute beginners, too.

One reason that anyone can mountain bike is that the bikes themselves may be the most user-friendly two-wheelers ever made. They have more gears for easier pedaling, simple shifting, flat handlebars (for an upright sitting position and more stability), and fat knobby tires (for a cushy and super-grippy ride). On the other end of the spectrum are the daredevil machines. If you're fit and you know what you're doing, you can take yourself to the edge of control in settings where your natural instinct is to be as careful as possible. You can shoot the rim of a hundred-foot drop-off, bomb down a rock-strewn trail at insane speeds, catch big air.

The number of operators offering mountain biking trips is increasing with the popularity of the sport. As with road tours, mountain-bike touring companies provide all sorts of support and expertise. But the biggest benefit to biking with an outfitter may be their knowledge of the terrain. Getting lost on the road can be an inconvenience. Getting lost in the wilderness is plain dangerous. Take a tour and you don't have to worry about your lousy sense of direction or how to read the trail network map.

You also don't have to worry about ancillary concerns: Do I have enough food and water to ride through that patch of desert? Will the trail empty out near an inn? How much equipment should I carry? All these problems are taken care of. You don't even need

Managing editor of *Bicycling* magazine, Bill Strickland pedals his way to work every day and races mountain bikes frequently. In more than 10 years of riding he's toured every corner of the United States.

to own a mountain bike, since most companies rent good models.

The format of off-road touring resembles that of road touring. Single track is a narrow trail, usually not more than a foot wide; double track is twice as wide, fit for two people to ride side-by-side. Double track is sometimes made by Jeeps. Most vacations are 2- to 10-day trips along preplanned routes. Trails include major points of interest and unique geographic features, as well as a variety of descents and ascents, and a few different types of terrain—from red rock to alpine meadows.

At least 2 accomplished outdoorsy guides lead each trip. One rides with you while the other drives a support van along the route. In some areas, such as stretches of narrow single-track, the support vehicle can't follow you. In these instances, it will parallel your route on the closest road or drive ahead to wait for you. The vans carry your gear, supply water and snacks, usually house mini bike shops for trailside repairs, and can even haul a few tired adventurers.

The going can be as tough or easy as you like. There are day-long treks over highly "technical" terrain (difficult to ride because of obstacles in the trail) on which it's not uncommon to walk your bike up and down slopes and over obstacles. And then there are casual jaunts on flat dirt roads that wind through forests or pretty backcountry. Easier trips usually spend a lot of time off the trail at attractions that include everything from museums to lakes.

This diversity means that there's a tour for everyone. What's more, there's variety even within a single tour. Most companies customize their routes slightly to allow you to ride more or less mileage, or to take different routes—so you can stay on the dirt road if you're unsure about that rocky trail.

There's a lot of diversity in the price of the trips, too. For example, a 5-day trip can range from $575 to $1,025. Prices can vary due to several factors: accommodations, food, amount of equipment provided, extra off-bike activities, demand for the trip.

More than road touring, mountain-bike trips seem to create a sense of comradery. The challenges are usually greater, or at least more obvious. Riders coach each other through the toughest parts, share advice, and swap war stories.

However, sometimes the group experience seems to work against the lure of the outdoors. Some people find it disconcerting to pick their way through an isolated forest with 10 other people. There are the practical inconveniences, too. Your schedule is tied to the group's. You wake when they do, begin riding when they do, and eat when (and probably what) they do. And when rain turns the trail to soup, don't think you can delay your trip for a day. Put on your foul-weather duds, pal, the group is heading out.

Still, most cyclists say the advantages of commercial off-road touring outweigh the disadvantages. The exception being getting stuck on an inappropriate trip.

I've talked to beginners who signed up for harsh, technical rides and spent most of their time dragging their bikes behind them or sightseeing from the seat of a van. Not exactly a peak outdoors experience. Neither is the trip where a true gnarly dude is confined to tame dirt roads. The trick is to match your physical ability and off-road experience to the right trip. It's okay to challenge yourself with a tour slightly over your head, or to take it easy on a relative snoozer. Just be honest with yourself about your ability.

Trip descriptions should give accurate pictures of how tough the riding will be, but don't get fooled by the mileage listings. Off-road miles are tougher than road miles. So don't think that 15 trail miles a day will be a snap compared to that 30-mile-per-day road trip you did once. A general rule for figuring your endurance is that one mountain bike mile equals at least 3 road miles. On tough single-track and technical slickrock, or in steep territory, it can be even harder.

Pay attention to other factors, too. The number of off-bike activities is a measurement of the difficulty of the tour (the more off-trail activities the less strenuous the tour). Weather can cook you or help you, and also affects the scenery. Spending a fall weekend on a New England mountainside is more beautiful and more comfortable than a summertime jaunt in the same area.

Right now, the best commercial rides are found in the Southwest and Rockies, and on the West Coast, where high-altitude ascents lead to overlooks of mind-boggling vistas. Any territory near canyons or mountain peaks is also guaranteed good riding. The east, especially New England, is loaded with trails, but commercial touring has yet to thoroughly invade the region. West Virginia and North Carolina are also ready to explode as hot spots. Once the touring companies expand into these areas you'll be able to find organized off-road thrills almost anywhere.

Don't kid yourself about your level of comfort when you're choosing a trip. The riding is tough, so don't feel foolish if you want to interrupt your days in the wilderness with nights of pampered comfort. Unlike a road tour, you're likely to get dirty and all-over tired. Tents and cold showers don't do much to alleviate this condition.

Mountain-bike touring isn't for everyone. This is because at its worst it can be jarring, difficult, and dirty. But at its best it can be jarring, difficult, and dirty. Know what I mean? If you do, I'll see you out there.

CHOOSING THE RIGHT TRIP

Everything associated with mountain biking—manufacturers, event organizers, and touring companies—has just begun the transition from niche sport to big-time popularity. There are some growing pains, which we try to help you avoid. To be included in these listings, each touring company has to meet these minimum criteria: offer trips along pre-planned, established routes; provide at least 2 mileage options each day; furnish some type of support (such as motorized route patrols, sag service for tired or injured riders, and luggage transport); supply or assist in arranging lodging and provide at least some meals; require the use of helmets (you never appreciate a skid lid until you need it).

But don't stop with the listings. Make a few phone calls to learn more about the companies you're considering. Don't be shy about asking these questions. You're about to spend a decent chunk of money. Think of it this way: For the cost of a 7-day tour, you could buy a trick new bike.

How tough is the trip? We offer as many details as we can, but the listings are just a guide to set you on your way. Describe your road-riding experience and your physical condition. Ask if the riding is technical or buff (smooth), on trails or dirt roads. You may be surprised to find that some of the riding occurs on pavement. This is sometimes necessary to link the off-road routes. It erodes the atmosphere, but provides a break from the rigors of the wilderness.

How much can the mileage be increased (or decreased)? The distances probably won't vary widely—off-road companies don't have as much leeway as road operations—but you'll get an idea if you can shorten a ride and stay on your bike, or if you'll be stuck in the van when you're tired.

What are the trail options? Can you find single-track spurs off the dirt road? Will you be stuck on the technical trail, or is there an easy parallel path for a break?

What are the accommodations like? Some trips are able to offer plush rooms even on truly wild excursions. This is because ski lodges and hunting inns are located near many trails. However most offer more rugged accommodations. If you'll be camping (as is common), check such details as rest-room arrangements and the availability of hot showers.

What are the meals like? Some campfire cooks are fit for the finest restaurants. Some serve up basic grub. Also, most companies skip at least one, lunch or dinner. We list these deletions, but changes may occur.

What's the cost and what's included? Prices in these listings are per person, double occupancy, and include gratuities, entrance fees to parks and attractions, and camping fees. Airfare and the cost of renting bikes or camping equipment isn't included in prices we quote, unless we note otherwise. Renting camping equipment (tent and sleeping bag) usually costs between $30 and $55 per trip. Sometimes there are extras. We tell you about as many as we could find, but always ask if there are others: $50 for the optional mule ride down the canyon or $30 for the massage.

What weather can I expect?

Will laundry service be available? It's usually not on off-road tours, but if so, it could save you a suitcase.

What extras are included? Many companies offer T-shirts, sweatshirts, water bottles, or other freebies.

What is the makeup of my touring group? You can find out ages, gender, marital status, home state, and sometimes even off-road cycling experience. This helps you predict the atmosphere of your entire trip. You should also ask about group size.

Is this same tour available for singles (seniors, women, and so forth)? We note as many of these as we can, but schedules may change. Some companies offer reduced rates for kids and families.

How extensive is the support? This could be the difference between walking out of the forest with a broken-down bike, or having it repaired on the spot. Some companies may make only one or two runs along a route. Others constantly patrol. Find out how many guides work each trip. The more the better.

What is the rental equipment like? Find out what brand of bike is offered, how many sizes are available, and how old the fleet is. A few companies offer you your choice of suspension or rigid bikes. If you're going on a camping trip, check the quality of the rental equipment. Gear is never more important than on a long mountain biking trip.

Do you offer free helmet use?

Who are the leaders, how old are they, and how are they trained? It may sound nosy, but in the wilderness you need guides who are not only expert cyclists but also expert outdoors types.

How long has the company been in business? This is especially important in such a newly popular field. You won't necessarily have a problem with an outfitter new to the sport, but an outfitter who's been running off-road trips for several years is probably more prepared to meet challenges and answer questions.

Can the leaders handle minor mechanical repairs (and is there a charge)? No type of cycling is tougher on equipment than mountain biking. You can count on at least one flat and something else that will need fiddling with. If it's just a quick brake adjustment, I'd expect a freebie. But be reasonable: If you do a biff and pretzel your wheel, cough up a tip for the guide who rebuilds it.

How far in advance do I need to book? Some trips are more popular than others and can fill up as much as a year in advance. So although 2 to 3 months is usually far enough in advance to book a trip, you should probably reserve as early as possible. If you find you've waited too long, don't hesitate to put your name on a waiting list, since cancellations may mean you get a spot on a trip even if you call only days in advance.

Do you have references from past guests? To be honest, I never call the telephone numbers I get. But if a company ever refused to give me some names, it would make me wonder why.

MAJOR PLAYERS

There are no gargantuans in this field. The sport is still young and small local companies match the free spirit of off-road cycling. The logistics are harder to handle than those of road tours, and the big outfitters aren't completely set up yet to develop a network of mountain-bike tours. Give them a few years.

Thankfully, small scope doesn't mean poor quality. Here are 7 off-road touring companies that offer consistent high quality, good variety, and an extra something special. The service at all 7 is exceptional. If you can't find exactly what you're looking for in our listings, give these touring experts a call and ask about their other offerings.

BACKCOUNTRY This company, founded in 1986, is known for its environmentally conscious touring programs and its exploration of new trails in the Southwest, Rockies, and on the West Coast. One of its owners, Doug McSpadden, is a former U.S. Forest Service employee and guide for The National Outdoor Leadership School. Most trips combine dirt and paved roads, and are highly supported.

Backcountry destinations include Montana, Utah, New Mexico, Colorado, Oregon, Washington, Wyoming, and Canada. A dozen trips are offered; each run up to 10 times a year. The company has 125 Trek 950 mountain bikes in its rental fleet, and customized vans and trailers provide trail support.

Accommodations include historic inns, lodges, resorts, hotels, and guest ranches. There are no camping options. The company also offers hiking, white-water rafting, and horseback riding (Box 4029, Bozeman, MT 59772–4029, tel. 406/ 586–3556, fax 406/ 586–4288).

BACKROADS This is the biggest touring company in the world. In business since 1979, it offers more than 90 road and mountain-bike trips each year. Although it's one of the best all-around bicycling outfitters, in the mountain biking world it's just about average. At press time 5 domestic mountain-bike trips were scheduled each year to destinations including California, Idaho, Utah, and Arizona. Foreign off-road trips are also offered in China, Mexico, Costa Rica, Thailand, Bali, Chile, and Argentina.

Backroads doesn't offer new or unique trails—you'll get the classics and well-

known routes on these trips—but it maintains the quality and first-rate service that made it such a powerhouse in road touring. The campfire menu, prepared by the guides using Backroads' fleet of custom-designed trailers, reads more like the bill of fare at a fancy big-city gourmet eatery: smoked salmon, homemade pasta with pesto, and fresh fruit cobblers. I've never eaten better than on a Backroads trip. The accommodations are often inns on the National Register of Historic Places, or comfortable lodges with regional flavor.

Backroads rents its own line of mountain bikes, made by Cannondale. The company also offers cross-country skiing, walking, hiking, trail-running and multi-sport trips, and custom-designed tours for groups (1516 5th St., Suite B122, Berkeley, CA 94710–1740, tel. 510/527–1555 or 800/ 462–2848, fax 510/527–1444).

ELK RIVER TOURING CENTER This is one of my favorites. The center is a former sheep farm in an area of Pocahontas County, West Virginia, that could become the next mountain biking mecca—at least for us East Coasters. It has mountain single-track without altitude problems, technical challenges as good as any of the rocky trails farther north in the east, and incredible valley vistas. Pocahontas was named by *Outside* magazine as one of the country's 100 best counties for experiencing the outdoors. The trail network needs development and grooming, but this will happen as the flow of grateful mountain bikers increases.

The company offers 6 tours, and runs about 39 trips per year. It also hosts the annual West Virginia Fat Tire Festival in June, a week of tours, races, riding clinics, blue grass music, and all-around fun. The owners, Gil and Mary Willis, are dedicated to providing instructional programs, such as mountain biking lessons for beginners. This is another idea waiting to blossom into a standard practice.

The food is delicious, and the high-carbohydrate, low-fat meals are perfect for the fitness minded. Specialties include whole-wheat French bread and trout from the Elk River. Vegetarian meals are always available. Accommodations are a comfortable mix of bed-and-breakfast rooms and cabins (Hwy. 219, Slatyfork, WV 26291, tel. 304/572–3771).

KAIBAB MOUNTAIN BIKE TOURS I like this outfitter for the feeling of confidence and competence inspired by every one of its guides. The company was established in 1987 to provide trips in southern Utah and the Colorado Plateau. It offers a good mix of classic trips—the White Rim Trail, the Maze District, Kokopelli's Trail—with extras such as half- or full-day treks into canyons on front- or full-suspension rental bikes.

Nine tours are offered, and about 50 trips are run each year. Support is provided by 3 custom-designed 4-wheel-drive trucks. The company started its own bike shop in 1990.

The tours are mainly dirt-road or rocky-surface trips, but some single-track options can be found. A high-carbohydrate menu emphasizes fish, chicken, pasta, fruits, and vegetables. It's mainly a camping-only company (Box 339, Moab, UT 84532, tel. 801/259–7423 or 800/ 451–1133, fax 801/259–6135).

RIM TOURS This was the first mountain-bike touring company in Moab, Utah. They're a fixture in the industry, and have a well-deserved reputation for doing the classic rides—Telluride to Moab, White Rim Trail, Colorado Trail, Tour of the San Juans, and the Maze—and doing them exceptionally well. Just saying that you took your tour with Rim or browsed in Rim Cyclery, the affiliated bike shop, will lend a certain hipness to your vacation tales.

The company offers more than 20 different trips, each of which is run at least twice a year. The food and lodging usually consists of camping and cooking out; the support van carries all the necessary equipment. A few trips have bed-and-breakfast accommodations (94 W. 1st North, Moab, UT 84532, tel. 801/ 259–5223 or 800/626–7335).

ROADS LESS TRAVELED Nobody does better Colorado trips than Roads Less Traveled.

Today, most organizers operating in Colorado share the same trails, but since 1988, this company has searched out commercially virgin single-track in the Rocky Mountain state. They also put together a better-than-average package including riding, off-bike adventures such as hiking and rafting, accommodations that range from plush mountain lodges to tents, and exceptional food. Even on camping trips the menu includes such dishes as grilled salmon and Thai curry chicken; vegetarian meals are always available.

Twenty-one tours are offered in Colorado, Arizona, Wyoming, Montana, New Mexico, Utah, and Canada. About 60 trips are run each year. My budget likes Roads Less Traveled, too. The prices are often slightly cheaper than those of other major operators, and trip quality doesn't suffer (Box 8187, Longmont, CO 80501, tel. 303/678–8750 or 800/488–8483, fax 303/678–5568).

WESTERN SPIRIT This is another one of my favorites, mainly because of the personnel. These people—from owner Lu Warner on down—have a knack for finding rarely used single-track and interesting new routes in the same old territory. The guides call this "unpublished" riding. They're also good at customizing their tours for special groups—so good that Ibis and other mountain bike–industry types go to Western Spirit for yearly company outings.

Established in 1989, Western Spirit offers 10 tours in Utah, Colorado, and Idaho. About 50 trips are run each year. They do camping trips with style (one of the company's mottoes is "Civilized tours in uncivilized terrain"), and the food is delicious and abundant.

This is also one of the most environmentally conscious touring companies. All tours are low impact, and each trip purchase includes membership in the International Mountain Bicycling Association, a group dedicated to promoting responsible land use and achieving fair land access policies for mountain bikes.

The company is also a pioneer in instructional programs for novices and intermediates—the equivalent of taking a tennis or golf lesson from a pro (Western Spirit Cycling, Box 411, Moab, UT 84532, tel. 800/845-2453, fax 801/ 259-2736).

FAVORITE TRIPS

THE NORTHEAST

MAINE **Mud in Your Eye.** You can't ride all there is to ride here. There's just too much. Back Country Excursions is run from a lodge outside the town of Limerick, in the middle of 12 acres of heavy forest and hills. Doesn't sound so big? This 12 acres is surrounded by 10,000 acres of a semi-wilderness preserve. And just across the New Hampshire border, close enough to cast a shadow on the trails, are the White Hills.

Each day you'll cover 20 to 35 miles of single-track and dirt roads that wind their way up to the ridges of the foothills (no murderous climbs here), around lakes, through bogs, rocky terrain, and forest so thick you can't get your bike off the trail. You can ride along the tops of several ridges without doing a lot of climbing, but there are great gradual descents and a few screamers. A fit beginner will learn a lot about mountain biking on these varied trails, while more advanced riders can bang away.

I like this area because it feels so out of the way, yet is only 2½ hours from Boston, and 6 from New York City. The lodge you'll stay in is comfortable but rustic. Accommodations here are your sleeping bag in one of the lodge's large common rooms, in bunks in one of two dormitory-style rooms, or in a tent (yours or a rental) at one of the abundant tent sites. Most cyclists opt to camp somewhere on the property, returning for meals, showers, a visit to the hot tub or sauna, and to meet their guide each day.

This trip is run 12 to 15 times a year. Trips ranging from a weekend to a week can also be arranged. *Back Country Excursions, Box 365, Limerick, ME 04048, tel. 207/625-8189. Mid-May–mid-Oct.: 2 days, $65. Price does not include lunch or dinner. Mountain-bike rental, $30 per day.*

VERMONT **Craftsbury Mountain Biking Center.** I like the concept of this trip. You show up, tell the veteran (and native) mountain biking guides what kind of riding you'd like to do, and they direct you to the perfect trail. Thorough maps are provided, but you go it alone on the trail. You get the best of commercial touring—someone else handles all the logistics—with the excitement of on-your-own exploration.

The center is sort of a sports resort. In winter it's got skiing. In summer there's hiking, horseback riding, and cycling, among other activities. It's on the shoreline of a lake, so you can swim, canoe, or sail when the your ride ends. Within a 10- to 15-mile radius of the center are more than 200 miles of dirt roads and a uncounted number of trails.

You'll bike 15 to 30 miles a day through typical northern Vermont terrain: hilly, technical, and rugged, with lots of potential resting spots for swimming, shopping, and chowing. There are dairy farms snuggled at the foot of the hills and quintessential whitehouse New England towns on top.

You need at least 4 people to set up a stay at Craftsbury—unless you get lucky and can piggyback with other stragglers. Lodging options include bed-and-breakfast rooms, suites with private baths, and cottages with kitchenettes. The food—the group decides how many meals a day are provided—is all homemade. The baked goods and home-grown vegetable dishes are so popular that Craftsbury has published its own cookbook. *Craftsbury Mountain Bike Center, Box 31, Craftsbury Common, VT 05827, tel. 802/ 586-7767 or 800/729-7751, fax 802/586-7768. May–Oct.: $96 a night for 2 people. Prices vary with dining and lodging selections. Price does not include guide ($60 per day). Mountain-bike rental, $25 per day or $35 for 2 days.*

THE MID-ATLANTIC

PENNSYLVANIA **Pocono White-water Gorge.**
I cut my teeth—and a few other body parts—
on these trails. This rich mountain biking
region centered in the town of Jim Thorpe
(he's buried there) has expert, near-vertical,
single-track; flat novice cruising territory,
with gorgeous river scenery; and everything
in between.

Pocono White-water, primarily a rafting
company, runs guided mountain-bike tours
through the area. They know the trails. Want
to catch a quick trip to the top of the mountain? Take a jaunt through the tiny tourist
town? Follow the Lehigh River for 30 flat
miles? Shake your bones on classic eastern
rock-track? No problem.

The town is a tourist hot spot: good food,
lots of shops, vintage buildings, and excellent inns. Combined with the closeness of
the trail network (almost all are directly
accessible from town), this makes the area
perfect for family getaways. You'll also get to
see some wildlife, including eagles and
hawks in migration season, lots of deer, and
maybe even a small black bear.

The company doesn't offer lodging, but
arranges package deals with inns in Jim
Thorpe. You can be out of your car and biking some of the East's sweetest single-track
within 2 hours of leaving either New York
City or Philadelphia. Many of the tours are
day trips, such as the popular 25-mile ride
through Lehigh Gorge.

The average daily distance covered is 25
miles. About 1,500 trips are run each year,
ranging from a weekend to a week. *Pocono
White-water Mountain Bike Tours, HC-2,
Box 2245, Jim Thorpe, PA 18229, tel.
717/325–3656 or 800/944–8392. Apr.–Oct.:
$35 per day. Price does not include meals or
lodging (lodging typically $65–$125 a
night). Shuttle service is $15. Mountain-bike
rental, $25 per day.*

WEST VIRGINIA **Cranberry to Canaan.** This
state makes me glad I'm an Eastern mountain biker. It has it all: smooth and technical

single-track, long climbs, heart-beater descents, grand views from atop mountains,
extended ridge rides, and valley cruises.
And Pocahontas County contains more than
302,000 acres of national forest. Everything
is greener than the West, and not quite as
high, so altitude sissies like myself can
climb, climb, climb, and never suck air.

This 5-day trip into the Monongahela
National Forest crosses a few passes before
flattening out into a nice valley ride. If you
tire, catch the shuttle back to the touring
center, which is surrounded by a network of
mapped and marked trails. Beginners will
fall in love with the sport; advanced mountain bikers new to this area will wonder why
they waited so long.

On one of your 15- to 25-mile daily rides, be
sure to check out Prop's Run, a 6-mile technical downhill that ranks high on my list of
favorite trails. The good old boys down there
tell me that there's even better riding over
the ridge.

Two nights are spent at Elk River Center, one
at a bed-and-breakfast inn, and two at a ski
chalet. This trip is run about 6 times per
year. *Elk River Touring Center, Hwy. 219,
Slatyfork, WV 26291, tel. 304/572–3771.
Late May–early Oct.: 5 days, $579. Moun-
tain-bike rental, $25 per day.*

WEST VIRGINIA **Twin Peaks.** West Virginia
is heaven for hard-core riders. I've ridden
the toughest trails this state has to offer.
These single-tracks are soupy, muddy,
treacherous launching pads that also happen to be a lot of fun.

This 4-day trip is full of those trails, beginning from the Elk River Touring Center and
heading into the vast Monongahela National
Forest. The days are long, and since the
shuttle van can't drive where you ride,
much of the ride can't be supported. This
means you have to carry some gear at times,
but if you're the right kind of rider, this just
adds to the fun.

You'll cover 20 to 30 miles a day, about 95%
of it on single-track—this is definitely one
for the overdrive crowd. But the accommo-

dations appeal to the lamb in all of us: lodges and bed-and-breakfast inns.

This trip is run about 5 times a year. If you need to rent a bike, ask for an Ibis with front suspension. You'll need it on these bumpy trails. *Elk River Touring Center, Hwy. 219, Slatyfork, WV 26291, tel. 304/572–3771. Late June–mid Oct.: 4 days, $495. Mountain-bike rental, $25 per day.*

THE MIDWEST

MICHIGAN **Lake Superior Wilderness Trek.** Michigan's upper peninsula may be the wildest and most undeveloped area in the Midwest. There aren't the incredible vistas, challenging climbs, and thrilling descents of the country's peak mountain biking areas; but off-roaders in this part of the nation can still find plenty of fun.

This 5-day tour is based in Big Bay, at an operating lighthouse that doubles as a bed-and-breakfast. From here, you'll explore double-track and single-track that twists through thick woods or winds down to Lake Superior. You'll also climb what locals call the Huron Mountains (which are more like big hills), on technical logging trails. The area has nearly 100 waterfalls, miles of shoreline, and thousands of small lakes. It's covered by second-growth forest, and is sparsely populated. It's a die-hard dirthead's dream.

Daily distances range from 10 to 25 miles. An experienced cyclist who's never ridden off-road will have a blast, but a true beginner could spend a lot of time befuddled. For those who need a break from the bike, there's a canoe trip, kayaking, and a nature hike. A chef on the premises cooks up a health-conscious mix of fresh vegetables and local game to keep guests' energy up. This trip is run twice a year. *Michigan Bicycle Touring, 3512 Red School Rd., Kingsley, MI 49649, tel. 616/263–5885. July–Aug.: 5 days, $799. Shuttle from Marquette, $25. Mountain-bike rental, $95.*

THE SOUTHWEST

ARIZONA **North Rim of Grand Canyon.** The south rim is the tourist-in-cars-looking-for-McDonald's magnet. This is the rim with the pine forest, awesome single-track, and dirt roads that border the big rip. It's the rim you can have practically to yourself.

This 4-day trip begins in the huge Kaibab National Forest, then follows the rim via a network of crisscrossing dirt roads and the single-track of the well-known (among mountain bikers, at least) Arizona Trail. After covering 20 to 25 miles each day, the guides set up a camp for the night. The food is gourmet campfire, with Dutch-oven specialties such as poached fish and pesto pasta. You'll sleep just 10 to 20 feet from the drop, sheltered and comfortable on a carpet of pine needles.

The single-track can be technical and tough, but because it parallels the dirt road, the less hardy can cruise the smooth surface for a while. There's some climbing, of course—and some descending. You'll be spending a lot of time at 8,000 feet, which can be hard if you're not used to altitude. On the 5-day trip you'll spend a day hiking down into the Grand Canyon. The trip is run about 10 times per year. Rent a bike if you go—they're Trek 970s or Kona Cinder Domes with front suspension. Cool. *Kaibab Touring Center, Box 339, Moab, UT 84532, tel. 801/259–7423 or 800/451–1133, fax 801/259–6135. June to Aug.: 4 days, $560; 5 days, $650. Free shuttle from St. George. Mountain-bike rental, $21 per day.*

ARIZONA **Northern Arizona's Red Rock Country.** This 6-day dirt-road ride covers 3 distinct areas of Arizona: the forested southern ridge of the Colorado Plateau, the huge red rock country of Sedona, and the high forest of Mormon Lake. Some of the riding is as remote as mountain biking ever gets.

The trip begins with a plummet off the southern rim of the Colorado Plateau, then heads downhill to the Verde River. The vistas of buttes, sandstone cliffs, and mesas are eye-poppers. By day 2 you're in among all those towering natural objects, spinning along easy dirt roads that thread between red-rock cliffs. Day three includes an optional Jeep ride to Indian ruins, or a tough ride up through the hills ringing the Los Abrigados Resort (a 20-acre Spanish-style estate with fountains, winding walkways, pool, tennis courts, and hot tub). There's also time to explore the village of Tlaquepaque, an artsy Southwestern shopping mecca.

The remainder of the trip is in forest and lake country—a dramatic change—and centers on the bluffs and woods surrounding Mormon Lake, Arizona's largest natural body of water. The trip ends in Flagstaff.

Meals include gourmet dinners (steak, seafood, the usual highfalutin' fare) or Southwestern cuisine at a mix of fine restaurants and small, funky eateries. There's a homestyle Arizona barbecue on the final day. Accommodations include the posh resort mentioned above, mountain-top cabins, and historic inns. The trip is run about 4 times per year. *Backcountry, Box 4029, Bozeman, MT 59772–4029, tel. 406/586–3556, fax 406/586–4288. May–June, Sept.: 6 days, $1,198. Mountain-bike rental, $129.*

ARIZONA **Sedona's Red Rock Country.** You won't find much single-track on this dirt-road trip, but you can't deny the beauty of this region. The 6-day tour begins in Flagstaff, atop the Colorado Plateau, and winds through the largest ponderosa pine forest in the world. Then it's on to Sedona and red rock heaven. Mesas, buttes, and cliffs surround the city. As you leave town, you'll pedal along the base of cliffs that hide ancient Indian dwellings (but you'll have to rent a jeep to get to them).

The accommodations include lodges and historic inns. Most meals are eaten at the inn restaurants, with picnic lunches packed for the trail. There are loads of shops and galleries at every stop. Daily rides range from 16 to 61 miles, some of them on pavement. Beginners may opt for the shuttle on some of the longer climbs—but it's all ridable. There

are no real technical challenges. This trip is usually run 9 times a year. Special dates are available for singles. *Backroads, Suite Q333, 1516 5th St., Berkeley, CA 94710–1740, tel. 510/527–1555 or 800/245–3874, fax 510/527–1444. May–Oct.: 6 days, $998. Mountain-bike rental, $119.*

NEW MEXICO **Off-Road Enchantment.** The general mountain biking public is just beginning to discover this trail-wealthy state, and this 6-day trip gives you a sample of some of the area's best riding.

The single-track and dirt roads of New Mexico rival the much-acclaimed routes of Utah, and the accommodations and off-bike activities are more plentiful here. For instance, at the end of a day of mondo trail climbing you can take your helmet off in a luxurious inn in Taos instead of bunking down in the dirt. The quirky, arty culture of the Taos area seems well-suited to the mountain biking mind-set, too.

This trip is offered 3 times a year for hardcore pedallers, and 7 times a year for beginners. The mileage is reduced for beginners, who bike from 20 to 25 miles a day as opposed to the 30 to 35 biked by advanced riders; and time spent on the trail is tempered with other activities such as a day of white-water rafting. A highlight of either trip is the dirt-road ascent of 13,161-foot Mt. Wheeler, the highest peak in New Mexico. This is the biggest climb of the trip, but not the only one. Ascension is a way of life in this region. *Roads Less Traveled, Box 8187, Longmont, CO 80501, tel. 303/678–8750 or 800/488–8483, fax 303/678–5568. June, Sept., and Oct.: 6 days, $999 for advanced, $1,075 for novice. Mountain-bike rental, $99.*

UTAH **Bryce and Zion National Parks.** Your first day on this trail you take a 2,000-foot descent. Enough said? Advanced riders will enjoy the trip the most, but novices can manage a shortened and shuttled version. The difficulty here is not the single-track, which isn't technically challenging, but the high level of fitness required to ride the entire trip.

You'll cover from 20 to 35 miles a day on this 5-day beauty, beginning at the Brian Head ski area and descending into Bryce on dirt roads. From the bottom of Bryce Canyon, you can either hike into the red-rock canyons or explore the single-track of the surrounding forests. Most first timers opt for the look at the natural amphitheater of the canyon.

There's climbing, too. Advanced riders can take a longer option and grunt up the mountains and through the alpine setting. Others continue their descent toward Zion, where you find yourself at the base of a sheer canyon. It's the opposite of Bryce, where you stood on top.

Accommodations are in rustic lodges. They're comfortable, but don't expect the plush resort-style comforts common in Colorado or New Mexico. The food, however, is up to Roads Less Traveled's usual high standards. The trip is run about 6 times per year. *Roads Less Traveled, Box 8187, Longmont, CO 80501, tel. 303/678–8750 or 800/488– 8483, fax 303/678–5568. June and Sept.– Oct.: 5 days, 995 advanced, $1,025 novice. Shuttle from Las Vegas, $40. Mountain-bike rental, $99.*

UTAH **Kokopelli's Trail.** This is the real thing—an isolated, 5-day trip on single-track and dirt roads that would be almost impossible to do on your own. You won't see anyone here but fellow adventurers.

The 150-mile trip travels along an established trail from Grand Junction, Colorado, to Moab, Utah. You start in big desert, spend a few days on the Colorado plateau with canyon scenery, and then move up into the mountains for some alpine riding. Finally, you drop back into Moab and civilization. This ride, with its climbs, long distances, and technical terrain, is tough—probably too tough for a lot of riders. But it's a mountain biking experience that can't be duplicated anywhere else in the country.

This is a camping trip, with one night's accommodation in a Moab hotel. You'll average 30 miles per day. The trip is run about 4 times per year. *Roads Less Traveled,*

Box 8187, Longmont, CO 80501, tel. 303/ 678–8750 or 800/488–8483, fax 303/678– 5568. May, Sept., and Oct.: 5 days, $685. Mountain-bike rental, $99.

UTAH **The Maze and Cataract Canyon.** You'd probably never bike the Maze on your own. This red-rock district, one of 3 in Canyonlands National Park, can be a logistical nightmare. But with the support van hauling your supplies, it's possible to explore its winding routes.

While you're pedaling among the rock pillars, looking for petroglyphs on the walls, you can test your skills on some of the technical slickrock and sandstone rides. There are a lot of ledge drops (natural stone steps) as well as easy cruising. Daily distances average about 27 miles, and veterans tell me the riding is rougher than the famous White Rim Trail, which doesn't have as many ledges or loose-rock sections.

The 3-day ride ends with a hike into Cataract Canyon. When you get to the Colorado River, you'll white-water raft out. The cost of the trip includes a round-trip flight from Moab to Lake Powell, where the trip begins. You can bring your own camping equipment or rent it from Kaibab. *Kaibab Touring Center, Box 339, Moab, UT 84532, tel. 801/259–7423 or 800/ 451–1133, fax 801/259–6135. May and Sept.: 5 days, $875. Mountain-bike rental, $21 per day.*

UTAH **Trail of the Ancients.** Follow the dirt roads and single-track of southern Utah into the Abajo Mountains, and you'll find the ruins of the ancient Anasazi Indians. It's not an easy trip—physically or logistically—but what's inaccessible to cars and hikers is within reach of mountain bikes. And this 5-day ride is sweet proof of that.

The journey begins about 50 miles south of Moab at the Natural Bridges National Monument with a 1,200-foot climb. Eventually you leave the red-rock canyons and enter alpine country, where you can look down on the desert and canyonlands. The ride ends in Monticello, just east of the 11,360-foot Abajo Peak.

Most of the riding is on dirt roads, and the company has some of the coolest rental bikes in the country—Ibis Mojo mountain bikes with Manitou front suspension forks. These rentals are better than most people's personal mounts.

The average daily distance is 20 miles. An intermediate rider should have no problem; beginners may suffer a little, but they'll survive. This is a camping trip and is run about 7 times per year. *Western Spirit Cycling, Box 411, Moab, UT 84532, tel. 800/845–2453, fax 801/259–2736. May, June, and Sept.: 5 days, $595. Mountain-bike rental, $125.*

UTAH **The White Rim.** This is a Canyonlands classic, run by one of the first (probably the original—but all kinds of companies are laying claim to the title now that mountain biking has taken off) off-road touring companies in the country.

The views from this 100-mile, 4-wheel-drive road are spectacular. It follows the Green and Colorado rivers from high atop Canyonlands National Park. The riding is rolling, with a lot of ledges and loose rock to test your technical ability. There are some short, way-steep hills and scary descents; but the trail can be mastered by beginners, who will find these small challenges a good introduction to the big-time drop-offs and descents found elsewhere on slickrock.

Why is this a classic? Many trails offer bits of the same scenery you'll catch here. But on a run of the White Rim, each day's vista seems to connect with the previous day's to make bigger and bigger—and more and more breathtaking—panoramas. It's like having a mural unrolled before you. The route's legend also stems from its whiteness. You cycle on a layer of white sandstone that seems to stretch endlessly along the ridge into the distance.

There are side hikes into the canyons on this 4-day camping trip, but you can expect to ride about 20 or 30 miles a day. About 17 trips are run each year. The company's stable includes thoroughbred mountain bikes from Jamis and Schwill, with front suspen-

sion. *Rim Tours, 1233 S. Hwy. 191, Moab, UT 84532, tel. 801/259–5223 or 800/626–7335, fax 801/259–3349. Late Mar., Apr., May, Sept., Oct.: 4 days, $515. Mountain-bike rental, $22 per day.*

THE ROCKIES

COLORADO **Colorado Single-track.** The area that includes Crested Butte, Gunnison, and Salida is is one of those must-ride regions for anyone aspiring to true mountain bikerhood. For instance, Crested Butte—part of the itinerary for this 4- to 5-day trip—is surrounded on 3 sides by mountains (13,000-footers) that are filled with single-track and dirt roads that provide some of the sweetest riding in the country.

Gunnison and Salida have a completely different character. For instance, "Gunny," as it's locally known, is dryer and rockier, more desert-like, with long, twisty downhills through sagebrush. It's all here in these 3 areas: the tech stuff, the buff stuff, screaming descents, big-altitude gaspers. And the views. Many towns in this state are stuck in box canyons, surrounded by mountain faces. But Crested Butte and Gunnison are more open. Long valleys stretch away with the big peaks in the distance.

The food and drink in the region is excellent, especially Crested Butte. Try to get to the Butte's "Donita's Cantina," owned by longtime fat-tire priestess Kay Peterson.

Because so many riding options are available, this tour that begins in Gunnison can cater to a mixed group of the rawest novice and the most die-hard dirthead. Accommodations are in inns or ski resorts in each town. Expect to average 20 to 30 miles per day, and to suck big wind if you're a flatlander. The altitude will get you by the third day. This trip is run about 2 times per year. *Rim Tours, 94 W. 1st North, Moab, UT 84532, tel. 801/259–5223 or 800/626–7335. July–Sept.: 4–5 days (depending on the group), $500–$650. Mountain-bike rental, $22 per day, with front suspension.*

COLORADO **Hut-to-Hut Biking.** This is real backcountry stuff, kids—a mountain-bike trip entirely apart from civilization, using a series of backwoods huts for support. OK, I'm stretching things. These "huts" are more like French chalets. They're 2-story log cabins with vaulted ceilings, varnished pine furniture, wood stoves, sundecks, and big windows.

The huts are linked by more than 300 miles of single-track and forested trails (including the famed "Tenth Mountain Trail"). You begin in Vail, then set out on a 6-day circuit of the unspoiled Holy Cross Wilderness. (Sorry, no riding in wilderness areas, though. It's the law.) You pedal along historic mining roads, abandoned railroad grades (great for climbing because the inclines are never too sharp), forest double-track, and true single-track. The scenery includes ghost towns, alpine lakes, Colorado summits, and deep forest.

Midway through the ride, you get to cheat a little and spend a refresher night at the Diamond Joy Guest Ranch, which has an outdoor hot tub and a wood-burning sauna. You'll ride 20-30 miles per day. The trip is run about 2 times per year. *Roads Less Traveled, Box 8187, Longmont, CO 80501, tel. 303/678–8750 or 800/488–8483, fax 303/678–5568. Late July–early Aug., late Aug.–early Sept.: $865. Mountain-bike rental, $99.*

COLORADO **Colorado Sampler.** My Colorado cycling buddies call this one "vistas for the lazy." Lazy is a relative term for these hammerheads, but it's true that this 5-day trip puts you amid incredible alpine scenery without requiring you to conquer the terrain. Beginners will never want to go home. If this trip doesn't make you into a mountain biker, nothing will.

You ride through the Arkansas River valley, paralleling the Continental Divide. Although you pass by 14,000-foot peaks every day, you'll be losing altitude—descending about 2,000 feet over the course of the trip. The riding is forest double-track, with one day of sweet single-track, and you'll average 25 miles a day. There's also a white-water raft trip on the Arkansas, and a visit to the hot springs on the last night. Accommodations are in cabins and bed-and-breakfast inns. The trip will be run 6 times in 1996 and 8 times in 1997. *Jun.–Aug.: 6 days, $1,050. Roads Less Traveled, Box 8187, Longmont, CO 80501, tel. 303/678–8750 or 800/488–8483, fax 303/678–5568. Mountain-bike rental, $99.*

IDAHO **Backcountry Hot Springs.** This is Western Spirit's most popular Idaho ride, because the wide-open scenery and riding are followed by a hot-springs soak every night. While the guides make camp (and great spinach lasagna and black-bean enchiladas) you soak away your trail aches. The 5-day ride begins in Ketchum and follows Warm Springs Road. Here fissures in the shore of Warm Springs River spill near-boiling water into the stream. You can control the temperature by using rocks to divert the water.

Daily rides average 12 miles, most of which is on dirt road. There is some single-track and some significant climbing, notably an 8-mile grind on the third day, but an athletic beginner should have no trouble, especially with the soothing therapy of the hot springs. Nearly 90% of Idaho is controlled by the Bureau of Land Management or the Forest Service, so maintained trails are everywhere. The area is so rural that, on the last day, you have to help chase deer from the airplane runway so your plane back to Ketchum can land!

If you go, rent a bike. The rentals are Ibis Mojo mountain bikes with Manitou front suspension forks. This trip is run about 8 times per year. *Western Spirit Cycling, Box 411, Moab, UT 84532, tel. 800/845–2453, fax 801/259–2736. July–Aug.: 5 days, $625. Mountain-bike rental, $125.*

IDAHO **Idaho Single-track.** Here's a rare gem. This 5-day trip is one of the few predominantly single-track mountain bike tours in the country. You begin at Elephant's Perch in Ketchum (literary pedal turners should be sure to ride a few loops around Hemingway's grave), then head into the wilderness. Because it's a camping trip, the leaders are free to alter the itinerary to find the best single-track and to steer you away from rain, overly dry areas, and other potential downers. The group can also decide whether to tackle tougher trails or take an easy spin.

Whatever the course, one almost-mandatory stop is at Galena Lodge, the site of the 1988 National Off-Road Bicycle Association national race course. Trail surfaces are usually clay or coarse soil packed with pine needles; and there are some tricky sections, some long grunts, and some easy climbs. Idaho is big country, and big fun on a bike.

This company rents Ibis Mojo mountain bikes with Manitou front suspension forks that are better than most people's personal mounts. Daily distances range from 15 to 30 miles, although a killer group might go up to 40. The trip is run about 3 times per year. *Western Spirit Cycling, Box 411, Moab, UT 84532, tel. 800/845–2453, fax 801/259–2736. July to Aug.: 5 days, $575. Mountain-bike rental, $125.*

MONTANA **Beartooth Bike.** This 6-day trek near the Montana–Wyoming border begins and ends in Bozeman, Montana, and covers portions of Yellowstone Park, and the Beartooth and Absaroka mountain ranges. You're cycling in the middle of about 900,000 acres of wilderness, which means the riding never gets boring. You'll spend time at 11,000 feet, in the bottom of canyons, and soaking in natural hot springs.

The distance covered each day averages from 23 to 43 miles. That's a lot on a mountain bike. The riding can get somewhat technical if you take the optional routes, with climbs up to 5 miles long, ridge rides, and wicked descents, spicing up what is otherwise an easy spin on dirt roads. Beginners may struggle because of the fitness- and skill-levels required for this trip. There's a one-day layover in Cook City, just outside Yellowstone, which you can use to rest (or to keep on riding as you explore the area).

The accommodations are in resorts and inns. The trip is run about 5 times per year.

Backcountry, Box 4029, Bozeman, MT 59772–4029, tel. 406/586–3556, fax 406/586–4288. July–late Aug.: 6 days, $1,028. Mountain-bike rental, $99.

MONTANA **Montana Off-Road.** This is what the hullabaloo is all about: true single-track mountain biking. The riding—everything from ridge running to crossing mountain passes and circling alpine lakes—is physically challenging, technically tough, and a fat-tire rider's dream. The single-track ranges from needle-carpeted buff to loose-rock slopes where almost everyone has to get off and walk. You'll only be able to average 15–20 miles per day on this 5-day trip: That's how demanding this one is. Hazards include wet, slippery, and rough terrain, steep slopes, embedded and loose rocks, tree roots, and fallen trees. Safety and teamwork are a big part of this ride, so expect to stop often to regroup, cheer each other on, and talk about how nuts you must be.

Starting in Bozeman, this trip runs south into the Gallatin and Madison mountain ranges. Many times there is no van support, but it will be there with your luggage at the end of the day. The accommodations are in resorts, lodges, and a guest ranch. The trip is run twice per year, and is for advanced riders only. *Backcountry, Box 4029, Bozeman, MT 59772–4029, tel. 406/586–3556, fax 406/586–4288. July–Aug.: 5 days, $1,035. Mountain-bike rental, $129.*

THE WEST COAST

CALIFORNIA **Haute Route.** This ride isn't for everyone, but if it appeals to you, it could be one of the best mountain biking excursions you'll ever make.

The trip is run on 2 separate weekends. The first begins at Big Bear Lake and descends to the Deep Creek Hot Springs, where you make camp, cook out (steak-and-potatoes fare), and soak away the trail. The terrain is tough—not yet extreme, but only for the hardy. There are a lot of up-and-down stretches, and a lot of technical challenges.

Water can be scarce as you ride through remote sections of the national forests and desertlike areas east of Los Angeles. The scenery changes as you move through pine forests into stretches of Joshua trees, then skirt the Mojave River and enter the desert, finally ending up amid patches of scrub oak. You may not have known there was this much wilderness left in the area.

The second weekend is harder. You'll climb back up to the Blue Ridge, then creep up and over 9,000-foot Mt. Baden-Powell (named for the man who founded the Boy Scouts). Once you conquer this peak, though, it's all screamer downhill back to Los Angeles. But even this section is technical, with some loose, rocky sections.

Expect to average 30 to 35 miles per day. This is a camping trip, run only once a year. You can also sign up for a single weekend. *Victor Vincente of America, 1582 Pride St., Simi Valley, CA 93065, tel. 805/527–1991. Apr. and May: 4 days, $220; 2 days, $110.*

CALIFORNIA **Otter Bar Lodge.** This resort is filled with water seekers during the peak kayak season, but in the late summer and fall, Otter Bar becomes mountain biking territory.

Klamath National Forest, where most of the guided rides take place, contains about 3,000 miles of dirt roads and 300 miles of trails. The lodge is remote (more than 2 hours from Eureka), and the surrounding fir trees and wildlife make it feel even farther from civilization.

Using Otter Bar Lodge as your base, you'll spend 7 days exploring the Trinity Alps and Marble Mountain wilderness areas. Jammers can make the climb from 1,200 to 6,000 feet, while a shuttle takes beginners up steep ascents. The riding runs from quick buff descents to bone-jarring technical roller coasters. Most trails are old logging roads, but the guides know where to find single-track.

Along with biking 15 to 40 miles a day, you'll spend time rafting on the Klamath River. Accommodations at the inn are pretty plush: The hot tub and sauna get high marks, as does the California haute cuisine. One night is spent in an old look-out cabin set on a 6,000-foot ridge, with a 360° view of the surrounding mountains. *Otter Bar Lodge, Box 210, Forks of Salmon, CA 96031, tel. 916/462–4772. Aug.–early Oct.: 7 days, $1,150. Price includes mountain-bike rental.*

WASHINGTON **Cascades Off-Road.** This 4-day bike-path (as opposed to tougher trails) trip is perfect for families or novice mountain bikers who don't feel comfortable on single-track or difficult terrain. Plus, it's accessible. You begin right in suburban Seattle, taking an abandoned railroad grade directly into the Cascades.

Railroad grades are good news for novices. For instance, you climb into the mountains—including Snoqualmie Pass—on a 1% incline, so gradual you'll hardly notice the effort. You go through tunnels (including a spectacular 2-mile long, pitch-black one), beside the Yakima River, down gentle descents, through woods, and across open pastureland.

You'll ride 15-40 easy miles per day. Any level of cyclist can hack the distance. There's one especially easy day that includes a shopping stop at Rosyln, the town where TV's *Northern Exposure* was filmed. Accommodations include hotels, lodges, and inns—nothing spectacular, all serviceable and comfy. You can get seafood, meat-and-taters, and pretty much any dish you'd want at the mix of restaurants. But remember, Seattle is espresso central. This trip is run about 4 times per year. *Bicycle Adventures, Box 7875, Olympia, WA 98507, tel. 206/786–0989 or 800/443–6060, fax 206/786–9661. June–Sept.: 4 days, $688. Mountain-bike rental, $136.*

SOURCES

ORGANIZATIONS **Adventure Cycling Association** (Box 8308, Missoula, MT 59807, tel. 406/721–1776) sells cycling maps and provides information about off-road touring. It publishes *The Cyclists' Yellow Pages* (including a special mountain biking supplement) and *BikeReport*. **American Youth Hostels** (Box 37613, Washington, DC 20013, tel. 202/783–4943) runs off-road tours and provides inexpensive accommodations.

The International Mountain Bicycling Association (Box 7378, Boulder, CO 80306, tel. 303/545–9011) advocates responsible trail use, and helps resolve land-access issues. It publishes *IMBA Trail News.* **The League of American Bicyclists** (Suite 120, 190 W. Ostend St., Baltimore, MD 21230, tel. 410/539–3399), a cycling enthusiast organization, runs events and provides touring information. It also publishes *Bicycle USA.* Although it's not heavily off-road oriented, it may be of some help. **Rails to Trails Conservancy** (Suite 300, 1400 16th St. NW, Washington, DC 20036, tel. 202/797–5400) promotes conversion of abandoned railroad land to cycling trails and provides touring information.

PERIODICALS The League of American Bicyclists (see above) publishes *Bicycle USA* 8 times a year and distributes it to members. Every issue contains at least one touring feature and lots of information on rides and events. *Bicycling* is a how-to magazine, with mountain-bike touring articles throughout the year and a special touring issue (Rodale Press, 33 E. Minor St., Emmaus, PA 18098, tel. 610/967–8093 for information, 515/242–0286 to subscribe). *The Cyclists' Yellow Pages,* an annual publication distributed to Adventure Cycling members (see above), lists sources of off-road touring information and maps. *Dirt Rag* lists off-road rides and events in New England, the East Coast, the Midwest, and the Southeast (5732 3rd St., Verona, PA 15147, tel. 412/795–7495). *Mountain Bike,* the sister magazine of *Bicycling,* has a special off-road touring issue each year and mountain bike-touring articles throughout the year (Rodale Press, 33 E.

Minor St., Emmaus, PA 18098, tel. 610/967–5171 for information, 515/242-0291 to subscribe). *California Cyclist* lists off-road rides and events in this region (Suite 304, 490 2nd St., San Francisco, CA 94107, tel. 415/546–7291). *Sports Etc/Northwest Cyclist* chronicles off-road rides and events in the Pacific Northwest (Box 9272, Seattle, WA 98109, tel. 206/286–8566).

BOOKS Pick up a copy of *500 Great Rail Trails* (Living Planet Press) to discover the U.S. rail-trail system, a series of abandoned rail lines that have been converted to bike trails. The 162-page guide tells you where the trails are and how long they run; it also gives highlights along the route and tells you where to get a map. Some of the best touring books available are those in the *Bicycling the Back Roads* series: *Northwest Oregon, Northwest Washington, Pacific Coast, Southwest Washington (The Mountaineers Books).* Each book has more than 200 pages compiled by local experts, with detailed route directions, sightseeing tips, and lodging and food recommendations. Some other excellent series include *America by Mountain Bike: Arizona, Central Appalachia, New Mexico, Northern California/Nevada, Northern New England, Smoky Mountain Country* (Menasha Ridge Press), which offers 230-page volumes of well-mapped and detailed off-road rides throughout the United States written by local experts; and *Mountain Bike Adventures: Four Corners Region, Northern Rockies, Washington's North Cascades and Olympics, Washington's South Cascades/Puget Sound* (The Mountaineers Books), whose 228-page volumes include many mapped routes along with good introductory material on mountain biking.

ALSO SEE If you enjoy the off-road bike tour experience, you may like surveying the country on road tours, too. See the Bicycling chapter for more information.

Race Car Driving Courses

By Michael B. McPhee and Jane E. Zarem

ere's a way to experience speed without first writing a will. Race-car driving courses are becoming enormously popular, as growing numbers of men and women are strapping themselves into powerful racing cars on wide-open tracks and safely driving well beyond speed limits that are legal on highways and country roads.

Elaina Litvak, a 40-year-old junior high school art teacher, finally agreed to try racing her boyfriend's souped-up Audi. "We had a short classroom session, then got in our cars and followed the instructor around several laps," she said. "The last laps we got up over 100 miles per hour.

"When you've never done this before," she continued, "the whole thing is overwhelming. But you settle down real quick. Soon, I tried catching a Corvette. I did everything I was told not to do, going for speed only. It really scared me. In the afternoon, I did a lot better."

Cindy Parmenter, a 39-year-old financial analyst, took up vintage-car racing with her husband. "It's a great feeling of power, the whining of the engine, the shifting, the tremendous exhilaration.

"Coming out of a corner into a straight, it takes guts not to take your foot off the gas or blip the brakes. But you do it, and God, it's great. When I spun out for the first time, I was filled with adrenaline; but I wasn't as scared as I thought I would be."

Both women say that, whether or not they ever race again, they now feel much more confident driving on the street—knowing the limits of braking, how to handle a corner better, how to avoid accidents.

Race-car driving courses cover a lot of driving techniques in a lot of different vehicles—including drag racing, go-cart, stock car, and ice driving. We've included a broad variety of course opportunities, but the main focus in this chapter is on racing courses—both road and Grand Prix racing—and street (defensive) driving courses.

Road racing and Grand Prix racing courses use the same squiggly, circular track, usually less than 2 miles long with 12 to 18 turns. Road racing is done in a car with fenders, like a sports car; and if you bump the other cars you don't do too much damage. Racing cars reach speeds of up to 120 miles per hour.

Grand Prix racing courses employ cars, such as those used at the Indianapolis Motor Speedway, with open wheels that stick out from the auto body and no fenders. These cars are much more powerful, traveling at speeds up to 160 miles per hour.

The street courses use regular street sedans, like Volvos, BMWs, and Toyotas. Some

Outdoors writer Michael B. McPhee has written for the *New York Times*, the *Washington Post*, and the *Boston Globe*. Jane E. Zarem, a travel writer and editor, is a regular Fodor's contributor.

schools let you bring your own car. In these defensive-driving courses, you learn skills that help you handle situations that could arise on any local street—skills like cornering, braking, skid control, or evasive driving to avoid a ball or a child. Some street courses are high-performance, concentrating on highway driving—how to handle a car at highway speeds, avoid sliding, pass, and handle curves.

Skids and slides are the bane of all driving, because they can cause you to lose control of the car. Consequently, these courses concentrate on avoiding slides or getting out of them once they start. All schools approach the problem differently, but they all have their own slide or skid cars equipped either with outriggers that prevent you from rolling over in a high-speed slide or with special suspensions that slide easily at low speeds. All schools also have their own skid pads—specially prepared sections of asphalt greased or oiled to cause cars to slide.

All driving schools are set up to teach you quickly. Most have half-day introductory courses that give you 10 or 12 laps of driving. Full courses are 1 or 2 days long; the more thorough ones last for 3 days. Some schools have 5-day courses for the serious wannabe racer. All the schools have surprisingly good safety records.

A typical day begins with a classroom session, where you learn the best line (the most efficient path) around a curve, how to exit a turn with the greatest speed and acceleration, and how to avoid or cope with sliding. Then you're on the track, either on foot or in a van or a car. Some schools have cars with twin seats that allow the instructor to sit beside you as you take laps.

Lunch may be catered by the school, but you are sometimes on your own. Afternoons are spent in the cars, applying what you've learned in class and practicing car control. You fend for yourself for dinner, but usually you get together with other students to talk about life in the fast lane. Nights are low-key, as a rule. Exhausted students hit the hay early for another day of driving.

Be prepared to spend $1,000 to $1,500 for a weekend and around $2,500 for a course that's 3 to 5 days long.

Many schools run courses we describe in other parts of the country and have additional courses to choose from—so inquire if you want to take a course in a certain area or take a different level or type of course in the same region.

CHOOSING THE RIGHT COURSE

In picking the right course, ask yourself why you're doing this. Do you want the sensation of driving an open-wheel vehicle at 150 miles per hour? Then sign up for a Grand Prix course for 1 or 2 days. Do you want to learn how to race? Then pick a 5-day racing course with certification at the end. Do you want to learn how to drive your car defensively in town? Choose a street-driving course. Or do you want simply to drive as fast as you possibly can? Then pick a drag racing or go-cart school.

Here are some other questions to ask to help you decide which course is right for you:

How long has the school been in business, and what is its safety record? A school that has been around for a while has a safety record you can evaluate. It also should have ironed out any problems in its curriculum and instructional routines.

What's the cost, and what's included? Always ask if the school supplies the car or if you must drive your own. Courses in which you use the school's vehicles generally cost more. You're usually on your own for accommodations and meals, although a few serve you lunch. Since there's no standard, we tell you what's included in the prices we list within the italicized service information at the end of each review. If you have any doubts, ask for clarification.

Even though driving schools don't usually put you up, they often know about the best deals in town. Sometimes a school works out a special rate for its students at a nearby hotel. Find out what the guest quarters are like and what facilities the property offers before you book.

Am I liable if I crash a car? Policies vary dramatically from school to school. At some schools, you are responsible for all damages to the cars you use; others sell insurance policies that limit your liability to a few thousand dollars, with or without a deductible; others never hold you responsible. (If you plan to use your own car, make sure that your regular insurance covers any damages incurred while in a race-car driving school.)

How many students are in the course, and how many students per instructor? The number of students in a class actually matters less than the number of students per instructor. A 4:1 student-to-instructor ratio is average for most courses.

How much driving time will I have? This depends on the philosophy of the school. Some courses split the time 50-50, in part because they don't have enough cars. Others provide plenty of time on the track—also known as seat time—on the principle that you learn by doing.

How fast can I go? Some schools limit your RPMs (and fine you if you rev the engine too high) or require you to stay together and wait for the slowest student. Others let you push the car as hard as you want on so-called hot laps.

Who teaches the courses? Are there any famous racers currently teaching? For the beginner, names don't matter much unless you want to meet your racing hero. Most schools share celebrity instructors. Celebrity drivers tied to schools don't mean anything unless they actually teach you, as they do, say, in Buck Baker's stock-car school. Just because so-and-so went there 10 years ago doesn't mean much. It's more important to find instructors actively involved in racing (not just in teaching).

Do you have references from past students? It's often more helpful to get a former student's description of his or her experience than it is to get one from a professional driver involved in the course.

What accreditation does the school have? Of the 6 groups that sanction automobile racing, only 2 are involved in racing schools: the Sports Car Club of America (SCCA) and the International Motor Sport Association (IMSA). Most of the schools mentioned below are sanctioned by one or the other. The curricula are developed by the schools themselves, who then apply to one of the two sanctioning groups. The instruction varies from school to school. Whether a school is accredited by the SCCA or IMSA, however, really matters only if you want to be licensed in order to race, since you can't participate in an organization's races without being licensed by it.

SCCA, the larger of the two, focuses primarily on road racing in a variety of cars, from full-bodied GT (Grand Tour) passenger cars to formula cars with open cockpits. It sanctions club racing, solo racing around pylons, and road rallies. SCCA is very social and is oriented toward beginners and amateurs. To be SCCA-licensed, you must complete a 3-day program at one of the 17 SCCA-accredited schools and take a 1- or 2-day course at one of the SCCA regionals listed in SCCA's monthly *Sports Car Magazine*. It costs $45 for a novice permit, plus $55 for club membership.

IMSA is much smaller, and its members are mostly self-styled professionals who also belong to the SCCA. IMSA licenses are awarded by all IMSA-accredited schools on completion of a 3-day course, a passing grade on an exam, and payment of a $225 fee. Keep in mind that the majority of races offer a minimal amount of prize money, and few pros ever break even.

MAJOR PLAYERS

SKIP BARBER RACING SCHOOL The Skip Barber Racing School, accredited by both SCCA and IMSA, is the largest racing and driving school in the world. After two decades of teaching, it also has the most celebrated alumni; in fact, each year since 1983, the average number of drivers starting the Indianapolis 500 who have Skip Barber training on their resumes is one-third—that's 11 of the 33 starters!

Courses are available at more than 20 different tracks throughout the United States, and the school is known for offering the same curriculum, the same cars, and the same instructor corps at each of its tracks. Programs run year-round on the West Coast, from April through October in the Northeast and Midwest, and from October through April in Florida and Georgia.

Courses are offered in both race-car driving/competition and defensive-driving techniques for street drivers. Racing instruction is top-of-the-line and ranges from a 3-hour introductory course ($395) to a 5- or 7-day Speedweek ($4,374–$4,970). The "classroom" is a fleet of Dodge vehicles, including Formula Dodges powered by 2.0 liter, 16-valve, four-cylinder stock engines. Class sizes range from 12 students with 4 instructors to 28 students with 8 instructors.

The 1- and 2-day street driving programs ($495–$975) teach such skills as skid control, decreasing braking distances, emergency maneuvers, and accident avoidance. Students are taught in Dodge vehicles in all driveline types: all-wheel-drive Stealths, front-wheel drive Stratus sedans, rear-wheel drive Dakota V-8 sport trucks, and the 410 h.p. Dodge Viper sports car.

Students are not liable for damage to cars for courses lasting up to 3 days. For longer duration courses, there is limited liability. Helmets and driving suits are provided. The school provides names of local hotels that offer students special rates. Meals are not included. (29 Brook St., Lakeville, CT 06039, tel. 203/435–1300, fax 203/435–1321; on the West Coast, Sears Point Raceway, 29355 Arnold Dr., Sonoma, CA 95476, tel. 707/939–8007, fax 707/939–8055.)

BERTIL ROOS DRIVING SCHOOL With almost 2 decades of experience, Bertil Roos Driving School is one of the old-timers. It offers both racing and street-driving courses and is accredited by both IMSA and SCCA.

The Roos Road Racing School is held at the Pocono International Raceway in Long Pond, Pennsylvania, about 30 minutes from Wilkes-Barre or Allentown. The Roos Oval Racing School is held at Nazareth Speedway, Nazareth, Pennsylvania, 5 miles north of Allentown. The Oval Racing School is on a 1-mile tri-oval with only 3 high-speed corners; you brake only once per lap and drive in top gear the entire time. Road Racing is on a 1.3-mile track with 8 corners: You're always busy braking, accelerating, shifting gears, and taking corners.

Roos is more wide open than most racing schools. It has no speed or rev limits, and its instructors encourage students to race and pass each other—students here end up driving faster (nearly 140 mph) than those at most other schools. The Roos school is also unique in that it stresses the eye, or ocular, driving technique, in which the student is taught to look always at the correct place on the course relative to the car, the track, and other cars. This is a help not only in racing but in ordinary highway driving. They also emphasize the line-recovery technique—keeping the car on the correct line through the track.

The 2-day Street Driving course ($795) is taught in Volvo 850 GLTs, which is no surprise since the school is sponsored by Volvo. Students also use specially engineered slide cars with pivoting rear wheels that are constantly sliding, creating ice- and snow-driving conditions more closely (the school claims) than do slide cars with outriggers.

Racing classes cover basic car-handling techniques, as well as racing in traffic, passing, and drafting (tailgating to reduce wind resistance). Some are Grand Prix courses. Bertil Roos offers half-day ($395) and full-day ($795) racing programs; the 3-day Grand Prix racing course and 2-day Competition course can be taken individually or in combination for a 5-day Race Week program (see below).

Racing classes can take up to 18 students, but the student-to-teacher ratio stays around 3:1. There's no liability for beginner courses, but in advanced racing courses you could be liable for up to $2,500 in damages. (Box 221, Blakeslee, PA 18610, tel. 717/646–7227 or 800/722–3669, fax 717/646–4794.)

BOB BONDURANT SCHOOL OF HIGH PERFOR- MANCE DRIVING From a base at the Firebird International Raceway, 20 minutes from downtown Phoenix, Arizona, this IMSA- and SCCA-accredited school offers a complete schedule of courses: Grand Prix Road Racing, Advanced Road Racing, High-Performance Driving, Highway Survival Training, Teenage Defensive Driving, and Executive Protection/Anti-Kidnapping programs. Classes are taught year-round on a 1.6-mile road course specially designed by Bob Bondurant for high-performance and race-driving instruction, as well as a 3.5 acre asphalt pad for advanced driver training. A 3:1 student-to-instructor ratio ensures individual attention.

Bob Bondurant has raced for Ferrari and Porsche and has won the World Manufacturers' Championship for Ford and the grand prize at Le Mans in 1964. The Bondurant school opened in 1968. Today, the fleet includes over 130 race cars: single-seat Crossle Formula Fords, 5.0 V8 Mustang GTs, Taurus SHOs, and Lightning F-150 pick-ups specially built for Bondurant by Roush Racing—the same company that prepares championship-winning race cars for the Ford Motor Company. Graduates have included numerous celebrities, such as Paul Newman, Tom Cruise, Gene Hackman, Clint Eastwood, Tim Allen, Crystal Bernard, and Candice Bergen.

The most popular program is the 4-day Grand Prix Road Racing course, during which you get plenty of track time in race-prepared Ford Mustang GTs and Formula Fords. Advanced Road Racing courses are available to graduates of the Grand Prix course or for drivers already certified by the SCCA or IMSA. The High-Performance courses, either 2 or 3 days, teach advanced street-driving skills.

All course prices include the use of a Bondurant School car. Students are liable for damage to vehicles, but optional insurance is available for a nominal charge. The school provides a list of nearby hotels and resorts that offer special rates and amenities to students. (Box 51980, Phoenix, AZ 85076, tel. 800/842–7223, fax 520/796–0660.)

FAVORITE COURSES

THE NORTHEAST

CONNECTICUT **Skip Barber's Speedweek.** If you want to become a pro, Skip Barber's Speedweek will take you from no experience at all to actually driving in a race in one week. Speedweek is a combination of the school's 3-day Competition Course—its most popular course—followed by two advanced lapping and/or practice sessions and two actual races. Speedweek is a 5-day course; Speedweek Plus, with additional advanced sessions, lasts a full week.

In the 3-day Competition Course segment, you're instructed in the techniques needed to compete against the best drivers in the world. You'll learn the fundamentals of racing—cornering, accelerating, shifting, and braking a race car—along with "race-craft" tactics and strategies, such as what all the racing flags mean and how to race in the rain. A lot of time is spent on the track in a professionally prepared Formula Dodge race car, steadily increasing your speed as skills are developed. You get instant and constant feedback from the instructors via walkie-talkie during and after each on-track exercise.

Lapping Sessions emphasize track time instruction and feedback. Students drive several multi-lap segments under the close scrutiny of instructors, so you can work on specific problem areas or simply gain experience. Practice Sessions are more intense—the laps are under race conditions, so you experience traffic and your laps are timed. The culmination of your week is participation in a Formula Dodge Race Series event.

To participate in Speedweek, you need no prior knowledge of cars or racing other than the ability to operate a manual transmission. Helmets and racing suits are provided. Students assume no liability for damage to cars through day 3; limited liability on days 4 through 7. Graduates of the 3-day Competition Course are eligible immediately to apply for SCCA or IMSA racing licenses, but most students simply are in it for the experience and the exhilaration. Courses are offered at more than a dozen race tracks around the country. *Skip Barber Racing School, 29 Brook St., Lakeville, CT 06039, tel. 203/435–1300, fax 203/435–1321. May–Dec.: 5-day Speedweek, $4,375; 7-day Speedweek Plus, $4,970; 3-day Competition Course only, $1,995).*

■NEW HAMPSHIRE■ 1-Day Arrive-and-Drive Course. Motion Dynamics/David Loring Drivers School is a small, SCCA-accredited school started in 1991 in the town of Loudon, about 30 minutes from Concord. It offers just one course on selected Thursdays, but the experience can add an exhilarating focus to a New Hampshire vacation.

The 1-day Arrive-and-Drive Course includes use of an SCCA spec racer, a road-racing sports car specifically designed to be used in SCCA-sanctioned road-racing competitions. These small sports cars are capable of racing up to 120 miles per hour. Because of their design, they are considered the ideal learning car—easy to handle and not too powerful.

Three hours of classroom instruction are followed by speed laps on the New Hampshire International Speedway. This class gives a maximum of 6 students a full day of driving. The level is determined by the students themselves. Students leave a $2,000 damage deposit on cars. No insurance is offered. Helmets and driving suits are provided. *Motion Dynamics of New Hampshire, Box 2245, Rte. 16, Conway, NH 03818, tel. 603/447–3543, fax 603/447–3296. Apr.–Oct.: 1-day course, $1,300.*

THE MID-ATLANTIC

■PENNSYLVANIA■ Bertil Roos 5-Day Race Week. This Race Week Program held at Pocono International Raceway in the mountains of northeastern Pennsylvania, is a combination of the school's 3-day Grand Prix road racing course and its 2-day Competition course that you can take on 5 consecutive days. No experience is necessary other than the ability to operate a manual-transmission vehicle.

In the 3-day course, instructors teach a step-by-step formula for driving a race car safely around a twisting road-racing circuit. You practice acceleration, braking, and cornering in one of the school's high-performance Volvo 850s. In a specially equipped Slide-car, you learn to maintain control when a racecar starts to slide. Then you get to drive one of the school's IndyStyle Formula 2000 Racecars, equipped with an in-car timing system that displays your lap time on the dash board every time you cross the finish line. There are no rev limits, and you're allowed to pass slower cars as you speed around the track.

The 2-day competition course teaches you actual wheel-to-wheel racing techniques. On the last day, you participate in a full-fledged race with other students. Upon completion of the Race Week program, students earn an IndyStyle Racing Challenge Competition License, which qualifies you to compete in special challenge races.

The school's 3:1 student-to-instructor ratio guarantees personal attention. Helmets and driving suits are provided; just bring sneakers and a pair of gloves. Information on nearby hotel and motel accommodations is provided when you enroll, and the school will make reservations for you if you wish. Lunch is available at the track for $10 per day. Students are liable for damages up to a maximum of $2,500 per incident during the last two days of Race Week only. *Bertil Roos Driving School, Box 221, Blakeslee, PA 18610, tel. 717/646–7227 or 800/722-3669, fax 717/646–4794. Apr.–May, July–Sept.: 5-day Race Week, $3,100; 3-day Grand Prix Racing Course, $1,995; 2-day Competition Course, $1,450.*

THE SOUTH

FLORIDA Frank Hawley's Dragster Courses. Drag racing is a sprint between 2 cars to see which one can accelerate faster. The vehicles are placed side-by-side, looking down a ¼-mile stretch of pavement. A series of flashing lights signal the drivers to start racing, and the first to cross the finish line wins. It sounds simple, but drag racers have taken this form of competition to a level that just a decade ago seemed inconceivable. Some cars use 4 engines, some burn especially flammable mixtures of alcohol, some even use jet engines. All are modified so severely that they may not be driven legally on the street.

The basic Gas Course offered by Frank Hawley's Drag Racing School gives you 2 days on the Gainesville Raceway, in a gas- or super-gas-powered dragster (the latter looks like a production model but runs with a high-performance engine and modified design). The school provides everything—dragster, driving suit, helmet. The first day includes classroom instruction, equipment fitting, and safety inspection. Then you're strapped into the car for warm-up exercises—practice with car control and burnouts (spinning the tires prior to racing)—at slow speed. The second day has more classroom work, then 6 runs, beginning with 4 short ones and working up to 2 down the length of the ¼-mile track. Students frequently reach speeds of 150 mph. If you want to try for your competition license or just want to make more runs, you can arrange to take Gas Course 2 immediately following the basic course. The fee is on a per-run basis, so you can do as few or as many runs—for as many days—as you wish.

Driving alcohol-powered dragsters is taught in a 3-day course. This is basically the same course given for the gas and supergas dragsters, except that cars that run on alcohol are much more powerful. You can reach speeds over 200 mph! These cars also require the driver to use a clutch, so more instruction is necessary. This course is not for novices.

The mechanics of the course are similar to the gas-powered dragster course, except that each session is videotaped and followed by a classroom review.

Classes are limited to 8 students for the gas dragster programs and 6 for the alcohol-powered dragster courses. Each class usually has one main instructor and a helper. Instruction is hands-on, and students progress at their own individual paces. No one is rushed or held back by the class, and everyone receives the same number of runs. Students are liable for up to $2,500 in damages if they crash or cause engine damage through over-revving. The gas dragster program is also offered in September at Bakersfield Raceway in Bakersfield, California, 90 minutes northeast of Los Angeles, and in July at Maple Grove Raceway in Reading, Pennsylvania. Driving suits and other equipment are provided. *Frank Hawley's Drag Racing School, Box 140369, Gainesville, FL 32614, tel. 904/373–7223, fax 904/338–1813. Year-round: gas and supergas 2-day course, $1,150; additional runs, $150 each; 3-day alcohol and funny-car course, $2,950.*

FLORIDA Southard's Racing Course. Southard's is the only stock car school in the country that teaches on both dirt and asphalt. The asphalt track is the New Smyrna Speedway in Smyrna Beach, Florida, about 60 miles northeast of Orlando. The dirt track is the Volusia Speedway, 20 miles west of Daytona Beach.

The 5-day Southard Racing Course includes 32 hours of classroom instruction—24 working hours of chassis training and one day in the shop applying what you've learned—followed by 8–10 hours behind the wheel. You may either bring your own car for track time or use one of the school's cars.

You must be able to drive a stick-shift car. Students are not liable for damages—unless, of course, it's your own car. Helmets and firesuits are available. Classes are limited to 8 students with 2 or 3 instructors. The school furnishes enrolled students with a list of motels and campgrounds in the area. *Southard's Racing School, Box 1810, New*

Smyrna Beach, FL 32170, tel. 904/428–3307; fax 904/428–3710. Year-round: 5-day course with your own car, $900; with the school's car, $1,700.

GEORGIA **Road Atlanta Road Racing Program.** About 45 minutes from the city, Road Atlanta Driver Training Center has an "arrive and drive" racing program that is taught on a long, 2½-mile, 12-turn road racing track. You reach speeds of 80 to 120 mph. in 300 ZX Nissans and 240 SXs (the school is sponsored by Nissan), with an instructor by your side. Because the racing is done in sedans, however, most of the techniques you learn can also be applied to street driving. Class sizes increase to meet the need, but the student-to-teacher ratio remains about 4:1. All programs are hands-on—the car is your classroom.

Road Atlanta's 3-day racing course is taught year-round and is accredited by IMSA and SCCA. Lapping Days, track sessions under the guidance of instructors, are offered to graduates (of this or other accredited road racing courses) and can be added on immediately after your racing course or scheduled separately. Students are liable for all damage to cars unless they take out the $75 insurance policy that cuts the liability to $3,000. Helmets and driving suits are included. You're on your own for meals and lodging. *Road Atlanta Driver Training Center, 5300 Winder Highway, Braselton, GA 30517, tel. 404/967–6143; fax 404/967–2668. Year-round: 3-day road racing, $1,595; lapping day, $450.*

GEORGIA **Buck Baker Basic Nascar Winston Cup Courses.** Stock-car racers are a breed of their own—rough-and-tumble guys (and a few gals), who drive modified American sedans with very large engines around an oval track at frightful speeds. Buck Baker Racing School is the place for those of you who want to drive in the fast lane. Within 2 or 3 days, students with no racing experience average 165 mph, with other cars on the track. (You must be able to drive a standard-shift car.) "We're into training here," they tell you, "not talking." And they back

up this boast: After 15 years of teaching like this, students are still not liable for damages.

Students use powerful 600 h.p. Winston Cup stock cars. You spend the first day in classes learning driving techniques, rules, and studying the chassis; then you're outside, inspecting the track and looking for the best line to steer into and out of the corners. For the next day, you're in the cars. An instructor rides with you as needed. There can be 4 or 5 cars on the track at any time. The third day is a chassis class, which shows you the hows and whys of the race car set-up.

A 2-day Basic Winston Cup stock-car training course is given at the 1½-mile Atlanta Motor Speedway (the third fastest track on the Winston Cup circuit). Three-day courses are given at the Richmond (Virginia) Raceway and at the 1-mile North Carolina Motor Speedway in Rockingham, about 90 minutes east of Charlotte. Of the 3 tracks, the Speedway is a bit slower (students average 140 mph) but more challenging. Expect 12 to 15 students per class, with 5 instructors. The school provides driver suits and helmets if you don't have your own. Graduate refresher classes and 2-day Advanced Winston Cup Training courses are available at all tracks. *Buck Baker Racing School, 1613 Runnymede Lane, Charlotte, NC 28211, tel. 704/366–6224 or 800/529–2825, fax 704/596–8931. Jun.–Dec.: 2-day basic course, $1,800; 3-day basic, $2,000; refresher course, $795 per day; 2-day advanced training, $2,000.*

THE MIDWEST

INDIANA **Fast Company's 3-Day Competition Driving Course.** Fast Company Racing School, founded in 1992, is the Official Racing School of Indianapolis Raceway Park. The school offers race-car driving programs on both oval tracks and road courses and is SCCA-accredited for race licensing.

Fast Company takes an aggressive approach to training and driving. Students have no speed limits, even in the introductory courses. Its 3-day Competition Driving course is the most aggressive program of it's kind—you get up to top speed as quickly as possible, with running starts and practice races with other cars on the track. The course culminates on the third day with a full-blown race between students. This 3-day program has a maximum of 14 students with 3 instructors. Nascar-style V8 stock cars will be offered on a limited basis.

Because you can drive as fast as you wish, you are liable for full damages. An optional insurance policy, offered for $25, limits liability to $2,000. Helmets and driving suits are provided. *Fast Company Racing School, Box 151, Greencastle, IN 46135, tel. 317/653–2532, fax 317/653–3046. Apr.–Oct.: 3-day Competition Driving School, $1,795; 2-hr. Introduction to Racing, $275.*

OHIO **Honda High Performance Courses.** If you either own a high-performance vehicle or want to learn the techniques of high-performance driving, this Mid-Ohio School course is for you. It's a comprehensive 1-day (weekday) program that will build your driving confidence so you will have more control of your vehicle on the road. The program focuses on maneuverability through cornering, skid car, braking, and slalom drills. An added attraction is that 3-time PPG Indy Car World Series Champion Bobby Rahal is a guest instructor during some classroom and course drills.

On selected dates, you can continue your instruction with the 1-day Honda Advanced High Performance course. Personal attention differentiates this advanced program from comparable driving-school programs. The curriculum is customized to your unique driving needs; the goal is to explore and realize your personal driving potential. You're observed on the track, then given a complete written evaluation of your driving skills. You can bring your own car or use one of the school's Hondas.

The Mid-Ohio School, founded in 1993, is endorsed by Bobby Rahal. It's based at the Mid-Ohio Sports Car Course, in Lexington,

Ohio, an hour north of Columbus and an hour south of Cleveland. Classes begin at 7 a.m. and end at 5 p.m. They are limited to 20-25, with a student-to-teacher ratio that never exceeds 4:1. Students are liable for all damage to cars up to $1,500. Helmets are provided (but not driving suits). Lunch is included in the price. *The Mid-Ohio School, 94 N. High St., Suite 50, Dublin, OH 43017, tel. 614/793–4615, fax 614/793–4624. May–Sept.: 1-day high performance, $525, or $575 using the school's car; 1-day advanced high performance, $550, or $600 using the school's car.*

OKLAHOMA **Stephens High-Performance Driving Course.** Founded in 1986 and approved by the SCCA, Stephens Racing School of High Performance Driving is a school for road racing only. It has its own facility, with 24 cars, at the Hallett Motor Racing Circuit in Hallett, Oklahoma (about 40 minutes west of Tulsa). The 1.8-mile circuit is a challenging track, with 10 turns and numerous elevation changes.

In the Stephens 2-day weekend course, you learn the techniques of how to drive your race car as fast as you are able, ending the day with a practice race. On the second day, you run the course counter-clockwise—giving you the experience of racing on two seemingly different circuits. Lapping sessions are videotaped and critiqued after each session to correct errors before they become bad habits.

Your classroom is an SCCA Enterprises Sports Renault: a single seat, open cockpit, closed-wheel sports racing car built specifically for racing. For an addition $200 per day, you can be equipped with an SCCA Spec Racer, a one-design, fixed-specification road course car for which only SCCA-specified components and parts may be used. They're tough and responsive, quite safe, and fun to drive.

Classes are limited to 18 students with 4 instructors. Students are liable for all damages, including over-revving the engine and not shifting properly. A $100 insurance policy limits liability to $1,000. Race cars, suits, and helmets are provided. Special weekend rates are available at the Downtown Double-tree Hotel, in Tulsa. Course prices include lunch. *Stephens Racing, 2232 S. Nogales, Tulsa, OK 74107, tel. 918/583–1134, fax 918/583–1135. Year-round: 2-day race school, $1,100.*

THE SOUTHWEST

ARIZONA **Bondurant Grand Prix Road Racing.** The Bob Bondurant School of High Performance Driving, based at the Firebird International Raceway in Phoenix, is for people who are considering professional motorsports or who just yearn to drive a race car. In this 4-day Grand Prix course, you're assigned your own race cars—a race-pre-pared V8 Ford Mustang GT and an open-wheel Formula Ford—and have plenty of track time. You're behind the wheel 80% of the time. Individual attention is stressed; instructors ride right along with you to cri-tique your moves as they happen. There's a 3:1 instructor-to-student ratio.

Graduates of the Grand Prix course (or other accredited courses) can follow up by enrolling in the Advanced Road Racing course (1-, 2-, or 3-day courses) to improve specific areas of driving and racing tech-niques. Students are assigned a school car or, for an extra fee, can use one of their For-mula Fords or World Challenge PROsearch Mustangs.

Classes are taught year-round on a 1.6 mile road course specially designed by Bob Bon-durant, as well as a 3.5-cacre asphalt pad for advanced driver training. All prices include helmets and driving suits. Students are liable for damages to vehicles, but optional insurance is available for a nominal charge. The school provides a list of nearby hotels and resorts that offer special rates to stu-dents. *Bob Bondurant School of High Perfor-mance Driving, Box 51980, Phoenix, AZ 85076-1980, tel. 800/842–7223, fax 520/ 796–0660. Year-round: 4-day Grand Prix, $2,695; 1-day Advanced Road Racing, $1,195; 2-day, $2,195; 3-day, $3,095.*

ARIZONA **Bondurant's High-Performance Driving Course.** This 2-or 3-day course is intended to teach skills and safety tech-niques of racing that you can apply to street driving. During classroom discussions, driving at high speed, and driving the Bon-durant skid cars, you learn accident-evasion techniques and skid control—and become a safer, more confident driver. You can bring your own car—sports, high-performance, GT, or garden-variety street car—or you can use one of Bondurant's specially prepared Ford Mustang GTs. You also get to drive the school's unique skid car. The skid car has a sub-frame with outboard wheels that can be hydraulically controlled to lift either the front or rear wheels to duplicate rain, snow, or ice conditions, as well as a complete loss of traction. In the skid car, you'll learn how to control both front-wheel and rear-wheel skids.

Graduates of the 3-day High Performance Driving course can combine—or come back for—Bondurant's 3-day High Performance Graduate–Grand Prix program to continue their training in an open-wheel Formula Ford. This special course is actually the last 3 days of the 4-day Grand Prix Road Racing Course (see above). You must have gradu-ated from the 3-day HPD course within the previous six months to be eligible.

Classes are taught year-round. All prices include helmets, driving suits, and the use of a school vehicle. Students are liable for damages, but optional insurance is available for a nominal charge. The school provides a list of nearby hotels and resorts that offer special rates to students. *Bob Bondurant School of High Performance Driving, Box 51980, Phoenix, AZ 85076-1980, tel. 800/ 842–7223, fax 520/796–0660. Year-round: 2-day High Performance, $1,395; 3-day, $1,995; 3-day Graduate–Grand Prix, $2,095.*

THE ROCKIES

COLORADO **Go 4 It Track Courses.** Mike Pettiford, a regular competitor on the pro-fessional racing circuit with numerous championships to his credit, operates a high-performance safety school called Go 4 It Services. Racing and street courses are given at four different tracks—but most of the action is at Second Creek Raceway, 15 minutes outside of Denver, and Mountain View Motor Sports Park in Mead.

Pettiford's road racing courses focus on driving rather than classroom study. He tailors the program to the needs of each student; in fact, you're asked on the registration form to suggest the subjects you'd like covered. Courses offered range from a ½-day beginner course to a full SCCA-accredited 3-day program, and each day builds upon the previous one. The one-day racing program concentrates on rules, braking, and turns. The 2-day course adds experience on a skid pad and emphasizes car control. The 3-day program continues with passing, lapping, race strategy and, of course, lots of track time.

Racing courses are restricted to no more than 4 people per instructor. The price does not include the use of a car, but you can rent a Chevrolet IROC-Z, Camaro, or Mazda RX7 from the school. Students are liable for all damages. *Go 4 It Services, 713 Grant Ave., Louisville, CO 80027, tel. 303/666–4113. Year-round: racing courses, 1/2 day, $250; 1 day, $350; 2 days, $650; 3 days, $950; car rental, $700 per day.*

COLORADO **Bridgestone Winter Driving Courses.** These courses, offered by the Bridgestone Winter Driving School in Steamboat Springs, will make you a more confident driver when the road glazes over. You'll develop better reflexes and learn how to drive with ease on snow- and ice-covered roads, avoid panic situations, and develop good reflexes. You'll also have fun sliding and spinning!

Courses are offered at three levels: ½ day, 1-day, or 2-days. Graduates range in age from 16 to 82; about 50% are women. The ½-day course gives you an hour of classroom theory and 2 hours on an ice track. The 1-day course offers more driving and a video analysis. The 2-day course is a comprehensive,

performance-oriented program and includes an Ice Driving Rally Course with individual instruction. If you still haven't had enough, you can continue training with a private instructor at an hourly rate.

A complete line of front-, rear-, and four-wheel-drive vehicles is provided by the school—Bridgestone doesn't use skid cars or artificial devices. The 1-mile circuit is a combination of frozen water and snow, a smooth, slippery surface specially designed with snowbank guardrails. Classes average 8 students, with 2 instructors. Liability is covered in the price of the course. Helmets and driving suits are not provided nor required. *The Bridgestone Winter Driving School, 1850 Ski Time Square Drive, Box 774167, Steamboat Springs, CO 80477, tel. 303/879–6104 or 800/949–7543, fax 303/879–6105. Dec.–early Mar.: half-day introductory course, $120; 1-day course, $240; 2-day course, $600.*

THE WEST COAST

CALIFORNIA **Jim Hall Kart Racing.** Race karts are deceptive in appearance. They look as if they would putter around a track at 15 miles per hour. Only about 3 feet wide and 5 feet long, with wheels 12 inches in diameter, a race kart sits just 1 inch off the ground. The advantage is in the kart's weight—averaging 140 pounds, including the motor. Drivers lower themselves into position with their knees sticking up about wheel level. A sprint kart travels from 0-60 mph. in less than seven seconds with a 175 lb. driver at the wheel. They can scream around a track at speeds approaching 85 miles per hour.

More than half the current Indy Car drivers began their racing careers in karts, primarily because of the relatively low cost. More important, though, is that a kart's vehicle dynamics and handling are comparable to a full-sized, formula-style race car.

Along the coast in Ventura, just one hour north of Los Angeles, Jim Hall Kart Racing Schools provide expert instruction with up-to-date racing equipment and safety apparel on two track circuits: A-Track is 0.3 miles long with 9 turns; B-Track is 0.4 miles long with 11 turns. Instruction in safety, track lines, vehicle dynamics, braking, passing, qualifying, and racing prepares the student driver for his or her in-kart, on-track driving experience.

Racing classes are offered in ½-day increments. Depending on your level of enthusiasm, modules can be taken separately or in sequence over a period of up to 5 days. Each class offers the student racer more driving sessions, with greater challenges, and culminating in actual racing competition among the student drivers on the 5th day.

The school is open year-round and has graduated more than 16,500 drivers since it opened in 1982. Ages 12 and up are accepted. A list of hotels, motels, and campsites convenient to the school is furnished to participants. Helmets and driving suits are supplied. *Jim Hall Kart Racing Schools, 1555-G Morse Ave., Ventura, CA 93003, tel. 805/654–1329, fax 805/654–0227. Year-round: first half-day module, $125; additional modules, $175–$225 each; 2-day package, $600; 3 days, $900; 4 days, $1,250; 5 days, $1,500.*

CALIFORNIA **The Russell Techniques of Racing Course.** Jim Russell opened England's first racing school in 1957. In 1980 he established The Russell Racing School, with headquarters at legendary Laguna Seca Raceway in Monterey. Russell's Techniques of Racing course is 3 days of intensive training to master driving on a challenging track with dips and hills—elevation changes equivalent to an 18-story building. Passing is permitted throughout the course as students work on their lap times. During the whole 3 days, you spend only 45 min. to 1 hour in class; the rest if the time you're on the track—either driving or being critiqued by an instructor. Graduates are eligible for regional SCCA licenses.

Students who complete the Techniques of Racing program may move on to the 3-day Advanced Racing Course, where you drive a high-powered, open-wheel Formula Russell car, with rotary engines, wings, slick tires, 5-speed gearboxes—and capable of 150 mph. Most people come back at a later time to take the advanced course, but the schedule can be arranged if you wish to take the two courses back to back. Graduates of the advanced class may compete in the 18-car USAC/Russell Championship Series, a 2-day race weekend run monthly at Laguna Seca.

In the techniques course, students have no liability for damage to Russell cars for the first accident. Advanced students have a $2,500 deductible for first-time damages. Courses are taught year-round, rain or shine. Class size is generally 15 students; some double classes have 30 students. The student-to-instructor ratio is about 5:1. Helmets and racing suits are provided. Meals are on your own except for the third day, when drivers are treated to a catered lunch. A list of hotels that offer discounts to Russell students is provided. *Russell Racing School, 1023 Monterey Hwy., Salinas, CA 93908, tel. 408/372–7223, fax 408/372–0458. Year-round: 3-day racing course, $1,895; 3-day advanced program, $2,495; race weekend, $1,395.*

OREGON **Pitarresi ProDrive Grand Prix Racing Course.** Pitarresi, a popular Portland school, offers one of the best hands-on racing programs—one of the few programs nationwide that is accepted by the SCCA, ICSCC, and IMSA. The school believes that to become a race car driver you need to be behind the wheel of a race car. So in their 3- or 4-day Grand Prix Competition Racing Course, you spend very little time in the classroom and a lot of time in the cockpit.

Students spend 3 hours in specially equipped Toyota Camry SkidCars before getting up to speed on the race track. Then you move to a brief classroom session, in which you learn how to apply the SkidCar principles (controlling your vehicle in slick road conditions at low speeds) to high-speed racing cars. You also learn basic racecraft—race rules and track courtesy. For the next two days, you're on the track with an instructor, driving your race-prepared, mid-engined, rear-drive Toyota MR2 on the same lines as champion race drivers. An optional fourth day puts you in a Formula sports racer, translating the skills you've acquired to a much quicker pace.

Pitarresi ProDrive is at Portland International Raceway, 10 minutes from downtown Portland. All the MR2s have roll cages and safety harnesses; instructors ride along to give instant help and encouragement. Helmets and driving suits provided. Information on Portland hotels and restaurants is available from the school. Grand Prix racing classes are small—from 1 to 4 people with one instructor. Students are liable for damage to cars. *Pitarresi ProDrive Racing School, 1940 N. Victory Blvd., Portland, OR 97217, tel. 503/285–4449, fax 503/285–3524. Mar.–Oct.: 3-day course, $1,995; 4-day course, $2,795.*

SOURCES

ORGANIZATIONS The two organizations that award accreditation to racing schools are the **Sports Car Club of America** (9033 E. Easter Pl., Englewood, CO 80112, tel. 303/ 694–7222, fax 303/694–7391) and the **International Motor Sports Association Inc.** (Box 10709, Tampa, FL 33679-0709, tel. 813/877–4672, fax 813/876–4604). Write to them for lists of other approved programs.

PERIODICALS *Racer* (Racer Communications Inc., 1371 E. Warner Ave., Suite E, Tustin, CA 92680, tel. 714/533–4083), a monthly magazine with color photos and high-quality graphics, includes articles on current racing issues and profiles of the sport's daring participants. Published twice a month, *On Track* (OT Publishing, Inc., Box 8509, Fountain Valley, CA 92728, tel. 714/966–1131, fax 714/556–9776) gives in-depth coverage of the international racing scene. *Super Stock and Drag Illustrated* (1655 Broadway, New York, NY 10023, tel.

800/333–3007 or 515/247–7631) is a monthly magazine for drag racing buffs—both those who do it and those who prefer to read about it. In addition to articles about racing, SCCA's *Sports Car* Magazine (see address above) lists race and driving-school schedules. It's published monthly, and you don't need to be a member of SCCA to subscribe.

BOOKS One of the best how-to books on racing is *Bob Bondurant on High Performance Driving,* by Bob Bondurant. It is available from Classic Motorbooks (Box 1, Osceola, WI 54020, tel. 800/ 826–6600, fax 715/294–4448). *Drag Racing: Drive to Win,* written by Frank Hawley, describes his own early racing career and gives inside information on the complexities of drag racing. *Drag Racing: How to Get Started,* also by Frank Hawley, gives all the details a novice needs to enter and enjoy his or her first race. Both books are available through Frank Hawley's Drag Racing School (Box 140369, Gainesville, FL 32614, tel. 904/373–7223). The Bridgestone Winter Driving School (Box 774167, Steamboat Springs, CO 80477, tel. 800/949–7543) publishes the *Winter Driving Manual,* a thorough booklet based on the same winter driving techniques that have made the school such a success.

VIDEOS Watching a video before you enroll will give you a good idea of what's involved in a racing or driving course. Southard's Racing School (Box 1810, New Smyrna Beach, FL 32170, tel. 904/428–3307) has dozens of technical videos on racing, such as *Short Track Asphalt Driving Techniques* and *Chassis Tuning for Oval Track Racing.* The Bridgestone Winter Driving School (Box 774167, Steamboat Springs, CO 80477, tel. 800/949–7543) has a video, *Winter Driving,* that illustrates the school's theory and techniques for driving safely and confidently on slippery roads. Those particularly interested in drag racing will enjoy *From Street to Strip,* produced by Frank Hawley's Drag Racing School (Box 140369, Gainesville, FL 32614, tel. 904/373–7223).

River Rafting

By Lee R. Schreiber

If the river is the highway into the wilderness, then the raft is the ideal mode of transportation. Rafts can take you places that roads, trails, and footpaths cannot. Then there are the white-water thrills: Spray that soaks your clothes and stings your face, the roar of rushing water that drowns out your screams, the rolls and drops that leave your heart somewhere back *there.* Unlike canoes, rafts are stable in these high or rough waters, and unlike kayaks, they can carry many passengers and their gear, not to mention the vegetables, fruits, and other ingredients that make for delicious open-air meals.

The United States has some of the most diverse and scenic river highways in the world, from mild to wild, particularly in the mountains of the West. Many people think the Colorado is the finest rafting river in North America, but there are many that are almost its equal. While some rivers are not dammed and raftable only during spring runoff, there are others, particularly in the Northeast, whose flow is maintained at runnable levels from spring through fall by regular water releases from the dams.

Many reputable outfitters can show you America's rivers on guided trips, which make even the rowdiest of this white water accessible to the inexperienced. On these trips, the greatest risks are banged shins, sprained ankles, and nasty sunburns. Today's rafts are designed to smack against waves or rocks and bend almost in two without breaking or flipping over, and only occasionally get "wrapped" (around a rock) or "Maytagged" (tossed and turned, as if in a spin cycle). Far from being the high-risk sport that it is often perceived to be, the odds of being seriously injured while white-water rafting on a commercial trip are about 25,000 to 1, and there is barely one death per million river runners.

Your rafting experience depends first of all on the river. Most provide serenity and the opportunity to catch wildlife unaware, to reach areas deep in the wilderness that would otherwise be accessible only by long hikes. Other rivers stand out for their white water. River rats classify white water as *Class I* (mild, with slow current and small riffles), *Class II* (beginner, with moderate waves and rapids, few obstructions, and easy maneuvering), *Class III* (intermediate, with swift current and more obstructions), *Class IV* (advanced, with powerful waves and numerous obstacles; previous experience recommended), *Class V* (expert, with complex and difficult rapids with very strong current and many obstructions). *Class VI* waters are considered unrunnable, entailing probable serious injury. In general, the steeper the river's drop in altitude, the faster the water and the wilder the ride. (When you encounter water too rough to tackle safely, outfitters either portage around

---

Outdoors writer Lee R. Schreiber, the founding managing editor of *Golf Illustrated* and *Backpacking Journal* and author of seven books, has traveled the world in search of a place to enjoy, simultaneously, his three passions: white-water rafting, poker, and a good cigar.

the rapid or resort to "lining"—that is, they empty each boat of all but cargo, then attach it to one or more ropes held by several crew members, who walk along the shore guiding the craft through the white water while you go around the rapid on foot.)

Outfitters run some terrific Class IV–V water in the East, including West Virginia's New, Gauley, and Cheat rivers, but almost all the runs are day trips. In the West, trips may last a week or two because western rivers themselves are longer, with longer rapids, longer stretches of flatwater, and more and bigger wilderness areas than those found in the East.

The craft you ride varies from outfitter to outfitter and even from trip to trip; sometimes you can bounce around from one kind of boat to another on the same trip. Some outfitters use *motorized rafts,* which allow you to cover more miles of river in less time. The downside is the intrusion of noise and modern technology into the wilderness. You may raft in a so-called *oar boat,* on which a guide takes the oars and does the work; no previous rafting experience is required, even on rivers with some serious white water. Or you can run the river in a *paddle boat,* where you and the other passengers wield the oars under the guidance of an experienced paddle captain; here you may need experience and a certain level of fitness, depending on the water you'll be covering. Some outfitters also give you the option of traveling in *inflatable kayaks* (called duckies or orange torpedoes); these usually accommodate a single person and require some skill and strenuous paddling. Still other outfitters use *dories*—flat-bottomed, splay-sided wooden row boats with upturned ends, which can usually hold 4 passengers plus a guide, and may come equipped with back rests and cushioned seats. Major John Wesley Powell used them to explore the Grand Canyon in 1869—but you can be sure that his craft didn't have padding.

Beyond that, every outfitter has its own style. Some take care of all the camp chores and discourage guest participation, while others invite it. Every trip has its own pace, though usually you spend 4 or 5 hours a day on the river and the rest of the time swimming in placid pools, picnicking, or hiking. Food on raft trips is invariably tasty (though the freshest foods, like Cornish hens or rack of lamb, come early on, and the vegetable lasagnas show up toward the end); but some outfitters have more interesting menus than others. On multiday trips, particularly down the great western rivers, expect to pay between $100 and $200 per day.

CHOOSING THE RIGHT TRIP

Outfitting your own trip is recommended only for experienced rafters. First pick the river you want to run, then ask several outfitters who run it the following questions:

Are you affiliated with any regional or national organizations? Most companies are; it lends a certain legitimacy and provides a higher authority in case a problem arises.

Are you licensed by the state? Licensing requirements vary from state to state, but, in general, they keep outfitters and guides alert to safety and environmental rules.

What is your safety record, and what are your safety procedures? All rafters should wear life preservers, and commercial outfitters require them (and provide them to all their guests). Helmets are a good idea on Class V and sometimes Class IV water; if you'll be rafting waters with those ratings, ask whether helmets will be provided.

How long has the company been in business? A company that has been in business for a few years is apt to have systematized its operations so that trips go smoothly.

What's the cost and what's included? Ask specifically about ground transportation, camping and personal gear, meals, and drinks, since policies vary widely from one outfitter to the next.

In general, outfitters provide all meals during the trip, as is true on all trips described below unless otherwise noted. However, if the itinerary has you overnighting in a town before your river journey begins or after it ends, you may be on your own for meals then. Once the journey has begun, most outfitters serve unlimited water, juice, lemonade, or punch both on and off the river; soda, beer, or wine is usually available at least off the river and sometimes on, and there may or may not be a charge.

As for camping gear, many companies provide a tent but charge extra to rent you a sleeping bag and pad (or ask you to make your own arrangements); unless otherwise noted, that's the case on all the trips described below. Personal gear is another matter. You may need a wetsuit, and it may or may not be included.

Usually included, but not always, is shuttle service to and from the put-in point—known more informally among river runners as, simply, put-in; when it is, it's usually from some central point and not from the airport. However, some firms shuttle you to put-in but not from take-out. Don't forget about your car and your luggage; some outfitters transport your luggage from put-in to take-out at no extra cost, but charge extra to bring your vehicle.

All prices quoted below are adult fares, per person; discounts are usually available for youngsters on trips appropriate for them.

What are your guides' qualifications? Ask how long they have been working with the outfitter and how many years of rafting experience they have. Make sure that they have first-aid certification, if not specialized wilderness first-aid and swift-water rescue training. Knowledge of the history, flora, fauna, and geology of the area is a decided plus.

What's the passenger-to-guide ratio? There is usually one staffer for every 3 to 6 passengers.

How many people will there be in your rafting party? The norm is between 20 and 25. If there are too many in your group, you lose a sense of wilderness that is one of the pleasures of river rafting.

How much white water will there be on the trip? If you are looking for rowdy white water, you don't want to end up on a sedate float trip—or vice versa. If you want to ride in an oar boat or an inflatable kayak, find out how much paddling experience is required. Most outfitters want paddlers to be in good physical condition, and some give a Class V paddler's test, with exercises to evaluate heart, grip, lungs, and mental adaptability; some even give a prerun oral and written white-water safety exam.

What kind of boats do you use? Find out whether the outfitter uses oar boats, paddle boats, motor-powered rafts, or other crafts. Ask about the maximum boat capacity, and find out how many people will be riding in each boat (some outfitters routinely don't fill boats to capacity). Find out whether the outfitter's boats are self-bailing. Most top companies have gradually replaced their fleets with self-bailing rafts, which are harder to flip than rafts that aren't; a boat full of water is unstable and hard to keep level. If you'd like to paddle part or all of the distance in an inflatable kayak, and you have the experience to do so, ask whether they're available.

What's the food like? Some outfitters stick to home-cooking, while others aim for Continental flair and ethnic accents; Dutch-oven cooking—that is, baking in a closed pot over an open fire—is fairly commonplace.

What kind of service do you provide? Some outfitters pamper guests and won't allow them to lift a finger; others let them help with camp chores and still others insist on it. Decide what type of service you want and then find the outfitter that provides it.

What are your days like? Find out how much time you spend on the river, and what passengers do the rest of the time. Ask whether people on this trip usually see wildlife, and what kind; and find out, if you're interested, whether there's fishing, what people catch, and whether rods are provided.

What conditions should I expect? Ask about the weather—and find out whether it'll be buggy. You don't want to find out only after put-in that it's the height of black fly or mosquito season.

Do you have a list of previous clients whom I can contact? Reputable outfitters are happy to share the names of previous guests. Talks with them may reveal things about the trip that'll make you decide for or against it.

How far in advance do I need to book? In most cases, it's between 2 and 6 months, but sometimes you must commit yourself even farther ahead, as much as a year in advance. If you have your heart set on going on a specific sold-out trip, you can always call at the last minute. Cancellations do occur.

MAJOR PLAYERS

AMERICAN RIVER TOURING ASSOCIATION

Known as ARTA, this nonprofit corporation, in business since 1963, offers about 20 different trips in 5 western states from April through October. Most runs have at least Class III water, appropriate for families and first-timers, while several trips have Class V stretches that challenge the expert paddler. ARTA boats include both 14-foot paddle boats that carry up to 6 guests and a guide, and 18-foot oar boats that accommodate 2 to 4 plus a guide; about half its guests ride in oar boats on longer trips (while most ride in paddle rafts on 1- to 3-day trips). You can choose an inflatable kayak on about half of ARTA trips; an equal proportion of the fleet is self-bailing—a little under half of the oar rafts, nearly three-quarters of paddle rafts, and all of the inflatables. Food is first-rate if not fancy, and guides are personable and well-educated, usually ecology-oriented or knowledgeable about local history, with an average 6 years' rafting experience. There is usually one guide trained in either swiftwater rescue or wilderness first aid on every trip, and the ratio of guests to staff ranges from 3:1 to 6:1 (the lower ratio applies to difficult trips where there are no paddle rafts and lighter boats are required). An ARTA trip is informal, and guides make a point of eating with guests. If you want to help in the kitchen, fine; if you want to read a book, that's okay, too. The staff, however, won't set up your tents (they show you how) or wash your dishes (that's up to you). Prices are $100 to $140 per day (24000 Casa Loma Rd., Groveland, CA 95321, tel. 209/962–7873 or 800/323–2782, fax 209/962–4819).

DVORAK'S KAYAK AND RAFTING EXPEDITIONS

Bill and Jaci Dvořák, whose family-owned outfit, founded in 1969, is one of the finest in the country, operate on 10 western rivers through 29 canyons from March through October. They use 12-foot paddle rafts that accommodate up to 5 passengers and a guide as well as 16-foot oar boats that accommodate up to 7 passengers and a guide; most of the fleet is self-bailing. Both inflatable and hard-shell kayaks are available for instructional purposes only. Guides have CPR, first-aid, and swift-water rescue training, and an average 3 years' rafting experience; on most rafting trips, there's a guide for every 5 passengers. The Dvořáks will take care of all the camp chores, but you're free to pitch in if you want. You'll find lots of fresh fruit and vegetables on the menu, along with western omelets at breakfast and chicken enchiladas and fajitas at dinner. Prices on the Green River, which are representative, average about $145 a day (17921 U.S. 285, Suite F, Nathrop, CO 81236, tel. 719/539–6851 or 800/824–3795, fax 719/539–3378).

ECHO: THE WILDERNESS COMPANY
One of the best among several strong California-based outfitters, this firm has been in business since 1971 and runs family trips, wine-tasting trips, fly-fishing trips, and classical- and bluegrass-music trips on some of the wildest, most scenic rivers in California, Oregon, and Idaho, from April through September. On every trip, you can opt for either an oar boat, which accommodates 2 to 4, or a paddle boat, which accommodates 4 to 6; single and double inflatable kayaks are available on the Middle Fork, Main Salmon, and Rogue, but not the American or Tuolumne. The outfitter has a reputation for hiring adaptable, experienced guides with strong personalities; all those on the Rogue,

Middle Fork, Main Salmon, and Tuolumne are certified in advanced first aid and swift-water rescue, while many are emergency medical technicians and several are paramedics. They have on average 8 years' experience on the Main Salmon, 4 years' on the Rogue. There is a guide for every 4 guests on the Middle Fork and Tuolumne—which require precision boat handling—and a guide for every 4½ guests on more forgiving rivers. Marinated leg of lamb, baked salmon, and vegetarian lasagna are signature dishes. Trip costs range from $100 to $180 a day (6529 Telegraph Ave., Oakland, CA 94609-1113, tel. 510/652-1600 or 800/652-3246, fax 510/652-3987).

FAR FLUNG ADVENTURES This outfitter, founded in 1975, operates year-round, mostly on well-traveled rivers such as the Salt in Arizona and the Rio Grande in northern New Mexico. But it is really known for its trips in Texas, in and around Big Bend National Park. Guides are friendly professionals with an average of 600 days' river-rafting experience; all are trained in emergency medicine and swift-water rescue. There's one for every 3 to 6 guests. You ride in 14- to 16-foot oar or paddle boats accommodating 4 to 6 passengers plus a guide, and all craft used in white water are self-bailing. Meals are hearty, not gourmet: breakfasts with bacon or sausage, dinners with steak and potatoes, and make-your-own-sandwich lunches. Average cost of a 7-day trip is $100 per day (Box 377, Terlingua, TX 79852, tel. 915/371-2489 or 800/359-2627, fax 915/371-2325).

GRAND CANYON EXPEDITIONS COMPANY Though most customers fly into and out of Las Vegas, there's no glitz in Mike Denoyer's relatively small operation. Yet this outfitter has been called the Rolls-Royce of Colorado River companies: Every detail of every trip is just a little bit better than on most other outfitters' excursions. You can opt for motorized raft runs that take 8 days, dory expeditions that take 14, or 8-day specialty trips for students of astronomy, geology, photography and the like. Though the capacity of all rafts is 20, there are never more than 14 people in a boat (four in a

dory). The 8-day trips run around $200 per day (Box 0, Kanab, UT 84741, tel. 801/644-2691 or 800/544-2691, fax 801/644-2699).

HOLIDAY RIVER EXPEDITIONS This operation, founded in 1966, runs 12 different sections of 8 rivers in 3 western states from May through September; the only constant is the high quality of the equipment, guides, and food. The outfitter uses oar or paddle boats, depending on the stretch of water they're running and the interests of the guests on the trip. Oar-powered boats carry from 4 to 6, paddle boats from 6 to 8; boats are 16 feet to 17½ feet long, and all are self-bailing. Inflatable kayaks are available on most trips. Guides are a diverse lot, but have an average 4½ years of rafting experience and are trained in river rescue, first aid, and CPR, some at advanced levels. They set up camp and cook the meals, but guests are responsible for setting up their own tents; if you want to help with the cooking, you're welcome to pitch in. The passenger-to-guide ratio averages 5:1. Most trips are geared for novice or intermediate paddlers and average $140 per day (544 E. 3900 S, Salt Lake City, UT 84107, tel. 801/266-2087 or 800/624-6323, fax 801/266-1448).

HUGHES RIVER EXPEDITIONS With nearly 30 years experience as a professional guide, Jerry Hughes runs a very tight ship at this family-owned operation, founded in 1976. He offers relatively few trips, most on Idaho and eastern Oregon rivers from May into September; the bulk of trips are on the Middle Fork of the Salmon and the Snake through Hells Canyon. On Hughes trips, the staff attends to virtually every detail, right down to hors d'oeuvres and dinner (roast Cornish hens and the like); by the time you reach camp at the end of each day, the Hughes crew has already pitched the tents, unloaded the gear, and organized the kitchen. Most guides are 35 to 45 years old with an average 12 years of rafting experience; everyone has first-aid and CPR training, and many have emergency medicine, advanced first-aid, or swift-water rescue training (and Hughes has a program of financial incentives to encourage all its guides to acquire the more advanced skills). Water conditions permitting, you can opt for paddle boats or inflatable kayaks as well as oar boats; small, more difficult streams like the Middle Owyhee require smaller and lighter craft, while larger streams are safe for larger oar rafts. All guest boats are self-bailing. The food includes steaks, lobster tail, halibut, and thick-cut pork chops, along with an array of fresh fruit and vegetables; baking-powder biscuits, whole-wheat cornbreads, muffins, coffee cakes, and layer cakes keep the Dutch ovens busy. The superb service comes at a price; most trips cost around $200 a day (Box 217, Cambridge, ID 83610, tel. 208/257–3477, fax 208/257–3476).

OARS This operation, whose name is an acronym for Outdoor Adventure River Specialists, has been leading trips on western rivers since 1968. Operating from April into October, it runs several trips in affiliation with other top companies, such as Holiday River, ARTA, and Mountain Travel-Sobek. You can opt for oar or paddle boats and, on some trips, dories and inflatable kayaks. Some 60% of the fleet is self-bailing. Meals always include fresh fruit and vegetables; cooks whip up hearty hot breakfasts, bring out sandwiches and salads at lunch, and bake lasagna or grill salmon steaks for dinner; one night, there's even a Mexican feast. Guides have first-aid and CPR training and an average of 7 years rafting experience. Passengers aren't routinely asked to help with camp chores, but it's always an option; about half the people on any given trip pitch in. There's usually one guide for every 4 passengers on oar trips, one for every 6 passengers on paddle trips. The 6-day run on the Main Salmon costs about $200 per day (Box 67, Angels Camp, CA 95222, tel. 209/736–2924, 209/736–4677, or 800/346– 6277, fax 209/736–2902).

and unlike most area operators—whose excursions last no longer than a weekend—it has a rafting package that keeps you on the water for 5 days, combining river runs and camping on the Penobscot with a night in cabins around a lakefront lodge. The West Branch of the Penob, as it's known among river rats, is one of the most scenic runs in the East, full of moose, osprey, eagles, and other wildlife. It's also one of the most challenging and dramatic runs in the region, thanks to such natural wonders as the awesome 2-mile-long Ripogenus Gorge, where the river descends a stomach-dropping 70 feet per mile over Class V rapids with names like the Exterminator and through the white water maze called the Cribworks. The water then smooths out beneath Mt. Katahdin, Maine's tallest peak, before challenging Nesowadnehunk Falls and the finale, Pockwockamus Falls. Except for one one-mile stretch on the upper Penobscot, which is not suitable for kids (they get shuttled around it), this is good for families. You ride in 14-foot, self-bailing paddle rafts with a guide in each; though each boat can handle up to 10, it usually carries only 8 passengers. The outfitter provides hearty meals, not gourmet fare; barbecued steak is the standard lunch, and lobster puts in appearances at dinner. Campsites are alongside pools where you can often swim—a possibility despite the latitude, since Maine's rivers drain from shallow lakes and run warmer than those in some other parts of the country. You may help with camp chores or just kick back. Expect mosquitoes at night, temperatures in the mid-70s to mid-80s, and water temperatures about 60°F. *Unicorn Expeditions, Box T, Brunswick, ME 04011, tel. 207/ 725–2255 or 800/864–2676. Mid-June–early Sept.: 6 days, $664. Sign up 2 months in advance.*

FAVORITE TRIPS

THE NORTHEAST

MAINE On the Penobscot. Unicorn Expeditions has been running trips on the wild rivers of New York and Maine since 1979,

---

THE SOUTHWEST

ARIZONA After John Wesley Powell on Motorized Rafts. Grand Canyon Expeditions covers in 8 days much of the same 300 river miles that it took Major John Wesley Powell a month to explore, a stretch of the Colorado that is probably unsurpassed in the world for its combination of white-water challenges, scenic virtues, and opportunities for off-river exploration. The grandest canyon of them all—from 4 to 18 miles wide and averaging a mile in depth—is just as incredible from water level. On its walls, nearly 2 billion years of the earth's past is visible, along with every color in the rainbow. In the desert that borders the river on both sides, cactus and wildflowers proliferate, while lush ferns blanket the glens into which magnificent waterfalls cascade. You are likely to see bighorn sheep, mule deer, coyote, and ring-tailed cats along the river as well as in the tributary canyons. Each day, you may spot hawks, golden eagles, falcons, great blue herons, or egrets. Deep within the "grand, gloomy depths" that Powell described, there is glorious white water—about 200 negotiable rapids in all—not to mention dozens of hikes to side canyons such as Havasu, the ancestral home of the Havasupai Indians. Here, the red cliffs, green vegetation, and turquoise water are truly spectacular. Some rafters are reluctant to ride a river in a motorized craft, but this outfitter's 37-foot, self-bailing rafts are spacious, seaworthy, and nonintrusive. From put-in at Lees Ferry in Grand Canyon National Park to take-out at Pearce Ferry on Lake Mead, the outfitter's attention to its guests is unflagging. The guides' Dutch-oven cooking is simple but superb. Campsites are diverse and scenic—from sugary sand beaches to a site of ancient Indian ruins. *Grand Canyon Expeditions Company, Box 0, Kanab, UT 84741, tel. 801/644-2691 or 800/544-2691, fax 801/644-2699. Mid-Apr.–mid-Sept.: 8 days, $1,700. Sign up 6 months in advance.*

ARIZONA **Grand Canyon by Dory.** The gorgeous, flat-keeled wooden dories used by Grand Canyon Dories (co-owned by OARS) are akin to those that Major John Wesley Powell took on one of the first expeditions through the canyon in 1869. They offer a totally different experience from conventional or motorized rafts. From the oarsman's perspective, they are more responsive than rafts while demanding better knowl-

edge of the intricacies of the current and the placement of the rocks. For passengers, the ride through riffles is friskier yet the pace of the trip is more leisurely: While motorized craft run the canyon in about 8 days and oar boats in 14, Grand Canyon Dories' trip takes 19 days in early spring and fall, 16 days from spring through late summer.

This company, founded in 1971, has a 3:1 guest-to-crew ratio—probably the lowest on the river—and the guides are among the most experienced in the canyon; their average age is around 38, and nearly a third are women. The food is basic American: hot breakfasts, sandwiches and salads for lunch, and lasagna, salmon, steak, or chicken for dinner. Campsites are on riverside beaches. *Grand Canyon Dories, Box 67, Angels Camp, CA 95222, tel. 209/736-0805 or 800/346-6277. Late Apr.–late Sept.: 16 days, $2,928. Apr. and Oct.: 19 days, $2,990. Sign up 12 months in advance.*

ARIZONA **Oar Boats Down the Grand Canyon.** Dick McCallum, the founder and owner of Expeditions, Inc., a small family outfit, has been running rivers throughout the world since 1957. Expeditions' trips down the Colorado are mainly on 18-foot oar-powered boats, though there is a paddle boat option for those who are willing to make that commitment and even a kayak for experienced paddlers. McCallum and company don't use motors, so the main sound is that of the river rushing through the canyon.

The 14-day trip covers the 226 river miles from Lees Ferry to Diamond Creek, a stretch offering varied experiences away from the river. Campsites might be on wide beaches or on cozy inlets. The guest-to-crew ratio is never more than 4:1, and the guides are all experienced hands who take pride in their knowledge of river lore and love to share it. Expeditions cuisine includes fresh produce throughout the trip. Dinners may be full-scale Mexican feasts, sautéed chicken breasts or pizza prepared in the Dutch oven; breakfasts are hot or cold, as lavish as you want; lunches are usually cold cuts, tuna, and egg salad.

Active people who like to hike take these runs, because there's plenty of time to explore off the river, and though McCallum encourages guests' participation in all aspects of the trip, he respects a preference to take it easy. *Expeditions, Inc., 625 N. Beaver St., Flagstaff, AZ 86001, tel. 520/779–3769, fax 520/774–4001. Apr. and Oct.: 14 days, $2,000. May–Sept.: 12 days, $1,875. Price includes sleeping gear but not tent; sign up 12 months in advance.*

ARIZONA **On the Salt River through the Sonoran Desert.** Winding deep in the White Mountains of Arizona, the Salt cuts through a series of rugged granite gorges in the Sonoran Desert wilderness. In early spring, when the snow at the headwaters melts and bright wildflowers dot the desert floor, Far Flung Adventures' rafting season comes into bloom.

Far Flung's 5-day, 52-mile trip down the Salt from the Highway 60 bridge to the headwaters of the Roosevelt Reservoir near the Highway 288 bridge is chock full of white water challenges and hiking opportunities in and around the side canyons, which reveal the many facets of the desert ecosystem. A portion of the trip passes through the White Mountain Apache Indian Reservation. Guides row you past woodlands of juniper, oak, and piñon into areas of arid desert vegetation. Most campsites are on wooded beaches and sandbars. If you have rafting experience, you can opt to paddle. Most of the white water is rated Class II–III, but there are at least a half-dozen tricky Class IV drops.

Temperatures on the Upper Sonoran desert can range from 70°F to 100°F during the day and drop as low as 40°F at night. March and April are considered optimal months for weather and white-water conditions. *Far Flung Adventures, Box 377, Terlingua, TX 79852, tel. 915/371–2489 or 800/359–2627, fax 915/ 371–2325; or Box 2804, Globe, AZ 85502, tel. 520/425–7272. Early Feb.–mid-May: 5 days, $700. Sign up 2–3 months in advance.*

TEXAS **Floating the Rio Grande's Lower Canyons.** Far Flung's 7-day trip through an 85-mile stretch in the Chihuahuan Desert, in 14- to 16-foot paddle or oar boats that accommodate 4 to 6 passengers and a guide, is not a run you make for unadulterated white-water thrills. Generally, the white water you encounter on the first 4 or 5 days is relatively mild, including Big Canyon (Class II–III), Palmas Canyon (Class III), and Rodeo (Class II–III); the sixth day brings the best run of white water on the trip, Burro Bluff rapid (Class III–IV). The attractions here are scenery and wildlife. Throughout the run, the river is lined with limestone cliffs with names like Las Vegas de las Ladrones (Outlaw Flat) and Complejo del Caballo (Horse Highlands); beyond them are spectacularly sculpted side canyons. Stay alert and you may catch a glimpse of a peregrine falcon, bighorn sheep, cougar, or even a bear; more than 400 different species of birds have been catalogued in the canyons, and close to 100 species may be sighted during spring and fall migrations. In the early spring, wildflowers abound, and in late summer you can gather prickly pear and pitaya—the fruit is ripe then and delicious. Autumn, with its cooler temperatures and higher water levels, is the peak time to explore the many tributary canyons, where you usually make camp. Group size ranges from a minimum of 4 to a maximum of 16. *Far Flung Adventures, Box 377, Terlingua, TX 79852, tel. 915/371–2489 or 800/359–4138, fax 915/ 371–2325. Monthly, year-round, coinciding with the full moon: 7 days, $650. Sign up 1 month in advance.*

TEXAS **Floating the Remotest Rio Grande.** This 65-mile, 7-day run through two magnificent limestone canyons, in the eastern part of Big Bend National Park along the Mexican border, is easily the most remote in Texas: Put-in at Talley is a 2-hour drive from Rio Grande Village along the eastern side of the Chisos Mountains, past the ruins of the Mariscal Mine. The scenery is the reward. After about 3 miles on the river, the expedition enters Mariscal Canyon within the Chihuahuan Desert and continues southeasterly between 1,600-foot cliffs to the Tight Squeeze, the only really challenging rapid on the entire trip: Here, the entire river flows through a narrow channel no wider than a raft. Subsequent miles bring you to the unusual Cactus Garden, across the border in Mexico, where you might find more than one of a half-dozen cactus varieties blooming simultaneously—not to mention many arroyos and canyons, 105°F hot springs you can soak in, and such picturesque Mexican villages as San Vicente and Boquillas. Among the most notable campsites is the broad, grassy stretch at Cross Canyons, where ancient Indian petroglyphs are displayed on a huge boulder. The Mexican-style egg dishes prepared at breakfast go right along with the scenery.

Conditions are usually best in spring and fall: Peak seasons are March and April, and October and November, when temperatures are 80°F to 90°F by day and 50°F to 60°F at night (down from summer highs that can reach a brutal 110°F). Water temperatures are generally at least 65°F in spring, more than 80°F in summer. Water levels are usually highest from August to October because of late-summer thundershowers. Far Flung uses 14- to 16-foot oar boats accommodating 3 to 6 passengers and a guide, but if there are at least 5 willing paddlers, you can opt for a paddle boat—and no experience is required. *Far Flung Adventures, Box 377, Terlingua, TX 79852, tel. 915/371–2489 or 800/359–4138, fax 915/371–2325. Year-round: 7 days, $600. Sign up 1 month in advance.*

UTAH The Colorado River through Cataract Canyon. Sheri Griffith Expeditions' 5-day run, named for the 36-mile-long canyon that is its major feature, actually covers 96 river miles in southern Utah's spectacular Canyonlands National Park. Anasazi and Fremont Indians lived here 700 to 1,500 years ago, and you can still see evidence of their existence along the river, along with 300 million years of geological history. Because of the canyon's diverse environments, many species of plants and wildlife thrive, including cacti and wildflowers, mule deer, bobcats, coyotes, muskrats, owls,

and eagles; the herd of desert bighorn sheep here is the largest in the West.

July, when the water level drops and the rapids become more moderate, is the best time for first-time river runners and youngsters, though the trip is never really suitable for children under 10. In May and June, you can experience some of the region's most challenging white water. In any season, the biggest thrills come on your third day out, when the Colorado flows into the Green, doubles in size, and drops precipitously over at least 24 rapids in 17 miles, including a Class V stretch that includes Big Drops, Little Niagara, Satan's Gut, and Mile-Long, a series of sheer drops and powerful white water. You spend the last day on Lake Powell, where you climb aboard a chartered aircraft for a 30-minute trip back to Moab, the trip's starting point and the site of the lot where guests' cars are parked. The trip is in 18-foot, 6-passenger oar-powered rafts; paddle boats are available by advance arrangement at some water levels (sometimes at additional cost). Campsites are on sandy beaches, and meals are western-style—grilled steaks with fried potatoes, southwestern barbecued chicken and steamed vegetables, fajitas and a Mexican casserole, with Dutch-oven cakes and crisps for dessert. All guides are trained in first aid, CPR, wilderness medicine, and river rescue. Griffith also offers luxury trips, with a fancier menu; staffers break and set up camp each day, so that all you have to do is sit back and relax. *Sheri Griffith Expeditions, Box 1324, Moab, UT 84532, tel. 801/259–8229 or 800/332–2439, fax 801/259–2226. May–mid-Sept.: 5 days, $763. Price does not include tent but does include flight and ground transportation from take-out to Moab; sign up 3–6 months in advance.*

UTAH Floating the Green River through Dinosaur National Monument. "Bus" Hatch, who built his first wooden boat in 1929, was one of the pioneers of the river-running industry. His heirs are still providing first-rate service on this 47-mile stretch of the Green River in Dinosaur National Monument—a relatively easy trip with mostly Class II–III white water.

Beginning near Maybelle, Colorado, at the northern border of the Monument, Hatch River Expeditions' 5-day run of the Green passes through Lodore, Whirlpool, and Split Mountain canyons—all serpentine, high-walled chasms, but each distinct: In Lodore, the bright green box elder trees contrast starkly with the vermillion-tinted cliffs; both Whirlpool and Split canyons have bone-white sandstone walls. En route, you're likely to see bighorn sheep, deer, beaver, and otter. Releases from the dam at Flaming Gorge Reservoir sustain the river at runnable levels throughout the season. Mostly, the Hatches use 18-foot, self-bailing oar boats with 5 passengers, but paddle options are available as well. Of the campsites, Rippling Brook, usually reached on the second or third day, is a favorite. In addition to a sandy beach and a scenic little swimming hole, it has a couple of good hiking areas nearby. Blueberry pancakes always appear during the trip at breakfast; rainbow trout and orange or teriyaki chicken are among the selections served at dinner. The passenger-to-guide ratio is usually 5:1 or less, and guests are usually required only to set up their own camp area, though they're welcome to help the guides with chores. *Hatch River Expeditions, Box 1150, Vernal, UT 84078, tel. 801/789–4316 or 800/342–8243. Mid-May–mid-Sept.: 5 days, $630. Price does not include tent or sleeping bag; sign up 2–3 months in advance.*

UTAH **Petroglyphs and Pottery Shards: Floating the San Juan.** The San Juan River—which runs through the San Juan Canyon, cutting and winding through the San Juan Goosenecks—is probably the least traveled of the forks that flow from the Grand Canyon on the Colorado River. That's the destination of a 5-day OARS trip, which uses oar rafts that accommodate 4 passengers and a guide. The waters are calm and usually warm in the canyon, and the surrounding area holds more archeological and geological interest than most of the Colorado River tributary trips: You see signs of the ancient Anasazi Indian culture and stunning rock formations and petroglyphs, and you may find pottery shards and ceremonial medicine sticks. The campsites are on broad, sandy beaches surrounded by tall, red-rock walls and cliffs. From put-in near Bluff, Utah, past Mexican Hat and on to take-out at Clay Hills Crossing, the 84 river miles move quickly but easily; the waters are fast-moving, but with no rapids above Class II. For that reason, this trip is excellent for novices and families with young children. *OARS, Box 67, Angels Camp, CA 95222, tel. 209/736–4677 or 800/346–6277, fax 209/ 736–2902. Late Mar.– Aug.: 5 days, $710. Price does not include tent; sign up 6–9 months in advance.*

UTAH AND COLORADO **Running the Green: White Water through Butch Cassidy Country.** Modern-day adventurers can follow in the path of such legendary figures as outlaw Butch Cassidy and explorer John Wesley Powell, who called the canyon wilderness covered by this 6-day, 86-mile Dvořák trip on the Green River "a region of wildest desolation"; it remains one of the most primitive desert wilderness areas in the United States, scattered with Indian petroglyphs, abandoned homesteads, and caves. On the river, there are more than 60 rapids, progressing from unnamed Class I riffles to Class III+ raft-rattlers such as Three Fords, Steer Ridge, and Coal Creek, which will give you a taste of white water but won't get you too wet. Though the river is navigable from April to October, Dvořák runs scheduled trips only from May into September (but will do custom trips before or after then if conditions permit). The experience is most exciting in late May and June, when the water is highest, while July and August runs provide hot weather, warm water, and good swimming; fall pairs the same warm water with crisp, clear air. You make the run in 14- to 16-foot paddle or oar rafts, most of which are self-bailing; inflatable kayaks are almost always available. Campsites along the Green are numerous and spacious. Most areas adjoin side canyons with good hiking; some are near streams and springs. Dvořák does a lot of baking, and whole-grain breads, brownies, and upside-down cakes make regular appearances, along with pancakes, French toast, and western omelets in the morning. One additional highlight to this run is worth mentioning: the flight to put-in. The air charter, which usually takes off at 8 AM on the departure day (and is included in the trip price), gives each passenger a 45-minute bird's-eye view of the entire stretch of raftable river. *Dvŏrák's Kayak and Rafting Expeditions, 17921 U.S. 285, Suite F, Nathrop, CO 81236, tel. 719/539–6851 or 800/824–3795, fax 719/539–3378. Apr.–Oct.: 6 days, $870. Price does not include tent or sleeping bag; sign up 3–6 months in advance.*

UTAH AND COLORADO **Floating the Yampa through Dinosaur National Monument.** The Yampa is the last major undammed river in the Colorado River system, and Holiday River Expeditions' 4- and 5-day trips on 46 miles of it are extraordinary, taking you through the rugged Dinosaur National Monument wilderness, and along 25 miles of the scenic Green River, notable for the exciting green waters of Whirlpool Canyon and Split Mountain Gorge. In May and June, the only months that waters are high enough for this trip, the Yampa reveals not only its several miles of Class I–III waters but also the daunting Class IV Warm Springs. En route, sheer, white tiger-striped sandstone cliffs rise to 2,000 feet and dizzying overhangs stand sentry over the fast-moving waters; you may glimpse bighorn sheep, deer, otters, beavers, golden eagles, and other birds of prey. The trip, usually made in 17½-foot self-bailing rafts that accommodate 4–6, is ordinarily an oar-powered affair because the water is so cold at this time of year, but paddle trips are available to those who have the right gear (wetsuits) and the right attitude (energetic). Both the 4- and 5-day trips allow plenty of time for hiking in and around side canyons ribboned with waterfalls or displaying ancient art on rocks and in cool caves. The campsites are well-used but well-maintained. Dinners include chicken fajitas, grilled salmon, and filet mignon plus potatoes and rice. Don't pass up the Big Drop Omelet for breakfast. *Holiday River Expeditions, 544 E. 3900 S, Salt Lake City, UT 84107, tel. 801/266–2087 or 800/624–6323,* *fax 801/ 266–1448. May–June: 4–5 days, $590–$665. Price does not include tent or sleeping bag; sign up 3 months in advance.*

THE ROCKIES

COLORADO **Classical Music River Journey on the Dolores.** Each June, musicians from the Los Angeles Philharmonic and the Santa Fe Symphony load their instruments onto one of Dvŏrák's rafts for an 8-day, 100-mile trip on the river the Spanish originally dubbed El Rio de Nuestra Señarret de Dolores (the River of Our Lady of Sorrows), through southwestern Colorado's remote Four Corners wilderness area. You ride in 14-foot paddle and oar rafts accommodating 5–7 people, over the Class III–IV torrent at Ponderosa Gorge and the Class II–III waters of Slick Rock Canyon downstream. En route, you and up to 16 other passengers are treated to 4 after-dinner fireside chamber concerts of Bach, Handel, Mozart, Ravel, Hindemith, and Dvŏrák (fifth cousin to outfitter Bill Dvŏrák) amid the tall sandstone cliffs and towering Ponderosa pines of huge natural amphitheaters. Great blue heron have been known to flock around these sessions, and Dvŏrák's symphonic journey has become something of a classic since it was first offered in 1984. Meals are appropriately highbrow, and include shrimp scampi and blackened salmon. Some say the trout fishing on the river is Colorado's best; off-river, you can explore 800- to 1,200-year-old Anasazi Indian ruins. *Dvŏrák's Kayak and Rafting Expeditions, 17921 U.S. 285, Suite F, Nathrop, CO 81236, tel. 719/539–6851 or 800/824–3795, fax 719/539–3378. June: 8 days, $1,525. Price does not include tent or sleeping bag; sign up 9–12 months in advance.*

IDAHO **Running the River of No Return: the Main Salmon.** This majestic stream, which flows through the 2.3-million-acre Frank Church River of No Return Wilderness Area—the largest designated wilderness area in North America outside Alaska—stands out for its mix of big white water and unspoiled wilderness. Everything about the Salmon is big. The river as a whole is the longest undammed river in the Lower 48, and during an average spring run-off, its white water is so fearsome that explorers Lewis and Clark decided to take another route when they saw it in 1805. (The same awesome white water prompted a 1935 National Geographic expedition to dub it "The River of No Return.") The Class III–IV Bailey Falls, Devil's Toe, Ludwig, Dried Meat, Chittum, and Vinegar are the most challenging rapids as well as some of the most colorfully named, and there are also several Class IV rapids.

ECHO's 6-day, 85-mile run, in paddle rafts, oar rafts, and inflatable kayaks, captures a big part of the Salmon's flavor, leading you from put-in at Corn Creek (a 2½-hour drive from the town of Salmon via a remote stretch of rather bad road) through a huge canyon with steep, sparsely forested walls and wide-open country of sagebrush and grass. Each day presents its bit of white water followed by stretches of calm water. Wildlife sightings are a constant, especially around the river's hot springs. Bighorn sheep wander to the river's edge, eagles swoop overhead, and an occasional moose stands in silent stateliness. On rare occasions, one of the estimated 5,000 extant mountain lions will show its face. Here and there is the evidence of human habitation: on cave walls, the handiwork of the Native Americans who called this canyon home for many centuries; as well as homesteaders' and miners' empty cabins, some of which are now museums. Among these is the former home of Jim Moore of Sylvan Hart—also known as Buckskin Bill, the last of the Mountain Men.

Campsites are among the finest on any river: wide, sandy beaches near clear side streams and hot springs. For dinner, there's vegetarian lasagna, grilled lamb, or chicken fajitas, with chocolate or lemon cake for dessert. *ECHO: The Wilderness Company, 6529 Telegraph Ave., Oakland, CA 94609, tel. 510/652–1600 or 800/652–3246, fax 510/652–3987. June–Sept.: 6 days, $910. Price in-*cludes sleeping bag, foam pads, and tent; sign up 2 months in advance.*

IDAHO **White Water and Rocky Mountain Kettle Cuisine: the Salmon's Middle Fork.** The primitive, awesome Middle Fork of the Salmon, one of the original 8 rivers to be designated Wild and Scenic by Congress in 1980, is still untamed and, for the most part, untouched; like the Main Salmon, it meanders through the Frank Church River of No Return Wilderness Area. Its white water is rated up to Class V in May and June, Class IV in July and August. It's an extraordinary stream, and the outfitters that run it are all topnotch. Even in that company, the 6-day, 105-mile trip run by Rocky Mountain River Tours (founded in 1978) stands out. Owners Dave and Sheila Mills use 2 paddleboats (accommodating 6), 4 oar boats (accommodating 4), and 4 inflatable single-passenger kayaks. There's one guide for every 4 guests.

In 1992, the Idaho Governor's Conference on Recreation and Tourism cited the Mills for their efforts to provide a quality white water rafting experience while preserving Idaho's environment. Sheila Mills's Dutch-oven cooking is an essential part of the experience, and after each trip many participants buy copies of her cookbook, *Rocky Mountain Kettle Cuisine II,* so that they can re-create, at home, her unusually interesting fare: sweet potato pancakes, fondue, or squash bread at breakfast; and for dinner, lemon-broccoli risotto with grilled catfish, Thai shrimp and Caribbean beans with papaya salsa, or crab-stuffed chicken breasts. Guides, most around 40 years old with a decade or more on the Middle Fork, are among the state's most experienced. Virtually every camp is spectacular, with a white sand beach, hot springs, and a stand of towering conifers. The Mills make camp early each day; you can help with camp chores if you wish, and there's ample opportunity to hike, fish for trout, swim, or just watch the deer, elk, mountain sheep, goats, otter, birds, and other wildlife. You can also explore caves with ancient pictographs and other Tukedeka Indian sites, old mines, homesteads, and hot springs—many accessible only by river. *Rocky Mountain River Tours, Box 2552, Boise, ID 83701, tel. 208/345–2400, 208/756–4808 June–Aug., fax 208/345–2688. May–Sept.: 6 days, $1,300–$1,500 (special rates in May). Prices include sleeping bags and pads; sign up 6 months in advance.*

IDAHO **Running the Snake River through Hells Canyon.** The Snake is one of America's Wild and Scenic Rivers, and Hughes River Expeditions' 83-mile trip down it runs through the rugged heart of the extraordinary Wallowa-Whitman National Forest straight into Hells Canyon, the country's deepest chasm (at one point, it's an incredible 8,032 feet from rim to river); the only people you're likely to see are other rafting parties, jet-boaters, and the occasional hiker, tramping the trail that skirts the river. The Snake runs high and fast between grass-covered slopes or stark basalt cliffs and beneath a scattering of ponderosa pines, producing some of the best Class III–IV white water in the Rockies. Water conditions permitting, rafts (all self-bailing) are normally 16- and 17½-foot oar boats accommodating 4 guests and a guide; 13- to 16-foot paddle rafts accommodating 4 to 6 guests and a guide; and, in less challenging waters, one-person inflatable kayaks. In between rapids, Hughes allows ample opportunity to explore abandoned homesteads and Native American petroglyphs, rock shelters, and house pits, and to look for mule deer, black bear, bighorn sheep, mountain goats, cougar, elk, golden eagles, and chukar partridge. Smallmouth bass, rainbow trout, white sturgeon, channel catfish, and steelhead proliferate in these waters, and fishing is excellent. However, since the river has been dammed, there are few beaches, so campsites are in scenic grassy clearings several yards off the water. Hughes's luxurious menu includes Cornish game hens and Dutch-oven desserts. *Hughes River Expeditions, Box 217, Cambridge, ID 83610, tel. 208/257–3477, fax 208/257–3476. Late May–Sept.: 5 days, $1,040. Price includes sleeping bags and pads; sign up 2–6 months in advance.*

IDAHO **A Wilderness Experience on the Wild Selway.** This river is one of the most remote in the Lower 48, and the surrounding 1.24-million-acre Selway–Bitterroot National Forest is among the most beautiful anywhere. To help preserve the Selway's unspoiled canyon, the Forest Service allows no more than one trip to launch each day. So ARTA's 5-day run down the Selway—which you make in 3 18-foot oar rafts and 1 paddle raft (12 guests maximum)—is among the very best wilderness experiences in the United States.

The Selway drops an average of 28 feet per mile (steep for navigable white water—the Colorado drops 8 feet per mile through the Grand Canyon), and during the river's rather short season (mid-June to mid-July), the Class IV+ white water flows up to an amazing 10,000 cubic feet per second; in one 5-mile stretch, the river falls 300 feet. In addition to such white-water challenges, the entire 47-mile trip provides top-notch catch-and-release fishing, superb campsites, scattered remnants of the great culture of the Nez Perce Indians, and extraordinary wildlife—eagles, hawks, grouse, deer, elk, bighorn sheep, mountain goats, moose, and black bear.

Campsites are small, sandy beaches edged with moss and ferns. Evergreens dominate the landscape; footpaths such as the Selway River Trail, which parallels the river, lead through the lush groves of fir and pine you can see from the river, and cedars 5 feet in diameter rise to 100 feet in the clear mountain air. *ARTA, 24000 Casa Loma Rd., Groveland, CA 95321, tel. 209/962–7873 or 800/323–2782, fax 209/962–4819. Mid-June–late-July: 5 days, $1080. Price does not include tent or sleeping bag; sign up at least a year in advance.*

WYOMING **The Grand Teton Float Trip on the Snake River.** On OARS's 5-day Snake River float trips from just south of Yellowstone, the scenery is some of the most dramatic in the United States: The ragged 10,000-foot saw-toothed granite peaks of the Grand Tetons loom above you like sentries.

This trip is perfect for kids and first-timers. Rapids are never above Class I, and for 3 days you're based at wilderness camps alongside Jackson Lake, a short float downstream and a 16-mile motor-powered ride from put-in at Flagg Ranch. En route, there are hidden estuaries and wildflower-carpeted meadows to explore, inevitably revealing moose, antelope, elk, killdeer, pelicans, bald eagles, osprey, great blue heron, beaver, sandhill cranes, or even, with luck, shaggy bison. A series of glacier-fed waterfalls is accessible by a vigorous hike; cutthroat trout are native to the waters; and the sunsets are amazing. The last 2 days are on the Snake with the motors turned off, gliding in front of the awesome Teton range. *OARS, Box 67, Angels Camp, CA 95222, tel. 209/736–2924, 209/736–4677, or 800/346–6277, fax 209/736–2902. Late May–early Sept.: 5 days, $770. Sign up 2–3 months in advance.*

THE WEST COAST

OREGON Floating the Free-Flowing Lower Owyhee. The 220-mile Owyhee is one of the longest wilderness rivers in the Lower 48, and probably one of the most obscure. That's because it winds through remote parts of northern Nevada, southwestern Idaho, and southeastern Oregon, and because it has such a short season: mid-April through May. However, it has great scenery—rugged canyons of basalt and reddish-purple rhyolite, with cliff walls rising 1,000 feet up to meet sagebrush plateaus. Since it is undammed, the Lower Owyhee, in southeastern Oregon, is only runnable when the high-mountain snows are melting and even then offers nothing more challenging than Class III waters. The 6-day, 63-mile trip from Rivers Odyssey West (ROW) shows off this wild, free-flowing stream at its best. You can opt for oar or paddle boats, or inflatable kayaks.

Enthusiastic, experienced river runners, cooks, naturalists, and entertainers all, ROW guides hold seminars on the area's natural history and varied wildlife daily. The passenger-to-guide ratio is 4:1. They happily do all the work, but encourage you to paddle, gather firewood, or help out around the campfire as the staff prepares dishes such as apple-pecan pancakes or eggs Benedict for breakfast, Thai tuna salad or the more usual cold cuts and peanut butter-and-jelly sandwiches at lunch, and, in the evening, hors d'oeuvres followed by platters of baked salmon or spinach lasagna, with double fudge brownies, pineapple upside-down cake, and other sweets for dessert. In the evenings you can go off for a soothing soak in one of the nearby hot springs, where only the occasional bighorn sheep and antelope will watch you. ROW is committed to what it calls "responsible stewardship" of the rivers on which it operates, and carries out everything that comes in, even campfire ashes. *River Odysseys West, Box 579, Coeur d'Alene, ID 83816, tel. 208/765–0841 or 800/451–6034, fax 208/667–6506. Mid-Apr.–May: 6 days, $1,100. Price includes transportation to and from Boise; sign up 2 months in advance.*

OREGON White Water on the Middle Owyhee. The Middle Owyhee has some of the Northwest's best runnable white water, as well as some of its most dauntingly unrunnable. You can see it on a 7-day, 95-mile run with Hughes River Expeditions in 16-foot oar rafts with 2 guests and a guide in each boat, or—water conditions permitting—in 13- or 15-foot paddle rafts accommodating between 4 and 6 guests and a guide, or in inflatable kayaks. There are usually 10 guests and 5 guides on Hughes's Middle Owyhee trips.

After a few hours of flatwater and gentle curves, you hit the rapids: a ¼-mile-long, Class IV+ S-turn, littered with boulders; about a half mile beyond, the Class V+ Cable, which you must line through or portage around; the notorious Class IV Ledge, a narrow gap punctuated with apartment-size boulders; and the grand finale, winding Class IV+ Half Mile and the ferocious Class VI Widowmaker, which you line—its scattered boulders are house-size. In between are seemingly endless miles of snappy little rapids punctuated by silent stretches, where you're floating between steep basalt and rhyolite cliffs and grassy slopes and past steep trails to magnificent overlooks, petroglyphs, and hot springs. Throughout the trip, you can expect to see lots of wildlife: Canada geese, mule deer, bighorn sheep, coyote, antelope, bobcats, cougar, prairie falcons, chukar, otter, and golden eagles.

The first night's camp—on a natural terrace surrounded by junipers—is typical of those on the Middle Owyhee. Here you get your first taste of the outfitter's hors d'oeuvres and excellent meals. *Hughes River Expeditions, Box 217, Cambridge, ID 83610, tel. 208/257-3477, fax 208/257-3476. Apr.–May: 7 days, $1,550. Price includes sleeping bags and pads; sign up 2–6 months in advance.*

OREGON **A White Water Expedition on the Upper Owyhee.** ROW's 7-day, 120-mile trip travels a section of this river so remote that only 200 rafters run it each year; it's one of the most remote rivers in the United States outside Alaska. The area is home to the Lower 48's largest breeding population of bighorn sheep and antelope and it's on the Pacific Flyway, which means that golden eagles, falcons, hawks, and waterfowl abound, and many nest in the area. In early spring, the only time the Upper Owyhee can be run, the desert canyon is bursting with bloom, and otter and beaver are hard at work. In keeping with the remote quality of the area, ROW's trips are more expedition-style than its trips on the Lower Owyhee. Camp comforts are at a minimum; you won't find little tables and chairs at mealtimes, as on other trips, for instance. Oar rafts predominate on these trips on the stream, which is rated up to Class IV.

Day hikes up the canyon take in Native American rock carvings and frontier settlers' abandoned stone cabins, many complete with cookstoves and whiskey bottles. The campsites are on white-sand beaches among twisted juniper trees and sagebrush. Food is about the same as on Lower Owyhee trips, but a bit simpler. *River Odysseys West, Box 579, Coeur d'Alene, ID 83816, tel. 208/765-*

0841 or 800/ 451-6034, fax 208/667-6506. Mid-Apr.–May: 7 days, $1,300. Sign up 2 months in advance.

OREGON **Running the Rowdy Rogue.** Named for a renegade band of Native Americans in the Siskiyou Mountains, the Rogue begins its run in central Oregon's Cascade Mountains and heads south and then west before emptying into the Pacific several miles north of the California border. Big, full, and fast, it is one of the most beautiful rivers in the Northwest, maybe in the entire country. ECHO's 4- or 5-day, 45-mile trip, using 15- to 17-foot oar rafts that accommodate 2 to 4, 14-foot paddle rafts that accommodate 4 to 6, and inflatable single and double kayaks, covers by far the wildest and most exciting section of the Rogue—a stretch so special that Congress designated it Wild and Scenic. It is especially satisfying for wildlife lovers, since you often sight deer, otter, osprey, great blue heron, raccoons, spawning salmon, and even black bear at night, and occasionally hear a coyote howl. But the waters challenge white-water enthusiasts; daily dam releases assure mostly Class III–III+ levels, with at least 3 especially challenging rapids at Rainey Falls, Mule Creek Canyon, and Blossom Bar. For an even wilder ride, you can opt for a kayak for part or all of the run.

ECHO's campsites on the Rogue are sandy, heavily forested, and isolated—perfect complements to a sunset drink and a hearty, well-prepared dinner of barbecued steak or chicken fajitas. The season runs from June through September, but July and August are probably optimal considering weather and water temperatures. *ECHO: The Wilderness Company, 6529 Telegraph Ave., Oakland, CA 94609, tel. 510/652-1600 or 800/652-3246, fax 510/652-3987. June–Sept.: 4–5 days, $570–$650. Price does not include tent or sleeping bag; sign up 2 months in advance.*

WASHINGTON AND OREGON **The Grande Ronde by Dory.** For solitude, wildlife, and lovely scenery coupled with the gentlest of thrills, an excellent choice is this 5-day, 75-

mile trip in the Blue and Wallowa mountains by OARS Dories, an affiliate of Grand Canyon Dories. As on the latter's trips, this one is in dories. Though the Grande Ronde moves swiftly, frequent stops for fishing and hiking keep the pace leisurely. Bird-watching is the order of the day, and you may spot nesting bald eagles and osprey, as well as deer, elk, beaver, geese, and bear. The canyon walls stair-step upward on either side, with small terraces where grass, flowers, and trees grow; occasionally you see bizarre basalt spires known as hoodoos.

The waters of the Grande Ronde rise to Class II at Red Rock, Vincent Falls, and Sheep Creek. Northwest Dories, unusual among area outfitters, tackles the rumbling Class III Narrows just above the confluence with Joseph Creek. Campsites are in wild wooded areas by the river, dinners often star fresh trout, and the guides tend to be older and more experienced than most on this river (with 30% of them women). There is normally one guide per 4 guests on this trip; you help load and unload the boats, but the guides do all the other camp chores, except washing your dishes. *OARS Dories, Box 67, Angel's Camp, CA 95222, tel. 800/877–3679, fax 209/736–2902. June: 5 days, $767. Sign up 3 months in advance.*

ALASKA

SOUTHEAST **Floating the Alsek River.** The people at Mountain Travel-Sobek have been known to call the Alsek the "most spectacular wild and scenic river in the world," and few who have made this 12-day, 180-mile run argue with that assessment. Fed by numerous side streams and glaciers, the river gathers force as it races toward the coast with exhilarating Class III–IV white water in the shadow of huge, stark peaks and ominous glaciers, between barren rock canyons, through sweeping forests, and across vast alluvial plains. Sometimes you can even glimpse a grizzly from the boats, and day hikes into the mountains offer splendid river views and long looks at moose, mountain goat, and red fox.

Midway through the run, which you make in 18-foot oar rafts, ultra-stable to avoid flipping into the icy waters, comes the encounter with 5-mile-long, 30-foot-wide Turnback Canyon. The huge rapids and low water temperatures here make it too dangerous even to line; instead, you ride over the rocky chasm via helicopter. On the other side, the terrain is palpably greener. Bald eagles perch along the mossy cliffs. Flowing down from the Fairweather Range are at least a dozen glaciers, a congregation of mammoth, fantastically shaped ice floes, whose huge chunks break off and fall into the clear water. One of these glaciers, the Walker, is a popular destination of hikers.

Each campsite is more ruggedly beautiful than the last. You might dine on shrimp-stuffed avocado or freshly caught salmon, and spend evenings around the campfire watching the Northern Lights. In summer, temperatures range from the 50°F to 75°F by day down to the 40s at night; rain is common. Group size is limited to 12. *Mountain Travel-Sobek, 6420 Fairmont Ave., El Cerrito, CA 94530, tel. 510/527–8100 or 800/227–2384, fax 510/525–7710. Early July–mid-Aug.: 12 days, $2,400. Price does not include 2 meals; sign up 6–9 months ahead.*

SOUTHEAST **Rafting the Tatshenshini River.** Alaska Discovery, which has plied these northern waters since 1972, offers an unmatched 10-day, 160-mile adventure on the legendary Tat, through some of the wildest and remotest river country in North America. Alaska Discovery runs the river in 18-foot oar rafts that accommodate 4 guests and a guide; up to 4 passengers can wield paddles on request.

The wildest rapids come soon after launch, plunging each raft into the whirling Class III waters of the Tatshenshini Gorge. The rest of the run includes mostly Class II white water. The real draw is the scenery, and sometimes you spend 2 nights in a single campsite because there is so much to explore. Near the river, hikes reveal moose, bear, mountain goat, lots of bald eagles, and, occasionally, wolves. At the confluence of the Tatshenshini and the Alsek, the outfitter's campsite offers a wonderful view of both river valleys bookended by glacier-encrusted peaks. The next site is near a glacier that, atypically, is good for hiking.

As you enter the rugged country where the Alsek divides the Fairweather and St. Elias ranges, you raft in view of dozens of other majestic glaciers, and in Alsek Bay, your view is filled by 7-mile-wide Alsek Glacier and behind it, 15,000-foot Mt. Fairweather.

From take-out at Dry Bay, a bush flight along the Gulf of Alaska conveys you to the town of Yakutat, where you catch a jet to Juneau. In summer, temperatures range from 50° to 75° by day, dropping to 45° to 55° at night.

Alaska Discovery invites all guests to help with camp chores, and for every 3 to 5 passengers there is one guide; some are specialists in natural history, fishing, or edible plants. You dine on salmon, halibut, or steak. Since put-in is in Yukon Territory, Canada, all guests need identification, such as a birth certificate or a passport. *Alaska Discovery, 5449-4 Shaune Dr., Juneau, AK 99801, tel. 907/780–6226, fax 907/780–4220. Early July–early Sept.: 10 days, $1,850. Price does not include 2 dinners; sign up 3–6 months in advance.*

SOURCES

ORGANIZATIONS **America Outdoors** (Box 1348, Knoxville, TN 37901, tel. 615/524–4814) is an advocacy group of outfitters. **American Rivers** (801 Pennsylvania Ave. SE, Suite 303, Washington, DC 20003, tel. 202/547–6900) is one of the country's leading river conservation organizations. **Friends of the River** (128 J St., 2nd Floor, Sacramento, CA 95814, tel. 916/442–3155, and Fort Mason Ctr., Bldg. C, San Francisco, CA 94123, tel. 800/374–8377) concerns itself with the environment and, among other activities, works on commission with outfitters to arrange rafting trips. The **Idaho Outfitters and Guides Association** (Box 95, Boise, ID 83701, tel. 208/342–1919) and the **Oregon Guides and Packers** (Box 10841, Eugene, OR 97440, tel. 503/683–9552) can provide information on outfitters in their areas. The **National Association of Canoe Liveries and Outfitters** (Box 248, Butler, KY 41006, tel. 606/472–2205 or 800/736–2256), which lobbies on behalf of outfitters, can send you lists of outfitters nationwide.

PERIODICALS The magazines *Men's Journal* (Box 57055, Boulder, CO 80322, tel. 800/388–2175) and *Outside* (1165 N. Clark St., Chicago, IL 60610, tel. 303/447–9330) regularly cover rafting.

BOOKS The Big Drops: Ten Legendary Rapids, by Robert O. Collins and Roderick Nash, gives a feel for white water. For ideas about other outfitters, consult *The Complete Guide to White-water Rafting Tours,* by Rena K. Margulis, or, perhaps better, the annually updated *Paddle America,* by Nick Shears (Starfish Press, 6525 32nd St. NW, Box 42467, Washington, DC 20015), which lists every outfitter in the country. Also providing good descriptions of the great river runs in the country are *Running the Rivers of North America,* by Peter Wood; *White-water Adventure: Running the Great Wild Rivers of America,* by Richard Bangs, one of the country's best-known adventure-travel writers; *White-water Rafting in Eastern North America* and *White-water Rafting in Western North America,* by Lloyd D. Armstead; *The White-water Source Book,* by Richard Penny; *Wild Rivers of North America,* by Michael Jenkinson; and *Wildwater: Exploring Wilderness Waterways,* by Buddy Mays.

ALSO SEE For more trips that kick spray in your face, see our chapters on Canoeing and Kayaking in White Water and Wilderness and Survival Schools.

Sailing Schools

By Michael B. McPhee

Updated by Beth Gibson

ailing is wonderfully democratic. You don't need to have exceptional strength, endurance, or wealth to enjoy it, or even to become quite good at it. Because this sport takes so many forms—day sailing, offshore cruising, racing—and is affected by the size of the boat, there are many "sub-sports" within the sport of sailing: one for every age and ability. Sailing, in fact, is one of the few sports you get better at as you get older.

There are an estimated 4.5 million sailors in the United States today, a number that's increasing from 5% to 8% each year. One reason for this growth is that boats are smaller, lighter, and faster than they were a decade ago. They're also easier to sail and more maintenance-free. But the main reason is that boats cost less, so people of modest income can own them without throwing themselves into debt. Today, a family can buy a small boat and everything needed to use it, from a trailer to life jackets, for as little as $2,500. For many, that's no more than the cost of a family vacation.

Sailors are also realizing that you don't have to own a yacht any more to sail in some of the more exotic waters of the world: You can easily fly to Tortola or Fiji and charter a boat, with or without crew. And, if you bring friends along to split the expense, the trip could end up costing less per person than if you stayed at a hotel.

The catch, of course, is that you can't just sail off alone, without training; sailing requires both knowledge and experience. The good news is that sailing schools are proliferating around the country. We have mainly listed schools according to the location of their headquarters; but many offer courses in other regions as well. There's a whole range to choose from, catering both to day sailors wanting to learn small boat sailing around a lake or bay to more ambitious sailors desiring to learn offshore sailing and navigation. Some new sailors enroll in advanced classes with the expectation of chartering a large boat without crew—called bareboat chartering—somewhere in the world.

Sailing has a strange vocabulary, and some of the concepts take getting used to. But, within a week, with good instruction, you can make sense of it all and be on your way. Most sailing school courses range from 1 to 10 days. Plan on 3 or 4 days of schooling and sailing to become confident about getting yourself back to the dock. People with mechanical aptitude learn faster, but nearly everyone can pick up the basic skills in less than a week.

If your goal is to learn sailing well enough to charter a boat, it's best to get some sailing

---

Outdoor writer Michael B. McPhee has logged more than 10,000 miles of offshore passages and has owned boats ranging from a Hobie Cat to a wooden Norwegian 8-meter sloop. Beth Gibson has competitively sailed in regattas such as the Vineyard Race and the Ft. Lauderdale–Key West Race on boats ranging from a one-design dinghy to a J-44.

experience after beginners' school. You should become very comfortable with boat handling, strong winds (over 15 knots), and emergency procedures, then take at least another 5 days of advanced instruction and sailing. It's one thing to make a sailboat go where you want it to go; it's another thing entirely to learn how to deal with storms, navigation, currents, and shipping lanes.

Some schools claim they can take beginners and prepare them for chartering in 3 to 5 days, but that's a tremendous amount to learn in such a short time. Furthermore, sailing is as much experience as it is knowledge, maybe more so, and I believe you can't expect anybody to learn how to sail in only 5 days and then go out where the weather can get seriously rough. Besides, sailing is meant to be relaxing—you're only going to go 6 miles or so an hour—so the journey should be as enjoyable as the destination. If you're constantly worried about the unknown because you don't have enough experience, you won't enjoy yourself.

Normally, schools for beginners are offered in 3 different formats—a week-long course, a 2-weekend course, or a course lasting one day or night each week for 4 or 5 weeks. Most of those programs last about 20 hours, with a combination of 3- or 4-hour sessions on midweek mornings or afternoons, and 6- or 8-hour programs on Saturdays or Sundays.

Training is on anything from small 14-foot skiffs to 30-foot cruising boats equipped with bunks. Some go inland—on lakes and rivers—others sail on open bodies of water, where tidal currents become a factor. Some stick close to shore, others take you out into the Great Lakes or open ocean, where learning navigation is a must.

Regardless of the format, you usually spend the first few hours of a basic course in a classroom or on a boat tied to the dock learning the nomenclature, safety procedures, and such elementary concepts as how a boat moves against the wind (called points of sail). During the remaining time, you're sailing—putting all that knowledge into prac-tice. If you're learning on a smaller craft, you can usually expect 2 students to a boat, with an instructor following alongside in a powerboat, shouting up to you as he or she pulls alongside, or addressing the entire fleet of boats with a bullhorn. Larger boats, of, say, 20 feet or longer, usually carry up to 4 students and an instructor.

With few exceptions, the day-sailing schools—the ones that teach the basics—offer no food or lodging. When classes end, you're on your own. More advanced students learning how to cruise usually sleep on the boats for up to a week in extremely tight quarters. Some of these boats stay under sail all night; others anchor in a bay or tie up at docks. Some return to the same port, others sail to a different one each night. But not every moment is spent sailing. There's often time for fishing, sunbathing, and swimming; in the evenings, the student crew sometimes takes dinghies ashore or sits around drinking and telling stories.

Friendships and animosities develop quickly in such close quarters, but learning how to cope with them is part of the training for bareboat chartering. In general, sailing schools are a great way to make new friends, since you're all thrown together in a challenging, confusing situation where everyone's learning and apt to make mistakes. Sometimes you show your vulnerabilities, but you all learn from each other's mistakes as well as from your own. That's the beauty of this sport.

Most schools realize that it takes time to remember that port is left and starboard is right, that you pull the tiller to windward in order to fall off to leeward, or that you need to harden the jib sheet (or "trim" the sheet) as you point higher into the wind. Don't worry if you get confused. The names and concepts take time to digest. Very soon, you'll be gliding out across the water agreeing with Rat in *The Wind in the Willows* that "there is nothing, absolutely nothing, half so much worth doing as messin' about in boats."

CHOOSING THE RIGHT SCHOOL

Pay a visit to a school you're considering, if it's nearby, and look at its boats. They should be clean and well maintained. If you see lots of patches on the boats and sails, if the ropes on the sails are frayed and worn, or if there is water sloshing around in the boats, the school probably doesn't take much pride in its fleet or in its program.

Once you've narrowed down the choices, ask each school:

Who are your competitors and what are their weak points? The answer to this may give you some insight into the strengths of the program you're considering. If you're also looking at one of the competing schools, you can ask them to respond to the criticism.

What type of boat does the school use? It makes sense to learn on a boat that's similar to one you hope to buy or rent someday, but ultimately the type of boat you learn on is much less important than the quality of the program. If you're taught well, you'll be able to apply the same principles to virtually any boat (except for catamarans and other multi-hulled craft).

If you're planning to sail small boats, you want to learn on one with a centerboard that can, and should, tip over. (Capsizing should be an important part of any day-sailing program, because you want to learn how to recover–called righting the boat–and continue on your way.)

If you're learning on a larger, heavier boat, you want one that's responsive, like a J-24, so you can feel every change as the boat responds to the wind, and learn how to react quickly and decisively.

Can I continue to take classes until I've mastered the course? Ask about performance (more popular in racing courses) and aptitude guarantees: Some schools offer extra lessons without additional cost or let you repeat a portion of the course. Others give a full or partial refund if you're unhappy with the results.

How many hours are spent not just in the boat but underway, with the sails up? A certain amount of classroom time is necessary so you can learn terminology, safety, and general principles. But you want as much time underway as possible—perhaps 70% of the program; that's when you're learning. The better schools get you in the boats right away, give you basic instruction, and shove you off under close supervision. Remember that some schools consider lunchtime or sleeping time as time spent in the boat.

If you're planning to go bareboat chartering, you want a learning experience as close to the real thing as possible, so try to sleep on a boat that remains under sail at least a few of the nights. You may have a more fun, relaxed time if you're tied up at a dock every night, but you won't learn as much.

How many students are in each boat, and how much time does each get to steer and work the sails? Expect 2 students on smaller boats and up to 4 students with an instructor on boats 20 feet or longer. Divide the hours sailing by the number in your boat to figure out how much time you get to steer or work the sails. Sailing is mostly experience, so make sure the school keeps you busy all the time and has small classes to ensure your constant participation.

Can I be certified on completion of the course? You'll frequently hear the word *certified*, as in, "This course will enable you to become certified." But the truth is, right now there is no single set of standards by which to judge the competency of a sailor other than professional coast guard licensing. However, various organizations are rushing to set those standards, including the United States Sailing Association (U.S. Sailing) and the American Sailing Association (ASA).

The private, profit-making ASA, based in California, has established a series of courses, exams, and 7 levels of certification for sailing students, ranging from beginning sailing through advanced coastal navigation and off-shore passage making. Successful completion of each course and a related exam certifies you at that level. ASA schools are concerned with providing a high-quality education, but they are not the final word in sailing schools. In fact, several of the best schools in the country, although very concerned with establishing standards and working hard toward that end, are not members of ASA. Be wary when ASA schools tell you that charter boat operators do not let you bareboat charter their vessels without an ASA certification. This is generally not true. U.S. Sailing is a nonprofit, nongovernmental body that for years set the standards for sailboat racing in the United States, under the authority of the International Yacht Racing Union (IYRU). U.S. Sailing is expanding beyond racing and moving into recreational sailing. They too have developed a series of certification courses and many are employed by some of the following schools.

What are the instructors' qualifications? Some of the small-boat sailing schools employ college-age students as teachers. There's nothing inherently wrong with this—but it does say something about the seriousness of the program, and you may want to ask if there are older instructors as well.

Some instructors claim a racing background. Don't settle for that as an explanation of experience; responsibilities on a racing boat can be very specialized. The more teaching experience a person has the better. Someone with, say, 10 years of teaching would be great, since poor teachers don't last. It's also a good idea to find someone with significant offshore experience, since offshore sailing requires well-rounded competence.

As for certification, the most universally accepted qualification is a coast guard license, which is common among instructors only in chartering courses. At that level, you should demand it. The ASA also has certification criteria for instructors as does U.S. Sailing.

What is the school's safety record? Most have stellar records. But don't be afraid to ask. Find out about the last 3 injuries and their outcomes. If you're day sailing, ask

how they plan to retrieve you when your boat tips. Do they have a support boat with an engine? Most schools have a supervisor in a powerboat right in the sailing fleet, ready for anything.

Don't let any school tell you nobody tips over. Schools teaching small boat and day-sailing courses intentionally capsize the students' boats at the beginning of the course. They test everyone's ability to swim in a life jacket and to recover the boat. You spend the rest of the day drying out. It's a great ice-breaker.

What's the cost and what's included? Most day-sailing classes provide nothing but instruction; you're on your own for meals and accommodations. Some day-sailing schools, however, let you sleep on boats at no additional charge, or offer packages that include room and board. Manuals, notebooks, and certification exams and certificates are usually extra, but not always.

Most live-aboard sailing courses include provisioning (meals and drinks), but not all. All day-sailing programs described below do not include food or lodging, unless otherwise noted. For live-aboard programs we tell you whether or not provisioning is included.

FAVORITE SCHOOLS

THE NORTHEAST

REGION-WIDE **Offshore Sailing School.** This huge Florida-based operation offers courses in the New York City area from April through early October—one in Jersey City, New Jersey; and one in Greenwich, Connecticut. Classes are taught in Newport, Rhode Island, from May through September; a 7-day live-aboard cruising course, a special offering of this branch, costs $1,395 (*see* The South, *below*).

CONNECTICUT **Women's Sailing Adventures.** Women's Sailing Adventures was founded in 1989 by Sherry Jagerson, an energetic woman who experienced her share of problems on male-dominated boats before striking out on her own. She's a veteran of 3 Bermuda Races ("I was hired as a cook, although I'd never even cooked on a boat before, and I wasn't even a good cook") and the disastrous 1979 Fastnet Race, where two dozen boats were lost in a storm. She has had a myriad of crew jobs, owned her own sail loft, and made on-board computers for race boats. Jagerson has been teaching women how to sail since 1980.

The mainstay of the school is the 20-hour, 4-day beginner course that is taught out of Westport, Connecticut. The typical boats are Cal 25s. All instruction is on board, and the boats are under sail about 75% of the time, usually with 3 students and an instructor.

During the warm months, there are also 7-day sailing trips through the San Juan Islands of Washington state. The student-to-instructor ratio is an impressive 4 or 5 to 2. Sailing is aboard 38- to 44-foot boats. Students live on board and anchor in different harbors off various islands each night. These cruising courses can be taught in Maine's Penobscot Bay, the San Juan Islands, and the British Virgin Islands. And Jagerson goes along on virtually every trip.

From February through April the school also offers beginner and intermediate courses in the Caribbean. *Women's Sailing Adventures, 39 Woodside Ave., Westport, CT 06880, tel. 203/227–7413 or 800/328–8053. May–Sept.: 20-hr., 4-day beginner course, $140; 7-day course, $1,095. Price includes all provisioning during the 7-day course.*

CONNECTICUT **Coastline Sailing School.** This school offers a wide variety of courses on Long Island Sound, some of the best sailing waters in the country. Based in Noank (near Mystic), it's primarily a big-boat school for sailors who have bareboat chartering in mind. Founded in the mid-'80s, Coastline today has 18 boats, primarily 30-foot Ericsons, and teaches roughly 100 students a year. There are 4 instructors, all of whom are ASA certified and have coast guard licenses.

The Basic Sailing Weekender course for beginners runs from 10 to 4 on a Saturday and Sunday. The first 2 hours are spent on the boat tied to the dock, learning terminology and safety procedures. The remaining 10 hours are spent sailing in the delightful Fisher's Island Sound. Each boat carries a maximum of 4 students and an instructor. The school can fill 5 boats on some weekends, and on those days you may sail together in a small fleet, or flotilla.

Coastline also teaches 3 ASA certifying courses with overnights on board, as well as several advanced courses.

Cruising courses are available for 2 to 5 days on several different, and comfortable, cruising yachts. They offer the sailor with basic sailing skills the chance to cruise with family or friends. There's a 5-day Bareboat Chartering Certification course designed for sailors with some experience who want to become competent to skipper a vessel over 30 feet. The emphasis is on crew safety and emergency procedures. There is a maximum of 6 students per boat, and you may sail as far as Martha's Vineyard or even Nantucket.

Finally, the school offers a 6-day sailing vacation to Martha's Vineyard, which with good weather can be one of the best sailing trips in the country. The vacation course is exactly the same as the 5-day bareboat course except it includes the ports of Edgartown and Vineyard Haven. *Coastline Sailing School, Eldridge Yard, Marsh Rd., Noank, CT 06340, tel. 203/536–2689 or 800/ 749–7245, fax 203/572–0778. Mid-Apr.–mid-Oct.: Weekender course, $265 ($25 extra to stay on board Saturday night); 2-, 3-, 4- or 5-day coastal cruising course, starts at $340; 5-day bareboat chartering course, $765; 6-day vacation course, $1,850 per couple.*

CONNECTICUT **Longshore Sailing School.** Based in Westport and founded in 1960, Longshore is one of the best organized day-sailing schools in the country. It uses boats under 16 feet long, so you don't get any chartering instruction, but you do receive a thorough education in how to sail. Its youth sailing program is one of the largest in the country.

Longshore has 25 counselors and 8 instructors, most U.S. Sailing certified, who teach nearly 1,400 students a year in more than 70 boats. You sail at the mouth of the Saugatuck River, at Westport, which gives you experience with salt water, tidal currents, and ocean buoys while affording a fair amount of protection from storms.

For adults, there are 4 levels of instruction: basic boating, which satisfies the State of Connecticut's requirement for skipper licenses for any boat either 20 feet or longer, with sail or engine; basic sailing; intermediate sailing; and advanced sailing. All courses have the same format: 12 hours of instruction in 4 sessions over 2 consecutive weekends. If you can't make one of these 3-hour periods, you must make it up in private instruction at $36 per hour.

Following basic classroom instruction on terminology and wind direction, students gather on the dock for a rigging demonstration. Then they break into pairs and rig the boats themselves. Longshore is unique in that it requires its students to swim 50 yards and tread water for 2 minutes.

On the second day students learn how to stop a sailboat and how to dock or beach it. They then shove off, 2 students per boat, and sail a figure-eight course over and over for the rest of the day. One instructor is at the dock with a bullhorn and others are in support power boats on the course. The third day focuses on sailing upwind and downwind, then out on the figure-eight course aligned into the wind. The fourth day is spent sailing a triangular course, practicing sail trim, reaching, tacking, and jibbing.

The intermediate course follows a similar format, concentrating more on why a boat sails, and adding additional sailing time. The advanced course offers more of the same at a higher level. Students sail solo on Lasers, which are very small, high-performance boats.

The school does not provide accommodations, but the nearby Inn at Longshore has attractive rooms as well as a restaurant and lounge. There's a snack bar near the school for burgers and fries. This is a very popular program, so sign up at least one month in advance. *Longshore Sailing School, Longshore Club Park, 260 S. Compo Rd., Westport, CT 06880, tel. 203/226–4646, fax 203/454–4120. Early May–mid-Sept.: 12-hour basic boating for adults, $155; all other adult courses, $175. Junior and private lessons are also available at $36 per hour. The school recommends 2-hour sessions.*

CONNECTICUT **Sea Sense.** Founded in 1989, New London–based Sea Sense is designed primarily for women. Founded by Patti Moore and Carol Cuddyer, two professional sailors with more than 50 years combined experience, the school has 10 licensed female captains and 5 student instructors who are working toward their captain's license. Moore and Cuddyer teach as well. The founders have spent much time and effort developing teaching methods to suit women, who usually have less upper-body strength than men. Scheduled courses are for women only, although they offer private lessons for men. The school handles about 200 sailing students each year, as well as about 50 powerboat students.

Acquiring skills to charter and bareboat is the primary goal here, with very little effort spent on day sailing, except on a student's own boat (instructors can be hired out for the day to drive to your marina and teach you privately on your boat). None of the courses follows a strict curriculum; instructors create a noncompetitive, non-threatening environment. The emphasis is on hands-on learning, but all students are given a thorough orientation, with a strong emphasis on safety. There are usually 2 instructors on board—at least one licensed—with no more than 6 students.

Courses of 3, 5, and 7 days are given for all levels—beginner, intermediate, and expert. You live on board the 35- to 45-foot boats, and sail to different ports each night, where you tie up, anchor, or pick up a mooring. Couples and men can request customized classes. The school also operates out of Wisconsin (June–Aug.) and Florida (Sept.–June). They also offer cruising packages in the fall and spring in the British Virgin Islands and in Greece in the summer. *Sea Sense, 25 Thames St., New London, CT 06320, tel. 203/444–1404 or 800/332–1404. May–Sept.: 3-day course, $470; 5 days, $730; 7 days, $980; private lessons on your boat, $250 a day, plus transportation. Cruising packages start at $1995. Prices include provisioning.*

MAINE **Bay Island Sailing School.** Founded in 1985, Bay Island runs a number of courses from beginning sailing through bareboat certification from its base at Journey's End Marina in Rockland, Maine. During these, you sail in some of the country's most scenic waters, with lighthouses and seals and ruggedly beautiful spruce-covered islands.

A Rhodes 19-footer and J-29s are used for the beginner classes, one of which is a 5-day course for 4 hours a day (the other runs a weekend). Both have a 4:1 student-to-teacher ratio and employ the boats and the bay as the classroom. The intermediate coastal cruising course, which uses J-24s or J-29s, has the same student-to-teacher ratio and schedule.

The bareboat charter certification class is taught on 36- to 40-foot boats. Called Bareboat I, the program runs Monday to Friday with the option to sleep aboard just on Thursday night or to stay aboard week-long. The student-to-teacher ratio is 6:1. *Bay Island Sailing School, 120 Tillson Ave, Rockland, ME 04841, tel. 800/421–2492 or 207/596–7550, fax 207/594–0407. June–mid-Sept.: 5-day beginner class, $395; 2-day beginner class, $395; 5-day bareboat course, $775; or weekend coastal cruising course, $395, with no provisioning.*

MAINE **WoodenBoat Sailing School.** This offshoot of the very successful *WoodenBoat* magazine offers one of the best and most thorough ways of learning to sail—using traditional methods, on board traditional wooden craft—while sailing the marvelous coast of Maine.

The school, founded in 1980, teaches some 700 students each year between June and mid-October. Beginners, intermediates, and advanced sailors are taught, on everything from 12-foot Beetle Cats to 170-foot topsail schooners. Most courses operate out of Brooklin, a 3-hour drive north of Portland, 5 hours north of Boston, and an hour from Bar Harbor. Some winter courses are given in the Caribbean.

Here you are taught theories of hull and rig balance, reefing, storm sailing, jury-rigging, knots, navigation, and sailing in fog. The school's focus is on instilling "sea sense"— the ability to tune in to the boat, the weather, and the crew, and apply good judgment so that they all work together harmoniously. Although the program does not offer ASA certification, it does follow the ASA course and exam guidelines and offers its own certificate of course completion.

Beginners and intermediates take the Elements of Seamanship course, which is about 30% classroom, 70% under sail in anything from 12-to 14-foot day sailers to 28-foot Friendship sloops. Classes are limited to 10, with no more than 3 students per boat. The 5-day program runs from Sunday night to Friday night. For an additional fee, the school can provide room and board on its "campus," which includes a campground and an inn.

Those with some experience on the water who want to learn about larger boats can take the 5-day Craft of Sail course, either on a 36-foot ketch or a 32-foot Friendship sloop. The 5-day Advanced Craft of Sail course is usually offered in September, when winds are heavier. Craft of Sail for Women, also 5 days, is designed for, and taught by, women.

The only live-aboard program is the 6-day Coastal Cruising Seamanship course taught on board larger boats. Students—no more than 5—sail from Sunday night to Saturday, anchoring at different islands each night. Knowing the boat, the backgrounds of the instructors, and the coast of Maine, I would say this is the ultimate week-long school in terms of knowledge gained, uniqueness of craft, location, and sheer pleasure. And it's probably the best value, too. *WoodenBoat, Box 78, Naskeag Rd., Brooklin, ME 04616, tel. 207/359–4651, fax 207/359–8920. June–mid-Oct.: 5-day Elements of Seamanship or 5-day Craft of Sail courses, $450 (room and board costs $300, camping site with meals, $165); 6-day Coastal Cruising Seamanship course, $925 with provisioning.*

MASSACHUSETTS **Community Boating.** This is the largest and oldest public sailing establishment in the United States, located on the beautiful tidal pool of the Charles River in Boston. Its staff teaches more than 3,000 adults and 1,500 children a year how to sail, many of them kids 10 to 17 who participate for $1 for the entire summer. The children's program runs late June through late August.

The adult program, run April through October, is too good to be true. For a basic membership fee you can sail on your own as often as you want or take as many lessons as you want on the school's fleet of 150 boats, which includes 15-foot Cape Cod Mercurys, Lasers, 470s, 23-foot Sonar keelboats, and 18-foot Typhoons among others. Most of the instructors are other members of the school who have achieved sailing competency and who volunteer their time. Classes, covering everything from rigging to advanced racing, meet for 1 to 2½ hours, usually on weekday evenings and weekends. If you want a private sailing lesson, just show up; there's usually an instructor ready to go off sailing with you. The boathouse is open for adults weekdays from 1 PM to sunset, and weekends from 9 AM to sunset. Membership includes unlimited sailing lessons (and kayaking and windsurfing), unlimited boat usage and classroom instruction, and free guest privileges. *Community Boating, 21 Embankment Rd., Boston, MA 02114, tel. 617/523–1038, fax 617/523–7699. Apr.–Oct.: 2-day visitor membership, $50; 30 days, $65; 75 days, $160; season, $215.*

NEW YORK **Oyster Bay Sailing School.** This relatively small school offers 3 courses

based exactly on the requirements for the 3 levels of ASA certification, covering everything from introductory boating to advanced coastal cruising.

The 3-day basic sailing course is taught on the waters of Oyster Bay Harbor on 23-foot Sonars, which are day sailors with no cabins. Each boat carries just 3 students and one instructor. On the first day, you're in the classroom learning knots, rules, safety, and other basic skills (for approximately 3 hours), and on the boats familiarizing yourself with the equipment (for the remaining 4 hours). The second day is spent sailing. The third day you take the boats out and follow a chase boat, then sail a course. Graduates are given 4 free hours in one of the Sonars. Lodging can be arranged at the nearby East Norwich Inn.

The coastal cruising course is taught over 2 full days on one of the following: a C&C 32, a Pearson 34, a 28-foot S2, a 30-foot S2, or a 30-foot Ericson, all capable, yet forgiving boats. Students can sleep on the boats, tied up at the dock, at no additional cost. No classroom instruction is given—the program starts right on board. Instruction includes maneuvering under power, engine maintenance, steering with a wheel, docking, and crew dynamics. Class is limited to 4 students.

The 3-day bareboat course is usually taught on weekends on a 35-foot Choy Lee or a 39-foot Beneteau. Instruction includes charts, navigation, weather, fog, night sailing, meal planning, engine maintenance, use of head and cooking systems, and on-board water handling. There's a limit of 4 students for this course. *Oyster Bay Sailing School, West End Ave., Oyster Bay, Long Island, NY 11771, tel. 516/624–7900 or 800/323–2207, fax 516/922–4502. Apr.–mid-Oct.: 3-day basic sailing course, $345 weekdays, $395 weekends; 2-day coastal cruising course, $395 without provisioning, but no extra charge for sleeping on board; 3-day bareboat course, $495 including provisioning.*

RHODE ISLAND **J World.** Founded in 1981, J World has grown steadily. It's named for a design of boat that the school uses in its courses (primarily J-24s, J-22s, and J-80s). J World has 4 domestic locations: Newport, Rhode Island, where its headquarters are; Annapolis, Maryland; Key West, Florida; and San Diego, California. The 4 schools offer the same programs and prices. Courses in Newport and Key West are taught on J-24s. Annapolis and San Diego offer courses on the new J-80s in addition to other Js.

There are 2 levels of recreational sailing courses—beginner and intermediate—and 3 levels of racing courses. Approximately 15 full-time instructors teach about 1,500 students each year. Student-to-instructor ratios are no more than 4:1.

The beginner course (Introduction to Sailing) is taught from 9 to 4 over 5 consecutive weekdays. After a one-hour lecture each morning, you're on the boats for the rest of the day. To qualify for the 5-day Intermediate Sailing course you need to complete the beginner program or be able to tack and steer a boat comfortably. This course teaches students how to dock and anchor, read charts, identify buoys, and plot courses, with the goal of preparing for bareboat chartering tests administered by chartering companies. J World, a member of the keelboat certification program, issues U.S. Sailing Certificates and diplomas including the course description that can be shown to charter companies.

For students with less time, there are also 2 weekend sailing programs, one for beginners and another for intermediates. There are no lectures; both have you out on the water 8 hours a day.

Three racing courses are offered Monday through Friday: Introduction to Racing and Advanced Racing include 2 days of boat handling, a third day practicing starts, and 2 days of short course racing. The 2-day Racing Boat Handling course, for the advanced sailor, covers crew work, advanced sail trim for racers, tacking and jibing drills, spinnaker sets, etc.

There are two weekend racing courses designed to improve tactics and strategy. These courses are for competitors who need to perfect their tactical skills. They include starting techniques, mark-rounding drills, downwind tactics and short race course strategy.

J World offers a 3-day live-aboard cruise for bareboat chartering. The live-aboard Cruising course covers all aspects of handling an auxiliary powered sailboat: engine operation; trouble shooting; coastal navigation; heavy weather and night sailing; on-board electronics, stoves, marine heads and holding tanks. This course is offered at all locations. *J World, Box 1509, Newport, RI 02840, tel. 401/849–5492 or 800/343–2255, fax 401/849–8168. Mid-May–Sept.: 5-day course, $695; weekend course, $295, 3-day live-aboard course, $825.*

THE MID-ATLANTIC

MARYLAND **Annapolis Sailing School.** With some 3,500 students, 50 instructors, and 65 boats, this school, founded in 1959, is one of the oldest and largest private sailing schools in the country. Its base is Annapolis, but it has branch schools in St. Petersburg and Marathon, Florida; and St. Croix in the U.S. Virgin Islands.

The school is unique in that it uses Rainbows, 24-foot keelboat day sailors for its basic courses. The Rainbow 24 was designed specifically for the school with an anti-capsizing design. Cruising classes are taught on live-aboard Newport 30s, Newport 41s, O'Day 37s, or Morgan 44s.

There are 4 formats for the beginner course: an extremely popular 2-day weekend course; a 3-day, Wednesday through Friday course; a more relaxed 5-day weekday course, and the new 4 consecutive Saturdays or Sundays course. The program for days one and two are the same for all 4 courses; the additional days are for supervised sailing, with an instructor in a support boat nearby. Students in the 3- and 5-day classes often sail across Chesapeake Bay to restaurants for lunch, or join together at anchor for a floating picnic.

The 2-day advanced beginner course uses boats 30 feet and longer to prepare students for bareboat chartering and is offered only as a weekend package.

There are two types of live-aboard cruising courses, both of them either 2 or 5 days long. The first type is a flotilla cruise for which couples or groups each have their own boat and cruise in a fleet, with an instructor following in a powerboat or sailboat. The other is a cruising course in which a group of students sail together on one boat with an instructor. On the flotilla course, at least one student must have skippering experience. Both courses are on 37- to 44-foot boats. *Annapolis Sailing School, Box 3334, Annapolis, MD 21403, tel. 800/638–9192 or tel. and fax 410/267–7205. Apr.–Oct.: 2-day beginner course, $225; 3 days, $340; 5 days, $475; 4-part beginner course, $190; 2-day advanced beginner course, $330; 2-day flotilla cruising course, $350 per boat without provisioning; 5 days, $1,390 without provisioning; 2-day cruising course without provisioning, $380; 5 days, $870 with provisioning.*

MARYLAND **Havre de Grace Sailing Services.** On the upper Chesapeake Bay, 30 miles north of Baltimore and 65 miles south of Philadelphia, family-owned Havre offers courses on the Chesapeake Bay. Havre de Grace has a standing policy of guaranteeing you'll learn to sail. If you don't get enough out of a course, you may attend as long as you need, at the school's expense, until you're satisfied that you've learn what you intended to in the course.

The 4-day, basic day-sailing course uses a 19-foot Flying Scot. The 3-day Learn to Charter course, for students who have a basic understanding of sailing and want to go on to bigger boats, uses 32- to 37-foot Hunters. Instruction covers all mechanical and electrical components of a boat, diesel maintenance, sail trim, reefing, man overboard procedures, anchoring, and navigation. You can take the course from Monday through Thursday, or do the work on two consecutive weekends.

Since you pay per boat, the cost is relatively low if you can gather a group of 4 persons or if you are willing to be paired with others. The boat docks each night and students generally eat in town and sleep on board. This is a limitation because you can't become totally proficient at bareboat chartering when you return to the same dock each evening. All instructors have coast guard captain's licenses and are ASA-certified to teach basic sailing. Some captains, but not all, are ASA-certified to teach bareboat chartering.

A 3-day Learn to Charter course is taught on Hunter 33.5s. The class is limited to 4 students. On the 5-day Ocean Cruising course, from Miami or Key West, students also leave Monday and return Friday. A few nights are spent sailing—which is as it should be—and a few are spent at anchor. *Havre de Grace Sailing Services, Tidewater Marina Bldg., Box 441, Havre de Grace, MD 21078, tel. 410/939–2869 or 800/526–1528, fax 410/939–2519. Apr.–Oct.: basic 4-day course, $290–$360; 3-day Learn to Charter course, $350–$450; 5-day Ocean Cruising course, $950.*

MARYLAND **Womanship.** Founded in 1984 in Annapolis, Womanship definitely has the most diverse course offerings of the women's schools. The school's motto is "Nobody yells."

Womanship's strength is in the quality of its staff: experienced female instructors, most on the far side of 30 and some in their 40s and 50s. The school emphasizes that teamwork and confidence are as important as the skills learned, and its instructors try to teach using support and encouragement. The school has less of an emphasis on qualifying for ASA certification than it does on teaching sailing and skippering, and students of any level of experience may join.

Womanship offers courses on the Chesapeake Bay from a base in Annapolis; out of various New England harbors, primarily Newport and Boston; in Washington's San Juan Islands; in Vancouver; along Florida's Gulf Coast and Biscayne Bay; and in the Virgin Islands. It also offers special courses in flotilla sailing throughout the world and passages between points of varying distances.

There are also a slew of customized courses, such as mother-daughter courses and courses for couples, families, and groups, even corporate or business empowerment courses. The scheduled courses are for women only; men may join in the customized or couples courses. All classes are taught on larger boats such as: Westerly, Beneteau, and Jeanneau boats ranging from 39 to 45 feet long. Womanship averages about 1,500 students each year.

The Chesapeake program includes 2- and 3-day beginner day-sailing courses. Most 3-, 5-, and 7-day programs, in Annapolis, New Zealand, Tonga, Tahiti, Greece, are live-aboard, with changing anchorages at night. Beginners, intermediates, and advanced students are usually grouped together on the same boats. *Womanship, The Boat House, 410 Severn Ave., Annapolis, MD 21403, tel. 410/267–6661 or 800/342–9295, fax 410/ 263–2036. Apr.–Nov.: 2-day day-sailing course, $248; 3-day day-sailing course, $358; 3-day live-aboard course, $464–$488 with provisioning; 5 days, $726–$784 with provisioning; 7 days, $984–$2,595 with provisioning.*

THE SOUTH

FLORIDA **Blue Water Sailing School.** This no-nonsense school gets you out on the water and gives you a solid lesson. All courses, from basic sailing to bareboat chartering, are from Saturday afternoon to Friday afternoon (weekend courses can be scheduled by appointment). The boats sail from Fort Lauderdale on Sunday morning and anchor each night at different harbors in the Florida Keys or Bahamas depending on course level. Exams and certifications are given on Friday afternoon. A maximum of 4 students are sent out with a coast guard licensed captain on 30- to 45-foot boats.

The basic sailing course is for students with no experience. The intermediate and char-

tering courses are for students with basic training. The advanced course offers coastal navigation and certification for chartering and includes a passage to the Bahamas.

This program is set up the way a sailing program should be—it gives students plenty of time to learn the intricacies of living on a boat; a chance to encounter storms, ships, and other unexpected hazards; and enough experience to gain a modicum of confidence. The school even tells prospective students with no experience that it's impossible to learn to charter in a week, except possibly for pilots or mechanics or persons with some of the knowledge required of a skipper. *Blue Water Sailing School, 1414 S. Andrews Ave., Ft. Lauderdale, FL 33316, tel. 305/768–0846 or 800/522–2992, fax 305/ 768–0695. Year-round: all 6-day courses, $899–$999 with provisioning.*

FLORIDA **Chapman School of Seamanship.** This school is referred to merely as Chapman's and is best known for the bible of all coastal piloting that was written by the school's co-founder, Charles F. Chapman. *Chapman Piloting Seamanship & Small Boat Handling* explains nearly every skill a skipper needs to safely cruise between ports. Most boats other than day sailors carry a copy. The school, like the book, has a military, no-nonsense feel to it, as it caters to those seeking a career in the marine industry.

Year-round Chapman offers standard 2-, 3-, and 5-day ASA certification classes on inland waters—mostly on the Intercoastal Waterway near St. Lucie Inlet. These are day-sailing programs, with no provisioning.

Chapman also offers a live-aboard offshore sailing course with up to 5 students and one instructor taking 40-foot boats to the Bahamas. The course is relatively unique in that all levels of students go out on the same boats for 6 days and 5 nights. You elect one of two levels of certification you want to work toward, and the licensed captain will work with you toward that end. Students may elect any of the ASA courses, from basic sailing through chartering, coastal navigation, and advanced coastal cruising. Prior to returning, the captain reviews all material with all students, then hands out the tests. You know whether you passed or not before you step back on the dock. This nonprofit organization has a tremendous reputation for its integrity and thoroughness. *Chapman School of Seamanship, 4343 S.E. St. Lucie Blvd., Stuart, FL 34997, tel. 407/ 283–8130 or 800/225–2841, fax 407/283–2019. Year-round: 2-day certification course, $245; 3-day basic coastal cruising course, $325 without provisioning; 6-day offshore sailing course, $1,025 plus port fees with provisioning.*

FLORIDA **Florida Sailing and Cruising School.** This school operates year-round along the barrier islands off the southwest Florida coast, from a base in Fort Myers. The program is designed exactly to the ASA requirements, so you can expect to learn what the ASA specifies.

The 2-day basic day-sailing course is taught on 24-foot keelboats in the Charlotte Harbor area. The 3- and 4-day courses, on 30- to 35-foot boats, combine basic sailing and coastal cruising, with 2 to 4 students on board.

The 5- and 6-day courses teach a combination of basic sailing, coastal cruising, and bareboat chartering. Boats usually spend at least one night at anchor, but tie up other nights. Students can sleep on boats or in area hotels. The school also offers a 10-day advanced cruising course which includes night sailing. *Florida Sailing and Cruising School, 3444 Marinatown Lane NW, North Ft. Myers, FL 33903, tel. 941/656–1339 or 800/262–7939, fax 941/656–2628. Year-round: 2-day basic sailing course, $295; 3-day basic sailing and coastal cruising course, $495; 4-day basic sailing and coastal cruising, $695; 5-day bareboat chartering course, $895; 6-day bareboat chartering course, $995; 10 days, $1,695. Prices do not include provisioning.*

FLORIDA **Offshore Sailing School.** This is one of the largest sailing schools in the country, and perhaps the best known, with more than 3,000 students attending each year. Founded in 1964 by Steve Colgate, a formidable ocean racer, the school has

developed into a year-round program of classes, cruises, and vacations. It has taught more than 75,000 students.

The school is affiliated with U.S. Sailing and offers its own certification for bareboat chartering in addition to U.S. Sailing certification. All instructors have U.S. Sailing certification, and instructors on boats with engines have coast guard licenses. Classes are taught at Captiva Island, Florida; at Newport, Rhode Island; at 2 schools in the New York City area; in St. Petersburg, Florida; and in Tortola.

Day-sailing courses are taught on 27-foot Solings, an Olympic-class boat. There may be as many as 20 students, but boats carry no more than 4 students and an instructor. Day-sailing classes last from 3 to 7 days, generally with 2 hours of classroom in the morning or evening and 3 hours of sailing in the afternoon (or vice versa depending on winds and tides). In a 7-day course, students arrive on Sunday for an evening classroom session, sail Monday through Thursday with instructors, and Friday and Saturday without instructors. The goal of the day-sailing classes is to get people comfortable handling a boat by themselves, with a crew standing by. In all but the 7-day bareboat chartering course from Newport, students sleep on shore each night.

The bareboat chartering courses are numerous; in Florida, 4- and 7-day courses are available. *Offshore Sailing School, 16731 McGregor Blvd., Ft. Myers, FL 33908, tel. 941/454–1700 or 800/221–4326, fax 941/ 454–1191. Year-round: 3-day day-sailing courses, starts at $375 without accommodations; 3-day bareboat course, starts at $375; 7-day bareboat charter course, $1,395 with accommodations including provisioning.*

FLORIDA **Sea Safari Sailing School.** Operating every week of the year out of St. Petersburg, Sea Safari teaches exclusively on catamarans—twin-hulled large sailboats with a cabin stretched on deck between them. Berths and heads are usually placed in the hulls.

Catamarans are wonderful boats—fast, stable, easy to handle. They don't heel (tilt) more than 10 degrees, and they're roomy and dry to sail. However, they sail much differently from mono-hull boats, so if you're not planning to buy or charter a multi-hull, it makes little sense to learn on one.

Sea Safari, run since 1990 by Captain Laurel Winans and her son Chip, offers 2-, 3-, 5-, and 7-day courses. The 5- and 7-day programs are for bareboat certification.

Much of the school's emphasis is on comfort and relaxation, unlike, say, the no-nonsense programs offered by Chapman or Blue Water. The brochure highlights all the sights that will be seen—the sandy beaches, the snorkeling, and so on—and even boasts that students will have their choice of great restaurants at night. This is a great schedule for beginners or intermediates or those interested in coastal cruising, but sailors seeking a performance or racing course would do best enrolling in courses elsewhere. But note that this is the only multi-hull school, so those looking for experience in catamarans cannot go wrong.

Up to 6 students can enroll in each liveaboard class; boats have only 3 queen-size berths. *Sea Safari Sailing, 11305 Jim Court, Riverview, FL 33569, tel. 800/497–2508. Year-round: basic multi-hull sailing course: 2-day course, $395; 3 days, $495; multi-hull coastal cruising: 5 days, $795; 7 days, $995. Prices include provisioning.*

NORTH CAROLINA **Water Ways.** Founded in 1992, Water Ways teaches some 400 students from April through November from its base in Wrightsville Beach. In addition to ASA-certified courses, it also teaches a waterway cruising course on the section of the Atlantic Intracoastal Waterway that runs from Norfolk, Virginia, to Miami, Florida. Many boaters prefer to use the waterway in transit north or south rather than sail in the open ocean despite the fact that the trip can be quite confusing and demanding when traffic is heavy, as you follow a series of fixed buoys with land on both sides. The course is 2 days and 1 night usually on

board a 35-footer, learning chart and buoy reading, and understanding sound and light signals, VHF radio, traffic, and other skills you need to sail here. Classes are limited to 3 students.

ASA courses come in several configurations. There's a 2-day basic sailing course, a 2-day basic coastal cruising course, and a 2½-day bareboat chartering course. The school uses 4 22- to mid-30-foot boats and has 4 coast guard-certified instructors. Mornings are spent in classrooms and afternoons, sailing.

Water Ways also offers a crash 6-day course designed to take a beginner through to bareboat certification. Mornings are spent in the classroom, afternoons sailing, and evenings ashore enjoying Wrightsville Beach's active nightlife. You're on board one night.

In addition, Water Ways offers a 7-day liveaboard course that cruises around the posh and exclusive Bald Head Island, a coastal navigation correspondence course, and a 3-day advanced coastal cruising course aboard vessels 30- to 50-feet in length. *Water Ways Inc., Box 872, Wrightsville Beach, NC 28480, tel. 910/256–4282 or 800/562–SAIL, fax 910/256–5898. Apr.–Nov.: 2-day waterway cruising course, $425 with provisioning; 2-day basic sailing course, $275; 2-day basic coastal cruising, $375; 2½-day bareboat chartering course, $425 with provisioning; 6-day (without provisioning) crash course in bareboat chartering, $895. 7-day liveaboard, $1,095 (with provisioning); coastal navigation correspondence course, $179; and advanced course in coastal cruising, $550 (with provisioning).*

THE MIDWEST

REGION-WIDE **Sailboats, Inc.** This well-established school offers a variety of facilities along the shores of Lakes Superior and Michigan from July through September. Although it's not affiliated with ASA, it's a member of the National Association of Sailing Instructors and Sailing Schools (NASISS) and offers its own bareboat certification, which it requires for chartering one of its own hundred-odd charter boats on the 2 lakes.

The basic program (Course I) takes beginners or novices with no open-water experience and teaches them the rudiments of charter sailing in 8 hours of classroom work and 16 hours on the water. Course II consists of classroom sessions the first 2 mornings, and sailing the first 2 afternoons and the entire third day. Course III, a variation of Course II, provides you with 8 hours of cassette and workbook lessons to be done at home, then 2 days of sailing. Classes meet once weekly for 3 weeks.

Classroom sessions are held in Minneapolis, Milwaukee, Superior, Madison, and Chicago. Sailing sessions, using 29- to 30-foot boats, head out to the Apostle Islands on Lake Superior from Bayfield and Superior, Wisconsin, and on Lake Michigan from both Chicago and Manitowoc, Wisconsin.

The school also offers an advanced, 4-day, live-aboard course called Blue Water Cruising to graduates of the basic chartering courses. The boat sails at night. New to the school's offerings are the beginner (Course I) and intermediate (Course II) courses scheduled for October and November in Longboat Key, Florida. *Sailboats, Inc., 250 Marina Dr., Superior, WI 54880, tel. 715/392–7131 or 800/826–7010, fax 715/392–7133. July–Sept., (Longboat Key, FL, Oct.-Nov.): Course I, $450–$495; Course II, $495; Course III, $450; 4-day Blue Water Cruising course, $895, including provisioning.*

ILLINOIS **Chicago Park District's Rainbow Fleet/Judd Goldman Adaptive Sailing Programs.** Since 1934, these programs have offered city dwellers, particularly beginners, a great way to learn to sail. The programs are particularly well-equipped for sailors with various disabilities.

The 35 instructors, many of whom are college students and about half of whom are certified by U.S. Sailing, teach up to 500 students a year on Lake Michigan. Among the 50-odd boats in the school fleet are Hobie 16

catamarans, Barnett 1400 dinghys, and Freedom 20s (keelboats designed specifically for sailors with disabilities and including swivel chairs, etc.).

The vast majority of classes are private, on a one-on-one basis. The private beginner course consists of 5 hour-long classes. Adult groups meet in 2-hour classes, usually on 5 evenings, spread out over 2½ weeks, or over 5 weekends. The first quarter of the course is spent in a classroom and the rest in the boats. Classes are taught at 3 lakeside locations, all within Chicago: North Shore Beach, Burnham Harbor, and South Shore Beach.

The program for people with disabilities is taught with 2 students and one instructor in each boat and only at the Burnham Harbor location and on a by-appointment basis. The 6 2-hour lessons are on Freedom 20s, which have special seats that slide from port to starboard so that students can easily change sides after tacking. About 50 students with disabilities take lessons each year, but over 500 students use the school's facilities. *Chicago Park District's Rainbow Fleet/Judd Goldman Adaptive Sailing Programs, 425 E. McFetridge Dr., Chicago, IL 60605, tel. 312/747–0737, fax 312/362–1005. Memorial Day–Labor Day: $35–$225.*

WISCONSIN **Milwaukee Community Sailing Center.** Since 1979, this private, nonprofit operation has been offering lessons to the public along the shores of Lake Michigan on property leased from the City of Milwaukee. The school has a strong interest in teaching people with disabilities.

The goal of the adult beginner course is to teach students to safely skipper a boat in up to 10 knots of wind. Beginning sailors have a choice of three formats. The daytime course meets for 3 hours, either mornings or afternoons, eight weekdays over a 2 week period. The evening course meets on 8 week-nights for 2 consecutive weeks. The intensive weekend course meets Friday evening, then all day Saturday and Sunday. Fees include unlimited use of boats for one calendar year.

Regardless of the meeting schedule, the first lesson is on dry land, where you learn terminology, rigging, and other basics. Subsequent lessons are all in the boats, 2 or 3 students in each, with a volunteer instructor. A staff instructor follows the fleet in a safety boat. All students must be able to swim 75 yards in a life jacket. Training includes capsize and man-overboard drills if one chooses to be rated and certified on center board boats (or dinghys). Eventually students sail alone, again with the staff instructor following.

Programs run from May through October and teach about 200 adults and 500 youths 17 and younger. Boats include Designers' Choices, Capri 14s, and Ensigns (23-foot keelboats). There are also a few Solings and J-24s. There are 14 instructors, most of them high-school and college-student age, all with their Level 1 U.S. Sailing certification.

An Introduction to Racing course meets for 5 consecutive weekdays or week-nights, and teaches basic racing rules and spinnaker sailing. There are a variety of other advanced courses as well as a full complement of youth courses, including a program for children 8 to 12 in which kids learn to sail using tiny dinghys, one student to a boat, in some of the lagoons around the city. You must be a member in order to take any course; it costs $75 to join if you live out of town and are using the center only to take a course. *Milwaukee Community Sailing Center, 1450 N. Lincoln Memorial Dr., Milwaukee, WI 53202, tel. 414/277–9094, fax 414/277–9124. May–Oct.: membership fee, $195 adults (for full calendar year); intensive weekend beginner course, $150; all other adult courses, $60–$65. Youth lessons: beginners, $75; intermediates, $50; advanced, $25.*

THE SOUTHWEST

TEXAS **Texas Sailing Academy.** Founded in the early 1960s, Texas Sailing offers a thorough training program with everything from day sailing to bareboat chartering on 65-mile-long Lake Travis on the edge of Austin, in a conference and vacation area. It has a variety of well-equipped boats from 14- to 42-feet long. The 4 instructors, all Coast Guard Master rated, teach about 100 students a year. The school, affiliated with U.S. Sailing, recommends that every student take its 8-hour boating safety class, taught completely in a classroom, before signing up for any of the sailing courses.

The 13-hour beginner sailing course is taught on Expo Solars, a 14-foot day sailer, with 2 students and an instructor per boat. Three sessions lasting 4 hours each are given on the water, and there's one hour in the classroom. An exam and sailing test are given at the end, and you are expected to tack, dock, and sail a short course proficiently.

The intermediate sailing course aims to have students comfortably handle a cruising sailboat under sail or power. It is taught on boats 26- to 35-feet long, and requires 8 hours in a classroom and 20 hours of sailing. Each boat has a maximum of 4 students and one instructor. All instruction is conducted during daylight hours, although students overnight on the boats for free. Coastal navigation and other advanced courses are available. *Texas Sailing Academy, 103-B Lakeway Dr., Austin, TX 78734, tel. 512/261–6193 or 800/864–7245, fax 512/261–8351. Year-round: beginner sailing, $275; intermediate sailing, $425.*

THE WEST COAST

CALIFORNIA **Crabtree Maritime Services.** This establishment is based about 4 hours (30 miles) by boat up San Francisco Bay from the Golden Gate Bridge. It's a one-person operation run by Sam Crabtree, a coast guard-licensed captain and owner of a well-equipped Cal 39-foot sloop, on which the courses are taught.

The thorough courses include lots of mileage at sea, some of which is at night under sail. This is the time when one really understands the romance of the sea: watching the sun rise and set while feeling the power of the wind. Crabtree takes sailors right out into the commercial fishing grounds, through the shipping lanes, into difficult harbors and anchorages. If I were shelling out good money for a sailing course, I'd want to be in a course like Crabtree's, learning navigational lights and radar rather than partying in some restaurant near the home dock.

Three-day courses for beginning sailors emphasize boat handling and coastal piloting en route to Drakes Bay or Half Moon Bay. Five-day courses travel to Monterey Bay, with students standing watch on one all-night sail. These two courses require some sailing experience. The 8-day courses travel from San Francisco to Noyo (Fort Bragg), sailing up to 100 miles offshore. Instruction includes everything needed to skipper a passage, such as radar, LORAN, traditional navigation with sextant, and sailing through fog.

Crabtree also offers a variety of 1- and 2-day sailing trips within San Francisco Bay. Of particular interest is his overnight course on piloting and seamanship in the Delta, an area thick with navigational hazards, buoys, currents, and other challenges. *Crabtree Maritime Services, 710 Shady Glen, Martinez, CA 94553, tel. 510/372-0144 or 800/959-4855. Year-round: 3-day course, $295; 5 days, $475; 8 days, $750; overnight courses, $195-$225 with provisioning.*

CALIFORNIA **Santa Barbara Sailing Center.** This small school founded in 1967 concentrates on day sailing; it has only one overnight course. The student-instructor ratio is 4:1.

The 16-hour, 4-day basic course uses 21- and 24-foot keelboats, which you can sleep aboard at no extra charge. Graduates can move on to the 2½-day, live-aboard, basic coastal cruising course, taught on a 30-foot boat that ties up at the dock at night.

The 2½-day bareboat chartering course is taught entirely on Catalina 30- or 36-footers. The boats sail 23 miles out to the Santa Cruz Islands, where they anchor for the night. Dinner and breakfast are cooked on board.

Students prepare meals for themselves and the instructor. *Santa Barbara Sailing Center, The Breakwater, Santa Barbara, CA 93109, tel. 805/962-2826 or 800/350-9090, fax 805/966-7435. Year-round: basic 4-day course, $259; 2½-day basic coastal cruising, $379 without provisioning; 2½-day bareboat course, $389 without provisioning.*

CALIFORNIA **Club Nautique.** Founded in the early '60s and affiliated with both U.S. Sailing and the ASA, Club Nautique operates out of Alameda and Sausalito on San Francisco Bay. Because sailing conditions are usually pretty strong on the bay, the school focuses on large-boat sailing and is considered one of the top schools in the country for teaching advanced offshore sailing. However, it has a strong program for beginners as well. Roughly 1,000 students sign up for classes each year. Its fleet includes some 45 boats ranging in sizes from 23 to 45 feet (including Hunters, Petersons and Ericsons), and there are some 20 instructors (all of whom have coast guard licenses).

The school offers all the ASA and U.S. Sailing courses and certifications. Beginning sailing (called basic keelboat) is taught over 4 days, consisting of mainly on-water participation with classroom presentations. Basic cruising is also a 4-day course that concentrates on sail trim, crew coordination, and boat mechanics. Coastal navigation, advanced coastal cruising, and offshore passage making are offered for those students desiring an in-depth study of distance cruising. If you don't understand the lessons, you can take either class as many times as you need to learn the material. Each boat carries a maximum of 4 students (more on the larger offshore boats) and an instructor. All students are welcome to overnight on the boats for free.

Bareboat cruising is taught in 4 straight days, usually Friday through Monday, with one night spent on board at anchor in San Francisco Bay or protected ocean waters. Students cook all meals. Some of the advanced classes sail all the way from Hawaii or Mexico back to San Francisco.

Club Nautique, 1150 Ballena Blvd., Suite 161, Alameda, CA 94501, tel. 510/865–4700 or 800/343–SAIL, fax 510/865–3851. Year-round: Basic keelboat, $595, basic cruising, $695, bareboat cruising, $895, advanced coastal cruising, $595, coastal navigation $295, offshore passage making, $1,195; all without provisioning; special rates and packages are often offered.

CALIFORNIA **Women for Sail.** Based in Oceanside, California, this is the only large-boat sailing school exclusively for women. It is owned by two women, run by women, and teaches only women. And it's doing well. Since 1985, it has averaged about 1,200 students a year. During the summer, the school expands to 30 staff and instructors, including Tania Aebi, who at 16 was the youngest woman ever to sail alone around the world.

"We are noncompetitive and teach in a non-threatening manner," says founder Jill London. The school has 5 boats, which it owns. This is often a good sign, because it usually means that the boats are well maintained and that the school can offer lower prices than schools that charter boats. Women for Sail emphasizes hands-on training right from the start, so it provides little classroom time.

The 3-, 5-, and 7-day live-aboard courses are taught on 43-foot Irwins and are offered in Key West, San Diego, Annapolis, Corsica and Sardinia, Thailand, Greece, and the Virgin Islands. During these cruises, boats anchor or tie up at a different port each night.

All North American courses, with 6 students and 2 instructors, are geared toward bare-boat certification. At least one of the instructors is a U.S. coast guard licensed captain. *Women for Sail, 537 Edgwater Ave, Oceanside, CA 92057, tel. 619/631–2860 or 800/346–6404. Year-round; 3- to 7-day cruises range from $845 to $2195 with provisioning, depending on location.*

WASHINGTON **San Juan Sailing.** Based in Bellingham, a 90-minute drive north of Seattle, this is a well-organized, family-owned sailing center.

There are 5 levels of weekend courses and a 6-day Learn-n-Cruise course. The 2-day weekend courses run from beginning sailing, for those who have never set foot on a boat before, to advanced sailing, including navigation and anchoring. All but the beginning course are live-aboards. ASA certification tests are given for an additional fee.

The 6-day course is an ideal way to learn to sail because it provides sufficient time and varying experiences for you to become relatively competent. The boats sail through the San Juan Islands with no set itinerary, going with the weather and currents. Aside from one dinner ashore, all meals are prepared and eaten on board, an important learning experience for a future charterer. The boats are either Pearson 38s or Nordic 40s, with up to 6 students and one instructor.

San Juan also offers offshore passages and a variety of advanced courses that follow ASA guidelines. *San Juan Sailing, 1 Squalicum Harbor Esplanade, Bellingham, WA 98225, tel. 360/671–4300, fax 360/671–4301. Year-round: 2-day weekend courses, $149–$275 without provisioning; 6-day course, $749 with provisioning.*

SOURCES

ORGANIZATIONS **United States Sailing Association** (Box 209, Newport, RI 02840-0209, tel. 401/849–5200, fax 401/849–5208), commonly referred to as U.S. Sailing, and the **American Sailing Association** (13922 Marquesas Way, Marina del Rey, CA 90292, tel. 310/822–7171, fax 310/822–4741) are the country's major sailing organizations. ASA has a free 2-page member list.

A recent trend has been for parks and recreation departments of larger cities to establish urban sailing programs, or at least to make city land available to private sailing schools at a nominal cost. (One of the largest and oldest of these schools is Community Boating, Inc., in Boston; *see* Favorite Schools, *above*.) So if you live in a city and need to stay close to home, check with your city's parks and recreation department.

PERIODICALS There are numerous sailing periodicals, virtually all of which are worth reading. The biggest difference among them is their target audiences—some are very technical, others are for cruising, and still others are purely for racing.

The monthly *Sail* magazine (Charlestown Navy Yard, 100 1st Ave., Charlestown, MA 02129, tel. 617/241–9500) is good on all aspects of sailing, from day sailing to ocean voyages. There's very little for the beginner sailor, but lots of sound, practical how-to articles, firsthand tales by fellow sailors, and boat want ads in the back for fantasizing. *Cruising World* (Cruising World Publications, Inc., 5 John Clarke Rd., Newport, RI 02840, tel. 401/847–1588) is a monthly magazine written for sailors who cruise on their sailboats, but it is highly readable for anyone with just an elementary understanding of sailing: Stories written from the decks of cruising boats all over the world, repair articles, recipes, and humor. *WoodenBoat Magazine* (WoodenBoat Publications, Inc., Box 78, Brooklin, ME 04616, tel. 207/359–4651) is a very high quality, bimonthly magazine written specifically for wooden-boat owners and lovers. *Sailing World* (5 John Clarke Road, Newport, RI 02840, tel. 401/847–1588) is the authority on performance sailing with helpful articles on crew organization, tactics and boat handling. This is a must-read for those interested in racing.

BOOKS In addition to the schools described above, there are hundreds of other reputable programs around the country, particularly for day sailing. The free *Where To Sail 1995*, published by the nonprofit United States Sailing Association (see above), lists nearly 900 programs across the country.

Your telephone directory (see "Boat Dealers" and "Marinas") can give you other options. These folks want you to start boating, so they're likely to know about local schools.

For how-to, try *The Craft of Sail* (Walker), by Jan Adkins. This is a well-written book for beginners, describing not only how a boat works but why as well, with lots of beautiful drawings. For good reading, try *Men At Sea* (Random House), by Brandt Aymar, a collection of the best sea stories of all time. *The Big Book of Sailing* (Barron's Educational Service), by Grubb and Richter, is an attractive book with great stories and chilling biographies of seafarers, richly illustrated in a large, coffee-table format. *Royce's Sailing Illustrated* by H.B. Warren (Fashion Press) is one of a kind. In publication since 1956, Royce's is a comprehensive guide to types of sailboats and rigging, especially dinghys; types of sails; wind direction; tacks and courses, anchors, reefing. You name it, Royce's covers it. It's a gem. *Chapman Piloting Seamanship & Small Boat Handling* in its completely updated edition by Elbert S. Maloney is known as the Bible of boating. And, although it is quintessentially a reference book, it's a fairly easy read. For those sailors who are comfortable in a boat and are concerned with performance sailing, the following books are the best on the market: *Advanced Racing Tactics* by Stuart Walker (Norton); *Championship Tactics* by Gary Jobson and Tom Whidden (St. Martin's Press), and *Sailing Smart* by Buddy Melges and Charles Mason (Holt Rinehart Winston). To learn more about wind and the resultant sail trim and sail construction, *Sail Power* by Wallace Ross (Knopf) is indispensable, covering everything from sail inventory and design to tuning of the rig.

ALSO SEE If you enjoy sailing boats, you may like sailing surfboards. The Windsurfing chapter tells you where you can learn.

Scuba Diving

By Lisa Skriloff

Updated by W. Lynn Seldon Jr.

ome divers like to see fish; they like to be surrounded by fish. For them, it's the marine life that makes scuba diving thrilling. Some divers like warm water, while others say warm-water diving is as adventurous as diving in your bathtub. They prefer the more rugged and challenging deep dives, where the water temperature is in the fifties. Or ice diving, or exploring underwater caves. Still others like the look at history that wreck diving affords, and go off in search of portholes, bottles, ammunition, or gold.

There are dive courses available in almost every state in the country, as well as places to go diving on one-day or weekend excursions. But if you've got a whole week and want to learn to dive, the warm water destinations of Florida, the U.S. Virgin Islands, and Hawaii are the ones that offer courses on trips of at least 5 days. In the Florida Keys you'll find warm water, schools of yellowtail snappers, sunken Spanish galleons, and a coral reef that extends north to Fort Lauderdale. In volcanic Hawaii there are caverns, underwater lava tubes, sea turtles, and octopus. Under Frederiksted Pier in St. Croix, U.S. Virgin Islands, you'll see seahorses and try night diving. And on the north side of St. Croix, where the reef drops off and descends vertically for hundreds of feet, there's wall diving.

Jacques-Yves Cousteau and Emil Gagnan started this sport in 1943 when they invented the Aqua-lung, the first self-contained underwater breathing apparatus (SCUBA). Since then, scuba diving has grown enormously—with 625,000 new divers worldwide in 1994 alone joining the estimated 4 million already certified. Couples are even getting married underwater! If you're over the age of 12 you can become a certified diver, no matter your level of physical ability, although you must be able to swim. The vast majority of divers are college-educated, fairly affluent, and work in professional or management positions.

Although scuba diving is open to all and is, statistically speaking, a safe sport, there are obvious dangers to being underwater, dependent on your equipment and your knowledge. Before you can dive (or even rent a tank of compressed air), you must have basic scuba certification (your C-card), which you earn in a course consisting of classroom work, pool instruction, and 4 or 5 checkout dives in open water (ocean, river, lake, quarry, etc.).

The courses are usually provided by dive shops and by YMCAs and YWCAs at night or on weekends over a period of a few weeks. At these local courses you meet like-minded people from your area—future dive buddies. After you have completed your class and pool work, the dive shop or Y arranges for you to take your checkout dives nearby. You can also take your class and

---

Lisa Skriloff holds a PADI Advanced Open Water certification card and has logged over 100 dives. Freelance travel writer and photographer Lynn Seldon has covered scuba diving for *Dive Training* magazine and has logged hundreds of dives throughout the world.

pool work near home, then request a referral letter and go to a resort for your checkout dives, after which you can spend the rest of your vacation diving.

On the other hand, you might want to take all your diving instruction at a resort and complete every aspect of certification while on vacation. The best place to start shopping for dive travel is your local dive shop. In addition to providing instruction, insight, and equipment, your dive shop can also normally prepare the perfect dive trip. While each shop is unique, they all share a love of scuba diving, instruction, and the travel that is inherent with loving to dive. Because dive shops and dive-travel wholesalers often book and buy packages in such large numbers the price to the consumer can be relatively low when compared to traditional bookings.

Another option is a resort course, an abbreviated version of a certification course (completed in about a day, as opposed to 4). This allows you to dive at the resort offering the course, but only that resort, for the remainder of your stay. A resort course does not certify you.

There are several major agencies that grant recreational scuba certification, and all dive shops are affiliated with one or more of them: the Professional Association of Dive Instructors (PADI), the National Association of Underwater Instructors (NAUI), Scuba Schools International (SSI), the YMCA National Scuba Program, and the National Association of Scuba Diving Schools (NASDS). About 70% of divers hold PADI cards, most of the rest have NAUI certification, and the balance is divided among the other agencies. PADI is definitely the most widely recognized worldwide. Sanction by an agency means that the affiliated dive center conforms to that agency's education methods and uses its diver manual. When you complete your course, your C-card is mailed to you by the national dive agency under whose auspices it was given.

Once you are certified, you can dive at any resort in the world, even if its agency affiliation is different from that on your C-card. How do you choose one over the other? If you're planning to take the course near home and then complete the checkout dives at a resort on vacation, it's best to choose a local dive ship affiliated with the same agency as the resort. You might choose a dive shop for its facilities (an on-site pool, perhaps), its programs (such as weekend getaways with cheap group airfare), the convenience of its schedule, its amenities (a repair shop), and its members' activities (meetings, parties, even a newsletter). If you will be learning to dive while on vacation, choose your destination first, based on the region and the characteristics of its dive sites; its agency affiliation makes little practical difference.

During the classroom sessions, the instructor gives lectures and teaches the material in the diver manual, which is required reading. Slides and videos are often used, and quizzes follow each chapter of the text, to help you prepare for the final, a multiple-choice written test. (It's really difficult to fail; after the final, any wrong answer is reviewed by the instructor until you know it.) The course material covers diving equipment, the effects of pressure on your body, and the dive tables—charts that tell you how long it's safe to stay submerged at various depths, and how long you must stay on the surface between dives on a single day. It also covers safety rules, such as not flying for 24 hours after a dive, and the buddy system. Much of this information is designed to prevent you from getting the bends, a serious condition that can occur if your body is subjected too quickly to changes of pressure.

The pool instruction usually starts with a brief test of your swimming ability. Then you learn to manage your equipment and master such skills as clearing your mask underwater (in case it fills with water or fogs up), communicating underwater with a companion, and using a compass. You also learn to snorkel. You can learn at your own rate and practice until you become comfortable underwater. You then move to open water, where you demonstrate these skills for your instructor's approval during your checkout dives.

The use of most necessary gear is normally included in the price of a scuba diving course, so you shouldn't buy it until afterward. You are lent a tank of compressed air; a buoyancy compensator (or dive vest), known as a BC; a regulator (through which you breathe the air in your tank); gauges that indicate your depth and the air remaining in your tank; a weight belt to help adjust your buoyancy; and a dive watch. A wet suit is provided if water temperature demands it. You also need a mask, a snorkel, and fins, which most courses don't supply. You should buy (or rent) these beforehand, to ensure proper fit. Expect to pay $45–$100 for a mask, $12–$45 for a snorkel, and $55–$135 for a pair of fins. Prescription masks can be made to order, but many people wear contact lenses. Some shops have rental/purchase plans, so if you decide to rent a few times before taking the plunge, your rental fees can be charged against the purchase price.

CHOOSING THE RIGHT COURSE

Following are some questions to ask about scuba diving courses. Some pertain to all certification courses, others only to courses taken at a resort.

How long have you been in business?

How many students are there in each class? How many instructors per student? In general, classes are limited to 8 people and there is at least one instructor per class. There are usually 2—an instructor and a divemaster (instructor-in-training)—for the open-water certification dives. A low student:instructor ratio is preferable, but the course may be more expensive.

What is the schedule of classroom sessions and pool sessions? Most courses take from 24 to 32 hours, divided between classroom study and pool work, plus 4 checkout dives (and sometimes an open-water snorkel dive). The 4- or 5-day courses given at

resorts generally cover classroom and pool work in 20 hours, plus checkout dives, but some let you study the manual in advance and cover pool work, checkout dives, and tests in 3 days.

What's the cost and what's included? Costs run $250–$500. The prices given here are for basic certification courses and include the diver manual and other course materials, rental gear used during class and pool sessions, checkout dives, and transportation to dive sites. They do not include mask, fins, snorkel, or the use of dive gear during checkout dives, unless noted. If you take your course at a resort, packages may be available that include lodging.

What kind of dive sites are used for the open water checkout dives? What will the diving conditions be like? New divers may feel more comfortable in shallower waters. And learning about the expected water temperature and visibility at different resorts at different times of year will help you choose where to go.

How demanding is the course? Do I need to be in good condition? It's best to be in good aerobic condition for diving, but you needn't be an overall athlete. For your swim test, you'll probably be asked to swim no more than 200 yards and float or tread water for 10 minutes. Although dive equipment is heavy, it's weightless underwater. For that matter, so is a neutrally buoyant diver, which means that an extra 10 pounds is not the hindrance it is, say, on a runner.

What is there to do in free time? At some resorts, there's nothing much to do but dive, while others have lots of activities or are located in or near lively towns. This is especially important if you're traveling with nondivers; you'll be fully occupied during the day and tired after a day's study and training.

What are the accommodations like? Is the hotel close to the course location? Weigh the advantages and disadvantages of luxury versus laid-back lodging; crossing an elegant lobby with wet dive gear can be intimidating (and frowned upon). Also consider the distance you must drag your gear bag, dripping wet, from the dock to your room if there are no lockers.

How far in advance do I need to sign up? People usually book 4 to 6 weeks in advance, but most schools can fit you in even if you decide to go on the spur of the moment.

Do you have references from past students? It's a good idea to ask the opinion of someone who knows from experience just how a school operates.

FAVORITE COURSES

THE NORTHEAST

NEW YORK **Hamptons Learn-to-Dive.** In the sometimes fast-food world of scuba instruction, Annie Libby's Bespoke Scuba is like a catered meal served on fine china. Bespoke means "custom-made," and this school offers just that: Top-of-the-line, learn-to-dive packages that may include a stay at local inns like the charming Maidstone Arms. Instruction is given at a local pool, and the checkout dives are done at nearby Fort Pond Bay, off Montauk, Long Island, or at an exotic location on a Bespoke trip.

Among the students here you'll find family groups, corporate executives and their clients, denizens of New York's Hamptons, and a variety of vacationers. If you have a group of 4 to 10 persons, Bespoke will also bring scuba gear and instructors to your pool. You must live within a 100-mile radius of the Hamptons, but the course price is the same. The student-to-instructor ratio is never greater than 8:1, and Libby is usually there, too. *Bespoke Scuba, 125 E. 63rd St., New York, NY 10021, tel. 800/537–2328 or tel. and fax 516/267–2169. May–Sept.: 4-day course, $885. Price covers use of equipment on open-water dives, including wet suit. Package accommodations average $200 per night.*

THE SOUTH

FLORIDA **Ft. Lauderdale Reef and Wreck Diving.** If you have any nervousness about learning to dive, it will soon be dispelled at Pro Dive. You get an immediate sense of the professionalism of the staff and instructors here, where novices are trained and where experienced divers learn to become instructors and dive-resort operators. You also get a sense of the fun you'll have when you see the photos of former student groups. Class size is 6 people maximum. Checkout dives are at offshore coral reefs and wrecks, including the Mercedes I. The wreck diving off Ft. Lauderdale is legendary.

Many divers stay right at the 16-story Bahia Mar resort (which caters to divers and has a special rate for them), where the retail shop, classroom, pool, dive boat, and your hotel room are all within steps of each other. Rooms reserved for divers are on the marina side, which means you don't have to lug your gear too far, and the hotel has a convenience store as well as 4 dining rooms. Nearby, on the Intracoastal Waterway, is Bahia Cabana, a small establishment with a casual air. Ft. Lauderdale's wonderful beach is right across the street, easily accessible by an overpass. *Pro Dive, Bahia Mar Yachting Center, 801 Seabreeze Blvd., Fort Lauderdale, FL 33316, tel. 305/761–3413 or 800/ 772–3483, fax 305/ 761–8915. Year-round: 4-day course, $295. Price includes equipment for checkout dives.*

FLORIDA **Key Largo Reef and Wreck Diving.** If you like diving in shallow, warm waters among schools of approachable fish, try Key Largo, in Florida's Upper Keys, only 50 miles south of Miami International Airport. Because the Florida Keys National Marine Sanctuary and the adjacent John Pennekamp Coral Reef State Park have been protected from spearfishing and coral collection for more than 30 years, divers will be surrounded by friendly fish. One dive site is Molasses Reef, home to yellowtail snappers, schools of barracuda, and giant rays. Another popular site is French Reef, notable for its swim-through caves.

The famous Christ of the Abyss, a nine-foot bronze statue standing in about 25 feet of water, is visible from the surface, so that both snorkelers and divers can see it. In fact, most dive sites in the Upper Keys are suitable for both, which means that snorkelers traveling with divers can go out on the same boat. One of the best dives in the world, to the US Coast Guard cutters *Bibb* and *Duane*, is here. These 327-foot cutters were sunk in 1987 as an artificial reef project. Learn-to-dive classes are available daily, as well as all PADI classes to instructor level.

Stay at the Marina del Mar Oceanside (or the slightly less expensive Marina del Mar Bayside) while you learn to dive with Ocean Divers, and you'll be immersed in scuba camaraderie—there are many avid and novice divers among the guests. Classes are held in the dive shop, and the hotel's pool is used. *Ocean Divers, 522 Caribbean Dr., Key Largo, FL 33037, tel. 305/451–1113 or 800/ 451–1113, fax 305/451–5765. Year-round: 4-day course, $395.*

FLORIDA **Key West Reef Diving.** Southpoint Divers, at the Hyatt Key West Resort, teaches a course you can complete in just 3 days, which allows more time for diving during your stay. The textbook is sent to your home, so you can do some reading in advance, and most classes have fewer than 4 students, so instruction goes fast. Not that the learning is unpleasant—classes usually take place at sunset at a table on the Hyatt dock. The checkout dives are done at shallow reefs, like Western Dry Rocks or Rock Key, where you see turtles, nurse sharks, spiny lobster, green eels, parrot fish, yellow jack, and rays.

Besides the reef dives, deep dives, and wreck dives around Key West, there's a museum exhibiting gold, silver, and artifacts from the wreck of the Spanish galleon Atocha. Key West makes a nice compromise destination if your traveling companion doesn't plan to scuba dive, since there's so much else to do. Dress is always casual; shorts and T-shirts go everywhere.

The hotel, too, has the laid-back atmosphere divers want, with rooms overlooking the pool or the ocean, a poolside café, and a more formal indoor-outdoor dining room. Southpoint Divers also has dive packages with lodging provided at reasonably priced guest houses nearby. *Southpoint Divers, 601 Front St., Key West, FL 33040, tel. 305/292–9778 or 800/ 824–6811, e-mail southpoint£aol.com. Year-round: 3-day course, $310; 6-day Hyatt dive package, $1,400, including 3-day course, mask, fins, snorkel, lodging, breakfasts, and sunset cruise.*

FLORIDA **Certification Course and Excursion to Dry Tortugas.** Lost Reef Adventures, an independent dive shop in Key West, and the Yankee Fleet's dive boat have teamed up to create a package that combines a 4-day certification course with a ferry to the Dry Tortugas for a day of diving there. The Dry Tortugas National Park is America's newest and farthest-at-sea national park. Lost Reef, which also rents and repairs equipment, gives its course under either PADI or NAUI guidelines and takes you out for your checkout dives in its own boat. Divers usually stay at the Days Inn (whose pool is used for classes) or at Island City House, a nearby Victorian bed-and-breakfast with tropical gardens and a pool. Both have doubles and housekeeping suites that sleep up to six, and you can explore the interesting town of Key West as you learn.

You spend the last part of your vacation doing nothing but diving in the Dry Tortugas, a pristine cluster of coral reefs 70 miles west of Key West. Here, in warm water with frequent 100-foot visibility, divers swim along the reefs and explore 16th-century shipwrecks. Some stops are made at virgin sites, where the fish are unafraid and curious.

The 100-foot-long, air-conditioned diesel cruiser *Yankee Freedom* (the Fort Jefferson ferry) takes only 12 divers on each trip. *Lost Reef Adventures, 261 Margaret St., Key West, FL 33040, tel. 305/296–9737 or 800/952–2749. Yankee Fleet, Box 5903, Key West, FL 33041, tel. 305/294–6963 or 800/ 634–0939 (July–Aug. 508/283–0313). Sept.–*

June: 4-day course, $300; 1 day aboard the Yankee Freedom, $125; price includes air, tanks, and weight belts, but not dive gear.

HAWAII

THE BIG ISLAND **Waikoloa Reef Diving.** When you take this course with Red Sail Sports at the Hilton Waikoloa Village, you're at a great diving location—a volcanic site where divers can see underwater lava flows and tunnels formed when the lava hit the sea. You might go to the Pentagon on one of your checkout dives, where lava formations make an interesting cave with five openings, and where there's a resident white-tip reef shark. Or perhaps you'll go to the Mauni Lani caves, home of Hawaii's famous green sea turtles.

At the Hilton, you get a luxury vacation, and you might even win a chance to buy a ticket to swim with dolphins in a pool (the dolphins can't handle all the people who want to do this, so numbers are restricted). The 1,241-room hotel sits on 62 acres, with interconnected canals, waterfalls, and swimming pools, 7 restaurants, plenty of water sports besides diving, and a program for kids. You might also stay at the Royal Waikoloan on the same property, or at the Ritz-Carlton or Mauni Lani, 3 miles away.

The 4-day course (PADI or NAUI) can start any day of the week, and the ratio of students to instructors is held to 4:1. Red Sail Sports is a large operator that also offers dive programs in Aruba, the Bahamas, and Grand Cayman. *Red Sail Sports, Hilton Waikoloa Village, 69-425 Waikoloa Beach Dr., Kamuela, HI 96743, tel. 808/885–2876 or 800/255–6425, fax 808/885–4169. Year-round: 4-day course, $395. Price includes mask, snorkel, and flippers and all equipment on checkout dives, including wet suit.*

MAUI **Lahaina Reef Diving.** Lahaina Divers is in the heart of Old Lahaina, a 19th-century whaling village. Beneath the surface, things are equally fascinating: There you see tropical fish, rays, octopus, eels, and white-tip

reef sharks against a volcanic terrain. Even in the shallow water off the coast of Lanai, on the checkout dives (which are usually conducted in an area chosen more for calm water than for visual interest), there are lava tubes and pinnacles.

The town has little gift shops, open-air cafés, and the casual feel of a beach town. Lahaina Divers puts up its clients at local condominiums and inns. Classes start twice a week for the 3-day PADI certification course, with instruction in English or Japanese. You're expected to pick up the textbook before the course starts and complete a required reading and study assignment. This gives you a jump-start on the training and allows maximum time for diving.

Lahaina Divers takes certified divers to Molokini Crater sites, where marine life and volcanic formations are plentiful, and where the water is shallow enough for snorkelers to enjoy. On these trips, both snorkelers and divers can spend the day together on the same boat. *Lahaina Divers, 143 Dickenson St., Lahaina, Maui, HI 96761, tel. 800/998–3483, fax 808/661–5195. Year-round: 3-day course, $95; does not include the $30 manual).*

U.S. VIRGIN ISLANDS

ST. CROIX **Year-round Reef Diving.** Cruzan Divers is in Frederiksted, on the quiet side of St. Croix, where the pace is more laid-back than it is on the more touristy Christiansted side. The diving is good year-round, with water temperature a warm 79°F to 80°F in winter, 82°F to 83°F in summer.

Classes are held in the dive shop, and pool work takes place in the shallow water of the harbor. For your open-water checkout, you might dive around and under the Frederiksted Pier, an easy shallow-water dive where you'll encounter sea horses; or go by boat to Rainbow Reef, Butler Bay wrecks, or King Reef.

Once you get certified, come back to the pier on a night dive, when the lobsters emerge from their hiding places, soft corals come out to feed, and you can touch the sleeping parrot fish. Cruzan Divers also takes boat trips to the north side of the island for wall diving. You slowly ascend from your maximum depth, examining, as you go, the sponges, frogfish, and elkhorn coral living along the wall. You might also spot parrot fish, angelfish, grouper, trunkfish, spotted drum, and eagle rays.

You can stay at the Frederiksted Hotel or at other local digs. In your off-hours, you'll find opportunities to go horseback riding in the rain forest and to enjoy the nearby beaches that are beautiful and clean. And if the bright lights call you, you can always drive or take a taxi-bus to Christiansted. *Cruzan Divers, 12 Strand St., Frederiksted, St. Croix, USVI 00840, tel. 809/772–3701 or 800/352–0107, fax 809/772-1852. Year-round: 5-day course, $600. Price includes equipment for checkout dives.*

SOURCES

ORGANIZATIONS Contact the following certifying agencies for the address of an affiliated dive shop in your area and for dive-travel package information: **National Association of Scuba Diving Schools** (1012 S. Yates St., Memphis, TN 38119, tel. 901/767–7265); **National Association of Underwater Instructors** (Box 14650, Montclair, CA 91763, tel. 909/621–5801); **Professional Association of Dive Instructors** (1251 E. Dyer Rd., No. 100, Santa Ana, CA 92705, tel. 714/540–7234), which awards its 5-star rating to shops that have repair centers and are qualified to train divers to become instructors; **Scuba Schools International** (2619 Canton Ct., Fort Collins, CO 80525-4498, tel. 303/482–0883); and **YMCA National Scuba Program** (6083-A Oakbrook Pkwy., Norcross, GA 30092, tel. 404/662–5172).

Divers Alert Network (Box 3823, Duke University Medical Center, Durham, NC 27710,

tel. 919/684–2948) is an international non-profit agency that promotes diving safety and sells low-cost diving insurance. The $25 annual membership fee provides an emergency hotline, medical-question line, emergency evacuation (if you're over 100 miles from home), a first-aid manual, and a subscription to *Alert Diver* magazine. **Handicapped Scuba Association** (116 W. El Portal, Suite 104, San Clemente, CA 92672 or 7172 W. Stanford Ave., Littleton, CO 80123, tel. 303/933–4864) certifies dive shops for teaching people with disabilities and provides a list of accessible resorts.

PERIODICALS *Dive Training* (1200 S. Federal Hwy., Ste. 301, Boynton Beach, FL 33435, tel. 407/731–4321 or 800/444–9932, fax 407/369-5882), published monthly, is the ideal publication for beginning divers or those considering getting certified. Rodale's *Scuba Diving* (Box 7589, Red Oak, IA 51591-0589, tel. 800/666–0016), published 8 times a year, covers the practice of diving, dive-travel, the marine environment, health, safety, and dive equipment. *Skin Diver* (Box 52595, Boulder, CO 80322-2595, tel. 800/800–3487) is a monthly with heavy advertising that covers the most popular dive destinations and lists dive shops by state. It's best for new divers. *Scuba Times* (Box 40702, Nashville, TN 37204-9905, tel. 800/950–7282), published bimonthly, has articles on destinations, diving news, and products. "Undercurrent" (Box 175, Great Neck Rd., Suite 307, Great Neck, NY 11021, tel. 800/237–8400, ext. 555) is a monthly newsletter (no advertising) that offers objective reviews of resorts, live-aboards, and equipment.

BOOKS Pisces' diving and snorkeling guides, a series of 24 guidebooks sold in dive shops, provide dive sites, history, and tourist information. Titles include: *The Hawaiian Islands, The Florida Keys, The U.S. Virgin Islands,* and *Northern California and the Monterey Peninsula. A Handguide to the Coral Reef Fishes of the Caribbean,* by Joseph Stokes, is a good fish identification book.

Sea Kayaking

By Rena Zurofsky

he first time I tried sea kayaking was in Currituck Sound, behind the Outer Banks of North Carolina. It was early morning, and before shoving off I'd received a life jacket and basic instruction on how to hold the paddle. The water was smooth as glass; it reflected the sky so particularly that when I dipped my paddle I was startled to see clouds waver apart. And as I glided forward, a fish leaped over the bow of my orange plastic boat and disappeared down the other side. I was the one who was hooked.

One of the country's fastest-growing sports, sea kayaking can be as thrilling or as peaceful as you make it. More stable than a whitewater kayak, more comfortable than a canoe, a sea kayak—even one loaded with a week's worth of gear—is maneuverable enough to poke into hidden crevices, explore side bays, and beach on deserted spits of sand. Designed by Inuit peoples for hunting, transportation, and swift travel through icy Arctic waters, kayaks are used today in open oceans, sounds, and large bays, as well as on lakes and slow rivers.

Anyone who doesn't mind getting a little wet and has an average degree of fitness can be a sea kayaker. The basic stroke is a surprisingly easy push-me-pull-you done with a double-bladed paddle; most people pick it up with a minimal amount of instruction. And you don't need that much in the way of basic gear to go sea kayaking, although you do need a kayak. These are made from many materials, including but not limited to seal skin (the original kayaks), wood, canvas, Kevlar, fiberglass, and plastic. Some designs are wide and very stable; others are narrow, fast-moving, and often quite tippy. Then there are collapsible, or folding, kayaks, which can be dismantled and packed into a large duffel bag. Most common are single and double kayaks, although there are custom multiples as well.

Kayaks generally have a fairly roomy cockpit; you sit with your legs comfortably stretched in front of you and your feet braced on adjustable pedals, which work the rudder of your boat. A spray skirt draped around your waist stretches to the rim of the cockpit. Although it can seem a touch claustrophobic, its function is to keep water out of your cockpit, not to keep you locked in. If you should happen to be knocked over by a wave, either the skirt will automatically come free or you can yank the escape cord and slide right out for a swim.

Don't assume that 10 minutes without tipping has adequately prepared you to circumnavigate Baffin Island. There's a lot to learn, and until you know your way around tides, currents, and nautical charts, you should go with an experienced guide who also knows what and how to pack and where to pitch a tent. A reputable outfitter can supply such a guide.

Freelance writer Rena Zurofsky has kayaked the waters of Maine, Central America, and the Canadian coasts. In her other life, she is a museum administrator.

Sea kayaking trips with an outfitter generally follow the same basic routine: You and 5 to 11 other paddlers meet 1 or 2 guides either at the put-in or at some other point from which you are shuttled to the put-in. On the first day you work on kayaking technique. You usually learn both the wet exit (how to fall out) and self-rescue (how to get back in). On succeeding days, paddling is interspersed with time to hike, play in the surf, improve your kayaking skills, or just lie around eating the M&Ms and peanuts that seem to be a staple of every mess kit. Itineraries are flexible; how far you paddle each day depends on the ability and stamina of the group as a whole. Although many intrepid sea kayakers do major open-water crossings, it is more common to make modest island crossings of up to, perhaps, 5 miles.

Different outfitters prefer different approaches to guiding, but most station one guide near the front of the group and another near the back to act as "sweep" to make sure the slowest paddlers don't fall behind. Kayaking guides are often trained biologists, botanists, or geologists; those who are not are usually extremely knowledgeable about the locations to which they escort you. Before you leave, you will be provided with reading lists: Use them to enhance your experience.

Most kayak outings are camping trips. You'll be surprised by how much gear can be wedged—with much planning and effort— through the waterproof hatches located in the front and rear of each kayak: clothes, tent, sleeping gear, cooking gear, food, fresh water, first-aid kit, cooking equipment, and more. Still, even fully loaded, a kayak rarely draws more than a few inches of water, and because of its low center of gravity, a packed boat is in fact a more stable craft.

The food on sea kayaking trips varies in quality. On a true expedition, you are expected to carry your share of the provisions in your boat. To keep weight and volume down, pasta, rice, and beans are usually a significant part of your diet, but some outfitters use miniature freezer packs to carry

meats, and many fish along the way. All of the outfitters listed below make a point of including as many fresh vegetables and fruits as possible; some stick to strictly vegetarian meals. Keep in mind that on longer trips, if there is no resupply point, you are eventually reduced to dried fruits and few vegetables.

Breakfasts usually consist of granolas, pancakes, oatmeal, or hot multigrain cereal, sometimes eggs and bacon. Lunches are often peanut butter, cheeses, salami, local jams, and homemade breads. Dinners are where an inventive guide can really go to town. Of course, there are the oh-so-familiar "Italian" or "Mexican" menus that are still tasty thanks to an appetite sharpened by a day's paddle. But you might also be served fish chowders, Thai chicken stews, and curried lentils that would be equally savory on shore. There's often wine, and always coffee, tea, and cocoa.

Food is usually prepared over a campfire or a camp stove. You sit where you can and use basic utensils. In our listings, guides tend to do the work unless chore sharing is specifically stated or unless you offer to help. Most people do.

Compared with bicycling or golf-school vacations, sea kayaking is inexpensive. Prices range from less than $100 to $200 per person per day, depending on whether the trip includes special transportation, such as an air charter, or hotel stays. Costs are kept low because camping is the norm and food supplies can be bought in bulk.

This is far from a complete listing of sea kayaking trips and outfitters. Furthermore, if you would rather design your own trip, most operators will customize a tour for your group.

CHOOSING THE RIGHT TRIP

In choosing an outfitter, your primary concern should be safety. An outfitter should be equipped with both the proper technical and first-aid gear, and should know what to do with them. Question every outfitter carefully so that you know what you're getting into.

How long has the company been in business? A couple of years of experience gives an outfitter time to work out problems with its operation and itineraries. All of the outfitters listed here have been in business a minimum of three years, although many have been leading trips for five or more.

How long have the guides been leading trips and how long have they been leading in the area where I want to go? The outfitters we list all use guides that have at least five years of kayaking experience, although not necessarily in a particular location. Sometimes it's best to have a guide who knows an area really well, but a guide's first visit can also be exciting. You decide.

What kind of training do the guides have? Look for outfitters whose guides have successfully completed a guiding course, such as those offered by Outward Bound, National Outdoor Leadership School, and Maine Island Kayak Company, or have been certified by either the American Canoe Association or the British Canoe Association.

Because organized sea kayaking is still very much in its infancy, no certification is usually needed to become an outfitter of guided tours. (The state of Maine requires that all outfitters be Registered Maine Guides, a license that involves considerable wilderness training, as well as the ability to make fish chowder.)

What is the participant-to-guide ratio? 5:1 is a recommended maximum, although some reputable outfits push to 6:1 or even 8:1 on calm waters.

How difficult, challenging, and scary is the trip? We've tried to give you an idea of how much skill and stamina you'll need to complete each of the following trips, but you should always ask for more information before you sign up. Keep in mind that if you're interested in a trip but are concerned that it is too advanced for you, most outfitters will happily give you extra instruction

(at a price) before you set out. You should also be sure to figure out your own fear levels. Again, be honest with yourself. Knowing how to handle surf is not the same as wanting to learn. At best, a novice among experts curtails everyone else's enjoyment; at worst, he can put himself in danger. I try to break through the next level with each trip, so I evaluate carefully how much I can handle at once—big waves *and* big marine mammals?

Is seasickness an issue? If you get seasick, some trips just won't be any fun. Watch for Hawaii's giant swells.

What will the weather be? It is important for you to evaluate honestly your own tolerance for heat, cold, and dampness. Nothing can ruin a trip faster than pervasive discomfort.

What are the accommodations like? Most of the time you sleep in tents, but sometimes there are huts or lean-tos and sometimes you sleep under the open skies. If tents are provided, ask how many people sleep in each one.

What's the food like? Some guides are terrific cooks; others just don't care about food. Ask for a menu, and, if you can, talk to someone who has taken the trip.

What kind of boats will you be using and is there a variety of boats to choose from? You'll often hear guides talking about "wearing the boat." That means that the kayak becomes an extension of its paddler, a state that makes the paddling experience not only more comfortable but also much more fun. Ask whether the outfitter stocks a variety of boats, so you can experiment until you find the kayak that best fits your weight, strength, ability, and paddling style.

What's the cost and what's included? The trips we list start at the point of put-in and include transportation back to that point. Transportation from and to the local airport is not included, although some outfitters provide it at a nominal fee. The trip fee also covers meals from lunch the first day to lunch the last. Unless otherwise stated, outfitters on these trips provide all kayaking gear (boats, spray skirts, personal flotation devices, wet suits, neoprene booties if necessary, and paddles), plus tents, cookware, and first-aid equipment, but *not* sleeping bags and pads.

How far in advance do you need to sign up? As you might expect, outfitters want you to sign up as far in advance as possible for a simple reason: If they don't get enough customers, it's not financially worth it to run the trip. For trips offered regularly, 30 days in advance might do. For trips offered infrequently or in faraway places, signing up anywhere from six months to a year in advance is not outrageous. There are, however, always last-minute cancellations.

Can you supply names of people who have taken this trip? This is one sure way to find out whether a good, safe time is usually had by all.

MAJOR PLAYERS

Sea kayaking is only lately becoming widely popular, so no organizations run trips throughout the nation. The following, however, do offer a host of trips in limited areas.

SIERRA CLUB OUTINGS DEPARTMENT This organization has a huge roster of expeditions and other trips, all run by leaders who are both members and volunteers. But unlike its selection of backpacking and hiking trips, which number in the hundreds, there may be only half a dozen sea kayaking trips. From year to year, destinations change, leaders change, trips to a particular area or with a particular leader may follow a different itinerary. Still, there are almost always a couple of trips to Alaska and off the coast of Georgia; Baja trips are offered fairly frequently; and trips in the Midwest, to destinations such as Wisconsin's Apostle Islands, put in an occasional appearance. Camping out and group participation in camp chores are the operative protocols, and costs are low to moderate (730 Polk St., San Francisco, CA 94109, tel. 415/923–5522, fax 415/776–4868).

ALASKA DISCOVERY This company holds the exclusive concession for sea kayaking trips in Glacier Bay National Park. In other words, these guys know what they're doing (5449-4 Shaune Dr., Juneau, AK 99801, tel. 907/780–6226 or 800/586–1911, fax 907/780–4220).

BLUE MOON EXPLORATIONS Blue Moon's Kathleen Grimbly combined her interest in cultural anthropology and nature studies with kayaking. As a result, you are as likely to dine on traditional Pacific Northwest Indian planked salmon on her trips as you are to paddle with migrating orca whales. Blue Moon specializes in customized tours, including corporate retreats and women's workshops; destinations onclude the San Juan Islands, Vancouver Island, and Hawaii. (Box 2568F, Bellingham, WA 98227, tel. and fax 360/856–5622).

MAINE ISLAND KAYAK COMPANY With more than 10 years of experience, MIKCO offers instructional seminars and island-camping trips all along the Maine Island Trail, as well as in Nova Scotia. Although the back office can be a little confused at times (sometimes they change put-in sites with little warning), MIKCO trips are professional and enjoyable, with camp food that's a revelation (70 Luther St., Peaks Island, ME 04108, tel. 207/766–2373 or 800/796–2373, fax 207/773–8601).

OUTWARD BOUND If you don't mind the constant emphasis on team-building and community, Outward Bound programs offer some of the best paddling-skills workshops and trips in the country. Be aware, however, that having fun is often second on the agenda, and food is even lower still. Outward Bound runs sea kayaking programs in Maine, North Carolina, Minnesota, and Oregon (Rte. 9D, R2, Box 280, Garrison, NY 10524–9757, tel. 914/424–4000 or 800/243–8520, fax 914/ 424–4280). For more about Outward Bound, *see* Wilderness and Survival Schools.

SOUTHWIND SPORTS RESOURCES This extremely professional operation places a strong emphasis on training and skills, for both beginner and advanced paddlers. It has a full complement of kayaks, so you're sure to find a model that suits you best (17855 Sky Park Circle #A, Irvine, CA 92714, tel. 714/261–0200 or 800/768–8494).

FAVORITE TRIPS

THE NORTHEAST

MAINE **Down East: Prospect Harbor via Jonesport to Machias.** Fog makes this trip an exercise in trust: Trust that the guide can read his or her compass; trust that he or she hears the big boats out there; trust that the shadow the guide is asking you to strain to see is in fact a granite-and-pine island where you can legally rest.

This trip is the quintessential tour of the Maine Island Trail, a 325-mile-long waterway in northern Maine that stretches from Casco Bay to Machias. You travel along the northern edge of the trail, which has the most demanding water, the most varied terrain, the most striking vistas, and the fewest signs of civilization.

You meet at 8 AM in the Prospect Harbor area, where you spend the entire first day developing your kayaking skills. Wet suits are distributed so that you can practice wet exits and self-rescues. Although the Maine coast has its calm moments, wind, rain, and waves are a real possibility; big-boat traffic and fog are virtual certainties—especially around the Petit Manan bar, an underwater ridge whose volcanic spires stretch 3 miles out into the sea. The spires force the cold Labrador current to the surface of the water, causing this area to have the reputation of second foggiest spot on the East Coast.

The island and mainland landscapes you paddle past are striking in their variety. Although much of the underlying rock is granite, you see everything from mile-long white sand beaches to imposing cliffs climbing out of the surf. At the southern end of the trip the vegetation is deciduous, but soon you see conifers, then subarctic jack pines. Many of these islands are owned by the

Nature Conservancy and are home to eagles, puffins, and other seabirds. On those that are not privately owned, you hike along cobble beaches and over grassy slopes. You may even attempt a stop on the island called Ladle Ledges, if Bojangles, the foul-tempered territorial black ram, allows it. You might also see seals, harbor porpoise, and minks.

As on most kayaking trips, the distances you cover are dictated by a combination of group strength and weather conditions. Assume you'll paddle anywhere between 8 and 15 miles per day, unless you are totally weathered in. Every few nights the group may opt to remain at a campsite for more hiking or kayaking instruction. Campsites are strictly wilderness, and you are expected to pack out everything you've brought in.

Food on this trip consists of fresh vegetables, home baked breads, grains, even pizza. Fish may be caught and lobster may be bought. Depending on the time of year, you may dig for mussels or forage for berries.

A maximum of 6 people are accompanied by 2 guides on this trip. Single kayaks are used. You should be in good physical shape with some previous paddling experience. *Maine Island Kayak Company, 70 Luther St., Peaks Island, ME 04108, tel. 207/766–2373 or 800/796–2373. July and August: 6 days, $900.*

THE SOUTH

FLORIDA **The Everglades and the 10,000 Islands.** Alligators, mosquitoes, and gnats—all are abundant in these swampy waters. But although every kayaker is sure to be bit by the latter two, as far as I know no kayaker has actually been eaten by an alligator. That's not to say that you won't be tense when one or more suddenly emerges from the quiet waters.

On this outing you just day-trip into the mangrove swamps of the Everglades, and reemerge to camp on the breezy, sandy beaches on the Gulf of Mexico. Some days you may not even venture into the mysterious mangroves. The group dynamic and the weather (if it blows out of the west) put you inland onto the 100-mile-long Wilderness Waterway (a marked water trail that runs from Flamingo to Everglades City) or keep you on the Gulf, where you can kayak from key to key, or back and forth between the mainland and the islands.

Beginning in Everglades City, the group heads south, camping in places with names like Pavilion Key and Turkey Key. These are sandy spots that are less atmospheric but more comfortable than the wooden stilt "chickees" and shell mounds available in the mangrove swamps themselves. Actually, sleeping on a sandy beach with the Gulf waters lapping the shores is not exactly lacking atmosphere, is it?

You paddle 5 to 6 hours a day. If the waters are clear you might see black-tips or nurse sharks. You're almost certain to spot dolphins. There are eagles, ospreys, swallow-tailed kites, the occasional flamingo, and alligators (only in the swamps). Some motorboat and sailing traffic is sure to be about, especially at Everglades City and Flamingo, but most beaches are absolutely pristine, framed by beach grasses and coastal palms.

The guide prepares your meals, but you are welcome to bring gear and fish for the group's dinners. Since you have to carry your whole week's worth of water in your boats, much of the food is freeze-dried, and pastas and beans are a significant part of your menu.

The maximum group size is 8, accompanied by one guide, in rigid single and double boats. This trip is suitable for all levels of paddlers. The best time to go is winter, and even then the days will be quite warm and moist, though cooler in the evenings. *Florida Bay Outfitters, 104050 Overseas Hwy., Key Largo, FL 33037, tel. 305/451–3018. Mid-Nov.–mid-Apr.: 7 days, $695. Price includes sleeping bags and foam pads.*

NORTH CAROLINA **The Outer Banks.** For those of you who have avoided Outward Bound because you don't *want* to lose your fear of rappelling, this sea kayaking venture is a way in. Okay, in order to build group spirit you and your 10 fellow paddlers have to discuss every move you make, but that isn't really a bad idea. And you spend one day doing some type of public service—working with wild ponies, studying dune formation, or hanging out with retired fishermen—but that isn't so bad either.

The North Carolina Outward Bound School offers 9 days of cruising the Outer Banks with 2 guides that have wilderness-survival expertise and are trained in basic communications and group facilitations. Their job is to "facilitate" good group interaction and to teach you skills like compass-reading and navigation. And to get you in shape for your solo camping experience—an Outward Bound must.

The trip starts at New Bern airport, and put-in is nearby, on the Neuse River. You paddle along the river and around the waters near Cape Lookout National Seashore, south of the Wright Brothers national monument. Happily, this area is well-removed from the heavily built-up beach towns of more northern Outer Banks. If conditions are calm, you may try ocean kayaking; otherwise, there is room enough and interest enough to stay on the inland side. It's pretty easy paddling, in and out of marshlands and tidal flats. You are challenged physically when you learn wet exits and self-rescues, but few crossings are more than a mile.

At night, you camp in the wilderness on remote beaches, with no facilities. You rise at dawn and spend the day in motion, paddling as many as 25 miles if conditions are excellent. But there are also days when you pass the time exploring dunes, acquiring map and compass skills, or engaging in service activities. At the end of the trip, you are left alone for 24 hours, an experience that is usually so peaceful that you wish it lasted longer.

The maximum group size is 10, accompanied by 2 guides, in single and double kayaks. The minimum age is 18. This trip is suitable for all levels of paddlers. *North Carolina Outward Bound School, 121 North Sterling St., Morganton, NC 28655-3443, tel. 704/437–6112 or 800/841–0186. May, Sept., Oct.: 9 days, $995.*

THE MIDWEST

MINNESOTA AND ONTARIO Lake Superior: **Sibley Peninsula and Pukaskwa Park.** Kayaking around these two island-dotted landscapes is like taking a trip into a fabulous canvas: Everywhere are bold strokes of bold colors, deep greens and blues, cut by the sharp gray of granite cliffs and boulders. The world's largest freshwater lake, Superior provides a kayaking experience that is just as varied as that offered by an ocean: still waters, wind and waves, fog and rain.

This trip begins at the University of Minnesota in Duluth, where you catch a van to a small inland lake, Marie Louise, on Ontario's Sibley Peninsula. You spend 2 nights camping here, with the first day devoted to improving your paddling skills while kayaking on Marie Louise, and then trying them out on an afternoon excursion on Lake Superior. There, the steep-banked, pebbly beached, rugged islands have quartz veins running through them, and if conditions are right, you can look down into the water where the quartz gleams through.

On the third morning you're driven to Canada's Pukaskwa National Park, on the northeast corner of the lake, for an afternoon put-in that begins 5 full days of paddling.

There's a lot to learn on this trip: You make open-water crossings, explore the interesting coast and rock outcrops, and tackle potentially wild river entries, made difficult to cross because of the runoff from upriver waterfalls. Caribou sightings are a definite possibility, and you may also see moose, white-tailed deer, black bears, river otters, osprey, and eagles.

Although this trip can be rough at times, it is an excellent introduction to different conditions and good for beginners: Open-water

crossings are minimal (less than 1 mile) and paddling distances are just 8 to 10 miles per day. Kayakers with more advanced skills enjoy the landscape and are challenged by the often-changing weather.

Just because the trip is school-sponsored doesn't mean that you travel with a young and rowdy crowd. The group tends to be mixed, with some teenagers and some middle-aged folks. Often a professor comes along. Sometimes no one in the entire group is affiliated with the university. Chores are assigned on this trip, which is offered every other year (the next trip being in 1996). The maximum size of the group is 8 paddlers, accompanied by 2 guides, in rigid single or double kayaks. *Kayak and Canoe Institute, University of Minnesota Outdoor Program, 121 Sports and Health Center, 10 University Dr., Duluth, MN 55812-2496, tel. 218/ 726–6533, fax 218/726–6529. Late July–early Aug.: 9 days, $521, $331 for UMD students. Price includes van transportation from Duluth.*

THE SOUTHWEST

UTAH Lake Powell. If you wanted to kayak much of the Colorado River, you'd need a white-water craft and a great deal of skill and nerve. But the imposition of the Glen Canyon Dam has rendered one part of that mighty river into a 186-mile-long lake that even a beginning kayaker can handle. And the desert Chinook winds make for an occasionally wavy good time.

Starting off from Hall's Crossing in the southeast corner of the lake, you paddle a mere 3 to 10 miles a day, maybe 15 if the group is really cooking. You must like heat and sun, because temperatures average in the low 80s and shade is hard to find. Under these conditions, falling out of your kayak is a welcome cold relief.

When you're not on the water, you have the opportunity to take hikes in the side canyons. Some hikes lead to Anasazi ruins; others take you past gleaming, sinuous slick-rocks, and desert flora and fauna—cacti and turkey vultures and rattlesnakes.

The downside of this trip is that the lake gets 3 million visitors annually, and most of them believe in motor boats and jet skis. And then there are the houseboats, which are moored in every scenic cove. Luckily, your kayak takes you into the shallow, narrow, out-of-the way places the houseboats can't go. And because Glen Canyon Dam's seasonal releases reveal or conceal caves, coves, and beaches along the lake's 1,960 miles of shoreline, the topography changes, affording plenty of quiet and solitude, if you know where to find it.

You camp in private red-rock canyons, or surrounded by gleaming white slick-rocks or sand, with the vivid blue of the water creating a landscape of stark contrasts in color and light. Although nights dip into the 30s, camping in this environment is an aesthetic tour de force, since the colors flattened by the light of day are often heightened by moonlight. The food is vegetarian, with a lot of pastas, soups, and chilies.

This company specializes in creating trips that can be joined by people with disabilities, who make up about half of most groups and participate in every activity.

Two well-trained guides accompany a maximum of 8 paddlers in triple kayaks. This trip is suitable for all levels. *Wilderness Inquiry, Inc., 1313 Fifth St. SE, Box 84, Minneapolis, MN 55414-1546, tel. 612/379–3858 or 800/728–0719, fax 612/379–5972. Mar.–Apr.: 8 days, $895. Price does not include $175 for round-trip van from Minneapolis (1½ days each way; be prepared to be driven through the night).*

THE WEST COAST

WASHINGTON San Juan Island, Orca Waters. The name of this trip says it all and should set your mood for 5 days with orcas, also known as killer whales. Despite their name and their size (adults generally reach about 25 feet in length), they have never been known to so much as dump a kayaker. Actually, the pods that revisit these waters tend to feast on salmon, herring, and other local fish.

The trip sets out from Friday Harbor, a port on San Juan Island that can be reached by a 4-hour ferry ride from Seattle. The San Juans are in the rain shadow of the Olympic and Cascade mountains, so they enjoy a mild, sunny climate, which means you just might stay dry while you're kayaking.

You launch from the west side of the island and head northwest. The trips vary in itinerary because the goal is to follow the whales, but you often cross into Canadian waters. An average day's paddling is 5 or 6 hours, depending on the winds, tides, and currents among the countless islands that make up the San Juan archipelago. As with most trips, wildlife sightings aren't guaranteed, but certain pods of orcas have returned again and again to these waters, and outfitters such as Sea Quest, which is run by a marine biologist, have long made it their business to know the best places to spot whales. In addition to the orcas, you may luck into the occasional loner minke whale, or some gregarious seals and sea lions. Birds in the area include bald eagles and the adorable, piping, orange-trimmed oyster catcher.

A maximum of 12 are taken in rigid double kayaks by 2 guides. Paddling instruction takes place on land, and you won't learn a wet exit and self-rescue, so it's comforting to be in the bigger double boats when whales surround you. It is also good to be in the bigger boats when some of the local motor boat traffic attempts to rush the whales. *Sea Quest Expeditions, Zoetic Research, Box 2424, Friday Harbor, WA 98250, tel. 206/378–5767. June–Sept.: 5 days, $449.*

ALASKA

SOUTHEAST Glacier Bay Grand Sea Kayak. It's a rare sea kayaker who hasn't gone or doesn't yearn to go to Alaska. Forget the cold. It isn't that cold in summer: 50°F to 80°F, although it gets colder once the sun actually sets (which can be quite late). Instead, picture deep icy bays in perfect blue stillness, interrupted by the great cracking sound of a glacier calving and huge chunks of ice thundering into the water. Imagine the sounding of whales, their breath almost welcomed for its heat (but not for its fishy odor). Although law dictates that you don't get too close to the whales, and the guides will do their best to have you all maintain respectful distances, the whales have been known to make their own approaches and surface as little as 20 feet away!

For this 7-day Alaska Discovery trip you begin in Gustavus and are flown into Glacier Bay National Park. You paddle the entire length of the east arm of the bay, a route that totals 60 miles of rigorous paddling.

There's the chance—the risk—that grizzly bears and wolves will share your sunlit nights. The guides choose your campsites for availability of water, protection from the weather, and accessibility to hiking trails. They lead beach and meadow walks, carrying bear mace for your protection. The food is not strictly vegetarian, but vegetarians are accommodated. Anglers can fish for salmon and halibut (bring your own gear). You move camp daily, and you're expected to share the chores.

You get basic paddle training, but no training for wet exits, because, frankly, you don't want to fall out in this water (and you probably won't—the double boats are pretty stable). Alaska hands may grouse that you won't see the variety of marine life that you might on a trip in nearby Icy Strait, but odds are you'll spot Stellar's sea lions, sea otters, harbor seals, and harbor porpoises.

The old growth rain forest at the entrance to Glacier Bay is 200 years older than the back of the bay, where the glacier is still retreating. As you head north, the vegetation alters, moving from conifers to cottonwood, finally to scrub brush and lichen before turning to barren rock. Birds abound, including bald eagles, an assortment of gulls, loons, horned and tufted puffins, cormorants, hawks, ptar-

migans, owls, kingfishers, and herons. Be aware, however, that as you travel north, the land and climate support life in less abundance. To see wildlife, you must be patient. The weather is likely to be wet, with rain falling at some point in the day, either in a heavy mist or a downpour, and skies often overcast. Consider in your planning that June gets 18 hours of light, but August gets the Northern Lights.

The maximum group size is 10 paddlers, accompanied by 2 guides. Energetic beginners will do okay, but you need to be fit because on some days you must work hard on the water to reach the desirable campsites. Note: Trips alternate paddling south-to-north and north-to-south, but all end in Gustavus. *Alaska Discovery, 5449-4 Shaune Dr., Juneau, AK 99801, tel. 907/780–6226 or 800/586– 1911, fax 907/780–4220. June–Aug.: 7 days, $1,800. Price includes round-trip air charter between Gustavus and Glacier Bay as well as all camping and rain gear.*

HAWAII

KAUAI **Na Pali Coast.** There are real reasons why the Hawaiian islands are called paradise: the ocean breezes, the wavering palms, the fast hard rains that cool you for the few minutes it takes to dry off. There are private pools and waterfalls, fragrant naupaka, beach morning glories, and dense vegetation from coconut palms to the multibranched, broad-leafed milo tree. But paradise comes at a price for paddlers, and the cost, in this case, is surf.

Hawaii is the surf capital of the world, and on this 6-day Na Pali Coast trip you may have to steer straight into a 6-foot wave that's just about to crash or, if you're lucky, ride it in. If the idea of eating sand fills you with fear, this is probably not the trip for you. But if you're daring and you don't get seasick, these ocean swells will float you to semiremote gleaming white sand beaches, such as the gorgeous crescent of Milolii.

Actually, you camp on only two beaches, Kalalau and Milolii, taking day trips out from each. So if you're rejected by the ocean, you can hike to deep pools and great sand dunes, or follow trails to waterfalls. And the sea conditions can't be too bad, anyway, since the outfitter regularly gets ice floated in (to Kalalau, at least). There aren't too many outfitters, except those in the Arctic, who can accomplish ice!

The trip puts in at Haena Beach Park early in the day, before the winds come up. Your days of kayaking—short hops of only about 6 miles—may take you exploring into sea caves that open into vaults of light or contain secret waterfalls. Although paddling instruction is strictly basic, fit beginners will do just fine. The primary concern is seasickness. You will probably learn a wet exit by doing one in the surf zone. On at least 2 days—if the group wants to—you paddle to good snorkeling spots. Free time is a Hawaiian specialty, and the guides give you as much as you'd like.

The beaches that are your base are equipped with open-air showers and very basic toilet facilities, but you still sleep in a tent or right out under the stars. Wild passion fruit, guavas, papayas, and bananas are on the menu, as are just-caught ahi (yellowfin tuna), fresh vegetables, local Portuguese breads, and wine. There's poi if you want it, too. Chores are shared.

Unfortunately, others know about this little bit of paradise, so you'll be buzzed occasionally by pleasure boaters and helicopter tours. The maximum group size is 12 paddlers in double or single kayaks, accompanied by 2 guides. *Kayak Kauai Outbound, Box 508, Hanalei, Kauai, Hawaii 96714, tel. 808/826–9844, fax 808/822–0577. May–Sept.: 6 days, $1,050. Price includes transport by van from Lihue or Princeville airports.*

SOURCES

ORGANIZATIONS There are many regional kayaking clubs, and most of them actively schedule trips throughout the United States. The best way to find out about clubs near you or about clubs that operate in the areas you wish to visit, is to contact the **Trade Association of Sea Kayakers** (Box 84144, Seattle, WA 98124, tel. 206/621–1018). TASK can also refer you to member outfitters. *Canoe* magazine's Club Hotline (tel. 800/692–2663) and the back pages of *Sea Kayaker* magazine are also good sources of information.

PERIODICALS A monthly magazine, *Canoe* (Box 316, Kirkland, WA 98083-3146, tel. 206/827–6363 or 800/678–5432) includes articles on canoeing and kayaking techniques, destinations, and resources. *Paddler* (Box 775450, Steamboat Springs, CO 80477, tel. 303/879–1450) covers canoeing, kayaking, and rafting; it contains a calendar of events and equipment reviews. The quarterly *Sea Kayaker* (6327 Seaview Ave. NW, Seattle, WA 98107-2664, tel. 206/789–9536) discusses equipment, technique, and journeys in-depth.

BOOKS *Sea Kayaking: A Manual for Long-Distance Touring,* by John Dowd, is a reference covering equipment, techniques, survival skills, and expedition planning. Fully illustrated, *The Essential Sea Kayaker,* by David Seidman, covers basic and advanced sea kayaking techniques, and tells you what to wear, how to travel to your put-ins, and more. You'll learn about safety and how to read charts and recognize sea conditions when you read *The Coastal Kayaker's Manual,* by Randel Washburne. This book also gives you information on what to wear and how to pack. Maps and descriptions of trips along the Northeast Seaboard can be found in *Sea Kayaking along the New England Coast,* by Tamsin Venn. Its Hawaiian counterpart is *Paddling Hawaii,* by Audrey Sutherland, and for information on the West Coast, try Joel Rogers's *The Hidden Coast—Kayak Explorations From Alaska to Mexico.*

ALSO SEE There are lots of other trips that you can take in a kayak. Canoeing and Kayaking in Flat Water tells you about the calm ones, and Canoeing and Kayaking in White Water puts you on the rapids.

Ski Schools

By Rosemary Freskos

Updated by Jordan Simon

hether you're an expert parallel skier or a beginner with a sense of adventure, a ski school vacation can be life-enhancing. It's not the same as simply going to a resort and taking one or two hour-long lessons. What we're talking about here is *intensive* skiing—skiing every day for up to 6 hours with an instructor watching you, drilling you and pushing you ahead. Not only do you learn how to ski better, you also learn that if you try harder, you can always improve your skills, on and off the slopes.

Nearly every ski resort in the United States has a ski school, but they are not all the same. Some small operations at small resorts offer only short group lessons and private lessons; others have 1,000 instructors teaching programs for every level.

The better (and usually bigger) ski schools hire only the most professional teachers, usually those who are certified by the Professional Ski Instructors of America, or PSIA. To get certified, a skier must first take a ski school instructor-training course and become an instructor. Then he or she can take a PSIA exam. Instructors commonly pass PSIA Levels I and II within two years; passing Level III is a rare achievement that takes from 5 to 8 years. (Most instructors teach for only 4 years before moving on to other professions.)

There are different methods of teaching people how to ski, but PSIA-certified instructors are trained in the organization's American Teaching System (ATS), which aims to make learning to ski as easy as possible. Following the ATS manual, instructors teach both novices and experts by breaking down the act of skiing into basic movement components: pressure control, edging, rotary, and balancing movements. The ATS allows an instructor to adapt his or her lessons to the particular terrain and to the students' level of skiing ability.

Although the ATS is most popular in the United States, some ski schools also use the Austrian, French, and Swiss teaching methods. With these methods you still need to learn the basic wedge turn, but you learn a different style of skiing. For example, the Austrian style is more rigid than the American; it emphasizes a stable upper body and strong counter rotation, with legs held together. On the other hand, the French style is to rotate the body and lean into the turns. Some resorts have their own teaching methods, usually variations on the ATS, and some are now using the Perfect Turn method, which was developed by Maine's Sunday River resort.

No matter what method is used, the quality of teaching at any school is greatly affected by the ski school director, who motivates

---

Rosemary Freskos has been writing about snow sports for some two decades. She took her first ski lessons on Ohio's modest slopes and has since skied at most of the world's major ski resorts. Jordan Simon is a regular contributor to Fodor's guides.

instructors and adapts the teaching system to best suit the area's terrain and clientele.

Once you're with an instructor what can you expect? If you're a "never ever" skier, your first hour will be spent learning how to balance, walk around and climb by side-stepping. Then you learn to slide down a very gentle incline, turn, and, hopefully, stop. The most important lesson is the one on how to fall and how to get up. By the second lesson you should feel secure enough to get that "whee" thrill of sliding while in control. You'll be making linked wedge turns and steering around obstacles. Those are the basics. Some skiers stay there for years; others get their skis together and make decent parallel turns in 3 or 4 days.

Age is no excuse to avoid skiing, but physical condition is. It's best to have all your parts working up to optimum level before tackling the slopes; this lessens the chance of pulled muscles and broken limbs. But even if you're in good shape, don't overdo it. Four to six hours of skiing is only for those in top condition; 2 to 3 hours of steady skiing is usually enough for the average person. If possible, avoid beginning your lessons on a weekend, since midweek classes are usually smaller and the slopes, less crowded. It's also less expensive to ski during the week.

Safety is a primary concern of ski areas as well as most skiers. The National Ski Patrol, a well-trained organization of volunteers and paid members is an important part of every ski area's staff. They help skiers in trouble and try to prevent accidents and promote safe skiing.

CHOOSING THE RIGHT SCHOOL

Many people plan their vacation and then ask about the ski school, but if you really want to *go to ski school* you must concentrate on asking questions about the ski school programs rather than about the resort. Start with these:

How long has the ski school been in business? The more experience the school has,

the more smoothly your lessons are likely to go.

Who are the instructors and what are their qualifications? Instruction costs the same no matter how well qualified or inexperienced the instructor. Although it's good to have an instructor who is PSIA certified, there are instructors who are not certified who are just as good.

If I'm not improving or communicating with my instructor can I request another one and another class at no extra charge? Sometimes you just don't feel comfortable with a particular instructor. Make sure you have the option of switching.

How large are the classes and if I'm the only one signed up for a group lesson will I still get the group rate? The maximum number of skiers for a good class is 10, but it's better to have just 6. At most schools you still pay the group rate if you're the only one who has signed up for a group class.

Do you use video for student analysis? Progressive schools film you while you're skiing and use the tape to show you what you're doing wrong (or right). Some even give you the tape at the end of the course.

What's the cost and what's included? Pricing for ski school programs varies in a big way. Some schools supply only lessons; others include lodging, meals, lift tickets, and rentals. Unless otherwise stated, prices given here include your lessons only; when lodging is included, prices are per person, double occupancy.

What are the accommodations like? Ski areas have hotels, inns, condos, and, sometimes, bed-and-breakfasts. If you're buying a package, ask for specifics about your room. If you need to book your own accommodations, make sure you know all your options.

What is the food like? Find out what kind of restaurants are on the mountain and if there is a grocery store nearby.

Do you have references from past guests? It's a good idea to talk with someone who has taken the course and can tell you more specifics about how it is run. Be sure to ask who the best instructors are.

How far in advance do I need to book? Special programs fill up quickly, so you may need to reserve a spot a few months in advance; other programs will take you on arrival at the resort.

FAVORITE TRAVELING PROGRAMS

Women's Ski Adventures. Kim Reichhelm, two-time World Women's Extreme Skiing Champion, personally runs these clinics geared specifically to women's needs and physical abilities. Kim's goal is to enable women of all ages to ski with confidence and enjoyment. All students, from first-timers to advanced, will learn to ski more aggressively in all conditions. Clinic sites change each year; in 1996 they'll be held in Aspen (January 6–10), $1,449; Crested Butte, January 24–28 and February 8–12 ($1,179); and Ruby Mountain Heli-Skiing in Nevada, March 21–24, $2,695. *Women's Ski Adventures, 237 Post Rd. W, Westport, CT 06880, tel. 203/454–2135 or 800/992–7700. Price includes luxury accommodations, skiing clinics with video analysis, airport transfers, welcome and awards dinners, fashion shows, fun races and awards, lift tickets, breakfast and lunch, product demos, and après-ski parties.*

Extreme Team Advanced Ski Clinics. The Des Lauriers brothers—Rob and Eric—and the Egan brothers—Dan and John—are perennially top-ranked extreme skiers, as well as genuine ski movie stars. Other top extremists, like Kristen Ulmer, Dean Decas, and Kristen Lignell, also participate in the fun. They run these hardcore extreme skiing schools at several U.S. resorts throughout the ski season; the goal is to ski as many different types of terrain and snow conditions (including off-piste) that the mountain has to offer, focusing on the specific skills and technique required. Intensive sessions include emphasizing balance and body position, speed acceptance, visualization, and such disciplines as mogul skiing, "air," and

powder. *In 1995–96: Bolton Valley/Sugarbush, VT, Dec. 15–18 and Mar. 17–20, $495–$587; Grand Targhee, WY, Dec. 9–13 and Jan. 19–23, $695–$741; Lake Louise, Alberta, Jan. 13–17, $658; Crested Butte, CO, Jan. 28–Feb. 2, $950; Squaw Valley, CA, Feb. 26–Mar. 3, $995; Whistler/Blackcomb, BC, and Mountain Heli-Sports, Apr. 15–22, $2,986. The Extreme Team, c/o Mountain View Travel, Box 368, Crested Butte, CO 81224, tel. 970/349–6168 or 800/782–6037. Clinics include lodging lift tickets, clinics with video analysis, welcome party, awards ceremony (everyone gets one).*

FAVORITE SCHOOLS

THE NORTHEAST

MAINE **Sunday River.** Janet Spangler's 5-day Women's Ski Experience focuses on self-empowerment: Women come together for a holistic approach to skiing—including lessons on nutrition, stress reduction, and massage—and they learn lessons applicable to life on the way.

Spangler, who designed the program, has been teaching at ski areas in the East since the mid-80s. Every member of her 20-woman staff is PSIA certified. Sunday River is where the Perfect Turn Skier Development Program began and all Women's Ski Experience professionals (as the ski instructors are called here) use this method. Although the Perfect Turn approach can be applied to novice and expert alike, it's specifically geared toward middle-of-the-road skiers whose learning curve has flattened. Skiers can select their own clinic level by watching a short video that allows them to match their ability with the skills demonstrated on the tape. Instructors stress skiers' strengths, rather than pointing out their weaknesses; this "reward" mentality gets students of on the right foot (or ski) psychologically.

The program starts off on Sunday afternoon, when the group of about 30 women gathers at a reception to check in and watch an "If

You Ski Like This" video. Each woman picks her skiing level with the assistance of a pro, and then identifies her personal learning style (i.e., experiential, analytical), and groups of 5 or 6 are formed.

A group headquarters is set up in a banquet room at the resort's Summit Hotel. This is where you eat your breakfast (a hot and cold buffet spread that changes daily), stretch, and change into ski clothes. Afternoon refreshments are served here, and this is where you come to see yourself skiing on video. Although rentals are not included in the price, students can try out ski gear and equipment specifically designed for women at no charge.

The 5-hour daily coaching sessions focus on group progress in the morning. You have lunch together every day at a different restaurant at the resort. The afternoons are more specialized—you may work on bumps, gates, or steep terrain. You will be filmed at some point in the week, and later you watch and critique yourself. The video is yours to keep. In the late afternoon you can attend seminars covering ski tuning, conditioning, and nutrition, or relax on your own.

The program ends after the Friday session, but there's a festive dinner on Thursday night at the Summit. Everyone gets some kind of award to wrap up the week.

Sunday River has consistently upgraded its facilities, added chairlifts, or cut new trails over the past several years. There are 95 trails serviced by 12 lifts (including 2 high-speed quads) spread over 5 peaks (the tallest has a vertical drop of 2,011 feet). Although much of the skiing could be classed as intermediate, there are a number of expert runs at the summits, including the aptly-named Shock Wave, Vortex, Agony, Obsession, and White Heat, billed as the longest, steepest, and widest trail in the East accessible by a lift.

Women can request a roommate to share hotel costs (not included) or bring a male guest who can make his own skiing arrangements. Regardless of gender or ability, skiers can also add a "Perfect Turn Premier Ski

Week" to their regular package for only $160. *Sunday River Resort, Box 450, Bethel, ME 04217, tel. 207/824–3000 or 800/543–2754, fax 207/824–2111. Dec.–Mar.: 5 days, $549; 3 days, $329. Price includes breakfasts, lunches, 1 dinner, and lift tickets.*

VERMONT **Killington.** Killington, like California's Mammoth, deserves superlatives: It's the largest ski resort in the East and one of the best. Its 6 different peaks, covered by 155 trails, would take a week to explore (take advantage of the free tours offered of the 6 mountains every morning at 9:45 AM). It has a total of 19 lifts, including the new Skyeship (the world's only heated—and fastest—gondola) and 2 high-speed quads. Because Killington makes snow—more than any other area in the world—it has the East's longest ski season, running from mid-October to June. The Rams Head area is beginners' Nirvana; Snowdown and Needle's Eye sections are ideal for intermediates; Skye Peaks, Killington Peak, and the Bear Mountain quad runs (including the fabled Volkswagen-size bumps of Outer Limits) will challenge the most jaded expert skiers.

A leader and innovator since its inception in 1958, the Killington Ski School is headed by John Okolovich, who has a staff of more than 250 full- and part-time instructors. Most are selected from the top graduates of Killington's Instructors' Training Program given each year in late November. The Killington Ski School uses the Accelerated Learning Method (ALM), and it has 99% of beginners skiing from Killington Peak by the third day.

If you've never skied before or you've only skied the so-called bunny hill, sign up for the Introduction to Skiing Program. This program begins with a half-hour film about the ALM, and then you are shuttled to Snowshed, where the elevation is 2,500 feet, and the slope is an open 300 feet wide with specially contoured terrain for teaching different techniques. It's separate from other parts of the mountain but open to all skiers (quite a few take advantage of the run, which is serviced by 4 lifts). Here you are introduced to exercises—stopping, wedge turns, side stepping, and getting on and off a lift—at learning stations. Each skier progresses through the stations at his or her own pace. When you are able to control your speed and direction, you are assigned to a compatible group, and the group continues as a whole through more advanced stations.

Students learn about chair lifts on an instructor-pushed model prior to their first ride. The 2-hour lesson is followed by coaching and skiing tips. This instructional program is available in 1- to 7-day formats to allow for different learning speeds. You could, for example, go through the stations for a few days, or you could work in a group with an instructor and skiers at your level after doing the stations just once.

In addition, Killington hosts several "Special Ski Weeks," ranging from race training to Mogul Clinics, Teen Ski Weeks to Women's Ski Escapes. Intermediate to advanced skiers might consider the Masters Ski School, which improves ability to ski any terrain and pushes skiers to achieve their peak potential. These specialized 2- to 7-day programs are limited to 5 skiers to ensure maximum attention.

Killington does not own lodging, but you can find out about a variety of packages from the Killington Lodging Bureau and Travel Service. *Killington Ski School, c/o Killington Lodging Bureau and Travel Service, Killington Rd., Killington, VT 05751, tel. 802/422–3333 or 800/621–6867, fax 802/422–4391. Oct.–June: $91 and up per day. Price includes limited lift pass and rentals.*

VERMONT **Okemo.** For several years Okemo has been making improvements that have placed it in the major resort category and attracted a lot of vacationing families. High-speed lifts, snowmaking on 95% of the runs, meticulous snow-grooming, mostly gentle intermediate slopes, especially off the Solitude Peak quad and Green Ridge triple, steeper slalom courses through the trees off the Glades Summit quad, and modernized day lodges are some of the draws. In addition, all facilities at the bottom of the mountain are easily accessed.

Okemo has developed a number of instruction programs, but one of the perennial favorites is the Women's Ski Spree, under the direction of Jennifer Speck and completely designed and run by women. Jennifer's philosophy is to let women advance at their own pace and have the best ski experience possible. The 5-day package includes lifts; 3 hours of instruction (by women) each morning; afternoon on-snow clinics with options on gates, bumps, fears, and more; indoor clinics on equipment; free ski tuning; and fitness conditioning. There's a bountiful breakfast and lunch daily, and a welcome party and farewell dinner. Programs start on Monday mornings, but Sunday arrivals can ski free.

The Cutting Edge Ski School offers various other programs as well, including snowboarding camps specially designed for children as well as adults, and intensive afternoon specialty clinics for more experienced skiers, ranging from bump lessons to mastering parallel turns.

Okemo has 72 trails serviced by 10 lifts, including 6 quads. The base elevation here is 1,150 feet, and the vertical drop is 2,150 feet. Lodging packages are available at the slope-side hotel and condos or at country inns in the nearby village of Ludlow. *Okemo Mountain Resort, R.F.D. 1, Ludlow, VT 05149, tel. 802/228–4041, fax 802/228–4558. Jan.–Mar.: 5 days, $475. Price includes lift tickets, breakfasts, lunches, and 1 dinner.*

VERMONT **Smugglers' Notch.** Smugglers' Notch is perennially rated one of America's top family resorts, not only by industry publications like *Snow Country* and *Ski*, but by such acknowledged experts in the field as *Family Circle* and *Parents*. Its Alice in Wonderland child care facility is the East's finest, the innovative "ski camps" appeal to all ages, and they even have an acclaimed Teen Central, which offers a disco and special programs from snow volleyball to chariot tubing. The raves begin with the model self-contained village development; everything from spa to indoor tennis courts and pool to ice rinks to restaurants and lodging is within walking distance.

Needless to say, the ski school excels in teaching children—and in instructing parents how to deal with them on the slopes. Peter Ingvoldstad and his over 200 instructors offer a variety of programs at the Ski Learning Center. While there are few multi-day programs, even daily classes include games, ski lessons and video analysis. All the children's ski programs incoroporate interactive games and well as informative information on everyting from equipment to weather conditions. In addition there are fun races and special themes held throughout the year open to all skiers. Perhaps the most innovative part of Peter's school is the Mom and Me, Dad and me learning program held for children 2-6 every Saturday in January, February and March. Parents of at least intermediate level work with instructors in a group lesson to learn game and techniques that make skiing fun. They can then take their kids out themselves and build upon this foundation. The cost for the 5-session program (any five Saturdays during a two-month period) is $149 for parent and child, including the child's equipment.

Smugglers' also offers a $39 day package for beginners of all ages that includes a group lesson, equipment rental and lift ticket to the easier Morse Mountain section. If you're not skiing after the first day, you receive a second free lesson. Children also have their pick of daily camps, ranging from Discovery (which includes cookie races, cocoa breaks and storytelling), and for older kids, Adventure and Snowboard Camps. Women have their choice of Wednesday seminars all season, including spa time after skiing, or a 3-day Women's escape weekend held three times during the winter for $139 (lift tickets, lessons and spa time included). There are also three intensive weekend Adult Ski Camps during the season, focusing on improving strong skiers' skills, for $189, not including lift ticket.

Smugglers' Notch is composed of three mountains; they provide something for the whole family, too, as well as northern Vermont's biggest vertical. Morse is for those mighty mites and novices of all sizes. Ster-

ling is the choice of savvy intermediates, including one mogul mine in Exhibition and an adult terrain garden that approximates variable snow conditions and terrain. And Madonna offers world-class steeps like F.I.S. and Freefall. It has surprising secret glade runs off the backside toward Stowe, along with posted tree gardens like Doc Dempsey's. *Smugglers' Notch, VT 05464-9599, tel. 802/644–8851 or 800/451–8752, fax 802/644–2713. Club Smugglers' and Family All-Inclusive Week packages start at $499 for a family of up to 4, and include, lodging and lift tickets for 7 days, evening entertainment, several parties including a torchlight parade, 5 group Ski Learning Center lessons, and more.*

VERMONT **Stowe.** Stowe ski school was founded in 1936 by one of the great Austrian ski teachers, Sepp Ruschp. It is now comprised of 3 ski schools, all under the direction of Ruschp's son Peter, assisted by David Merriam, the only member of the 10-person PSIA Demonstration Team who is now working in the East.

About 60% of the 135 instructors here have some level of PSIA certification. The schools use the ATS but make an effort to customize the method to students' individual goals and learning styles. Classes are skill-taught, meaning that instead of being taught how to turn, you learn the skills involved in making a turn, enabling you to make the actual turn with your own knowledge. Class size is limited to 8.

Stowe's Mt. Mansfield Ski School offers the Mountain Experience Week, designed to acquaint intermediate skiers with the different terrain and conditions on Mt. Mansfield and then teach them how to master it. You're in the same group and with the same coach all week, for a 2-hour daily lesson in the morning or in the afternoon.

Other fine programs offered include Racing Clinics, special Extremely Teen camps, for experts a Front Four Workshop (learning to master 4 of the East's gnarliest runs), and the Children's Adventure Center. The Nordic Ski Center is equally renowned.

The mountain's base is at 2,000 feet, and the vertical drop is 2,360 feet. There are 10 lifts, including a high-speed gondola, serving 45 trails, 59% of which are intermediate, including the smooth-as-silk cruisers of Spruce Peak. The legendary Front Four— Goat, Starr, Liftline, and National—are mogul steeps that have long separated great skiers from the merely good.

The 200-year-old town of Stowe is a picturesque New England village, with clapboard and saltbox houses and churches tucked into the mountains. Stowe Mountain Resort, the only slopeside lodging, has 5-day packages with lift tickets; some packages also include meals. *Stowe Mountain Resort, 5781 Mountain Rd., Stowe, VT, 05672, tel. 802/253–3000, fax 802/253–8756. Jan.– Apr.: 5 days, $104 for Mountain Experience week; weekdays lessons only.*

VERMONT **Stratton.** Skiers at this sophisticated resort have been signing up for the Tyrolean Ski Week (now called the Ultimate Ski Week, and lasting for 3–5 days), a program of instruction that can accommodate skiers of all levels, since the early 70s. The goal in this informal program is a close instructor-student relationship. In addition to helping to improve your skiing ability, your instructor acts as a host and guide for the week, giving you tips about what to do on and off the mountain. The staff of 150 is directed by Austrian-born Alois Lechner, who has been at Stratton for more than 20 years.

You arrive Sunday in time for a half-day of skiing, but the champagne welcome party isn't until Monday. Monday through Thursday there is instructor-escorted skiing from 9:30 AM until noon, when everyone breaks for a hearty, complimentary lunch with the instructors, and then more skiing until 4 PM. Daily activities are determined by the group, but usually there aren't many drills. Instead, you may learn more about how to find good trails or snow. Thursday night is the Tyrolean dinner and awards party, and Friday is a free skiing day. Equipment rental is included as is Continental breakfast (week-

days), a group photo, free child care for non-skiing tots under 5, and video analysis. Other top-notch programs include Womens Ski Weeks (similar to those at other resorts described above) and KidsKamp.

The village at the base of the mountain has covered parking for 700 cars, a condo-hotel, restaurants, and a minimall with about 25 shops. The lower mountain is accessible to beginners and intermediates from the 8 lifts at the base lodge. A high-speed gondola serves the upper, more difficult and expert runs, and there are 4 quad chair lifts as well. Stratton has 92 runs, base elevation is 1,900 feet, and the vertical drop is 2,000 feet. The area is nicknamed "Yuppie Hill," thanks to the sleek modern facilities and slopes as manicured as the largely upscale clientele. Snowboarders also regard Stratton as a mecca, since this is where shred guru Jake Burton tested the first boards. As a result, the snowboarding lessons may be the best in the country. Stratton has undergone a major overhaul to retain its position atop the ski hill: $5 million dollars of improvements for the 1995/96 season include increased snowmaking and installation of the East's first 6-person high-speed chairlift.

Despite its image as an easy mountain, Stratton has opened more demanding terrain like Bear Down and Freefall, which feature mammoth moguls. The upper half provides more advanced cruisers like Lift Line, and narrower traditional runs off the Grizzly Chair. The flowing Sun Bowl is another fave, especially on bitter days since it's on the leeward side with a southern exposure. Novices have their own 45-acre Ski Learning Park.

There's plenty to do in the town of Manchester, a factory outlet haven that bustles year-round. *Stratton Corp., Stratton Mountain, VT 05155, tel. 802/297–2200, 802/297–4000, or 800/843–6867, fax 802/297–2939. Dec.–Mar.: 5 days, $199. Price includes breakfasts, lunches, 1 dinner, lift tickets, and rentals.*

VERMONT **Sugarbush.** More than 15 years ago Denise McCluggage and Sigi Grottendorfer set out to change the way people thought about moving downhill and developed the Centered Skiing method. Using Eastern philosophy with Western psychology, as well as visualization techniques, the 5-day Centered Ski Week aims to help primarily intermediate and advanced skiers who have reached a plateau and are frustrated by their inability to ski more challenging terrain.

Each day begins with a round-table breakfast with informal ski-talk. This is followed by a 2-hour workshop led by Paul McKinnie, the "Zen ski master." Using books, music, and illustrations, he tries to teach you GRACE— that is how to be Grounded, Relaxed, Aware, Centered, and Energized. You go through stretching and aerobic movements from yoga and aikido, and you participate in games that promote trust and confidence.

Once on the slopes, you join a group of no more than 5 skiers per instructor. This program involves a bit of New Age thinking. They might tell you to surround yourself in a white light to protect yourself from collisions with other skiers, or have you and other group members concentrate your psychic energy to pull someone gracefully down the mountain. Equipment such as the new Elan parabolic skis, whose unique shape enables skiers to carve better turns, are used to learn balance and centering.

The program begins on Monday (you ski free on Sunday afternoon) and includes daily lift tickets, 7 hours of instruction and workshops each day, breakfast, lunch, and video analysis and review. Sugarbush has also incorporated the Perfect Turn method into all its programs now that Les Otten (the owner of Sunday River, which inaugurated Perfect Turn) has purchased Sugarbush.

Sugarbush is comprised of Sugarbush South and Sugarbush North. The base elevation is 1,535 feet at Sugarbush North, 1,575 feet at Sugarbush South; the vertical drops are 2,600 feet and 2,400 feet, respectively. Sugarbush completed the largest single-season lift and snowmaking expansion in ski history for 1995/96, including 7 new lifts (4 of them high-speed quads) that increased uphill capacity by 60%. There are 18 lifts

serving 6 mountains with 111 trails, of which roughly 30% are expert and 50% intermediate, with diverse terrain. Intermediates should head for the North section, which has stunning views of Lake Champlain as a bonus. Sugarbush South is a giant bowl, with a vast novice area to the right, and plenty of thigh-burning stomach-churning runs to the left side of the mountain.

The luxurious Sugarbush Inn is most convenient to the slopes. A car is helpful even though free shuttles circulate the area. *Sugarbush Resort, R.R. 1, Box 350, Warren, VT 05674, tel. 802/583–2385, ext. 340 or 800/ 537–8427, fax 802/583–3209. Jan.–Mar.: 5 days, $895. Price includes lift tickets, breakfasts, and lunches.*

THE MIDWEST

MICHIGAN **Boyne USA Resorts.** The venerable Boyne Ski School, founded in 1947, has taught more than 600,000 people how to ski. Midwesterners, especially those from Chicago and Detroit, consider it the best place to ski within the region. The resort's all-inclusive old-fashioned Ski Weeks are based on the premise that you have come for a week's skiing vacation and that everything should be taken care of—lodging, lifts, lessons, full breakfast, lunch, dinner, and evening entertainment.

Many of the ski schools' 100 instructors are Austrian-born, as is director Toni Sendlhofer. He requires that all instructors attain American certification, and the school uses the Austrian-American Teaching Method, established in 1948. Instructors teach 4 hours daily and stay with the same class throughout the week. During lessons, instructors introduce and demonstrate a new drill or skill, after which skiers try it themselves. There's also time for questions and answers as well as free skiing. Skiers can opt for a specialty seminar that may focus on moguls, snowboarding, or racing technique. A goal for repeat visitors is improving racetime at the Thursday fun race, which takes place on a modified giant slalom course.

A welcome reception and dinner on Sunday night begin the week. Evening activities include seminars on equipment and safety, the latest Warren Miller ski film, and dancing to live music at the Zoo bar. Thursday everyone wins prizes at the awards banquet, where ski instructors in Austrian garb entertain. The official week ends after lunch on Friday, but you can ski the rest of the day on your own. You are videotaped throughout the week and receive a customized video souvenir at the end of the program. They also offer a Ski Party and Instructional Weekend, which include 7 hours of lessons, 2-day lift ticket, 2 nights' lodging, 2 breakfasts, 1 buffet dinner, and parties Friday and Saturday evenings.

What Boyne Mountain's runs lack in length and vertical drop (500 feet), they make up for in sheer numbers: There are 17 runs, and the longest is over 5,200 feet. With 10 lifts, including one of America's first 6-place, high-speed chair lifts, skiers of all levels will find challenges, especially experts who enjoy bumps and narrow chutes. Beginners have their own new section off the Ramshea lift. Both lodging and dining offer the greatest elegance and comfort in the Midwest. *Boyne Mountain, Boyne Falls, MI 49713, tel. 616/549–6000. Boyne Highlands, Harbor Springs, MI 49740, tel. 616/526–3000 or 800/462–6963. Dec.–Feb.: 5 days, $375 and up per person. Price includes lodging, breakfasts, lunches, dinners, and lift tickets. Ski Party and Instructional weekends: $145–$180.*

THE SOUTHWEST

NEW MEXICO **Taos Ski Valley.** Advanced skiers come to Taos not only because more than 51% of the runs are for experts but also because they can learn how to ski those runs at the renowned Ernie Blake Ski School. The school, which has been under the direction of Jean Mayer since 1957, is constantly changing its teaching methods to keep up with advances in technology and technique.

One of the best packages available here is the Super Ski Week, designed by Alain Veth,

a former French National Ski Team member and technical representative on the U.S. Ski Team. The focus of this program is to make strong intermediate skiers better by going back to the basics. You go through drills and exercises that teach you how to maneuver, using gates, and you take seminars that cover various technical topics such as avalanche awareness and ski technique (historic skiers and their techniques).

On the first day you break into groups of up to 7 skiers and free ski on the easier, groomed slopes paying attention to balance, flexibility, stance, and the basic turn. Day 2 is a challenge: Advanced skiers are asked to slow down to a beginner's wedge in the fall line, and this helps them to feel the turn and appreciate it as a new skier would. The third and fourth days see more advanced drills on moguls and a slalom course. A race is held and a test is given on day 6, but competition is underplayed. The course ends with the class free skiing with the coach and a guest coach, usually a celebrity instructor. There is much camaraderie in this intensive course.

An option for skiers of lesser ability is the Ski Better Weeks, which offer classes of no more than 8 people, morning lessons, lift tickets, video analysis, NASTAR race, and après-ski parties daily. Women's Ski Weeks (all instructors and students are women) and Masters Ski Weeks (all instructors and students are over 50) are also highly acclaimed, as are the one-day Mogul Workshops and Yellowbird Programs for first-timers.

With groomed beginner and intermediate runs on 49% of Taos's slopes, and expert mogul slopes making a total 72 runs, served by 11 lifts, Taos has something for everyone, and it sees itself as a family place. But there's no question Taos has a mystique for experts; the famed Kachina Ridge, and other ridges, plummet precipitously from the summit, accessible only after hour-plus hikes.

Lodging and dining options are numerous. If you stay in one of the 5 lodges or 7 condo complexes at the Ski Valley, you won't have to travel far to the slopes, but lodging at the nearby historical town of Taos is cheaper.

Taos Ski Valley, Box 90, Taos Ski Valley, NM 87525, tel. 505/776–2291, fax 505/776–8596. Dec.–Mar.: 5 or 6 days, $240–$360 for Ski Better Weeks, $463–$548 for Super Ski Weeks. Price includes lift tickets.

UTAH **Park City Ski Area.** Home to the U.S. Ski Team, Park City is one of the most accessible large ski resorts, just a 40-minute drive from Salt Lake International Airport. Because Pacific storms have lost much of their moisture by the time they reach Utah's high Wasatch Mountains, the snow here is true champagne powder—light and dry.

You don't have to want to be an instructor and you don't have to be an expert to join the 3-day Fall Ski College, which is essentially a Ski Instructors Training Program: This is an opportunity for solid intermediate and advanced skiers to get better without paying for private lessons. But book early, because these camps have proven extremely popular with locals, so much so that Park City has stopped promoting them.

You ski in a group of 10 with one instructor for about 6 hours most every day, less on the two days when there's video analysis. You rotate among three instructors if you're taking the program to be hired; otherwise you stay with the same instructor the whole time. This is a back-to-basics approach with an emphasis on balance and stance.

Top women's slalom skier Kristi Terzian started her Women's Challenge Camps in 1994 and they're already acclaimed as one of the industry's best. Her philosophy is that women can ski just as well as men can, given the chance to learn at their own pace and in a supportive all-women environment that improves self-confidence and reduces fear. Kristi and her crackerjack team take participants through a variet of ski-related subjects, from which equipment is ideal for women, mental preparation, ski tuning and physical conditioning to the basics of balance and technique, moguls and powder, even racing.

The mountain has 89 runs and 15 lifts, including a 4-passenger gondola, as well as 5 bowls and one 3½-mile green run. The base is at 6,900 feet, and the vertical drop is 3,100 feet. As the terrain suggests, this is an intermediate paradise. Beginners can join in the fun, taking the lazy circuitous Claim-jumper/Bonanza route from the top, or slipping down the sunny Pioneer lift trails; experts will find steep mogulled beauties in Thaynes Canyon and still more precipitous drops off the Ski Team lift. But Park City's crowning glory is the series of bowls serenely perched up top. If you're not sure you're ready, check out the equally steep but much shorter Blueslip Bowl. Jupiter boasts the widest variety of terrain from chutes to glades. Jupiter whet your appetite? Head further right off the lift to the elevator shafts called Portuguese Gap and Scott's. Not enough? Take a hike to McConkey's and Puma Bowls. There's something for everybody at Park City. The only complaint is that it's virtually impossible to ski that 3,100-foot vertical interrupted (that's the price you pay for diversity).

Park City itself is the only true ski town in Utah, and retains charming vestiges of its 19th century mining town origins. It's filled with interesting shops, restaurants, and hotels, many within easy walking distance of the ski lifts. Because the program runs in the early season, you pay less for lodging. *Park City Ski Area Ski School, Box 39, Park City, UT 84060, tel. 801/649–8111 or 800/227–2754, fax 801/649–5964. For lodging, Park City Ski Holidays, tel. 800/222-7275. Early Nov.–Dec.: 3 days, $225. Women's Challenge Camps, held 8 weekends mid-Dec.–mid-Mar.: 3 days, $255. Prices do not include lift tickets, lodging, or meals.*

THE ROCKIES

COLORADO **Aspen.** Thomas Crum, Aspen Ski School instructor and author of *The Magic of Conflict,* uses aikido to teach skiing. His week-long program, the Magic of Skiing, is open to skiers of all levels; its aim is to help you develop a better mind-body relationship. There are usually between 20 and 40 participants in each session. Check-in is in the late afternoon, on either Saturday or Sunday depending on the session. Participants meet each other, set goals for the week, do exercises, and see an aikido demonstration.

You eat breakfast at your hotel, then meet the group for stretching, warm-up, and breathing exercises. Groups of 5 or 6 students of similar ability are formed. You can switch groups if your needs change during the week. Each day your group decides where to ski. You hit the slopes before 10 and ski until the lifts close at 3. Crum decides a theme for the day's lessons, such as balance or steering. Your group stays together for breaks and through lunch (not included), which you have at one of the on-slope restaurants. Video feedback is used at different times; you watch the instant replay on the mountain and again off the slopes if you'd like. Every afternoon there is a meeting for review and questions. You have a day off from lessons in the middle of the week. (Price includes 5 days of lessons and a lift ticket that's good for 6 of the 7 days.)

The 4 mountains at Aspen have a total of 270 trails and 42 lifts. Aspen Mountain is the most challenging, with no beginner trails. Its base is at 7,945 feet, and its vertical drop is 3,267 feet. Tiehack, with a base at 7,870 feet and a vertical drop of 2,030 feet, is preferred for beginners. You can also ski Snowmass (base 8,223 feet, vertical drop 4,087 feet), known for its powder and variety of terrain, and Aspen Highlands (base 8,000 feet, vertical drop 3,800 feet).

Highlands is the self-styled "maverick" ski area. Welcome changes when the Aspen Skiing Company took over includes replacing two notoriously slow lifts with high-speed quads. But the new owners promise its anti-establishment spirit will live on, in such enduring traditions as the freestyle competition held every Friday and the death-defying leap of the Ski Patrol over the Cloud Nine Picnic Hut deck (and startled skiers) daily at noon, weather permitting. Highlands has a lot more to offer: the best views of the four

Aspen ski areas, Colorado's longest vertical, great powder days, the hair-raising steeps of Steeplechase and Olympic Bowl, and equally fine intermediate terrain.

Snowmass is often dismissed as Aspen's "family" area. All ages do enjoy the self-contained modern development, whose amenities and facilities are beginning to rival those of her chic sister. With over 50% of its terrain rated intermediate, Snowmass is considered a premier cruising mountain; the broad, silky runs off the Big Burn lift are justly famous. But people forget that this sprawling area is four times the size of Ajax, with nearly triple its double diamond terrain. One look at the plunging chutes of Hanging Valley should settle (or unsettle) the matter once and for all. Recent improvements feature two more high-speed quads and a snowboarding transition park. It's part of an ambitious five-year plan that will include a gondola and still more terrain (you can already get lost between its five mountains if you don't study the trail map carefully).

Ajax (the local name for Aspen Mountain itself, after the original silver mine) remains a definitive test of skiing ability, quickly separating the great from the merely good. The narrow mountain is really a series of fearsomely precipitous ridges and gullies requiring the utmost concentration and pinpoint navigation. Intermediates should head for the knob circling the summit and the valleys between the ridges, where they can practice on Ruthie's Run, Buckhorn, International or Copper Bowl. The Ridge of Bell, Kristi's. Hyrup's, Cone Dump and the ironically named Trainer Hill provide enough thrilling—and chilling—descents for even the most jaded expert.

Buttermilk still sets the standard by which beginners' areas measure themselves (Homestead Road is a classic glide through shillering aspen stands that makes hundreds of converts yearly); thoughtful touches include the Max the Moose express, which picks kids up at Aspen area hotels, leaving their parents to fend for themselves. But the Tiehack side features some beautifully cut advanced intermediate runs (as well as lingering powder dumps), enough to make that "sissy" reputation undeserved. All three additional mountains offer equally notable, if more traditional, ski school programs for all ages and abilities.

If you sign up for the early January program, you will stay at the Little Nell Hotel, a grand hotel with fireplaces and oversized feather quilts in every room. At other times, you'll be housed at Aspen Meadows, a historic hotel on 40 acres of mountain meadows. Both are in Aspen and convenient to its après-ski and nighttime activities. *Magic of Skiing, Aiki Works, Inc., Box 7845, Aspen, CO 81612, tel. 303/925–7099 or 716/924–7302, fax 303/925–4532. Jan.: 7 days, $2,095; Feb.: 7 days, $1,695. Price includes lodging, breakfasts, and lift tickets.*

COLORADO **Crested Butte.** If you've never skied before or you aren't sure you want to ski again, consider Crested Butte's early-season Learn to Ski Free Program. From mid-November to mid-December, beginning beginners get free instruction and free lift tickets as well as discounted lodging packages.

The Crested Butte Ski School uses learning stations scattered over the lower mountain to teach first-timers the basics. You start off inside at Station 1 watching a video that gives safety tips and explains how to put on boots and snap into bindings. When you're ready, head for Station 2, where you sidestep up a slight incline and learn to snowplow down. At this point the group breaks up: Those that are ready head for the next learning station; those that aren't continue side-stepping and snowplowing. At every station there's a ski school instructor who teaches you a different technique. You proceed through the stations at your own pace, repeating each one until you are skilled enough to move on to the next. After 2 days you should be riding the Keystone Lift and skiing down the easy slopes, though theoretically, you could continue with the stations for the entire month at no charge. Companions with more skiing experience also ski free during this time period. Crested Butte

also sparked the "rediscovery" of telemarking in the 1970s and is one of the best places to learn that graceful yet demanding discipline, as well as extreme skiing (for those who always wanted to jump off cliffs and live to tell about it.

Crested Butte is a laid-back resort on the other side of a mountain it shares with Aspen. Base elevation here is 9,375 feet. The resort has 85 runs with a vertical drop of 2,775 feet (3,062 feet if you hike to the peak) and is served by 13 lifts, including one high-speed quad. Known for its double black diamond extreme skiing ("The Butte" hosts the U.S. Extreme Skiing Championships on the heart-stopping runs on The North Face and Extreme Limits), Crested Butte also has plenty of gentle terrain for beginners and moderate steeps for intermediates. Don't come here for glamour and glitz; Crested Butte views itself as the downhome alternative to more upscale resorts. (The area once had the audacity to call itself "Aspen like it used to be and Vail like it never was.") Indeed, Crested Butte is a countercultural haven. Part of its charm is the quirky juxtaposition of a Victorian, Old West ambience with a nonconformist attitude. Not many furs here; bellbottoms and tie dyes are more likely in this low-key, friendly resort. The town of Crested Butte is a National Historic Landmark District (the buildings' hot pink and chartreuse facades attest to residents' sense of warmth and whimsy), with a surprising number of fine boutiques and galleries, plus some of Colorado's best restaurants. The mountain village—three miles away—is standard functional '60s architecture. So are the lifts; thankfully they replaced the creaky old Silver Queen with a high-speed quad (another is on the way).

Crested Butte offers another surprise (unaffiliated but often marketed with the resort). The Irwin Lodge touts itself as the "best-kept secret in the Rockies," and it's no idle boast. Talk about seclusion: in winter you must take a thrilling snowmobile ride around several switchbacks to reach this aerie, nearly 1,000 feet above (and eight miles from) Crested

Butte. The lodge sits 10,700 feet above sea level, on a remote ridge overlooking Lake Irwin and the Sangre de Cristo range. The weathered wooden structure cannily looks much older than it is: it was built in 1976 as a snowcat ski lodge by former owner Dan Thurman. Current co-owner/manager Rich Curtis preserves the informal, homey feel. Several cozy lounge areas circle a magnificent stone fireplace in the expansive lobby, where guests mingle throughout the day, exchanging anecdotes about their adventures, playing pool, darts and foosball or watching a video from the extensive library on the big-screen TV.

The smallish, charmingly rustic rooms are tastefully appointed, with pine walls and mahogany furnishings. A hearty breakfast is included in the rate; fine continental lunch and dinner, served family style, are available for a nominal surcharge. The heavy repeat clientele knows this is the premier place in America to learn powder skiing, as the surrounding area boasts an average of over 500 inches of fluffy white stuff a year. A snowcat will take you up to 12,000 feet, accessing a 2,000-foot vertical drop, which can be negotiated by strong intermediates. (Nonguests can make arrangements on a limited basis). Instructors have included gold medalists in the World Powder Championships. The lodge also offers fun snowmobiling tours. *Crested Butte Mountain Resort, Box A, Mt. Crested Butte, CO 81225, tel. 303/349–2252, 800/754–3733, or 800/544–8448, fax 303/349–2397. Mid-Nov.–mid-Dec.: unlimited days, free. Lodging, from $95 per person for 3 nights. Irwin Lodge (tel. 970/349–5140): 23 doubles with baths, 1 suite. Dining room. 2 hot tubs; snowcat skiing, snowmobiling, horseback riding, fishing, canoeing (the latter 3 in summer). $220–$260 per person, all-inclusive Nov.–Apr. MC, V.*

COLORADO **Keystone.** Phil and Steve Mahre, Olympic medalists and professional racing champions, have been hosting the Mahre Training Center at Keystone since it began in 1984. At these instructional camps, beginners to experts learn through a 5-step system of progression developed by the Mahres.

The technical progression is based on balance, weight transfer, and fluid vertical motion. Learning these skills gives you a foundation upon which to build. The goal is to develop better control and more efficient skiing by practicing a variety of drills. Gate drills and video feedback are part of the program.

The staff for these camps are Keystone Ski School instructors who have been working with the Mahres since the program's first year. Each session takes 25 to 90 skiers, who are then broken into groups of up to 8 skiers according to ability. Classes run from 9 AM until noon, break for lunch, and then from 1 PM until 2:30 or 3:30.

The 5-day camp begins with an orientation and welcome party held at the Keystone Lodge the day before skiing begins. Indoor evening sessions include a question-and-answer period with either Phil or Steve and seminars on ski technique and ski equipment. During the day, one of the Mahres is available for hands-on demonstration and pointers. The camp ends with a fun race and an evening awards party.

Keystone is a family-oriented resort, with 89 runs on 3 mountains. Keystone is the gentlest, North Peak is steeper with more moguls, and the Outback has mostly gladed trails. Base elevation is 9,300 feet, and vertical drop is 2,340 feet. There are 19 lifts, including 2 gondolas and 3 high-speed quads.

Keystone Corporation (parent Ralston Purina) is one of the industry giants now that it owns three Summit County areas, all of which can be skied on one ticket (hardcores can start at A-Basin and finish up with America's largest night skiing operation on Keystone Mountain). Keystone itself is a self-contained, ultramodern development, designed to blend harmoniously with its surroundings. In terms of apres skiing, the restaurants are Summit County's finest.

A-Basin is America's highest ski area, with a *base* of 10,800', opened in 1945; some carp it hasn't changed since (the lifts *are* ancient). A-Basin's devoted fans couldn't care less.

They love the short lift lines, breathtaking views, above-timberline skiing, and wide-open bowls seemingly on top of the world. This legendary, gnarly area is not for beginners. The howling winds and menacing clouds atop the mountain make for some heart-pounding adventures, as does the east wall with its plunging chutes and gullies. Intermediate and advanced skiers can push themselves on those lovely, stark, expansive bowls, which stay open well into June.

Since purchasing Breckenridge in 1993, Ralston Purina has linked it more closely with Keystone/A-Basin. This megaresort offers eight mountains, 276 trails and 4,142 acres of skiing. Breckenridge itself had already completed expansion to a fourth mountain, Peak 7, which offers steep bowls, twisting chutes and bumptious bumps. This complements the expert terrain of the Back Bowls off Peak 8, the North Face of Peak 9 (with the infamous, Devil's Crotch, Hades and Inferno), and the bucking moguls of Mustang and Dark Rider on Peak 10. But Breck isn't for experts only: Peak 10 also offers some great cruisers and Peak 8's varied terrain includes a sizable beginner's area.

Settled during the gold rush of 1859, Breckenridge is the oldest continuously occupied town on the Western Slope (save for a brief stint on the offical ghost town itinerary in the 1950s). It comprises one of Colorado's largest National Historic Districts, though today it's hard to imagine the pretty pastel Victorian false fronts and gingerbreads once housed gambling parlors and bordellos. But Breck also prides itself on looking forward: it was the first major Colorado area to welcome snowboarders and hosts the World Snowboarding Championships annually. Known for its friendly, approachable bars, Breck's apres ski scene is considered top-notch.

A fourth, separately owned option is Copper Mountain. Its modern development may be an eyesore to some, but it's admirably compact and completely self-contained, with enough variety of lodging, dining and activities to suit all ages and pocketbooks. The area's award-winning design is creatively contoured to the natural terrain; the layout separates the beginner, intermediate and expert sections (right, center and left respectively as you face the mountain), meaning experts needn't slalom around beginners, who can't get into trouble. Copper also offers 350 acres of guided adventure skiing for die-hards who can't get enough thrills and spills in Spaulding Bowl or the Enchanted Forest. Copper is also completing a 500-acre expansion on the back side of Union Peak.

The Keystone Lodge, with restaurants, lounge, and indoor-outdoor pool, is the most convenient place to stay, but there are plenty of other options at the resort. A group lodging rate is available to students of the camp, and the resort has packages that include lodging, lift tickets, and airfare from major cities. *Keystone Resort, Box 38, Keystone, CO 80435, tel. 303/468–2316 or 800/222–0188, fax 303/468–4007. Mahre Training Center, tel. 800/255–3715. Nov.–Mar.: 5 days, $645. Price includes lift tickets.*

COLORADO **Steamboat.** Steamboat is becoming an increasingly hot destination, providing the trappings of a world-class resort while avoiding the traps. While the mountain village is a plastic collection of deluxe condos, trendy boutiques and fern bars, the town itself, a ten-minute drive away, offers a refreshing change-of-pace from glitzier resorts. Despite attempts to gussy it up, Steamboat Springs remains a cowtown at heart, a ranching community where Stetsons and studs are sold for use and not as souvenirs. The rodeo circuit is still a big draw in summer and galleries showcase Western art and collectibles.

The terrain is extremely varied, especially for beginners and intermediates, with Storm Peak and Sunshine Bowl being favorites. Experts won't find many true steeps, but connoisseurs of tree skiing agree Steamboat's ranks among the best in America, creating a natural slalom course on such runs as The Ridge and Crowtrack. Afterwards, you can soak your weary bones in one of the many revivifying hot springs that give the town its name.

Steamboat is also known as "Ski Town USA" for the more than 30 athletes it has sent to the Winter Olympics. The most famous is undoubtedly Billy Kidd, silver medalist in the 1964 slalom, who conducts tours of the mountain when he's around. Following in his tracks (and that bobbing ten-gallon hat) is tremendous fun. His Kidd Center for Performance Skiing is one of the best places to learn disciplines like powder, mogul (with the help of world champion freestyler Nelson Carmichael) and tree skiing, as well as racing techniques. The area also earns raves for its comprehensive children's programs, including Kids Ski Free.

The center offers racing camps, the Nelson Carmichael Bump Camps, and a program called Billy Kidd Challenge, in which groups of skiers with similar abilities set out with a coach looking for the biggest challenges the group can handle, whether it be mogul fields, black diamond terrain, or race courses.

All Billy Kidd programs are taught using Kidd's own teaching method, one that relies heavily on video. Every coach carriers a portable video camera and playback equipment so that you can see how you did immediately following a run. Classes of no more than 6 skiers are taught by one coach, who stays with the group throughout the program. You meet early on the first day to discuss the program before heading for the slopes, where you meet the other days. Up to 7 hours are spent on snow, with a lot of instant replay, and you watch videos in a classroom at the end of the afternoon. You work on the skills required for racing, bumps, and powder skiing. Lunch is with your coach, but breakfast and dinner are up to you. At night there are ski-related seminars, such as a ski and boot analysis, held at the round-up room in Gondola Square.

At the end of the program you get a copy of your group's video, which you can use in the future to monitor your advancement. You also get a 30-page profile of your skiing, telling you what you do well, what you need to work on, and how your equipment fares.

The report also includes a fitness program, photo, and diploma. If you don't see an improvement in your skiing, you get your money back.

The coaching staff roster here is impressive: among the rotating pros are Jace Romick, former U.S. Ski Team member and number one downhiller in 1982; Jon Smalley, former U.S. Ski Team freestyle coach; Jarle Halsnes, 3-time World Pro Racing Champion; and 15 other skiers with similar credentials. Steamboat is also highly rated for its children's programs, including "Rough Riders Ski Weeks," and its Learn to Ski Weekends for all ages.

The 107 trails at Steamboat are served by 20 lifts, including the 8-person Silver Bullet gondola. Base elevation is 6,900 feet with a 3,668-foot vertical drop. There are a number of upscale condos at the mountain, hotles with ski-in, ski-out access, and cheap but comfortable motels and B&Bs downtown (all serviced by a skier's shuttle to the lifts). *Billy Kidd Center for Performance Skiing, Steamboat Ski School, 2305 Mt. Werner Circle, Steamboat Springs, CO 80487, tel. 303/879–6111, ext. 543, fax 303/879–7844. Early Dec.–early Apr.: $155 adults; $140 teens; $125 kids 6–12 per day for 2 or 3 days. Nelson Carmichael Bump Camps are per day: adults $200, ages 13–17 $150, ages 6–12 $135. Price includes lunch and lift ticket.*

COLORADO **Vail.** One of the best reasons to start skiing early in the season is Pepi's Wedel Weeks for intermediate to advanced skiers. Four sessions of this 7-day ski program are given from November to early January. The program is designed to get skiers warmed up and focused for the season and to build skiing friendships that might continue throughout the year.

The word *wedel* (pronounced vay-*del*) refers to the short stylized ski turn made famous by the Austrians, but this turn is only one of the techniques you learn during the week. You get the personal attention of Pepi Gramshammer, a former member of the Austrian Ski Team and the Professional Ski Racers Association, and his partner, John Horan-Kates, owner of East West Outdoors, an outfitter that specializes in sports vacations; they ski with every group at least once during the week.

Wedel Week starts with a Sunday reception and buffet and ends with a farewell dinner and awards ceremony. Vail's top instructors teach groups of 7 skiers, divided by ability into 9 different levels, in morning and afternoon sessions, covering wedel turns, carved turns, slalom and giant slalom as well as moguls and sometimes powder skiing. They use the ATS. Instructors stay with the same group the whole week.

Vail has the largest ski school in the world, with more than 1,200 instructors, but Wedel Weeks are limited to 100 skiers, 75% of whom are repeat participants. The mountain's base is at 8,120 feet, and the vertical drop is 3,300 feet. There are 121 runs served by 26 lifts, including one gondola and 8 high-speed quads. Vail's regular ski school programs are superb as well, including the new "SKE-COLOGY." This innovative educational program uses Vail's resources to teach children about the environment. Kids are taken to various "SKE-COLOGY sites," including hibernating bear caves and abandoned gold mines. The lessons teach kids how to develop and utilize natural resources responsibly. Other notable program are the Delaney Adult Snowboarding Camps (see Aspen, above), Technique Weeks for Women, and a two-day Mogul camp run by 5-time Pro Mogul Champion Scott Kauf and 2-time women's champion Patti Sherman-Kauf.

Vail is Valhalla for skiers, annually ranked the number one ski resort in America. The reasons are obvious: the thoroughly professional service, the sophisticated ambience, and of course, the phenomenal skiing. It's a model resort and mountain development. Despite the mountain's enormity, it's easy to negotiate, thanks to the intelligently designed layout and connecting series of lifts. The variety of terrain is impressive, with the famed Back Bowls like China, Siberia and Mongolia and the classic bump

runs off Prima Ridge the stuff of strong skiers' dreams. Beginners have their own areas at Golden Peak and Lionshead, while intermediates can romp almost at will over that astonishing expanse. Shredders enjoy the Boardertown Park, with its half-pipe and 300-foot berm.

Of course, Vail *is* congested (*never* tell someone to meet you at mid-Vail around lunchtime). It hosts 20,000 skiers on an *average* day, after all. But you can pop down I-70 to Vail's sister resort, Beaver Creek (which merged with the small next-door Arrowhead in 1995/96 to create another mega-area). Elegant Beaver Creek is crafted to anticipate a guest's every need, with some of the USA's finest on-site dining and lodging. Lacking Vail's mystique, Beaver Creek's slopes are often wonderfully deserted even on the valley's busiest days. It also has tremendous family appeal, with such model developments as "Children's Adventure Zones," where kids slalom around Old West sets like ghost towns and Indian villages. The area built its reputation on immaculate grooming and snowmaking, making skiing here the stuff of ego massage. The link to Arrowhead added still more intermediate terrain to the lovely gladed Harriet and Grouse Glade Areas. as well as such classic cruisers as Latigo, Centennial and Larkspur Bowl. But don't overlook the challenging ungroomed skiing on Grouse Mountain and the aptly named Birds of Prey—mogul heaven on powder days.

Lodging choices for the program are first-class: the Gasthof Gramshammer, Lodge at Vail, Sonnenalp Resort, and Christiania— all in the center of the village. There's a raclette party and fashion show on Wednesday and a farewell dinner on Saturday, but other evenings are free. The ski groups eat breakfast together. *Pepi's Wedel Weeks, 231 E. Gore Creek Dr., Vail, CO 81658, tel. 303/476–5626. Nov.–Jan.: 7 days, $1,755–$1,950 for 1 person, $1,475–$1,640 per person based on double occupancy. Price includes lodging, breakfasts, 3 dinners, and lift tickets.*

COLORADO **Winter Park.** Colorado's oldest major ski area, Winter Park, is unusual in that it is owned by the city and county of Denver and operated by volunteer trustees. Under this successful partnership, it has evolved from its beginnings in 1940 as a small day area to a top resort with more than a million skier visits annually.

The Winter Park Ski School, headed up by former PSIA president Jerry Muth, has 200 instructors, 95% of whom are certified by PSIA at various levels. The school has programs for all skiers, but one of the most flexible for beginners is the Discover Skiing Package, which includes 4 nights lodging, 3 days of rentals and lift tickets, and a couple of 4½-hour lessons.

As a beginner skier, you are first taught the basics, using the ATS, at the resort's new learning area, Discovery Park. This area consists of a 30-acre nonthreatening environment that allows weaker skiers to sample varied conditions, including bump and tree skiing. It is best to take your first lesson on the day you arrive, but you can take your second lesson on either day 2 or day 3. Whether or not you move out of Discovery Park on your second lesson depends on the ability of your group as a whole. In addition to its highly regarded children's program, Winter Park is noted for its pioneering National Sports Center for the Disabled. Women's programs and Style and Technique Workshops are among the other fine clinics available.

Skiers will find plenty of terrain to their liking, whatever their level of ability, spread out over three mountains. Winter Park Base area accesses primarily beginner and lower intermediate trails, with the Alice in Wonderland section a standout. Vazquez Ridge and the recently opened Parsenn's Bowl are cruising heaven, while the steeper runs off Zephyr in the West Portal area hint at the fun to come on the Mary Jane peak, with some of Colorado's most awesome steeps and moguls (those on the backside are the most difficult).

Winter Park has 121 trails served by 20 lifts, including 5 high-speed express quads. The base elevation is 9,000 feet, and it has a vertical drop of 3,060 feet. Accommodations range from motels to condominiums to mountain inns where breakfast and dinner are included in the cost. Central Reservations can help you with lodging, which ranks among the most affordable in Colorado. *Winter Park Resort, Box 36, Winter Park, CO 80482, tel. 303/725–5514, fax 303/892–5823. Central Reservations, tel. 303/447–0588 or 800/453–2525. Nov.–Apr.: 3 days, $75 for lessons alone. Call for special package deals.*

WYOMING AND IDAHO **Grand Targhee.** The spirited energy of the WomenSki the Tetons program comes from its one-woman staff: Patricia Karnik, who personally guides each workshop. A free-style competitor in the 1970s, she has been teaching people to ski for more than 20 years. Using visualization, discussion, video, and "kinesthetic awakening" (exercises that help you isolate individual body parts to become aware of their movements), women in Patricia's classes not only learn to turn their skis properly, they also learn to stretch their limits.

Patricia accepts no more than 7 women at a time in any of three group levels—WomenSki I, novice; WomenSki II, terminal intermediates stuck in a stem christie; and WomenSki III, advanced skiers who want to cover more difficult terrain.

The skiing day begins with breakfast at 7:30, after which you participate in an hour-long session of kinesthetic awakening exercises, such as writing your name with your big toe or balancing on one foot and slowly turning parts of your leg, which aim to train your muscles into skiing action. By 9:30 you're on the slopes. Competence, confidence, power, and versatility are covered over the 4 days. At the end of each day, you may watch a video and discuss what you've learned. You are filmed the first and last day for comparative analysis, and you also watch a video of "perfect skiing" done by others.

Even though lunch and dinner are not included in the cost of a workshop, you usually eat with the group, and lots of friendships are formed. There aren't many distractions at this small resort, just three lodges, five places to eat, and a self-contained village at the base. Driggs, a tiny town 12 miles away, provides additional nightlife.

Groups II and III go to the town of Jackson and Jackson Hole Resort for a change of pace. Group III includes a day of skiing Targhee's 1,500 acres of untracked slopes reached by Sno-Cat (called Peaked Mountain).

In fact, Targhee is the best place to learn powder skiing in the West (rivalled only by Colorado's Irwin Lodge); it also offers some of the finest intermediate terrain anywhere. Most of the runs are above-treeline open bowls and ridge lines, with plenty of elbow room. If you need some ego massaging, the mountain grooms about 300 acres of runs. And despite its growing reputation, Targhee remains both unpretentious and uncrowded since experts usually opt for the macho terrain at Utah's Alta or Snowbird. One of the friendliest areas around, Targhee is even developing a quietly arty reputation, thanks to dynamic owners Carol and Mory Bergmeyer. Escapees from the city rat race, they ensure that development takes a back seat to the surroundings. Talk about natural splendour: The Tetons seem right in your face and there are views of three states from its summit. On the sunny side of the Tetons, it is usually warmer than neighboring Jackson Hole and has lots of open, intermediate terrain without the terrifying pitches of Jackson's slopes. Base elevation is 8,000 feet. There are 45 trails with a vertical drop of 2,600 feet, served by 4 lifts. *Patricia Karnik, Box 25011, Jackson, WY 83001, tel. 208/ 354–8586 or 800/TAR–GHEE, fax 307/353– 8148. Dec.–Apr.: 5 nights/4 days, $1,250– $1,500. Price includes lodging, breakfasts, lift tickets, and airport shuttle.*

THE WEST COAST

CALIFORNIA **Squaw Valley, Lake Tahoe.** Another program for intermediate and advanced skiers aiming to ski tougher terrain, the Squaw Valley Ski School's 5-day Advanced Skiing Clinic (ASC) has been dubbed Marine Corps Boot Camp Revisited by former students. The resort's best instructors lead small, well-matched groups through 5½ to 6½ hours of intensive skiing daily.

French champion Emil Allais started the Squaw Valley Ski School in 1949, but the French method of teaching has given way to the ATS. The ASC program gets an equal mix of men and women, with husbands and wives, fathers and sons, and daughters and mothers, but you must be over 18 years old. ASC started as an instructor training course; it was the first of any ski week to focus on the intermediate skier, and one of the first to use on-hill video feedback.

The program begins Sunday evening with an orientation, and by 8:30 Monday morning, before the lifts officially open, you are on the hill being evaluated for placement in smaller groups of up to 5 skiers. Your skiing is videotaped every day, and the tape is viewed during lunch, which is included in the cost of the clinic. Afternoons are spent skiing with the instructor until the lifts close. The same instructor stays with the group all day. You spend one evening at a local ski shop learning the art of fine-tuning your equipment, and one evening at a workshop tuning your skis to match the snow type. You learn about waxing, filing, and more. On Thursday you concentrate on racing and gate training, getting ready for the big Friday morning race. There's a banquet on Thursday evening, and after the race on Friday, awards are given, you watch the week's video, and your instructor gives you a written evaluation of your progress.

In addition to the ASC, Squaw offers highly rated "Just for Women" ski clinics, a fine "Children's World" program, and one-day mini workshops on skiing moguls or powder. All are similar in quality and approach to programs described at other areas.

Not content to coast on its reputation, Squaw Valley (host of the 1960 Winter Olympics), has undergone a huge expansion the past few years, adding several high-speed quads and more luxury amenities and facilities, including the Resort at Squaw Creek. None of this really mattered to regulars, because Squaw is one of those ultimate ski experiences: if you think you're good, you come here to find out just how good. Squaw has no cut trails, rather over 4,000 acres of open fields that range from expansive bowls to some of North America's tightest, most forbidding chutes, glades and cliffs—a mecca for extreme skiers. Base elevation is 6,200 feet, and there's a vertical drop of 2,850 feet. The 32 lifts include one gondola and one cable car.

If you like air, head for gladed Poulsen's Gully off the new Big Red chair, Eagle's Nest and the Palisades. Mere experts will find thrills aplenty on the KT22 side. Chute 75 is reputedly the steepest trail in Tahoeland (a piddling 10-20' jump from a cornice gets you to its mega-bumps). Then there are the aptly-named Funnel, Waterfall and Elevator Shaft. Another challenge for good skiers is that the six separate peaks that comprise Squaw offer different exposures and snow conditions. No way can you get bored here. For the rest? Actually, 70% of Squaw's terrain is rated blue and green. Intermediates will have a snowfield day on Chicken (unfairly named) and Sun Bowls (the latter a black diamond challenge with perfect spring conditions), as well as the runs in the Shirley Lake, Newport, Gold Coast and Mainline areas. Beginners have their own gorgeous bowl called Bailey's Beach. Boarders can enjoy all those nasty bumps and pitches, as well their own half-pipe. The nordic system offers similar challenge, with hills vaulting over 500 feet, as well as gentler terrain.

Lodging is not included in the cost of the ASC; most students stay at the Resort at Squaw Creek, but the village at Squaw Valley has a variety of condos and hotels. *Squaw Valley Ski School, Squaw Valley, CA 96146, tel. 916/583–0119 or 800/545–4350. Early Dec.–Mar.: 5 days, $725. Price includes lunches and lift tickets.*

CALIFORNIA **Mammoth Mountain.** For the past 40 years, owner, founder, and true mountain man Dave McCoy has shaped Mammoth into a world-class skiing area. At 79, he continues to be a dominant and creative force in all facets of the community, so it is no surprise that the 5-day Senior Ski Camp here is superb.

You must be an intermediate or advanced skier over 50 years old to join a senior camp, where you work on your basic technique without the pressure of competing with young daredevils. The ski school staff, under the direction of Jack Copland, tries to identify the goals of each student and work with that student on creating a program to attain those goals. You spend 6 hours daily with your instructor in groups of no more than 6 skiers. The ATS is used. In the morning you warm up with exercises and visualization before you start skiing. There's a lunch break, and you are videotaped every afternoon. Viewing is indoors.

Senior Ski Camp includes instruction and one social evening in a bar. If you're interested in racing, there is one chance to race toward the end of the week. Mammoth is also notd on the other end of the spectrum for its children's and first-timers' programs.

As for the skiing, Mammoth's name is apt: it's a behemoth in every sense of the word. Imagine a volcano that blew its top, leaving a series of ridges, canyons and endless bowls. No place in California, perhaps America, offers such remarkable variety of terrain. Of course, every skier has heard the horror stories about weekends at Mammoth, when it becomes worse than the Santa Monica Freeway after the latest Big One. But with all that terrain, and a state-of-the-art lift network, it's not as bad as legend has it. At Mammoth you don't use names: you use numbers, the chair numbers to be exact. Real experts should head for 22, whose ridges and chutes empty out into pristine bowls. 1 gets you some bumptious bumps on The Wall; the gondola gets you the Cornice and Hangman's (as forbidding as they sound). Intermediates should chant "2, 4, 6, 8, who do we appreciate?" They'll also like 3, 10, 16 and 24. 7 and 11 are lucky for beginners.

And for avoiding crowds? 19, 22, 25 are locals' favorite numbers.

Even though Los Angeles is 300 miles to the south, Mammoth Mountain is where Angelenos and other Southern Californians come to ski. It has 3,500 skiable acres (200 with snowmaking), with 150 runs served by 30 lifts capable of moving 43,000 skiers per hour. The base is at 7,953 feet, and the vertical drop is 3,100 feet. It also has big, comfortable day lodges with well-stocked restaurants and bars and an assortment of lodging options. The Mammoth Mountain Inn, with both condominiums and hotel rooms, is the only lodging located at the base of the lifts, so it is generally used for optional lodging packages with instructional programs. Despite its convenient location, however, some skiers prefer to stay in town, where there are more than 50 restaurants, lots of shops, and lodging to fit all budgets. A free shuttle bus makes the 4-mile trip every 15 minutes. *Mammoth Mountain, Box 24, Mammoth Lakes, CA 93546, tel. 619/934–2571, fax 619/934–0603. Dec.– Apr.: 5 days, $238 for lessons only.*

OREGON **Timberline.** Lots of the skiers at the Timberline Summer Ski Race Camp are under 18, but everyone over 6 is welcome. The program, begun in 1956, is designed to increase your confidence, perfect your skills, and teach you slalom and giant slalom racing techniques and tactics. Training takes place at 8,500 feet on the Palmer Snowfield, which is reached by two chair lifts, including a high-speed detachable quad.

The 12-day camps are co-ed and designed for parallel skiers and above, including recreational, high school, college, and United States Ski Association level racers. Although adults can attend all sessions, those who want to ski just with other adults should sign up for the shorter, 6-day Masters Camps for 21 and over only.

You and 15 to 35 other skiers eat breakfast together at 6:30 AM then hit the snowfield by 7:15 and ski until 1 PM. The area where you ski is an open 160 acres. The base is at 6,000

feet, and the vertical drop is 2,500 feet. After lunch, camp instructors lead the group through various exercises and games, including off-slope slalom drills, weight training, hiking, soccer, swimming, and volleyball. Adults may play golf or tennis. In the evening there are informative seminars covering tuning, boot fitting, and race strategy. There's also video review and other movies. Rossignol sponsors the camp and provides free demo skis for participants. The camps attract would-be Olympians from around the world, creating a wonderfully cosmopolitan mix on the mountain. And it's a great opportunity to meet tomorrow's ski stars.

All camps include dormitory-style lodging at the magnificent Timberline Lodge, a National Historic Landmark built in the 1930s; adults can upgrade to a private room by paying a supplement. This WPA lodge is a veritable shrine to Americana. You'll find glorious handcrafted furniture and wainscoting, including intricate wrought iron chairs upholstered in rawhide, crocheted rugs and hand-hewn wood beams. Breakfast and lunch are served in the ski area day lodge, and dinner is in the Cascade Dining Room. Lifts, coaching, lodging, meals, and Portland Airport shuttle are included in the cost. *Timberline Summer Ski Race Camp, Timberline Lodge, OR 97028, tel. 503/231–7979 or 503/231–5402, fax 503/272–3710. June– Aug. 12-day camp, $1,690; 5-day camp, $820. May, June, and Aug.: 6-day Adult Masters Camp, $1,040. Price includes lodging, meals, and lift tickets.*

SOURCES

ORGANIZATIONS Most large cities have local ski clubs and councils that sponsor trips and outings; check the telephone directory or the bulletin boards at local ski shops. State and regional associations publish brochures promoting ski tourism. Among the biggest of these groups are the **California Ski Industry Association** (340 Townsend St., San Francisco, CA 94107, tel. 415/543–7036, fax 415/777–0383), **Colorado Ski Country/USA**

(1560 Broadway, Suite 1440, Denver, CO 80202, tel. 303/837–0793, fax 303/837–1627), **Ski New Mexico, Inc.** (Box 1104, Santa Fe, NM 87504, tel. 505/982–5300, fax 505/984–1184), **Ski Utah** (150 W. 500 S, Salt Lake City, UT 84101, tel. 801/534–1779, fax 801/521–3722), and **Vermont Ski Areas Association** (26 State St., Montpelier, VT 05601, tel. 802/223–2439, fax 802/229–6917).

Skiers who are 50 and over might consider joining the **Over the Hill Gang** (3310 Cedar Heights Dr., Colorado Springs, CO 89090, tel. 719/685–4656), a national organization with local chapters that sponsor ski trips and other year-round outdoor activities for members.

PERIODICALS News, highly opinionated views, and recommendations on skiing can be found in the "Insiders' Ski Letter" (Editor/Publisher, Greg Berry, 1550 Sherman St., Denver, CO 80303, tel. 303/863–7865), a newsletter with no ads and no photos. *SKI Magazine* (Box 55533, Boulder, CO 80322, tel. 800/678–0817), which has articles on all aspects of the sport, is published 8 times yearly. *Skiing* (Box 54189, Boulder, CO 80322, tel. 800/825–5552), published 9 times annually, also has articles focusing on all aspects of the sport. *SnowCountry* (Box 2072, Harlan, IA 51593, tel. 800/333–2299), published 8 times a year, includes stories on mountain people and lifestyles; it also has technical and instructional articles for all winter sports. *Ski Impact* (2 Main St., Man-chester Center, VT 05255, tel. 802/362–5066) is published 2–4 times each winter and distributed free at several major ski areas across the country; it offers resort and celebrity profiles, as well as instructional and equipment tips. *Skier News* (11 Clive Court, Ewing, NJ 08638-1709, tel. 609/882–1111) is a hard-news-oriented paper published 4 times yearly.

BOOKS *Handbook of Skiing* (Borzoi/Alfred A. Knopf), by British writer Karl Gamma, is a well-illustrated volume covering all aspects of learning to ski. It is especially good for beginners. *Inner Skiing* (Bantam), by Timothy Gallwey and Bob Kriegel, focuses on the psychological aspects of the sport. *SKI Magazine's Managing the Mountain* (Fireside/Simon & Schuster), by Seth Masia, covers terrain-specific problems and tactics for skiers of all levels. *Ski Taos Style* (Market Relations Press), by Jerome Gladysz and Taos's instructors, explains the Taos ski school teaching methods, aiming to improve the skills of intermediate and expert skiers. *Breakthrough on Skis* (Vintage), by renowned skier/mountaineer Lito Tejada-Flores, is subtitled "How to Get Out of the Intermediate Rut," and Tejada-Flores utilizes some unorthodox methods, as well as as clever psychology to enable middle-level skiers to accomplish that goal.

ALSO SEE Once you've mastered the downhill, it's time to test your stamina. Turn to Cross-Country Skiing to see how it's done.

Skydiving

By Erik Fair

Just take one step—out of a perfectly good airplane—and you instantly become a member of an ultra-exclusive club. Considerably less than one-tenth of 1% of the earth's population skydives.

Within a few seconds of exiting the airplane, you will find yourself immersed in the flap and roar of terminal velocity—plummeting, at 120 miles an hour, toward the hard earth 10,000 feet below. Sound terrifying? The simple truth is that the psychological requirements of skydiving are harder to meet than the physical requirements. Tandem jumps have been enjoyed by all kinds of people, including the elderly and people with developmental, physical, hearing, and visual impairments. If you weigh over 250 lbs. or have significant back or joint problems, you may want to pass. Otherwise, all you really need is an attitude.

Thirty seconds into your 50- to 60-second free-fall you will remember the skydiving instructor and *two* parachutes buckled to your back. Your brain will flash: "Salvation!" and you will open your mouth to shriek, "This is great!" But your cheeks won't work because they'll be plastered against your cheekbones.

After you lose your staring contest with the ground and get a brief look at the breathtaking scenery all around you, you will suddenly feel you've been jerked blindfolded up a 300-foot chimney. A split-second later you'll be floating along in a soft and noiseless world, dangling beneath a beautiful canopy, headed for the landing zone (the LZ). Just about 5 minutes later, you'll be on the ground grinning and reveling in the knowledge that you have just experienced raw speed—the purest rush that thrill-sports have to offer.

It is the speed reversals that will stand out in your memory. When you exit an airplane you go from zero to 120 mph in just seconds. The acceleration simply takes your breath away, mainly because you think you're about to die. But once you stabilize in free-fall it's as if speed slows down. You say to yourself: "Wow, I've never gone so fast this slowly before!"

When it's time to throw your parachute, you feel like you've been catapulted upward. The sensation reverses, and you say to yourself: "Wow, I've never slowed down this fast before!" The next thing you know you're floating through space like a bubble. It all happens in less than a minute, and you're left dangling under a canopy wondering, "How many time zones did we go through? Is this the same planet?"

That's why they call skydiving "the granddaddy of all thrill-sports."

Adventurer and writer Erik Fair is the author of *California Thrill Sports*. Fair's awe of skydiving is the result of one tandem jump, one Accelerated Free Fall jump, and a lifelong love affair with blue space.

The style of jumping is changing, too. When you employ the original static-line jump, you dive alone from 3,000 to 4,000 feet, and your chute is immediately jerked open by a steel cable attached to the airplane. Using a one-way radio your instructor coaches you through canopy-check, approach, and landing. Many schools still offer static-line jumps for those who treasure the solo experience above all else, or who fear 50 to 60 seconds of 120 mph free-fall. But these jumps are being replaced by tandem and Accelerated Free Fall (AFF) jumps, both of which enable you to experience the thrill and angst of free-fall, from up to 13,000 feet, on your very first jump.

A tandem jump, which typically costs about $150, is the hair-raising experience described at the beginning of this chapter. You can expect 30 to 60 minutes of ground school before your jump. This will include a briefing on jump procedures, familiarization with equipment (especially the location and grasping of the rip cords), a walk-through of the exit sequence, and practice of free-fall body positioning. Pay attention! Ground school is where you learn how to remain calm and do something besides pass out if the certified tandem instructor buckled to your back dies of a heart attack the instant you leap out of the airplane. If that happens, *don't worry:* You don't need the instructor nearly as much as you need the two parachutes buckled onto his or her back.

You see, the rip cords for both the main parachute and the emergency reserve parachute are strategically mounted on the front of your harness, where they can easily be reached by either you or your instructor. Structural failure of both parachutes is practically unheard of in skydiving, but one fact remains: When you're headed toward the earth at 120 mph, *somebody* has to pull the rip cord before the ground arrives! Ergo, the bottom-line rules of tandem skydiving: (1) If you think you're going to pass out, first make sure your instructor hasn't died of a heart attack, and (2) If your instructor is unconscious, or looks the slightest bit woozy, don't pass out!

There are two key differences between the Accelerated Free Fall and the tandem jump. First, an AFF jump is twice as expensive, about $300, because you jump with two instructors. Second, you're not buckled to either of them, so you have considerably more responsibility.

The two instructors grab onto your hip straps and dive right alongside you when you leap from 9,000 to 13,000 feet, give you hands-on help stabilizing your body during free-fall, and don't let go until a split-second after you deploy your main parachute. Through radio contact, the first jump-master will coach you through a sequence of checks to confirm that you are dangling safely underneath a flyable (and "landable") canopy. He or she also coaches you through maneuvers necessary for a safe approach and landing.

One other difference between an AFF jump and a tandem jump is the length of time you spend in ground school: 4 to 7 hours as opposed to 30 to 60 minutes. This preparation includes more extensive familiarization with equipment, including the automatic deployment device; memorization of jump procedures; and repeated practice of the exit sequence, free-fall body positioning, and deployment techniques, including cut-away of a failed main parachute and deployment of the reserve chute. You'll practice everything until it's second nature, so you'll know what to do instantly if both your instructors get struck by lightning.

If skydiving sounds a little overwhelming, you may want to look before you leap (literally) by attending a Boogie. This is a day or weekend when skydiving addicts flock together to fall through the sky. Many schools listed below have regular Boogies that are great opportunities to sop up some of the skydiver's hari-kari culture without actually jumping out of an airplane.

On the other hand, if skydiving sounds like the sport for you, you should know that it takes 25 jumps to earn an A License in skydiving, the minimum license you need to hurl yourself through space under your own supervision. Because it takes 1 or 2 months and $1,500 to $2,000 to do 25 jumps, you're not likely to earn a license over your vacation. Go for a single tandem or AFF jump. If it really turns you on, call the United States Parachute Association (USPA) for a list of their members near you. All of the schools listed here offer full instructional programs. If you commit to becoming a skydiver, you will have student status for your first 8 tandem or AFF jumps, then you'll jump alone as a supervised novice, until you've logged 25 jumps.

CHOOSING THE RIGHT SCHOOL

Selecting a skydiving school worthy of your trust is a relatively straightforward proposition, because skydiving is well regulated. The United States Parachute Association (USPA) develops training techniques and standards, and certifies instructors, schools, and drop zones. The Federal Aviation Administration (FAA) works cooperatively with the USPA and the Parachute Industry Association to regulate the testing of skydiving harnesses and reserve parachutes for strength, reliability, and rate of descent under maximum load. The FAA also regulates the packing and periodic repacking of reserve parachutes and governs the operations of the pilots and airplanes that transport skydivers. When choosing a trip, be sure to ask the following questions:

Are you a member of the USPA? Make sure the school and its instructors are certified. All of the schools described here have USPA certification.

How long has the school been in business, and how long have the instructors been teaching? A good track record is a good sign that a school is doing something right.

What types of jumps do you offer? If you are interested in a particular jump experience— for example, the solo sensation of a static-line jump—make sure that the school you choose offers it. The schools listed here offer tandem, AFF, and static-line jumps unless otherwise noted.

What facilities are available at your drop zone? A drop zone is any area that the FAA has declared legal for skydiving, and many are nothing more than obscure runways or big patches of dirt. Many schools in this chapter offer unusually well-equipped drop zones, with extras such as classrooms, snack bars, observation areas, swimming pools, and camping sites.

What kind of planes do you use? Remember this rule of thumb: Bigger, faster airplanes (especially twin-engine or turbine airplanes) can carry more people to higher altitudes faster than conventional single-engine airplanes. That usually translates into higher jumps, longer free-falls, lower costs per jump, and less time to sweat bullets on the way to your "moment of truth." Cessna 182s, which seat 4 to 5 people, are usually the smallest plane used for skydiving.

When is the best time of year to jump? Interesting scenery and a comfortable climate are important to consider when choosing a school, and both can vary seasonally. For example, Minnesota may be particularly beautiful in the fall foliage season but is probably too cold for comfort in the winter months.

What other attractions are in the area? This is especially important if you're bringing nondivers on your trip—give them something to keep their minds off of how crazy they think you are!

How far in advance do I need to book? Although some schools will accept walk-in jumpers when not fully booked, it's best to make reservations two weeks in advance. In these listings, chamber of commerce telephone numbers are given for assistance in finding accommodations near the schools.

Do you have references from past students? It helps to talk with someone who has already made the jump.

FAVORITE SCHOOLS

THE NORTHEAST

MASSACHUSETTS **Pepperell Skydiving Center.** As you slice through the air over Sports

Center Airport (about 50 minutes northwest of Boston), you can take in excellent views of the Atlantic Ocean, downtown Boston, and the mountains of southern New Hampshire, including Mt. Monadnock. And all of these places can be reached in less than two hours by those who choose to remain on the ground. Tony Carbone, the director of Pepperell as well as the Northeast Conference of the USPA, has been skydiving since 1976 and instructing since 1980. The center uses 4 airplanes, including a 23-passenger De-Havilland Twin Otter. Drop-zone facilities include a swimming pool, snack bar, and electrical hook-ups for RVs. The Greater Boston Soaring Club operates at the same airport so family members who would enjoy a little tamer air adventure can get a ride in a sailplane for $79–$99. Nearby Nashua, New Hampshire ("If we screw up, we land there," jokes Carbone), has numerous hotels and restaurants. *Pepperell Skydiving Center, Rte. 111, Pepperell, MA 01463, tel. 508/433–9222 or 800/759–5867. Nashua Chamber of Commerce, tel. 603/881–8333. Mar.–November: tandem (from 12,500 ft.), $185; AFF (from 12,500 ft.), $300; static-line (from 3,500 ft.), $225.*

NEW YORK **Blue Sky Ranch (a.k.a. "The Ranch").** This popular school and drop zone, nestled in the Hudson River Valley near Gardiner, New York, is 80 miles from Albany, 30 miles from the Catskill Mountains, and just 4 miles from the Shawangunk Mountain range, known internationally as "The Gunks" (See rock climbing chapter). Billy Richards, who started skydiving over 25 years ago at age 16, is head honcho of The Ranch Parachute Club, which supervises operation of the school.

As you might suspect, the scenery from the jump altitude of 13,500 feet is an awesome array of mountains, lakes, rivers, valleys, and orchards. The fall foliage of October is especially stunning from jump altitude.

The Ranch aircraft include two Super Otters (capacity 22 each) and an 8 seat Pilatus Porter. Boogies on Memorial Day, The Fourth of July, and Halloween are great opportunities to watch experienced skydivers fall through the sky in droves. The Ranch will host the 1996 United States National Skydiving Championships. "The Rats," a four-person dive team headquartered at the ranch, will compete for the "four-way" title.

The Ranch draws most of its upscale clientele from four states: New York, New Jersey, Pennsylvania, and Connecticut. Facilities include showers, camping, bathrooms, volleyball, basketball, and a pond to cool off in. The snack bar serves health-conscious breakfast, lunch, and dinner on weekends only; the snack bar owner also provides horse rentals for those who would rather trot on the ground than scream through the sky. Nearby tourist towns, such as New Paltz, and a number of local apple orchards, provide other diversions for non-jumping family members. The Catskills, an hour's drive from the Ranch, offer great mountain biking and swimming. Kids love inner tube rides on the Esopus River, 40 minutes away. *Blue Sky Ranch (a.k.a. "The Ranch"). Sand Hill Road, Box 121, Gardiner, NY 12525, tel. 914/255–4033. Accommodation referrals available. Hudson Valley Tourism, tel. 800/232–4782. Open mid-Apr.– mid-Nov., daily; Dec.–Mar., weekends: tandem (from 13,500 ft.), $175; AFF (from 13,500 ft.), $265; No static-line jumps.*

THE MID-ATLANTIC

WASHINGTON, D.C. **The Skydiving Center of Greater Washington, D.C.** This D.C. center has a microclimate perfect for skydiving. Storm fronts that roll through D.C. seem to run out of rain before they get to this rural airport 55 minutes from the Beltway, and it's cooler here in the summer and warmer in the winter. Though they've only been in business since 1990, co-owners Kevin and Cindy Gibson have 25 years of drop-zone experience between them. Kevin is former editor of *Parachutist Magazine* and one of the first USPA-certified tandem jump-masters. He spent many years teaching tandem-jump techniques to other instructors all over the United States. Cindy gives instruction for accelerated free-fall and static-line jumping. Her forte is teaching women body-positioning techniques that take advantage of their lower center of gravity and encouraging them to rely more on technique than force in steering an open canopy. The school has a Cessna 182 and a 22-seat Twin Otter that lets you jump from 13,500 feet. The views of the Patuxent River, Chesapeake Bay, and Maryland's eastern shore include sandy shorelines, rocky cliffs, lush tide marshes, and several bird estuaries. The drop-zone facilities are modest—indoor and outdoor observation areas, picnic facilities, and a snack bar—but that doesn't stop the school from gathering a crowd of young thrill-seekers. It is, as Kevin admits, "A real yuppie hangout, with polo shirts and everything."

In addition to the traditional tourist sights of D.C., you can visit Solomon's Island, a well-preserved old seafarer's town with cozy bed-and-breakfasts, several nightclubs, and fishermen who still go out to sea each morning. St. Mary's City, one of the oldest settlements on the coast; the Maritime Museum; and the Patuxent Naval Air Station and Museum are also nearby.

In 1995 The Skydiving Center began offering tandem jumps from a Cessna 182 at 10,000 feet from the Ocean City, Maryland airport. When you exit the airplane you'll be treated to views of the Ocean City Boardwalk, miles of surf, and Assateague Island. Kevin himself is the tandem master between April and October. Prices are the same at both locations. *Skydiving Center of Greater Washington, D.C., St. Mary's County Airport, 315 Airport Dr., Suite 600, California, MD 20619, tel. 301/870–3686. St. Mary's County Chamber of Commerce, tel. 301/884–5555. Year-round (winter jumping only as weather permits): Ocean City location, tel. 410/213–1319. Apr.–Oct.: tandem (from 9,000 ft.), $195 for 1st jump, $175 per additional jump; AFF (from 9,000 ft.), $295–$315 for 1st jump, $145–$175 per additional jump; static-line (from 3,000 ft.), $180–$200 for 1st jump, $50 per additional jump.*

THE SOUTH

FLORIDA **Air Adventures Florida.** You'll feel like an astronaut re-entering the atmosphere when you leap out at 12,500 feet and see both coasts of Florida and Lake Okeechobee below. Nonjumpers will also appreciate the ideal location of this school in South Central Florida, two hours from Miami and Naples, and 1½ hours from Palm Beach. Judging from the high volume of students here (100–125 new jumpers a week), the scenery isn't the only thing Air Adventure has going for it. Owner Marty Jones has been skydiving for 32 years (since he was 13) and instructing for more than 27 years. He employs up to 20 instructors at a time, depending on demand. Winter is the busiest season for the school, since that's when most tourists hit the area. The excellent array of aircraft—two Cessna 195s, and a Turbine Pilatus Porter—translates into inexpensive high-altitude jumps for first-timers. The school has also gone out of its way to design a drop zone to attract families and vicarious-thrill seekers. There's a restaurant and snack bar, electrical hook-ups for RVs, a comfortable waiting room with a well-stocked video library, and a game room.

Nearby Clewiston offers classic Florida airboat rides (for those who like their sports a little closer to the ground) and Roland Martin's Marina, which hosts numerous bass-fishing tournaments. *Air Adventures Florida, Airglades Airport, Rte. 27, Clewiston, FL 33440, tel. 813/983–6151. Clewiston Chamber of Commerce, tel. 813/983–7979. Year-round: tandem (from 12,500 ft.), $150; AFF (from 12,500 ft.), $250; static-line jumps (from 3,500 ft.), $65.*

FLORIDA **Skydive DeLand.** It's not surprising that skydiving has flourished in De-Land: The school's hangar is surrounded by leading manufacturers of skydiving equipment, including Bill Booth's Relative Workshop, one of two companies that pioneered the development of tandem parachutes and training techniques. The close proximity of the manufacturers attracts some of skydiving's most innovative instructors, such as Rob

Laidlow, author of the instructional book *Sky-dive University*. This school hosted the 1993 Skydiving National Championships and, according to Manager Mike Johnston, 20 of DeLand's employees participated in the filming of the movie "Drop Zone," starring Wesley Snipes. Tom Cruise did his first jumps here while filming *Days of Thunder* in Daytona Beach, and Ronald Reagan, Jr., has jumped here, too. It's like a little skydiving community, and local skydivers even open their homes (for a fee) to out-of-town students.

You can afford to do high-altitude jumps here, because the aircraft (2–5 Twin Otters, depending on the season) can seat 22 jumpers apiece and there are often enough students to fill them. Ground facilities are also first-rate. There's a restaurant, a souvenir shop with T-shirts to advertise your experience, bathrooms, showers, classrooms, an equipment shop, tent sites, and a few electrical hook-ups for RVs. About the only thing that's less than superlative here is the free-fall view of the airport and several small lakes. The best time to dive is from late October through May, because, as the local saying goes, the best summer you'll ever have is winter in Florida.

DeLand is only 45 minutes from Walt Disney World and 30 minutes from Daytona Beach. The legendary Fountain of Youth, at nearby Ponce De Leon Springs State Park, is a great place to take loved ones who have worried themselves gray over your skydiving escapades. *Skydive DeLand, DeLand Municipal Airport, Box 3077, DeLand, FL 32723, tel. 904/738–3539. List of local accommodations and local skydivers (who are sometimes willing to rent you a room) available upon request. Year-round: tandem (from 13,500 ft.), $150; AFF (from 13,500 ft.), $275. No static-line jumps.*

GEORGIA **Sky Dive Monroe.** Forty-five year-old co-owner Bill Scott has logged move than 3,500 skydives since taking up the sport in 1978. He is a USPA Safety and Training Adviser, and a Tandem Examiner, which means that he not only give tandem jumps but he also trains and certifies other tandem instructors. Scott operates out of a

hangar at Monroe Walton County Airport, 40 minutes from Atlanta and 25 minutes from Athens. Facilities include shower, bathroom, and 6-person bunkhouse, but the nearest sources of sustenance are fast food franchises about two miles down the road. Camping is permitted on airport grounds.

Two Cessna 182s and a 10-seat Navajo fly students to 10,000 feet for tandem and AFF jumps. From there you can see trees, farmlands, nearby Stone Mountain, and (on clear days) downtown Atlanta and Athens. Fall foilage (mid-September through mid-October) provides colorful splashes of reds, browns, and yellows.

For nondiving family members, The Six Flags Over Georgia Amusement Park and Stone Mountain State Park are about an hour away. Nearby High Falls State has a natural rock water slide that kids love. Jackson Lake Marina offers boating and fishing. *Sky Dive Monroe, Box 1204, Monroe, GA 30655, tel. 770/207–9164. Walton County Chamber of Commerce, tel. 770/267–6594. Year-round (by appointment only), Wed.–Fri. noon–sunset, weekends 9:00 AM–sunset: tandem (from 10,000 ft.), $130–$150; AFF (from 10,000 ft.) $230–$250. No static-line jumps.*

THE MIDWEST

MISSOURI **Missouri River Valley Skydivers.** This drop-zone is just two miles north of the Missouri River and, according to owner Tom Dolphin, it was under water for a month during the great floods of 1993. Dolphin has completely rebuilt his operation, which now includes camping, shower, and laundry facilities as well as a bunkhouse that sleeps up to 16. Dolphin also has a full-service pro shop that stocks all kinds of equipment, apparel, and souvenirs. Three powerful, high-capacity Cessna 182s, an E-50 Twin Bonanza, and a Pilatus Porter Turbine were flown to safety before the flood reached them.

When you jump here you can see the Kansas City skyline, the Missouri River running north to Iowa and south to St. Louis, and a bucolic patchwork of farm fields, small towns, and flood plains. The drop zone is 3 miles from Lexington, Missouri, home of a Civil War Museum and battleground, and 30 miles from Liberty, site of Jesse James's first bank robbery. Nearby Kansas City has a great zoo and the Worlds of Fun amusement park. *Missouri River Valley Skydivers, Rte. 1, Box 46, Henrietta, MO 64036, tel. 816/494–5315 or 800/776–5315. Lexington Chamber of Commerce, tel. 816/259–3082. Mar.–Oct.: tandem (from 9,500 ft.), $145; AFF (from 10,000 ft.), $285; static-line (from 3,200 ft.), $125. Package deals available for groups.*

WISCONSIN **Sky Dive Osceola.** Gino Broom and Karen Zarnstorff run this school which is in an airport in the heart of the St. Croix River Valley. Broom owns the airport, and since he uses it only for skydiving, there's no competing air traffic. Facilities include a clubhouse with a VCR and tons of skydiving videos, showers, and campsites. The school has two Cessna 182s which take students as high as 12,500 feet. From that altitude, you really get the full impact of the beauty of the surrounding countryside. The river bluffs of St. Croix Valley National Park, the Minneapolis skyline, Cedar Lake, and lush Wisconsin farmland are breathtaking. The fall foliage is particularly stunning. Addressing pertinent seasonal issues, Broom admits "it gets cold around here—we usually stop student jumps in November because we can't trust 'em to pull the right handles with ski gloves on."

Nearby, there's inner tubing on the Apple River, canoeing on the St. Croix, miniature golf, and a water theme park. *Sky Dive Osceola, St. Croix Valley Airport, 2248 40th Ave., Osceola, WI 54020, tel. 715/294–4262. Somerset Chamber of Commerce, tel. 715/247–3366. Apr.–Oct., daily: tandem (from 10,000 ft.), $150; AFF (from 12,500 ft.), $250; static-line (from 3,500 ft.), $150.*

THE SOUTHWEST

ARIZONA **Skydive Arizona.** This may be the best place in the country to observe gangs of skydivers at their zaniest. Sky-

dive Arizona hosted the 10th World Championships of Formation Skydiving in 1993, and Boogies take place on most major holidays (Easter, Halloween, Thanksgiving, Christmas, and New Year's Day). Former *Parachutist Magazine* editor Kevin Gibson says the Arizona weather and superb equipment here make this the best skydiving facility in the country. And judging from the crowds at the Boogies, a lot of people agree with him.

In business since 1979, the school moved to its new drop zone, adjacent to the Eloy Municipal Airport, in 1991. Extras at the new site include a swimming pool, shaded observation area with picnic tables, and several freelance "videographers" on hand to record your free-fall for posterity. The impressive array of aircraft—3 Super Otters, and a DC-3—enables the school to take a large number of students up for high-altitude jumps.

The clear desert skies here offer visibility of up to 60 miles year-round, but the views are best at certain times of the year. In March, the land is cool and green from the winter rainy season; April brings yellow, white, and purple desert flowers; and in May, the cacti add their bright red and yellow blooms. Summers—June through August—can be scorchers.

Eloy is an hour from both Phoenix and Tucson. Casa Grande Ruins National Monument is on the road to Phoenix, and the Arizona-Sonora Desert Museum is just outside Tucson. *Skydive Arizona, Eloy Municipal Airport, 4900 N. Taylor Rd., Eloy, AZ 85231, tel. 520/466–3753. Eloy Chamber of Commerce, tel. 520/466–3411. Year-round (closed Tues. and Wed. June–Aug.): tandem (from 12,500 ft.), $125; AFF (from 12,500 ft.), $250; static-line (from 3,500 ft.), $105.*

TEXAS **Skydive Dallas.** Stop screaming and smile for the camera! A unique feature at this ultramodern facility, founded in 1991, is the video that's included in the price of a tandem jump. An instructor wearing a helmet camera does the filming, and you can choose background music from a library of 50 songs, including such apropos titles as Tom Petty's "Free Falling." The school was opened by two local entrepreneurs, Dr. Lee Schlichtemeier and his wife, Carol, who fell in love with skydiving after a couple of tandem jumps. Now they own Tri-County Airport, about an hour northeast of Dallas, and a 15,000-square-foot hangar that holds student classrooms, a pro shop, a restaurant, and a lounge. Kids can romp in indoor and outdoor play areas with slides, swings, and games.

Manager Alphonse Trone will be the first to say that this is already one of the premier skydiving facilities in the United States. And he'll back up his claim by showing you the star of the hangar—a million-dollar Cessna 208 Caravan single-engine turbine. The plane can unload 15 jumpers at 13,000 feet two or three times an hour! Other aircraft include: two Cessna 182's, a 9 seat Pilatus Porter, and a 22 seat Twin Otter. No matter which aircraft you jump from, you'll find yourself flying over the Red River, Lake Texoma, and the brown-and-green geometric patterns of plowed farm fields. On clear days you also get a view of the Dallas skyline. *Skydive Dallas, Rte. 2, Box 15, Whiteright, TX 75491, tel. 903/364–5103, or 800/688–5867. Accommodation referrals on request. Year-round: tandem (from 13,000 ft.), $175; AFF (from 13,000 ft.), $250. No static-line jumps.*

THE ROCKIES

MONTANA **Skydive Lost Prairie.** Lost Prairie owner Fred Sand has been skydiving for 24 years. During the summer of 1995 he blew past the 6,000 jump milestone on the way to an anticipated 10,000 jumps. The views at Sand's little patch of Montana paradise start on the ground and only get better when you take to the sky in one of the school's two Cessna 182s. This get-away-from-it-all drop zone in northwest Montana is in a secluded valley that was first homesteaded fewer than 100 years ago. It's accessible only via a gravel road that winds through a pine forest for 4 miles before the trees part to reveal Lost Prairie, tucked in the foothills of the Rockies. Aerial views here include the Rocky Mountains, McGregor Lake, and (on a clear day) glaciers at Waterton/Glacier National Park. Each fall, the larch trees claim the distinction of being the only pines to turn yellow as they drop their needles. It's a spectacular scene.

The Skydive Lost Prairie Jump Meet, held each year in the last week of July or first week of August, is the largest gathering of divers in the northwestern states. Many of the divers fly their own planes to this meet just to enjoy the spectacular scenery on the way in and out. During the rest of the year, the school's isolation and low number of jumpers make it a peaceful retreat. Sand teaches here year-round but most students are accommodated in spring, summer and fall. Winter diving in Montana is so cold that Sand says it's "for addicts only."

The school is about 35 miles west of Kalispell. It has its own bar, café, and great places to camp. Cabin accommodations and plenty of fishing and hiking are available at McGregor Lake Resort, just 10 minutes away. Glacier National Park is a 2-hour drive. *Skydive Lost Prairie, 3175 Lower Lost Prairie Rd., Marion, MT 59925, tel. 406/858–2493. McGregor Lake Resort, tel. 406/858–2253. Apr.–Oct.: tandem (from 9,000 ft.), $139; AFF (from 10,500 ft.), $249; static-line (from 3,500 ft.), $139.*

THE WEST COAST

CALIFORNIA **Perris Valley Skydiving School.** The lake town of Perris, California, along with neighboring Elsinore, is part of skydiving history. These were two of the first places in the country where people made nonmilitary jumps—where jumping suddenly became recreation. Perris Valley Skydiving School is one of the biggest schools in the nation. This school's new owner is Melanie Conatser, who has owned the Perris Valley Drop Zone for the past twenty years.

The school has a very popular instruction program, graduating more than 200 AFF students per year. It also has excellent aircraft: a King Air, two Twin Otters, and a Sky Van that can drop 21 jumpers from 13,500 feet. During jumps on clear days you can see north to Los Angeles and south to San Diego. Even the everyday scenery is far from mundane, with snowcapped mountains (San Gregonio and San Jacinto) to the east, and the Ortega Mountains, Pacific Ocean, and Catalina Island to the west. Perris and Elsinore Lakes also stretch out below. Those who like their air adventures a little tamer can enjoy the scenery from a hot-air balloon.

There's a trailer where free-fall videos are produced and another large trailer housing classrooms and offices. There's also a swimming pool, and a newly built restaurant-bar called "The Bomb Shelter" that serves breakfast, lunch, and dinner. Laundry, and shower facilities are provided and tent camping is allowed. One new feature is a shallow "Swoop Pond" where you can see experienced skydivers swoop in under canopy and drag their feet through the water like a bunch of geese. Perris's Orange Empire Railway Museum provides rides on antique trains pulled by real steam engines. *Perris Valley Skydiving School, 2091 Goetz Rd., Perris, CA 92570, tel. 909/657–1664 or 800/832–8818. Perris Chamber of Commerce, tel. 909/657–3555. Year-round: tandem (from 12,500 ft.), $160 weekdays, $175 weekends; AFF (from 12,500 ft.), $275 weekdays, $299 weekends; static-line (from 4,000 ft.) $160.*

CALIFORNIA **Sky Dance Skydiving.** This was the first school in California to offer tandem jumps; the quality of instruction makes it the premier school in the Bay Area. Co-owner Dan O'Brien is an accomplished competitive skydiver; and his partner, Ray Farrell, is a master parachute rigger and one of the few instructors in the country qualified by the USPA to train other tandem instructors. A host of other experienced instructors pitch in to carry the heavy student load.

Sky Dance hosted the 1992 National Skydiving Championships, and with Boogies on Memorial Day, July 4th, and Labor Day, it's another great place to watch experienced skydivers hurl themselves through space in clusters. The school has standard ground facilities with a few extras, such as the observation lawn with picnic tables and a snack bar open on weekends. Dan and Ray take their students up in a Cessna 182, a Beechcraft King Air, and a Twin Otter. The thrill of the jump will have to suffice here, because the scenery is on the average side— farm fields, barns, and the town of Davis. Summer and winter temperatures here are extreme, so spring and fall are your best bets.

Sky Dance is 1½ hours from San Francisco, 25 minutes from Wooz Amusement Park in Vacaville, and just 20 minutes from historic (if touristy) Old Towne Sacramento. For more thrills, drive an hour to run the white water of the south fork of the American River, from Chile Bar to Coloma, in a raft. *Sky Dance Skydiving, 24390 Aviation Ave., Yolo County Airport, Davis, CA 95616, tel. 916/753–2651. Davis Chamber of Commerce, tel. 916/756–5160. Year-round, Wed.–Sun.: tandem (from 9,000 ft.) $128, (from 13,500 ft.) $158; AFF (from 10,500 ft.–13,500 ft.), $286; static-line (from 3,000 ft.), $188.*

OREGON **Skydive Oregon.** This is the home of the highest altitude jumps in the country. Joe Webber, Skydive Oregon's owner and operator, uses his Beechcraft Westwind Twin Turbine to drop you off at 14,500 feet! In fact, the plane can carry 14 jumpers to this height three times an hour. You appreciate the extra seconds of soaring through space when you see the views: Mt. St. Helen, Mt. Rainer, Mt. Hood, the Columbia and Willamette River gorges, the Portland skyline, and the Pacific Ocean. Although the area is lovely all year, in April and May the flowering of local orchards turns the ground pink, white, and lavender.

Weber, who has been skydiving since 1972, declares, "I built this airport and drop zone because I wanted the best place to skydive—

and I got it." Indoor facilities include three classrooms, bunk rooms for 30, and a video lounge with a wood-burning stove. Outside, you can sit on the porch and gaze at the Cascade Mountains, beyond the picnic tables and barbecue. Portland is only 45 minutes away, and Mt. Hood National Forest, with camping, hiking, and fishing, is right next door. *Skydive Oregon, Skydive Oregon Airport, 12150 S. Rte. 211, Molalla, OR 97038, tel. 503/829–3483 or 800/934–5867. Molalla Chamber of Commerce, tel. 503/829–6941. Year-round (by appointment only): tandem (from 10,000 ft.–14,500 ft.), $139–$169; AFF (from 10,000 ft.–14,500 ft.), $229; static-line (from 4,000 ft.), $139.*

SOURCES

ORGANIZATIONS United States Parachute Association (1440-P Duke St., Alexandria, VA 22314, tel. 703/836–3495) will supply you with a complete list of all USPA Group Members (schools, programs, clubs, and drop zones) in the United States and general information on ratings and certifications. Membership includes a subscription to its monthly publication, *Parachutist Magazine.*

PERIODICALS *Parachutist Magazine,* the official publication of the United States Parachutist Association (*see* Organizations,

above), has equipment reviews, "there I was" stories, competition reports, and inspirational pictures of people plummeting through space. *Skydiving Magazine* (Box 1520, DeLand, FL 32721, tel. 904/736–4793) is similar, but it's more tailored to the leading-edge or advanced sky diver.

BOOKS *Parachuting, The Skydiver's Handbook,* by Dan Poynter, is the most definitive text on skydiving for basic- to intermediate-level enthusiasts. It's detailed, accurate, and entertaining. *Skydiving, a Dictionary,* by Bill Fitzsimons, is full of humorous skydiving terminology. *Parachuting's Unforgettable Jumps III,* by Howard Gregory, gives a historical view of both military and sport jumping. *Skies Call,* by Andy Keech, is three volumes of outstanding color photos by a gifted parachuting photographer. *Parachuting Manual with Log,* by Dan Poynter, is a pocket-sized, first-jump-course logbook that's full of excellent illustrations and essential information. It's the least expensive way to learn a lot about skydiving. A *Parachuting Manual With Log for Accelerated Free Fall* is also available.

ALSO SEE If you like hanging out in the skies with a giant tarp over your head, you may like gliding through them with your own wings. Check out the Hang Gliding chapter for more information.

Snowmobiling

By Rosemary Freskos and Jane E. Zarem

he secret is finally out: Snowmobiling is one of the most exciting and comfortable ways to experience America's backcountry in winter. Driving one of today's light, nimble snowmobiles is a cross between riding a motorcycle, driving a car, and steering a sled with handlebars (except that you control the speed). An extensive network of marked and often groomed trails throughout the United States and Canada means that the average rider can explore hundreds of thousands of acres of spectacular territory too remote to be easily reached by any other means. You can snowmobile wherever snow and terrain permit, and there are trails for every ability: packed and groomed tracks that soothe nervous beginners, rolling terrain for intermediates, and thrilling steep trails and deep powder for experienced drivers. No wonder snowmobiling is such a fast-growing sport in North America's snowbelt—Maine and Quebec, Minnesota and Wisconsin, the Rockies, and Alaska.

Once you're hooked, a day trip doesn't offer nearly enough time to explore the wilderness, swoop through the evergreens, blast over hilltops, and create rooster tails in meadows of fresh powder. That's where snowmobile tours come in. A number are available, ranging in length from a weekend to a week or longer. Outfitters take care of all the arrangements. A trip can involve camping or bedding down in a comfortable inn, hearty campfire cooking or elegant feasts. It might run at a relaxed pace of about 100 miles a day, hitting top speeds of 30 to 40 miles per hour with time for photography and exploration, or it could be a haul of up to 200 miles a day with speeds topping 50 miles per hour. A snowmobile tour is definitely the best way to get into the sport, and prices generally run a reasonable $100 to $200 per person per day, including lodging, meals, clothing rental, and a guide.

Some of the best areas for riding don't have organized tours. To visit them, contact snowmobile associations, state tourism boards, local chambers of commerce, and regional and local national park and forest offices for lists of lodges with rental equipment and areas with extensive snowmobile trails. Some rental services offer only detailed trail maps, but others can fix you up with a guide for around $100 to $150 per day per group. Depending on the area and the amount of competition there, the average snowmobile rental fee ranges from $65 to $100 for single riders and $80 to $125 for doubles (sleds that can hold a pair of riders). A deposit of $70 to $200 is usually required. If you have a choice of machine, opt for more power at higher altitudes, because the engine's performance is hampered by the thinner air of the mountains. And be sure it has heated handle grips!

Rosemary Freskos has been writing about snow sports for some two decades. Jane E. Zarem, a travel writer and editor from Connecticut, had her most thrilling snowmobile experience buzzing the Arctic Circle on a safari in Finnish Lapland.

When you plan your trip, try for February and March rather than December and January: The days are longer, so you'll get more time on the trail. Perhaps more to the point, the weather is warmer. Even die-hard winter lovers appreciate a few extra degrees.

CHOOSING THE RIGHT TRIP

You're better off asking lots of questions before signing up than being surprised after the fact.

How long has the operator been in business? Longer is better, especially if you're new to snowmobiling. An outfitter who has been in business for a while has experience answering a range of questions and resolving problems.

What are the guides' qualifications? They should be very familiar with the area and know how to fix mechanical breakdowns on the trail. If you will be far from civilization, they should have first-aid training, including CPR, if not more advanced training in emergency and wilderness medicine.

What is the ratio of customers to guides? The standard is generally one guide for every 5 customers.

How many people are on each tour? Many outfitters sign up a large number of people and then break the crowd into smaller groups. Others—especially outfitters who run customized trips only—limit the number of guests. The optimal size is 5 to 10 riders of similar abilities.

How much riding will be done each day, and what is the average speed? What kind of terrain will be covered? As in any sport, snowmobiling has its experts and its novices and a wide range of intermediates. It's important to choose your comfort zone, whether it involves easy riding on groomed trails or long-distance bushwhacking in the backcountry. Novices might shoot for 100 miles a day, with speeds ranging 30 to 40 miles per hour; aggressive riders can cover twice the distance in a day and handle 50 miles per hour.

What's the cost, and what's included? Most prices include lodging and meals, snowsuits, gloves, boots, helmets, snowmobiles, gas, and oil. On all the trips described below, unless otherwise noted, prices are per person based on double occupancy. Question operators carefully to determine their specific policies. Snowmobiles are sometimes included in the price; if not, figure on $65 to $100 per day for rental. Also, find out who pays for any necessary repairs during the trip and for trailering machines to the starting point, whether you're bringing your own sled or using the operator's. If trail fees are required where you'll be riding, make sure they're included as well. Always inquire whether you are eligible for a refund if there's no snow. If gas and oil are not included, get an estimate of the cost for the trip.

Similarly, if you are not driving to the group assembly point, ask whether transfers from the airport are included—and if not, find out how much they will cost. Airfare is almost always extra.

What are the accommodations like? Most operators use comfortable, moderately priced lodging. Make sure you know what to expect.

What are meals like? Don't look for fancy cooking. Plain fare is the rule—meat and potatoes, chicken and salads—except in more luxurious packages.

What kind of equipment does the outfitter supply? Whether a snowmobile is provided or you rent one, get its make, model, and year. Be sure the sled is light and easy to maneuver, and find out whether it comes with heated hand grips, an electric starter, automatic oil injection, or other conveniences. If the sled in question has an electric starter, make sure that it is also equipped with a backup manual starter to use if the battery is weak. If you don't like what's being provided, ask whether upgrades are available at additional cost. If the outfitter is providing the snowmobile, either as part of the package or as a rental at extra cost, ask what damages you are liable for in the event of an accident. If your own homeowner's policy does not cover such damages, you may want to purchase a snowmobile accident policy, particularly on trips that involve riding off established trails; such a policy costs between $10 and $15 a day and covers damage to your snowmobile and to the one in front of you should you run into it—above a set deductible, normally $250 to $300.

What kind of clothing is provided? The right clothing is absolutely essential. You'll need an insulated snowsuit, a full helmet, special gloves, and waterproof, insulated boots. If you don't already have your own, this can represent a sizable outlay of money. Typically, outfitters do not provide silk or polypropylene long johns, thermal boot inserts, and other essential underpinnings.

Will a support vehicle accompany the tour? Lodge-to-lodge and other long-distance trips are typically accompanied by a van or truck, which tows a trailer that can be loaded with two or more snowmobiles and carries luggage, parts, food, and other supplies—as well as snowmobilers who decide not to ride on a given day.

Do you have references from past guests? They may be able to articulate strengths and weaknesses of a given operator that would be hard to find out about on your own.

How far in advance do I need to book? If your destination is a popular one or you visit during a holiday, reserve at least a couple of months ahead.

MAJOR PLAYERS

DECKER'S SNO-VENTURE TOURS Decker's, in business since 1980, offers a diverse schedule of snowmobile vacation packages to prime destinations in Wisconsin, Michigan, Minnesota, Wyoming, Oregon, Montana, Alaska, and Yellowstone National Park.

The trips, with some exceptions, include meals, accommodations in lodges or motels, guiding, and a support vehicle. Rental snow-mobiles and gear (boots, suits, helmets, gloves) are available and priced separately, as some people have their own machines and gear; double units are available. Prices range from $100 a day with lodging, meals, and guides to $220 a day with snowmobiles added. (Hwy. 45 North, Box 1447, Eagle River, WI 54521, tel. 715/479–2764, fax 715/479–9711).

INTERNATIONAL SNOWMOBILE TOURS This company was formed in 1980 by Dick Squiers who, with his tour coordinators, Don Bole, Bob Thornburg, and John Stegemoller, claim some three quarters of a century of combined snowmobiling experience. IST runs 10 to 12 tours per season in Minnesota, Michigan, Yellowstone, and Ontario; some are for aggressive riders with high skill levels who can maintain speeds of 50 miles per hour and travel 200 miles a day. Clothing and snowmobile rentals are not included in the prices but Polaris liquid-cooled snowmobiles may be rented for $100 per day. Group size is usually about 20, and IST guides are all experienced deep-snow riders, with outgoing personalities and training in first aid, wilderness and emergency medicine, and CPR. A support vehicle is present only on tours that involve motel transfers. Some meals are included. Lodging is provided primarily in Best Westerns, Holiday Inns, and similar hostelries. Prices range from $95 to $110 per day (427 Sycamore St., Chesterfield, IN 46017, tel. 317/378–5074).

SENIOR WORLD TOURS Owner-operator Roger Matthews has been active in the industry since 1967, much of the time promoting snowmobiling in his home state of Michigan. His most popular tours, however, are to Jackson Hole, Yellowstone National Park, Alaska, and Ontario. Tours are geared mainly to beginners and intermediates, most at the upper end of the age spectrum who don't want to spend all their time sledding; seniors-only groups are their specialty. There is one guide for each group of 10 snowmobilers, with no more than 30 riders per tour. Each guide has at least 10 years' experience, as well as rescue and emergency medical training. Meals of basic fare (steaks, plain seafood, roast beef, or the like), and lodge or log cabin accommodations are included in the prices. On some trips, snowmobiles are included in the package; on special senior trips, personal gear is included. (3701 Buttrick Rd. SE, Ada, MI 49301, tel. 800/676–5803, fax 616/676–5898).

YELLOWSTONE ADVENTURES If you want to visit this national park on a snowmobile, Yellowstone Adventures is one of the top outfitters. Take two days or two weeks to explore the 2.2 million-acre park's natural wonders on the country's most extensive trail system. Trails begin right in town, where snowmobilers share city streets with motorists. Founded in 1973, Yellowstone Adventures is the town's exclusive Ski-Doo dealer, and their rental fleet of 110 sleds is replaced every year. They also put together custom packages that include lodging, snowmobile rental, clothing, dinner discounts, and complimentary gifts—but not meals. Lodging is in modern, comfortable motels with hot tubs and/or indoor pools. Guides tend to be personable, outgoing, and knowledgeable about the area, with 8 to 10 years of experience and emergency medical training. There's usually one guide for every 10 riders and 5 to 10 snowmobiles per group. Packages range in cost from $65 to $125 per person per day, depending on the duration and room occupancy. (131 Dunraven St., Box 669, West Yellowstone, MT 59758, tel. 406/646–7735 or 800/231–5991, fax 406/646–9608).

FAVORITE TRIPS

THE NORTHEAST

MAINE Aroostook County. The northeastern tip of Maine, called simply "The County" by natives, is a vast land of small communities set among forests, lakes, streams, and farms. Local snowmobile clubs maintain over 1,500 miles of groomed trails, all marked for gas, food, lodging, mileage, and directions. Towns are just far enough apart along the trails to make it easy to escape civilization without leaving the comforts of a gas station too far behind.

Kent and Kathie Forbes's operation specializes in custom trips in this area. You decide the number of nights, the type of lodging and dining, and how many miles of riding, and the Forbeses set it up. Kent Forbes accompanies small groups and has a staff of guides to help him out with groups larger than 5. Favorite routes explore the Fish River chain of waterways, known for its great ice fishing for salmon and trout; the historic town of Fort Kent, on the banks of the St. John River, known for its role in the Aroostook War of 1839 between the United States and British Canada; and tiny Eagle Lake, a former logging hub now catering to snowmobilers, where you might spot moose, deer, coyote, and fox. Presque Isle, about an hour's ride from Caribou, has good shopping and dining. Polaris snowmobiles are used. Prices vary according to the package you choose and the number of people in your party. *Crystal Snowmobile Tours, Box 1448, Caribou, ME 04736, tel. 207/498–3220 or 207/492–7471. Dec.–Mar.: about $350 per day per couple including snowmobile rental and lodging, but not meals, clothing, gas or oil; sign up 1–2 months in advance.*

THE MIDWEST

MICHIGAN Superior Tour. This 6-day International Snowmobile Tours program takes you across Michigan's Upper Peninsula, along the Lake Superior shore to Copper Harbor, on some of the best groomed trails in the area. Overnight stops are at Marquette, Baraga, and Gwinn—areas noted for their snowfall. A support vehicle brings your luggage, so all you have to do is enjoy the drive, the hearty meals, and the socializing. You need moderate skills to handle the trip: You should be able to maintain speeds of 35 miles an hour for prolonged periods, usually 135 miles a day and about 8 hours out; ice riding may be necessary. Breakfast is a buffet of pancakes, French toast, and cereal; dinner is prime rib, steak, or seafood. Accommodations for the 20 tour participants and the guide who accompanies them are Best Western properties or the equivalent. *International Snowmobile Tours, 427 Sycamore, Chesterfield, IN 46017, tel. 317/378–5074 or 800/378–8687. Feb.: 6 days, $650. Price does not include snowmobiles, gas, oil, or lunch; sign up 6 months in advance.*

MICHIGAN AND WISCONSIN **Winter Wonderland.** This 6-day tour from Decker's Sno-Venture starts in Eagle River, Wisconsin, and loops to Copper Harbor, Michigan, and back—a total of 660 miles. Distance traveled varies from 75 to 120 miles per day at speeds averaging 25 miles an hour.

The terrain and scenery change as you go: The first day, you ride through forests sprinkled with lakes to the foothills of the Porcupine Mountains (a.k.a. the Porkies) and into White Pine, Michigan, to rustic Konteka Lodge. The next day's highlights include a ride to the magnificent Lake of the Clouds overlook and across a 300-foot-high trestle bridge. Pushing on, you follow the bend of the Keweenaw Peninsula, a historic mining area; stop en route to admire copper craft work; and picnic trailside on wine and meat-filled turnovers known as pasties, traditional miner's fare. Your destination is the tiny resort town of Copper Harbor, nestled on the shore of Lake Superior. The tour continues through other historic towns, such as Calumet, then back through Houghton to Bruce Crossing and a farewell banquet. The group size is anywhere from 6 to 30, with the number of guides dependent on the group size. *Decker's Sno-Venture Tours, Box 1447, Eagle River, WI 54521, tel. 715/479–2764, fax 715/479–9711. Feb.: 6 days, $595. Price does not include clothing, snowmobiles, gas, or oil; sign up 2–3 months in advance.*

MINNESOTA **North Coast Grand Tour.** Every year since they opened in 1983, Scott Borland has driven the North Shore and Gunflint Snowmobile Trails that follow the forested ridge line of the rugged hills overlooking Lake Superior. Borland is the leader of this trip out of Duluth. He's also an expert snowmobiler with some 30 years' experience.

This trip includes four days of snowmobiling, first-class lodging, delicious meals, and stunning scenery. You drive your machine along trails that cut through lowland meadows, swamps, and thick forests, and pass cascading rivers and waterfalls plummeting into the lake. You'll find no towns along the main route, but there are shelters with firewood and outhouses every 10 miles. Gas, food, and lodging are accessible via groomed side trails. Traveling in a group of 4 to 8 riders and your guide, you cover 75 to 100 miles a day on Ski-doo Safari 377s.

Every day, Scott prepares a hot lunch of grilled trout or steak. Accommodations vary night to night: Little Ollie, a remote but modern cabin accessible only by snowmobile or skis; the rustic Trestle Pine Inn, a favorite gathering place of sledders; luxurious condos at Blue Finn Bay, where you can swim in a pool, soak in a hot tub, and have a hearty dinner of lake trout or herring. Most days allow time for hiking. A special event is the Mongolian firepot dinner, a sort of meat-and-vegetable fondue served in the traditional Mongolian tent known as a yurt. Other dinners range from basic burgers to fresh lake trout, elegantly presented. With luck, you'll get a glimpse of the northern lights. *Boundary Country Trekking, 590 Gunflint Trail, Grand Marais, MN 55604, tel. 218/388–9972 or 800/322–8327, fax 218/388–4487. Feb.: 4 days, $1,200. Price does not include gas; sign up 3 months in advance.*

THE ROCKIES

COLORADO **Colorado to Wyoming Cross-border Tour.** Some of the country's best snowmobiling terrain is in Colorado, but multi-day tours are hard to find. This tour from American Wilderness Experience combines great snow, spectacular mountain scenery, quality equipment, first-class lodging, delicious meals, and fun-loving guides. The Inn at Steamboat Lake, one-half hour north of Steamboat Springs, is your primary base for this 4-day snowmobile safari. The first day is unstructured, leaving time to relax, join the group for a happy-hour orientation and a sumptuous dinner.

In the morning, after being outfitted and assigned a factory-fresh Polaris Indy snowmobile, you're off on a full day-exploration of the countryside surrounding the Steamboat Lake area, which has 300 miles of groomed and virgin trails, and an average annual snowfall of 325 inches. That night, a hot tub, good meal, and cozy room will be most welcome.

On the third day, you'll lash your overnight gear onto your machine and head north through spectacular mountain passes and forests of aspen and pine. After lunch, you'll cross the border to Wyoming and drop down into Water Valley. Water Valley Ranch, your lodging for the night, is a secluded working ranch on the banks of the wooded Encampment River, adjacent to an elk refuge. During the return trip back into the Colorado high country the next day, you may wish to try off-trail riding on untracked powder in a wide-open meadow. This tour is suitable for beginners, but experienced riders will also find it enjoyable. Snowmobiles, gas and oil, clothing, lodging, and all meals are included in the price. *American Wilderness Experience, Box 1486, Boulder, CO 80306, tel. 303/444-2622 or 800/444-0099, fax 303/444-3999. Dec.–Mar.: 4 days, $895. Sign up 6 months in advance.*

MONTANA **Montana Mountains.** This 6-day tour in the Montana Mountains offers great scenery and terrain that's challenging for accomplished snowmobiliers and manageable for beginners. You're picked up at Missoula's western-style airport and transported to Lola Hot Springs, your home for the next six days. There's a genuine hot spring here and a marvelous indoor-outdoor swimming pool. No miraculous cures are claimed, but it's certainly nice to know that there are "healing waters" available at the end of the day's ride. Accommodations are very comfortable; meals are tasty, generally American

or Continental fare. Riding here, as anywhere, depends on conditions; routes can change daily. But one thing is certain: Each day will reveal another new scenic panorama. A trio of guides (Buster and his two sons, Charles and Greg) are top-rated on account of their considerate guiding style. *Decker's Sno-Venture Tours, Box 1447, Eagle River, WI 54521, tel. 715/479-2764, fax 715/479-9711. Mar.: 5 days, $499. Price does not include snowmobiles, gas, oil, or clothing; sign up 2–3 months in advance.*

MONTANA **Yellowstone National Park out of West Yellowstone.** Having catered to snowmobilers ever since the sport emerged on the scene in the late 1960s, this town is widely known in the field as the Snowmobile Capital of the World. Every year in winter, the place bustles with the sledding crowd, especially on weekends. You can rent snowmobiles in any number of places and ride them around town, where nearly a dozen feet of snow fall every year. The town border the park, which has nearly 200 miles of groomed trails. Wildlife abounds: Bison and elk may even decide to share your trail. In the nearby Targhee National Forest, in Idaho, and the Gallatin National Forest, in Montana, there are hundreds of miles of groomed trails and thousands of acres of powder fields—snowmobile playgrounds par excellence.

One of the best resort motels in the area, the Stage Coach Inn, has complete 3- to 7-day packages. Snowmobiles are new, and all makes are available. Guides are not included but can be arranged at additional fees. Otherwise, you explore with a trail map— trails are well-marked. The inn is modern, with custom touches like the sweeping staircase in the lobby and antler lamps and willowlike chairs in the guest rooms. *Stage Coach Inn, 209 Madison Ave., West Yellowstone, MT 59758, tel. 406/646-7381 or 800/842-2882, fax 406/646-9575. Dec.–Mar.: 3– 7 days, $520–$970. Prices do not include meals or gas after the first tank; sign up 6 months in advance for February and busy holiday periods (or call for a cancellation exactly 30 days in advance).*

WYOMING **Continental Divide Trail.** This exhilarating high-country tour departs from Jackson and crisscrosses the Divide through portions of three mountain ranges: the Wind Rivers, Gros Ventre, and Absaroka. The Continental Divide Trail is a recently established groomed system of backcountry trails, lookouts, and loops that offer spectacular vistas and great opportunities for free-style snowmobiling. On the first day, after a hearty breakfast at the Wort Hotel, participants are outfitted and shuttled by van 50 miles to the trailhead. During three full days of touring, you'll visit Green River Lake, an elk refuge, hot springs, and countless mountain passes high above the tree line. The two nights are spent relaxing at cozy, remote guest ranches along the route; they differ with each trip.

This trip is suitable for novices, although experienced snowmobilers will find it appealing due to the nature of the terrain and the off-trail snowmobiling opportunities. Groups are limited to just six participants, accompanied by a guide. New Arctic Cat snowmobiles with handwarmers are provided. The price also includes two nights' lodging, all meals, clothing, guide, permits, gas and oil, and ground transfers. *American Wilderness Experience, Box 1486, Boulder, CO 80306, tel. 303/444–2622 or 800/444–0099, fax 303/444–3999. Feb.–Mar.: 5 days, $800. Sign up 6 months in advance.*

WYOMING **Togwotee Mountain, the Continental Divide, and Yellowstone.** Northern Wyoming's high mountain valley, which starts at 6,200 feet and rises to 13,000 feet, contains some of the country's finest deep powder—about 500 inches a year—and some of its steepest mountains. The mountains dare hard-core riders, while the well-groomed trails of the national park welcome novices. Senior World's basic tour of this area, designed for under-the-hill riders as well as older clientele, begins in Jackson Hole. A 50-mile van trip puts you at Cowboy Village Resort at Togwotee nestled in jack pines. The resort is 8,500 feet on the Continental Divide Trail, which encompasses some 330 miles of groomed, interconnected

trails from Pinedale north. The rest of the package involves guided day-tripping out of the lodge in late-model snowmobiles. Some days, you cover 100 to 125 miles on groomed trails and cross-country; other days, there's time to play in the powder, with only 40 to 60 miles on the itinerary. The challenges are the pleasures: high peaks, deep valleys, and flat trails where you can jump, side-hill, or simply cruise past mountain sheep, moose, elk, and coyote. Speeds range from 35 to 40 miles per hour for slower groups to 60 miles per hour for faster ones.

Six 6-day and four 7-day tours for seniors only include a lesson the first day, as well as a sleigh ride in the National Elk Refuge—home to 10,000 elk. Accommodations are in comfortable lodges or log cabins, and meals are buffet-style—breakfasts of eggs, bacon, pancakes, and cereal, and dinners of seafood or roast beef. All tours include lodging, breakfast, and dinner each day, some lunches, snowmobiles with all gas and oil, guides, clothing, and airport transfers. Prices vary depending on the choice of accommodation. *Senior World Tours, 3701 Buttrick Rd. SE, Ada, MI 49301, tel. 800/676–5803, fax 616/676–5898. Dec.–Mar.: 8 days, $1,399–$1,859; 6 days, for seniors only, $1,089–$1,419; 7 days, for seniors only, $1,279–$1,619. Some lunches are not included.*

WYOMING **Yellowstone from the East.** Pahaska Tepee, a rustic resort at the eastern entrance to Yellowstone and 50 miles west of historic Cody, Wyoming, makes a totally different base from the motels in busy West Yellowstone, 85 miles west. You spend your time playing in the powder close to the lodge—following the Gibbon River, where coyotes sometimes fish for trout; heading off to Norris Junction, with its own spate of geysers and fumeroles a bit smaller than those around Old Faithful, 69 miles away; and to Artists' Point, for a view of 200-foot Yellowstone Falls, a cascade of ice in winter. Carry cross-country skis on your sled, and you can enjoy silent, remote trails that are off-limits to snowmobiles. Guides are not provided, since the routes are well-marked.

The 50-unit Pahaska Tepee resort dates back to 1905, when Buffalo Bill Cody, called Pahaska by the Indians, built a hewn-log hunting lodge near the banks of the Shoshone River. Now a National Historic Landmark, it is the most distinctive structure on the property. Current guest quarters are scattered around the grounds in small, basic A-frame cabins with private baths but no phones or TVs. Rooms are also available in the resort's hillside Reunion Lodge, a 7-bedroom, 8-bath log building decorated with original Southwestern art and anchored by a massive 36-foot-tall fireplace.

Pahaska offers 3- and 5-day snowmobile packages, which include lodging, breakfast, dinner, a new Polaris snowmobile, snowmobile suit, gloves, helmet, and the option to stay in West Yellowstone for a couple of nights. Menus offer such hearty fare as mountain man skillet at breakfast (home fries topped with fried onions, ham, mushrooms, tomatoes, cheese, and eggs); chili, soup, and burgers and other sandwiches at lunch; and, at dinner, steak and seafood. *Pahaska Tepee Resort, 183-R Yellowstone Hwy., Cody, WY 82414, tel. 307/527–7701 or 800/628–7791, fax 307/527–4019. Dec.– Mar.: 5 days, $850; 3 days, $495. Price does not include lunch, gas, or oil; sign up 6–12 months in advance.*

THE WEST COAST

CALIFORNIA **Tahoe National Forest.** The 175 miles of uncrowded trails that Eagle Ridge Snowmobile Outfitters owner David Ceruti uses on his tours are some of the best groomed in the state. They wind past Jackson Meadows reservoir and frozen Webber Lake and through deep-powder Pirazza Meadows and pristine forests with the majestic Sierras as a backdrop. There are 650 square miles to explore here, so the specific terrain you visit is selected for its interest and challenge. You might indulge in a relaxing trail ride at 5,000 feet in the Plumas National Forest or, if you're an expert, climb to 8,500 feet in the Sierras. Each group includes 2 to 6 snowmobilers, accompanied

by an experienced guide. Snowmobiles are new every year; high-performance vehicles are available for experienced riders.

Because this is '49er country, overnight stops are in old mining towns, including Sierra City, the northernmost of the Gold Rush towns, and Bassett's Station, a boomday stagecoach stop and now a peaceful hamlet with a B&B, motel, general store, and a total population of 8. Lodging at Bassett's Station is in an elegant B&B. As we go to press, another B&B is being built on Webber Lake. Meals are in restaurants, where you can order basic burgers and sandwiches; your B&B breakfast, of course, is included. *Eagle Ridge Snowmobile Outfitters, Box 1677, Truckee, CA 96160, tel. 916/747– 1902. Nov.–Apr.: 2 days, $350. Sign up 1 week in advance.*

ALASKA

SOUTHEAST **Eureka Lodge and the Iditarod Dog Sled Race.** Much more than just snowmobiling, this 9-day trip combines a look at the most famous dogsled race in the world and the chance to explore untamed backcountry.

The tour kicks off in Anchorage on Friday, with a visit to the Iditarod mushers in their motels. On Saturday, you're first in line to see the start of this famous race. Then you and the dogs part ways as you make the run to Eureka Lodge, your base for the next 5 days in this wide-open region. Here, you run cross-country toward the Horse Pasture area, notable for its scenery; sled on scenic rivers like the Caribou, Alfred, Squaw, and Nelchina; and explore deserted gold-mining camps. About 100 miles of groomed trails in the immediate area of the lodge give you access to open meadows, challenging mountains, and rolling valleys—the sheer size of the area is enough to take your breath away.

Typically, you average 75 to 125 miles a day, at speeds of between 40 and 70 miles per hour, depending on the group. On an optional 105-mile trip to Valdez, experienced drivers with extensive mountain and sidehill experience can cross the Nelchina, Stephens, and Valdez Glaciers; traverse the 6,000-foot-high Scott Ice Field; overnight in Valdez; and return the next day.

This is a true frontier adventure through untracked wilderness that few snowmobilers ever see, but it's for the experienced snowmobiler only. The group size is limited to 10, with 2 guides. *Senior World Tours, 3701 Buttrick Rd. SE, Ada, MI 49301, tel. 800/676–5803, fax 616/676–5898. Mar.: 9 days, $1,845. Price does not include snowsuits, helmets, boots, or air transportation; sign up 6 months in advance.*

CANADA

ONTARIO **Canadian Adventure Via the Snow Train.** In the 10,000-square-mile Nordaski region of northern Ontario, hundreds of miles of groomed trails link Hearst, the area's principal town, with other communities distinctive for their mix of French-, Ojibway-, and Cree-speaking residents. Because downtown Hearst is open to snowmobile traffic, you can ride directly from your lodging to the trails. Here, and on the numerous old logging roads into the bush, you experience true deep snow country, where up to 4 feet of powder is present all winter.

Dick Squiers developed his tour of the area in the 1970s and has been running it 3 to 4 times a year since then. Groups of 30 converge in Sault Ste. Marie, Canada, over the bridge from Sault Ste. Marie, Michigan, where you board the Algoma Central Railway's Snow Train for a day-long, 297-mile ride north over ice-bound rivers, across high trestles, past Bridal Veil and Black Beaver falls, through spectacular Agawa Canyon, and over two "floating bridges" to the end of the line—Hearst—where you're based for the duration of the trip. You break up into smaller groups of riders of similar abilities and spend the week daytripping around the area with your guide. Daily treks surpass 100 miles over rolling terrain at speeds of 30 to 50 miles per hour, depending on the

group. Lodging is in modern motels with comfortable rooms. Sunday dinner and a Friday evening banquet are included in the price. *International Snowmobile Tours, Inc., 427 Sycamore, Chesterfield, IN 46017, tel. 317/378–5074 or 800/378–8687. Feb.–Mar.: 6 days, $675. Price includes train fare, 6 nights lodging, guides, and trail permits, but not snowmobiles, clothing, gas, oil, or most meals; sign up 6 months in advance.*

ONTARIO **Via the Snow Train to Wawa.** Embarking at Sault Ste. Marie, Michigan, Senior World Tours also makes use of the Algoma Central Railway but, after 5 hours, you jump off in the town of Wawa. Usually there are 10 to 15 people per group, and each group is accompanied by a guide.

The snowmobiling around Wawa is as good as it is farther north, with plenty of groomed trails, snow cover, and scenery of frozen lakes and rolling meadows interspersed with thick forest. The sheer size of the area is enough to overwhelm even experienced sledders. Daily runs range from 75 to 125 miles, depending on the speed of the group. Although high speeds are not encouraged, a faster group will average 40 to 50 miles per hour; a slower one, only 20 to 30. Lodging is in motels, with hot tubs and swimming pools. Sunday dinner, Monday breakfast, and an awards banquet on Friday evening are included. You also have the option of traveling an extra 180 miles north to Hearst—the trip is included in the price. *Senior World Tours, 3701 Buttrick Rd. SE, Ada, MI 49301, tel. 800/676–5803, fax 616/676–5898. Feb.: 8 days, $759. Price does not include snowmobiles, clothing, gas, oil, and some meals; sign up 6–8 months in advance.*

SOURCES

ORGANIZATIONS The **International Snowmobile Manufacturers Association** (ISMA, 271 Woodland Pass, Suite 220, East Lansing, MI 48823, tel. 517/332–1760; fax 517/332-0856) is a central source for general information. The ISMA publishes a trail map directory to 20 states and 8 Canadian provinces, a guide to publications about snowmobiling, a complete list of products, and a safety handbook. In the Northeast, the **Vermont Association of Snow Travelers** (Box 839, Montpelier, VT 05601, tel. 802/ 229–0005; fax 802/223–4316) is a nonprofit group of volunteers, that operates a trail system and publishes a newsletter and vacation information. The **Western Maine Mountains International Snowmobile Network** (Western Maine Mountains Chamber of Commerce, Box 934, Wilton, ME 04294, tel. 207/864–3932) is a 260-mile marked and groomed loop partly in Quebec. Five member chambers of commerce can help you plan a tour with overnight stops in each of their towns. In the Rockies, the **Utah Travel Council** (Council Hall/Capitol Hill, Salt Lake City, UT 84114, tel. 801/538–1030) publishes a free brochure and trail maps on snowmobiling throughout the state. The **California/Nevada Snowmobile Association** (Ken Nelson, Bucks Lake Lodge, Box 236, Quincy, CA 95971, tel. 916/283–2262; fax 916/283–5008) can also be helpful.

PERIODICALS The quarterly *Snowmobile Magazine,* which concentrates on product evaluation and destinations, and *SnowGoer Magazine,* which focuses on snowmobile technology, are both published by Ehlert Publishing Group (319 Barry Ave. S, Way-zata, MN 55391, tel. 612/476–2200); *Snow-Goer's* December issue is a comprehensive annual vacation guide that details every snowmobile area in the East, Midwest, and Canada but covers the West only sketchily. *Snowest Magazine* (Harris Publishing Co., 520 Park Ave., Idaho Falls, ID 83402, tel. 800/638–0135) discusses snowmobiling in the West; an annual subscription includes the *Western Guide to Snowmobiling,* a state-by-state guide to hot spots and guide services in 12 western states and British Columbia.

VIDEOS Two practical guides include the International Association of Snowmobile Administrators' *Snowmobiling Safety and You: Snowmobile Operations and Tracks of Winter: Guide to Responsible Snowmobiling* (Outdoor Empire Publishing, 511 Eastlake Ave. E, Seattle, WA 98109, tel. 206/624–3845). *Snowmotion: The Art of Sledding* (Petersen Production, Inc., 314 West Pender St., Vancouver, B.C. Canada V6B 1T3, tel. 604/669–8890) captures powder bashing, grabbing air, racing, and incredible mountain scenery—in a jazzy, adventure-flick format.

ALSO SEE If you like a blue-and-white color scheme in the wilderness and the feel of icy wind on your cheeks, see the Cross-Country Skiing and Ski Schools chapters.

Surfing Schools

By Erik Fair

xperienced surfers call beginning surfers Kooks. The plight of the Kook is summed up by the East Coast editor of *Surfer Magazine,* Amy Van Sant, who says: "Anyone who has surfed for over a year instantly hates anyone who has surfed for less than a year." Van Sant and her West Coast counterpart Ben Marcus laugh at this. Although they admit that it's at least partially true, they insist that the rewards of surfing far outweigh all the kookiness you'll endure as you evolve into a special kind of being—one who can compete for the most magical and natural commodity on earth: a ridable breaking wave. "The first time you stand up on a breaking wave," says Marcus, "you'll feel like a supreme being who has conquered a whole ocean. You'll think you're moving much faster than you really are, and the sound of the water peeling off the rails [sides] of your board is unbelievably crisp." But the biggest thrill for any beginning surfer, says Marcus, is "the personal satisfaction of mastering something that is very difficult and very frustrating."

For the raw beginner, just balancing on a surfboard while lying down is awkward. The idea of reading waves seems as unfathomable as the ocean itself; and the chances of simultaneously catching a breaking wave and standing up are slim and none. Throw in the indignity of starting at the absolute bottom of a rigid pecking order, and it's easy to understand why 90% of all surfers seem to be confident young men with thick skin.

In reality, surfing can be enjoyed by anyone of any age—as long as he or she realizes that surfing's learning curve is as personally defined as it is limitless. If you have average strength, stamina, and flexibility, coupled with above-average patience, tenacity, and humility, you can learn to surf. Naturally, the more fit and philosophical you are, the faster you'll negotiate the metamorphosis from Kook to Surf God or Goddess.

First things first: Before you can catch a wave, you need to understand it. The formation of a wave begins when breezes blowing hundreds or even thousands of miles away from shore sweep unobstructed across the ocean. Their force is absorbed by the surface of the ocean and translated into an ocean swell. Eventually the long bands of swell encounter shallower waters and, ultimately, the shoreline where you eagerly await your first surfing lesson. As each band nears the shore, friction from the rising ocean bottom slows down the lower part of the swell. The upper part of the swell keeps moving at the swell's original speed, and water piles up until something has to give. When it does, the wave breaks. The steepness and composition of the ocean bottom combine with the size, shape, direction, and speed of the swell to determine just where and how that happens. Other variables include tides, changes

Adventurer and writer Erik Fair is the author of *California Thrill Sports.* He has been marinating in southern California's surfer-dude culture for most of his adult life.

in the contour of the ocean floor caused by the force of breaking waves, and local breezes, which can knock a perfectly surfable swell into a useless chop.

From a beginner's perspective there are 3 types of breaking waves: (1) waves you can have fun with, (2) waves that will scare the bejabbers out of you, and (3) waves that will eat you for breakfast. What an instructor is looking for is a gradually sloped sandy ocean bottom and relatively slow-moving 1- to 3-foot waves with a soft (sometimes called crumbly) break. He or she will also look for waves that break as far as possible from the shoreline, in water shallow enough for you to stand up in. Stay away from big, fast, steep waves that break with a cool-looking curl and a bone-rattling "WHOMP!"

Once you understand the natural forces you're dealing with, it's time to get familiar with the equipment involved in surfing: the board. A board is a magical planing device that allows you to scoot, perfectly balanced, along the face of a breaking wave and carve elegant turns by subtly shifting your weight.

As a beginner you need a relatively big board that has plenty of flotation and is stable enough to withstand your clunky initial attempts at weight-shift control. You'll probably want a board that is at least a foot taller than you are, about 3 inches thick, and 19 to 22 inches wide in the middle. Avoid the short, thin, cool-looking Tri-Fins or Thrusters that most experienced surfers use. Some schools use soft surfboards, made out of plastic foam, that float well and won't hurt if they hit you. Other schools use traditional hard boards carved out of polyurethane foam blocks and coated with fiberglass. These can definitely hurt you if they hit you, but this won't be a problem as long as you observe normal safety procedures. Most schools use a "leash," which attaches a hard board to your ankle to prevent it from shooting out of a wave like a missile aimed at someone's head.

Once you have a good beginner's board, an experienced instructor, and suitable surf conditions, it's time to learn a few skills.

First, you learn how to lie down on the board and stay balanced, in both side-to-side and front-to-aft positions. Next, you learn how to rotate your arms in a smooth paddling motion and stay balanced while being pitched on your way to the spot where waves are breaking.

Once you're in the water, you'll need to be able to read the waves, so you can match the wave's speed and catch it at the exact moment it breaks. Unfortunately, your biggest problem at this point is still staying balanced while being pitched up and down by a rolling sea. During your first few lessons count on your instructor to read waves for you, pushing you into position to actually have a chance of catching a few waves. To catch a wave you have to shift your weight slightly to the rear, so the nose of your board doesn't "pearl" (dive into the wave and flip you over like a piece of driftwood). This is relatively easy to do the first few times because, hey, no one's asking you to stand up yet. That will come after you develop a feel for all the above techniques.

The motion you'll use to stand up is called a pop-up, which is a sudden, smooth motion from a face-down, lying-down position to a side-straddle crouched position with one foot in front of the other. Practicing a pop-up on dry land is one thing. Doing it while catching a wave and balancing on a speeding surfboard is quite another. With good instruction you can expect gradual progress from your belly to your knees to a nervous crouch to a full Bronze Surf God stand-up. It takes most beginners from 1 to 4 lessons (2 to 10 hours) to stand up in the water. It all depends on the surf spot, surf conditions, your ability, and your instructor's ability.

Private or group lessons given by the hour or half-day are the most popular type of surfing school option for adults. Costs typically range from $25 to $70 an hour for private lessons and from $15 to $30 an hour for group lessons. These lessons are usually tailored to the age and level of the students.

Most 3- to 7-day surf camps are designed for and run by a younger crowd, with most participants between the ages of 10 and 16. However, some schools, such as those listed here, reserve one session for adults. A week will give you the chance to progress from just balancing efficiently to learning to catch better waves more quickly and to angle across the face of a wave rather than taking it straight into shore. Virtually all camps take place between June and August, and most involve camping out in tents, telling tall tales around a campfire, and surfing your brains out during the day. Costs range from $200 to $800 per camp, depending on number of days and type of accommodations, if any, offered.

CHOOSING THE RIGHT SCHOOL

Lots of folks learn how to surf by trial and error, or from buddies or freelance instructors loosely affiliated with a local surf shop. The risks and rewards of trial and error are obvious. Be wary of informal referrals from surf shops; salespeople may confuse your best interests with their own. Ask these questions before choosing an instructor:

How long have you been teaching, and what certifications do you have? Because there is no official instructor certification in the world of surfing, you should look for an instructor with a lot of experience and other certifications, such as CPR and first aid, for proof that he or she is worthy of your trust. Beyond that, find an instructor whose personal style you feel comfortable with.

What's the cost and what's included? Prices for camps in these listings are per person and include food, lodging, and surfboards. Prices for lessons also include use of a board. Find out what kind of board is offered (soft or hard), because you might want to bring your own. Also ask if you need to bring your own leash or water wear (such as a wet suit).

What are the accommodations like? Accommodations at most surf camps are camping or dorm style, so make sure you know what you're getting into. In these listings, cham-

ber of commerce telephone numbers are given to assist you in finding lodging near surf schools that offer only daily lessons.

What is the food like? Food at the camps listed here is basic camping fare. If you're not prepared to dine on the likes of hot dogs and simple Mexican dishes, surfing school may not be your ideal vacation.

Do you have references from past students? This is one way to get the scoop on how well a surfer teaches.

How far in advance do I need to book? You may need to sign up 2 months in advance for surfing camps and 2 weeks in advance for private lessons.

FAVORITE SCHOOLS

THE MID-ATLANTIC

DELAWARE **Surf Sessions.** Bret Buchler is a true surfing addict—just ask his children, Baptiste, Abi, and Jake, all of whom were surfing by the time they were 3. Bret started at 22 when he caught his first wave in Ocean City, Maryland, in the summer of 1976. By that fall the charm of the waves had lured him to California. Three months later, still not satisfied, he took a 6-month surfing safari to Hawaii. From there it was a stint as a crew member on a ship making a round-the-world voyage, during which he surfed in Tahiti and other South Pacific Islands as well as France and Israel. He finally returned to Fenwick Island, Delaware (half a mile from Ocean City, Maryland), where he founded Surf Sessions in 1988. Buchler combines his passion for the sport with his skill as a teacher (he teaches geography in a junior high school) to come up with a great program.

Surf Sessions, one of only 2 established surfing schools on the East Coast, offers week-long overnight camps from June through August, and day lessons from May through October. Although most of the camps are for kids (ages 12–18), the last one each summer is for adults (usually between 21 and 50).

Your week starts on Sunday evening with a 30-minute orientation session on water safety, followed by 30 minutes of stretching exercises and pop-up practice on the beach. Sunday evening Buchler and his 2 assistants take you into the water, guide you to the right spot, and push you into a few small waves.

For the first day or so, until you no longer need pushing, you ride straight into shore in white water. Then the instructors give verbal cues—"paddle hard," "keep paddling," "watch the wave," "go left," "go right"—to help you catch some waves on your own. By the third day you can leave the little white water behind and get into the line-up where slightly larger waves are breaking. Here you learn to read the waves and how to angle across the face of a wave rather than riding it straight into shore. The days are intense: You stay in the water as long as waves are breaking and your energy level holds up.

Each night you return to camp headquarters in a house 50 feet from the beach. Two bedrooms with bunk beds house 10 campers. They may not be the most luxurious accommodations, but you'll be too tired to care. Meals are catered, and there's a fireplace where sleepy surfers gather to swap stories about the day. *Surf Sessions, Rte. 3, Box 275 D, Fenwick Island, DE 19944, tel. 302/539–2126. June–Aug.: 7-day camp, $450. May–Oct.: 2-hour lesson, $20 for first lesson and $15 for subsequent lessons.*

THE SOUTH

FLORIDA **Cocoa Beach Surfing School.** Craig Carroll has been surfing for 29 of his 37 years, and in 1993 he started the only surf school in Cocoa Beach. In 1995 Carroll was honored by being selected as a member of the United States Surfing Team. The warm water temperatures (no wet suits needed here) and gradually sloping, sand-bottom beaches make Cocoa Beach the most comfortable spot on the East Coast for beginning surfers. Cocoa Beach is also a top vacation spot for non-surfers; it's only an hour east of

the Orlando area and half an hour south of the Kennedy Space Center.

Although he teaches surfing to all ages—he started his son Corey at 6 months—Carroll's week-long day camps in June, July, and August are usually attended only by children (ages 7–15). He gives adults 1-hour private lessons and 2-hour group lessons year-round. Carroll has had great success with his adult pupils, and says he hasn't had one yet who couldn't stand up at least once by the end of his or her first lesson. The 2- to 3-foot waves characteristic of the summer make it the best season to make your first attempts. Carroll provides only soft boards and leashes, so if you want to learn on a fiberglass board you'll have to bring your own.

Carroll has a special arrangement with the Wakulla Motel in Cocoa Beach, which is one block from the beach and two blocks from the famous Ron Jon Surf Shop. At this motel with two-bedroom suites that normally go for $79 per night, Carroll's students receive an automatic 10% discount just for mentioning his name. *Cocoa Beach Surfing School, 490 Tina Place, Merritt Island, FL 32952 tel. 407/452–0854. Wakulla Motel, tel. 800/992–5852. June–Aug.: 5-day summer day camp, $135. Year-round: 1-hour private lesson, $25; 2-hour group lesson, $20 per person (4-person minimum). Sign up 2 weeks in advance.*

THE SOUTHWEST

TEXAS **Riding a Wave Machine.** You definitely need an ocean to learn how to read wave conditions, but you no longer need one to catch a breaking wave. Not since Thomas Lochtfeld invented a million-dollar machine called a Flow Rider that can pump out a perfectly ridable simulation of a 5-foot wave—one with a true shoulder that breaks continuously, as long as the machine is turned on. This effect is created by shooting a 3- to 4-inch sheet of water up the machine's foam-coated, wave-shaped concrete structure. The water's 10 to 14 mile-per-hour upward flow can support a surfer. Even pro surfers rave about how realistic the Flow Rider feels and how useful it is for practicing difficult maneuvers.

The Texas incarnation of Lochtefeld's invention is at a wave pool dubbed the Boogie Bahn. It's the first artificial wave pool in the country to offer waves big enough and well-shaped enough to allow you to catch a breaking wave, drop into it, and do turns back and forth across its face. You can practice the physical skills and timing of catching a wave without having to deal with the mysteries and inconsistencies of an ocean.

The safe environment created by the machine gives you the freedom to experiment away, without much risk of hurting yourself. You are not allowed to stand up or use hard surfboards, because the water-park owners are not ready to assume the risk of beginners falling into 3 or 4 inches of water from a standing position or sending hard surfboards flying around the relatively small area. Instead, you ride the wave lying down or kneeling on a soft body board—not exactly Surf God position, but still a blast. You also get a chance to watch exhibitions by experienced surfers who *are* allowed to stand up and show off their skills.

There are no instructors here, so most people come with a friend who knows at least a little about how to ride a wave. Bring your own body board, or rent one. *Schlitterbahn at the Rapids, The Boogie Bahn, 370 W. Lincoln, New Braunfels, TX 78130, tel. 210/625–5510, or 210/620–4000 (ask for Rick Faber or Sherry Brammel). For an updated list of other Flow Riders write or call Thomas J. Lochtfeld, 5508 Pacifica Dr., La Jolla, CA 92037, tel. 619/273–0307. New Braunfels Chamber of Commerce, tel. 210/625–2385. Year-round: 1-day pass at Boogie Bahn, $25. Price does not include board rental.*

THE WEST COAST

CALIFORNIA **Paradise Surfing Lessons.** Malibu Point is one of the finest and most consistent point breaks in the world. And— blame it on the Frankie and Annette *Beach Blanket Bingo* surfing movies of the fifties and sixties—it's also the best-known surfing spot in the continental United States. Throw in the glitter of nearby Hollywood, and it's easy to understand why Ted Silverberg hit a gold mine in 1983 when he decided to start a surf school here.

Silverberg, now 36, has been surfing since he was 13. He worked his way through law school by renting surfing equipment to Hollywood movie studios and teaching stars and stuntpeople how to surf well enough to perform their roles without drowning. His school offers private instruction to people of all ages and abilities, ranging from custom-tailored lessons for adults to an annual special outing for students from the Braille Institute. Silverberg says some of his most rewarding moments have come while taking one of these children for an exhilarating tandem ride.

Although he no longer teaches, Ted supervises a staff of 4 to 5 instructors who give around 25 private lessons a week. All equipment is provided, and, because Silverberg keeps 65 surfboards and 125 wet suits in stock to accommodate the whims of Hollywood Studios, you are virtually assured of a perfect fit. Most of Paradise Surfing's private lessons take place at Pointe Dume, the private beach where Silverberg makes his home—along with Barbra Streisand, Johnny Carson, Julie Andrews, and Sylvester Stallone. *Paradise Surfing Lessons, 28128 Pacific Coast Hwy., Malibu, CA 90265, tel. 310/457–9829. Malibu Chamber of Commerce, tel. 310/456–9025. Year-round: 2-hour private lesson, $50. Sign up 2 weeks in advance.*

CALIFORNIA **Paskowitz Surfing Camps.** This school has a family history. Director Moses Paskowitz is one of 9 children in an 11-member surfing family. As a teenager, he learned to surf at his father's school in Tel Aviv, Israel, and since 1977 he has headed up his family's surf camp in San Onofre, California. The Paskowitz's camp is the longest-running and largest surf camp in Southern California. Between the 10 summer surf camps and year-round private lessons, Moses and his 7 brothers, archetypal surfer dudes, introduce more than 200 people per year to the sport.

Taking one of Paskowitz's surf camps is like spending a week or 2 with your favorite cousins. The brothers teach, while matriarch Juliette and sister Navah run the camp headquarters. Although luxury accommodations are available at hotels nearby, the vast majority of the Paskowitz's students prefer sleeping bags under the stars or the 2-person tents the school sets up at San Clemente's San Mateo campground.

The family works hard to minimize Kook talk and instead preaches the Aloha spirit, which Moses defines as "Hey, do unto others as you would like them to do unto you." In addition to delivering top-flight one-on-one instruction during 2 daily surf sessions, Moses and the boys dispense philosophical tidbits ranging from "Hey, no one owns the waves" to "Hey, the ocean always forces you to go forward" and "If Elvis surfed, he'd be alive today."

Each of the week-long summer surf camps run between June and August draws between 15 and 25 campers from all over the world. The number of adults at the camps has grown annually, and currently about 25% of the campers are 18 or older. The rest of the crowd is between 12 and 17. Your fee includes tent; chow; all surfing equipment, including traditional fiberglass boards, wet suits, and leashes; and video teaching sessions (you're filmed by one of the brothers). During the week most students progress from a beginning site called Blue Lagoon to Old Man's, a popular intermediate site adjacent to Lower Trestles, an advanced site dominated by highly territorial local surfers. *Paskowitz Productions, Box 522, San Clemente, CA 92674, tel. 800/998–3475. June–Aug.: 7-day camp, $795. Sept.–May: 1-hour private lesson, $50. Sign up 2 months in advance for camps, 2 weeks in advance for lessons.*

CALIFORNIA **Richard Schmidt Surf Camp.** This Santa Cruz camp is one of only a few in Northern California. Cold water and a shoreline exposed to winds make most of the area a tough place to surf. A notable exception is the Monterey Bay coastline near Santa Cruz. This extraordinarily beautiful and pristine area (also known as the Monterey Bay National Marine Sanctuary) is protected from oil drilling and other sources of pollution. The bay protects the beaches from swell-busting wind, thus offering a wide variety of beaches that are open to swells from almost any direction.

Richard Schmidt's school is a cut above many others for a number of reasons. First, he has been surfing for more than 27 years, teaching surfing for upwards of 17 years, and running surf camps for a third of that time. As a lifelong resident of Santa Cruz, he is intimately familiar with the area's beaches and ocean conditions. And he teaches nearly as many adults as teenagers. Finally, he has developed a unique teaching technique that allows him to guarantee stand-up surfing by the end of the first lesson.

Schmidt doesn't just get you into position to catch a wave and shove you in the right direction at the right time like most instructors. He actually catches the wave right alongside you. "That way I'm right there when the wave breaks," says Schmidt, "and I can stabilize your board with one hand, while yanking you to a standing position with the other." He has even developed a harness with a handle on the back to facilitate these yank-ups.

Schmidt runs 6 1-week camps between July and August. Approximately 5 of the 15 participants each week are adults, many of whom take lessons with their kids. Tents are provided at a local KOA campground with a grocery store, hot showers, batting cage, whirlpool, and in-ground swimming pool. The cost of the camp includes food; camping fees; transportation to and from surf sites; all equipment, including wet suits, leashes, and soft boards; plus special "yank-up" instruction from Schmidt and 2 other instructors. A video of you surfing is also included in the price. *Richard Schmidt Surf Camp, 236 San Jose Ave., Santa Cruz, CA 95060, tel. 408/ 423–0928. July–Aug.: 7-day camp, $700. Year-round: 1-hour private lesson, $50; 2-hour group lesson (maximum of 4 students per instructor), $70. Sign up 1 month in advance for camps, 1 week in advance for lessons.*

HAWAII

OAHU **Oahu Hawaii Beach Boys Association.** According to surfing industry insiders, the beaches of Waikiki may be the best place in the United States to learn how to surf. Minimum tidal currents coupled with wave-breaking areas several hundred yards offshore mean two things. Waikiki waves are among the safest for beginners to learn on, and they provide the longest rides possible. Waikiki is also one of the most reliable surfing areas in the world because there are very few days when there are no ridable waves. That's because Waikiki Beach develops surfable waves from swells approaching from a number of directions: South and southwest swells come in from the South Pacific, and northeast and easterly tradewind swells wrap around Koko Head Point to become surfable waves.

The Beach Boys Association is a loose alliance of the area's top surfing instructors who get their customers from the numerous hotels on the beach. Rabbit Kekai, Blackout Whalex, Clyde Aikau, and Captain Bob are 4 of the association's most colorful and experienced instructors. Rabbit Kekai, for instance, has been surfing and teaching for most of his adult life. Now in his 70s, he is still going strong. The epitome of surfing spirit and informality, the Beach Boys Association headquarters is nothing more than a desk under a beach umbrella behind the statue of Hawaiian surfing legend Duke Kahanamoku. Just go to the Hyatt Hotel on Kuhio Beach in Waikiki and ask for directions to the "Duke" statue. *Hawaii Beach Boys Association, Inc., Clyde Aikau, President, 41-703 Mekia, Waimanalo, Hawaii; or*

call George Downing, tel. 808/732–4563. Year-round: 1-hour private lesson, $50–$75 (depending on instructor); 1-hour group lesson (minimum 3 students), $25. Half-, full-, and multi-day lesson fees are negotiable.

SOURCES

ORGANIZATIONS The **United States Surfing Federation** (7104 Island Village Dr., Long Beach, CA 90803, tel. 310/596–7785) and the **Surf Industry Manufacturer's Association** (3334 E. Coast Hwy., #416, Corona Del Mar, CA 92625, tel. 714/760–0784) can provide the latest information on the sport and its equipment.

PERIODICALS *Surfer Magazine* (Surfer Publications, Inc., Box 1028, Dana Point, CA 92629, tel. 714/496–5922) and *Surfing Magazine* (Western Empire Publications, Inc., San Clemente, CA 92672, tel. 714/492–7873) are the two major surfing magazines in the United States. Both feature hot surfers and surfing spots, new maneuvers, contest results, political surfing issues, and surfing heritage. They celebrate the sport with top-flight graphics and photography.

BOOKS *Surfer's Start-Up: A Beginner's Guide to Surfing* (Pathfinder Publishing), by Doug Werner, is an easy-to-read book that arms the beginning surfer with solid knowledge about equipment and technique. Werner's book also captures the spirit of surfing and gives a bunch of inside tips on how to survive localism (surfing's rigid pecking order) during the first year. The black-and-white illustrations are excellent. *How to Surf*, compiled by *Surfing Magazine* editor Nick Carroll, is actually part of a special collector's series published by the magazine. It provides excellent information on the natural elements of surfing. Successive short articles read like chapters and take you from selecting your first surfboard to learning various turns.

ALSO SEE There are other ways to ride the surf: How about putting a sail on your board? Turn to Windsurfing for schools that will show you how it's done.

Tennis Camps

By Susan Farewell

Updated by W. Lynn Seldon Jr.

hether you've just taken up the sport or you're a top seed at your club, time at a tennis camp can do wonders for your game. (Just imagine spending several hours each day with someone whose job is to help you play better.) There are dozens of places where you can do this around the country—so many, in such a wide range of styles, that you can afford to be choosy.

Some tennis camps colonize college campuses or ski resorts in summer, others are held at posh resorts in glamorous locations, and a few were designed and built exclusively for teaching tennis. A handful are under the auspices of some tennis great, while others are run by pros who have built their reputation by teaching.

Some camps will give you a week-long, 6-hour-a-day tennis-a-thon, while others offer a vacation with tennis as the primary—but not the only—activity.

Most camps aim to refine and improve your existing style of play. Others—they're rare—have you re-learn the game their way. There is a host of teaching styles, and each camp has its own repertoire of drills.

No matter where you go, you should be beyond beginner level, and you need to be in good condition. After all, you're just cheat-ing yourself if you can't keep up with the drills.

Five- to 7-day tennis camp programs usually involve working over all aspects of the game, from serves, strokes, and net shots to strategy for both singles and doubles play. Nearly all begin by evaluating your ability and grouping you with others at your level. Depending upon the camp, you either move from pro to pro during the day or stay with one pro for the duration. At some point during your stay, the staff videotapes you and analyzes your game during the playback. (Sometimes you get to keep the tape.) Most tennis camps have ball machines; sometimes you use them under the instructor's eye and sometimes they're for extracurricular practice. Instructors might be former pros, new-to-the-tour pros, people who've developed some particular method, or, occasionally, a superstar teacher—someone who achieved fame and fortune for his or her teaching abilities and methods alone. You will sometimes see it mentioned that a camp's instructors are members of the USPTA, and while this does signal their status as professional tennis players, it isn't an endorsement of them as teachers.

A big selling point at many schools is the number of hours you're on the courts each day and the ratio of students to instructors. Generally speaking, the more hours on the

---

Susan Farewell, a Connecticut-based travel and fitness writer, has an eclectic style of play that comes from a dozen years of visiting tennis camps and resorts the world over. Freelance travel writer and photographer Lynn Seldon played high school and college tennis and still plays at some of the best resorts in the United States.

court and the fewer students per instructor, the better. But 5 hours on the court at a program with a 6:1 ratio may be no more rewarding than 3 hours in a program with twice the number of instructors.

Off court, most tennis camps fall somewhere on the comfort spectrum between courtside boot camps and exclusive private clubs. Accommodations vary dramatically—sometimes even within the same camp. At tennis camps on college campuses, you usually sleep in no-frills dormitories, where you share a room with at least one fellow camper and use a bathroom that's down the hall. When the camp is held at a resort, you may wind up in anything from your standard hotel room with two double beds to a luxurious suite with a fireplace, patio, and amenities galore. Most resort camps offer a tuition-and-lodging package; if you don't like the basic quarters it includes, you can usually pay extra for an upgrade. When the camp is on a college campus, you eat institutional cafeteria fare; when you're at a fancy resort, menus are fancy, too. Resort programs usually include access to other recreational facilities as part of the package.

Although tennis camps can cost anywhere from less than $500 to more than $2,000 for 5 to 7 days, most run between $700 and $1,200.

CHOOSING THE RIGHT CAMP

Asking a few key questions will help you find the best camp for you.

What are the accommodations like? They could be anything from Spartan dorm to posh resort hotel. Know what you're getting into.

What is the food like? A camp's cuisine takes its cue from the setting: you eat institutional fare on college campuses and feast on more ambitious dishes at luxury resorts. Whatever the case, also find out what your options are if you feel like a change of pace.

What's the cost and what's included? Unless otherwise noted, prices given in the reviews below are per person and include lodging, based on double occupancy, and meals.

What are the teachers' credentials? Even at a camp run by a well-known player or teacher, you spend lots of time with other instructors; find out who they are, and what their playing and teaching experience is.

What's the ratio of students to instructors? And how many hours each day do you spend on the court with your instructors?

How long has the camp been run? If the program is new, be particularly careful to find out about the people in charge and their plans for the camp. Make sure that their teaching experience is credible, and that the instruction program seems well-conceived and well-organized.

What's the ratio of students to courts? Even with a good student-to-instructor ratio, too few courts means lots of time spent waiting around for your turn. The ideal ratio would be 2 players to each court, but don't count on seeing that too often; 4:1 should be fine, since not every student will be on the courts at all times.

How physically demanding is it? Find out what drills are involved, and how many hours a day you spend in strenuous physical activity. Then decide whether you want to commit yourself to the level of work.

Are courts covered in case of rain? You don't want to risk losing tennis time to inclement weather.

What are the court surfaces? Trying out all the different surfaces is important, but you may want to hone your skills on the surface you play on at home.

Is there unlimited access to tennis facilities during free time? You want to be able to try out your new moves while the lessons are fresh.

Are courts lighted for night play? This extends the amount of time available for extracurricular play. You'll also appreciate lighted courts if you're there when the weather is hot.

What's the clientele? Some camps attract mostly singles, others are more popular with couples and groups of friends traveling together, or people of a similar age. The more expensive the program, the older the crowd. Unless otherwise noted, all of the camps listed here attract a varied group from 20s to 60s.

How social is the program? Some programs have a lot of planned, off-court socializing, and some don't. If you want to play all day and party into the night, don't choose a program whose campers regularly turn in early.

How far in advance do I need to sign up for camp? Few camps have a strict deadline, but all recommend reserving as early as possible. This is especially true for traditional holiday or vacation times and for camps held only seasonally. Still, if they've got the room, they'll sign you up at the last minute.

Is laundry service available? The answer to this determines how many complete tennis outfits you need to pack.

Do you have references from past students? To clarify your ideas about instruction, accommodations, and food, there's no substitute for a talk with someone who has done the drills, slept in the beds, and eaten the meals.

FAVORITE CAMPS

THE NORTHEAST

MASSACHUSETTS **Amherst Tennis Camp.** The most impressive statistic about this operation at Amherst College in western Massachusetts is not its number of tennis courts (36) but the percentage of students who come back for more (40%). This probably has a lot to do with the good value you get from your tennis camp dollar: your room, 3 meals a day, at least 5 hours of instruction daily, a 4:1 student-to-instructor ratio, and 3 half-hour private lessons during the week. There are also dozens of instructors, a mix of USPTA players, college tennis instructors, and foreign pros.

Amherst offers advanced clinics, designed for those wanting to refine their game; doubles clinics, which pay special attention to ball placement, strategy, and team communication; clinics for single people, which include fun tournaments, softball and volleyball games, and other social activities; and open sessions, which address both the basics and more advanced techniques.

In all the clinics, you work on strokes and strategy for both singles and doubles play. After 35 or 40 minutes with one instructor, another instructor arrives to go over a different aspect of the game. You're videotaped a couple of times so that you can see your progress, and you can take home the tape, along with your private instructor's written assessment of your game, with suggestions for ways you can improve your game at home.

Off court, this is a sociable program, popular among professional men and women in their 30s and 40s. Lodging is in single dormitory rooms; you make your own bed and share baths and rec rooms. You can opt for less spartan accommodations off-campus, but then you'd miss out on the camaraderie that develops among campers. Meals are buffet-style in the school's cafeteria: One night you may get spareribs, and another spaghetti, but there are usually calorie-wise and vegetarian options. You have access to the college's indoor swimming pool, cushioned outdoor running track, and other facilities. *Amherst Tennis Camp, Box 2271, Amherst College, Amherst, MA 01002, tel. 413/542–8100, fax 413/542–5789. Mid-June–mid- or late Aug.: 7 days, $790. Sign up at least 1 month in advance.*

MASSACHUSETTS **Total Tennis.** Held on the campus of Williston-Northampton prep school in the heart of the Pioneer Valley, just 20 minutes from Amherst, Total Tennis is close to Tanglewood, the summer home of the Boston Symphony Orchestra, and Jacob's Pillow Dance Festival. It's easy to reach from New York and Boston, and draws heavily from both cities.

One of the distinguishing features of Total Tennis is that you work with a single pro throughout the program: Each is assigned to a quartet of students for the duration in the interest of fostering group spirit and allowing an instructor to get to know each student's game. The goal is ultimately to make you comfortable with the fundamentals before you work on other aspects of the game. Although there are instructional guidelines and goals, all Total Tennis pros have considerable latitude to use the methods they think will work with their group.

You have at least 5 hours a day on the court plus 2 half-hour private lessons. There are 10 red-clay courts and another 5 with all-weather hard surfaces. If it rains, you use the indoor courts at the Ludlow Tennis Club, about 20 miles away. In free time, you can work with the ball machine, play round-robin matches, or practice with other campers. There's also a pool, a fitness center, a gym where you can play volleyball or basketball, and a ¼-mile track.

Unlike many college dorms in the Northeast, those used by Total Tennis are air-conditioned and have daily maid service. Most single campers share a double room, but single rooms are available ($25 per night surcharge). Meals, served in the school's cafeteria, consist of standard cafeteria fare—hearty, healthful, and American. On Wednesday and Saturday evenings, predinner cocktails are served on the lawn.

Usually, about half of Total Tennis's campers are traveling solo, and off-court hours mean cocktail parties, mixed-doubles round-robins, volleyball games, and dancing at local nightclubs on nights when the camp hasn't scheduled instructional films or lectures on topics ranging from rackets and strings to sports psychology. *Total Tennis, Box 1106, Wall Street Station, New York, NY 10268, tel. 718/636–6141 or 800/221–6496. Early June–Labor Day: 6 days, $750; 7 days, $800. Sign up 2–3 months in advance.*

VERMONT **Bolton Valley Resort/International Tennis School.** With its location in the mountains of northern Vermont, Bolton Valley Resort's tennis school is a good choice if you prefer playing tennis where the weather is fresh and cool. It also is a good bet for families; there's day care for children 3 months and older, and an all-day children's tennis camp for kids 3 to 12 years old.

The program, which admits absolute beginners as well as more advanced players, is run by Anthony Boulle, a native of South Africa and former nationally ranked touring pro in the United States, who has worked with such tennis luminaries as Fred Stolle, Harry Hopman, and Vitas Gerulaitis. Boulle's style is relaxed and easygoing, and you take home solid, uncomplicated advice that's easy to remember and put into effect back on your home court.

Each day there are 3 hours of instruction: Lessons are videotaped and analyzed. The program spends about half of the lesson time every day on one specific point—ground strokes, net play, serving and returning serves, overheads, drop shots, lobs, strategy—and the other half going over the other fundamentals and playing matches. There's a 5:1 student-to-pro ratio, and there are 10 courts (2 indoors). Outside class, you get unlimited court time and use of a ball machine.

Breakfast and dinner are served at Lindsay's, a small restaurant on the resort's grounds. Dinners include pasta, seafood, and vegetarian dishes, cooked with a continental flair. You stay at the Swiss chalet–style Bolton Valley Lodge just up a hill from the courts or, for an extra charge, you can opt for one of the resort's condos. Off-court, you can explore the resort's 6,000 acres of mountains and woods on foot, or work out in the sports center, which has 2 pools (1 indoor, 1 outdoor), saunas, a whirlpool, and an exercise room. *Bolton Valley Resort/International Tennis School, Bolton Valley, VT 05477, tel. 802/434–2131 or 800/451–3220. July and Aug.: 5 days, $423. Price does not include lunch; sign up any time.*

VERMONT **Killington School for Tennis.** The Accelerated Tennis Method, developed at this big ski-and-summer resort, is a step-by-step approach that starts you at the net, working on volleys, and gradually moves you back toward the baseline, expanding your repertoire of moves and strokes as you work with more of the court.

Upon arrival your game is analyzed, and you are given drills specifically chosen for your game and then paired off with others of similar ability. The program here is highly structured and organized. You get 5 hours of instruction daily, and the 4:1 student-to-teacher ratio allows for considerable personal attention. Practice sessions are videotaped and replayed in slow motion for detailed analysis. Each session focuses intently on one aspect or skill of the game.

Killington emphasizes achieving ball control—direction, pace, and spin, including top spin. Once you've worked over the various strokes, you move on to singles and doubles strategies. Pros make themselves available for optional hitting sessions for an hour or so in the evening, and there are round-robin and mixed doubles tournaments throughout the week. At the end of your stay, you get a personal critique of your game and an Accelerated Tennis Method manual. Tennis facilities include 8 clay and cushion courts, 5 of them lighted for night play, and 8 enclosed ball lanes with ball machines.

Accommodations are courtside at the resort's Villager Motor Inn, which has terrific views of the surrounding mountains. Three meals a day are included in the package, and the menu offers varied choices and always plenty of healthful options. Tuesday dinner is an outdoor barbecue.

Off-court diversions include an 18-hole golf course, hiking, and mountain biking, and the towns of Woodstock and Manchester are a short drive away. *Killington School for Tennis, Killington, VT 05751, tel. 802/422-3101 or 800/343-0762, fax 802/422-3283. Late May–late Sept.: 5 days, $890. Sign up at least 2 weeks in advance.*

VERMONT **Stratton Tennis School.** Stratton is an especially good choice if you're vaca-

tioning with someone who doesn't play tennis. There's golf, mountain biking, hiking, and horseback riding in the cool Green Mountains, and the galleries, antiques shops, theaters, concerts, and restaurants of Manchester are a 20-minute drive away.

Not that the tennis at Stratton isn't serious: It was rated one of the top 50 tennis resorts by *Tennis Magazine.* There are 15 outdoor and 4 indoor courts. Tennis director Kelly Gunterman started his teaching career working for John Newcombe. Gunterman and his staff build on your skills and help you overcome your game's weaknesses. The 5-day program includes a 3-hour clinic every morning, each focusing on a different aspect of the game: volleys and overheads, ground strokes, serve and returns of serve. On the fourth day you review what you've learned and play doubles with the pros, and on the last day you get individualized attention and more doubles with the pros. There are video critiques of your game throughout the program, and you get unlimited access to the outdoor courts after classes. Additional 2-hour afternoon clinics are available at an extra charge.

Breakfast is at the sports center and lunch is served at the resort's Sage Hill restaurant, and there's no shortage of dinner options nearby. You lodge in the chalet-style Stratton Mountain Inn, a 125-room hotel just a short walk from the tennis courts. Other recreational facilities include a fitness center with racquetball, a 75-foot lap pool, whirlpool, steam rooms, aerobics classes, and massage, and trails for hiking, mountain biking, and horseback riding. *Stratton Tennis School, PO Box 163, Manchester Center, VT 05255, tel. 802/297-4230 or 800/843-6867. May–early Oct.: 5 days, $355–$395. Price does not include dinners; sign up any time.*

VERMONT **Sugarbush Tennis School.** Also ranked as one of the country's top 50 tennis resorts by *Tennis Magazine,* Sugarbush has a tennis program that attracts both beginners and highly competitive advanced players who come for the resort's plush accommodations and pristine mountain setting as well as its full-throttle tennis instruction. Under new tennis director Cons Moundalexis, who was the head pro for 10 years at the Killington School for Tennis, Sugarbush is emphasizing pro involvement on the court.

You can sign up for 2, 3 or 4 days of half-day group lessons (2½ hours) or full-day lessons (5 hours), with a 3:1 student-to-pro ratio. All packages include round-robin tournaments, and, during your evening free time, use of the 5 red clay and 10 Har-Tru courts, 7 hard courts (3 of which are lighted), ball machines, and the resort's swimming pools, fitness rooms, racquetball courts, steam baths, and saunas. Sugarbush staffers will fix you up with other campers for extracurricular matches.

Lodging is in the tony Sugarbush Inn or in 1-, 2-, or 3-bedroom condos with fireplace or wood stove, private sun deck, and kitchen. A Modified American Plan option includes a breakfast and dinner daily at one of the resort's three restaurants. *Sugarbush Tennis School & Club, R.R. 1, Box 350, Warren, VT 05674, tel. 802/583–2391 or 800/ 537–8427, fax 802/ 583–3209. Mid-May– late Sept.: full-day program, $149 per day; half-day program, $125 per day. Price does not include lunch or dinner; sign up at least 6 weeks in advance.*

THE MID-ATLANTIC

PENNSYLVANIA **Tennis Camps Ltd. at Swarthmore College.** The programs held on the 325 manicured acres of this 127-year-old college, 12 miles from Philadelphia, are especially popular with singles wanting to meet other singles while improving their tennis. But this isn't the Love Boat, and the meeting and mixing happens off the court.

The 5-day clinics include 5 hours of instruction daily (with a 4:1 student-to-instructor ratio) and 3 half-hour private lessons. After your game is evaluated and you've been grouped with others at the same level of play, the instruction focuses on game-sharpening drills and strategy, with the emphasis

on improving consistency and increasing power. You're videotaped and your strokes are analyzed, and there are supervised matches between campers as well as exhibition matches between instructors.

Accommodations are on campus in single or double rooms in the Dana Dormitory, the luxurious Ashton House (a beautiful Victorian stone mansion on campus), or the Strathavan condominium hotel. Meals are hearty, well-balanced, and planned by the college dietician. You have access to the school swimming pool, Nautilus equipment, outdoor track, and (by appointment) its masseuse. *Tennis Camps Ltd. at Swarthmore College, 444 E. 82nd St., Suite 31D, New York, NY 10028, tel. 212/879–0225 or 800/ 223–2442, fax 212/879–0226. Mid-June– mid-Aug.: 5 days, $675 ($795, but excluding dinners, if you opt to stay at Ashton House). Sign up 2–4 months in advance.*

THE SOUTH

FLORIDA **Harry Hopman Tennis Academy.** The late Harry Hopman was the most successful captain and coach in Davis Cup history, winning 16 times over 21 years. The Australian teams he led included Ken Rosewell, Rod Laver, Fred Stolle, John Newcombe, and Tony Roche. Hopman was known as a strict disciplinarian who demanded the best of his players, and usually got it.

Hopman's tough ways prevail at Saddlebrook, a 480-acre resort north of Tampa, whose tennis program he started. Now run by Tommy Thompson and Howard Moore, this camp is for all levels of players looking to tune up their game.

Your group stays with the same pro for the week, and there are never more than 4 players to an instructor. You do 5 hours of imaginative, fast-paced, hard-hitting drills a day, all created by Hopman and all meant to make you react instinctively to the ball.

In addition to the on-court training, you do fitness and agility exercises prior to morning and afternoon sessions.

Not surprisingly, Saddlebrook's tennis facilities are top-of-the-line. The 45 courts represent every Grand Slam surface—clay, Har-Tru, even grass—and 5 of them are lighted for night play. Players of all ages come to Saddlebrook from around the globe, from all walks of life. Because it is one of the United States Tennis Association's National Training Centers, players on the way up occasionally train here. (When you see them, take note: They're doing the same drills you are.)

You can lodge in standard hotel rooms or 1- and 2-bedroom suites; meals are available in several restaurants at the resort and nearby. You have use of the resort's enormous swimming pool and its two Arnold Palmer–designed golf courses, elaborate fitness center, and jogging and bicycle trails—in case you have energy left over after the tennis. Rates are highest from late December through April, and January, February, and March are the busiest months. *Harry Hopman Tennis Academy, 5700 Saddlebrook Way, Wesley Chapel, FL 33543-4499, tel. 813/973–1111, ext. 4211 or 800/729–8383, fax 813/973–2936. Year-round: 5 days, $822–$1,152. Price does not include meals; sign up at least 1 month in advance.*

FLORIDA **Nick Bollettieri Tennis Academy.** This is the world headquarters of the tennis school that produced Andre Agassi, Monica Seles, Pete Sampras, and Jim Courier; it is the largest tennis training operation in the world. Although Nick Bollettieri, who currently trains Boris Becker and Mary Pierce, is best known for his years of coaching professional players and top juniors, non-pro adults will benefit from his extensive years of teaching players within their own style of play. The adult camps have programs aimed at both recreational and advanced players.

Each day starts with stretching, strength, and aerobic exercise followed by a warm-up on the court composed of intensive drills designed to cover all strokes. You spend an average of 4 to 5 hours a day on the court, broken into two sessions that each highlight a specific stroke. Breaks allow the player to watch tennis videos featuring top players, listen to lectures, study the aspects of the mental game or watch demonstrations on strokes, strategies, strength, and conditioning. Match play and doubles strategy is also offered. Your play on clay courts, but the Academy boasts 71 courts in all, with a variety of surfaces—clay, hard, supreme, and Florida's only 4 indoor courts. If you still feel like you need more tennis, there is one-on-one special help available.

Campers stay in 2-bedroom, 2 bathroom condominiums equipped with a kitchen, cable TV, and a living room. Meals are served buffet-style. The million-dollar fitness center has a private pool and sauna, Hammer strength, Bodymaster, Life-Cycle and Life-Steps equipment—everything you'd need for an optimal workout. Massage therapy is available.

Programs are offered year round on a weekly, mini-weekly (any 3 consecutive days) or daily basis. Discounts are offered at various times throughout the year. All prices include meals, accommodations and tennis instruction. Special help and massage therapy are extra. For those who can't make it to Florida, adult sessions are held in satellite locations throughout the world. *Nick Bollettieri Tennis Academy, 5500 34th St. West, Bradenton, FL 34210, tel. 941/755–1000 or 800/872–6425, fax 941/756–6891. Year-round: 7 days, $1,095. Sign up 1 month in advance.*

SOUTH CAROLINA **Litchfield Racquet Club & Tennis School.** This is yet another school with a location at one of America's top 50 tennis resorts, according to *Tennis Magazine.* The club has 17 Har-Tru surface courts (3 lighted) as well as an indoor facility with two hard-surface courts. It is in this facility that the Litchfield Tennis School is set. The school includes 3-day/9-hour weekend programs, as well as a 4-day/12-hour weekday program. The staff of USPTA and USPTR certified tennis professionals offer excellent instructional programs and many all-inclusive packages. In the midst of the Myrtle Beach golf mecca, Litchfield has many diversions for nonplaying guests. A variety of lodging options are available and may be packaged with the tennis school. *Litchfield Tennis School, Litchfield Beach & Golf Resort, PO Drawer 320, Hwy 17, Pawleys Island, SC 29585, tel. 803/237–3411 ext. 2 or 800/845–1897, fax 803/237–3282. Year-round 4 days: $175, not including accommodations and including only 1 meal.*

SOUTH CAROLINA **Van der Meer Tennis-University.** Although he was a top-rated player in his native South Africa, Dennis Van der Meer is best known as "the pro who teaches the pros." He coached Margaret Court and Billie Jean King and has taught hundreds of tennis teachers and thousands of players, from 3-year-olds to senior citizens, from beginners to touring pros.

Of the 6 Van der Meer Tennis University facilities worldwide, the main location is the Tennis Center on Hilton Head Island. Most sessions of the 5-day adult program are for intermediate and advanced players, though beginners can be accommodated. The 6:1 ratio of players to pros may sound high, but with 6 hours of instruction each day, you get your share of coaching and hitting. In addition to providing video analysis and an evaluation of your strokes and tactics, Van der Meer's method works on your consistency, agility, and footwork, and teaches you how to concentrate, overcome tension, and keep from choking.

Van der Meer is completely involved in his program. He is personally on hand several weeks a year and leads clinics when he's around (the center will provide a list of dates on request). He's as amusing as he is well-informed, and his enthusiasm for helping players makes it clear why he is so successful as a teacher and why people return to this camp. The Tennis Center has 28 courts—25 hard and 3 clay—of which 8 are lighted, and 4 of those are covered. The nearby Shipyard Racquet Club, which Van der Meer recently took over, has 14 clay and 6 hard courts.

Packages include lodging at the Players Club Resort, next to the Tennis Center, which has a Nautilus equipment center, pool, whirlpool, sauna, and restaurant, and

is within walking distance of the beach. There are also many other hotels, resorts, and restaurants nearby. *Van der Meer Tennis Center, Box 5902, Hilton Head Island, SC 29938, tel. 803/785–8388 or 800/845–6138, fax 803/785–7032. Year-round: 5 days, $315–$425 depending on the season ($100 more for clinics personally led by Dennis Van der Meer). Price does not include meals; sign up 3–6 months in advance; 6 months for Van der Meer-led clinics.*

THE SOUTHWEST

ARIZONA **Gardiner's Resort on Camelback.** John Gardiner invented the concept of tennis clinics; his Carmel Valley resort in California (see below) was the very first, and this Tennis Ranch, just outside Scottsdale, Arizona, may just be the ultimate, providing comprehensive tennis instruction in luxurious, resortlike surroundings on 53 landscaped desert acres.

The Tennis Clinic Week includes 21 hours of clinic instruction, 4 hours of optional round-robin play, complimentary court time, and 2 half-hour-long massages.

Gardiner's emphasizes doubles play, especially for intermediate players. There are more campers here in the 45-to-60 age range than there are at many camps. About 35 people usually participate in each session, more during holiday periods and in February and March.

There are 24 tennis courts and 30 instructors. Two of the courts have computerized ball machines, which can be programmed to fire off a random sequence of lobs, serves, and shots of varying spins.

You stay in standard rooms; 2-bedroom, 2-bath suites; or casitas, adobe-colored brick structures with arched windows and doorways. There are also 2- to 5-bedroom homes. Each room has a private patio or enclosed sun room, with a spectacular view of the valley. Each of the larger houses has a private swimming pool, and many have private tennis courts and spas.

A carafe of freshly squeezed orange juice and the *Arizona Republic* are delivered to your doorstep every morning, and there are coffeemakers in each room. Breakfast and lunch are buffet-style (lunch can also be à la carte) and quite lavish. Dinner, served in a room with views of Paradise Valley, is New American cuisine—local fare with a Continental or Pacific Rim influence. Men are required to wear jackets (but not ties) after 7 PM.

The ranch has a large pool at the clubhouse, and several smaller pools throughout the grounds, along with whirlpools and saunas. There is also a fitness room with top-of-the-line workout equipment, and hiking and jogging trails. *Gardiner's Resort on Camelback, 5700 E. McDonald Dr., Scottsdale, AZ 85253-5268, tel. 602/948-2100 or 800/245-2051, fax 602/483-7314. Mid-Apr.–mid-Dec.: 7 days, $2,530. Mid-Dec.–mid-Apr.: 7 days, $2,875. Sign up 6 weeks in advance.*

TEXAS **The John Newcombe Tennis Ranch.** The one thing you learn here—if nothing else—is that although tennis should be played well and taken seriously, it's a game, and it should be fun.

John Newcombe (a.k.a. "Newk"), a U.S. Open and Wimbledon champion and Australian Davis Cupper, along with Trinity University tennis coach Clarence Mabry, converted this onetime dude ranch into a tennis school, and the two still run the place, with the help of several other tennis greats.

The program here begins with a preview of the stroke of the day and a video with tips by the various pros. Then you get 2½ hours of drill work on the courts. You're videotaped in action and critiqued just before lunch. You go back to the court in the afternoon for more drills, strategy sessions, and supervised match play. Clinics use the station-to-station method, whereby participants move as a group from court to court, and from pro to pro. Spring and fall (when the weather's not too hot) are the most popular seasons, and clinics during this period can fill up with as many as 80 participants, but the student-to-pro ratio rarely exceeds 4:1, and is often less.

Packages include accommodations in apartment units with fireplaces, kitchens, and patios or balconies, all with court views. There's an Old West feel to this place, and it still looks very much like the dude ranch it once was. Meals are a big part of the fun here. Breakfast, lunch, and dinner are lavish buffet spreads with plenty of nutritionally balanced choices, but the kitchen staff takes special pride in its Western-style dinners, such as mesquite-grilled rib-eye steaks, roast prime rib, and smoked and barbecued meats. Other cuisines—including French, Italian, Oriental, and Mexican—are also offered. The socializing doesn't end after mealtime. There are parties, dancing, and live entertainment in the evening—anything from a movie to "blooper" videos of campers on the court to a stage show or comedy routine put on by the staff. The gregarious staff create an infectiously collegial atmosphere. The week ends with a doubles tournament and an awards banquet.

There are 28 hard outdoor courts, 8 of them lighted and 4 covered. There are also a swimming pool and whirlpool on the premises, and nearby are horseback riding, golf, river rafting, and bungee jumping, as well as such regional attractions as the Alamo and Sea World. *The John Newcombe Tennis Ranch, Box 310469, New Braunfels, TX 78131, tel. 210/ 625-9105 or 800/444-6204, fax 210/ 625-2004. Year-round: 5 days, $755-$875. Sign up 1 month in advance.*

THE WEST COAST

CALIFORNIA **John Gardiner's Tennis Ranch.** This 25-acre Carmel Valley ranch was the first American tennis camp, started in 1957 by John Gardiner, a local tennis teacher who was convinced that people would take a vacation where the main activity was playing tennis.

He was right, and even three decades later this is still one of the most sought-after—and exclusive—tennis camps around. It is also the only one with one court per guest room—14 of each.

The basic clinic runs 4 hours a day, supplemented by optional sessions and as much recreational tennis as you can play (the watchwords around here are "Repetition is the law of learning" and "Never have so many tennis balls been hit by so few"). The student-to-instructor ratio is 4:1, so you get plenty of individual attention, and you can pretty much set your own pace.

During the session there are also mixed doubles tournaments and various social events. At the end of the week, there is a "graduation" ceremony with champagne, prizes, and diplomas.

Guest rooms are in cottages of varying sizes in a woody setting just steps away from the courts. All have private patios and fireplaces. They fill up quickly, especially with repeat guests—often celebrities, politicians, and corporate executives. The ranch tends to attract very well-to-do couples, generally over the age of 50. This is a very traditional, almost old-fashioned, sort of place, where guests are requested to wear predominantly whites on the courts (not that everyone does).

The food at John Gardiner's is a big part of the experience. The elaborate breakfast buffet is served on the glass-walled sun porch, and lunch is a selection of hot and cold entrées served poolside. Dinner is formal; it begins with drinks and hors d'oeuvres in the elegant clubhouse, then moves to the dining room. Gardiner's specialties are lamb dishes and soufflés. There are also lots of local fruits and vegetables as well as fresh Pacific seafood.

The ranch has 2 heated swimming pools, an outdoor whirlpool, and saunas. Golf is nearby. *John Gardiner's Tennis Ranch, Box 228, Carmel Valley, CA 93924, tel. 408/659–2207 or 800/453–6225, fax 408/659–2492. Late Mar.–late Nov.: 5 days, $1,800–$1,900. Sign up 1–2 months in advance.*

CALIFORNIA **Vic Braden Tennis College.** Winning isn't everything to Vic Braden.

"Remember," he says, "fifty percent of all tennis players who played today lost." Still, he's also the first to point out that playing well and winning cheers people up. Braden became famous through his "Tennis for the Future" TV series, his 5 tennis instruction books, and 40 years of teaching everyone from beginners to pros.

Braden's teaching method mixes upbeat humor and high-tech gadgets, such as a video analysis of your game that helps you spot imperfections. Probably the toughest thing about this school is that you're taught ways to change your bad habits, even if they're your best shots. Braden suggests that each shot be hit in a particular way. "Tennis is an engineering problem," he says. "We teach you how to teach yourself to play tennis."

Braden's Tennis College facilities are among the most extensive and sophisticated anywhere. In the classroom, Braden—in person or on video—presents a daily lecture, and courtside viewing rooms allow for instant-replay videotape analysis. There are 17 hitting lanes with ball machines, and 17 hard courts, 14 with lights. The surfaces of the main 3 teaching courts have been painted with targets, Xs, and dotted lines, so you can work through the school's different drills even without an instructor. Although the student-to-pro ratio can reach 6:1, you're on the courts with your pro for a minimum of 6 hours a day.

In addition to being a tennis instructor, Braden is a psychologist, and he puts a lot of emphasis on getting you over the mental hurdles of the game and becoming more comfortable on the court.

Guest rooms are in modern structures and come in a variety of sizes and configurations (and prices), from basic hotel room to suites with kitchens and patios. All are adjacent to the tennis courts and within walking distance of the 2 swimming pools and whirlpool. The on-site restaurant offers burgers, pizzas, and pasta dishes; other dining options are a short drive away. *Vic Braden Tennis College, 23335 Avenida La Caza,*

Coto de Caza, CA 92679, tel. 714/581–2990, 800/225–5842 in CA, or 800/422–6878 outside CA. Year-round: 5 days, $650. Price does not include lodging or meals; sign up 2–3 weeks in advance.

SOURCES

ORGANIZATIONS **United States Tennis Association** (Membership Department, 70 West Red Oak Lane, White Plains, NY 10604, tel. 914/696–7000) is a volunteer, nonprofit organization established in 1881. Membership benefits include USTA league and tournament programs; discounts on apparel, publications, videos, and travel packages; and annual subscriptions to the monthly newsletter "Tennis USTA" and *Tennis Magazine.*

PERIODICALS *Tennis* (5520 Park Ave., Box 395, Trumbull, CT 06611-0395, tel. 203/373–7000) is a monthly magazine with how-to tips, features on professional players, tennis resort information, fitness tips, and more. *Tennis Week* (341 Madison Ave., #600, New York, NY 10017, tel. 212/808-4750) is a fortnightly magazine covering professional tennis news, racquet roundups, book reviews, how-to information, and more. *Tennis Magazine* (available through the USTA, address above) prints a comprehensive list of tennis camps and clinics every year in its February issue.

BOOKS There are many tennis instructional books available. A current favorite is *Winning Ugly,* by Brad Gilbert (with Steve Jamison), which details Gilbert's technique for outsmarting an otherwise superior opponent. A great read is W. Timothy Gallwey's *The Inner Game of Tennis* (Bantam Books).

Van and 4-Wheel-Drive Tours

By Sandra Widener

Updated by Steven R. Adang

ould you like to take off into the wilderness on a cross-country off-road camping trip? How about a month-long van trip through an entire region, stopping in cities and camping along the way? Outfitters have trips to fit anyone's desires, most in two categories: 4-wheel-drive tours (aka Jeep tours) and van tours.

A Jeep tour can be a painless jaunt through spectacular country, punctuated by the witty insights of a knowledgeable guide, with nights spent in relative luxury in charming bed-and-breakfasts. Or it can be a rugged vacation where you cover a lot of breathtaking ground by day on death-defying trails a horse would blink at, and camp by night, cooking over a fire.

In the Rockies, the western national parks, the Southwest, Alaska, and Hawaii, 4-wheel-drive trips are common, and often take travelers into backcountry locations dedicated hikers could reach only with days of effort. Four-wheel-drives go down trails and up rocky riverbeds that are normally inaccessible; they make it easy to visit remote places like Alaska, where seeing a lot on your own is difficult.

Four-wheel-drive trips often entail walking and optional activities such as rafting and horseback riding, but you don't need to be in top physical shape. Vehicles carry the equipment and undertake the heavy-duty travel, which is great if you like wilderness but aren't up for hiking a mountain with a 40-pound pack.

Some companies that offer 4-wheel-drive trips cater to their clients' every whim, with luxurious lodgings and restaurant meals; some use guides who are consummate experts on the area, who can spout the Latin names of flora and fauna and explain the significance of prehistoric rock art. Other outfitters design their trips around a special interest, such as geology or photography.

Many of the guides take pride in knowing places their guests would never have found on their own; their ability to take you off the beaten track, away from the herd, and show you spectacular hidden places is one of the best things these trips have to offer. It's worth paying for the enthusiasm and knowledge of someone who is passionate about the area, rather than muddling about on your own.

Costs of 4-wheel-drive trips range widely, but you can expect to spend from $500 for a basic week-long camping trip to $2,000 and more, if you're led by a well-known expert and stay in good hotels. Alaskan trips tend to cost more (to cover higher prices in the Last Frontier) and can often run to $3,000 for 10 days. A week's trip in Hawaii will cost in the neighborhood of $1,000.

Sandra Widener, a freelance writer who lives in Denver, takes Jeep trips into the mountains with her family. Steven Adang currently does his four-wheeling in the concrete jungle of New York City, where he is a graduate student.

Van trips are common on the East Coast and in the Midwest and the South, all places where 4-wheel-drive trips are almost impossible to find. Van trips use vehicles that comfortably seat a dozen people. Travel is mainly on paved roads; tours often cover whole regions, visit cities and famous landmarks, and emphasize national parks and natural settings. Over the past 20 years or so, a platoon of van-touring companies has sprung up, aimed at showing groups of mainly foreign young people the United States.

On van tours, everyone contributes to a food kitty and takes turns cooking and cleaning up. Lodging is primarily in fairly civilized campgrounds with hot showers, and most operators supply the tents gratis, though sleeping bags must be rented. The cost, pared down for student budgets, runs about $400 per week: This includes everything but the bill for the moderate hotels where you stay when visiting cities. You're not paying for exquisitely educated guides or attentive service; though often bilingual and even foreign-born, most of the guides are glorified van drivers with guidebooks.

Despite these considerable differences, there are three things that 4-wheel-drive and van trips have in common: Small children often don't do well on them, and many outfitters require participants to be 18 or older. Almost all have no more than 18 people (on most trips, you rub elbows with fewer than 10 people). And for those with a little taste for adventure, both types of trip can make a wonderful vacation.

CHOOSING THE RIGHT TRIP

Here are some questions that will help you pick the right outfitter and the right trip.

How many years has your company been in business? Longevity is evidence that somebody's doing something right.

What are the guides' qualifications? For off-road trips, degrees in botany, zoology, geology, anthropology, and the like are desirable, but local knowledge and experience are a must. For van trips, local knowledge is a frill; what counts is organizational skill and experience in leading groups.

What is the client-to-guide ratio? Will I be expected to do any chores? A client-to-guide ratio of between 10:1 and 13:1 is likely to mean the clients do a lot of the work, but on camping trips that's often part of the fun.

What kinds of people take this trip? How large is the group? It's comfortable to be among your peers, but a little variety adds spice. A small group travels quickly and efficiently, with less waiting around. A larger one offers more possibilities for making friends or just finding congenial companionship. The cost of any trip often determines the age of the participants; the more expensive, generally, the older the clientele.

What are the accommodations like? Find out if you'll be camping or staying in hotels or B&Bs. If camping, ask if there are cabins or tents and if hot showers will be available. If you'll be staying in a B&B, ask if there are private baths.

What are the meals like? Even when you're camping, there's a wide spread between hotdogs and hamburgers cooked over a fire by you and carefully thought-out Dutch-oven dishes prepared by a guide who's a good cook.

What will the weather be like? So you like hot weather—but if you don't ask, you won't know how humid it can be in the South, or how buggy. Or how cold it can get in the mountains, even in July.

What's the cost and what's included? Unless otherwise noted, hotel accommodations (per person, double occupancy), meals, guides, and transportation are included, but participants must get themselves to the trip's jumping-off point. In addition, on camping trips, camp tents and other necessary gear are included, but not sleeping bags (often available for rent). In some cases, you are expected to contribute a set amount to the food kitty. Find out in advance about any hidden costs: meals or hotels or desirable options that cost extra. Will you just have to pay for a bite of lunch, or are you responsible for dinner in a hotel? Is there equipment you must rent?

How much free time will there be? Are any local events happening before or after the tour? If you find out in advance, you can take advantage of what the area has to offer.

Do you have references from past guests? Sometimes they can articulate important strengths and weaknesses that a tour operator can't or won't point out.

How far in advance do I need to book? You may be able to sign up just a month before departure, or you might have to give an outfit 6 months notice.

MAJOR PLAYERS

ALASKA WILDLAND ADVENTURES Established in 1977, this company runs natural-history van tours in Alaska. It houses guests in tents at campgounds, in its own rustic riverside cabins, and in its more upscale lodge within Denali National Park. Some members of its staff have been around for years: guides in their forties who love to show off Alaska and college students who have been guiding for several seasons. The guest to guide ratio is about 6:1. The food ranges from campfire cooking and family-style meals on the deck at the cabins to desserts prepared by a pastry chef at the lodge. These tours are at the high end of the scale; the outfitter also offers a trip designed for families and one for seniors. For travelers interested in 7 to 12 day package tours, the Alaska Wildland Safaris would be of most interest (Box 389, Girdwood, AK 99587, tel. 907/783–2928 or 800/334–8730, fax 907/ 783–2130).

AMERICAN ADVENTURES This van-camping operator runs dozens of low-priced trips throughout the United States, Canada, and Mexico (some even cross borders). Trips range from 6 to 68 days; participants travel in large vans in groups of 11 to 13 and camp in state and national parks and, occasionally, KOA campgrounds. Everyone helps cook and clean up. Cooking gear and tents for 2 are provided; bring your own sleeping bag. This tour group's guides are exclusively North Americans, which distinguishes them from the competition. Many of them are teachers, others simply have a yen for adventure; their leadership skills are honed by a 6-week training course. Most guests are from overseas, and their average age is about 30 (6762A Centinela Ave., Culver City, CA 90230, tel. 310/390–7495 or 800/864–0335, fax 310/390–1446).

CAMPALASKA TOURS This company's philosophy is simple: Alaska is a huge, beautiful place where hotels are extremely expensive. The solution? Travel by maxi-van and camp out. Everyone takes a turn with cooking, camp chores, and food shopping, which is done every day or so. Camping is in established campgrounds, although a hot shower may be only an every other day event. Groups, often mixed equally by sex, are never larger than 12. The guides all have at least several years of experience. Camp-Alaska offers 16 different moderately priced tours throughout Alaska (Box 872247, Wasilla, AK 99687, tel. 907/376–9438 or 800/376–9438, fax 907/376–2353).

GREEN TORTOISE This outfit appeals to those who never lost their love for the '60s—it's been around since 1972. The mood is togetherness, the mode of transportation is bus-turned-camper, the group size is up to 38, and the meals are vegetarian. The clientele is youngish, poor (a 9-day trip around the Southwest costs $310, including food), obviously gregarious, and doesn't mind not taking a shower every day. Either you fit in or you don't. Each trip has a pair of drivers, who trade off sleeping and driving and whose primary qualifications are love of nature and regard for safety. The lead drivers assist in writing company guidebooks, and use them to identify sights. Green Tortoise runs its fleet of buses on trips throughout the United States, Mexico, Costa Rica, and Guatemala. It runs 8- to 14-day loops around the western national parks, trips that head south from San Francisco to Guatemala and Baja and back, 2-week cross-country trips, and a 35-day trip to Alaska (494 Broadway, San Francisco, CA 94133, tel. 415/956–7500 or 800/867–8647, fax 415/956–4900).

NATURE EXPEDITIONS INTERNATIONAL Education is the focus here, with guides trained to a fever pitch in natural history and anthropology. The company, which also runs trips around the world, considers itself an eco-touring pioneer. In the United States it tours Alaska, Hawaii, the Southwest Native American country, and the Pacific Northwest. Traveling in vans, groups of about 10 hike between 3 and 5 miles a day. Clients, who are 35 to 70 years old, tend to be as interested as the guides in ecosystems. They also tend to have money; all that expertise can get expensive, and the accommodations and food are generally first-class. The 1- and 2-week tours run about $1,200 per week, except Alaska which is $1,500 (Box 11496, Eugene, OR 97440, tel. 503/484–6529 or 800/869–0639, fax 503/484–6531).

EYE OF THE WHALE Mark and Beth Goodoni were formerly naturalists guides for Pacific Quest, which they bought and absorbed into Eye of the Whale, the company they formed in 1986. The Goodonis design itineraries for people who want to get past the plastic leis and find Hawaii's secret waterfalls and rain forests. In addition to their sailing itineraries, Eye of the Whale offers non-camping, land-based hiking adventure vacations in Hawaii. Participants explore the wild parts of the islands yet come back to the comforts of home every evening: Guests stay in scenic inns and cozy B&Bs. Each trip reflects the company's philosophy of blending relaxing pleasures of vacations while fostering an appreciation and understanding of Hawaii's natural wonders. Groups are small (4 to 10 people). Trips range in length from 6 to 10 days; costs average $1,000 per week (Box 1269, Kapa'au, HI 96755, tel. 808/889–0227 or 800/659–3544).

SUNTREK This adventure camping-tour operator, in business for 23 years, runs dozens of trips that range in length from 1 to 13 weeks. You share experiences with up to 13 people (about 18 to 38 years old) on trips to the Pacific Coast, the western national parks, from San Francisco to New York, down the East Coast, and around the Northwest. You'll stay in campgrounds whenever possible, or in inexpensive hotels, which cost extra. Camping gear is provided, except for sleeping bags, and everyone contributes to a food kitty and takes turns cooking. Two people sleep in each of the company's 4-person tents, so there's plenty of room for gear. Suntrek advertises largely to the European market, and most clients come from abroad. There's a good mix of men and women, singles and couples (singles get paired with tentmates of the same sex). The guides— who are as likely to be European as they are American—have passed an intensive training program and are usually bilingual. Don't expect detailed knowledge of the terrain. A part of each day is usually spent traveling, and the trips usually include such extras (at additional cost) as whale-watching expeditions or visits to famous sights. Prices typically start at $399 for a 1 week trek (Sun Plaza, 77 W. 3rd St., Santa Rosa, CA 95401, tel. 707/523–1800 or 800/786–8735, fax 707/523–1911).

TAG-A-LONG EXPEDITIONS This Utah operator offers Jeep treks with hiking and occasional white-water rafting. The outfit is based in Moab, a center for 4-wheel-drive trips, and the camping and touring is done in the scenic red rock land of Canyonlands National Park. Tag-A-Long prides itself on the leadership as well as the cooking skills of its guides; it's been in business since 1963 and has been hired by *National Geographic,* Walt Disney Productions, and television networks to help them get around the Canyonlands wilderness. Most participants are urban professionals, ranging in age from 30 to 60. Expect gourmet camp cooking: A typical dinner is a fruit plate, Caesar salad, chicken Cordon Bleu done in a Dutch oven, wild rice pilaf, and flaming cherries jubilee. Tag-A-Long's 4-wheel-drive vehicles take you to wilderness trailheads and, on other trips, go into the canyon country to focus on geology, archaeology, and natural history. On the rafting segments offered on some trips you will see the stark, beautiful desert terrain from a different perspective. Trips range from half a day to 11 days in length and cost between $34 and $1,095. The staff sets up portable restrooms at each camp; you can rent sleeping bags and tents. (452 N. Main St., Moab, UT 84532, tel. 801/259–8946 or 800/453-3292, fax 801/259–8990).

TREK AMERICA This outfitter offers 52 trips (38 in summer, 14 in winter) throughout the United States that last 1 to 9 weeks and cost about $450 per week. Groups of 13, plus a guide, travel in vans around the western national parks, on a southern route across the country, in Alaska, in Florida, and up and down the West Coast: There's not much that Trek America misses. Everyone shares cooking and cleanup duties in camp, and you bring only a sleeping bag; everything else is supplied. Nights are spent in campgrounds with showers and, occasionally, pools. Americans are a rarity on these trips, which draw young visitors (ages 18 to 38) from all over the world. Guides are at least 23, but they are more drivers than dedicated biologists; most are American (Box 189, Rockaway, NJ 07866, tel. 201/983–1144, fax 201/983–8551).

FAVORITE TRIPS

THE NORTHEAST

REGION-WIDE **Van Camping Across the Northeast.** Would you like to camp from New York City to Niagara Falls to Maine and back with a group of international travelers? Suntrek's Mayflower, a 2-week loop trip, caters to the 18–38 age group and is informal in style, with group cooking and cleanup. Transport is by a specially-equipped maxi-van, which holds up to 13 people (the limit per trip) plus a driver-guide, who is as likely to be European as American. On this trip, starting in New York City, you travel about 4 hours a day, visiting Pennsylvania Dutch country, Niagara Falls (where you ride the *Maid of the Mist*), Adirondack Park, White Mountains National Forest, Acadia National

Park, Boston, Cape Cod (with a whale-watching trip), and then return to New York. Optional activities include canoeing, hiking, and bicycle riding. Nights are spent in two-person tents at campgrounds. *Suntrek, Sun Plaza, 77 W. 3rd St., Santa Rosa, CA 95401, tel. 707/523–1800 or 800/786–8735, fax 707/523–1911. Early June–late Sept.: 14 days, $814–$837. Price includes a whale-watching tour, use of camping gear (except sleeping bag), campsite fees, entrance fees to national park, and boat ride. An additional $25–30 per week food kitty covers most meals; sign up 1–2 months in advance.*

THE SOUTH

NEW YORK-FLORIDA **Van Camping Down the Confederate Trail.** On this 14-day trip, you start in New York with an international group of 11 to 13 people, most single and in their mid-20s, and travel in maxi-vans up the coast, through the nation's capital and the Deep South before moving on to sun and fun in Florida. A wide range of activities are offered—a White House visit, a tour of Graceland, and a Mississippi River cruise (optional activities are not included in the cost of the trip)—before the trip winds down in Miami. You camp every night in 2-person tents and help cook and wash the dishes. The leader-drivers are all Americans or Canadians; they're chosen more for their ability to keep a diverse group together than for their encyclopedic knowledge. Expect fairly pedestrian camping facilities, though they usually have hot showers. *AmeriCan Adventures, 6762A Centinela Ave., Culver City, CA 90230, tel. 310/390–7495 or 800/ 864–0335, fax 310/390–1446. May–Oct.: $659–$769. Sign up 2–3 months in advance.*

THE SOUTHWEST

REGION-WIDE **The National Parks Loop.** On this keep-the-cost-down trip, Green Tortoise's converted bus is not only transportation, but home for up to 38 people. Guests, who are usually in the 25 to 30 age range, are prepared to become very chummy and often sleep in their bunks en route. There are seating areas with tables that convert to bunks, and platforms that become dormitories. On this 16-day trip, half the nights are spent on the bus, the others at campgrounds along the way. The trip starts in San Francisco, and covers a lot of ground, skimming through the cream of the West's national parks and recreation areas: Grand Tetons, Yellowstone, Flaming Gorge, Arches, Canyonlands, the Grand Canyon, and Zion. The bus also makes stops at some hot springs. Food (mostly vegetarian) is communally cooked, the campsites are primitive, and the pair of guides, who trade off on driving, are no scholars, but they know the territory. *Green Tortoise, 494 Broadway, San Francisco, CA 94133, tel. 415/956–7500 or 800/867–8647, fax 415/956–4900. June–Aug.: 16 days, $499. Price does not include $121 food fund, meals eaten in restaurants (about 25%), or camping gear; sign up 1–2 months in advance.*

ARIZONA **Photographing the Canyonlands.** Paul Lazarski, a professional nature photographer and avid adventurer from Vancouver, runs this 7-day combination tour and photography workshop. You'll be able to capture highlights of four of the most spectacular areas of the desert Southwest. Snapping opportunities include the vertical walls and monolithic peaks of Zion National Park, the rock pillars and narrow canyons of Bryce Canyon, and the colorful petrified wood and sensuous hills of the Painted Desert. The tour's highlight is the famous Navajo sandstone formations of Antelope (Corkscrew) Mountain. A resident of Arizona who's also a photographer comes along as an additional guide, and groups are held to 15; two vans are used, if needed. You also travel by horseback and helicopter (included in price) to reach some of the remote locations. *Ecosummer Expeditions, 936 Peace Portal Dr., Box 8014-240, Blaine, WA 98230, tel. 604/669–7741 or 800/688–8605, fax 604/669–3244. Mar. and Nov.: 7 days, $1,895; sign up 4 months in advance.*

UTAH **Rafting and Jeeping in Canyonlands.** For 6 days and 5 nights, you and 7 companions are off the road—either rafting in the famous Cataract Canyon in Canyonlands National Park or traveling by 4-wheel-drive vehicles on tough roads to see the desert valleys and towering rock monuments of the national park. Two Toyota Land Cruisers are driven by guides who specialize in the natural and human history of the park and provide running commentary. They also cook the food, which can include everything from pan-fried trout to pineapple upside-down cake. The wilderness campsites are pristine, and everything is set up by the guides, from the portable sanitary facilities to the occasional solar-heated shower. The 3½-day rafting part of the trip sweeps you through 25 significant rapids and whets your imagination for seeing the spectacular, harsh scenery close up. You then fly from Lake Powell to an outpost in Canyonlands. Participants tend to be 30- to 60-year-old professionals. *Tag-A-Long Expeditions, 452 N. Main St., Moab, UT 84532, tel. 801/259–8946 or 800/453–3292, fax 801/259–8990. Apr.–Oct.: 6 days, $1,095. Price does not include tent or sleeping bag; sign up 1–2 months in advance.*

UTAH **Prehistoric Rock Art of the Fremont.** Patricia and Gary George, a husband and wife team, deeply love the wild Colorado Plateau where they grew up; they know its history, wildlife, archaeology, and geology, and think showing its beautiful, harsh countryside to others is a blast. They've been leading Jeep tours since 1975, both scheduled and custom-designed, hotel-based and camping, (camping is their specialty). Their favorite is a 5-day tour that takes 6 to 12 people aged 30 to 60 to sites to view the rock art of the Fremont Indians (ca. AD 700–1300). You are surrounded by gorgeous country: red rock spires reach toward a powder blue sky, and there's an oasis of brush green in the valley. Plan on about 6 hours of activity a day, riding and walking. Meals, cooked over the campfire, feature such local fare as trout and Southwestern specialties like deep-dish enchilada pie. The Georges set up camp, with sanitary facilities and camp showers, in isolated, beautiful spots, and they'll help you put up your tent. Take the May trip if possible; August can be gruelingly hot. *Hondoo Rivers and Trails, Box 98, Torrey, UT 84775, tel. 801/ 425–3519 or 800/332–2696, fax 801/425–3548. May and Aug.: 5 days, $785. Price includes 1 night lodging and all camping gear; sign up 1–3 months in advance.*

THE ROCKIES

COLORADO **Over the Continental Divide.** Burt Green, who holds Colorado Off-Road Scenic Permit No. 1, personifies his company, the Mountain Men. For some 30 years he's been sharing his hidden Colorado— the off-the-asphalt spots with spectacular views; the secrets of gold panning; where to go for great fishing. His is a personalized service: You tell him what you want to do and for how long, and he will create the trip accordingly. One of his favorite itineraries takes you along the catch-your-breath, off-road Jeep trails that crisscross the Continental Divide. Because you design the tour, you decide the level of of dining and lodging. Remember, however, that you'll be paying for your guide to eat and sleep where you do, and that will set your group back about $50 per night and around $20 per day for meals. *Mountain Men, 3003 S. Macon Circle, Aurora, CO 80014, tel. 303/750–5200, fax 303/750–2949. June– Oct.: $400 daily for groups of up to 14 on custom trips. Price does not include lodging, meals, or staff expenses; sign up 1–2 months in advance.*

COLORADO **The Switzerland of America.** Ouray, Colorado, has a romantic mining history and equally romantic views of the red mountains that snuggle up against the town. Marv Dimond's Switzerland of America has been running Jeep tours here for 28 years, and if you ask him why the terrain is special, he gets as enthusiastic as a greenhorn from the East. He'll design multi-day journeys to order, but his choice trip would take his awed guests (7 passengers plus guide in a Jeep Scrambler) on a 5-day outing up and down several rugged 13,000-foot mountains for the 360° views on top, past the remains of old ghost towns, and over passes where riots of wildflowers compete with waterfalls as photographic subjects. Marv and his guides cook sturdy campfire meals such as grilled steak, baked potatoes, and green beans. You stay in wooded mountain campsites, where the staff sets up sanitary facilities, but not showers. *Switzerland of America, Inc., 226 7th Ave., Box 780, Ouray, CO 81427, tel. 970/325–4484 or 800/432– 5337, fax 970/325–4059. Memorial Day– Labor Day: 5 days, $875 per person (minimum 4 people); $1,200 (3 people); $1,500 (2 people). Price does not include sleeping bag; sign up 1–2 months in advance.*

MONTANA **Wildlife and Creature Comforts.** This is the less-traveled Rockies, where deer, moose, bear, elk, wolf, bald eagles, and other wildlife are more common than people. Although you're surrounded by such wilderness on this package with John and Carma Sinerius, a pair of avid naturalists, it may be just the trip for those whose love for the outdoors doesn't extend to camping out in it. After a day of mountain scenery, wildflower meadows, and historic sites, you head for the comforts of home and dinner in the Sinerius's own Virginia City B&B: a main house furnished with antiques, plus a cabin for 6 that's full of the town's Old West atmosphere. The food is "homestyle gourmet," with entrées that include barbecued chicken and grilled trout, and for dessert, homemade pie. Full breakfasts of fresh seasonal fruit, homemade muffins, and sourdough pancakes are served with coffee or tea. You travel in groups of three and four per vehicle, each with a guide to share the wonders of the area. The daily itinerary may include a trip to pan for gold, a day of mountain biking through meadows, or hiking around historic mining sites and ghost towns. *Just an Experience, Box 98, Virginia City, MT 59755, tel. 406/843–5402. Memorial Day–mid Oct.: 4 days, $560. Sign up at least 3 weeks in advance.*

THE WEST COAST

CALIFORNIA–ARIZONA Yosemite and the Grand Canyon. The Explore Company, an English outfitter, runs van tours throughout the United States primarily for Britons. This 20-day tour, as you'd expect, hits the tourist high spots: San Francisco, the Napa Valley, Death Valley, Yosemite, Los Angeles, the winding drive up the coast on Highway 1, Las Vegas, the Grand Canyon, and Zion National Park. A maximum of 12 people travel by van from campground to campground, most of them in national parks; in L.A., San Francisco, and Las Vegas you stay at hotels. Everyone helps cook and clean up. Among various optional excursions, you can take a rafting trip ($60) on the American or the Merced rivers, rent a bicycle ($12 per hour) or a horse ($45 for 2 hours) to cover Yosemite, and take a helicopter ride over the Grand Canyon ($90). Those who don't take these options can explore a gold-mining town and do more hiking in the Grand Canyon area. The guides, mostly Americans, are chosen more for their ability to keep a group happy than for comprehensive knowledge of the area. Tour participants range in age from their twenties to their sixties, and everyone should be able to handle some serious hiking. *Explore Adventure Center, 1311 63rd St., Suite 200, Emeryville, CA 94608, tel. 510/654–1879 or 800/227–8747, fax 510/654–4200. June–Sept.: 20 days, $1,500. Price does not include frame backpack, 6 lunches and 10 dinners, or optional activities; sign up 3 months in advance.*

CALIFORNIA–WASHINGTON Up the Pacific Coast. If you have 2 weeks, you can do the Pacific Coast with Trek America, traveling by van, camping out (except in San Francisco, where you stay at a budget hotel), and sampling everything from Disneyland to Big Sur, Mount Rainier to the Puget Sound. The groups are limited to 13 and cooking and cleaning tasks are shared. Most driverguides are Americans, with at least 4 years of guiding experience but less botanical or naturalist expertise. You stay at established campsites (most equipped with showers),

many of which are in national parks such as Yosemite. The food depends on the whim—and skill—of that night's guest-chef. *Trek America, Box 189, Rockaway, NJ 07866, tel. 201/983–1144, fax 201/983–8551. Apr.–Sept.: 2 weeks, $648–$750. Price includes Disneyland admission. An additional food kitty of $35 per week covers most meals. 2 nights' lodging in San Francisco is an additional $25–$30 per night (multiple share); sign up 2 months in advance.*

OREGON–WASHINGTON Natural History in the Pacific Northwest. Understanding the ecosystems of the magnificent forests and coasts of Oregon and Washington is the focus on this 16-day trip by passenger van. Nature Expeditions International's guides, all with college-level teaching experience in anthropology, biology, or natural history, comment on the local wildlife and explain such arcana as the Native American use of plants. You might take a raft trip down the McKenzie River, travel from high desert country to rainforest, see moose or elk as you hike through Olympic National Park, and savor the Oregon's craggy coastline. Accommodations are in lodges, first-class hotels, and inns, where you also eat your meals—except for the salmon bake beside a river. This trip attracts people with an avid interest in natural history and the average group size is 9. There are no small group surcharges. *Nature Expeditions International, Box 11496, Eugene, OR 97440, tel. 503/484–6529 or 800/869–0639, fax 503/484–6531. July–Sept.: 9 days (Oregon only), $1,690; 16 days (includes Washington), $2,490. Price includes all meals and accommodations.*

ALASKA

CENTRAL From Kenai Peninsula to Denali. "This is a little wilder, a little more Alaskan," says owner Tim Adams, contrasting this 2-week van-camping trip on little-traveled dirt roads with others available in the area. Guides with several years' Alaska experience take you into the stunning mountains of Denali National Park. You also see the breathtaking Kenai Peninsula's glaciers and wildlife, visit the towering Wrangell Mountains, and fly to Kodiak Island for 2 days. There's a maximum of 12 people per trip and half of the clientele is international. Participants take turns cooking and cleaning. Campsites are in state and national parks, and some have showers. *Camp Alaska Tours, Box 872247, Wasilla, AK 99687, tel. 907/376–9438 or 800/376–9438, fax 907/376–2353. June–Sept.: 14 days, $1,350. Price includes flight to and ferry (with cabin) from Kodiak. An additional $115 food kitty covers most meals; sign up 4 months in advance.*

CENTRAL **Cabin Safari to the Fjords and the Bush.** Those who want their Alaska wild but like to sleep indoors will be attracted to these tours. Here you're housed in both a rustic, comfortable cabins with shared baths and in a restored lodge, both run by the outfitter. You're met at the Kenai Airport and taken to the cabins by the Kenai River that are home for the next 5 days. You usually have meals on a riverside deck under a tarp, and salmon is a sure bet. Guides take you by van to trailheads one day; on another you take a raft trip on the Kenai. There's a day trip by yacht to the Kenai Fjords National Park to watch for sea otters, puffins, seals, sea lions, and whales. From there, it's on to Talkeetna, a bush town, to stay for a night before heading north for 3 days at a carpeted, refurbished lodge in Denali National Park. The lodge has private baths, and the cook specializes in homemade bread and pastries. On the last day, bid farewell to your trip guide and board the world-famous Alaska Railroad (cost included) for your ride back to Anchorage. Groups are never larger than 18, and the 2 or 3 guides are extremely well versed in the natural history of this wild state. Participants are usually ages 35 to 60. *Alaska Wildland Adventures, Box 389, Girdwood, AK 99587, tel. 907/783–2928 or 800/334–8730, fax 907/783–2130. June–Sept.: 10 days and 9 nights, $3,095. Sign up 4 months in advance.*

HAWAII

THE BIG ISLAND **Earth, Fire, & Sea.** This tour is designed for those with only a few days to spend on the is[...] sneaking suspicion th[...] than deluxe resorts. [...] vans transport you to [...] waterfalls, down specta[...] and to unknown beache[...] the whole time, where [...] morning to the smell of [...] include lots of fish and tropical fruit and vegetables. On the last day on land you embark on an all day exploration of the botanical and geological wonders of Volcanoes National Park. Tropical rainforest yields to steaming vents and frozen forms of lava as the group hikes into Kilauea, the world's most active volcano. This 6-day tour of the Big Island also includes day sailing, whale-watching (in the winter months), and snorkeling. There is a group minimum of 2 persons and a maximum of 10. *Eye of The Whale, Box 1269, Kapa'au, HI 96755, tel. 808/889–0227 or 800/659–3544. Year-round: 6 days, $975 (includes 3 meals per day except for two dinners.). Sign up 4 months in advance.*

HAWAII, MAUI, AND KAUAI **Islands of Aloha.** On a 10-day trip, Mark and Beth Goodoni's company takes small groups (6 to 9 is usual; 10 is the max) to Hawaii, Maui, and Kauai, flying between islands and traveling by van to little-visited destinations. Clients hike to volcanoes on Maui, drive to an old fishing village on Hawaii, and snorkel along the Pali coast on Kauai. You spend the nights in off-the-trail B&Bs, whose hospitable owners are as much an attraction as the rooms, most of which have private baths. Mark and Beth (who leads the Earth, Fire & Sea trip), are both trained naturalists with an intense interest in the islands; they can introduce you to such birds as the elepaio, i'iwi, and apapane. Although you eat some meals in the B&Bs and small inns, Mark and Beth also cook in parks and make a point of serving Hawaiian seafood and native produce. Participants tend to be well-educated 35- to 50-year-olds who are in good shape—the hiking is strenuous. *Eye of the Whale, Box 1269, Kapa'au, HI 96755, tel. 808/ 889–0227 or 800/659–3544. Year-round: 10 days, $1,550.*

does not include 3 dinners; sign up 4 months in advance.

SOURCES

ORGANIZATIONS **United Four Wheel Drive Associations** (4505 W. 700 S, Shelbyville, IN 46176, tel. 317/729–5862 or 800/448–3932, fax 317/729–5930) publishes a newspaper 5 times yearly with advocacy information, news about trails, and lists of local associations. For California, contact the **California Association of 4-Wheel Drive Clubs** (c/o Pat Horvath, 3104 O St. 313, Sacramento, CA 95816, tel. 916/332–8890 or 800/494–3866, fax 916/332–1730).

PERIODICALS *4-Wheel & Off-Road* magazine (Petersen's Publishing, 6420 Wilshire Blvd., Los Angeles, CA 90048, tel. 800/800–4294) is geared to the do-it-yourself off-road enthusiast. *Off-Road* (12100 Wilshire Blvd., No. 250, Los Angeles, CA 90025, tel. 310/820–3601) is a monthly magazine of general interest to owners of 4-wheel-drive vehicles.

BOOKS Spiral-bound *Backroad Tips & Trips,* by Harry Llewellyn (Glove Box Guides), is available in RV and off-road specialty shops.

ALSO SEE Want other ways to get around in the wilderness without expending too much energy? See Horse Packing, Trail Riding, and River Rafting.

Wilderness and Survival Schools

By Naomi Black and Jane E. Zarem

ake part in a wilderness skills or survival school, and you'll learn how to take care of yourself and feel confident in nature. The schools and courses available to you, however, vary considerably. Survival schools teach the basics of living outdoors *without* or with a minimum of gear. You navigate cross-country and live without tents or sleeping bags. You learn to make a shelter, build a fire, fashion tools, and forage for food and water. Outdoor skills schools, on the other hand, teach some of these same lessons but put more emphasis on minimum-impact recreational camping *with gear.* You learn how to manage in the wilderness so you can avoid survival situations.

Either type of program may include a solo—a day or more when you're on your own in the wilderness with a minimum of equipment and food. It's a time to practice what you've learned, reflect on who you are, and think about where you're going.

Underpinning all these programs is solid, basic instruction in conservation, environmental protection, and safety skills. Most courses teach the rudiments of navigation, food planning and preparation, equipment maintenance, water purification, wilderness first aid, and wilderness safety. Natural history and local history and culture may come up, as well. All the programs incorporate

some sort of personal growth activities; some help you acquire leadership skills, learn teamwork, and build character. After all, when you're traveling with a group in an unpredictable environment—and nature is always unpredictable—you must rely on each other to complete whatever task is given you, whether navigating safely to a destination or making sure everyone is fed.

Depending on the location of the program, personal development happens while you're hiking or backpacking, river rafting, whitewater canoeing, sea kayaking, sailing, mountaineering, rock climbing, horse packing, backcountry skiing—even dogsledding. Courses take place all over the country, in all kinds of surroundings, and may last anywhere from one week to several months.

Although it helps to be moderately fit, there is really just one requirement: You must be willing to throw yourself into the wilderness situation. Some courses are hard-core survival experiences, with no camping equipment, no sleeping bags, no mattress pads, no change of clothes, and no toilet paper. Meals are to fuel the body, not the soul, and you may have only two per day. Whether you travel from place to place or spend a week or more in a single location, you'll be learning every day and practicing what you're taught: fire building, shelter building, navigation with a map and compass, or plant lore, for

New York City–based Naomi Black encountered her first survival skill, making soup in a cow's stomach, as a child in summer camp. Jane E. Zarem, a freelance travel writer and editor from Connecticut, has managed to survive in the wilderness—so far. She is a regular Fodor's contributor.

example. Free time is at a minimum. And since you will be with instructors or other students almost all the time, there's little room for privacy.

The program fees vary considerably, ranging from Reevis Mountain School's rock-bottom rates of about $28 per person per day to Alaskan forays that cost more than $150 per person per day.

CHOOSING THE RIGHT PROGRAM

There are a lot of questions you need to ask the staff at the programs you're considering—and many questions to ask yourself, too.

What's the school's safety record, and how long has the school been in business? Most wilderness skills schools and survival schools have excellent safety records; you don't want to get involved with one that has a history of accidents. A long track record can be an indication that you'll be in good hands.

What are the leaders' qualifications? At least one instructor in each course should have first-aid training. Wilderness first-aid training, which is slightly different, is an even better qualification. A leader who's an expert on leadership training may not be an expert on winter conditions or on local flora and fauna, history, geology, and ecology. Make sure that your instructor is knowledgeable about areas that interest you.

What is the student-to-teacher ratio? To get the most out of a course, look for a small student-to-teacher ratio. Smaller groups are better because you'll learn more. In courses that move from point to point, 5 students per instructor is a good number. For base camp or classroom courses, the number can be higher.

What are food and accommodations like, and what's the creature-comfort quotient? Some courses allow more creature comforts than others. Think carefully about what you're willing to do without for the dura-

tion, and make sure the program doesn't ask more of you. Most schools forbid alcohol and recreational drugs and recommend kicking the caffeine habit before you leave home. Some courses limit your food intake or give you a diet made up largely of grains and legumes. Such draconian measures are not intended to starve you but to simulate either a camping experience where you're carrying as little as possible or a survival situation where food is not abundant. Depending on the terrain, weather, insects, and course philosophy, sleeping arrangements vary from wind-tight tents to dozing under the stars without so much as a blanket. Some courses don't allow you to bring a change of clothes, and you use local plants or sand as toilet paper.

What is the focus of the school and what is its approach? Some schools emphasize survival skills; others teach basic outdoor skills. Survival skills courses teach you how to get by in the wild without gear. They tend to be tougher than outdoor skills courses, which primarily teach you how to camp responsibly with gear. Some curricula encourage students to become leaders or team members. If you want to learn the geology or biology of an area, ask in advance if those topics are covered. Some schools expect students to undertake service work, such as maintaining trails in a national forest.

The itinerary of many programs varies from one session to another, depending on the weather and participants' fitness levels and skills. At some schools, students and instructors work out a plan together; at others, the instructors alone know the distances—that safety is so many hours or miles away—to simulate a more realistic survival situation.

What kind of people participate? Some trips bring people of all ages together, and some are age specific; that is, designed for those under 18, over 30, over 50, and the like.

Does the school offer a solo? Not all courses include a solo. The solo experience is a period of reflection, abstinence, and consolidation of your newly learned skills. You're settled in one spot and monitored regularly by an instructor. If you don't know how you feel about spending time alone in the wild, talk to a staff member from the school. Many people regard the solo as the best part of the trip.

What's the cost, and what's included? Prices for the programs listed below, unless otherwise noted, include instruction, meals while in the wilderness, and basic camping equipment (including tarps or tents and sleeping bags if you will be using them). Sometimes outdoor clothing can be rented. Transportation to and from the staging area is not included.

How fit do you have to be to participate? Daily exercise and some aerobic activity a few times a week is excellent training for these trips. If you don't exercise regularly, you can still go on most courses; you'll just have to work harder.

Do you have references from past guests? If you have doubts or questions that program spokespeople don't address, there's no substitute for talking to past students.

How far in advance do I need to book? Sign up ranges from one month to a full year ahead.

MAJOR PLAYERS

BOULDER OUTDOOR SURVIVAL SCHOOL This well-regarded school, known informally as BOSS, has been teaching primitive survival skills since 1980 and offering desert courses since 1965. Without the dependency on the high-tech gear that some outdoor schools utilize, BOSS programs, as you might expect, are rugged. BOSS's reliance on knowledge and technique, rather than gadgets and technology, has people coming back again and again to learn more about the natural world and the skills needed to live in it confidently and comfortably.

BOSS programs are divided into two formats: Skills Courses and Field Courses. Skills Courses are 5 to 7 days in length and focus on the physical skills and techniques you need to be proficient outdoors. All aspects of outdoor survival are covered, from shelters and fires to preparing food and making tools. BOSS also offers specialty courses that focus on a specific aspect or skill, like animal tracking, hide tanning, or celestial navigation. Since the emphasis for all Skills Courses is on learning, meals and primitive accommodations are provided. Students bed down in wickiups (teepees) in forest settings and in caves and under overhangs in canyon locations. You may bring sleeping bags and pads.

Field Courses are for people looking to challenge themselves. The BOSS Standard Field Course—27 days in the desert, with blanket, knife, and minimal food—has been attracting adventurers for more than 30 years. While students certainly learn the skills necessary to create a natural living environment (shelter, fire, water, plantlife, trapping, etc.), the physical challenge of hiking rugged trails and going without food and water for days at a time can do more for some people than all the skills in the world. For those who may be short on time, this same format is offered in 7- and 14-day versions.

BOSS has offices in both Boulder, Colorado and in Boulder, Utah, halfway between Bryce Canyon and Capitol Reef national parks. The student-to-staff ratio is usually 6:1 with, typically, 12 students per section (Box 1590, Boulder, CO 80306, tel. 303/444–9779; fax 303/442–7245).

NATIONAL OUTDOOR LEADERSHIP SCHOOL People have been hiking, climbing, skiing, and paddling through the wilderness classrooms of NOLS since 1965; the alumni of this school, a nonprofit educational corporation, number more than 30,000. The basic wilderness, water, and mountaineering courses last a month or longer, but a number of special courses are offered to adults 25 and over who have less time available. These courses are easier than the longer versions but do not lose the focus for which NOLS is known: minimum-impact camping, outdoor safety, and gear-oriented outdoor skills. Not a survival school, NOLS emphasizes that you can avoid a survival situation by learning to camp responsibly.

The school's magnificent settings include Alaska's Gates of the Arctic National Park, Baja California, the Arizona desert, and the Pacific Northwest. The longer courses go even farther afield. NOLS has international branches in Canada, Kenya, and Patagonia.

Although the technical skills and safety courses are formal and demanding, there's less structure to the overall expedition than, for instance, Outward Bound or the Boulder Outdoor Survival School walkabouts, whose expeditions have several specific stages. (NOLS courses have no solo or marathon, for example.) Most NOLS programs, however, do encourage each person to become leader for the day.

Students set up and sleep in 3- to 4-person tents (or tarps) and, with their tent mates, form a group that eats, cleans up, and usually travels together. You eat pasta, lentils, beans, bulgur and other grains, and cook everything from scratch—bread, pizza, soup, salads of wild greens. No freeze-dried or dehydrated prepared foods here.

To sign up, you must usually be at least 16; special sessions are available for 14- and 15-year-olds, educators, and adults 25 years and older. Sign up at least 6 months in advance for the 25 and over courses. Average cost per day is often less than $100, and the student-to-teacher ratio is about 5:1 (288 Main St., Lander, WY, 82520-0579, tel. 307/332–6973, fax 307/332–1220).

OUTWARD BOUND The best-known of the wilderness skills schools, Outward Bound is also the oldest. Founded in 1941, it has some 350,000 alumni in the U.S. alone. Actually, OB calls itself an adventure-based education program; the objective is training people as leaders, helping people learn more about themselves, building self-confidence, and instilling compassion for others. Schools are in Denver, Colorado; Rockland, Maine; Minneapolis, Minnesota; Morganton, North Carolina; and Portland, Oregon. Each is an independent operation, with its own man-

agement and roster of courses. But whether you travel to the Cascade Mountains of the Pacific Northwest or the southern Appalachians, and whether you study backpacking, mountaineering, or rock climbing; canoeing, kayaking, or rafting; bicycling or sailing; dog-sledding, skiing, or winter camping—you go through several distinct stages.

You spend the course with a group of 8 to 12 other students. Once you've packed your gear and sat through a short orientation period that includes safety instruction, you set out on an expedition. You carry your own packs, prepare your own food, and bed down at night in sleeping bags laid out under tarps (or, occasionally, in tents). En route, you learn the skills appropriate to the course. You encounter situations in the wild that the leaders recognize as goals, and the group works as a team to accomplish them. About midway through the course, you separate for your solo, 1 to 3 days in an assigned spot with ample water but a minimum of food; some students choose to fast. Instructors monitor each person at least once a day to ensure their safety. The trip ends with a marathon—either a 26-mile run or some other long, exhausting, and celebratory race that proves how far each student has come. The student-to-staff ratio is 4:1.

OB is a nonprofit, tax-exempt, educational institution. In addition to its wilderness schools, it has urban centers to reach out to inner-city kids, special programs for professional development, and college-semester programs. The wilderness schools also offer special programs for women, 14- to 17-year-olds, parents and their children, couples, and health and education professionals. All gear except clothing, boots, and personal items is included in the cost, which averages between $75 and $150 per day. A physical examination is required. Sign up at least 3 months in advance (Rte. 9D, R2, Box 280, Garrison, NY 10524-9757, tel. 914/424–4000 or 800/243–8520, fax 914/424–4280).

TOM BROWN TRACKING, NATURE, WILDERNESS SURVIVAL SCHOOL Tom Brown earned a reputation for himself as one of the country's foremost trackers. Simply by looking at the track that a person or animal has left behind, he can tell more about that individual's behavior than most people can by direct observation. Brown has written 15 books, and students are encouraged to read them before registering. The school he founded in 1978, now with some 4,000 alumni, is so popular that prospective students sign up 6 months or even a year in advance.

Each of Brown's courses cover equally what he considers the three major categories of survival: tracking, nature awareness, and the ancient philosophy of the Earth. The core of the school's curriculum is the week-long Standard Course, which emphasizes skills, techniques, and workshops for surviving in pure wilderness. The Standard Course is required regardless of a student's background or experience. Once you have taken it, you are eligible to sign up for a number of other 7-day courses. The Advanced Standard Course includes more difficult skills and pure survival living. Then there's an Advanced Tracking and Nature Observation course and a philosophy workshop, which covers ancient Native American customs, traditions, and ceremonies (such as the vision quest, storytelling, and the sacred pipe). Also available are 10-day winter survival courses and a 7-day course that recreates the Apache Scout experience, traveling on a mission away from the tribe and surviving; to take these, you must have already taken the Advanced Standard and Advanced Tracking courses.

Brown himself gives about half of the lectures in any given course, and his instructors have all studied with him for years. Since there isn't time to absorb all the information Brown covers within the context of an arduous hiking trip, most courses stay in one place—at either the Pine Barrens, near Tom's River, New Jersey, or at the Tracker Farm, about an hour west of the Pine Barrens in Asbury, New Jersey. Whether indoors or out, the classes draw everyone together into an almost tribal community in which people look out for others. This group spirit and the oneness with nature that is emphasized are focal points of the school. Learning to rely on your instinct and trained inner vision is as important in The Tracker classes as learning to start a fire with a bow drill. Although you will not test your physical limits, this is hardly a vacation. You'll be rising early and practicing your skills until late at night. The minimum age is 18. Average cost per day is between $95 and $100, and the student-to-instructor ratio is usually 12:1 (Box 173, Asbury, NJ 08802, tel. 908/479–4681, fax 908/479–6867).

FAVORITE COURSES

THE NORTHEAST

MAINE **Winter Backpacking.** The presence or absence of snow determines the itinerary of this 8-day course in Maine's Mahoosuc Mountains, part of the White Mountain National Forest near the New Hampshire border. No leisurely cross-country ski trip this. Whether or not the ground is white, this is a day-to-day match with the elements, all the more rigorous because almost everyone participating is a neophyte. If there's no snow, the focus is on hiking and winter ecology. If you do have snow, you also go cross-country skiing and snowshoeing.

Heaping portions of oatmeal, pasta with dried spaghetti sauce, real butter, sausage, and other goodies fuel these exertions. Your daily intake is a whopping 6,000 calories: You need the extra fats and carbohydrates to manufacture and sustain warmth. To further ensure that everyone is toasty, Outward Bound provides all the winter equipment, from parkas and boots to sleeping bags and, because this is Outward Bound, tarps instead of tents. You have a typical Outward Bound solo (you may have to break through a stream or melt snow to get more water than you have brought), followed by a marathon—a 6-mile snowshoe race and 11-mile cross-country ski dash. Courses begin in Newry, Maine. Minimum age is 16. *Outward Bound, Rte. 9D, R2, Box 280, Garrison, NY 10524-9757, tel. 914/424–4000 or 800/243–8520, fax 914/424–*

4280. Dec.–Mar.: 8 days, $795. Sign up 3 months in advance.

THE MID-ATLANTIC

NEW JERSEY The Tracker's Standard Course. For 7 days, you get up every morning at 5, turn in at 10 or 11, and spend the hours in between listening to lectures on nature observation, tracking, survival, and Native American philosophy—and practicing what you've learned. Even the simplest walk between buildings becomes a learning experience: You can practice fox-walking, a balanced gait that allows you to move soundlessly through the forest and should induce a dynamic meditation (like tai chi).

The instruction—mostly in the classroom—revolves around how to recognize the abundance that surrounds you outdoors. You learn how to make a fire with a bow drill, set traps, tan hides, stalk animals, make simple tools out of rocks, and identify edible plants. There is also a sweat lodge, a sort of Native American ritual sauna. Because the course is only a week long, however, you are *not* out in the woods: You bundle up in your own sleeping bag in the hay barn at night or bring your own tent and camp.

Expect oatmeal for breakfast and vegetarian or meat stew for lunch and dinner, with peanut butter and jelly or spaghetti as special treats. One of the week's culinary highlights is fish you've gutted and cleaned yourself. Courses are held in Asbury, New Jersey; about 80 students participate. *Tom Brown, The Tracker, Inc., Box 173, Asbury, NJ 08802, tel. 908/479–4681, fax 908/479–6867. Mar.–Sept.: 7 days, $650. Sign up 6–12 months in advance.*

NEW JERSEY The Tracker's Advanced Standard Course. Like the Standard Course, Tom Brown's Advanced Standard Course requires its students to rouse themselves before dawn and work until well after nightfall. Out in the sandy-soiled, brushy, pine- and oak-dominated Pine Barrens, all 60 novices build their own debris shelter, a simple, efficient hut that can save your life

in a survival situation. Instruction takes place in a group hut or under a tarp.

During this course, you rarely venture far from the base camp. Instead, you spend your time under the tutelage of Tom Brown, 5 full-time teachers, and visiting instructors, all of whom coach you in how to make water bowls, utensils, and grass tepees, and other elaborate survival skills. By the end of the week, you are using the chipping stone and blankets you've made instead of the knife and sleeping bag you brought.

Brown advises sleeping in a cool environment and getting in shape before attending this class, which makes the transition from recreational camping to full survival living. The Standard Course is a prerequisite. *Tom Brown, The Tracker, Inc., Box 173, Asbury, NJ 08802, tel. 908/479–4681, fax 908/479–6867. July and Oct.: 7 days, $700. Sign up 3–4 months in advance.*

THE SOUTH

NORTH CAROLINA Appalachian Mountain Adventures. In a very short distance, the North Carolina landscape changes from lowland rhododendron forests near gushing waterfalls to 5,000-foot mountain areas above the tree line where it's just rocks and horizon. The state also has some of the nation's best white-water rafting and rock climbing. The North Carolina OB School takes advantage of this terrain for its courses. In programs that range from a 4-day immersion course (the shortest) to a 4-week adventure, you do backpacking, rappelling, ropes work, rock climbing, and canoeing.

Just as the terrain changes, so does the weather. Summer, the most consistent season, tends toward daytime highs in the 80s and nighttime lows in the 60s—but it rains. Spring and fall are beautifully clear most of the time but cooler—in the 50s to 70s by day, into the 30s to 50s at night. Flowers are in bloom from late April through early June, and fall puts on its show from mid-September to late October.

This course includes a service project, underscoring the school's commitment to helping others. Projects range from trail maintenance to helping return peregrine falcons to the wild. Special courses are available for women or parents with children. All courses begin in Asheville, NC. *Outward Bound, Rte. 9D, R2, Box 280, Garrison, NY 10524-9757, tel. 914/424–4000 or 800/243–8520, fax 914/424–4280. Mar.–Nov.: 8 days, $895; 16 days, $1,795; 23 days, $2,195; 28 days, $2,495. Sign up 3 months in advance.*

THE SOUTHWEST

ARIZONA **Vision Quest Trek.** Although the nonprofit Reevis Mountain School is small, its reputation extends throughout the world of wilderness skills and survival school teachers. Founder Peter Bigfoot, so-called because of his size 15 feet, is an expert on medicinal and edible plants.

The school, 3 hours east of Phoenix, offers more than a dozen weekend courses that focus on self-reliance skills and natural healing, everything from stone masonry and Oriental touch-healing to one called Zen and the Art of Land Navigation. You are provided 2 meals a day. Bring your own camping equipment or pay $5 extra a night to sleep in Reevis tepees. After taking weekend courses on plant identification, natural healing, and desert survival, or the like, you become eligible to join the Self-Discovery Club ($680). The 7-day Vision Quest Trek, where you put these skills to the test as you hike along Native American trails dating from America's early mining days, is free to members.

Trek participants start each day with meditation before sunrise, then pack up camp and walk several miles before breakfast. You hike from 4 to 14 miles a day (sometimes walking on even after dark), and climb a 5,800-foot mountain pass. Peter, who is always personally on hand, allows a pound of food per person in the communal cache, which includes mainly rice, pasta, oatmeal, and the like. You learn to find sources for water and other food, foraging for prickly pear and hedgehog cactus, small rodents and snakes, agave and onion bulbs in spring, and mesquite tree leaves and cactus fruit in fall. You sleep in sleeping bags under the stars. Vision Quest Treks are limited to 10 people, with one instructor per group. Participants must be in good physical shape. *Reevis Mountain School, HCO2, Box 1534, Roosevelt, AZ 85545, tel. 602/467–2675; writing is preferable, since the phone rings 10 miles away from the school. Apr., Oct.: 7 days, $680. Sign up 2–3 months in advance.*

TEXAS **White-Water Canoeing and Desert Backpacking.** An indigenous myth tells the story that God made the world and put all the leftovers in Big Bend. The stark southern Texas landscape boasts beautiful combinations of white, yellow, and red volcanic soil mixed with basalt. Fossil-filled limestone cliffs and adobe buildings that predate East Coast settlements mark this land that served as a hunting ground for nomadic tribes, such as the Comanche and the Apache.

Set against this background is a 14-day course from the Voyageur Outward Bound School, a week of white water followed by a week of backpacking. Part of the time, since the river runs alongside a road, cars may be within sight. Sometimes, however, all you'll see is the 500-foot canyon wall or the 8,000-foot Mexican mountains in the background.

The first week, while not physically difficult, demands your attention as you master the art of reading the water and learn to recognize from the patterns on its surface the location of rocks and other obstacles. In this Outward Bound program, the water is the place you confront your fears, so the very first thing your instructor makes you do is to dump your boat and learn to swim in the current.

On the backpacking segment, climbers typically scale a 50- to 80-foot cliff. While exact hiking routes vary, most ascend into high piñon pine and juniper forests or traverse rugged mesas. Packs on this trip are on the heavy side because of the extra water—up to 2 gallons—that you must carry.

Throughout the course, you use tarps, not tents, except when the bugs are out—which is not often, at least while you're backpacking. Weather varies with the season: October can be quite hot; in December and January temperatures often drop below freezing at night and in March, the mercury might top 102°F—or you might have a light snow. Some sessions include a service day—when, for example, you help out in a Mexican orphanage. If you're interested in this, be sure you make it clear on your application. Courses begin in El Paso, TX. *Outward Bound, Rte. 9D, R2, Box 280, Garrison, NY 10524-9757, tel. 914/424-4000 or 800/ 243- 8520, fax 914/424-4280. Dec., Jan., Feb., Mar., Oct.: 14 days, $1,495; 21 days, $1,695. Sign up 3 months in advance.*

UTAH **Earth Skills in Forest and Canyon.** The BOSS Earth Skills I Course doesn't test your mettle against the elements on an extended trek; instead, it teaches you self-sufficiency out of 2 base camps. The first camp sits among the sagebrush and cottonwood of a desert canyon; the second, in an aspen forest on a mountaintop. You sleep in sleeping bags in natural caves in the desert, and in wickiups in the forest. Staff members do the cooking—BOSS meals emphasize natural grains and unprocessed foods, so you can remain healthy and concentrate on the lessons at hand: setting traps, making fires without matches, building shelters, creating tools of bone and stone, learning about local flora and fauna, and much more.

Earth Skills II picks up where you left off and teaches more advanced arts: bow and arrows, atlatls, hafted tools, etc. After that, there's Aboriginal Living Skills, a 2-week course which give you 1 week of skills and preparation followed by 1 week in the desert with only the items you've made previously: no knives, blankets, or water bottles.

Although there's no extensive travel during Skills Courses, you do move about and must be prepared to hike between 3 and 6 miles to gather materials needed for instruction. The courses are kept small, with about 12 participants and 2 instructors per section. Courses

begin and end in Boulder, Utah. If you want to use your skills on an expedition, sign up for a BOSS Field Course (*see below*). *BOSS, Inc., Box 1590, Boulder, CO 80306, tel. 303/444-9779, fax 303/442-7245. June– Aug.: 7 days, $675. Sign up 6 weeks in advance.*

UTAH **BOSS Field Course.** Imagine leaving behind the world of fast food, cell phones, talk shows, and crowded cities for a 27-day primitive desert expedition. Traveling light and fast, you will hike through canyon rivers, climb slickrock mountains, and experience some of America's most astounding backcountry using the skills and knowledge developed by traditional cultures around the world.

Regardless of its length (whether 7, 14, or 27 days), each BOSS Field Course is highly structured with 5 or 6 components: orientation, impact, group expedition, solo, student expedition, and a final expedition or celebration. During the impact phase, you hike over rugged terrain with only the clothes on your back, drinking the water you come across on the trail, and sleeping wherever night finds you. It's an acclimatization period, a time for getting used to the local alkaline water, natural foods, and the cold desert nights. The experience shows every student how well people can adapt and overcome strenuous situations. By the middle of the course, everyone thoroughly appreciates the luxury of having a blanket.

During the next phase, the group expedition, each student carries only a small blanket pack, a water bottle or two, a knife, extra clothing, and a little food. You soon begin to feel a bit run down, just enough to recognize what a little deprivation feels like and how it affects problem-solving abilities. Learning to find solutions to challenges despite the strain builds self-confidence.

Your band travels from food cache to food cache, setting up base camp occasionally on the longer Field Courses. To make the experience feel more like a real-life survival situation, only the instructors know how far away the next cache is. Foraging for food is encouraged but must be kept in check to maintain a balance in the fragile desert ecosystem. BOSS students prepare meals from the 1,500-calorie-per-day food packs that the school supplies—using rice, wheat flakes, mixed flours, and amaranth, you prepare meals that resemble those consumed by the ancient peoples of the canyons. On the 14- and 27-day courses, you slaughter a sheep, scrape its hide, and use all the parts for food, basic material, and/or tools.

The group expedition is followed immediately by a solo period which gives you a chance to relax, practice the skills you've recently acquired, and work on a gift you must make for another student. Some students opt to try a vision quest—a Native American rite of passage conducted in solitude. While participants are alone in both cases, a subtle monitoring system insures everyone's safety.

On 14- and 27-day Field Courses, the final celebration, at which students present each other with their creations and discuss the impact of the past 4 weeks, is preceded by an extended hike and night run. On most BOSS programs, the student-to-staff ratio is 6:1. Courses begin and end in Boulder, Utah. *BOSS, Inc., Box 1590, Boulder, CO 80306, tel. 303/444–9779, fax 303/442–7245. June–Aug.: 7 days, $725; June, Aug.: 14 days, $1,275; July: 27 days, $1,925. Sign up 6–8 weeks in advance.*

UTAH **Rainbow Bridge Hiking.** The food is good on this trip from Earth Treks, a small adventure travel company founded in 1990: You're served bagels with almond butter or cream cheese, granola with fruit, or oatmeal for breakfast; tuna salad, hummus in pita bread, or dips and chips for lunch; noodles, burritos, chili, or spaghetti and fruit rolls for dinner. Among wilderness skills schools, whose fare is notoriously basic, this makes Earth Treks a luxury operation.

Still, you get the instruction you need to camp safely and feel comfortable in the wild. Earth Treks proprietor Buck O'Herin, who leads the trips, has been doing this for more than 15 years and has advanced wilderness first aid and rescue training under his belt. Although you're welcome to pitch in, he and his co-cook are the ones to thank for the food. Groups usually number only 9 people, most in their 30s and 40s. Some are newcomers to the great outdoors, and some are simply eager to acquire enough skills to go backpacking on their own.

The group assembles in Flagstaff for the long drive into Utah, where you pick up a trail on the Navajo reservation that you follow for 26 miles during the next week. No experience is necessary. Hiking is rated easy to moderate: usually you cover from 3 to 5 relatively level miles per day at a leisurely pace. There's normally plenty of time to explore the beautiful sandstone canyons and creek beds en route. The ultimate destination is Rainbow Bridge, 300 feet high with a span of about 200 feet and one of the largest natural stone arches in the world. Bring a bathing suit to swim in the lake by the arch or to splash around in one of the area's many small pools. *Earth Treks, RFD 2, Box 785, Thorndike, ME 04986, tel. 800/489–4770 or 207/589–4311. May and Oct. trips: 8 days, $740. Sign up 2 months in advance.*

THE ROCKIES

COLORADO **Winter Skills and Simple Comforts in the San Juans.** High in the San Juan Mountains, at 11,500 feet between Ouray and Silverton and a mile's ski from civilization, a cozy lodge created from recycled materials sits in the shell of an 1889 mine building. The lodge, owned by Chris George, is your base for a trip that's a total immersion in backcountry skiing. It has composting toilets and no electricity, but you do have hot water, a sauna, and you sleep in either private or shared rooms. You must bring your own sleeping bag. The chef, who once cooked for Charlie Chaplin, dishes up hearty fare to warm body and soul: Breakfasts are hot cereals and eggs and bacon or pancakes; lunches are soups and sandwiches; and dinners, cooked on an antique propane stove, incorporate fresh vegetables into dishes such as tarragon chicken and lasagna. Whole-grain bread is baked fresh every day. Wine is permitted, but its consumption is not recommended—at least early in the program, since it interferes with acclimatization.

Ski outings are scheduled twice daily, one each in the morning and in the afternoon. Tours may go to old mining camps, up to the high passes, or to a summit. The group splits up according to ability, so beginners usually spend mornings in classes going over basics, while more experienced skiers might learn the nuances of telemark or downhill parallel turns. Every day, after the afternoon outing, leaders Bill Donahue and Dana Densmore offer a different hour-long lecture on wilderness skills. Their 6-part program covers hypothermia and how to treat it, proper clothing and equipment, navigation during white-out conditions, how to build a snow cave, and, if you have time, how to get a fire going in the snow. Chris George, who serves as one of the guides, is also an avalanche expert. He instructs on the physics of avalanches and avalanche safety, based on the teachings of the well-respected Silverton Avalanche School. The price includes use of skis, boots, and poles, as well as food and lodging. Maximum group size is 12, and no experience is necessary. Departure is from Montrose, Colorado. *Earth Treks, RFD 2, Box 785, Thorndike, ME 04986, tel. 800/589–4770 or 207/589–4311. Mar.: 7 days, $925. Sign up 2 months in advance.*

WYOMING **Range Backpacking and Wilderness Skills in the Wind River.** Pack animals, either horses or goats, lighten your load on this program, which treks along at 8,000 to 10,000 feet in the spectacular Wind River Wilderness that bridges the Shoshone and Bridger-Teton national forests. The area, known for its glacially sculpted U-shaped valleys, is thick with wildlife. It's possible to spot deer, elk, pronghorn antelope, marmots, hawks, maybe even moose and bear.

Since you have just 2 weeks, the course concentrates on basic skills, such as minimum-impact camping, rather than the compass

work and cross-country travel that are keystones of most NOLS courses; but you usually learn a few unusual techniques, including the Tyrolean traverse—a thrilling river-crossing method. The trek goes into boulder fields and dense forests and along some not-so-well-trodden trails. The first days out, you average a few miles each day with a lot of ups and downs. By the end of the course, you may cover over 6 miles on an average day. Depending on the group, the season, and the weather, the trip may include the ascent of a peak, fly-fishing, rock climbing, or snow travel.

While there's not a lot of free time, the instructors do try to schedule layover days when you can sleep past the usual 6 AM wake up. Layover days also give instructors a chance to lead a morning bird class or help those who fish practice their casts. Most of the leaders know their natural history well and teach wildflower identification, basic geology, tracks, and animal signs.

Lunches and dinners are typical NOLS fare, with the occasional freshly caught trout (if you're lucky) and salads of spring beauty, mountain bluebell, or other wild edibles. The weather in the northern Rockies is variable, with occasional great fluctuations between daytime and nighttime temperatures. It can snow at any time, or it could be a balmy 80°F out of the wind. In general, weather is wetter for courses earlier in the year, making stream crossings more challenging. The warmer weather later on brings its own problem: bugs. Course departs from Lander, Wyoming. *NOLS, 288 Main St., Lander, WY 82520-0579, tel. 307/332–6973, fax 307/332–1220. June–Aug.: 14 days, $1,750. Sign up 3–4 months in advance.*

THE WEST COAST

CALIFORNIA **Desert Backpacking and Bouldering in Joshua Tree.** Boulder-choked canyons, craggy rock formations, and the eerie, spiky, spare silhouettes of the Joshua tree mark the national monument named for the unusual tree yuccas, a kind of succulent. Because of the solidity of the rock and the reliability of the weather, it's one of the world's best-known climbing sites—and the Pacific Crest Outward Bound School uses it to good advantage. This exploration course, which follows OB's standard structure, mixes backpacking, rock climbing, and bouldering (climbing over big boulders). Joshua Tree National Monument, because its terrain is so unusual, nurtures a profound sense of solitude that's different from that of a forested area. Because the mountains are low (about 5,000 feet) summit ascents are a possibility; alternatively, if the weather's not good, it's easy to drop lower into the desert to stay warm. January, for instance, can be cold—or warm enough to be in short sleeves out of the wind. Because the dates do not coincide with school summer vacation periods, the course attracts an older crowd. The average age ranges from mid-20s to late 40s. Courses begin at Palm Springs, California. *Outward Bound, Rte. 9D, R2, Box 280, Garrison, NY 10524-9757, tel. 914/424–4000 or 800/243–8520, fax 914/424–4280. Mar., Apr., Sept., Oct., and Dec.: 7 days, $995. Sign up 3 months in advance.*

ALASKA

NORTHEAST **By Canoe through the Brooks Range.** The Arctic National Wildlife Refuge, the locale of this course, is home to more caribou than canoers and kayakers. On some days, 500 of the animals may loom ahead; on other days, only one or two. And although the group rarely runs into people, a noticeable number of small planes drone across the sky. It's the primary method of transportation in this remote area north of the Arctic Circle.

Though experienced paddlers do sign up for this 125-mile canoe journey on the Sheenjek River, it is designed for beginners. The route, which begins at the tree line in the mossy tundra, moves south through the cool boreal forest. Spruce and willows give way to alder, aspen, birch, and poplars. Blueberries, cranberries, and cloudberries sometimes grow along the riverbank. July usually brings tundra flowers; August, the changing of the seasons. Unfortunately, the long nights of twilight don't guarantee summer weather: A calm, sunny 65°F day may be followed by a run of freezing nighttime temperatures. Gentle afternoon showers with rainbows are more common than downpours.

During the first few days, along with basic camping how-to, you learn about paddling, equipment care, paddle signals and communication, and bears. You find out how rivers flow and how to pack a boat. The hardest part, at first, is staying in water deep enough so wading isn't necessary. But then, the Sheenjek is joined by tributaries that increase its water volume and transform it from a relatively easy Class I stream into a waterway with some reasonably demanding Class II waters. Then, the challenges begin. (*See* River Rafting for definitions of classifications.) Waking and sleeping times that vary with the weather, paddling under the midnight sun, and 6-hour day after 6-hour day on the river, push students to their limit. Layover days offer a chance to hike or fish for grayling. Campfires are permitted in certain places. So unlike many wilderness courses, there's a certain romance intact here—especially if you hear the wolves howling in the night. Courses begin in Fairbanks. *NOLS, 288 Main St., Lander, WY 82520-0579, tel. 307/332–6973, fax 307/332–1220. July–Aug.: 14 days, $2,650. Sign up 5–6 months in advance.*

NORTHWEST **A Backpacking and Rafting Expedition in the Gates of the Arctic.** Lying entirely north of the Arctic Circle in the Brooks Range, the Gates of the Arctic National Park and Preserve boasts hundreds of square miles without trails except animal tracks. It's an area that's as rugged as it is remote. And it's one of the few areas where Outward Bound students routinely sleep in tents, primarily because of bears, insects, and the unpredictability of the weather.

The whole course is modified to the environment, so instead of the standard OB rock-climbing activities or ropes work, students focus on the expedition skills necessary to get safely from one place to another. The solo is also altered: You stay out for only part of a day, in the high country away from known bear territory. There's no standard marathon at the end of the course, either. The food tends to be a little better, too; you'll eat corn-bread biscuits, tortillas, pizza, and other baked goods.

The first 10 days of this 18-day program have you trekking across the tundra, both cross-country and on trails that are used regularly but not marked or officially maintained, into an area of low peaks, where the views are truly amazing. Tree line begins at about 2,500 feet in this part of the world. Because you are so far north, the sun barely dips below the horizon; the nighttime twilight allows you to hike long past the hour that OB students elsewhere have turned in. As the hike ends, you descend to the Koyukuk River to learn river skills and, off-river, natural history. In drier and warmer July, insects can be numerous, but so are the tundra flowers. By August, the flowers thin out and the treed landscape looks like a miniature autumn forest; it can snow at any time. You may spot Dall sheep and wolves in the high country and ptarmigan, moose, caribou, and foxes on the river. Courses begin in Fairbanks. *Outward Bound, Rte. 9D, R2, Box 280, Garrison, NY 10524-9757, tel. 914/424-4000 or 800/243-8520, fax 914/424-4280. June–Aug.: 18 days, $2,995. Sign up 3 months in advance.*

SOURCES

ORGANIZATIONS The nonprofit **Wilderness Education Association** (20 Winona Ave., Box 89, Saranac Lake, NY 12983, tel. 518/891-2915, ext. 254) promotes wilderness education at the college level. Membership includes a subscription to "WEA Legend," a quarterly newsletter.

PERIODICALS "Compass: The Outward Bound Alumni Newsletter" (Rte. 9D, R2, Box 280, Garrison, NY 19524-9757, tel. 800/243-8520, fax 914/424-4280) is a slim, 16-page newsletter published 2 or 3 times a year and distributed free to alumni. It is devoted to alumni news, instructor profiles, updates on land use, course descriptions, and journal entries. Many wilderness education instructors read the *Journal of Experiential Education* (2885 Aurora Ave. #28, Boulder, CO 80303, tel. 303/440-8844, fax 303/440-9581), published three times a year by the Association for Experiential Education (whose members are people involved in wilderness and other outdoor programs).

BOOKS *The New Wilderness Handbook,* second edition, is edited by Paul Petzoldt—founder of NOLS and considered the grand old man of wilderness education. The *Outward Bound Map & Compass Handbook,* by Glenn Randall, teaches you how to get from here to there and back again. Although it can't substitute for actually taking the course, the *Outward Bound Wilderness First-Aid Handbook,* by Jeff Isaac and Peter Goth, is a good reference guide. Not a guidebook but a thoughtful exploration of the area and its people, *The Pine Barrens,* by John McPhee, is definitely worth reading if you're planning to take one of The Tracker's courses. To get an idea of what you've signed up for, read *Tom Brown's Field Guide to Wilderness Survival,* by Tom Brown, Jr., a good introduction to his philosophy of survival in the outdoors. Its sequel, *Tom Brown's Field Guide to Nature Observation and Tracking,* by Tom Brown, Jr., focuses more on The Tracker's methods. Feeling inspired? *The Tracker,* by Tom Brown, Jr., as told to William Jon Watkins, is Tom Brown's autobiography of his early years—from meeting his mentor, Stalking Wolf, to the time he left home.

ALSO SEE Many of the skills you acquire in wilderness and survival schools can be used on other trips into the backcountry. Check out the chapters on Canoeing and Kayaking in Flat Water, Canoeing and Kayaking in White Water, Climbing and Mountaineering, River Ráfting, Sea Kayaking, and Cross-Country Skiing.

Windsurfing Schools

By Melissa Rivers

If you haven't tried windsurfing yet, you haven't been left behind. Also known as boardsailing and sailboarding, windsurfing was invented in California in the late 1960s and is still in its infancy, with new equipment, maneuvers, and teaching methods emerging almost every day. While the sport looks easy, it is actually quite tricky: You need balance and stamina, much as you do in surfing and skiing, and an understanding of wind, current, and wave variables, as in sailing.

Too many sports in one? The easiest, quickest, and least frustrating way to pick up skills is through professional lessons at one of the many outstanding schools around the country. Most people who try to teach themselves the sport get frustrated and quickly lose interest. A professional instructor will get the basics across and have you up and sailing in no time so that you get more experience on the water and more enjoyment out of your vacation. That's where inclusive learning packages come in. These packages provide everything from professional instruction to equipment rental, ground transportation, accommodations, dining, and alternative activities to fill those windless days.

Instructors, who have been trained to teach by a variety of equipment companies such as Mistral and Bic, follow different methods, but most break down windsurfing skills into easily understood components learned on a dry-land simulator (a sailboard mounted on a swiveling platform that simulates the experience of being on water). You'll get a feel for proper stance and learn to uphaul the sail, tack and jibe, and perform a self-rescue before ever touching the water. And in a very short time, you'll be out there, zipping back and forth on your own, enjoying the thrill of controlling wind in your sail. An average of 3 hours of daily instruction, both on land and water, often includes being videotaped while you're testing your skills in the surf. This is followed by practice, solo, for as long as your strength holds out. Class size is often limited to 4 or 5 participants at the beginning and intermediate levels; advanced techniques are generally taught on a one-to-one basis.

When there is some breeze, you can sail in virtually any body of water, from inland lakes—ideal for learning because of their warm, flat waters—to open ocean, where swells and chop offer bump-and-jump challenges for experienced sailors. In selecting a windsurfing program, most people look for one in a destination that is appealing as a vacation spot and that offers conditions suitable for their particular sailing level. Beginners look for easier areas such as inlets and coves or calmer waters protected by a reef. Intermediate and advanced sailors need the challenges of big winds and waves to increase their knowledge of advanced maneuvers.

Melissa Rivers is a freelance writer who makes her home not far from one of the world's top windsurfing destinations, the Gorge.

In the Columbia River Gorge, mecca of boardheads the world over, there are more than 50 sailing locations and a variety of conditions, from heavy winds and large, choppy waves off expert locations like Swell City to calmer, shallower waters such as the Hood River Marina, where beginners will feel comfortable getting their feet wet. The Gorge (as it's known in the windsurfing world) is a research, manufacturing, and production zone for windsurfing equipment, and many school operators there purchase new equipment every season, giving you access to the hottest new boards, sails, and other paraphernalia.

Maui, another world-class windsurfing destination, offers warm waters and strong sideshore winds in a lush tropical setting. Because of rulings prohibiting concessions on the beach, you're generally required to pick up equipment in one location and transport it to the water yourself to meet instructors.

Although the Gorge and Maui top the lists, there are many other windsurfing destinations to choose from. Puerto Rico, one of the best-kept secrets in the industry, has consistent trade winds and clear waters sheltered by barrier reefs. The U.S. Virgin Islands are equally inviting, with similarly conducive conditions suitable for year-round sailing. Hidden surfside locations in Northern Baja that used to be known only to the pros are "in" now; there's an operator who takes intermediate and advanced sailors on weeklong journeys to enjoy the tremendously challenging waves and winds. Protected inland lakes and waterways in Florida and California are easier for learning, while the challenging wind and wave conditions of the Atlantic and the Pacific offer something for advanced sailors.

For the most part, instructors are in their 20s or 30s, certified to teach windsurfing, and have had several years of instructional experience, as well as Red Cross lifesaving, first aid, and CPR training. It may be an odd picture to see them teaching the average student, who is a fairly well-to-do professional between 30 and 50, but the enthusiasm that brought them to the sport is contagious and forms a bridge between the generations. They, like their students, are physically active, and usually aficionados of biking, skiing, snowboarding, rollerblading, and other solo outdoor sports.

The cost of a trip like this varies greatly, but on the average a week of windsurfing costs around $700. Ground transportation is usually part of the package: A bus or van is used to carry gear and shuttle students between the learning site and lodgings, out for meals, and to slack-day activities when they are included in the package.

CHOOSING THE RIGHT SCHOOL

In picking a windsurfing school, it's important to ask these questions:

How long has your school been in operation? You want an experienced outfit with a good reputation, not a fly-by-night school with inexperienced instructors. There are no industry regulations for windsurfing schools, but those around for at least 3 years are generally your best bet.

Do you have references from past guests?

What is the location like? Is your lesson site good for beginner, intermediate, or advanced students? Intermediate and advanced students should look for challenging conditions (high winds, big waves) needed to increase skill level. Beginners, however, will do better on flat, calm waters with steady but mild breezes. Warm water and a sandy bottom add to your comfort when just starting out.

Are lessons available for all skill levels?

What are the teacher's qualifications? It's much better to have a professional teacher, rather than the school's temporary summertime helper, instructing you. The professionals are certified, meaning that they have been trained to teach all levels of skill and specifically introductory techniques.

Are land simulators used? Land simulators are boards and rigs set up on land to give you the feel of a particular movement (or set of movements) before you get in the water. Practicing the basics on a simulator cuts the learning time down considerably.

How much time is spent on land and on water learning? Beginners usually spend about a third of the class time on land getting a feel for the basic skills before hitting the water. Intermediate and advanced students should look for a school that emphasizes in-water instruction.

Is the equipment current? Equipment changes frequently—with modifications in designs to make sailing easier and faster—so it's best to learn on the latest gear rather than old gear that will just slow you down.

Must I rig and carry the equipment? Several schools rig the equipment themselves to get you on the water as soon as possible; others want you to learn to rig and have you do it yourself each time.

What's the cost and what's included? All prices listed are per person, double occupancy, and include lodging, equipment, meals, and airport transfers unless noted otherwise. Every program, however, is run slightly differently, so check carefully before booking your trip. Occasionally, personal gear (harness, wetsuit, gloves, booties or sailing shoes, and so on) is included in the package. Several schools are moving away from inclusive packages, but do provide assistance in booking nearby accommodations, often at discounted rates; if the school you're interested in no longer offers an inclusive package, you'll be on your own for meals and transportation as well.

Is a rental car necessary? Most outfitters transport the gear to the water, but there are schools that require you to have a car to transport the equipment. Obviously, this will add to the expense of your trip; however, renting a car gives you the flexibility to have a meal on your own or go sightseeing.

Are alternative activities available on windless days? You don't want to waste your vacation just because there's no wind, so pick a school that provides alternative activities to fill those slack days.

Do you have child-size equipment? If you plan to travel with children, make sure that smaller boards are available.

What is the food like? There is a huge variation in the dining options on these trips— from hamburger cookouts to homecooked buffet meals to eating in restaurants.

What are accommodations like? Some schools put you up in tents, others in hotels or bed-and-breakfasts. Each outfitter does things differently so ask ahead so you know what to expect.

Will laundry service be available?

How far in advance do I need to book? All operators will sell space as available up to the last moment, but you should try to book at least 60 to 90 days ahead to make sure you get a spot, especially during peak seasons.

FAVORITE SCHOOLS

THE SOUTH

FLORIDA **The Sailboard School.** Fast tack, flare, carved jibes, water-starts, and beach-starts are covered in this 5-day program that uses 3 types of teaching simulators and extensive video analysis. The school maintains a fleet of current Bic and Fanatic boards and sails suited for varying ability levels, giving even experienced sailors an opportunity to test their skills on equipment they've never tried before.

Since there are typically only 4 students per session, you receive lots of personal coaching from Burr and Patty Hazen and their assistant, all Mistral-trained instructors, who spend the entire day with you. You learn to rig your own equipment, and before heading out into the shallow waters of Indian River Lagoon, they equip you with a radio receiver so that you can clearly hear instructions and advice while executing turns and other maneuvers. On-shore winds of 10 to 15 knots provide plenty of power for your sails, and as Patty can attest, there are virtually no flat days here.

Burr dropped out of Wall Street banking to open the Sailboard School in Portland, Maine, in 1981. After developing a 6-step teaching process to make learning the sport and its skills easier and quicker, he relocated the school in 1983. By moving to the east coast town of Sebastian near Vero Beach (about an hour and a half southeast of Orlando), the Hazens extended the sailing season.

Burr and Patty completely renovated the Florida Inn, a turn-of-the-century roadhouse, outfitting it as "ground school," where you'll review videos shot the day prior before heading outside to practice on dry-land simulators. Next it's on to the lagoon, where students pile into the water for lessons and free sailing for the remainder of the day. Most students are professionals (predominantly from the medical field) and are between the ages of 30 and 50; children under 18 are not accepted.

Lodging, meals, and local transportation are no longer part of the package here, but Patty, who is also a travel agent, can handle all the arrangements for you, short of packing a daily lunch. *The Sailboard School, 9125 U.S. 1, Sebastian, FL 32958, tel. 407/589–2671 or 800/253–6573, fax 407/589–7963. Year round: 5 days, $575; accommodations start at $50 per night. Sign up 2 weeks in advance.*

THE WEST COAST

CALIFORNIA ABK Rio Vista Camps. Following the precedent set by ski racing camps, ABK Sports began sending world-class windsurfers around the country in 1982 to teach multiple-day clinics. The company now runs about 30 very affordable sessions per year. Of those, 10 take place in Rio Vista, a well-known beginner-to-advanced sailing spot about 1½ hours north of San Francisco, in rolling delta country. New sailors may find the river location intimidating because of the winds and currents, but ABK does teach novice courses during the 4-day camp by using a protected, sand-bar site. Novice courses cover balance and stance, sail trimming, tacking, and jibing. If you already know the basics, you can learn to sail more confidently in a variety of conditions and work on advanced skills such as jumping, high-wind sailing, carved jibes and racing techniques. Up to 40 students attend each session.

Everything is provided, from tents and meals to instruction and use of up-to-date demo equipment (including booties, wetsuits, harnesses, and state-of-the-art Bic boards and UP sails). Days can begin early with a warm-up stretch followed by in-line skating, running, or mountain biking, or you can choose to sleep in. After a hearty breakfast, you're off to class on a protected grassy area across from the campground just above Windy Cove, a location with constant winds and a gradually dropping sandy floor. Lectures, demonstrations, and rigging practice fill the morning. Students are then divided into small groups (generally 5 per instructor) according to ability level for on-water instruction and practice. Afternoon lectures follow lunch, with the topic tailored to the day's conditions, then it's back to the water for practice drills and races. The day on the water is videotaped so that you can analyze your technique with the instructors after dinner.

There is a tremendous return rate here among students, who come back to hone skills and spend a fun holiday with like-minded friends. Kids are welcome, but those under 14 must be accompanied by a parent and all under 18 must have a signed release form. ABK also offers camps at other California sites and multiple east coast locations. *ABK Sports, 101 Casa Buena Dr., Suite F, Corte Madera, CA 94925, tel. 415/927–8835 or 800/996–2267, fax 415/927–7634. Late June–Aug.: 4 days, $385. Sign up at least 1 month in advance.*

OREGON Camp Surf–the Gorge. Despite the quaint name, Camp Surf, which offers one of the few all-inclusive windsurfing packages in the Gorge, is a full-service outfit; no hot dogs and camp outs on this trip. Owned and operated by Tom and Pam Wright, locals who know the Gorge inside and out, Camp Surf is a week-long program suitable for all skill levels. The camp accommodates no more than 15 students per week, allowing for plenty of personal attention from certified instructors who are good enough to take you from beginning lessons to water-starts before the week is out. The Wrights provide top-of-the-line equipment, including Bare wetsuits, Ezzy sails, and customized Hi-Fly boards; equipment is replaced every year.

To let you experience the wide variety of conditions in the Gorge, vans transport you to different windsurfing spots each day, including the Hook, the Wall, Maryhill, the Hatchery, and Doug's Beach. Instruction is unlimited—they stick with you until you learn it—and personalized, though you may share an instructor with 3 or 4 other students. Dry-land hook-and-foot simulators are used to teach beginners the basics before they enter the water. Once you do get wet, instructors stay right with you. Experienced sailors spend most of their time in the water perfecting techniques and picking up new skills while trying out Gorge Animal boards and other cutting-edge sailboarding equipment. Videos are taken and analyzed to help you learn. Days with little or no wind are filled with other group activities, including white-water rafting, mountain biking, and guided hikes—all covered by the package.

Guests stay at the waterfront Hood River Inn, a Best Western property remodeled in 1994. There's a swimming pool, a grassy area above the beach for land instruction, and a launch site for beginners. Most meals are covered in the package price, from hearty breakfasts at the inn and catered lunches on the road to full-service dinners in a different Hood River restaurant on five of the seven nights. Older teens (usually post-high school) are welcome when accompanied by a parent, but this program is really for adults. While visits to the River City Saloon and popular North Shore on the Washington side aren't included in the package, you might wrangle a van ride to these locations to take in the Gorge's active night scene. Camp Surf also offers a similar package that focuses on a different adventure sport each day, from windsurfing to snowboarding to rock climbing. *Camp Surf, Box 1526, Hood River, OR 97031, tel. 503/386–9090 or 800/927–3768, fax 503/386–9090. June–early-Sept.: 8 days, $1,050–$1,200; nonsailor 8-day package $300 less. Sign up at least 1 month in advance.*

OREGON **Heavy Air Gorge.** Intermediate sailors find their place at Joe and Lucy Field's Heavy Air Gorge. Based in Rowena, their waterfront property is a mile and a half down from the mouth of the Clickitat River, where the world speed-sailing records were set, and a mile and a half up from the swells and expert conditions of Doug's Beach. In other words, there are plenty of challenges here. An array of high-end equipment—Neil Pryde and Rush Wind sails, Dynafiber masts, Watson custom and Seatrend epoxy boards—waits pre-rigged for you on Joe and Lucy's private (and therefore uncrowded—unlike most in the Gorge) beach, so you can hit the water the moment the wind is up. This bonus allows you to try out a variety of equipment and to change gear rapidly and easily as the sailing conditions change.

Radar is used to clock your speeds, and a high power video camera puts you on tape. Daily coaching on land is part of the package; Joe will analyze your moves on video and give you pointers each evening, but he doesn't spend time with you on the water unless you request it (personalized water instruction may incur additional cost). Joe's Zodiac chase boat is on standby if you need a rescue, but advanced sailors seldom do.

Up to 10 guests per week can be accommodated in airy guest rooms in the detached guest lodge or in the main house on the waterfront. Meals are not included in the package (thus the low price), but there is a fully equipped kitchen for you to use and plenty of fine little restaurants a quick car ride away in Hood River. Children of all ages are welcome, so this is a viable option for sailboarding families. Those who don't windsurf can hike, relax in the beachside hot tub, or use the mountain bikes to explore the area. White-water rafting, horseback riding, and summer skiing and snowboarding outings can be arranged at additional cost. *Joe & Lucy Field's Heavy Air Gorge, 6005 Rowena River Rd., Rowena, OR 97058, tel. 503/298–1513 or 800/544–7211, fax 503/386–7077. May and Oct.: 8 days, $619. June and Sept.: 8 days, $719. July and Aug.: 8 days, $819. Prices do not include in-water instruction or meals; sign up 1–4 months in advance.*

OREGON **Vela's Ultimate Gorge Tour.** Established in 1986, Vela Windsurf Resorts was the first, and is now the largest, windsurfing vacation company in North America, operating windsurfing centers in 8 locations. In 1993, the company joined the ranks in the Gorge, and it now offers 1-week inclusive packages for advanced beginners to expert sailors. These include accommodations, equipment, instruction, and off-water activities. Under the watchful eye of manager Ernesto Monroy and his 4 instructors, each with years of Gorge experience, up to 14 students learn or perfect their skills in the sport using F2 and Seatrend boards and Neil Pryde sails. You'll need to bring your own wetsuit and harness.

Morning seminars on land are followed by on-the-water sessions with personal coaching and remote-assisted lessons at sites that offer the best wind and other conditions for your ability level. Instruction is given 3 or 4 hours each day and is usually followed by 2 to 4 hours of practice. Videos are taken and daily critiques of them accelerate your learning. To let you experience the wide variety of conditions in the Gorge, vans transport you and your gear to different locations—including the Hook, Maryhill, the Hatchery, and Doug's Beach—during the week. There's at least one white-water rafting trip per week, and flat days are filled with other group activities, such as mountain biking, wine-tasting tours, and a Mt. Hood scenic train ride, all included in the package price.

Guests stay at the waterfront Hood River Inn, a Best Western property remodeled in 1994. There's a swimming pool and a grassy area above the beach for land instruction. Most meals are covered in the package price, from hearty breakfasts at the inn and catered lunches on the road to full-service dinners in a different Hood River restaurant on four of the seven nights. Older teens (14 and up) are welcome when accompanied by a parent, but this program is really for adults. While visits to the River City Saloon and popular North Shore on the Washington side aren't included in the package, you might wrangle a van ride to these locations to take in the Gorge's active night scene. *Vela Windsurf Resorts, 351C Foster City Blvd., Foster City, CA 94404; tel. 415/525–2070 or 800/223–5443, fax 415/525–2086. Mid-June–mid-Sept.: 8 days, $1,195–$1,295. Prices do not include some meals; sign up at least 2–3 months in advance.*

HAWAII

MAUI **Excursions Extraordinaires on the North Shore.** Keith Nelson and Greg Young, owners of Excursions Extraordinaires, have been organizing windsurfing vacations since 1986 at centers in the Gorge, Maui, Baja, Costa Rica, Margarita, and Tobago. Surprisingly, their company is the only operator that provides an all-inclusive windsurfing vacation in Maui. The week-long package includes unlimited use of pre-rigged equipment, a private North Shore launch, ranch-style beachside lodging, breakfast and lunch, daily clinics, and personalized instruction. The program is better suited for intermediate and advanced sailors who want to pick up high wind and short-board skills, but is open to "determined beginners" as well.

The waterfront location between the famous sailing spots of Kanaha and Spreckelsville gives you the opportunity to experience the best of Maui's sailing conditions using the latest Bic Sport and Hi-Tech boards, Chinook booms, light carbon masts, and Ezzy sails. Afternoon trade winds blow at least 20 knots, especially April to September. Early mornings, fairly calm on Maui, are dedicated to hiking, biking, and snorkeling (rental gear is available). Late mornings and early afternoons are devoted to group instruction, private sessions, and free sailing time. Beginner and high-wind simulators are used on land, and instructors join you in the water. Special guest instructors such as Rhonda Smith-Sanchez, five-time world champion in women's windsurfing, are brought in a few times each season to conduct clinics.

Meals are served alfresco on the large, ocean-view deck of the guest house. There are theme lunches throughout the week with Western barbecue, Polynesian, Thai, Italian, and Mexican specialties; vegetarian options are always available. You sleep in one of the small, private cottages with narrow lanais that look out on the North Shore or in one of four simply furnished bedrooms (two with private bath) in the guest house. Just outside is a roomy hot tub to help you relax tired muscles after a long day on the water. Airport pickup is included in the price. Smaller equipment and special kids clinics make this suitable for families. *Excursions Extraordinaires, Box 5766, Eugene, OR 97405, tel. 503/686–4265 or 800/678–2252, fax 503/343–7507. Mid-Apr.–mid-Sept.: 7 days, $949. Price does not include dinners; sign up at least 2–3 months in advance.*

MAUI **Vela and Cort Larned Windsurfing School.** Unlike its packages in the Gorge, Vela Windsurf Resort's Maui packages are not all-inclusive. Vela explains your options and puts together the lodging and transportation portions of your trip; the equipment and teaching is left to Cort Larned Windsurfing School, based at the Maui Windsurf Company. Cort Larned and head instructor Keith Holland have a highly effective system of teaching that takes into consideration the high-wind conditions of the island and employs a number of high-tech devices to facilitate learning. Lessons are broken down into concise, logical components that are easy to understand, and class

size is kept to an average of 3 or 4 students per instructor.

Cort Larned Windsurfing School has produced a series of instructional videos that are used along with simulators for the on-land lessons. The expert staff (all with five or more years of teaching experience) use instructor-to-student radios to provide simultaneous guidance and feedback in novice sailing classes. Beginners are usually sailing back and forth within the first hour of practice. Instructors join intermediate students in the water for classes in high performance sailing, jibing, and water-starts (the latter guaranteed within 3 days or you continue lessons free of charge). Skilled sailors who rent equipment from Maui Windsurf Company can trade off as often as they like to experience all the hottest new boards and rigs including F2, Seatrend, and Maui-Built custom boards and Neil Pryde sails. The school also teaches children using smaller rigs, but kids must weigh at least 75 pounds and parents must remain on site during the lesson.

First you pick out equipment suitable for your size and ability at the school's headquarters about a half-mile from the beach. The staff there will outfit your rental car with racks and load up the equipment before sending you on to Kanaha Beach Park to meet your instructor. Classes actually take place on Cook's Beach, the longest and most upwind stretch of sand in Kanaha. There is a grassy staging area for rigging and shallow, flat water for learning on the calm side of the reef. Open sea beyond the reef is suitable for polishing wave-sailing techniques. Winds are light each morning (best for beginners) and pick up in the warm afternoon (a challenge for intermediate and advanced sailors). The 3- and 5-day lesson packages include 3 hours of morning or afternoon instruction (1 hour on land, the rest in the water) and unlimited use of equipment. Lessons do not have to be taken on consecutive days, so you can take time off to rest and sightsee. *Vela Windsurf Resorts, 351C Foster City Blvd., Foster City, CA 94404; tel. 415/525–2070 or 800/223–5443, fax 415/525–*

2086. Year-round instruction: 3- and 5-day packages, $170–$260; 7 days' lodging from $450. Prices do not include meals; sign up at least 2–3 months in advance.

BAJA CALIFORNIA

NORTHERN BAJA **Advanced Sailing and Camping in Northern Baja.** Advanced sailboarders looking for a new challenge should get ready for the playful surf of Northern Baja, where Kevin Trejo, owner of Solo Sports Excursions, teaches wave-sailing. For years the sailing spot featured on this trip remained a carefully guarded secret known only to an elite group of top windsurfers who were drawn to shred and jump in the wind and waves. Word has spread over the years, and now you run into determined sailors from around the world, but the spot's inaccessibility still keeps crowds away—it's a long haul on rough dirt roads, and since there are no services on this remote stretch of Baja Coast, you must bring everything you need with you. Solo Sports Excursions takes the work out of getting here, supplies all the basic necessities (tents, meals, equipment), and offers informal instruction in wave-sailing techniques during 6 full days.

Kevin has been visiting the same Baja location for over a decade; he learned wave-sailing here from pros like Kevin and Matt Pritchard and Bennett Williams. Once or twice a month, one of the top sailors on the professional circuits will take a break from his or her travels to join these trips and help out with instruction. The teaching method is fairly hands on, with dry-land, verbal explanations of the moves followed by work on the waves, where you watch and copy the instructor. Advanced sailors who can already water-start, complete 50% of their jibes, and swim safely in the surf without a personal flotation vest should have no problem picking up several new tricks in the brisk side-offshore winds and long, mellow breaking waves of the site.

The 8-day trip begins and ends in Irvine, California, and includes overnight accommodations at each end of the journey. Sturdy shuttle buses are used to haul a maximum of 10 sailors and their equipment to the site; you can either bring your own gear or use the Tiga and Hi-Tech boards, wave-sails by Ezzy and Neil Pryde and other top-notch gear that Solo Sports Excursions supplies. Tents are set on a desert bluff overlooking the surf, and solar showers are available to rinse off the saltwater. Camp meals are very hearty, from yogurt, cereals, fruit, pancakes, and eggs in the morning to deli-style sandwiches and salads for lunch and chicken, steaks, fish, or pasta dishes with vegetables and breads for dinner. This is not a trip for kids or beginners. *Solo Sports Excursions, 78 Blazewood, Foothill Rand, CA 92610, tel. 714/837–1396, fax 714/588–8356. Mid-Apr.–Oct.: 8 days, $1,095 ($200 less if you bring your own equipment). Price does not include airport transfers; sign up at least 30 days in advance.*

THE CARIBBEAN

PUERTO RICO **Ventolera School.** Eddie Rodriguez, presently ranked among the top windsurfers in Puerto Rico, runs a windsurf school through Ventolera Watersports in Lajas. In 1990, he started offering instruction and lodging packages from 5 days to one month. Instruction is at all levels, from the basics of rigging, balance, and turns to advanced slalom sailing, jibing, and water starts. His lessons are easy to understand and his equipment (Mistral boards and Raf and North rigs) is first-rate, but there's no doubt that it's the warm waters and sunny skies of this tropical paradise that are the main draw of this program.

While the shop and various guest-house accommodations are based in the quaint village of La Parguera in Lajas, actual instruction takes place on the first of three barrier reefs, about a mile off shore. Here steady trade winds blow at 12 to 15 knots across the crest, providing ample wind for sailing away from the reef. The back-reef lagoon, an ideal site for novices, seldom gets large waves and has an average depth of 3 feet of crystal clear water. Eddie and one other instructor teach a maximum of 8 students per session. They follow students by boat, calling out instructions as the group sails. Most students are professionals around 35 years old, but the school accepts children 10 and over who can swim (smaller rigs are available). Non-sailors are welcome.

Following morning simulator practice and a critique of your performance on the previous day, you leave the dock with board and rig and head out to the reef by boat. There you receive 3½ hours of instruction and practice time before returning for some relaxation. Free-time activities such as scuba diving, snorkeling, fishing, kayaking, and biking (all at additional cost) fill the afternoon.

There are numerous seafood restaurants and cafeterias in the village, but you need a rental car to get from the international airport in San Juan to Lajas and to do any sightseeing. Guest-house rooms are simply furnished, but very neat; all have private bath, several have air-conditioning, and one has a small kitchen and living room. A camping package is also available for those on a budget. Nightfall brings an impressive display put on by the area's unique bioluminescent organisms, so finish up dinner early and gather with locals and tourists to watch at the nearby bay. *Ventolera Windsurfing School, Box 386, Lajas, PR 00667, tel. 809/899–3030, fax 809/899–4698. Year-round: 5 days, $500; $150–$400 per day for nonsailors. Price does not include meals; sign up at least 1 month in advance.*

SOURCES

ORGANIZATIONS You can write to each of the following organizations for information on the best schools, instructors, and equipment rental shops in the vacation destinations of your choice: **Board Sailing USA** (Box 2157, Citrus Heights, CA 95611), the

International Windsurfer Class Association (1955 W. 190th St., Box 2950, Torrence, CA 90509), the **National Association of Sailboard Retailers & Instructors** (1000 E. Shore Dr., Ithaca, NY 14850), and the **United States Windsurfing Association** (Box 978, Hood River, OR 97031).

PERIODICALS *New England Windsurfing Journal,* published 10 times a year, covers sailboarding in the Northeast, with articles on destinations, schools, equipment news, and current events (Buzzwords Publishing, Box 2120, Southbury, CT 06488, tel. 203/264–9463). *Performance Windsurf Reports,* published six times a year, lists performance ratings on equipment and includes a travel directory for windsurfing schools and resorts in the western hemisphere (MBA Publishing, 2710 Belmont Dr., Hood River, OR 97031, tel. 503/386–3522). For distribution to subscribers, MBA also puts out *3.5: Windsurfing Guide to the Gorge* once a year. *The Gorge Guide* is a publication that describes the area's rental and retail shops, restaurants, and lodging (Gorge Publishing, Inc., Box 918, Hood River, OR 97031, tel. 503/386–7440; $3.95 plus postage). *WindSurfing Magazine* profiles equipment, destinations, and occasionally lists schools. It comes out eight times per year (World Publications Inc., 330 W. Canton Ave., Winter Park, FL 32789-3195, tel. 407/628–4802).

BOOKS *The Complete Guide to Windsurfing* (Facts On File Publications), by Jeremy Evans, is an instructional book on sailing and racing techniques that lists a few top windsurfing destinations. For coverage of sailing techniques, equipment selection, advice on where to go for the sport, even instructions on building your own board, try *The Windsurfing Funboard Handbook* (Barron's Educational Series, Inc.), by Clive Boden and Angus Chater.

ALSO SEE If, after getting your feet wet, windsurfing appealed to you, take a dip in the Sailing Schools and Surfing chapters.

Working Farms, Ranches, and Cattle Drives

By Erik Fair

f you picture yourself in a cowboy costume eating country cookin' or in bib overalls wringing milk out of a cud-chewing heifer while spinning yarns, you want a dude ranch or country-inn farm vacation.

But if you want something more—like a sore butt from riding too hard, bleary eyes from waking up with crowing roosters and bellowing cows, or the bone-deep satisfaction of bunking down at night knowing you've worked like hell and had the time of your life doing it—you may be hankering for a more challenging adventure: like a working farm vacation, a working ranch vacation, or even a real live cattle drive.

Each of the working farms and ranches listed in this chapter produces something for market. And each offers you either the possibility or the guarantee of hard, soul-satisfying work in extraordinarily beautiful surroundings. Most ranches and farms are relatively small family-owned operations run by family members or trusted hands in traditional or semitraditional ways, which means anything from preserving and using their own natural water resources to using their own fertilizer. All of this is more time-consuming and expensive than modern methods, so if the farm or ranch is to remain profitable, something (or someone) has to give.

One of those someones is you. The deal is more or less this: You become a temporary member of a hard-working American family that has at least partially preserved the romance of traditional farm and ranch life in this country. They get some of your honest labor and several hundred of your hard-earned dollars per week—anywhere from $300 to $1,200—to help make ends meet.

The kinds of farms and ranches that can give you a memorable vacation are not to be confused with the ultra-big, ultra-scientific farms and ranches that produce the majority of this country's meat, produce, and dairy products. From most vacationers' point of view, there is nothing earthy about fleets of million-dollar farm machines rolling over endless expanses of row crops that have been fertilized by tons of chemicals. There is nothing romantic about the stench of barren feedlots where thousands of cattle drink from metal troughs and consume vast amounts of high-nutrient grain that bring them to market weight as quickly as possible.

Some working farms are in rich agricultural areas like Kansas or Wisconsin. Others are nestled in the beautiful rolling hills of New England. Farmers raise every kind of produce under the sun and may also generate other products, such as milk, cream, eggs, chickens, hogs, and wool. Although riding horses is a part of farm life, learning how to

---

Adventurer and writer Erik Fair is the author of *California Thrill Sports*. He had his share of the farming life during several summers at High Valley Camp, a working farm near Mount Pisgah in North Carolina.

drive tractors, slop hogs, or use wooling shears is a bigger part. And hands-on exposure to the ageless interaction of land, weather, farm plants, farm animals, and sunup to sundown hard work is the biggest plus of all.

Most working ranches are out west, in valleys near the Great Rocky Mountains, or on the spectacular plains and foothills of Montana and Wyoming. Put most simply: Working ranches raise grass to feed cattle and cattle to feed humans and that's it. But don't underestimate what that entails. Cattle has to be rounded up for inspection, then there's grouping the cattle, calving, branding, pregnancy testing, castrating, and other stuff too gross to mention. Riding horses is a huge part of ranch life and the ability to use a horse is mighty useful when it comes time to inspect vast pastures, build or repair fences, or move the herd (or parts of the herd) from one place to another.

Moving cattle from pasture to pasture within the ranch itself is not to be confused with a cattle drive, when ranchers drive cattle to market or—more commonly—between summer and winter grazing areas. Cattle eat tons of grass all year. A rancher has to grow and store enough hay in the summer to feed the whole herd all winter long, but because ranchers can't grow winter feed on land that's being grazed by cattle in the summer, they need a gang of special cowboys called wranglers to drive the herd to a different "summer range" every spring. After the ranchers have grown, cut, and stored enough hay to feed the herd throughout the winter, they need another gang of wranglers to drive the cattle back home to their "winter range" every fall. Cattle drives vary a great deal depending on the distance between the winter and summer ranges and the type of terrain that separates them or the location of the best market.

Almost everything on a ranch or farm is constructed, arranged, and scheduled according to the day-to-day, season-to-season realities of caring for, growing, and delivering a product to market. Everything else has to do with

maintaining, improving, or preparing the ranch or farm to assure future production. Consequently, there is always the anticipation of the next big job at hand. The daily schedule is subject to last-minute changes, depending on the needs of the crop or animals—so there is the excitement of knowing you have to be on your toes, ready for anything. Best of all, there is the right-now intensity of knowing that certain jobs just have to get done no matter how long it takes or how bad the conditions. This is especially true if you've signed up for a multiday cattle drive with overnight camp outs.

The activities that you participate in almost always have a purpose beyond your personal pleasure. You may catch a brilliant sunset on your way back from a late ride to check fences, but odds are good you won't even think about riding out just to see the next sunset after a full day of taking part in the miracle of calving.

The bottom line is that a sense of purpose—a sense of productive participation in an age-old process that is far bigger than yourself—is what ultimately separates working farms and ranches from "farm theme" country inns and "cowboy spa" dude ranches.

Every farm, every ranch, and every cattle drive is different. Some offer basic accommodations and commitment to rugged work, while others offer plush accommodations and the opportunity to take the work or leave it, depending on your mood or preference. Some programs encourage participation by the whole family and provide baby-sitting services and kids' activities to prove it. Others merely tolerate children and leave child care and supervision entirely up to you. Take these options into consideration when choosing your trip—and get a good night's sleep before you go.

CHOOSING THE RIGHT TRIP

By and large, each farm, ranch, or cattle drive reflects the tastes, idiosyncrasies, and personalities of the owners or operators. The only way to know exactly what you're getting into is to ask detailed questions before you sign up.

What do you call yourself? Most places that identify themselves as working farms or working ranches really are, but the variation on the experience is limitless. Some places call themselves dude (or guest) ranch, guest farm (or farm inn), ranch (or lodge) resort, farm (or ranch) bed-and-breakfast, wilderness lodge, or rural hideaway. You might find a wonderful vacation at any of these places but odds are overwhelming that you won't be permitted to soil yourself with honest, productive work.

What do you produce? Potatoes or tomatoes? Hay and 500-pound calves? Chickens and eggs? Hogs and hams? All, some, or none of the above? Once you know the answer you can decide if you want to be an enthusiastic working part of that mission for a week or two.

Season by season, what tasks will I perform as one of your guests? The experience of working the same farm or the same ranch is radically different depending on the season. Let's say you've selected the Hargrave Cattle and Guest Ranch in Montana. If you like the idea of helping out when all the baby calves are born you'll need to schedule your visit for March or April. If you loathe the idea of "burning butts" you'd better stay away from branding season in May. If you want to participate in the spring cattle drives, you're looking at June and part of July. Choose the time of year that you take your trip carefully—your activities depend on it.

Is work required or optional? This question, more than any of the others, will give you clues as to the nature of the farm or ranch and the personalities, goals, and expectations of your hosts. Some are low key, others are more driven. The ones who can't wait to give you a sore butt from riding too hard say things like "After three days on horseback, honey, you can't tell the difference!"

How many head of cattle do you have? How many wranglers do you have at one time? A cattle head count helps you judge the size of the ranch: 200 head is an enormous, serious operation. If your host makes a big distinction between guest wranglers and real wranglers—and there are more than 20 guests at a time—chances are that you will be treated like part of the herd rather than part of the work force. If you're looking for a working ranch experience, smaller usually means better.

How many horses do you have? Working ranches often have nearly two horses for every wrangler. A one-horse-per-wrangler ratio sometimes indicates overworked and dispirited horses or extremely short rides.

How long are the cattle drives? You'll want to find out the answer in miles, days, and nights. A one- or two-day drive covering 10 to 25 miles is a much different experience from a five-day, five-night drive covering 70 miles.

What kind of riding experience do I need to participate? A long ride over rough or hilly terrain requires better horsemanship and tougher buns than a short ride over flat terrain. Also, the amount of experience you need depends on what tasks you participate in.

Do we come back to the ranch at the end of each day or do we camp out? The variations are endless. Some places bring you back to your warm bunk at the ranch every night, even if the drive covers 60 miles. On other drives you'll camp out just one night and on still others you'll sleep under the stars for as many nights as the drive takes.

What are the accommodations like? When you stay on the ranch or farm, your quarters may be a cozy private cottage with a host of modern conveniences, a private room with shared bath in a bunkhouse, or the previous bedroom of an older sister in the main house. When you're away from the ranch or farm (either on the trail, on a cattle drive, or at a distant pasture or feeding area), the roughing it can get a little rougher. Trail accommodations usually mean private tents (possibly with cots), portable outhouses, and primitive bathing facilities. Wood-stove-heated cabins with outhouses and without electricity or running water are sometimes used at distant pastures and other areas away from the main ranch.

What are the dining options? Actually, the better question is **How's the chow?** Home cookin' is the norm, but the location and ambience of where it gets served varies immensely depending on the tasks you're involved in. If you're doing chores in and around the ranch, you can expect home-cooked meals either in the main ranch house where your hosts live or in a central guest dining area. Picnic lunches or outdoor bar-becues (usually called steak fries) are com-mon, especially when the work takes you to a distant pasture or a particularly scenic area. If you're camping out on a cattle drive, expect your meals from an old-fashioned chuck wagon or a modern equivalent such as a van.

Will laundry service be available? This could save you a suitcase.

What's the cost and what's included? Prices listed include lodging, meals, and whatever camping equipment is necessary (tents, cots, cooking equipment, and portable toilet), although you'll probably be asked to bring your own sleeping bag and personal items. Most places provide horses and riding equipment as part of the service, but some do charge extra. Be sure to ask.

Pickup and drop-off services usually are available at the airports and bus stations that are closest to the ranch or farm, but because of the remote locations of most ranches and farms, don't be surprised if you are asked to pay a nominal fee for pickup and drop-off—just enough to cover your host's costs.

How long have you been accepting guests? Putting up guests might be a recent addition; the more experience with guests, the easier the time the management has solving prob-lems.

Do you have references from past guests? In this case, straight from the horse's mouth can give you the exact information you're looking for.

FAVORITE TRIPS

THE NORTHEAST

NEW YORK **Merrill's Farm.** New Yorkers looking for a convenient, inexpensive farm vacation where children are more than wel-come need look no farther than the country home of the Merrill family. Just three hours from New York City on the border of the Catskill Forest Reserve near Beaverkill River, Merrill's Farm has hosted guests from all over the world for nearly 30 years. The farm has been in the family since 1868 and is currently run as a family corporation, with matriarch Vivian Merrill and a number of grown children and grandchildren acting as hosts.

Although the family lost its milk market nearly 15 years ago, the Merrills still raise cattle and produce their own maple syrup. The highlight of the farm, however, is the opportunity to learn how to preserve jams, jellies, and all the vegetables that grow in the garden. The planting starts with frost-resistant onions, peas, radishes, and lettuce, followed by string beans, beets, carrots, corn, potatoes, and—after the last frost in late May or early June—tomatoes. A natural spring supplies the Merrill Farm with all the water it needs.

You can work the garden as much or as little as you wish here. Naturally, all meals, with guests and hosts eating together at a 10-foot dining table, feature homegrown vegetables. Along with the beef, pork, and chicken dishes, Vivian Merrill's famous cinnamon buns and other homemade pastries are always available. Visitors stay in a one-and-a-half-story guest house that has wood-pan-elled rooms—five with double beds, two with singles—and shared baths. All the rooms have dressers, chairs, and central heating that ensures toasty nights.

If you have a car, Cooperstown, New York, with the Farmer's Museum and the Major League Baseball Hall of Fame, is 70 miles away. Nearby Howe Caverns (an under-ground cave) also makes an excellent day trip. There are lots of antiques stores, good hiking and fishing, and—with just 10 guests at a time—lots of opportunity to putt around in the Merrills' classic 1924 Dodge. Picking wild strawberries, raspberries, and blackberries is another favorite activity of farm guests. *Merrills Farm, 829 Horton Brook Road, Roscoe, NY 12776, tel. 607/498–4212. Early May–mid Oct.: weekly rate, $240 adults, $180 children under 10; daily rate, $40 adults, $30 children.*

VERMONT **Berkson Farms.** "The cows are machine milked at 5:00 AM and 4:00 PM seven days a week, 365 days a year," says Connie Rand, manager of Berkson Farms, "and a surprising number of guests are willing to take turns helping out with the morning milking." Milk is far and away the chief product here. Owner Sidney Berkson's 600-acre dairy farm is in the heart of the small town, quaint covered-bridge section of northern Vermont, just 40 minutes from Stowe, the famous Vermont ski resort, and an hour from downtown Montreal.

The heart of the farm is a century-old farmhouse and a sugarhouse for boiling maple sap into maple syrup; its soul is the 250 head of Holstein dairy cows. You can learn machine-milking and the lost art of hand-milking. Rand, who runs the farm for owner Sidney Berkson, says "some guests even like to help muck out the stalls but most have more fun with the haying that goes on between June and August." This farm produces all the hay and silage the cows need to get through the winter.

The best time of all to visit may be the period between mid-February and mid-March, and not just because of the excellent opportunities for cross-country skiing, ice-skating, snowshoeing, and snowmobiling right on the farm. "We have our own sugarhouse here," says Rand. "We tap plastic lines into each maple tree and drain off the sap into 300-gallon central tanks. When those fill up we haul them by tractor to the sugarhouse and use a huge wood-burning stove to boil the sap into maple syrup." Rand says that 10 to 15 guests at a time can

help and most are so amazed that it takes 52 gallons of sap to make one gallon of maple syrup that they don't mind paying $28 a gallon for it. Berkson Farms produces 100 to 150 gallons of syrup a year using this method and also teaches its guests how to gather sap the old-fashioned way, bucket draining.

Chickens, ducks, rabbits, and sheep keep the kids busy, and a large garden, which guests are welcome to work in, produces all the vegetables consumed on the farm. Rand, who prepares all the meals, describes her culinary style as "country comfort cooking, with kind of an emphasis on vegetarian and chicken dishes." One of her special dishes is chicken and broccoli in a creamy pesto sauce. Homemade soups, including daily versions of "garden surprise," are flavored with herbs from the garden. Rand's desserts include traditional homemade apple pie, chocolate mousse cake, and Death by Chocolate with raspberry sauce. Guests gather to eat around a huge round dining table on the first floor of the large, two-story, 100-year-old farmhouse. Rand occupies half of the upstairs and give the other half over to four guest bedrooms, one with private bath and the others sharing two bathrooms.

Hop in your car and take advantage of the nearby auctions, flea markets, antiques stores, theater, boating, riding, tennis, and 9-hole golf course. Other activities include swimming in a mountain brook near Jeffersonville (a 25-minute drive followed by a 20 minute hike to the brook), and nature hikes around Lake Carmi, which is just 3 miles from the farm. *Berkson Farms, Enosburg Falls, VT 05450, tel. 802/ 933–2522. Year-round: weekly rates, $330 adults, $180 children.*

THE MIDWEST

KANSAS **Prairie Star Guest Ranch.** Stan Greene's 6,500-acre ranch is in the Flint Hills of Kansas, a cattleman's paradise with miles of undulating bluestem grass–covered prairie meadows that are ideal for fattening cattle. Stan and his family pride themselves on their top-quality cow horses, horses specially trained to move cattle around. According to Greene, his horses are particularly good at making up for any inadequacies beginning riders have. Which is good because you ride right alongside working cowboys and help them tend to the herd's needs. The ranch typically has 150 cows and 2,200 yearling cattle to look after so there is always plenty to do, most of it on horseback, from moving them from pasture to pasture to inspecting mile after mile of pasture and fences. The prairie comes alive with its prairie chicken, beaver, deer, duck, quail, pheasant, wild turkey, antelope, and eagles. Take your camera along: The wildlife and the vast panoramas of one of the world's richest grazing lands make for some excellent photographic opportunities.

Stan Greene assures that you will get the real old-time experience by eliminating modern distractions such as telephones, televisions, and non-working pets. The goal is to maintain a lifestyle that, as technology advances and economics becomes burdensome, is becoming less realistic and feasible to practice.

Guests stay in a rustic 4-bedroom cabin with stone fireplace, hot tub, and bathhouse. You can either take your meals at the new centrally located cookhouse or barbecue your own food right outside your cabin door. A new 15-acre watershed (artificial lake) is about 150 feet from the cabin. It is stocked with bass and other species of fish and is plenty big enough in which to swim or canoe. Off-site leisure activities include fishing and water sports at nearby El Dorado Lake, hiking along the Teter Nature Trail near the lake, hayrides, and old-fashioned barbecues. Groups and organizations are welcome. *Prairie Star Guest Ranch, RR 1, Cassoday, KS 66842, tel. 316/ 735–4295 or 316/735–4480. Late Apr.–Oct.: daily rate, $125. Price does not include trip from Kansas City Airport.*

NEBRASKA **Meadow View Ranch.** Meadow View Ranch is in northwestern Nebraska in the Sandhills area, particularly well suited

for cattle ranching because of excellent grassed-over topsoil and naturally sub-irrigated meadows. "The water table is so high that the roots of the grass are fed by it," says owner Clyde Lefler. "We get excellent grazing and economical hay crops that the cattle do real well on in the winter."

Clyde and wife Billie host one family or group in a 2-bedroom guest house that sleeps seven. As Clyde says, "I can't keep an eye on more than about six city slickers at a time." New guests join the Leflers between May and September. After they get to know you, they'll let you come around in the spring for calving and branding.

This 2,000-acre ranch is home to about 400 pair (cow and calf) of cattle. The Leflers rotate about 100 pair at a time among various pastures on the farm itself. These rotations last the better part of a day and you're back in your own bed at night. The 8-mile-long, 2-mile-wide ranch has 3 lakes (one of them covers a square mile), which can be seen on a 4-wheel-drive tour. Guests love the tour because of the abundant antelope, deer, beaver, blue heron, trumpeter swans, and geese. Rental horses are available for those who want to ride. Lefler agrees that "only about six of our twenty horses are gentle enough for guests and that's the way I like it." *Meadow View Ranch, HC 91, Box 29, Gordon, NE 69343, tel. 308/282–0679. June–Sept. (new guests), Apr.–Oct. (repeat guests): daily rate, $60 per couple, $17 additional adult, $15 children 12–18, $9 children 6–12. Horse rentals: $17 per hour, $50 per day. 4-wheel-drive tour of the ranch: $20.*

THE SOUTHWEST

NEVADA **Cottonwood Ranch.** Horace Smith has spent 41 years raising cattle and hosting guests on 1,200 owned and 20,000 leased acres in the O'Neil Basin of Elko County, Nevada. Smith runs 500 head of cattle and 100 horses on the spread, near the beautiful and isolated Jarbidge Wilderness. One of two primary attractions at Cottonwood is the 40-mile, 4-day "horse drives" in mid-May and September, complete with camping out around campfires, cowboy poetry, and sing-alongs. A "horse drive" is like a cattle drive only faster and more fun because horses are smarter than cattle. It serves the same pur-pose—moving the animals between summer and winter grazing ranges. In the summer, you can work with the cattle and sleep in the 7-bedroom lodge, which has private and shared baths. But, starting in July after the mountain snows melt, most guests opt for Cottonwood's other attraction—the 4- to 7-day horseback pack trips into the Jarbidge Wilderness.

On these guided trips you take all your food and equipment on packhorses, and ride past dramatic views of mountains with names like Cougar, Matterhorn, and Jumbo Peak. Ride across aspen- and willow-covered hills, and meadows filled with sunflowers and lupines. Photographic and trout-fishing breaks give your sore buns an occasional rest during the day, and at night you camp out in the wilder-ness. These wilderness pack trips, where you just have to look out for yourself and maybe a few pack animals, may be the ultimate trial run for those who are ambivalent about sign-ing up for a working cattle drive.

Cottonwood is an especially attractive place for environmentalists and others who philo-sophically support what the Smith family calls its "Holistic Resource Management Program." This program features frequent rotations of animals among numerous graz-ing areas in order to preserve natural condi-tions and help maintain wildlife.

Whether you go for the horse drives or the pack trips, all you need to bring is your sleeping bag and personal gear. Food, guides, horses, and tents are provided. Gen-tle horses are available for children 12 or older. *Cottonwood Ranch, O'Neil Basin, HC 62, Box 1300, Wells, NV 89835, tel. 702/ 752–3604. Mid-May–Sept.: daily rate, $100; horse drive, $1,000 for 4 days; pack trips, $150 per day, 3-day minimum; 1-week wilderness pack trip, $995.*

TEXAS **Y.O. Ranch.** About 100 miles north-west of San Antonio at an elevation of 2,200 feet, Y.O. Ranch is one of the largest working ranches in Texas and one of the largest exotic game ranches in the world. It is famous for its herd of 2,000 Texas Long-horns, the largest such herd in the country. Folks come from all over the world to spend time in the saddle mixing it up with the rare Longhorns and eyeballing the giraffe, wil-debeest, scimitar-horned oryx, fallow deer, red sheep, black buck antelope, zebra, and watusi cattle that roam the ranch's 40,000 acres. Over 10,000 animals representing over 35 species are at home on this range.

It's not surprising then that horseback riding is perhaps the biggest pastime on the ranch. Rides go out twice a day for 1 to 3 hours. The daily guided wildlife tours are a good way of acquainting yourself with the ranch, and at extra cost there is an excellent photographic safari. Of course, you can always relax by the pool and hot tub. Thirty-four guests stay in five 100-year-old renovated log cabins, each with a fireplace, heat and air-condi-tioning, and a front porch on which to kick back. There are four additional rooms in the main house, but none of the rooms have either telephones or TVs.

Every spring during the last week of April and the first week of May, Y.O. stages a 3-day "cattle drive" and steer-branding involving 60 to 80 Texas Longhorns and 150 to 225 guest wranglers on horseback.

You have plenty of opportunities for hard work with the cattle and sheep, including branding, moving, castrating, and shearing, but because this is not part of the ranch's regular service, it must be pre-arranged with Walter Schriener, manager of Y.O.'s Long-horn division. Schriener will question you to make sure you're up to the work at hand. If you pass muster, you're in for a rare oppor-tunity to work with Texas Longhorns and you'll also gain insight into the care and feeding of the ranch's exotic animals. *Y.O. Ranch, Highway 41 West, Mountain Home, TX 78058, tel. 210/640–3222. Year-round (except Christmas Eve and Christmas Day): daily rate, $75 adults weekdays, $85 week-ends; cattle drive, $300–$350 with your own* horse, $400–$450 with horse provided. Pick-up from airport not included.

UTAH **Rockin' R Ranch.** Burns Black is the current patriarch of a family that has been raising cattle in Southern Utah for more than 100 years. He currently runs about 1,000 head of cattle on 1,000 owned and 50,000 leased acres of grazing land in a beautiful valley surrounded by mountains near the spectacular Rainbow Canyons. Lake Powell, Dixie National Forest, Bryce Canyon, Zion and Capitol Reef National parks are all within striking distance for day trips.

In 1970, Burns and wife, Mona, realized that the best way to survive in the cattle business was to diversify into the guest business. The main lodge has a 3-story fireplace and 41 spacious rooms, all with private baths with either showers or tubs. Children under 4 stay free. There are even supervised activities for youths that make Rockin' R great for families. The ranch's tennis court, gift shop, hot tub, weight room, library, and restaurant make it a community within itself. Full- and half-day horseback rides and riding instruction make your days fly by. Rockin' R also has an authentic 1853 Vintage Stagecoach for guests to ride around in during their stay. Otter Lake, just 5 miles from the main lodge, offers great fishing, sailboarding, canoeing, sailing, inner tubing, and waterskiing for family members who would rather play in the water than work with cattle.

You are invited to help out with as much summer cattle work as you wish. This includes roundups at the ranch's cow camp 10,000 feet up at the summer range in the mountains. Burns and Mona even have a special coordinator for the 3-, 5-, and 7-day cattle drives that take place between late June and October.

All in all, Rockin' R is the ideal place to get your feet off the ground with cattle work without leaving out family members who would rather spend their vacations enjoying a host of recreational pursuits amidst spectacular Utah scenery. *Rockin' R Ranch, 1021 North University Ave, Suite 205, Provo, UT 84604, tel. 801/344–8588 or 800/767–4386.*

Year-round: daily rate, $120 adults, $69 children; cattle drive, $195 per day.

THE ROCKIES

COLORADO **Focus Ranch.** Aptly named, the focus of this ranch is working with cattle on the ranch itself. Owner Terry Reidy runs 1,000 head of cattle on his spread, which sits at 7,000 feet in the mountains near the northwest corner of Colorado, about 50 miles north of the famous Steamboat Springs ski resort. As a guest on Terry's ranch you are more or less expected to saddle up every morning and ride with him, but you'll want to. You pass through high country, aspen forests, and lush alpine meadows as he rounds up cattle, moves them between forest grazing areas and salt licks, repairs fences, checks irrigation ditches, or busts up beaver dams. Nearby Medicine Bow National Forest offers unlimited space for pleasure riding and hiking if you want a day off from the work-related rides, and the Little Snake River, dotted with great trout fishing and swimming holes, flows right through Terry's property. At the end of the day you can fry steaks next to the river, play volleyball or baseball, square dance, or just sit back and relax. There's also excellent cross-country skiing in the winter.

Focus Ranch's mission is fattening up yearlings, so there are no cattle drives here. New stock arrives every May and guests help move them among various grazing pastures on the ranch until final roundup days in mid-September. This place definitely isn't snooty or luxurious, but accommodations in the lodge with private and shared baths, plus the five rustic log cabins, are homey and comfortable. All the food is homemade. Terry will tell you that this is a meat, potatoes, and vegetables kind of place, but the bread is baked fresh daily—homemade French rolls are a lunchtime favorite—and the desserts are mouthwatering.

Focus Ranch is the place to go if you want to ride along with a devoted and experienced rancher as he goes about the daily business of caring for his herd. Plus, for better or for worse, there's none of that vagabond feeling you'll get on a cattle drive. After a hard day in the saddle, you'll eat like a king every evening, and sleep in the same warm bunk every night. *Focus Ranch, Box A, Slater, CO 81653, tel. 303/583–2410. Year-round: weekly rate, $950 adults, children under 4 free, ages 4–9 $400, ages 10–13, $500, ages 14–17, $600.*

MONTANA **Hargrave Cattle and Guest Ranch.** Leo and Ellen Hargrave own 1,400 acres in the Thompson River Valley, 42 miles southwest of Kalispell, Montana. This beautiful mountain valley is shouldered by tall pines with the Thompson River flowing through the ranch's broad green meadows. Bordered by Lolo National Forest to the south, it is also only an hour and a half drive north to Glacier National Park and the Canadian border. The same distance to the southwest is the National Bison Range. There are 6 lakes within 10 miles of the ranch for those who would rather swim, canoe, or fish than work with the cattle. Alpine skiing at Whitefish Mountain Resort and cross-country skiing at Glacier National Park and on the ranch itself make this a great place to come in the winter.

The Hargraves' product is 500-pound calves. They run 300 pair (calf and mother) between their ranch and various grazing areas on 86,000 acres of leased range. This means a lot of horseback riding on the spread, which is always done with a purpose. "If we're not out checking the cows, we're out checking and mending fences," explains Leo, "or we're out checking the pastures and creeks to make sure they haven't been damaged by the cattle, which tend to trample them." Because so much of your activities involve riding, and the group's riding skills and experience can vary tremendously, the Hargraves routinely provide riding and horsemanship lessons. This means that folks with little or no time in the saddle can end up having as much fun as experienced riders.

In addition to all the seasonal work with the cattle, the Hargraves offer a number of one-day cattle drives that are included in the price of your stay. The drive in June moves the herd approximately 15 miles to its summer range. Drives in July and August are up to ten miles, shifting the herd among various pastures in the summer grazing area to assure proper grass and water utilization and protect pastures from excessive damage by the herd. The final drive in September or October involves rounding up the herd and returning it back to the home valley for the winter. Ellen Hargrave points out, "our guests come home every night to hot showers and real beds."

Alternatively, the Hargraves usually offer one night per week, weather permitting, for camping out somewhere on the ranch. This way you get a taste of chuck-wagon cooking (barbecued beef, beans, and biscuits), campfire storytelling, and sleeping out under the stars. Additional activities and services include: skeet shooting one night a week, target practice with a 22 rifle one night a week, and the option to enjoy a professional massage from a massage therapist who drops by one night a week. *Hargrave Cattle and Guest Ranch, 300 Thompson River Rd., Marion, MT 59925, tel. 406/858–2284 or 800/933–0696. Year-round: weekly rate, $980 adults. Price includes riding lessons, overnight camp out, and a tour of Glacier Park.*

WYOMING **Two Creek Ranch.** Talk about the real thing. For the past several years Dennis and Nancy Daly have taken guest wranglers on 75-mile spring and fall cattle drives between the winter and summer grazing areas at Douglas Meadows and Laramie Plains in Wyoming. Now they invite riders to join them throughout the year to find out what cattle ranching is all about. They're not kidding either: Depending on the time of year you go, you'll have completely different experiences. In calving season from mid-February to mid-April you help separate expectant cows and monitor their health and condition as they prepare to calve, then help with the normal births. In late April to early May, you round up 1,000 head of cattle on the winter range and sort them into two groups for the relatively short (17-mile) drive to the spring range. Branding Weekend, the first weekend in May, includes plenty of riding to gather, brand, and release three separate groups of calves. Keep in mind that branding is hard, dirty work and you've got to be ready for the stench of burning cowhide and the bleating of frightened calves. The spring cattle drive in the last 10 days of May is the big one for wranglers with cabin fever who kinda like the constant bleating of growing calves and nervous mama cows. You trail 1,000 head of cattle 75 miles from the spring range at 5,000 feet to Laramie Peaks, the high-country pasture, at 7,000 feet. You're looking at 11 days and 10 nights with all but 2 nights camping out next to the herd. The fall cattle drive is the same 75 miles in reverse, which takes place in the last 10 days of October. Other activities include anything from pregnancy testing the heifers in early August to separating and weighing the calves for market. *Two Creek Ranch, 800 Esterbrook Rd., Douglas, WY 82633, tel. 307/358–3467. Year-round: daily rate, $65. Late May and late Oct.: 75-mile cattle drive, $1,100.*

THE WEST COAST

CALIFORNIA **Hunewill Circle H Guest Ranch.** This 4,500-acre spread on the Northeast edge of California's Yosemite National Park has been in the Hunewill (pronounced Honey-will) family since 1861. It sits at 6,500 feet in the Bridgeport Valley North of Mono Lake hard against the eastern slopes of the Sierra Nevada mountain range. The Hunewills opened their white-frame ranch house to guests in 1931 and have such a loyal following that the ranch is usually booked solid in the summer months. That's okay though, because most of the work involving cattle and riding horses takes place in spring and fall.

The highlight from a prospective wrangler's point of view is the November cattle drive from Circle H to the winter range at the Hunewills' other ranch in Nevada, 60 miles to the northeast. The 5-day fall drive starts at Circle H, goes past canyons and piñon-cov-

ered mountains to the Bridgeport Reservoir. From there you'll cross the East Walker River and go over Sweetwater Summit on the middle day of the drive. The last leg of the drive into Nevada is past more canyons that eventually open up into a wide, high desert. The bad news is that the weather in November can be anything from bright sun to rain or snow. The good news is that you return to Circle H—and your nice warm bed in a cottage with private bath or in a shared room in the ranch house—every single night of the drive.

Riding horses is the biggest part of life here. There is lots of riding associated with the care, feeding, and moving of the herd, but there are also regular morning and afternoon rides just for fun and practice. The Hunewills' pride and joy are their 100 horses, which serve both ranch hands and the up to 40 guests. You get to keep the same horse for your entire stay and you're encouraged to ride as much as possible. Ride leaders will show you how to lope with a partner for a mile at a time, perform figure eights, do controlled "serpentine" weaving maneuvers in a group, and perform a timed group crossing maneuver called "thread the needle." Don't worry, there are rides for every age and experience level. The highlights for more experienced riders are the all-day Wednesday rides into the high country in Toiyabe National Forest and special "fall color" rides. Kids over 6 get their own horses and, during the peak summer season, Circle H provides 24 hours per week of free baby-sitting services so you can enjoy your rides. *Hunewill Circle H Guest Ranch, Box 368, Bridgeport, CA 93517, tel. 619/932–7710 (summer) or 702/465–2201 (winter). May–late Sept.: weekly rate, $795–$934, 5-day cattle drive, $670; 3-day Fall Color Ride, $427.*

SOURCES

ORGANIZATIONS **The Dude Ranchers' Association** (Box 471, LaPorte, CO 80535, tel. 303/223–8440) represents more than 100 ranches in the western United States and

Canada. The association's annual *Dude Rancher Magazine* is essentially a detailed directory of member ranches, the services they offer, and descriptions of the surrounding areas. The directory costs only $3 and is especially useful because the listings are coded to identify the type of ranch listed— from working ranches to resort dude ranches.

BOOKS *Eugene Kilgore's Ranch Vacations*, by Eugene Kilgore, though somewhat outdated, has detailed listings of hundreds of ranches throughout the United States and Canada. Most are strictly guest or resort ranches, but the ones that do offer work programs are easy to find, thanks to an easily accessible appendix. New editions of *Pat Dickerman's Farm, Ranch & Country Vaca-*

tions, by Pat Dickerman, were printed most years between 1949 and 1989. The listings of farms, ranches, lodges, and inns are slightly outdated (especially the prices), but the book has an excellent 6-page introduction. A variety of sections do a great job of conveying the spirit of farm and ranch vacations. Other sections help you with the nuts and bolts of choosing the vacation that's right for you. On the downside, although the working farms and ranches are clearly identified, there are precious few of them buried in a sea of bed-and-breakfasts, guest farms, wilderness lodges, and ranch resorts.

ALSO SEE If your saddle isn't too sore from all this riding, and this hard-working, outdoor life appeals to you, see the Covered Wagon Trains chapter.

Appendix: Where the Programs Are

Fodor's Travel Publications

Available at bookstores everywhere, or call 1–800–533–6478, 24 hours a day.

Gold Guides

U.S.

Alaska

Arizona

Boston

California

Cape Cod, Martha's Vineyard, Nantucket

The Carolinas & the Georgia Coast

Chicago

Colorado

Florida

Hawaii

Las Vegas, Reno, Tahoe

Los Angeles

Maine, Vermont, New Hampshire

Maui

Miami & the Keys

New England

New Orleans

New York City

Pacific North Coast

Philadelphia & the Pennsylvania Dutch Country

The Rockies

San Diego

San Francisco

Santa Fe, Taos, Albuquerque

Seattle & Vancouver

The South

U.S. & British Virgin Islands

USA

Virginia & Maryland

Waikiki

Washington, D.C.

Foreign

Australia & New Zealand

Austria

The Bahamas

Barbados

Bermuda

Brazil

Budapest

Canada

Cancún, Cozumel, Yucatán Peninsula

Caribbean

China

Costa Rica, Belize, Guatemala

Cuba

The Czech Republic & Slovakia

Eastern Europe

Egypt

Europe

Florence, Tuscany & Umbria

France

Germany

Great Britain

Greece

Hong Kong

India

Ireland

Israel

Italy

Japan

Kenya & Tanzania

Korea

London

Madrid & Barcelona

Mexico

Montréal & Québec City

Morocco

Moscow, St. Petersburg, Kiev

The Netherlands, Belgium & Luxembourg

New Zealand

Norway

Nova Scotia, New Brunswick, Prince Edward Island

Paris

Portugal

Provence & the Riviera

Scandinavia

Scotland

Singapore

South Africa

South America

South Pacific

Southeast Asia

Spain

Sweden

Switzerland

Thailand

Tokyo

Toronto

Turkey

Vienna & the Danube

Fodor's Special-Interest Guides

Branson

Caribbean Ports of Call

The Complete Guide to America's National Parks

Condé Nast Traveler Caribbean Resort and Cruise Ship Finder

Cruises and Ports of Call

Fodor's London Companion

Gay USA

France by Train

Halliday's New England Food Explorer

Healthy Escapes

Italy by Train

Kodak Guide to Shooting Great Travel Pictures

Shadow Traffic's New York Shortcuts and Traffic Tips

Sunday in New York

Sunday in San Francisco

Walt Disney World, Universal Studios and Orlando

Walt Disney World for Adults

Where Should We Take the Kids? California

Where Should We Take the Kids? Family Adventures

Where Should We Take the Kids? Northeast

Fodor's
Special Series

Affordables

Caribbean

Europe

Florida

France

Germany

Great Britain

Italy

London

Paris

Fodor's Bed & Breakfasts and Country Inns

America's Best B&Bs

California's Best B&Bs

Canada's Great Country Inns

Cottages, B&Bs and Country Inns of England and Wales

The Mid-Atlantic's Best B&Bs

New England's Best B&Bs

The Pacific Northwest's Best B&Bs

The South's Best B&Bs

The Southwest's Best B&Bs

The Upper Great Lakes' Best B&Bs

The Berkeley Guides

California

Central America

Eastern Europe

Europe

France

Germany & Austria

Great Britain & Ireland

Italy

London

Mexico

Pacific Northwest & Alaska

Paris

San Francisco

Compass American Guides

Arizona

Canada

Chicago

Colorado

Hawaii

Idaho

Hollywood

Las Vegas

Maine

Manhattan

Montana

New Mexico

New Orleans

Oregon

San Francisco

Santa Fe

South Carolina

South Dakota

Southwest

Texas

Utah

Virginia

Washington

Wine Country

Wisconsin

Wyoming

Fodor's Citypacks

Atlanta

Hong Kong

London

New York City

Paris

Rome

San Francisco

Washington, D.C.

Fodor's Español

California

Caribe Occidental

Caribe Oriental

Gran Bretaña

Londres

Mexico

Nueva York

Paris

Fodor's Exploring Guides

Australia

Boston & New England

Britain

California

Caribbean

China

Egypt

Florence & Tuscany

Florida

France

Germany

Ireland

Israel

Italy

Japan

London

Mexico

Moscow & St. Petersburg

New York City

Paris

Prague

Provence

Rome

San Francisco

Scotland

Singapore & Malaysia

Spain

Thailand

Turkey

Venice

Fodor's Flashmaps

Boston

New York

San Francisco

Washington, D.C.

Fodor's Pocket Guides

Acapulco

Atlanta

Barbados

Jamaica

London

New York City

Paris

Prague

Puerto Rico

Rome

San Francisco

Washington, D.C.

Rivages Guides

Bed and Breakfasts of Character and Charm in France

Hotels and Country Inns of Character and Charm in France

Hotels and Country Inns of Character and Charm in Italy

Short Escapes

Country Getaways in Britain

Country Getaways in France

Country Getaways in New England

Country Getaways Near New York City

Fodor's Sports

Golf Digest's Best Places to Play

Skiing USA

USA Today The Complete Four Sport Stadium Guide

Fodor's Vacation Planners

Great American Learning Vacations

Great American Sports & Adventure Vacations

Great American Vacations

National Parks and Seashores of the East

National Parks of the West

Before Catching Your Flight, Catch Up With Your World.

Fueled by the global resources of CNN and available in major airports across America, CNN Airport Network pro-

vides a live source of current domestic and international news, sports, business, weather and lifestyle program-

ming. Plus two daily Fodor's features for the facts you need: "Travel Fact," a useful and creative mix of travel trivia; and

"What's Happening," a comprehensive round-up of coming events in major cities around the world.

CNN Airport Network, you'll never be out of